The Epistle of Forgiveness

Volume One

Letter from the General Editor

The Library of Arabic Literature is a new series offering Arabic editions and English translations of key works of classical and premodern Arabic literature, as well as anthologies and thematic readers. Books in the series are edited and translated by distinguished scholars of Arabic and Islamic studies, and are published in parallel-text format with Arabic and English on facing pages. The Library of Arabic Literature includes texts from the pre-Islamic era to the cusp of the modern period, and will encompass a wide range of genres, including poetry, poetics, fiction, religion, philosophy, law, science, history, and historiography.

Supported by a grant from the New York University Abu Dhabi Institute, and established in partnership with NYU Press, the Library of Arabic Literature will produce authoritative Arabic editions and modern, lucid English translations, with the goal of introducing the Arabic literary heritage to scholars and students, as well as to a general audience of readers.

Philip F. Kennedy
General Editor, Library of Arabic Literature

رسالة الغفران

لأبي العلاء المعرّيّ

المجلّد الأوّل

LIBRARY OF
المكتبة
ARABIC
العربية
LITERATURE

To dear Marcelle —
With my love & admiration —
Jamie
Jan 27 2016

The Epistle of Forgiveness

or

A Pardon to Enter the Garden

by

Abū l-ʿAlāʾ al-Maʿarrī

edited and translated by

GEERT JAN VAN GELDER

and

GREGOR SCHOELER

Volume One: A Vision of Heaven and Hell

preceded by

Ibn al-Qāriḥ's Epistle

NEW YORK UNIVERSITY PRESS

New York and London

NEW YORK UNIVERSITY PRESS
New York and London

Library of Congress Cataloging-in-Publication Data

Abu al-'Ala' al-Ma'arri, 973-1057.
The epistle of forgiveness or, A pardon to enter the garden / by Abu l'Ala al'Ma'arri ; edited and translated by Geert Jan van Gelder and Gregor Schoeler.
volumes cm
Bilingual English and Arabic edition.
Includes bibliographical references and indexes.
ISBN 978-0-8147-6378-0 (cl : alk. paper) -- ISBN 978-0-8147-6899-0 (e-book) -- ISBN 978-0-8147-7197-6 (e-book) -- ISBN 978-0-8147-7194-5 (cl : v. 2) -- ISBN 978-0-8147-6896-9 (e-book : v. 2) -- ISBN 978-0-8147-6970-6 (e-book : v. 2)
I. Gelder, G. J. H. van, translator editor. II. Schoeler, Gregor, translator editor. III. Abu al-'Ala' al-Ma'arri, 973-1057. Risalat al-ghufran. IV. Abu al-'Ala' al-Ma'arri, 973-1057. Risalat al-ghufran. English. V. Ibn al-Qarih, 'Ali ibn Mansur, b. 962. Risalat Ibn al-Qarih. VI. Ibn al-Qarih, 'Ali ibn Mansur, b. 962. Risalat Ibn al-Qarih. English. VII. Title. VIII. Title: Pardon to enter the garden.
PJ7750.A25R513 2013
892.7'134--dc23
2013007519
CIP

New York University Press books are printed on acid-free paper, and their binding materials are chosen for strength and durability.

Series design by Titus Nemeth.

Typeset in Tasmeem, using DecoType Naskh and Emiri.

Typesetting and digitization by Stuart Brown.

Manufactured in the United States of America
c10 9 8 7 6 5 4 3 2 1

To our spouses, Sheila and Christa, asking their Forgiveness for spending so many hours in al-Maʿarrī's company instead of theirs.

Table of Contents

Acknowledgments

We are grateful for the encouragement and help we received from the LAL editors, in particular Philip Kennedy, Shawkat Toorawa, and James Montgomery. Our labors were alleviated by the great efficiency and expertise of the LAL managing editor, Chip Rossetti; of the digital production manager Stuart Brown; of Carolyn Brunelle, who extracted a Glossary from our endnotes; and from the copy editor, Kelly Zaug. Of all these it was James Montgomery who contributed most, with his countless stylistic and linguistic improvements and his editorial accuracy. If, on very rare occasions, we disagreed with him and stuck to our own ideas, we hope for his forgiveness—which is, after all, the leitmotiv of the present work.

Abbreviations used in the Introduction and Translation

EI2	*Encyclopaedia of Islam*, New [= Second] Edition
Gh	*Risālat al-Ghufrān / The Epistle of Forgiveness*
IQ	*Risālat Ibn al-Qāriḥ / The Epistle of Ibn al-Qāriḥ*
L	(in prosody) long syllable
O	(in prosody) overlong syllable
Q	Qur'an
S	(in prosody) short syllable

Introduction

The lengthy, mocking reply by a cantankerous maverick, obsessed with lexicography and grammar, to a rambling, groveling, and self-righteous letter by an obscure grammarian and mediocre stylist: this does not sound, prima facie, like a masterwork to be included in a series of Arabic classics. It is even doubtful whether it firmly belongs to the canonical works of Arabic literature. The maverick author, Abū l-ʿAlāʾ al-Maʿarrī, was certainly famous, or infamous, as we shall see, but in the entry on him in the biographical dictionary by Ibn Khallikān (d. 681/1282),[1] who calls him the author of "many famous compositions and widely known epistles," the present work is not even mentioned; in the very long entry on him in a somewhat earlier, similar work by Yāqūt (d. 626/1229) it is merely listed in a long list of works, without commentary.[2] It is true that the same Yāqūt has an entry on the rather obscure author of the original letter, the grammarian Ibn al-Qāriḥ, whom he describes as "the one who wrote a well-known letter to Abū l-ʿAlāʾ, known as 'the Epistle of Ibn al-Qāriḥ',"[3] which suggests that Abū l-ʿAlāʾ's reply was famous. However, the work is not often mentioned or discussed in pre-modern times, unlike Abū l-ʿAlāʾ's poetry.

As happens occasionally in the history of Arabic literature, the *Risālat al-Ghufrān* (*The Epistle of Forgiveness*), owes its present fame mostly to the rediscovery in modern times, by a western Arabist. Reynold A. Nicholson, in a letter to the *Journal of the Royal Asiatic Society*,[4] describes a collection of manuscripts gathered by his grandfather, to which, as he writes, "I would call special attention, because it is, as I believe, a genuine work, hitherto unknown and undescribed, of the famous blind poet and man of letters, Abū 'l ʿAlā al-Maʿarrī." Over the following few years, between 1900 and 1902, he published a partial edition with a summary and at times paraphrasing translation of the contents in a series of articles in the same journal.[5] The *Epistle*'s subsequent rise to fame is mainly due to the fact that it seemed to prefigure Dante's *Commedia Divina* and that misguided attempts were made to prove the influence of the Arabic work on the Italian. This thesis has now been abandoned and one can appreciate *Risālat al-Ghufrān* in its own right.

Abū l-ʿAlāʾ al-Maʿarrī

The earliest appearance of al-Maʿarrī in Arabic literature is found in a work by a contemporary, one of the greatest anthologists of Arabic literature, al-Thaʿālibī (d. 429/1038). In the supplement to his *Yatīmat al-dahr*, he quotes a certain poet, Abū l-Ḥasan al-Dulafī al-Maṣṣīṣī, who told him:

> In Maʿarrat al-Nuʿmān I came across a true marvel. I saw a blind man, a witty poet, who played chess and backgammon, and who was at home in every genre of seriousness and jesting. He was called Abū l-ʿAlāʾ. I heard him say, "I praise God for being blind, just as others praise Him for being able to see. He did me a favor and did me a good turn by sparing me the sight of boring and hateful people."[6]

Our author is usually called Abū l-ʿAlāʾ al-Maʿarrī,[7] the first part (literally "Father of Loftiness") not being a teknonym[8] in this case—for he never had children—but an added honorific name or nickname, and the second part derived from his place of birth, Maʿarrat al-Nuʿmān, or al-Maʿarrah for short, a town in northern Syria, between Aleppo and Homs. The medieval biographical dictionaries, usually arranged alphabetically, list him under his given name, Aḥmad, and supply not only the name of his father, ʿAbd Allāh, and grandfather, Sulaymān, but also some twenty to thirty further generations, tracing him back to the legendary realm of pre-Islamic Arab genealogy; he belonged to the famous tribal confederation called Tanūkh, entitling him to the epithet al-Tanūkhī. He was born toward sunset on Friday, 27 Rabīʿ Awwal, 363 (26 December AD 973) in a respectable family of religious scholars and judges. At the age of four he lost his eyesight due to smallpox. He made up for this disability by having a truly prodigious memory, about which several anecdotes are related; apparently he had the aural equivalent of a photographic memory and he stood out in a milieu that was already accustomed to memorization on a large scale. His blindness meant that he wrote his numerous works by dictating them; his pupil al-Tibrīzī mentioned that al-Maʿarrī at one stage had four well-qualified secretaries and a servant girl (*jāriyah*), who wrote down his dictations.[9] As a boy he studied with several teachers, including his own father, in his hometown and Aleppo; his main interest was poetry and he became an ardent admirer of the great poet al-Mutanabbī (d. 354/965), on whose poetry he was to write a commentary, entitled *Muʿjiz Aḥmad* (*Aḥmad's Miracle*), exploiting not only the fact that he shared his given name with the poet but also, rather daringly, alluding to the Qurʾan, which was the prophetic "miracle" (*muʿjizah*) of the Prophet Muḥammad, who is sometimes called Aḥmad.

It seems that his own poetic efforts date from an early age, when he was eleven or twelve. Normally the poetry of a poet is collected in a single *dīwān*, in which poems are arranged alphabetically on rhyme letter, or chronologically, or thematically. Most of al-Maʿarrī's poetry however, as far as it is preserved (for many of his works are lost), is contained in two very distinct major collections; yet more poems are found in some minor works. His early poetry, in a *dīwān* called *Saqṭ* (or *Siqṭ*) *al-zand* (*The Spark of the Fire Stick*[10]), shows the influence of al-Mutanabbī. The second collection contains his later poetry and it is very different. Instead of more or less conventional odes, it offers nearly sixteen hundred mostly short pieces. Thematically and stylistically the collection is unusually coherent: it is a sustained invective on mankind in general, a glorification of wisdom and reason, and it expresses skepticism to a degree that made the poet very suspect in pious circles. Dogmatically, however, it cannot be called coherent, for doubts about the Resurrection and afterlife or the value of prophethood alternate with professions of orthodox belief. The title, *Luzūm mā lā yalzam*,[11] literally "the necessity of what is not necessary," could also be translated as "the self-imposed constraints," one of these being a form of rich rhyme, involving two rhyme consonants instead of one and using all the letters of the alphabet as rhyme consonant. Another constant trait is the sustained use of figures such as paronomasia. The poems are riddled with allusions and studded with rare words and recondite expressions.[12] In order to refute allegations of unbelief detected in this collection he wrote a work called *Zajr al-nābiḥ* (*Chiding Away the Barking Dog*), parts of which are extant.[13]

Al-Maʿarrī's gloomy outlook on the world probably has something to do with his unsuccessful attempt to settle in Baghdad in 399/1008. He returned to al-Maʿarrah after some eighteen months, partly, it seems, because he was unable to secure suitable patronage and because he fell out with a leading personality in the cultural and literary life of the metropolis, al-Sharīf al-Murtaḍā. They quarreled about the merits of al-Mutanabbī; when al-Murtaḍā made a disparaging remark about the poet, al-Maʿarrī retorted with a cleverly allusive and insinuating quotation, after which he was unceremoniously dragged by his feet from the literary gathering. Henceforth, for the rest of his long life, with only one brief exception, he remained in his birthplace, describing himself as *rahīn* (or *rahn*) *al-maḥbisayn*, "hostage to two prisons," meaning his blindness and his seclusion; in an epigram he mentions a third prison, his soul being confined to his body.[14] Although contemporaries mention that he was wealthy and greatly esteemed in his town, he lived like an ascetic. He was obviously fond of various forms of self-imposed constraints. He abstained from marriage and sexual intercourse; the inscription on his grave says "This is my father's crime against me, | a crime that I did not commit to anyone."[15] His diet was extremely frugal, consisting chiefly of lentils, with figs for sweet;[16] and, very unusually for a Muslim, he was not only a vegetarian, but a vegan who abstained from meat, fish, dairy products, eggs, and honey, because he did not want to kill or hurt animals or deprive them of their food. This was an attitude he had to defend when he was attacked by the famous Ismāʿīlī ideologue and "chief propagandist" (*dāʿī l-duʿāh*), Abū Naṣr al-Muʾayyad fī l-Dīn al-Shīrāzī, a kind of Grand Mufti of the Fāṭimids in Cairo (whose influence extended to Syria). This attack branded him as a heretic who tried to pose as someone "more merciful than the Merciful," i.e., God, who, after all, allowed the consumption of meat. The interesting exchange of letters between the theologian and Abū l-ʿAlāʾ has been preserved.[17] It is not clear from where he derived his ideas; his critics speculated that he might have adopted the vegan lifestyle from the Indian Brahmans.[18]

In spite of his ascetic attitude, Abū l-ʿAlāʾ was no true recluse, someone who cuts himself off from society. On the contrary, people flocked to him and scholars and viziers visited him, paying their respect and hoping to learn from him. Among his pupils were famous philologists such as the poet and critic Ibn Sinān al-Khafājī (d. 466/1074) and Abū Zakariyyā Yaḥyā ibn ʿAlī al-Tibrīzī (d. 502/1109). The latter reported that when Abū l-ʿAlāʾ died, after a short illness at the age of eighty-four in the month Rabīʿ al-Awwal of 449 (May, AD 1057), eighty-four poets recited elegies at his grave;[19] whether or not this is true, several such elegies have been preserved. Abū l-ʿAlāʾ also took a lively interest in the intricate politics of his own time and place (involving several dynasties and realms, such as the Ḥamdānids, Būyids, Mirdāsids, Fāṭimids, and the infidel Byzantines); an interest that is apparent from references in his poetry and from some of his letters and prose works. Probably the most interesting work in this respect is his *Risālat al-Ṣāhil wa-l-shāḥij* (*The Epistle of the Neigher and the Brayer*), a lengthy work in which the main characters are animals, notably a horse and a mule. Speaking animals had been familiar to the Arabs since the famous collection of animal fables, *Kalīlah wa-Dimnah*, was translated from the Pahlavi into Arabic by Ibn al-Muqaffaʿ (d. ca. 139/756),[20] but Abū l-ʿAlāʾ's book, composed around the year 144/1021, does not contain fables; it is a commentary on contemporary politics involving the Mirdāsid and Fāṭimid dynasties and the Byzantines. It also discusses matters such as taxation. At the same time, like other works of his, it is full of digressions on highly technical matters in the fields of grammar, lexicography, poetics, prosody, and rhyme.

Abū l-ʿAlāʾ ranks as one of the great poets in Arabic literary history. Unlike most poets of the first rank he also excelled as a prose writer. In addition to the present work and the *Epistle of the Neigher and the Brayer*, mention should be made of a controversial work of his: *al-Fuṣūl wa-l-ghāyāt* (*Paragraphs and Periods*). It is composed in an exceptionally difficult idiom (the author regularly interrupts his text with a commentary and explanation of obscure words and expressions), but once one has grasped the sense the work is, at first sight, not shocking: it is a series of homiletic, sermon-like texts, containing praise of God, which call for piety, asceticism, and submission to Fate. The controversy that arose about the book is on account of its style and its form, together with the suspicion that the author's intention was to outdo the Qurʾan. It is composed in an intricate form of rhymed prose, with rhymes interwoven on two text levels: short range within the various sections or paragraphs (*fuṣūl*), and long range, because the last words ("ends", *ghāyāt*) of successive sections also rhyme in an alphabetic series. It uses many idioms that have a Qurʾanic flavor. Altogether, it is not surprising that some thought that its author intended to surpass the Qurʾan, an attitude clearly blasphemous to orthodox Muslims, who believe that the style of the Qurʾan, God's literal words, is inimitable and unsurpassable. When someone rhetorically asked how *al-Fuṣūl wa-l-ghāyāt* could possibly be compared to the Surahs and *āyāt* ("verses") of the Qurʾan, Abū l-ʿAlāʾ reputedly replied, "Wait until it has been polished by tongues for four hundred years; then see how it is,"[21] an answer that would not endear him to the pious.

Although he has been called "the poet among philosophers and the philosopher among poets," it does not do him justice to consider him a philosopher. It is probably wrong to see a consistent world view in his works. He is a humanist who generally hates humanity and loves animals, a Muslim who expresses many unorthodox thoughts (such as his frequently expressed doubts about a bodily resurrection), a rationalist, a skeptic, and a stoic, a precursor of Arthur Schopenhauer. But above all he is a witty and erudite man of letters, a satirist and moralist, with an incredible command of the Arabic language.

Among his other works that have been preserved is a treatise on morphology (*Risālat al-Malāʾikah*); a "prosimetrical" work, *Mulqā l-sabīl*, in which each section consists of a very short ethical paragraph in prose followed by a versification;

a collection of letters in ornate style; and commentaries on the collected poetry by famous Abbasid poets: Abū Tammām, al-Buḥturī, and al-Mutanabbī. Many other works listed in the ancient sources are no longer extant.

Al-Maʿarrī lived at the end of what has been called "the Golden Age" of Arabic literature.[22] Whether or not this qualification and this periodization are justified, he firmly belongs to the "classic" Arabic authors. But his reputation has always been mixed throughout the pre-modern period. "People have different opinions about Abū l-ʿAlāʾ," says Yāqūt, "Some say that he was a heretic (*zindīq*) . . . , others say that he was a pious ascetic who subsisted on little and who imposed on himself a harsh regimen, being content with little and turning away from worldly matters."[23] Against the many admirers there are as many detractors. One of the latter, a certain Abū Ghālib ibn Nabhān, apparently had a dream shortly after al-Maʿarrī's death:

> Last night I had a dream in which I saw a blind man with two vipers on his shoulders, dangling down to his thighs. Each of them raised its mouth toward his face, biting off the flesh and devouring it. The man was yelling and crying for help. Shocked and frightened as I was by seeing the man in this state, I asked who he was. "This is al-Maʿarrī, the heretic (*mulḥid*)," was the reply.[24]

With this fancy about the afterlife of a presumed heretic we turn to the present work, al-Maʿarrī's imaginations about life in heaven and hell, much of which is devoted to heresy. It also has several passages about snakes.

Risālat Ibn al-Qāriḥ and *Risālat al-Ghufrān*

Around the year 424/1033 Abū l-ʿAlāʾ received a long and somewhat rambling letter from a grammarian and Hadith scholar from Aleppo, called ʿAlī ibn Manṣūr ibn al-Qāriḥ, also known as Dawkhalah.[25] The elderly writer, already in his seventies, obviously tries to ingratiate himself with the famous inhabitant of al-Maʿarrah. He complains at length of his infirmities and indigence, apologizes for his foibles, and attempts to impress the addressee in the customary ornate style, employing rhymed prose (*sajʿ*) with much display of erudition and orthodoxy, in the course of which he digresses with a discussion of a number of notorious heretics.[26] One of the aims of the letter to Abū l-ʿAlāʾ, whom he praises volubly, is to exculpate himself of allegations, which he knows Abū l-ʿAlāʾ has heard about him: he had been accused of ingratitude toward a family that had patronized him, a family some of whose members had close links with al-Maʿarrī. Abū l-Ḥasan al-Maghribī (d. 400/1009–10) was a man of letters who became state secretary, serving under the Ḥamdānids in Aleppo and later under the Fāṭimids in Cairo. He made Ibn al-Qāriḥ the tutor of his children, in particular Abū l-Qāsim (d. 418/1027), who later became vizier. When the family fell into disgrace and several were executed at the orders of the notorious Fāṭimid caliph al-Ḥākim, Abū l-Qāsim was the only prominent member of his kin who escaped. Ibn al-Qāriḥ not only disassociated himself from his former patron but even composed invective poems lampooning him.[27] One might expect that in his letter to Abū l-ʿAlāʾ, Ibn al-Qāriḥ would apologize for his vicious attacks on al-Maʿarrī's friend. Instead, he goes to some length in trying to justify his views, by describing Abū l-Qāsim as a madman, and a very unpleasant one at that.

It is easy to imagine Abū l-ʿAlāʾ being not a little irritated by this rather incoherent and self-righteous appeal and the attacks on a friend. Apparently he took some time before replying, and when he did it was in the form of this strange book known as *Risālat al-Ghufrān, The Epistle of Forgiveness.* Formally it is a *risālah*, a letter, but it is longer than many a book, and like many Arabic "epistles" addressed to one person it is obviously meant to be read by many. Abū l-ʿAlāʾ does not openly refute or rebuke his correspondent; he remains as polite and respectful as Ibn al-Qāriḥ. Both epistles are brimful with pious wishes and blessings, parenthetically added whenever the other is addressed or mentioned (in the polite epistolary style of the time, the third person is used instead of direct address, to refer to the recipient). Abū l-ʿAlāʾ's work opens with sections expressing his affection for Ibn al-Qāriḥ and praise of his letter, and the second part of *al-Ghufrān* opens with a discussion of hypocrisy, of which Ibn al-Qāriḥ is said to be wholly free. The reader will not be fooled, however: it is clear that all this is ironical. The very difficult preamble of Part One (usually omitted by translators)[28] ostensibly expresses al-Maʿarrī's affection for Ibn al-Qāriḥ, but it is an exercise in double entendre, where words, said to refer to the writer's "heart," are closely linked to words for "black" and "snake." It is an odd way to open a friendly letter, and Bint al-Shāṭiʾ has suggested that al-Maʿarrī, with these snakes and the blackness, obliquely refers to what he really thinks of Ibn al-Qāriḥ's hypocrisy and malice.[29] There is a problem with this interpretation, because al-Maʿarrī is speaking of his own heart in this preamble, not that of Ibn al-Qāriḥ;[30] but in any case the ambiguous and punning diction seems to suggest that the fulsome praise is not to be taken at face value: al-Maʿarrī's epistle is steeped in sardonic irony, even though it is not always clear when he is being ironic.

When Abū l-ʿAlāʾ extols the qualities of Ibn al-Qāriḥ's letter, his irony takes a different direction. He imagines that this letter will help the writer to secure God's favor and forgiveness. Taking the theme of forgiveness as his starting point and as a leitmotiv for his text, he then embarks on a lengthy and extraordinary flight of fancy, which takes all of Part One of his *Epistle*. He imagines that on the Day of Resurrection, at the end of the world, Ibn al-Qāriḥ is revived like all mortal beings. He is admitted to Paradise, but not without difficulty. He has to cope, even at the Last Day, with what one could call the hardships of bureaucracy: one cannot be admitted without a document stating one's true repentance of sins. Unfortunately, the Sheikh (as Ibn al-Qāriḥ is often called) has lost this crucial document amidst the hustle and bustle and he must find someone to testify for him. When at last he has taken this hurdle and someone has duly attested that Ibn al-Qāriḥ showed true repentance in the nick of time, he still needs the intercession of the Prophet and the help of the latter's daughter and son. Having arrived in Paradise, after crossing the narrow Bridging Path in a rather undignified manner, riding piggyback on a helpful girl, he decides to go on an excursion. He meets with poets and grammarians—he is, after all, himself a grammarian with a great knowledge of poetry—and asks them how they have been able to attain eternal bliss. Some poets died before the coming of Islam; others composed verses of a dubious, irreligious nature, and one may wonder why they have been forgiven. The conversations are often about points of morphology, syntax, lexicography, and matters of versification, such as irregularities of meter and rhyme; in general, the Sheikh's interest is keener than that of the poets themselves, many of whom have forgotten, on account of the terrors of the Last Day, what they produced in the "Fleeting World."

The blessings and pleasures of Paradise are also described: the quality of the wine, at last permitted, and hangover-free; the food (a banquet is depicted), and the heavenly singing of beautiful damsels. Ibn al-Qāriḥ meets some ravishing girls who tell him that they were ugly but pious on earth and have been rewarded. Not all paradisial females had a worldly pre-existence: other black-eyed beauties emerge from fruits that can be plucked from a tree; Ibn al-Qāriḥ acquires his personal houri in this manner. Before settling with her he leaves for another excursion. He visits the part of Heaven reserved for the jinn or demons (for some of them are believing Muslims). There he meets the extraordinary demon called Abū Hadrash, who boasts in long poems of his devious exploits, but who has been forgiven because of his repentance. Then the Sheikh heads for the spot where there is (as the Qur'an states) a kind of peephole, through which one can look into Hell and gloat. Our Sheikh converses with poets who have been consigned to Hell for various reasons; he pesters them with queries about their poetry, but mostly meets with a less than enthusiastic response. He also talks to the Devil, who in turn asks him some perplexing questions about Paradise. On his way back the Sheikh visits yet another region: the relatively dusky and lowly Paradise of the *rajaz* poets, *rajaz* being an old and rather simple meter that is deemed inferior. Finally he rests, seated on a couch, carried by damsels and immortal youths, surrounded by fruit trees, the fruits of which move toward his mouth of their own accord.

This concludes Part One of the *Epistle of Forgiveness*. The author admits that he has been rather prolix and says, "Now we shall turn to a reply to the letter." This he does in Part Two, which is a point-by-point discussion of Ibn al-Qāriḥ's epistle. The bulk of this part is devoted to the various heretics and schismatics mentioned by Ibn al-Qāriḥ, after which al-Maʿarrī turns to the Sheikh's "repentance" and other matters. He concludes by apologizing for the delay in replying. This second part will appear in a second volume in the Library of Arabic Literature. The first part can be read on its own; indeed, most existing translations do not even contain the second part.

Yet the two parts hang together. Al-Maʿarrī's irony is present on a deeper level. There are strong indications[31] that the true purpose of his *Epistle* is to enjoin Ibn al-Qāriḥ to repent of his insolent and ungrateful behavior toward a former patron, of his self-confessed self-indulging in the past, of his hypocrisy in his own *Epistle*, of his sometimes tactless and self-righteous condemnation of poets and heretics, and of being generally obsessed with himself. The fictional Ibn al-Qāriḥ, in *al-Ghufrān*, only acquires forgiveness and reaches Paradise with much difficulty; it turns out that he only truly repented of his sins at the last moment: it may still happen in reality, implies al-Maʿarrī, if God wills. He also implies, therefore, that in his view Ibn al-Qāriḥ's own letter does not amount to true repentance. He mocks Ibn al-Qāriḥ's obsession with himself and his own profession (grammar and poetry) by imagining him in Paradise as being interested only in poets and philologists; even when he meets others, such as Adam, Abū Hadrash the jinn, or the devil, the conversation is mostly about poetry. Part One is therefore an elaborate and extremely lengthy introduction to the proper reply to the original letter. In Part Two several points reappear, such as the importance of true repentance. The fictional Ibn al-Qāriḥ had seen the poet

Bashshār in Hell, but al-Maʿarrī says in Part Two that he will not categorically say that Bashshār's destination will be Hell; God is merciful and kind.

While *Risālat al-Ghufrān* did not receive as much attention from pre-modern authors as his *al-Fuṣūl wa-l-ghāyāt* or the poems of *Luzūm mā lā yalzam*, it met with some mixed criticism. A note by al-Dhahabī (d. 748/1348) encapsulates it all: "It contains Mazdakism (*mazdakah*) and irreverence (*istikhfāf*); there is much erudition (*adab*) in it."[32] Ibn al-Qāriḥ's imagined experiences in Heaven (with glimpses of Hell) as told by al-Maʿarrī form an interesting kind of fiction. Overt fiction was often frowned upon in pre-modern Arab literary culture; hence, for instance, the condemnation of fairytales and fantastic stories such as are found in *The Thousand and One Nights*. But al-Maʿarrī did not pretend that his fantasies about his correspondent actually happened: the events are set in the future and the Arabic present tense (which can refer to the future, for events that will or merely might happen) is used consistently, rather than the perfect tense normally employed in narrative texts. If he cannot be accused of writing fictions or lies, one might think that his apparently irreverent descriptions of Paradise border on the blasphemous. There can, in fact, be no doubt that he is mocking popular and pious beliefs about the hereafter; after all, he himself frequently questioned the reality of bodily resurrection, one of the central dogmas of orthodox Islam. Yet he does not introduce anything in his descriptions of Paradise and Hell that has not been, or could not be, imagined or written by pious Muslims. As is well known, Qur'anic descriptions of the Last Day and the Last Things (Heaven and Hell) are vivid and full of concrete images; popular pious literature greatly expanded and elaborated the Qur'anic images, turning Paradise into a Land of Cockayne, where birds fly around asking to be consumed, not unlike the peacock and the goose in the *Epistle of Forgiveness* that are instantly marinated or roasted as desired, and are then revived again. The Qur'an (56:20–21), after all, promises the believers "whatever fruit they choose and whatever fowl they desire."

Eschatological tourism is known from several literatures, notably through Dante's *Divine Comedy*. That the latter was inspired partly by al-Maʿarrī was a hypothesis put forward by several scholars, notably Miguel Asín Palacios, and eagerly embraced, naturally, by some Arab scholars such as Kāmil Kaylānī, whose abridged edition of *Risālat al-Ghufrān* also contains a summary of Dante in Arabic, and who provides Part One of *al-Ghufrān* with the subtitle *Kūmīdiyā ilāhiyyah masraḥuhā l-jannah wa-l-nār*, "A Divine Comedy, Staged in Paradise and Hell."[33] One Arab writer even argued that Dante, having stolen al-Maʿarrī's ideas, produced a greatly inferior work, in which he should have made al-Maʿarrī his guide rather than Virgil.[34] The hypothesis that Dante was influenced by al-Maʿarrī has now been largely abandoned; if there is an Islamic root to Dante's *Commedia*, it is more likely to have been inspired by popular ideas about the Prophet's celebrated short excursion, his ascension to heaven (*al-miʿrāj*) after his "nocturnal journey" to Jerusalem (*al-isrāʾ*); a European translation of the anonymous *Kitāb al-Miʿrāj* (of which Latin, French, and Castilian versions were popular) was probably known to Dante. It has also been suggested that Dante may have been inspired by a Hebrew version of a work by Avicenna, *Ḥayy ibn Yaqẓān*, describing an imaginative "cosmic" journey.[35]

Nicholson rightly remarks[36] that while the *Risālat al-Ghufrān* "faintly" resembles the Sixth Book of Virgil's *Aeneid*, where Aeneas visits the Underworld, the *Divine Comedy*, or the Zoroastrian, Middle Persian *Book of Ardā Vīrāf*, a more significant parallel can be found in Lucian (d. ca. AD 180), who like al-Maʿarrī was a Syrian, though Greek-educated. In his ironically entitled *True Histories* (or *True Fictions*) Lucian describes his fantastic journeys on earth and even to the moon. He visits a Blessed Isle, the delights of which are depicted in some detail; there he meets not only ancient worthies such as heroes of the Trojan War but also Homer, whom he questions about his poetry.[37] All this is written in a lively and very irreverent style, altogether akin to that of al-Maʿarrī, who shared Lucian's rationalism, skepticism, and pessimism. It must not be supposed, however, that al-Maʿarrī knew Lucian's work, for he was not translated into Arabic and al-Maʿarrī did not know Greek. But Lucian was popular with the Byzantines: his works were much copied, annotated, imitated, and taught in schools[38] and one could imagine that some of Lucian's themes reached al-Maʿarrī orally. One also notes that the motif of the tree woman, exploited in *The Epistle of Forgiveness*, admittedly known in Arabic popular lore,[39] is also found in Lucian's *True Histories*.[40]

It has been suggested[41] that *Risālat al-Ghufrān* was inspired by *Risālat al-Tawābiʿ wa-l-zawābiʿ* by the Andalusian Arab poet and prose-writer Ibn Shuhayd (d. 426/1035), who composed it only a few years before al-Maʿarrī wrote his work. In this short, incompletely preserved work, translated by James T. Monroe as *The Treatise of Familiar Spirits and Demons*,[42] the author takes as his starting point the ancient Arab idea that a poet is inspired by a demon or genius, an idea that survived in Islamic times even though many would not take it more seriously than European poets would literally believe in the existence of the Muses or a personal muse. Ibn Shuhayd describes his imagined conversations with the demons of some famous poets: the pre-Islamic Imruʾ al-Qays, Ṭarafah, and Qays ibn al-Khaṭīm, and the Abbasid poets Abū Nuwās and Abū Tammām; he boldly expands the idea by assigning similar demons to prose writers such as ʿAbd al-Ḥamīd ibn Yaḥyā, Badīʿ al-Zamān al-Hamadhānī, and al-Jāḥiẓ (who no doubt would have been surprised by the fancy), and by describing some animal genii: a mule and a goose. It is not impossible that al-Maʿarrī (who in fact composed a short epistle on the same topic)[43] was aware of this work, but one would underestimate his powers of invention if one assumed he was unable to compose his *Epistle* without such inspiration.

The *Epistle of Forgiveness* builds to some extent on his own *Risālat al-Malāʾikah* (*The Epistle of the Angels*), mentioned above as a work on morphology. In this work, composed probably a few years before the *Epistle of Forgiveness*, al-Maʿarrī imagines that he himself discusses oddities of the Arabic lexicon with angels in the afterlife. He surprises the angels with his analysis of the word for "angel" (*malak*, pl. *malāʾikah*),[44] and he discusses other words with them. He argues that those who end up in heaven enjoying the *ḥūr* (black-and-white-eyed damsels) and other delights such as the *sundus* and *istabraq* ("silk and brocade") should at least be aware of the morphology and etymology of these words.[45] The imagined conversations are at times very similar to those in *al-Ghufrān*, for instance when al-Maʿarrī quotes poets and grammarians to prove a point, whereupon an angel exclaims, "Who is this Ibn Abī Rabīʿah, what's this Abū ʿUbaydah, what's all this nonsense? If you have done any pious deeds you will be happy; if not, get out of here!"[46] There is clearly some self-mockery here.

Similarly, although al-Maʿarrī is clearly mocking Ibn al-Qāriḥ in *al-Ghufrān*, one suspects that many of the philological concerns of the latter were also his own. Ibn al-Qāriḥ's fictional persona often uses obscure and rare words, which he immediately explains in plainer language; it looks as if he is being mocked for his pedantry. However, al-Maʿarrī does the same when he writes in his own voice; he appears to flaunt his extraordinary knowledge of the Arabic lexicon. A passage in Part Two hints at another, practical reason why he added his glosses: our blind author fears that his dictations, with their recondite diction, may be misunderstood or garbled by his scribes.[47] Likewise, one assumes that some of the criticism voiced by Ibn al-Qāriḥ on points of grammar and versification is shared by al-Maʿarrī. A similar preoccupation with philology is found in other works by him, such as *The Epistle of the Neigher and the Brayer*. It is clear that for al-Maʿarrī and, as he imagines, for Ibn al-Qāriḥ the expected delights of Paradise are not primarily sensual but intellectual. The various delights provided by pretty girls, music, food, and drink are generally described in a somewhat ironical vein and the comparisons of heavenly substances with earthly equivalents are couched in ludicrously hyperbolic expressions; but the pleasures of poetry and philological pedantry are taken, on the whole, rather more seriously, even though here, too, a modicum of mockery is not altogether absent.

It is not surprising that in almost all translations of *The Epistle of Forgiveness* such passages about grammar, lexicon, and prosody have been drastically curtailed or omitted altogether, for a combination of reasons: they will not greatly interest those who do not know Arabic, they will seem an annoying interruption of the narrative to those who read the text for the story, and not least because they are rather difficult to translate and in need of copious annotation. When Bint al-Shāṭiʾ published her adaptation of Part One of the *Epistle of Forgiveness* for the stage, as a play in three acts,[48] she naturally excised much of the philology, even though she lets the actors discuss some matters regarding grammatical case endings and poetic meters on the stage. It is not known if the play has ever been performed and one cannot but have some doubts about its viability.[49]

Al-Maʿarrī's rationalist critique of religion has influenced and inspired neoclassicist and modernist Arabic writers and poets, such as the Iraqi poets Jamīl Ṣidqī l-Zahāwī (1863–1936) and Maʿrūf al-Ruṣāfī (1875–1945). The former wrote a verse epic, *Thawrah fī l-jaḥīm* (*Revolution in Hell*, 1931) in which he offers an interesting and subversive interpretation of the *Epistle of Forgiveness*, involving many well-known figures from Western and Arab history and culture. Heaven is the place for the establishment, Hell for the maladjusted and the socially ambitious, who are punished for their courage. Finally, supported by the angels of Hell, they storm Heaven, claiming it as their rightful place since it is they who have advanced mankind.[50] *Ḥadīth ʿĪsā ibn Hishām* (*The Story of ʿĪsā ibn Hishām*), a well-known work of fiction first published serially between 1898 and 1902 by the Egyptian author Muḥammad al-Muwayliḥī (1858?–1930), is often linked with the *Maqāmāt* of Badīʿ al-Zamān al-Hamadhānī (d. 398/1008) but it has several things in common with *Risālat al-Ghufrān*: a protagonist who is resurrected from the dead before an imaginary journey, implicit and explicit criticism of contemporary beliefs and customs, and a style in which rhymed prose alternates with ordinary prose.

The varied fate of the text, with its incomplete, truncated translations and its transformation into a play, clearly shows how difficult it is to classify it, to those who love neat classifications. Although called a *risālah* and addressed to one person, it is not an ordinary letter, nor is it intended to be read only by the addressee. While containing a narrative complete with a lengthy flashback it is not a normal story, *qiṣṣah, ḥadīth, khabar*, or *ḥikāyah*. It incorporates much of what normally belongs to the genre of philological "dictations," *amālī*. It contains, in al-Dhahabī's words quoted above, "much *adab*," which here has all its meanings of erudition, literary quotations including much poetry, moral edification, and entertaining anecdotes. Searchers for the "organic unity" of this heterogeneous literary work will have an arduous task. One could argue that part of its originality and its attractiveness lies precisely in the impossibility of pigeonholing it; but not every reader, critic, or publisher will be charmed by this.

A Note on the Text

Language, Style, and Translation

The present translators originally harbored some doubts about translating the text in full. However, it is the admirable purpose of the Library of Arabic Literature to present complete texts, in the original Arabic and in an English translation. We consented and took on the task as a daunting but stimulating challenge. The present translation, for the first time in any language, is complete, for the sake of the integrity of the text and in order not to distort its actual character, which reflects the author's character, as far as we can know it. Abū l-ʿAlāʾ is not first-and-foremost a storyteller: he is a satirist, a moralist, and a philologist who, in his physical blindness and linguistic insight, lives in a universe of language to such an extent that one could even say that, in addition to the two or three "prisons" mentioned above, he also lived in the admittedly very spacious prison of the Arabic language. It was a prison in which he felt at home like no other. The reader should be warned that *The Epistle of Forgiveness* is not exactly an easy read; but the philological passages can be skipped by impatient readers.

Telling a story could be done in a simple, unadorned style. The stories in *al-Faraj baʿd al-Shiddah* (*Relief after Distress*) by al-Muḥassin al-Tanūkhī (d. 384/994), for instance, are written in a relatively plain Arabic, and so are innumerable anecdotes and stories in various collections and anthologies. However, the aim of epistolary prose, in al-Maʿarrī's time, was not always primarily to express one's meaning clearly: that would be paramount to an insult, as if the recipient could only understand plain speech. One ought to employ a flowery style, rich in metaphors, allusions, syntactical and semantic parallelism, recondite vocabulary, and above all *sajʿ* or rhymed prose, usually in the form of paired rhyme (*aabbccdd*...). Such an ornate style is found especially in preambles of letters and books, and in descriptive, "purple" passages, or on any occasion where the author wishes to display his erudition and stylistic prowess. Already in al-Maʿarrī's lifetime interesting experiments had been done to introduce *sajʿ* into narrative prose texts continuously rather than on specific occasions, Badīʿ

al-Zamān al-Hamadhānī (d. 398/1008) being a pioneer in this field, as the "inventor" of the *maqāmah* genre.

Al-Maʿarrī, in Part One of his *Epistle*, does not use *sajʿ* throughout but only at certain points. Since it is such a characteristic and striking element of classical Arabic prose, it has been imitated in the translation, at the risk of sounding somewhat quaint.[51] The same has not been done, except very occasionally, in the translation of Ibn al-Qāriḥ's epistle; likewise, the frequency of *sajʿ* in Part Two of *Risālat al-Ghufrān* will make it impossible to imitate it in English. The reader should be aware that many a strange expression could have been caused by an Arabic rhyme; as Nicholson says, perhaps too harshly, "Abū'l-ʿAlā seldom escapes from his artificial prose with its forced metaphors and tyrannous rhymes."[52] Often, especially in Part Two, he is not content with ordinary rhyme but employs the "rich rhyme" that also marks the poems in his *Luzūmiyyāt*. Where al-Maʿarrī uses an obscure word, the translation also uses an unusual English word, if possible. Fidelity to the text therefore overrides readability at times. The translators have stayed as close as possible to the Arabic text and have never resorted, unlike predecessors such as Brackenbury, Meïssa, and Monteil, to summary, large-scale paraphrase, and blatant glossing over difficulties by simple omission (Brackenbury and Meïssa cannot be blamed for this, since they relied on Kaylānī's edition, which leaves out everything that is difficult or obscure). Some concessions to English style and usage had to be made, of course. Thus we have not hesitated to make pronouns (the ubiquitous and often confusing "he," "him," and "his" of Arabic narrative) explicit in order to make it clear who or what is meant, wherever this seemed desirable. Very often, when al-Maʿarrī refers to Ibn al-Qāriḥ, we have rendered "he" as "the Sheikh." Al-Maʿarrī's language is difficult and not all problems have been solved. Arab editors and commentators can ignore them, or pretend they do not find them problematical rather than confess their ignorance (we suspect this is often the case); a translator cannot hide in the same manner. In the notes we have discussed some of our difficulties and doubts or professed our inability to understand the text.

Many such problems are found in the poetry quoted in the text. Both epistles contain much of it, most of it by other poets, although the poems recited by the demon Abū Hadrash in *Risālat al-Ghufrān* are obviously by al-Maʿarrī himself. Classical Arabic poetry always rhymes (normally with "monorhyme": *aaaaaa*...), but our translations, with very few exceptions, do not use rhyme, which would normally be incompatible with accuracy; instead of the Arabic quantitative meters (not unlike those of ancient Greek, Latin, or Sanskrit) a loose English meter (e.g., iambic) has generally been chosen. In view of the difficulties of many verses and the fact that they do not contribute to the bare narrative, it is not surprising that all earlier translators drastically cut the verse. Needless to say, in the present translation nothing has been cut.

The two translators have collaborated closely. The English text of the translation, annotation, and introduction, was made by van Gelder, who was helped, in varying degrees, by predecessors such as Nicholson, Brackenbury, Meïssa, Dechico, and Monteil,[53] by Bint al-Shāṭiʾ's excellent annotation, by Schoeler's published, partial, German translation, and by his unpublished rough draft of the complete German translation of Part One. Van Gelder's drafts were thoroughly revised by Schoeler and difficulties were discussed in frequent and fruitful email exchanges. The final English version was polished by two native speakers, Sheila Ottway and especially James Montgomery, our project editor at LAL. Translations from the Qur'an are by van Gelder; they are marked by angle brackets (French quotation marks) to distinguish them from other quotations, just as in Arabic they are customarily given in special decorative "bow brackets." English and Arabic titles of the various chapters have been added.

After the completion of Part One, the translators were made aware of a new translation into Italian of Part One, by Martino Diez, who kindly sent a copy. Unlike its predecessors, it is virtually complete and includes the various digressions on grammar, lexicon, and prosody; it is provided with informative notes. We could make only limited use of this excellent translation.

A Note on the Edition

Reynold A. Nicholson may have been the pioneer in studying *The Epistle of Forgiveness* and making scholars acquainted with it, but the towering figure in the field is without question the Egyptian scholar ʿĀʾishah ʿAbd al-Raḥmān (1913–98), who named herself Bint al-Shāṭiʾ ("Daughter of the Riverbank"[54]), and whose doctoral dissertation at the University of Cairo in 1950 became the basis for the first scholarly edition of the epistles by al-Maʿarrī and Ibn al-Qāriḥ. Her richly annotated edition, a monument of scholarship, appeared in 1954 (Cairo: Dār al-Maʿārif) and was republished several times with minor revisions. For the present bilingual edition it was decided not to duplicate her efforts, but to rely for the most part on her edition. The ninth edition that appeared in Cairo in 1993 forms the basis of the Arabic text offered here; we have also used some of her earlier editions, notably the third (Cairo, 1963) and fourth (Cairo, n.d.), because even though the later edition corrects some mistakes and inaccuracies, some new typographical errors have crept in occasionally. Furthermore, we have consulted other printed editions, all of them uncritical. Nicholson's articles contain only selected parts of the Arabic text. The oldest of these printed texts is that by Ibrāhīm al-Yāzijī (Cairo: al-Maṭbaʿah al-Hindiyyah, 1903); rather fully voweled, the edition is devoid of annotation and does not contain Ibn al-Qāriḥ's letter. Kāmil Kaylānī, in an undated volume published in Cairo (Dār al-Maʿārif) in 1943, entitled *Risālat al-Ghufrān li-l-shāʿir al-faylasūf Abī l-ʿAlāʾ al-Maʿarrī* (*The Epistle of Forgiveness by the poet-philosopher Abū l-ʿAlāʾ al-Maʿarrī*), offered a shortened version of the epistles of Ibn al-Qāriḥ and al-Maʿarrī, stripped of most of the difficult passages, together with much relevant and sometimes irrelevant annotation and a selection of other epistles by al-Maʿarrī. Later editions, all uncritical, are obviously (but only rarely explicitly) dependent on Bint al-Shāṭiʾ: the lightly annotated one of Mufīd Qumayḥah (Beirut: Dār Maktabat al-Hilāl, 1406/1986, no indexes) and the more fully (but often erroneously) annotated one by Muḥammad al-Iskandarānī and Inʿām Fawwāl (Beirut: Dār al-Kātib al-ʿArabī, 2011/1432, provided with indexes).

In her critical edition of the two epistles Bint al-Shāṭiʾ explains that for Ibn al-Qāriḥ's *Epistle* she relied on two manuscripts from the Taymūriyyah collection in the National Library (Dār al-Kutub) in Cairo and one printed edition, the one incorporated by Muḥammad Kurd ʿAlī in his collection *Rasāʾil al-bulaghāʾ*.[55] The older, undated manuscript was apparently the basis for both the later one (copied in 1327/1909) and the edition in *Rasāʾil al-bulaghāʾ*, and Bint al-Shāṭiʾ took it as the basis for her own edition. We have also benefited from the only other critical edition of Ibn al-Qāriḥ's epistle, part of the unpublished doctoral dissertation by Michel Dechico, which also contains a study and a translation.[56]

For her edition of *Risālat al-Ghufrān*, Bint al-Shāṭiʾ used seven manuscripts, as well as Nicholson's publication and earlier printed editions. The most important manuscript, preserved in Istanbul, seems to date from the seventh/thirteenth century; its copyist remarks that he collated the text with a manuscript corrected by Abū Zakariyyā l-Tibrīzī, mentioned above as a pupil and great admirer of al-Maʿarrī, and an important scholar himself. The other manuscripts used by Bint al-Shāṭiʾ are obviously of less importance, being later, sometimes incomplete, and offering a less reliable text.

Bint al-Shāṭiʾ provides two kinds of footnotes. One supplies textual commentary, including meticulous, detailed information about variant readings in the manuscripts and parallel texts, occasional emendations, and glosses that explain difficult words. At times she cites Nicholson's readings and interpretations, often with gratuitously scathing remarks when he was wrong. The other set of footnotes gives basic information on persons and places mentioned in the text. Even though her editorial practice has been criticized,[57] altogether her notes display stupendous learning and she is almost always right. In our own annotation we have relied much on her notes, but we have not slavishly followed her and it would have been impossible simply to translate her annotation. The textual notes to the present Arabic edition only provide the main variants and those instances where we decided to deviate from Bint al-Shāṭiʾ's text; variants that are obviously scribal errors have been ignored. For detailed information about manuscript variants the reader is referred to Bint al-Shāṭiʾ's edition. Where needed, explanations and justifications of our choices are found in the annotation to the English translation.

The original guidelines of the Library of Arabic Literature recommend that annotation be kept to a minimum. We are grateful to the editors for approving the increased volume of annotations included in the present work. Because of the difficulty of the present text and the plethora of names and allusions it contains, a great deal more explanation was considered essential; there would have been yet more if we had done full justice to the text. Instead, we have limited the annotation to a minimum. A full list of the names of individuals, places, tribes and dynasties which occur in the text is given in the Glossary of Names and Terms.

الرموز

إف	محمد الإسكندراني وإنعام فوّال (٢٠١١)
ب	بنت الشاطئ ط. ٩ (١٩٩٣)
٤	بنت الشاطئ ط. ٤ (دون تاريخ)
د	Michel Dechico (1980)
ك	كامل كيلاني (١٩٤٣)
كع	محمد كرد علي (١٩٥٤)
ن	R. A. Nicholson (1900–2)
ق	مفيد قميحة (١٩٨٦)
ي	إبراهيم اليازجي (١٩٠٣)

Notes to the Introduction

1 Ibn Khallikān, *Wafayāt*, i, 113–16; the same in al-Ṣafadī, *al-Wāfī*, iv, 94–111.

2 Yāqūt, *Muʿjam al-udabāʾ*, iii, 107–217; see p. 161.

3 Yāqūt, *Muʿjam al-udabāʾ*, xv, 83.

4 Nicholson, "Persian Manuscripts."

5 Nicholson, "The Risālatu 'l-Ghufrān by Abū 'l-ʿAlāʾ al-Maʿarrī," *Journal of the Royal Asiatic Society* (1900): 637–720; (1902): 75–101, 337–62, 813–47.

6 Al-Thaʿālibī, *Tatimmat al-Yatīmah*, p. 16; also in Yāqūt, *Muʿjam al-udabāʾ*, iii, 129–30; Ibn al-ʿAdīm, *Bughyat al-ṭalab*, p. 897; al-Ṣafadī, *al-Wāfī bi-l-Wafayāt*, vii, 96. Ibn al-ʿAdīm, always keen to defend al-Maʿarrī, doubts that he ever played games or even jested. Al-Maʿarrī's jesting cannot be denied but it is admittedly always of a serious kind.

7 Following Arabic usage, in this introduction he will be called either al-Maʿarrī or Abū l-ʿAlāʾ, for the sake of variety.

8 The Arabic term is *kunyah* (incorrectly translated as "patronymic" in the *Encyclopaedia of Islam*, New [= Second] Edition, v, 395).

9 Ibn al-ʿAdīm, *Bughyat al-ṭalab*, pp. 896–97.

10 An allusion to making fire by means of the friction between two pieces of wood, one hard and one soft.

11 The collection is often called *al-Luzūmiyyāt*.

12 For a good selection, with English translations, see Nicholson, "The Meditations of Maʿarrī."

13 Abū l-ʿAlāʾ al-Maʿarrī, *Zajr al-nābiḥ: Muqtaṭafāt*.

14 Al-Maʿarrī, *Luzūm mā lā yalzam*, i, 188 (rhyme *-īthī*): "I see myself in my three prisons | (so do not ask me about my secret story) || Because of my loss of sight, being homebound | and my soul's residing in an evil body."

15 See, e.g., Ibn Khallikān, *Wafayāt*, i, 115.

16 Al-Qifṭī, *Inbāh al-ruwah*, i, 85.

17 Yāqūt, *Muʿjam al-udabāʾ*, iii, 176–213; see Margoliouth, "Abū 'l-ʿAlāʾ al-Maʿarrī's Correspondence on Vegetarianism."

18 e.g., Yāqūt, *Muʿjam al-udabāʾ*, iii, 125.

19 Yāqūt, *Muʿjam al-udabāʾ*, iii, 126; Ibn al-ʿAdīm, *Bughyat al-ṭalab*, p. 910 mentions "seventy poets from al-Maʿarrah."

20 On speaking animals, see Wagner, "Sprechende Tiere in der arabischen Prosa."

21 There are several versions of this anecdote, see, e.g., Ibn al-ʿAdīm, *Bughyat al-ṭalab*, pp. 879–80.

22 Gibb, *Arabic Literature: An Introduction*, whose "Silver Age" begins two years before al-Maʿarrī's death, with the Seljuqs entering Baghdad.

23 Yāqūt, *Muʿjam al-udabāʾ*, iii, 142; cf. e.g. Ibn al-ʿAdīm, *Bughyat al-ṭalab*, p. 865.

24 Ibn al-ʿAdīm, *Bughyat al-ṭalab*, p. 909, al-ʿAbbāsī, *Maʿāhid al-tanṣīṣ*, i, 52. The two snakes growing on the shoulders are reminiscent of al-Ḍaḥḥāk/Zahhāk/Zuhāk, the evil Arabian king of Iranian lore; see, e.g., E. Yarshater, "Zuhāk." Ibn al-ʿAdīm gives the dream an interpretation that is favorable to al-Maʿarrī: the snakes are the false accusations of heresy and unbelief; the dream describes the sheikh's life, not his afterlife.

25 *Dawkhalah* or *dawkhallah* means "date basket made of palm leaves."

26 On Ibn al-Qāriḥ see Yāqūt, *Muʿjam al-udabāʾ*, xv, 83–88; shortened in al-Ṣafadī, *Wāfī*, xxii, 233–35; al-Suyūṭī, *Bughyat al-wuʿāh*, ii, 207. It is said that he died after 421/1030 (al-Ṣafadī, xxii, 234; Yāqūt, implausibly, has "after 461/1068").

27 For a fragment of four verses, see Yāqūt, *Muʿjam al-udabāʾ*, xv, 84.

28 For a German translation and study, see Schoeler, "Abū l-Alāʾ al-Maʿarrīs Prolog zum *Sendschreiben über die Vergebung*."

29 ʿĀʾishah ʿAbd al-Raḥmān "Bint al-Shāṭiʾ," *Qirāʾah jadīdah fī Risālat al-Ghufrān*, pp. 52–54; *eadem*, "Abū ʾl-ʿAlāʾ al-Maʿarrī," p. 337.

30 Schoeler, "Abū l-Alāʾ al-Maʿarrīs Prolog," p. 421.

31 Schoeler, "Die Vision, der auf einer Hypothese gründet: Zur Deutung von Abū ʾl-ʿAlāʾ al-Maʿarrīs *Risālat al-Ġufrān*."

32 Al-Dhahabī, *Tārīkh al-Islām: Ḥawādith wa-wafayāt 441–50, 451–60*, pp. 199–200; the Arabic words are *mazdakah*, *istikhfāf*, and *adab*. The term *mazdakah*, instead of the normal *mazdakiyyah*, is unusual but found elsewhere, e.g., al-Ṣafadī, *Wāfī*, xv, p. 426. Since Mazdak is not mentioned in *Risālat al-Ghufrān*, Nicholson suggests (*Journal of the Royal Asiatic Society*, 1900, p. 637) that *mazdakah* could be a corruption of the common word *zandaqah*, which has a related meaning. The former is derived from Mazdak, who was the leader of a pre-Islamic revolutionary religious movement in Sassanid Iran in the early sixth century AD, while *zandaqah* is derived from *zindīq*, "heretic," often implying Manichaeism.

33 He is followed by Brackenbury in his English translation, which is based on Kaylānī's edition.

34 Qusṭākī l-Ḥimṣī, in articles published in *Majallat Maʿhad al-Lughah al-ʿArabiyyah* (Damascus), 7 (1927) and 8 (1928); see Hassan Osman, "Dante in Arabic."

35 See Strohmaier, "Chaj ben Mekitz – die unbekannte Quelle der Divina Commedia."

36 "The Risālatu'l-Ghufrān," p. 76.

37 *True Histories*, in Lucian (trans. Keith Sidwell), *Chattering Courtesans*, pp. 308–46; see esp. pp. 330–39.

38 Introduction to Lucian, *Chattering Courtesans*, p. xx.

39 See e.g. Tibbets and Toorawa, section "The tree" in the entry "Wāḳwāḳ," *EI2*, xi (2002), pp. 107–8.

40 Lucian, *Chattering Courtesans*, p. 312.

41 See e.g. J.M. Continente Ferrer, "Consideraciones en torno a las relaciones entre la *Risālat al-Tawābiʿ wa-l-Zawābiʿ* de ibn Šuhayd y la *Risālat al-Gufrān de al-Maʿarrī*," in *Actas de las jornadas de cultura árabe e islámica*, 1978, (Madrid, 1981), pp. 124–34; ʿAbd al-Salām al-Harrās, "*Risālat al-Tawābiʿ wa-l-zawābiʿ* wa-ʿalāqatuhā li-*Risālat al-Ghufrān*," *al-Manāhil*, 9:25 (1982): 211–20.

42 Ibn Shuhayd, *The Treatise of Familiar Spirits and Demons*.

43 *Risālat al-shayāṭīn*, published in Kāmil Kaylānī's edition of *Risālat al-Ghufrān*, pp. 475–506 (only the beginning of the epistle deals with the demons of poets).

44 Al-Maʿarrī, *Risālat al-Malāʾikah*, pp. 5–8.

45 Al-Maʿarrī, *Risālat al-Malāʾikah*, pp. 26–28, 36–38; for *sundus* and *istabraq* see Q Kahf 18:31 and Dukhān 44:53.

46 Al-Maʿarrī, *Risālat al-Malāʾikah*, p. 8.

47 *Risālat al-Ghufrān*, p. 382.

48 *Qirāʾah jadīdah fī Risālat al-Ghufrān* (*A New Reading of The Epistle of Forgiveness*), subtitled *Naṣṣ masraḥī min al-qarn al-khāmis al-hijrī* ("A Dramatic Text of the Fifth Century of the Hijra"), see pp. 65–186; cf. "Moreh", *Live Theatre and Dramatic Literature in the Medieval Arabic World*, pp. 112–13.

49 There is no drama in the classical Arabic "high" literary tradition; the texts employed in popular slapstick acting were almost never written down.

50 See Wiebke Walther's review of Schoeler's translation of *Risālat al-Ghufrān* in *Zeitschrift der Deutschen Morgenländischen Gesellschaft*, 157 (2007): 225–28, her article "Camīl Ṣidqī az-Zahāwī," her entry "az-Zahāwī, Ǧamīl Sidqī" in *Kindlers Neues Literatur Lexikon*, Bd. 22 (Suppl.) 1998, p. 741, and the German translation by G. Widmer in *Welt des Islams*, 17 (1935): 1–79.

51 Recent examples of prose rhyme in English translations from the Arabic may be found in Paul M. Cobb's translation (2008) of *al-Iʿtibār*, the memoirs of Usāmah ibn Munqidh (d. 584/1188), as *The Book of Contemplation*, and in Humphrey Davies' translation

(2007) of a seventeenth-century work, *Yūsuf al-Shirbīnī's Brains Confounded by the Ode of Abū Shādūf Expounded.*

52 *Journal of the Royal Asiatic Society*, 1902, p. 75.

53 Monteil's "translation" is full of wild guesses that are often wrong and without any solid basis in the Arabic text, even though they seem to produce a plausible sense.

54 She grew up in Dimyāṭ (Damietta).

55 Fourth ed. Cairo, 1954 (first ed. Cairo, 1908); for the *Risālah* see pp. 254–79.

56 "La Risāla d'Ibn al-Qāriḥ: traduction et étude lexicographique," Thèse pour le Doctorat de 3e Cycle, Paris: Université de Paris III, Sorbonne Nouvelle, 1980.

57 See Hellmut Ritter's review in *Oriens*, 6 (1953): 189–91.

رسالة ابن القارح

The Epistle of Ibn al-Qāriḥ

بسم الله الرحمن الرحيم

استفتاحاً باسمه، واستنجاحاً ببركته. والحمدُ لله المبتدي بالنعم، المنفرد بالقِدَم، الذي جلّ عن شَبَه المخلوقين، وصِفات المحدَثين، وليّ الحَسَنات، المُبَرّأ من السيّئات، العادل في أفعاله، الصادقِ في أقواله، خالق الخلق ومُبديه، ومُبقيه ما شاء ومُفنيه. وصلواتُه على محمد وأبرار عِترته وأهليه، صلاةً ترضيه، وتقرّبه وتُدنيه، وتُزلفُه وتحظيه: ١،١

كتابي – أطال الله بقاء مولاي الشيخ الجليل، ومَدّ[١] مُدّته، وأدام كفايته وسعادته، وجعلني فداءه، وقدّمني قِبَلَه[٢] على الصحة والحقيقة، وبعد القصد والعقيدة، وليس على مجاز اللفظ ومجرى الكتابة، ولا على تنقُّص وخِلابة، وتحبُّبٍ ومسامحة، ولا كما قال بعضُهم وقد عاد صديقاً له: كيف تجدك جعلني الله فداك، وهو يقصد تحبُّباً، ويريد تملُّقاً، ويظنّ أنه قد أسدى جميلاً يشكره صاحبه إن نهض واستقلّ، ويكافئه عليه إن أفاق وأبلّ، عن سلامة تمامُها بحضور حضرته، وعافية نظامُها بالتشرّف بشريف عِزّته، وميمون نقيبته وطلعته. ١،٢

ويعلم الله الكريم – تقدّست أسماؤه – أنّي لو حننتُ إليه – أدام الله تأييده – حنينَ الواله إلى بكرها، أو ذات الفرخ إلى وكْرها، أو الحمامة إلى إلفها، أو الغزالة إلى خِشْفها، لكان ذلك مما تُغيّره الليالي والأيام، والعصور والأعوام، لكنّه حنين الظمآن إلى الماء، والخائفِ إلى الأَمن، والسليم إلى السلامة، والغريقِ إلى النجاة، والقَلِقِ إلى السكون، بل حنين نفسه النفيسة إلى الحمد والمجد، فإنّي رأيتُ نِزاعَها إليهما نِزاعَ الاستُقُصّاتِ إلى عناصرها، والأركانِ إلى جواهرها. فإن وهَبَ الله لي مَلاءً من

١ ب: (ومُدّ). ٢ ب: (قبْلَه).

In the name of God, the Merciful, the Compassionate

We commence in His name, seeking success through His benediction. Praise be to God, the originator of blessings, Who is alone in being pre-eternal; Who is exalted above any likeness to His creatures and above the attributes of those who have been brought into being; Who bestows benefactions but is not responsible for malefactions; Who is just in His acts and truthful in His words; the Creator and Originator of creation, who makes it last and annihilates it as He wills. His blessings be on Muḥammad and his pious family and relations, with a blessing that may gratify him, bring him nearer and closer to Him, and give him favor and good graces with Him. 1.1

Ibn al-Qāriḥ's hopes for a meeting with al-Ma'arrī[1]

I am writing—may God lengthen the life of my lord the venerable Sheikh and prolong his time; may He give him lasting protection and happiness; may He make me his ransom and may He present me before him[2] in truth and in reality, having been moved by good intention and firm belief, not only by way of speech and writing, without disrespect or guile, without the affectation of affection or complaisance; not as somebody said when visiting a sick friend of his: "How are you? May God make me your ransom!," merely intending to show affection and wanting to flatter, thinking that he had done a good deed for which his friend would thank him were he to get up and recuperate, and reward him were he to regain his health and recover—I am writing in a state of well-being that would be complete with being in the Sheikh's presence, and in a state of prosperity that would be in perfect order by being honored by his noble person, his blessed mind, and his countenance. 2.1

God, the most Noble—His names be sanctified—knows that if I had yearned to meet him—may God always support him!—as a bereft mother camel yearns for her calf, or a bird with chicks for its nest, or a dove for its mate, or a gazelle for its fawn, it would have been one of those things changed by the course of nights and days, years and ages; rather, it is the yearning of the thirsty for water, the fearful for safety, the snake-bitten for recovery, the drowning for rescue, the perturbed for quiet of mind—nay the yearning of the Sheikh's precious soul for God's praise and glory; for I have seen how it is drawn toward these things as components are drawn toward their elements and basic principles toward their substances.[3] If God grants me a fullness of life that enables me to delight in seeing the Sheikh and to hold fast on to the

العمر يؤنسني برؤيته، ويعلقني بحبل مودّته، صرتُ كساري الليل ألقى عصاه، وأحمدَ[1] مَسراه، وقرّعينا ونَعِمَ بالاً، وكان كمن لم يمسَسه سوءٌ، ولم يتخوّنه عدوٌّ، ولا نهكه رواحٌ ولا غُدوّ. وعسى الله أن يمُنَّ بذلك، بيومه أو بثانيه، وبه الثقة.

٢،٢ وأنا أسأل الله على التّداني والنوى والبعاد، إمتاعَه بالفضل الذي استعلى على عاتقه وغاربه، واستولى على مَشارقه ومَغاربه، فمن مرّ على بحره الهيّاج، ونظر في لألاء بدرِه الوهّاج، خليقٌ بأن يكبُوَ قلمُه بأنامله، وينبُوَ طبعُه عن رسائله، إلا أن يُلقِيَ إليه بالمقاليد، أو يستوهبه إقليداً من الأقاليد، فيكون منسوباً إليه، ومحسوباً عليه، ونازلا في شِعبِه، وأحد أصحابه وحِزبه، وشرارةَ ناره، وقُراضةَ ديناره، وسَمَلَ بحره، وثَمَد غمره. وهيهات!

ضاق فِترٌ عن مَسيرِ

ليس التكحُّل في العينين كالكَحَلِ

خُلقوا أسخياءَ لا متساخيـ ـنَ وليس السخيُّ من يتساخى

لا سيّما وأخلاقُ النفس تلزَمُها لزومَ الألوان للأبدان، لا يَقدِر الأبيض على السواد، ولا الأسود على البياض، ولا الشجاع على الجُبن، ولا الجبان على الشجاعة، قال أبو بكر العَرْزَميّ:

يَفِرُّ جبانُ القومِ عن أُمّ رأسِه ويحمي شُجاعُ القوم مَن لا يناسبُهْ
ويُرزَقُ معروفَ الجوادِ عدُوُّه ويُحرَم معروفَ البخيلِ أقاربُهْ
ومَن لا يكُفّ الجهلَ عمّن يوَدُّه فسوف يكُفّ الجهلَ عمّن يواثبُهْ

٣،٢ ومن أين للضَّباب صوبُ السحاب، وللغُراب هُوِيُّ العُقاب! وكيف وقد أصبح

[1] ب: (وأحْمِدَ).

rope of his affection, then I shall be like the nocturnal traveler who lays down his staff, praises[4] his nightly journey, and whose heart and mind are gladdened and delighted; he is like someone untouched by evil, not betrayed by an enemy, not worn away by setting out at night and returning in the morning. Perhaps God will grant me this, today or tomorrow—in Him is our trust.

I ask God, despite the need to come closer, the distance, and the remoteness, 2.2
to let the Sheikh enjoy the excellence that has risen high upon his shoulders and which has conquered East and West. For if one traverses his raging sea of knowledge and considers the brilliance of his radiant full moon, one's pen is apt to falter in one's fingers and one's natural talent will fail to impress itself[5] on one's epistles, unless one hands to him the keys or asks him to bestow one of the keys of his knowledge, so that one could be affiliated to him, in his debt, as someone who has come down to his mountain path, one of his associates and his party; a spark of his fire, a sliver of his gold dinar, a drop of his ocean, a puddle of his flood—Alas, how remote!

A span is too short for a journey;[6]

Applying kohl to the eyes is not like having coal-black eyes;[7]

They were created generous, not feigning to be generous:
the generous is he who does not feign generosity;[8]

—especially since the characteristics of the soul cleave to it like colors to bodies: white cannot turn black, nor black white. Nor can a brave man be cowardly, or a coward brave. Abū Bakr al-ʿArzamī says:

The coward among men flees, abandoning his nearest and dearest,[9]
while the brave among men will defend those unrelated to him.
A munificent man's favor will be granted to his enemy,
while the favor of a miser will be denied to his relatives.
He who does not refrain from brutishness to those who love him
will refrain from brutishness toward those who assail him.

How could a fog compare with a downpour from the clouds? How could the 2.3
crow swoop like the eagle? How to compare oneself to the Sheikh, whose name, when mentioned in the sessions of recollection, has become a call to

ذِكْرِه في مواسِمِ الذكر أذانًا، وعلى مَعالم الشكر لسانًا! فَمَن دافع العِيان، وكابَرَ الإنْس والجان، واستَبَدَّ بالإفْكِ والبُهتان، كان كمَن صالَبَ بوَقاحتِه الحجر، وحاسن بقَباحتِه القمر، وهذَى وهذَر، وتعاطى فعقَر، وكان كمحموم بُلسِم فعفر، ونادى على نفسه بالنقص في البدو والحضر، وكان كما قال من يعنيه ولا يشكّ فيه:

كنـاطِحٍ صخرةً يومـًا لِيَـفلقَها   فلم يَضِرْها وأَوْهَى قَرنَه الوَعِلُ

ورُوي أنّ رسول الله – صلّى الله عليه وسلّم، وزاده شرفًا لديه – قال: لعن الله ذا اللسانين، لعن الله كلّ شقّارٍ، لعن الله كلّ قتّات.

وردتُ حلب ظاهِرَها – حماها الله وحرسها – بعد أن مُنيتُ بِربَضِها بالدُرَخْمين ٤،٢
وأُمّ حَبَوْكَرَى والفُتَكْرِين، بل رُميتُ بآبِدة الآباد والداهيةِ النآد، فلما دخَلتُها – وبعدُ لم تستقرّ بي الدار، وقد نكرتُها لفقدان معرفةٍ وجار – أنشدتُها باكيًا:

إذا زُرتُ أرضًا بعد طولِ اجتنابها   فقـدتُ حبيبًا والبـلادُ كما هيا

كان أبو القَطِران، المرّارُ بنُ سعيد الفَقْعسيّ، يهوى ابنةَ عمه بنجدٍ، واسمُها وحشيّةُ فاهتداها رجلٌ شاميٌّ إلى بلده. فغمّه بُعدُها، وساءه فِراقُها، فقال من قصيدة:

إذا تركتْ وحْشيّةُ النجدَ لم يكنْ   لعينيك مما تبـكيان طبيبُ
رأى نظرةً منها فلم يَملكِ البُكا   مَـعاوِزُ يَـربو تحتـهن كثيبُ
وكانت رياحُ الشام تُكرَه مرّة   فقد جَعلتْ تلك الرياحُ تطيبُ

فحصلتُ من الرياح على الرياح، كما حصل لأبي القطران من وحشيّة.

prayer, a tongue to express the landmarks of gratitude?[10] He who rejects the evidence of the eyes, who treats both mankind and jinn haughtily, and who clings to calumny and falsehood obstinately is like someone who in his insolence vies with the hardness of the stone in his obdurateness, who seeks to rival the beauty of the moon with his ugliness, who raves and babbles, who «takes in hand and hamstrings it».[11] He is like someone afflicted with fever who is delirious and who looks jaundiced,[12] like someone who proclaims his own shortcomings among the dwellers of the desert and the towns. He is—and this is unquestionable—like the person the poet meant:[13]

Like one that butts a rock, one day, hoping to cleave it,
but does not harm it, and the ibex only hurts his horns.

It is transmitted that the messenger of God—God bless and preserve him and increase him in honor with Him—said, "God curse him who speaks with two tongues, God curse every liar, God curse every slanderer!"

I reached the periphery of Aleppo—may God protect and guard it—after 2.4
having been smitten in its outskirts with catastrophe, calamity, and casualty; nay, I was stricken with the rarest misfortunes and a crushing disaster. When I entered the town, not yet having a fixed abode, I did not recognize it, for I could not find any acquaintance or neighbor; then I recited to it, weeping:

When, after long avoidance, I pay a visit to a land,
I miss a loved one, though the place is still the same.

Abū l-Qaṭirān al-Marrār ibn Saʿīd al-Faqʿasī was in love with his cousin in Najd who was called Waḥshiyyah. A man from Syria took her as his wife to his country. He was grieved and afflicted by her being far away and by being separated from her. In a poem he said:

Since Waḥshiyyah has left Najd, no doctor
can cure your eyes of what they weep for.
He saw a glance from her and he could not hold back his tears:
her clothes, with underneath a rising sand dune![14]
The winds that blow from Syria were once[15] disliked,
but now those same winds have turned sweet.

What I had gained is gone with the wind, as happened to Abū l-Qaṭirān with Waḥshiyyah.

ثم . . . وثم . . . وثم . . . [1]

ثم أُجري ذكرُه – أدام الله تأييده – من غير سبب جرّه وغير مقتضٍ اقتضاه، فقال: ٥،٢
الشيخ بالنحو أعلمُ من سيبويه، وباللغة والعَروضِ من الخليل.

فقلتُ والمجلس يأذن: بلغني أنه – أدام الله تأييده – يُصَغِّر كبيرَه، ويُنَزِّر صغيرَه، فيصير تصغيره تكبيرًا وتحقيره تكثيرًا. هكذا شاهدتُ من شاهدتُ من العلماء رحمهم الله أجمعين، وجعله وارث أطْولِ أعمارِهم وأنضرِها وأرغَدِها. وما ثمّ له حاجةٌ دعَتْ إلى هذا: قد تَفَتَّحَ النَوْرُ وتَوَضَّحَ النُور، وأضاءَ الصبحُ لذي عينين!

كان أبو الفرج الزَهْرَجيّ كاتبُ حضرةِ نصرِ الدولة – أدام الله حراستَه – كتب ١،٦،٢
رسالةً إليّ أعطانيها، ورسالةً إليه – أدام الله تأييده – استَوْدَعَنيها، وسألني إيصالها إلى جليلِ حضرته، وأكون نافِقَها لا باعِثَها، ومُعجِّلَها لا مُؤجِّلَها. فسرق عديلي رحلاً لي، الرسالةُ فيه، فكتبتُ هذه الرسالةَ أشكو أُموري وأبثُّ شُقُوري، وأُطلِعُه طِلعَ عُجَري وبُجَري، وما لقيتُ في سفري من أَقْوام يدّعون العلم والأدب، والأدبُ أدبُ النفس لا أدبُ الدرس، وهم أصفارٌ منها جميعًا، ولهم تصحيفاتٌ كنت إذا ردَدتُها عليهم، نَسبوا التصحيف إليَّ، وصاروا إلبًا عليّ.

لقيتُ أبا الفرج الزهرجيّ بآمدَ ومعه خِزانة كُتُبِه، فعرضها عليّ فقلتُ: كتبك هذه ٢،٦،٢
يهوديّةٌ، قد برئت من الشريعة الحنيفيّة، فأظهر من ذلك إعظامًا وإنكارًا، فقلت له: أنت على المُجَرَّب، ومثلي لا يَهْرِف بما لا يعرف، وابلُغْ تَيَقَّنْ. فقرأ هو وولدُه وقال: صغَّرَ الخُبرُ الخَبَرَ. وكتب إليّ رسالةً يُقَرِّظُني فيها بطبعٍ له كريمٍ وخُلُقٍ غير ذميم.

[1] كذا في النسخ.

And then... and then... and then...[16]

2.5 Then the Sheikh's name was mentioned—may God always support him!—without any cause or occasion requiring it; and someone said, "The Sheikh knows more about syntax than Sībawayh and more about lexicography and metrics than al-Khalīl."

I replied, as the assembly gave ear, "I have heard that he—may God always support him!—belittles what is great in him, and even minimizes what is little in him; thus his belittling becomes a form of aggrandizement and his deprecation becomes an augmentation. I have witnessed the same thing in some other scholars I have met personally—may God have mercy upon them all, and may He make the Sheikh the inheritor of their longest, most flourishing, and most prosperous lifetime!—but there is no need for this: the flowers have blossomed, the light is bright, and dawn is shining for those with sight!"

2.6.1 Abū l-Faraj al-Zahrajī, state secretary at the court of Naṣr al-Dawlah—may God always protect him!—wrote a letter to me, which he gave me, and another letter to the Sheikh—may God always support him!—which he entrusted to me, asking me to deliver it to the venerable Sheikh, as speech, rather than as a dispatch, and quickly convey it and not to delay it. But my traveling companion robbed me of one of my saddlebags, which had the letter in it, so I wrote this letter instead, complaining of my state of affairs and explaining my needs, to inform the Sheikh of all my foibles and failings and of my experiences, during my travels, with all the petty people who pretend to have knowledge and erudition. True erudition is that of the soul, not that of study; but they are devoid of both. They commit errors when they read or write[17] but when I point them out, they gang up against me and impute the errors to me!

2.6.2 *Criticism of heresy and heretics*

I met Abū l-Faraj al-Zahrajī in Āmid. He had a library that he showed me. I told him, "These books of yours are Jewish and devoid of the Shariah of the True Religion!" He showed his annoyance and disapproval of this remark. So I said to him, "You are talking to an experienced man; someone like me does not talk rubbish about things he does not know about. Verify and you will be certain!" He and his son began to read, and he said, "First-hand knowledge has belittled reported knowledge!" He wrote me a letter, eulogizing me, for such is his good nature and unblemished character.[18]

قال المتنبّي: ١،٧،٢

أذمُّ إلى هذا الزمان أُهَيلَهُ

صغَّرَهم تصغيرَ تحقيرٍ غير تكبير، وتقليل غير تكثير، فَنَفَثَ مصدوراً، وأظهر ضميراً مستوراً. وهو سائغ في مجاز الشعر، وقائله غير ممنوع من النَظْم والنثر ولكنه وضعَه غير موضِعِه، وخاطَب به غير مستَحِقِّه. وما يستَحِقّ زمانٌ ساعدَه بلقاءِ سيف الدولة أن يُطلِق على أهلِه الذمَّ. وكيف وهو القائل:

أَسيرُ إلى إقطاعِهِ في ثيابِهِ   على طِرْفِهِ من دارِهِ بحُسامِهِ

وقد كان من حقّه أن يجعلهم في خِفارته، إذ كانوا منسوبين إليه محسوبين عليه. ولا يجب أن يشكو عاقلاً ناطقاً إلى غير عاقلٍ ولا ناطقٍ، إذ الزمان حركاتُ الفلك إلا أن يكون مِمَن يعتقد أن الأفلاك تَعقِل وتعلَم وتفهم، وتدري بمواقع أفعالها، بقصود وإرادات، ويَحمله هذا الاعتقادُ على أن يُقرِّب لها القرابين ويُدخِّنَ الدُخن، فيكون مناقضاً لقوله

فتَبّاً لدينِ عبيدِ النجومِ   ومَن يدّعي أنها تعقِلُ

أو يكونَ كما قال الله تعالى في كتابه الكريم: ﴿مُذَبْذَبِينَ بَيْنَ ذَٰلِكَ لَا إِلَىٰ هَٰؤُلَاءِ وَلَا إِلَىٰ هَٰؤُلَاءِ﴾ ويوشك أن تكون هذه صفته.

٢،٧،٢ حكى القُطْرَبُّلِيّ[١] وابن أبي الأزهر في كتابٍ اجتمعا على تصنيفه - وأهلُ بغداد وأهلُ مصر يزعمون أنه لم يُصنَّف في معناه مثله، لصِغَرِ حجمه وكِبَرِ علمه - يحكيان فيه أن المتنبّي أُخرج ببغداد من الحبس إلى مجلس أبي الحسن عليّ بن عيسى الوزير - رحمه الله. فقال له: أنت أحمد المتنبي؟ فقال: أنا أحمد النبي، وكشف عن

١ ب: (القُطْرُبُّلي) بضمة الراء وتشديد اللام، والصحيح ما أثبتناه.

Al-Mutanabbī[19] says: 2.7.1

> I blame the manikins of these our times.

using the diminutive ("manikin" of "man"), out of deprecation and not veneration, and by making them few and not many; thus spitting out his words like someone with a disease of the chest,[20] by which his hidden mind was expressed. This is possible in the figurative language of poetry, and one is not forbidden to say such things in verse or prose, but he said it inappropriately and addressed it to people who did not deserve it. A time in which he has had the good fortune to meet Sayf al-Dawlah does not deserve to have its people blamed. How could it, when he himself said,

> I go to his fief in his clothes
> on his steed from his house with his sword.

He should have considered that these people are under Sayf al-Dawlah's protection; they were affiliated to him and his protégés. And one should not complain to a reasonless, dumb object about persons possessing reason and speech: for "time" is no more than the movements of the celestial sphere—unless he is one of those who believe that these spheres possess reason and have knowledge and understanding, aware of the effect of their actions, with intentions and volitions, and who by their belief are induced to bring sacrifices and burnt offerings to them. In that case he would contradict his own words:

> Perish the religion of the worshippers of stars
> and those who claim that these have reason.

Or he would be as God the Exalted says in His noble Book:[21] «Wavering between this, not to these, not to those»; he all but answers to this description.

In a book on which they collaborated—the people of Baghdad and Cairo claim that nothing like it was ever written on the subject, on account of its slim size and its great learning—al-Quṭrabbulī[22] and Ibn Abī l-Azhar[23] tell how al-Mutanabbī was taken from prison in Baghdad, to the court of Abū l-Ḥasan ʿAlī ibn ʿĪsā, the vizier (God have mercy upon him).[24] The latter asked, "Are you Aḥmad, the would-be prophet (*al-mutanabbī*)?" Al-Mutanabbī replied, "I am Aḥmad the prophet (*al-nabī*)!"[25] He bared his stomach and 2.7.2

بطنه فأراه سَلْعة فيه وقال: هذا طابع نُبُوّتي وعلامة رسالتي. فأمر بقلع جَمَشَكه[١] وصَفَعَه به خمسين، وأعاده إلى محبسه.

ويقول لسيف الدولة:

وتغضبونَ على مَنْ نال رِفْدَكُمُ حتى يُعاقِبَه التنغيصُ والمِنَنُ

وكذب والله، لقد كان يتحرّش بالمكارم ويتحكّك بها، ويحسد عليها أن تكون إلا منه وبه. وهذا غيرُ قادحٍ في طُلاوة شعره ورَونَق ديباجته.

ولكني أغتاظ على الزنادقةِ والملحدين الذين يتلاعبون بالدين، ويرومون إدخال الشُّبَهِ والشكوك على المسلمين، ويستَعذِبون القدح في نبوّة النبيّين، صلواتُ الله عليهم أَجمعين، ويتظرّفون ويبتدئون إعجاباً بذلك المذهب: ١،٣

تِيهُ مُغَنٍّ وظَرْفُ زنديقِ

وقتل المهديّ بشّاراً على الزندقة، ولما شُهر بها وخاف، دافع عن نفسه بقوله:

يا ابن نِهْيَا[٢] رأسي عليّ ثقيلُ واحتمالُ الرأسين عبءٌ ثقيلُ
فادْعُ غيري إلى عبادةِ ربَّيْـ ـنِ فإنّي بواحدٍ مشغولُ

وأحضر صالح بن عبد القدّوسِ وأحضر النطع والسيّاف، فقال: عَلامَ تقتلني؟ قال: على قولك: ٢،٣

رُبَّ سِرٍّ كتمتُه فكأني أخرسٌ أو ثَنَى لساني عَقلُ
وَلَوَ انّي أَظهرتُ للناسِ ديني لم يكنْ لي في غيرِ حَبْسِيَ أَكْلُ

١ ب: (جُمْشُكِهِ)، والصحيح ما أثبتناه. ٢ ب: (نَهْيا)، والصحيح ما أثبتناه.

showed him a wen.[26] "This," he said, "is the stamp of my prophethood and the sign of my mission." The vizier gave orders that his shoe be removed and his head be slapped with it fifty times. Then he sent him back to his prison.

Al-Mutanabbī also said, addressing Sayf al-Dawlah:

You are angry with him who has obtained your support,
so that annoyance and gifts[27] torment him.[28]

He lies, by God! He had been badgering him about these acts of generosity and rubbing him up about them, jealously wanting them to come only from him and through him. But this does not detract from the polish of his poetry or the splendor of its fine style.

But I am furious about those heretics[29] and apostates[30] who make fun of religion and wish to instill doubts and skepticism among the Muslims, those who take delight in detracting from the prophethood of the prophets, God's blessings be on them all, and who are so satisfied with their sophistication and invention: 3.1

The conceitedness of a singer and the sophistication of a heretic.[31]

Al-Mahdī had Bashshār killed for heresy. When the latter attracted notoriety for this and began to be afraid, he defended himself by saying,

Ibn Nihyā,[32] my head is heavy for me,
and carrying two heads would be a heavy load!
Let others call for worshipping two Lords:
One is enough to keep me busy!

Al-Mahdī also summoned Ṣāliḥ ibn ʿAbd al-Quddūs. He called for the execution mat and the executioner. Ṣāliḥ asked, "Why are you sentencing me to death?" The caliph replied, "Because you said: 3.2

Many a secret I have hidden, as if I
were dumb, or my tongue were tied.
If I had exposed my religion to the people
the rest of my meals would be taken in prison.

ياعَدِيَّ اللهِ وعُدَيَّ نَفسِه:

السِتْرُ دون الفاحشاتِ ولا   يَلْقاكَ دونَ الخيرِ من سِتْرِ

فقال: قد كنت زنديقاً وقد تُبت عن الزندقة. قال: كيف وأنت القائل

والشيخُ لا يَتركُ عاداتِهِ   حتى يُوارَى في ثَرى رمْسِه
إذا ارْعَوى عادَ إلى غَيِّه   كذي الضَنَى عاد إلى نكْسِه

وأخذ غَفلته السيّافُ، فإذا رأَسه يتَدَهدأُ على النطع.

وظهر في أيامه في بلد خلف بخارى وراء النهر رجل قصّار أَعور، عمل له وجهاً ٣،٣
من ذهب وخوطِبَ بربّ العِزَّة، وعمل لهم قمراً فوق جبلٍ ارتفاعُهُ فراسخُ فأنفذ المهديّ إليه فأُحيط به وبقلعته، فحرق كل شيء فيها، وجمع كل مَن في البلد وسقاهم شراباً مسموماً، فماتوا بأَجمعهم، وشرب فلَحِق بهم، وعجّل الله بروحه إلى النار.

والصناديقيّ في اليمن كانت جيوشه بالمُدَبْخِرَة وسَفْهَنَةَ وخوطب برب العِزَّة، وكوتِبَ ٤،٣
بها، فكانت له دار إفاضة يجْمَعُ إليها نساء البلدة كلها ويُدْخِلُ الرجالَ[١] عليهن ليلاً. قال مَن يُوثَقُ بخبره: دخلت إليها لأَنظُر، فسمعتُ امرأَةً تقول: يا بُنيَّ! فقال: يا أُمَّهْ، نريد أن نمضي أمر وليّ الله فينا!

وكان يقول: إذا فعلتم هذا لم يتميّز مال من مال ولا ولد من ولد، فتكونوا كنفس واحدة. فغزاه الحَسَنيّ من صنعاء فهزمه، وتحصّن منه في حِصْنٍ هناك، فأنفذ إليه الحسنيّ طبيباً بِمِبْضع مسمومٍ ففصده به فقتله.

١ ب: (ويُدْخِلُ عليهن ليلاً). د: (ويَدخُل الرجالُ). وفي ق و إف ما أثبتناه.

"Enemy of God, and enemy of yourself!

A fine reputation veils scandalous deeds;
but you'll find no veil that covers good deeds."[33]

Then Ṣāliḥ said, "I was a heretic but I have repented and renounced heresy!" But al-Mahdī said, "How can that be! You yourself said:

An old man will not abandon his habits
until he is buried in the earth of his grave.
Though he may mend his ways, he will return to his error,
just as a someone chronically ill will relapse."

The executioner struck before he knew what was happening, and his head rolled on the mat!

In his reign, in a town beyond Bukhārā in Transoxania, there lived a one- 3.3
eyed man, a fuller, who made himself a gold mask and who was addressed as Lord Almighty.[34] He also erected a moon on a mountain several parasangs high for his followers.[35] Al-Mahdī dispatched an army to him, which laid siege to him in his fortified town. Then the heretic burned everything in it, gathered all the townspeople and gave them poisoned wine to drink; they all died. He too drank and joined them; and God hastened his spirit to Hell.

Al-Ṣanādīqī, in Yemen, had his troops in al-Mudaykhirah and Safhanah. 3.4
He was addressed as Lord Almighty, also in writing. He had a "House of Abundance," to which he brought all the women of the town, and he would let the men come and sleep with the women[36] at night. A trustworthy souce said: "I entered that place, to have a look. I heard a woman say, 'My dear son!' and he said, 'Mummy, we want to perform what God's Friend has commanded us!'"

He would say, "If you do this, private possessions will cease, and child will no longer be distinct from child. Thus you will become like one soul." Al-Ḥasanī conducted a campaign against him, from Sanaa, and routed him; he then entrenched himself in a citadel in that region. Then al-Ḥasanī sent to him a physician with a poisoned lancet. He used it to let his blood and thus killed him.

والوليد بن يزيد أقام في المُلكِ سنةً وشهرين وأياماً وهو القائل: ١،٥،٣

إذا متُّ يا أُمَّ الحُنَيكِل فانكحي   ولا تأْملي بعدَ الفراقِ تلاقِيا
فإنّ الذي حُدِّثْتِه من لقائِنا   أَحاديثُ طَسْمٍ تتركُ العقلَ واهيا

ورمى المصحف بالنشّاب وخرقه وقال:

إذا ما جئتَ ربَّكَ يومَ حشْرٍ   فقلْ: يا ربّ خَرَّقَني الوليدُ

وأنفذ إلى مكّة بَنّاءً مجوسيّاً ليبني له على الكعبة مَشرَبَة، فمات قبل تمام ذلك. فكان الحُجّاجُ يقولون: لَبَّيْكَ اللّهمَّ لبيك، لبيك يا قاتل الوليد بن يزيد، لبيك!

وأحضر بُنابِجة[1] من ذهب وفيها جوهرةٌ جليلةُ القدر، على صورة رجلٍ. فسجد له وقبّله وقال: اسجُدْ له يا عِلج! قلت: ومن هذا ؟ قال: هذا ماني. شأنه كان عظيماً، اضمحلَّ أمرُه لطولِ المدّة. فقلت: لا يجوز السجود إلا لله. فقال: قُمْ عنا.

وكان يشرَبُ على سطحٍ وبين يديه باطية كبيرةٌ بِلَّور وفيها أقداحٌ، فقال لندمائه: أين القمر الليلة؟ فقال بعضهم: في الباطية. فقال: صدقتَ، أتيتَ على ما في نفسي، والله لأَشربَنَّ الهَفتَجَة، يعني شُرْبَ سبعة أسابيع متتابعة.

وكان بموضع حول دمشق يُقال له البَخْراء[2] فقال:

تَلَعَّبَ بالنبوّةِ هاشميٌّ   بلا وحْيٍ أتاه ولا كتابِ

فقُتِلَ بها، ورأيت رأسه في الباطية التي أراد أن يُهَفتِجَ بها.

---

١ ب٤، إف، ق: (بنايجة). ك: (بُنابَجَة). د: (بِنا جِّة).   ٢ ب، إف، ك، ق، د: (البحرا).

Al-Walīd ibn Yazīd reigned for one year, two months, and a few days. He is the one who said: 3.5.1

When I die, mother of the little dwarf, marry
  and do not hope to meet after the separation!
For what you have been told about our meeting
  is but "tales of Ṭasm," which leave one's reason feeble.[37]

He once shot arrows at a copy of the Qur'an, piercing it, and saying,

When you come to your Lord, on Resurrection Day,
  then say: O Lord, I have been pierced by al-Walīd!

He sent a Zoroastrian builder to Mecca, to build him a chamber to drink in on top of the Kaaba; but he died before its completion. The pilgrims would cry,[38] "Here we are, O God, here we are! Here we are, O Thou who hast killed al-Walīd ibn Yazīd, here we are!"

Once he called for a vessel(?)[39] made of gold which contained a jewel of great value, in the shape of a man. He prostrated himself before it, kissed it, and said, "Prostrate yourself before it, you lout!" I said,[40] "Who is this?" "Mani," he replied, "He was once great but his cause has dwindled with the passing of time." "One is not permitted to prostrate oneself," I said, "before anything but God!" He replied, "Leave us!"

Once[41] he was drinking on a rooftop with a large crater made of crystal set before him, which contained several cupfuls. He said to his drinking companions, "In which sign of the zodiac is the moon tonight?" One of them said, "In the crater!" "True!" he replied, "You have said what I had in mind, too. By God, I shall drink a hebdomad!"[42] i.e., drinking for seven consecutive weeks.

Once he was in a place called al-Bakhrā',[43] in the environs of Damascus; then he said,

A Hāshimite played at being a prophet,
  without a revelation that came to him, nor a book.

He was killed in that place. I saw his head in that crater, with which he intended to "hebdomadize."

وأبو عيسى بن الرشيد القائل: ٢،٥،٣

دهَاني شَهرُ الصَوْمِ لا كان من شهرِ ولا صُمتُ شهراً بَعْدَهُ آخِرَ الدهرِ
ولو كان يُعْديني الإِمامُ بقدرةٍ على الشهرِ لاستعديتُ دهري على الشهرِ

عرض له في وقته صَرَعٌ فمات ولم يُدرِك شهراً غيره والحمد لله.

والجنّابيّ قتل بمكة أُلوفاً، وأخذ ستة وعشرين ألف جمل[1] خِفّاً، وضرب آلاتهم وأثقالهم بالنار، واستملك من النساء والغلمان والصبيان من ضاق بهم الفضاء كثرةً ووفوراً، وأخذ حجر الملتزَم وظنّ أنها مغناطيسُ القلوب، وأخذ الميزابَ. قال: وسمعت قائلاً يقول لغلام دُحسُمانَ طُوال يرفل في بُردَيْه وهو فوق الكعبة: يا رَخْمة، اقلعْه وأسرعْ، يعني ميزاب الكعبة. فعلمتُ أن أصحاب الحديث صحّفوه فقالوا يقلعه غلام اسمه رَخْمة، كما صحّفوا على عليّ رضي الله عنه قوله: تهلك البصرة بالريح. فهلكت بالزنج، لأنه قتل علويُّ البصرة في موضع بها يقال له العقيق أربعة وعشرين ألفاً، عدُّوهم بالقَصَب، وحرق جامعها، وقال في خطبته يخاطب الزنج: إنكم قد أُعِنتُم بقُبحِ مَظْهَر فاشفعوه بقبح مَخْبَر: اجعلوا كل عامرٍ قفراً وكلّ بيتٍ قبراً! قال لي بدمشق أبو الحسين اليزيديّ الوَرْزَنينيّ[2]: على نَسَب جَدّي دخل وإيّاه ادّعى. ١،٦،٣

وقال أبو عبد الله بن محمد بن عليّ بن رِزام الطائيّ الكوفيّ: كنتُ بمكّة وسيف الجنّابيّ قد أخذ الحاجَّ، ورأيت رجلاً منهم قد قتل جماعةً وهو يقول: يا كلاب، أليس قال لكم محمد المكّيّ: ﴿وَمَن دَخَلَهُ كَانَ آمِنًا﴾، أيُّ أمنٍ هنا؟ فقلت له: يا فتى العرب تؤمّنني سيفَك أفسّر لك هذا؟ قال: نعم. قلت: فيها خمسة أجوبة، الأول: ومَن دخله كان آمناً من عذابي يوم القيامة، والثاني: مِن فَرْضي الذي فرضْتُ عليه، ٢،٦،٣

١ ب٤، ك: (حملٍ). ٢ ب، ق، د: (الوزريني). ك: (الوزير بن).

Abū ʿĪsā, the son of al-Rashīd, is the one who said: 3.5.2

The month of fasting has come to me as a disaster; may that month cease to be!
And may I never fast for another month!
If the caliph were to aid me and give me power over that month
I would appeal for aid against that month as long as I live.

Instantly he was struck with a fit and he died before he lived to see another month, God be praised!

Al-Jannābī killed thousands of people in Mecca. He took twenty-six thousand camels easily,[44] he set fire to their equipment and baggage, and seized so many women, youths, and small children, that the area was crowded with them. He took away the "stone of the place of attachment,"[45] thinking that it was the "magnet of the hearts," and he took the waterspout.[46] I[47] heard him say to a tall, bulky, black servant, who, dressed in his two mantles, was strutting on top of the Kaaba, "Rakhamah, wrench it off, be quick!"— meaning the waterspout of the Kaaba. Then I became aware that the Hadith scholars had made a mistake when they said, "A boy called Raḥmah will wrench it off,"[48] just as they misspelled ʿAlī's words—God be pleased with him—when he said, "Basra will perish through the wind," but it perished with the Zanj,[49] for the Alid pretender of Basra killed twenty-four thousand people there at a place called al-ʿAqīq; they counted them by tallying with reeds. He set fire to its great mosque. He addressed the Zanj in a sermon: "You have been helped by your ugly physique; to follow it up, an ugly reputation you must seek! To every habitation bring doom; turn every room into a tomb!" Abū l-Ḥusayn al-Yazīdī al-Warzanīnī[50] said to me in Damascus, "He attached himself to my ancestor's family and claimed to be related to him."[51] 3.6.1

Abū ʿAbd Allāh ibn Muḥammad ibn Rizām al-Ṭāʾī al-Kūfī reports: "I was in Mecca at the time when the sword of al-Jannābī had wrought havoc among the pilgrims. I saw one of them who had killed a number of people, saying, 'You dogs! Has Muḥammad, the man from Mecca, not told you that «Whoever enters it will be safe»?[52] But what safety is there here then?' I replied, 'Arab warrior, if you guarantee that I will be safe from your sword, I shall explain this to you.' 'Very well,' he said. I continued, 'There are five answers. First, it means: whoever enters it will be safe from My torment at the Resurrection. Secondly: safe from the religious duty that I have imposed 3.6.2

والثالث: خرج مَخرَج الخبر وهو يريد الأمر كقوله: ﴿وَٱلْمُطَلَّقَٰتُ يَتَرَبَّصْنَ بِأَنفُسِهِنَّ﴾، والرابع: لا يقام عليه الحدّ فيه إذا جني في الحِلّ، والخامس: مَنَّ الله عليهم بقوله: ﴿أَنَّا جَعَلْنَا حَرَمًا ءَامِنًا وَيُتَخَطَّفُ ٱلنَّاسُ مِنْ حَوْلِهِمْ﴾ فقال: صدقتَ، هذه اللحية إلى توبة؟ فقلت: نعم فخلاني وذهب.

والحسين بن منصور الحلاج من نيسابور وقيل: من مَرْو، يَدَّعي كل علم، وكان ١٠،٧،٣
متهوّراً جَسوراً يروم إقلاب الدوَل ويدّعي فيه أصحابُه الإلهية، ويقول بالحلول، ويُظهِر مذاهب الشيعة للملوك، ومذاهب الصوفيّة للعامّة، وفي تضاعيف ذلك يَدَّعي أن الإلهية قد حلّت فيه. وناظَره عليّ بن عيسى الوزير فوجده صِفراً من العلوم وقال: تَعَلُّمُك لطهورك وفَرْضِك أجدى عليك من رسائل أنت لا تدري ما تقول فيها، كم تكتب إلى الناس: تبارك ذو النور الشَعْشَعاني الذي يلمع بعد شَعْشعته! ما أحوجك إلى أدب!

حدّثني أبو علي الفارسيّ قال: رأيت الحلاج واقفاً على حلقة أبي بكر الشِبْليّ . . .[1] أنت بالله ستفسد خشيته.[2] فنفض كُمَّه في وجهه وأنشد:

يا سِرَّ سِرٍّ يَدِقُّ حتى ... يَجِلّ عن وصفِ كلِّ حَيّ
وظاهراً باطناً تبَدَّى ... من كلِّ شيءٍ لكلِّ شيّ
يا جُملَةَ الكُلِّ لستَ غيري ... فما اعتذاري إذاً إليّ

وهو يعتقد أن العارف من الله بمنزلة شُعاعِ[3] الشمس، منها بدأ وإليها يعود، ومنها يستمدّ ضَوءَه.

---

١ النص ناقص على ما يظهر. ٢ في نسخة: (ستفسد خشبته)، وفي نسختين: (ستفسد خشبة)؛ وفي العبارة غموض.
٣ كلمة (الشعاع) مأخوذة من هامش نسخة الأصل.

on him.[53] Thirdly: it is expressed as a statement but a command is intended, as in God's words:[54] «and divorced women will wait by themselves». Fourthly: The prescribed punishment shall not be applied when someone commits a crime in a non-sacred territory.[55] And fifthly: God has granted it to them with His words:[56] «We have made a secure sanctuary, though around them people are being snatched away».' The man answered, 'You are right! Will this beard of mine[57] be forgiven?' I said, 'Yes!' Then he let me go and off he went."

Al-Ḥusayn ibn Manṣūr al-Ḥallāj from Nīsābūr—some say from Marw— 3.7.1
claimed to possess all knowledge. He was a reckless, insolent man who wanted to overturn dynasties. His followers claimed that he was divine; he preached the doctrine of divine indwelling. To rulers he made an outward show of the teachings of Shi'ism, to the masses he made a show of the ways of the Sufis, and implicitly in all this he claimed that divinity dwelled in him. The vizier 'Alī ibn 'Īsā questioned him in a dispute and found him to be devoid of any knowledge. He said to him, "You would have derived more profit from learning about your ritual purity and your religious duties than writing treatises where you do not understand what you say in them. How often have you not written to the people: 'Blessed be He with the glittering light that still gleams after its glittering!'[58] You are so much in need of education!"

Abū 'Alī al-Fārisī told me: "I saw al-Ḥallāj when he was standing in the circle of Abū Bakr al-Shiblī. [. . .][59] 'You, by God, will one day corrupt the fear of Him!'[60] Al-Ḥallāj shook his sleeve in his face and recited:

O secret secret, subtle to the point of being
exalted beyond description by any living being;
Outwardly, inwardly, you manifest yourself
in every thing to every thing.
O whole of All, you are not other than I,
so why excuse myself then to myself?"

He believed that someone with mystic knowledge stands in relation to God as rays are to the sun: from it they appear, to it they return,[61] and from it they derive their light.

أنشدني الظاهر لنفسه: ٢،٧،٣

أَرى جِيلَ التصوُّفِ شرَّ جيلٍ   فقـل لهـمُ، وأَهْوِنْ بالحـلولِ
أَقـال اللهُ حـين عَشـقـتُـموه   كُلُوا أَكْلَ البهائِم وارقصوا لي؟

وحرّك يوماً يده فانتثر على قومٍ مسكٌ، وحرّك مرةً أُخرى فانتثر دراهم، فقال له بعض مَن حضر ممن يفهم: أَرِني دراهم غير معروفة، أُومنْ بك وخلقٌ معي إِن أَعطيتَني درهماً عليه اسمك واسم أَبيك. فقال: وكيف هذا وهذا لا يُصنَع؟ قال: مَن أحضر ما ليس بحاضر، صنع ما ليس بمصنوع.

وكان في كتبه: إني مُغرِقُ قوم نوح ومُهلِك عادٍ وثمودَ.

فلما شاع أمرُه وعرف السلطان خبَرَه على صحّة، وقّع بضربه[١] ألفَ سوط، وقطع يديه، ثم أحرقه بالنار في آخر سنة تسع وثلاثمائة. وقال لحامد بن العبّاس: أنا أهلِكك. فقال حامد: الآن صحّ أنك تدّعي ما قُرِفْتَ به.

٨،٣ وابن أبي العَزاقِر أبو جعفر محمد بن علي الشَلْمَغاني أهله من قرية من قرى واسط تُعرف بشلمغان، وصورته صورة الحلاج ويدّعي عنه قوم أنه إله، وأن الله حلّ في آدم ثم في شِيث ثم في واحدٍ واحدٍ من الأنبياء والأوصياء والأئمة حتى حلّ في الحسن بن عليّ العسكريّ وأنه حلّ فيه. وكان قد استغوى جماعةً منهم ابن أبي عَونٍ صاحب كتاب التشبيه، ومعه ضُربت عنقه. وكانوا يُبيحونه حرمهم وأموالهم يتحكّم فيهم، وكان يتعاطى الكيمياء، وله كتب معروفة.

٩،٣ وكان أحمد بن يحيى الراوَنْديّ من أهل مرْوِ الرُّوذ حسن السِّتر جميل المذهب، ثم انسلخ من ذلك كله بأسباب عرضت له، ولأن علمه كان أكثر من عقله، وكان مثله كما قال الشاعر:

١ ب٤: (بضربةٍ).

Al-Ẓāhir[62] recited to me these verses of his own: 3.7.2

I think the Sufi kind is the worst kind;
so ask them (how contemptible is this "divine indwelling!"):
"Has God then told you, when you fell in love with Him,
'Eat like beasts and dance for Me'?"

One day al-Ḥallāj moved his hand, whereupon the odor of musk spread to the people. Another time he moved it and dirhams were scattered. One of those present, someone with understanding, said to him, "Show me unfamiliar dirhams, then I shall believe in you, and other people will join me: how about giving me a dirham struck with your name and that of your father!" Al-Ḥallāj replied, "How could I, since such a coin has not been made?" The man answered, "He who presents that which is not present can make that which has not been made!"

In his writings one finds: "I am he who drowned the people of Noah and who destroyed 'Ād and Thamūd." When his fame spread and the ruler[63] had gained reliable intelligence about him, he signed the sentence of one thousand lashes and the amputation of his hands, after which he had him burned in the fire, at the end of the year 309 [922]. Al-Ḥallāj said to Ḥāmid ibn al-'Abbās, "I shall destroy you!" Ḥāmid replied, "Now there is proof that you claim what you have been charged with."

The case of Ibn Abī l-'Azāqir Abū Ja'far Muḥammad ibn 'Alī al-Shalmaghānī,[64] 3.8
whose family is from a village near Wāsiṭ called Shalmaghān, was similar to the case of al-Ḥallāj: people claimed that he was a god, that God had dwelt in Adam, then in Seth, then in each successive prophet, legatee,[65] and imam, until He dwelled in al-Ḥasan ibn 'Alī al-'Askarī, and finally in himself. He had led a number of people astray, including Ibn Abī 'Awn, the author of *The Book of Simile*, who was beheaded along with him. They allowed him free use of their women and their property; he ruled over them according to his whims. He dabbled in alchemy, and he wrote some books that are well known.

Aḥmad ibn Yaḥyā al-Rāwandī, from Marw al-Rūdh, had a good reputation 3.9
and was doctrinally sound. Then he divested himself of all this, for various reasons, and because "his learning was greater than his intellect."[66] He was like the one described by the poet:[67]

ومَنْ يُطيق مَرَدًّا عند صَبْوته   ومَن يقومُ لمستورٍ إذا خَلَعا؟

صنّف:

كتاب التاج، يحتجّ فيه لِقِدَم العالَم، فنقضه أبو الحسين الخيّاط.

الزمُرُّذ، يحتجّ فيه لإبطال الرسالة. نقضه الخيّاط.

نعت الحكمة، سفّه الله – تعالى – في تكليف خَلْقه أمره، نقضه الخيّاط.

الدامغ، يطعن فيه على نظم القرآن.

القضيب، يُثبتُ أنّ علم الله مُحْدَث، وأنه كان غير عالم حتى خلق لنفسه علماً، نقضه الخيّاط.

المرْجان، في اختلاف أهل الإسلام.

علي بن العباس بن جُرَيج الرُّوميّ، قال أبو عثمان الناجم: دخلتُ عليه في علّته ١،١٠،٣
التي مات فيها، وعند رأسه جام فيه ماء مثلوج وخنجر مجرّد لو ضُرب به صدر خرج من ظهر، فقلت: ما هذا؟ قال: الماء أَبلّ به حلقي فقلّما يموت إنسان إلا وهو عطشان. والخنجر، إن زاد عليّ الألم نحرتُ به نفسي. ثم قال: أقصّ عليك قِصّتي تستدلّ بها على حقيقة تَلَفي: أردتُ الانتقال من الكَرْخ إلى باب البصرة، فشاورتُ صديقنا أبا الفضل وهو مُشتَقٌّ من الإفضال، فقال: إذا جئتَ القنطرة فخذ على يمينك – وهو مشتقّ من اليُمْن – واذهبْ إلى سِكّة النعيمة – وهو مشتقّ من النعيم – فاسكنْ دار ابن المُعافَى – وهو مشتقّ من العافية – فخالفتُه لتعسي ونحسي. فشاورتُ صديقنا جعفرًا – وهو مشتقّ من الجوع والفرار – فقال: إذا جئتَ القنطرة فخذ على شمالك – وهو مشتقّ من الشؤم – واسكن دار ابن قِلابة. وهي هذه لا جَرَمَ، قد انقلبت بي الدنيا، وأضرّ ما عليّ العصافير في هذه السِّدرة تصيح: سِيقْ سِيقْ: فها أنا في السياق، ثم أنشد:

And who is able to repel someone in his youthful folly?
Who can stand up to a decent man when he casts off restraint?

He wrote the following books: *The Book of the Crown*, in which he argues for the pre-eternity of the world; it was refuted by Abū l-Ḥusayn al-Khayyāṭ. Also, *The Emerald*, in which he argues the invalidity of prophetic mission, also refuted by al-Khayyāṭ. In *In Praise of Wisdom* he declares that God the Exalted had been foolish to impose His command on His creatures; it was also refuted by al-Khayyāṭ. In *The Brain-Basher*[68] he attacks the composition of the Qur'an. In *The Rod* he establishes that God's knowledge is not temporally originated, and that He did not have knowledge until He created knowledge for Himself. It was refuted by al-Khayyāṭ.[69] *The Coral* deals with the differences of opinion among the Muslims.[70]

'Alī ibn al-'Abbās ibn Jurayj al-Rūmī: Abū 'Uthmān al-Nājim says, "I visited him when he was ill with the disease that would carry him off. Near his head he kept a bowl of ice-cooled water and an unsheathed dagger so long that, struck in one's chest, it would have come out at one's back. I asked him, 'What is this?' and he replied, 'With the water I moisten my throat, for people seldom die unless they are thirsty. If my pain gets so bad I'll cut my throat with the dagger.' He added, 'I'll tell you my story, from which you can infer the true cause of my demise. I wanted to move from al-Karkh to Basra Gate. I consulted our friend Abū l-Faḍl, "Father of Favor," whose name is derived from "bestowing favor." He said, "When you come to the bridge, turn right"—"right" (*yamīn*) is derived from *yumn*, "right good fortune"—"Then go to Na'īmah (Bliss) Street"—whose name derived from "bliss"—"Then live in the house of Ibn al-Mu'āfā, 'Son of Healthy'"—which is derived from "well-being." But, to my misery and misfortune, I did not follow his advice but went on to consult our friend Ja'far—whose name is derived from *jū'*, "hunger," and *firār*, "fleeing."[71] He said, "When you come to the bridge, turn left"—"left" (*shimāl*) is derived from *shu'm*, "ill omen"—"And live in the house of Ibn Qilābah"—and sure enough, my world has been overturned (*inqalabat*)! And the worst thing of all: the birds on that lotus tree, chirruping *sīq sīq*, and here I am—sick!'[72] Then he recited:[73] 3.10.1

أبا عثمان أنت قريعُ قومِكْ وجُودُك للعشيرةِ دونَ لَومِكْ
تمتّعْ من أخيك فما أُراه يراك ولا تراه بعد يومِكْ

وألَحّ به البَوْل فقلتُ له: البول مُلِحٌّ بك. فقال: ٢،١٠،٣

غداً ينقطعُ البولُ ويأتي الويلُ والعَوَلُ
ألا إنّ لقاءَ اللّـهِ هولٌ دونه الهولُ

ومات من الغد.

فأرجو أن يكون هذا القول توبةً له مما كان اعتقده من ذَبحِه نفسه، والرسول عليه الصلاة والسلام يقول: من وَجَأَ نفسه بحديدة حُشِرَ يوم القيامة وحديدته بيده يجأ بها نفسه خالداً مخلّداً في النار، من تردّى من شاهقٍ حُشر يوم القيامة يتردّى على مِنخرَيه في النار خالداً مخلّداً، من تحسّى سُمّاً حُشر يوم القيامة وسمُّه بيده يتحسّاه خالداً مخلّداً في النار.

١١،٣ قال الحسن بن رَجاء الكاتب: جاءني أبو تمّام إلى خراسان فبلغني أنه لا يصلّي، فوكلتُ به من لازَمَه أياماً فلم يره صلّى يوماً واحداً، فعاتبته فقال: يا مولاي، قطعتُ إلى حضرتك من بغداد، فاحتملت المَشَقّة وبُعْدَ الشُّقّة ولم أره يثقُل عليّ، فلو كنت أعلم أن الصلاة تنفعني وتركُها يضُرّني ما تركتُها. فأردتُ قتله فخشيت أن يُحمَل على غير هذا.

١٢،٣ وفي تاريخٍ كثيرةٍ أنه أُحضر المازيار إلى المعتصم وقبل قدومه بيومٍ سخط على الأفشين لأنّ القاضي ابن أبي دُواد قال للمعتصم: أَغْرَلُ ويطأ امرأةً عربية! وهو كاتب المازيار، وزيّن له العصيان.

Abū ʿUthmān, you are the leader of your people;
You're above blame through your generosity toward the tribe.
Enjoy the presence of your friend, for I don't think
you'll see him or he'll see you after today.

"He found it difficult to stop urinating, so I said to him, 'You find it difficult to stop urinating!' He recited: 3.10.2

Tomorrow there will be an end to urinating
and there will be wailing and howling!
Indeed, meeting with God
is terror upon terror.

"He died the following day."

I hope that these words were an act of atonement for his idea of committing suicide. God's messenger (on whom be blessing and well-being) said, "He who stabs himself with a knife will be resurrected on the Day of Resurrection with his knife in his hand, and he will stab himself with it forever and ever in Hell. He who throws himself from a height will be resurrected on the Day of Resurrection and be thrown on to his nostrils in Hell forever and ever. He who drinks poison will be resurrected on the Day of Resurrection with his poison in his hand, drinking it forever and ever in Hell."

Al-Ḥasan ibn Rajāʾ, the state secretary,[74] said, "Abū Tammām came to me in Khorasan. I had heard that he did not perform the ritual prayer, so I appointed someone to stay close to him for some days, and he did not see him perform the ritual prayer one single day. I reproved him, but he said, 'My lord, I have come all the way from Baghdad to visit your eminence, I have borne hardship and suffered a long journey, which I did not find burdensome. If I had known that ritual prayer would benefit me, and omitting it would harm me, I would not have omitted it!' I intended to have him executed but I was afraid that this would be ascribed to the wrong motive." 3.11

It is mentioned in many historical works that al-Māzyār was brought into the presence of al-Muʿtaṣim one day after the latter had become enraged with al-Afshīn, when the judge Ibn Abī Duʾād had said to al-Muʿtaṣim, "An uncircumcised fellow, and he sleeps with an Arab woman! Also, he has corresponded with al-Māzyār and encouraged him to rebel!" 3.12

فأحضر كاتبه، وتهدده المعتصم فأقرّ أنه كتب إلى المازيار: لم يكن في الأرض ولا في العصر بَليَةٌ إلا أنا وأنت وبابَك، وقد كنت حريصاً على حقن دمه حتى كان من أمره ما كان، ولم يبق غيري وغيرك، وقد توجّه إليك عسكرٌ من عساكر القوم، فإن هزمته وثَبَتُ أنا بمَلِكهم في قرار داره، فظهر الدينُ الأبيض. فأجابه المازيار بجوابٍ هو عنده في سَفَط أحمر. فجمع بين الأفشين والمازيار، فاعترف المازيار بما حُكي عنه. وقيل للمعتصم: إن وراء المازيار مالاً جليلاً، فأنشد:

إن الأُسودَ أُسودَ الغابِ هِمَّتُها   يوم الكريهة في المسلوب لا السَلَبِ

وذكروا أن اثنين قتلوا[1] ثلاثة آلاف ألف وخمسمائة ذبّاحٍ بالثياب الحُمر والخناجر الطوال، وأنهم وجدوا أسماءهم في وقعةٍ وقعةٍ وفي بلد وبلد، وكانوا يأخذون من كل واحد علامةً: خاتمَه أو ثوبَه أو منديلَه أو تِكّتَه: أتى الوادي فطَمَّ على القَرِيّ.

قد لقيتُ مَن يجادلني أن علياً، رضي الله عنه . . .[2] وكذلك الحاكم. ١٣،٣

وقد ظهر بالبصرة من يدّعي أنَّ جعفرَ ابنُ محمد عليهما السلام، وأنه متّصِلٌ به وروحه فيه ومُتصلةٌ به. ولو استقصيتُ القول في هذا الفنِ لطال جدّاً ولكن:

لا بُدّ للصدور أن ينفثا   وللذي في الصدر أن يُبعَثا

بل لو قلتُ كل ما أعلمه، أكلتُ زادي في محبسي، بل كنت أُنشد:

أحمِلُ رأسًا قد مللتُ حمْلَه   ألا فتًى يحمل عنِّي ثِقلَه

وأستريح إلى أن أُنشد:

---

١ كذا في ب؛ وفي ق، إف: (قتلا)؛ وفي العبارة غموض ولحن.   ٢ في النص نقص واضح.

Al-Afshīn's secretary was summoned; when al-Muʿtaṣim threatened him he confessed to having written on behalf of al-Afshīn to al-Māzyār as follows: "In this world and at this time there is no scourge other than I, you, and Bābak. I was keen not to have Bābak's blood shed, but his fate was otherwise. Now there is no one left but you and me. One of the armies of the Abbasids is heading for you. If you defeat it I shall attack their king, in his 'fixed abode,'[75] and the 'white religion'[76] will prevail." Al-Māzyār had written a reply, which he had with him in a red basket. The caliph confronted al-Afshīn with al-Māzyār and the latter confessed to what had been reported of him. Someone said to al-Muʿtaṣim, "Al-Māzyār has lots of money!" But the caliph recited,

The lions, the lions of the thicket, are intent,
on an evil battle day, on the despoiled, not on the spoils.[77]

It is said[78] that two men killed three million and five hundred *dhabbāḥ*(?) in red clothes and with long daggers, and that they found their names in every individual encounter in every individual location; from each they took a token: his signet ring, his cloak, his kerchief, or his waistband. "The torrent reached the wadi and flooded the riverbed."[79]

I have met somebody who disputed with me, arguing that ʿAlī—God be pleased with him— . . . and likewise al-Ḥākim . . . [80] 3.13

In Basra there appeared someone who claimed that Jaʿfar[81] was the son of Muḥammad—on both of whom be peace—, that he had a close connection with him, and that his spirit was in him and connected with him.

If I were to treat this topic exhaustively it would be very lengthy. However,

He who suffers from a chest infection must spit;
What his chest contains must be ejected.

In fact, if I mentioned all I know, "I would eat the rest of my meals in my prison,"[82] or rather I would recite:[83]

I carry a head I am tired of carrying:
Is there no lad who'll carry its load for me?

And I would rest and finally recite:[84]

ليس يشفي كلومَ غيري كلومي   ما بهِ ما بهِ، وما بيَ ما بي[1]

١،٤ إن شكوتُ العصر وأحكامه، وذممتُ صروفه وأيامه، شكوتُ مَن لا يُشْكي أبداً، وذممتُ مَن لا يُرضي أحداً، شيمتُه اصطِفاءُ اللئام، والتحامل على الكرام، وهمّته رفع الخامل الوضيع، ووضع الفاضل الرفيع إذا سمحَ بالحِباء فأَبْشِرْ بوَشْكِ الاقتِضاء، وإذا أَعار فأحسبه قد أَغار، فما بين أن يقبل عليك مستبشراً، ويولّي عنك متجهماً مستبسراً، إلا كلَمْح البصر واستطارة الشرر. لم يخترق ذكرُ الوفاء مَسامِعَه، ولم يَمْسس ماءُ الحياءِ مدامعه، ظاهره يسرّ ويؤنِس، وباطنه يسوء ويوئس، يُخيّب ظنّ راجيه، ويُكذّب أمل عافيه، لا يسمع الشكوى ويشمتُ بالبلوى.

٢،٤ قد ذممت شيئاً ووقعت فيه أنا، كالغريق يطلب مَعْلَقاً، والأَسير يندب مطلقاً. وأستحسن قول عليّ بن العبّاس بن جُرَيج الروميّ:

أَلا ليس شيبُكَ بالمنتزَعْ   فهل أَنتَ عن غيّهِ مُرتَدِعْ؟
وهل أَنت تاركُ شكوى الزمانِ   إذا شئتَ تشكو إلى مُستمِعْ؟
فشَيبُ أَخي الشيبِ أُمنيّةٌ   إذا ما تناهى إليها هَلَعْ

٣،٤ كنت في حال الحداثة أقربُ الناس إليَّ، وأعزّهم عليّ، وأقربُهم عندي وأجلُّهم في نفسي مرتبةً، من قال لي: نسأ اللهُ في أَجَلِكَ، جعل اللهُ لك أمدَّ الأَعمار وأطولها. فلما بلغتُ عشرَ الثمانين جاء الجزعُ والهلع. فمِمَّ أرتاع وألتاع، وأخلد إلى الأَطماع، وهو الذي كنت أتمنّى ويتمنّى لي أهلي؟ أمن صدوف الغواني عنّي؟ فأنا واللهِ عنهنّ أصدفُ، وبهنّ وأدوائهنّ أعرف، إذا لست ممّن ينشد تحسُّرا عليهنّ:

[1] ب: (ما بى بى)، والصحيح ما في سائر الطبعات.

My wounds cannot heal another's wounds:
he has his and I have mine.

If I complain of the time we live in and its decrees and blame its vicissitudes and evil days, I complain to someone who never heeds a complaint, and I blame someone who makes none content. His habit is to favor the ignoble and to maltreat the noble; he is bent on raising the lowly and obscure, and on debasing the virtuous and high-minded. If he grants a gift, look forward to being soon asked to return it! If he lends a thing (*aʿāra*) I think he has carried out a raid (*aghāra*). Between turning toward you with a cheerful face and turning away from you with a glum frown lies but the wink of an eye, the flying of a spark. His ears have never heard of fidelity to promises, his eyes have never been touched by tears of embarrassment. His appearance gives joy and delight, but his inner self causes evil and despair. He disappoints those who expect his favors, he thwarts the hopes of those asking for support. He does not listen to complaint and gloats at people's torment. 4.1 *On fate*

For this I once cast blame, but now I do the same,[85] having fallen into it like a drowning man clutching at straw, or a prisoner lamenting his freedom. I think ʿAlī ibn al-ʿAbbās ibn Jurayj ibn al-Rūmī said it well: 4.2 *Ibn al-Qāriḥ's complaints of old age*

Ah, the grayness of your hairs will not be snatched away:
will you forswear the foibles of old age?
And will you stop complaining of the times,
complaining to a listener whenever you want?
To live to be gray-haired is everyone's desire,
but having gained it, one desponds.[86]

In my youth, my closest friend and dearest fellow, the man I deemed nearest to me, and the person I held in highest esteem was anyone who would say to me, "May God postpone your term, may God extend your life and grant you the longest of lives!" But now, with my eighth decade, come dismay and despondence. But why should I feel anxiety and agony, cherish ambitions in perpetuity, when I have attained what I desired and what my family wished for me? Because pretty women shun me? But, by God, I shun them more than they shun me, and I know them and the illnesses they bring only too well, for I am not one to recite, in grief over them: 4.3

للسودِ في السودِ آثارٌ تركنَ بها   لُمعاً من البيض تثني أعينَ البيضِ

وقول الآخر:

ولما رأيتُ النسرَ عزَّ ابنَ دايةٍ   وعشّش في وكرَيْه جاشت له نفسي

ولا أنشد لأبي عُبادة البحتريّ:

إن أيّامه من البيض بيضٌ   ما رأين المفارقَ السودَ سودا
وإذا المحلُ ثارَ ثاروا غيوثاً   وإذا النقعُ ثار ثاروا أُسودا
يحسن الذكرُ عنهمُ والأحاديـ   ـثُ إذا حدّثَ الحديدُ الحديدا
بلدةٌ تنبت المعالي فما يثـ   ـغرُ الطفلُ فيهمُ أو يسودا

٤،٤ وهذه صفة مَعرّةِ النعمان به - أدام الله تأييده - لا خلتْ منه ومن النعمة عليه وعنده، فقد وجدتُ أهلَها معترفين بعوارفه، خلا أبي العبّاس أحمدَ بنِ خلف المُمتّع - أدام الله عزّه - فإني وجدتُ آثار تفضُّلِه عليه ظاهرةً، ولسانه رطباً بشكره وذكره، قد ملأ السماء دعاءً والأرض ثناء.

١،٥ قالت قريشٌ للنبي عليه الصلاة والسلام: أتباعك من هؤلاء الموالي بِلالٍ وعَمّارٍ وصُهَيب، خيرٌ من قُصَيّ بن كلاب، وعبد مَناف وهاشم وعبد شمس؟ فقال: نعم، والله لئن كانوا قليلاً ليكثُرُنَّ، ولئن كانوا وُضعاءَ ليَشرُفُنَّ حتى يصيروا نجوماً يُهتدى بهم ويُقتدى، فيقال: هذا قول فلان وذكر فلان. فلا تُفاخروني بآبائكم الذين مُوّتوا في الجاهلية، فلَمَا يُدَهْدِه الجُعَل بِمَنخره خيرٌ من آبائكم الذين مُوّتوا فيها. فاتّبعوني أجعلكم أنساباً، والذي نفسي بيده، لتَقْتَسِمُنَّ كنوز كِسرى وقيصر.

Black [nights] have left their mark on black [hairs],
gleamings of white, by which the eyes of the white[-skinned women]
are turned off.[87]

Or some other poet's verse:

But when I saw the vulture overcome the crow,
and settle in two nests, my soul grew agitated.[88]

Nor shall I recite Abū ʿUbādah al-Buḥturī:[89]

Its days were white, because of white-skinned women,
so long as they saw that my black hair stayed black.
Whenever a drought came on they rose as showers of rain,
whenever a dust cloud rose in battle, they would rise as lions.
It's good to mention them and tell their stories,
of iron swords that, clashing, talked to iron swords.[90]
A place[91] where lofty deeds grow; as soon as the young child among
them sheds his milk teeth, he becomes a leader.

4.4 And this is how Maʿarrat al-Nuʿmān may be described, while the Sheikh is there—may God always support him, and may it never be parted from him, never cease to bring him blessings and to be blessed in his presence! I have found that its inhabitants acknowledge his acts of kindness, to say nothing of Abū l-ʿAbbās Aḥmad ibn Khalaf al-Mumattaʿ[92]—may God give him lasting vigor!—for I found clear evidence of his beneficence toward the Sheikh, while the latter's tongue is voluble with his approbation and his laudation, having filled heaven with prayer and earth with praise.[93]

5.1 *The Prophet at the beginning of his mission*

The men of Quraysh said to the Prophet—blessing and peace upon him—: "Your followers who are freedmen—such as Bilāl, ʿAmmār, or Ṣuhayb[94]—are they better than Quṣayy ibn Kilāb, ʿAbd Manāf, Hāshim, or ʿAbd Shams?"[95] He replied, "Yes, by God, though they be few they will be many; though they be lowly, they will be noble, to the point of becoming stars by which one is guided and that are followed. Then people will say, 'This was said by So-and-so, or mentioned by So-and-so.' So do not boast to me of your ancestors who died in pre-Islamic ignorance.[96] Truly, what the dung beetle rolls about with its nose is better than your ancestors who died then! So follow me and I shall

فقال له عمُّه أبو طالب: أبقِ عليّ وعلى نفسك. فظنَّ عليه الصلاة والسلام أنه خاذلُه ومُسْلِمه، فقال: ياعمّ، والله لو وضعوا الشمس في يميني والقمر في شمالي على أن أترك هذا الأمر حتى يُظهره الله أو أَهلِك فيه ما تركتُه. ثم استعبر باكيًا، ثم قام. فلمّا ولّى ناداه: أقبِلْ يا ابن أخي. فأقبل. فقال: اذهبْ وقل ما شئتَ، فوالله لا أُسلمتُك لسوء أبدًا.

٢،٥ فكان عليه الصلاة والسلام يذكر يوماً ما لقي من قومه من الجهد والشدة، قال: لقد مكثتُ أياماً وصاحبي هذا - يشير إلى أبي بكر - بضع عشرة ليلة ما لنا طعامٌ إلا البرير في شُعَب الجبال. وكان عُتبة بن غَزْوان يقول إذا ذكر البلاء والشدّة التي كانوا عليها بمكّة: لقد مكثنا زمانًا ما لنا طعامٌ إلا ورق البَشام أكلناه حتى تقرحت أشداقُنا، ولقد وجدتُ يوماً تمرةً فجعلتُها بيني وبين سعد وما منا اليوم أحدٌ إلا وهو أمير على كُورة. وكانوا يقولون فيمن وجد تمرةً فقسّمها بينه وبين صاحبه: إن أسعدَ الرجلين من حصلت النَّواةُ في قسمه، يلوكها يومَه وليلته، من عَدَم القوت. وكذا قال رسول الله صلّى الله عليه وسلّم: لقد رَعيتُ غُنيماتِ أهل مكّة لهم بالقراريط.

وابتداء أمره أنه وقف على الصَّفا ونادى: يا صباحاه، يا صباحاه! فجاءوا يهرعون فقالوا: ما دهَمك؟ ما طَرَقَك؟ قال: بم تعرفوني؟ قالوا: محمد الأمين. قال: أرأيتم إن قلتُ لكم إن خَيلاً قد طَرقَتكم في الوادي، وإن عسكرًا قد غشيكم من الفَجّ، أكنتم تُصدّقوني؟[١] قالوا: اللّهمَّ نعم، ما جرّبنا عليك كذبًا قطّ. قال: فإن الذي أنتم عليه، ليس لله ولا من الله ولا يرضاه الله، قولوا: لا إله إلا الله، واشهدوا أني رسوله، واتبعوني تُطِعْكُم العرب وتملكوا[٢] العجم، وإن الله قال لي: استخرِجْهم كما استخرجوك،

١ ق، إف: (تصدقونني). ٢ في النسخ: (تملكون).

give you worthy lineages! By Him who holds my soul in His hand, you shall divide among yourselves the treasures of Chosroes and Caesar!"

Abū Ṭālib, his paternal uncle, said to him, "Spare me and yourself!"[97] So he thought—blessing and peace be upon him—that his uncle was deserting him and forsaking him, and he said, "Uncle, I swear by God that even if, on condition that I abandon this, they put the sun in my right hand and the moon in my left, I shall never give it up until either God makes it prevail or I die!" Then he burst into tears and sobbed. He stood up and as he turned away, his uncle called him, "Come here, my nephew!" He did so and then Abū Ṭālib said, "Go and say whatever you want, for, by God, I shall never forsake you and let you come to any harm!"

One day the Prophet—blessing and peace upon him—mentioned the trouble and hardship he had experienced at the hands of his fellow tribesmen: "For days I went with no food but the fruit of the *arāk* tree in the mountain clefts. My companion here (pointing at Abū Bakr) went for more than ten days." ʿUtbah ibn Ghazwān, speaking of the distress and hardship they had suffered in Mecca, said, "We stayed for some time with nothing to eat except leaves of the balsam tree, which we ate until our jaws were sore. One day I found a date and I divided it between myself and Saʿd; and now every single one of us is a governor of a province!" They used to say that when someone found a date and divided it between himself and his friend, the luckier of the two was the one who got the stone, for he could chew it day and night, so scarce was food. The messenger of God—God bless and preserve him—also said, "I used to shepherd the small herds of the Meccans for a trifling sum."[98] 5.2

His mission began when he stood at al-Ṣafā and called out, "O dawn! O dawn!" They came hurrying toward him and said, "What has happened to you? What has come over you?" He asked them, "How do you know me?" "As Muḥammad, the trusted one," they said. He continued, "Do you think that if I said to you that horsemen are coming against you in the wadi, or that an army is attacking you coming from the mountain road, you would believe me?" "Yes, by God!" they said, "We have never known you to utter a lie." He said, "Your conduct is not for the sake of God, nor is it from God, nor is God pleased with it. Say: there is no god but God, and testify that I am His messenger! And follow me, and then the Arabs will obey you and you will reign over the non-Arabs. God has said to me, 'Draw them out, as they have drawn you out, and I shall send an army five times its size.' He guaranteed to

وابعثْ جيشاً أبعثْ خمسة أمثاله، وضمن لي أنه ينصرُني بقومٍ منكم، وقال لي: قاتلْ بمن أطاعك من عصاك. وضمن لي أنه يغلب سلطانيْ سلطانَ كسرى وقيصر.

٣،٥ ثم إنه عليه الصلاة والسلام غزا تبوك في ثلاثين ألفاً، وهذا من قِبَل الله الذي يجعل من لا شيء كلَّ شيء، ويجعل كل شيء لا شيء، يُجمّد المائعات ويُميع الجامدات، يُجمّد البحر ثم يفجّر الصخر. وما مَثَله في ذلك إلا كمثل من قال: هذه الزجاجة الرقيقة السخيفة، أَحكُّ بها هذه الجبال الصلْدة الصلْبة المُنيفة، فترضّها وتفُضّها، وهذه النملة الضعيفة اللطيفة، تهزم العساكر الكثيرة المُعَدّة!

وكذا حقيقة أمره عليه الصلاة والسلام، حتى لقد قال عُروة بن مسعود الثقفيّ لقريش، وكان رسولهم إليه صلّى الله عليه وسلّم بالحُدَيْبِيَة: لقد وردتُ على النجّاشي وكسرى وقيصر ورأيتُ جندهم وأتباعهم، فما رأيت أطْوع ولا أوقَرَ ولا أهْيب من أصحاب محمد لمحمدهم، هم حوله وكأن الطير على رؤوسهم، فإن أشار بأمرٍ بادروا إليه، وإن توضّأَ أقتسموا وضوءه، وإن تنخّمَ دَلكوا بالنُخامة وجوهَهم ولِحاهم وجلودهم. وكانوا له بعد موته أطوع منهم في حياته، حتى لقد قال بعض أصحابه: لا تُسُبّوا أصحاب محمد فإنهم أسلموا من خوف الله، وأسلم الناس من خوف أسيافهم.

٤،٥ فتأمّلْ، كيف استفتحَ دعوته -وهو ضعيفٌ وحده- بأن هذا سيكون، فرآه العدوّ والوليّ. وما كان مَثَله في ذلك إلا مَثل من قال: هذه الهباءةُ تعظُم وتصير جبلاً يُغَطّي الأرض كلّها، ثم أنذر الناس بها في حال ضعفها.

وجاء صلّى الله عليه وسلّم يوماً ليدخل الكعبة، فدفعه عثمان بن طَلْحة العبْدَريّ فقال: لا تفعل يا عثمان، فكأنك بمفتاحها بيدي أضعه حيث شئتُ. فقال: لقد ذَلّت يومئذ قريشٌ وقَلّتْ. قال: بل كثُرت وعزّت.

me that He would grant me victory by means of some fellow tribesmen of yours, and He said to me, 'Join with those who obey you in fighting against those who disobey you,' and He guaranteed to me that my power would overcome the power of Chosroes and Caesar."

Then—blessing and peace be upon him—he carried out the raid of Tabūk 5.3
with thirty thousand men.[99] This was due to God, who makes everything from nothing, and who makes everything into nothing; He solidifies liquids and liquefies solids, He causes the sea to solidify and then He cleaves rocks. All this is as if someone said, "With this thin, insignificant piece of glass I shall scratch these hard, lofty mountains and they will be crushed and broken thereby; and this weak, tiny ant will rout many well-equipped armies."

This is how it really was with the Prophet—blessing and peace be upon him. 'Urwah ibn Mas'ūd al-Thaqafī said to Quraysh, being their emissary to the Prophet—God bless and preserve him—at al-Ḥudaybiyah: "I have visited the Negus, Chosroes, and Caesar; I have seen their troops and their followers. But I have never seen people more obedient, more dignified, and more awe-inspiring than Muḥammad's companions when it comes to their Muḥammad! They stand around him 'as if birds were perched upon their heads.'[100] At the mere gesture of a command from him they hasten to act. When he performs the ritual ablution they divide the water among themselves. When he expectorates they rub their faces, their beards, and their skins with his sputum!" They were even more obedient after his death than they were during his lifetime, to the point that one of his companions said, "Do not revile the companions of Muḥammad, for they became Muslims for fear of God, whereas other people became Muslims for fear of their swords."

Consider, therefore, how he began his mission, when he was weak and 5.4
alone, claiming that all this would happen. Friend and foe saw him, while his situation could only be likened to someone saying, "This speck of dust will grow and become a mountain that will cover all the earth!" Then he warned people about this, while as weak as the speck of dust. One day he—God bless and preserve him—wanted to enter the Kaaba, but 'Uthmān ibn Ṭalḥah al-'Abdarī stopped him. "Don't do that, 'Uthmān," he said, "soon you will see me holding the key in my hand, which I shall put where I please!" Then 'Uthmān said, "Quraysh will be humbled that day, and few in number." But the Prophet said, "On the contrary, they will be many and mighty!"

١،٦ وأنا أستعين بعصمة الله وتوفيقه، وأجعلهما مُعِينَيَّ على دفع شهواتي، واشكو إليه عكوفي على الأماني، وأسأله فهماً لمواعظ عِبَرِ الدنيا، فقد عميتُ عن كلوم غِيَرِها، بما جَثَمَ على خواطري من الشعف بها. ولست أجد مُنصفاً لي منها، ولا حاجزاً لرغبتي فيها عنها، وأين ودائعُ العقول وخزائن الأفهام يا أولي الأبصار؟ صفحنا عن مساوئ الدنيا إغماضاً لعاجل مُوبِقِ[1] التنغيص، وتومئ إليه يد الزوال، وتكمن له الآفات. قال كُثيّر:

كأنّي أُنادي صخرةً حين أَعرضَتْ   من الصُّمِّ لو تمشي بها العُصْمُ زلَّتِ

٢،٦ وأقول على مذهب كُثيّر: يا دنيا، في كل لحظة لطرْفي منك عبرة، وفي كل فكرة لي منك حسرة! يا مُرنِّقةَ الصفا ويا ناقضة عهد الوفا؛ ما وُفق لحظة من عرَجِ نحوَك، ولا سعِد من آثر المُقام على حسن الظن بك، هيهات يا معشر أبناء الدنيا، لكم في الظاهر اسم الغِنى، وفي الباطن أهل التقلّل لهم نفس هذا المعنى. كم من يوم لي أغرّ كثير الأهلّة، قد صحَتْ سماؤه وامتدّ عليّ ظلّه، تمدّني ساعاته بالمُنى، ويضحك لي عن كل ما أهوى، حتى إذا اتّصل بكلّ أسبابي[2] نَفِسَت عليّ به الدنيا فسعت بالتشتيت إلى أُلفَته، والنقص إلى مُدّته، فكسفت بهجتَه كسوفاً، وأرهقت نضرتَه وحشيةُ الفراق، وقطّعتنا فرقاً في الآفاق، بعد أن كنّا كالأعضاء المؤتلفة، والأغصان اللدنة المنعطفة:

واحسرتي في يوم يجـ   ـمعُ شِرّتي كفَنٌ ولَحْدُ
ضيّعتُ ما لا بُدَّ منـ   ـه بالذي لي منه بُدُّ

وأُنشد قولَ ابن الروميّ:

---

١ ب٤، إف: (مُونِقِ). ب: (مونِقٍ). ق: (مونق). ورجحنا أن الصحيح ما أثبتناه.   ٢ كع، د: (بكل أسبابي وامتزج سروره بفرحي وروحي وأترابي).

I ask protection and success from God, making them my helpers in subduing my passions; I complain to Him about my indulging in my desires; and I ask Him to make me understand the admonishing lessons of the world. For I have become blind to the wounds inflicted by its vicissitudes, by the burning desire for it that has perched on my thoughts. I find nobody who will give me justice against it, no one who can restrain my longing for it. Where are the storerooms of reason and the treasuries of understanding, O ye with insight? We have condoned the evils of this world, shutting our eyes because of fleeting, obnoxious[101] troubles, to which the hand of extinction already points, and for which evils lie in hiding. Kuthayyir said: 6.1

Ibn al-Qāriḥ's weaknesses and self-reproach

It is as if I'm calling to a rock when she averts herself,
hard rock, where mountain goats, if walking there, would lose their footing.

And I say, following Kuthayyir: O world, at every glance you fill my eyes with tears, at every thought you cause me grief! O you who make turbid any purity, O you who breach any pact of loyalty: he who turns toward you has never prospered for a single instant, and he who prefers to remain well-disposed toward you has never been happy. Far from it! O children of this world, outwardly you are called rich, but inwardly and truly it is those happy with little who are rich in the true sense of the word. So many splendid days have I known, with many new moons, the sky bright, the shade stretching over me, the hours providing me all I desired, smilingly offering me all I longed for. But once it had attached itself to me in all my affairs,[102] the world begrudged me all this; it strove to break up my intimacy with it and to shorten its extent. Its splendor was eclipsed to gloom and the desolation of separation blighted its bloom. It has scattered us, dispersed to the horizons, after we had been like limbs held together, like bending, pliant branches; 6.2

O my grief, the day my youthful zeal
was gathered in a shroud and grave!
I've squandered what I needed
for what I did not need.[103]

I quote a verse by Ibn al-Rūmī:[104]

أَلا ليس شيبُكَ بالمنتزِعْ فهل أَنتَ عن غَيِّهِ مرتدِعْ

فأَقلقُ وأَبكي بكاءً غير نافع ولا ناجع، ويجب أن أبكي على بكائي وأُنشد:

لساني يقولُ ولا أَفعلُ وقلبي يريدُ ولا أَعملُ
وأَعرِف رُشدي ولا أَهتدي وأَعلَمُ لكنّني أَجهلُ

عرض عليّ بعض الناس كأس خمر، فامتنعتُ منها وقلت: خلُّوني والمطبوخَ على ٣،٦
مذهب الشيخ الأوزاعيّ. وقلت لهم: عَرَض إبراهيم بن المهديّ على محمد بن حازم
الخمرة فامتنع وأنشد:

أَبعدَ شيبيَ أَصبو والشيبُ للجهل حَرْبُ
سِنٌّ وشيبٌ وجهلٌ أَمرٌ لعمرُكَ صَعْبُ
يا ابنَ الإمامِ فأَلّا أَيامَ عُودِيَ رطْبُ
وإِذ مَشيبي قليلٌ ومَنهلُ الحبّ عذبُ
وإِذ شفاءُ[١] الغواني مِنّي حديث وقُربُ
فالآنَ لما رأى بِيَ الـ ـعُذّالُ ما قد أَحبّوا
وآنَسَ الرشدَ منّي قوم أُعابُ وأَصبو؟
آليتُ أَشربُ خمرًا ما حَجّ لله ركْبُ

وأقبلت على نفسي مخاطبًا، ولها معاتبًا، والخطاب لغيرها والمعنى لها: ١،٤،٦
لقد أَمهَلكم حتى كأنه أهملكم! أما تستحيون من طول ما لا تستحيون! فكنْ
كالوليد تُقلِّبُه يد اللطف به على فراش العطف عليه، تُصرَف إليه المنافع بغير

١ د: (شفاه).

Ah, the grayness of your hairs will not be snatched away:
will you forswear the foibles of old age?

I am perturbed, I weep though weeping is neither useful nor beneficial, and I should rather weep for my weeping and recite:

My tongue speaks but I do not act;
My heart desires but I do naught.
I am aware of the right path but do not let myself be guided;
I know, but act in ignorance.[105]

Some people offered me a cup of wine. I refused and said, "Leave me with boiled wine, according to the doctrine of Sheikh al-Awzāʿī!"[106] I told them that Ibrāhīm ibn al-Mahdī once offered wine to Muḥammad ibn Ḥāzim, who refused and recited: 6.3

Shall I, with my gray hair, be foolish like a child?
Gray hair is at war with brutish ignorance.
Old age, gray hair, and ignorance:
upon your life, they're hard to reconcile.
O caliph's son, O for the days
when I was strong and fresh,
When my gray hairs were few
and drinking from love's spring was sweet,
When I was cured by pretty girls
by conversation and proximity!
But now, when those who chided me
see in me all they yearned to see,
And people see me taking the right path:
shall I once more be chided and be foolish like a child?
I swear that I shall never drink wine
as long as pilgrims ride to go on hajj for God!

I turned to myself, addressing and reproaching my soul; the address is phrased as if to others but is in fact to it:[107] 6.4.1

"He has given you respite as if He has neglected you. Are you not ashamed of how long you have been unashamed!"[108] Be like a newborn child, turned by a gentle hand in its cot, surrounded by affection, on whom benefits are showered without asking, because of his infancy, and from whom harm is

طلب منه لصغره، وتُصرف عنه المضارّ بغير حذر منه لعجزه. أما سمعتَ الرسول عليه الصلاة والسلام إذ يقول في دُعائه: اللّٰهم اكلأني كلاءةَ الوليد الذي لا يدري ما يُراد به ولا ما يريد. ألا متعلق بأذيال دليله؟[١] ألا مُعدٌّ مطيّةً ورَحلاً ليوم رحيله؟ يا هلاه! الدُلجةَ الدلجةَ! إنه من لم يسبق إلى الماء يَظمَ. إنما منعتُك ما تشتهي ضنّاً بك وغيرةً عليك، قال الرسول عليه الصلاة والسلام: إذا أحبَّ اللّٰه عبداً حماه الدنيا، وأنت تشكوني إذا حميتُك، وتكره صيانتي إذا صُنتُك. ألا لائذٌ بفنائنا ليعزّ؟ ألا فارّ إلينا لا فارّ منا؟ يا من له بدّ من كل شيء، أرحم من لا بدّ له منك على كل حال! اللّٰه يُغني بشيء عن شيء، وليس يغنَى عنه بشيء، فلهذا قال جبريل للخليل: ألك حاجةٌ؟ قال: أما إليك فلا، اللّٰه يستحقّ أن يُسأل وإن أغنى، لأنه لا يُغنَى بشيء عنه. أطِعْه لتطيعه ولا تطعه ليطيعك فتفتر وتملّ. من ترك تدبيره لتدبيرنا أرحناه! جلّ من لَوالِب القلوب والهمم بيده، وعزائم الأحكام والأقسام عنده:

أَنسِيتَ ذِكْرَ أَحِبّـةٍ ... ينسَونَ ذنبكَ عنـد ذكرِكْ؟ ٢،٤،٦
وجـفوتَـهم ولطالمـا ... كانوا خِلافَكَ طوعَ أَمرِكْ
وصبرْتَ عنـد فراقِهم ... ما كان عذرُكَ عند صبرِكْ؟

تترك من إذا جفوتَه ونسيتَ ذكره وتعدّيتَ حدّه وتركتَ نهيه وضيّعتَ أمره، وتُبتَ إليه وعوّلتَ في تفضّله عليك عليه، وقلت: يا ربّ، قال لك: لبّيك

١ ب: (ألا مُتعلِّقٌ والإذلالُ أذيالُ دليلِه). ق، إف، د: (ألا مُتعلِّقٌ والأذيالُ أذيالُ دليلِه).

averted without his being on his guard, because of his infirmity. Have you not heard the messenger of God— blessing and peace upon him—when he said in his prayer, "O God, guard me as a newborn child is guarded, who neither knows what is wanted from him nor what he wants himself!" Is there no one who will hold on to the shirttails of his guide?[109] Is there no one who readies a mount and a saddle for the day of his departure? You people! Departure at daybreak! Departure at daybreak! He who does not arrive before the others at a watering place will suffer burning thirst. I have refused to give you what you desire only in order to spare you and to protect you jealously. The messenger of God said— blessing and peace upon him—, "When God loves someone He protects him against the world." You complain about me when I protect you; you dislike my guarding you when I guard you. Is there no one who will seek refuge in our courtyard so that he may be achieve glory? Is there no one who flees to us, rather than from us? O Thou who canst dispense with everything, have mercy on him who cannot dispense with Thee in any circumstance! God is all-sufficiient, but one cannot do without Him in anything. It is for this reason that when Gabriel said to the Friend:[110] "Do you need anything?" he replied "Not from you." God deserves to be asked, even though He has already given sufficiently, because one cannot dispense with Him in anything. Obey Him in order to obey Him and do not obey Him in order that He may obey you and you grow lazy and bored. To him who abandons looking after his own affairs and leaves them to Our providence We shall give ease. Exalted is He whose hand holds the winding coils of the human hearts and human ambitions, who controls the decisions of decrees and apportionments.

Have you forgotten to think of loved ones 6.4.2
    who forget your sins when they remember you?[111]
You treated them unkindly, even though so often,
    unlike you, they have been at your beck and call.
And you endured it calmly when they left:
    what was then your excuse when you endured it thus?

You abandon Someone whom you have treated unkindly, whom you forgot to remember, whose limit you have transgressed, whose prohibition you have abandoned, whose commands you have ignored; then you turned to Him in repentance, relying on His grace toward you, and saying: "O Lord!" Then He will say to you, "Here I am! «And when My servants ask you about

﴿وَإِذَا سَأَلَكَ عِبَادِي عَنِّي فَإِنِّي قَرِيبٌ﴾ إن كان الذُباب بوجهك فاتّهمْك، وإن قطّعت أنا أعضاءك فلا تتّهمْني، أنت الذي إذا أعطيتك ما أمّلت تركتني وانصرفت: ﴿وَإِذَآ أَنْعَمْنَا عَلَى ٱلْإِنسَٰنِ أَعْرَضَ وَنَـَٔا بِجَانِبِهِۦ﴾ . يا واقفاً بالتّهم كم كم؟ أليس يقول لك: ما غرّك بي؟ تقول حِلمك، وإلا لو أرسلتَ عليّ بَقّةً لجمعتني عليك إذا أردتَ أن تجمعني:

أَمِنْ بعدِ شُربِكَ كأْسَ النُهى وشَمّكَ ريحانَ أَهلِ التُقى
عشقتَ فأَصبحتَ في العاشقيـ ـنَ أَشْهرَ من فرَسٍ أَبْلَقا؟
أدنيايَ من غَمْرِ بَحْرِ الهوى خُذِي بيدي قبل أَن أَغرقا
أنا لكِ عبدٌ فكوني كمَنْ إذا سرّه عبدُه أعتقا

كان ببغداد رجل كبير الرأس فِليّ الأُذنين اسمه فاذوه رأسه في الأزمنة الأربعة ٥،٦
مكشوفٌ، لا يتورّع عن ركوب مُخزِية، يقال له: يا فاذوه، ويْلك! تُب إلى الله. فيقول: يا قومِ، لِمَ تدخلون بيني وبين مولاي وهو الذي يقبل التوبة من عباده؟

فكان في بعضِ الشوارع يوماً ذاهباً، والشارع قد اتّسع أسفله وضاق أعلاه والتقى جَناحانِ فيه، فناولَت جارةٌ جارتَها مِهْراساً، انسَلّ من يدها على رأس فاذوه فهرس رأسه، وخُلِطَ لحمُه بالهريسة، وأعجله عن التوبة. وكان لنا واعظ صالح يقول لنا: احذروا مِيتة فاذوه.

قال جبريل في حديثه: خشيتُ أن يتمّ فرعون الشهادة والتوبة، فأخذت قطعةً من حال البحر فضربتُ بها وجهه - يعني طينه، والحال ينقسم ثمانية أقسام منها الطين - فكيف يصنع من عنده أن التوبة لا تصِحّ من ذنب مع الإقامة على آخر؟ فلا حول ولا قوة.

Me I am near».[112] If you have a fly on your face, accuse yourself; but if I sever your limbs, you must not accuse Me. You are the one who abandoned Me and turned away, after I had given you what you hoped for. «And when We bless man he recoils and turns aside».”[113] O you who stands with these accusations—how many! How many! Will He not say to you, “What has deceived you about Me?”[114] and you will say, “Your forbearance! Or else, if Thou wouldst send a tiny bug against me, it would gather me unto Thee if it were Thy wish thus to gather me.”[115]

After drinking from the cup of understanding,
and smelling the sweet herbal fragrance of the pious,
Have you fallen in love and turned a passionate lover, more
conspicuous than a piebald horse?
O world of mine, please take my hand before I drown
In the deluge of the sea of love!
I’ll be your slave; so be then like the master who,
pleased with his slave, will set him free![116]

There was a man in Baghdad with a large head and elephantine ears, called 6.5
Fādhūh. His head was uncovered during all the four seasons; he had no scruples about doing disgraceful things. People would say to him, “Hey Fādhūh, shame! Turn to God in repentance!” But he would reply, “People, why do you come between me and my Lord? It is He who accepts repentance from His servants!”

One day he was going along a certain street that was broad at the bottom but so narrow further up that the opposing houses nearly met. A woman handed her neighbor woman a mortar, but it slipped from her hand and fell on Fādhūh’s head, pounding it to a pulp as if it were a *harīsah*. It fell too fast for him to repent! We had a pious preacher who used to say us, “Beware of a death like Fādhūh’s!”

Gabriel says in a tradition: “I feared that Pharaoh[117] would complete professing the creed and his repentance, so I took some of the mud (*ḥāl*) of the sea and struck his face with it.”—*ḥāl* here means “mud;” the word has eight meanings, including “mud”—So how can someone act who believes that repenting of a sin is not valid if one persists in another sin? There is neither might nor power . . . [118]

بلغني عن مولاي الشيخ - أدام الله تأييده - أنه قال وقد ذُكِرتُ له: أعرفه خَبَرًا، هو الذي هجا أبا القاسم بن عليّ بن الحسين المغربيّ. فذلك منه - أدام الله عزّه - رائع لي، خوفًا أن يستشرّ طبعي، وأن يتصوّرني بصورة مَن يضع الكفر موضِعَ الشكر. وهو بتعريف التنكير أنفع لي عنده، لجلالة قَدره ودينه ونُسكه، وأنا أُطلِعه طِلعه، ليعرف خفضه ورفعه، وفُراداه وجمعه. ١٫٧

كنت أدرس على أبي عبد الله بن خالَوَيْه رحمه الله، وأختلف إلى أبي الحسن المغربيّ، ولما مات ابن خالويه سافرت إلى بغداد ونزلت على أبي علي الفارسي وكنت أختلف إلى علماء بغداد: إلى أبي سعيد السِيرافيّ، وعليّ بن عيسى الرُمّانيّ، وأبي عبيد الله المرزُبانيّ، وأبي حفص الكَتّانيّ صاحب أبي بكر بن مُجاهِد. وكتبت حديث رسول الله صلى الله عليه وسلم، وبلّغتُ نفسي أغراضها جهدي والجهد عاذر. ثم سافرت منها إلى مصر، ولقيت أبا الحسن المغربي فألزمَني أن لَزِمته لزوم الظلّ، وكنت منه مكان المِثل، في كثرة الإنصاف، والحنو والتحافّ. فقال لي سرًا: أنا أخاف هِمّة أبي القاسم أن تَنْزُوَ به إلى أن يوردنا وِردًا لا صَدَر عنه. وإن كانت الأنفاس مما تُحفَظ وتُكتَب، فاكتُبْها واحفظها وطالِعْني بها. ٢٫٧

فقال لي يومًا: ما نرضى بالخمول الذي نحن فيه. قلت: وأي خمول هنا؟ تأخذون من مولانا - خلّد الله مُلكَه - في كل سنة ستّةَ آلاف دينار، وأبوك من شيوخ الدولة وهو معظَّمٌ مُكرَّم. فقال: أريد أن تُصار إلى أبوابنا الكتائبُ والمواكبُ والمقانبُ، ولا أرضى بأن يُجرَى علينا كالوِلدان والنِسوان! فأعدتُ ذلك على أبيه فقال: ما أخوفَني أن يَخضِبَ أبو القاسم هذه من هذه، وقبض على لِحيَته وهامته. وعَلِمَ أبو القاسم بذلك، فصارت بيني وبينه وَقْفَةٌ.

وأنفذ إليّ القائدُ أبو عبد الله الحسين بن جوهر فشرفني بشريف خدمته، فرأيتُ الحاكم ٣٫٧

I have heard about my lord the Sheikh—may God always support him!—that he said when I was mentioned to him, "I know of him by hearsay. He is the one who lampooned Abū l-Qāsim ibn ʿAlī ibn al-Ḥusayn al-Maghribī." These words are alarming to me, for I fear that he thinks ill of my character, and that he imagines me as someone who replaces gratitude with ingratitude. By acquainting him with what he does not know I would enhance my standing with him, with the greatness of his worth, his religion, and his pious asceticism. And so I shall inform him so that he is aware of the long and the short of it, and the high and the low of it.[119] 7.1

The Sheikh exculpates himself

I studied with Abū ʿAbd Allāh ibn Khālawayh—God have mercy on him—and I often went to see Abū l-Ḥasan al-Maghribī. When Ibn Khālawayh died I left for Baghdad and stayed with Abū ʿAlī al-Fārisī. I frequented the scholars of Baghdad, such as Abū Saʿīd al-Sīrāfī, ʿAlī ibn ʿĪsā al-Rummānī, Abū ʿAbd Allāh al-Marzubānī, and Abū Ḥafṣ al-Kattānī, the companion of Abū Bakr ibn Mujāhid. I wrote down the Traditions of the messenger of God—God bless and preserve him—and achieved the goals I had set myself, to my best efforts (one is exculpated by giving one's best effort). Then I traveled from there to Egypt, where I met Abū l-Ḥasan al-Maghribī. He compelled me to stick to him like his shadow; I became like an equal, through the abundance of his equity, his affection, and our mutual friendship. He told me, in confidence, "I am afraid that the ambition of Abū l-Qāsim will draw him, and us with him, toward a watering place from which there is no return. If you can memorize and keep an accurate tally of even the breaths he takes, then do so and keep me informed!" 7.2

One day Abū l-Qāsim said to me, "We do not like how we live in obscurity." "What obscurity?" I replied, "You receive six thousand dinars each year from our lord—may God make him reign forever!—and your father is one of the leading men of the state; he is revered and honored." He said, "I want battalions and processions and squadrons to defile at our gates! I don't like being treated like boys and women!" I repeated these words to his father, who said, "I am really afraid that Abū l-Qāsim will dye this (he grasped his beard) blood-red with this (he touched his head)!" Abū l-Qāsim got to know this, and this brought about an estrangement between us.

General Abū ʿAbd Allāh al-Ḥusayn ibn Jawhar sent for me and honored me by employing me in his service. I saw that, whenever he had a leading person 7.3

كلما قتل رئيساً أنفذ رأسه إليه وقال: هذا عدُوّي وعدوّك يا حسين فقلت:

مَنْ يَـرَ يَوماً يُرَ بـهِ والدهـرُ لا يُغـتَرُّ بـهِ

وعلمت أنه كذا يُفعَل به. فاستأذنته في الحج فأذِنَ، فخرجت في سنة سبع وتسعين، وحججتُ خمسة أعوام وعدتُ إلى مصر وقد قتله، فجاءني أولاده سراً يرومون الرجوع إليهم، فقلت لهم: خيرُ ما لي ولكم الهربُ، ولأبيكم ببغداد ودائعُ، خمسمائة ألف دينار، فاهربوا وأهرب. ففعلوا وفعلتُ، وبلغني قتلُهم بدمشق وأنا بطرابلس.

٤،٧ فدخلتُ إلى أنطاكِيَة وخرجت منها إلى مَلَطْية وبها المايَسْطرِيّة، خَولة بنت سعد الدولة، فأقمت عندها إلى أن وَرَدَ عليّ كتابُ أبي القاسم فسِرت إلى ميافارقين فكان يُسِرُّحَسْواً في ارتغاء.

قال لي يوماً من الأيام: ما رأيتُكَ! قلت: أَعرَضَت حاجةٌ؟ قال: لا، أردت أن ألعنك. قلت: فالعنّي غائبا! قال: لا، في وجهك أشفى! قلت: ولمِ؟ قال: لمخالَفَتِك إياي فيما تعلم. وقلت له ونحن على أنس بيني وبينه: لي حُرُماتٌ ثلاث: البلدية، وتربية أبيه لي، وتربيتي لإخوته. قال: هذه حُرَمٌ مُهتَّكَةٌ: البلدية نسب بين الجدران، وتربية أبي لك مِنّةٌ لنا عليك، وتربيتك لإخوتي بالخِلَع والدنانير.

أردت أن أقول له: استَرَحْتَ من حيث تَعِبَ الكرام فخشيت جنون جنونه، لأنه كان جنونُه مجنوناً، وأصحُّ منه مجنونٌ، وأجنُّ منه لا يكون. وقد أُنشد:

جنونُك مجنونٌ ولستَ بواجدٍ طبيباً يداوي من جنونِ جنونِ

بل جُنَّ جِنّانه، ورقص شيطانه:

executed, al-Ḥākim would send his head to him, with the words "Ḥusayn, this is my enemy and your enemy!" I said to myself,

He who sees something will one day be seen himself:
One should have no illusions about Fate.[120]

I knew that he would be treated in the same manner. I asked leave to go on pilgrimage, which he permitted. I left in the year ninety-seven.[121] I went on pilgrimage, staying away for five years, and when I returned to Egypt he had been executed. His sons came to me in secret and wanted me to return to their service; but I said to them, "The best thing we all can do is to run away. Your father has deposited goods in Baghdad worth five thousand dinars, so run and I shall run too." They did so, as did I. I heard that they were killed in Damascus when I was in Tripoli.[122]

Then I went to Antioch and left it again for Malatya, where Mistress Khawlah,[123] the daughter of Saʿd al-Dawlah resided. I stayed with her until I received a letter from Abū l-Qāsim. Then I traveled to Mayyāfāriqīn. He was "secretly drinking the milk while pretending to sip the froth."[124] 7.4

One day he said to me, "I do not want to see you ever again!" I asked, "Has something happened?" "No," he said, "I want to curse you!" I answered, "Then curse me in my absence!" "No," he said, "it gives me more satisfaction to do it in your face!" "Why?" I asked. He replied, "Because you act against me, as you know very well!" Since there had been such a bond of close intimacy between us, I told him that there were three reasons why I deserved respect: the fact that we came from the same place, that his father had educated me, and that I had educated his brothers. But he retorted, "These reasons are to be torn to shreds. Coming from the same place is merely sharing walls. Being educated by my father was a favor we did you, and your education of my brothers was done in return for robes of honor and dinars!"

I wanted to say to him, "You had a comfortable life when noble people toiled!" However, I was afraid of the madness of his madness, for his madness was in fact mad. A madman was sounder in mind than he! One could not be madder than he. It has been said:

Your madness is mad and you won't find
a doctor who's able to cure the madness of madness.[125]

Even the jinn who possessed him were mad[126] and his devil danced!

بـه جِنّـةٌ مجـنونةٌ غيرَ أنـها إذا حصلَتْ منه أَلَبُّ وأعقلُ

وقال لي ليلةً: أريد أن أجمع أوصاف الشمعة السبعة في بيت واحد وليس يسنح لي ما أرضاه. فقلتُ: أنا أفعل من هذه الساعة. قال: أنت جُذَيلها المحكَّك وعُذَيقها المُرجَّب. فأخذتُ القلم من دواته وكتبت بحضرته: ٥،٧

لقد أَشبهتْني شمعةٌ في صبابـتي وفي هَوْلِ مـا أَلقى ومـا أَتوقَّـعُ
نحولٌ وحرقٌ في فَنـاءٍ ووحـدةٍ وتسهيدُ عَيْنٍ واصفرارٌ وأَدمُعُ

فقال: كنتَ عملت هذا قبل هذا الوقت! فقلتُ: تمنعني سرعةَ الخاطر وتُعطيني عِلم الغيب؟ وقلت: أنت ذاكرٌ قول أبيك لي ولك وللبَتّيِّ الشاعر وللمحسّن[1] الدمشقيّ، ونحن في الطارمة: اعملوا قطعةً قطعةً، فمن جوّد جعلتُ جائزته كَتْبَها فيها، فقلت:

بَلَغَ السـماءَ سُـمُوُّ بيـ ـتٍ شَـيدَ في أَعلى مكانِ
بيتٌ عـلا حـتى تغوَّ رَ في ذُراه الفـرقـدانِ
فـانعَمْ بـه لا زلتَ مِنْ ريْبِ الحوادثِ في أمـانِ

فاستجاد سُرعتها وكتبها في الطارمة، وخلع عليّ.

وكان أبو القاسم ملولا، والمَلول ربما ملّ الملالَ، وكان لا يملّ أن يملّ، ويحقد حقد من لا تلين كَبِدُه، ولا تنحلّ عُقَدُه. ٧،٦،١

وقال لي بعض الرؤساء معاتباً: أنت حقودٌ ولم يكن حقوداً. فقلت له: أنت لا تعرفه، والله ما كان يُخنى عُودُه، ولا يُرجى عَوده. وله رأيٌ يُزَيِّن له العُقوق،

١ في النسخ: (ولمحسن).

In him is a mad madness; yet, when it occurs,
It's more intelligent and sensible than he's himself!

He said to me one evening, "I want to combine seven attributes of a candle in one verse, but nothing that comes to my mind pleases me." I said, "I'll do it now!" He said, "You are the well-rubbed little tree-trunk[127] and its well-propped palm-bunch!" So I took the pen from its inkwell and wrote in his presence, 7.5

A candle resembles me, in my passionate love,
in my terror at what I encounter and what I expect:
Thin, and burning, and dwindling, and lonely,
with wakeful eye, being pale, and tearful.

Then he said, "You composed this earlier!" I replied, "You deprive me of my quick wit and credit me with knowing the future! You will remember," I continued, "what your father said to us, to al-Battī the poet, and to al-Muḥassin al-Dimashqī, when we sat in the pavilion:[128] 'Compose an epigram, each of you! I shall reward the best by having his poem inscribed on this pavilion.'" Then I said:

The sky has been reached by the height of a house
raised on the loftiest place;
A building so high that its roofs
make the Little Bear's stars[129] sink beneath them.
So be happy in it and may you from bad
turns of fortune forever be safe.

"He liked my quick response and wrote it on the pavilion, also giving me a robe of honor."

Abū l-Qāsim was easily bored. Someone easily bored is sometimes bored with his own boredom; he, however, was never bored of being bored! He was full of resentment, like someone whose liver never softens[130] and whose joints are never relaxed. 7.6.1

A high official once reproached me, saying, "You are the one who is resentful; not him!" I said to him, "You do not know him. By God, he is inflexible and one cannot hope for any favors from him.[131] He has a frame of mind that encourages him to be disrespectful and that makes respect for

ويُمِقّت إليه رعاية الحقوق، بعيد من الطبع الذي هو للصد صَدود، وللتآلف أَلوفٌ وَدود. كأنه من كِبْره قد ركب الفلك واستوى على ذاتِ الحُبُك. ولست ممن يرغب في راغبٍ عن وصْلَته، أو ينزع إلى نازعٍ عن خُلّته. فلما رأيته سادراً، جارياً في قلة إنصافي على غُلَوائه، محوْتُ ذكره عن صفحة فؤادي، واعتددتُ وُدَّه فيما سال به الوادي:

فَفِي الناسِ إن رَثَّت حِبالُكَ واصلٌ وفي الأَرضِ عن دارِ القِلى مُتحوَّلُ

وأنشدت الرجلَ أبياتاً أعتذر بها في قطعي له: ٢،٦،٧

فلو كان منه الخيرُ إذ كان شَرُّه عتيداً، لقلنا: إن خيراً مع الشرِّ
ولو كان – إذ لا خيرَ – لا شرَّ عنده صَبَرْنا وقُلنا لا يَريشُ ولا يبْري
ولكنه شرٌّ ولا خيرَ عنده وليس على شرٍّ إذا دام من صَبْرِ

ونُغضي له – شهد الله – حيّاً ومَيْتاً، أوجبه أخذُه محاريبَ الكعبة، الذهب والفضّة. وضربها دنانير ودراهم وسمّاها الكعبية، وأنهب العرب الرَّملة. وخرّب بغداد وكم دمٍ سفك، وحريم انتهك، وحُرّة أرمل، وصبيّ أيتم!

٨ وأنا معتذر إلى الشيخ الجليل من تقريظه مع تفريطي[١] فيه، لأنه قد شاع فضلُه في جميع البشر، وصار غرّةً على جبهة الشمس والقمر. خلُد ذلك في بدائع الأخبار، وكُتِبَ بسواد الليل على بياض النهار. وأنا في مكاتبة حضرته بمنظومٍ ومنثور، كمن أمدّ النار بالشرر، وأهدى الضوء إلى القمر، وصبّ في البحر جُرعةً، وأعار سير الفلك سُرعة، إذ كان لا يحلّ النقص بواديه، ولا يطور السهو بناديه.

١ في النسخ: (تقريظي).

people's rights seem hateful to him. He is far from having a character that rejects rejection but is amiable and loves mutual affection. It is as if he, in his arrogance, rides the celestial sphere and has seated himself on the galaxy-striped sky. Yet I am not the type to seek out anyone who seeks disassociation from his companionship, or to draw toward anyone who inclines toward withdrawal from his friendship.[132] When I saw how thoughtlessly he acted without doing me justice in his excessive pride, I wiped away his name from the page of my heart and considered my affection for him as something swept away by the river's flow.

For if the bonds with you are frayed, others will make ties;
There are places I can turn to on earth, away from an abode of hate."[133]

I recited some verses to the man, justifying myself in them for breaking off my contact with him: 7.6.2

If any good thing came from him, whose badness comes so readily,
then we could say: the good comes with the bad!
And if he had no bad, as well as nothing good,
we could endure it, saying: "he's no fletcher and no trimmer!"[134]
But he is bad and there's no good in him;
and badness, when it lasts, can't be endured.

My hatred of him, whether alive or dead—God is my witness—is the inevitable result of the fact that he appropriated the gold and silver niches of the Kaaba and coined them into dinars and dirhams, which he called "Kaaba coins."[135] He made the Bedouins plunder al-Ramlah and he laid Baghdad in ruins. So much blood did he shed, and so many women did he ravish, widowing free women and orphaning little children!

Praise of al-Maʿarrī

I ask the venerable Sheikh to excuse me when I laud him, even though I fall short of doing him justice, because his excellence has spread among all people and he has become a bright light on the brow of the sun and the moon. This has been immortalized in wonderful reports and has been written night-black on day-white. In writing to his noble person in verse and in prose I am like someone who fuels a fire with a spark, who presents the moon with a gift of light, who pours a mouthful into the sea, or who lends speed to that of the celestial sphere; for no shortcoming settles in his valley and no inadvertence nears his assembly. 8

ولقد سمعتُ من رسائله عقائل لفظٍ إن نعتُّها فقد عِبتُها، وإن وصفتُها فما أنصفتها. وأطربتْني - يشهد الله - إطراب السماع. وبالله لو صَدَرَت عن صدر مَن خِزانتُه وكتبه حوله، يُقلّب طرْفه في هذا ويرجع إلى هذا - فإن القلم لسان اليد وهو أحد البلاغتين - لكان ذلك عجيباً صعباً شديداً. ووالله لقد رأيت علماء، منهم ابن خالَوَيه إذا قُرِئَت عليهم الكتب، ولا سيما الكبار، رجعوا إلى أصولهم كالمقابلين يتحفظون من سهو وتصحيف وغلط.

والعجب العجيب والنادر الغريب، حِفْظُه - أدام الله تأييده - لأسماء الرجال والمنثور، كحفْظ غيره من الأذكياء المبرّزين المنظوم، وهذا سهل بالقول صعب بالفعل، من سمعه طمع فيه، ومن رامه امتنَعَت عليه معانيه ومبانيه.

١،٩ حدّثني أبو علي الصِقلّيّ بدمشق قال: كنت في مجلس ابن خالَويه إذ وردت عليه من سيف الدولة مسائل تتعلّق باللغة، فاضطرب لها ودخل خِزانته وأخرج كتب اللغة، وفرّقها على أصحابه يُفتّشونها ليجيب عنها. وتركتُه وذهبت إلى أبي الطيّب اللُغَوي وهو جالس وقد وردت عليه تلك المسائل بعينها وبيده قلم الحُمْرة، فأجاب به ولم يُغَيّره، قُدرةً على الجواب. وقال أبو الطيِّب: قرأت على أبي عُمَرَ الفصيح وإصلاح المنطق حفظاً. وقال لي أبو عمر: كنت أُعلّق اللغة عن ثعلب على خَزَف، وأجلس على دِجلةَ أحفظها وأرمي بها.

٢،٩ وأنا تعبت وحفظت نصف عمري، ونسيت نصفه. وذاك أني درست ببغداد وخرجت عنها وأنا طَريُّ الحفظ، ومضيت إلى مصر فأمرجتُ نفسي في الأغراض البهيمية، والأعراض المُوثِمية، وأردت برَغْمي وخديعة الطبع المُلِيم أن أذيقها حلاوة العيش، كما صبرتُ في طلب العِلم والأدب، ونسيت أن العلم غذاء النفس الشريفة

I have heard the Sheikhs's epistles being read, which contain expressions so exquisite that if I extolled them I would have disgraced them, and which if I described them I would not have done justice to them. I was enraptured by them—God is my witness—as if enraptured by music. By God, if they were produced by someone who had his library and his books around him, turning his eyes now to this, and then to that—for "the pen is the tongue of the hand and one of the two kinds of eloquence"—it would be an amazingly difficult feat. By God, I have seen scholars such as Ibn Khālawayh who, when books were studied under their supervision, especially large ones, would consult their exemplars, like those who collate copies of texts in order to guard themselves against slips, misspellings, or errors.

But what is a truly amazing and an extraordinary and rare thing, is the Sheikh's memory—may God always support him!—of people's names and prose texts, just as other intelligent and eminent people memorize poetry. It is easy to say but hard to do; he who hears of it aspires to it, but if he aims for it, he finds it impossible to achieve it in meaning and form.[136]

Abū ʿAlī al-Ṣiqillī[137] told me in Damascus: "I was sitting in Ibn Khālawayh's assembly when he received some queries from Sayf al-Dawlah concerning lexicography. He became agitated about this, went into his library and got out dictionaries, distributing them among his companions, so that they could consult them and he could find the answer. I left him and went to Abū l-Ṭayyib al-Lughawī, who was holding a session and who had received the very same queries. He was holding a reed pen with red ink, with which he was writing the answers, without making any changes, such was his skill in replying. 'I recited from memory *The Pure Language* and *The Correction of Speech*[138] with Abū ʿUmar,' said Abū l-Ṭayyib, 'and Abū ʿUmar told me, "I would take notes in lectures on lexicography from Thaʿlab, writing the notes on pieces of pottery; I would sit on the bank of the Tigris memorizing them and then throwing them away."'" 9.1

On memorizing and forgetting; Ibn al-Qāriḥ complains again

I have exhausted myself spending the first half of my life memorizing things, and the second half forgetting them. I studied in Baghdad and left it when my memory was still fresh. I went to Egypt, letting myself indulge in animal desires and sinful designs. I wanted, in my eagerness, deceived by my blameworthy nature, to taste the sweetness of a life of pleasure, just as I persevered in seeking knowledge and erudition. I forgot that knowledge is the food of a 9.2

وصيقل الأفهام اللطيفة. وكنت أكتب خمسين ورقة في اليوم، وأدرس مائتين، فصرت الآن أكتب ورقة واحدة وتحكّني عيناي حكًّا مؤلمًا، وأدرس خمس أوراق وتكلّ.

ثم دُفعتُ إلى أوقات ليس فيها من يرغب في علم ولا أدب، بل في فضّة وذهب، فلو كنت إياساً صرت باقلاً. وأضع كتاباً عن يميني وأطلبه عن شمالي، وأريد مع ضعفي أرتاد لنفسي معاشاً بظهيرٍ غير ظهير، بل كسير عقير، وصُلبٍ غير صليب، إن جلستُ فهو كالدُمّل، وإن مشيت فجُملتي دماميل. ومعي بقيّة نزرة يسيرة من جملة كثيرة، لو وجدت ثقة أعطيته إياها ليعود عليّ بما أُرفّه به عن جسمي من الحركة، وقلبي من الشغل. وأنا أجد من أدفعها إليه وبقي أن يرُدّها إليّ!

دفع رجل إلى صديقٍ جاريةً أودعها عنده وذهب في سفره، فقال بعد أيام لمن يأنس به وتسكن نفسه إليه: يا أخي، ذهبتْ أمانات الناس، أودعني صديق لي جارية في حسابه أنها بِكرٌ، جرّبتُها فإذا هي ثيّب! ٣،٩

ومن طريف[١] الأخبار أن بنت أختي سرقت لي ثلاثة وثمانين ديناراً، فلما هدّدها السلطان – أطال الله بقاءه، ومدّ مدّته، وأدام سموّه ورفعته – وأخرجت إليه بعضها قالت: والله لو علمتُ أن الأمر يجري كذا، كنت قتلته فاعجبوا من هرستي وزَبوني!

والله لولا ضعفي وعجزي عن السفر، لخرجت إليه متشرفاً بمجالسته ومحاضرته، فأما مذاكرته فقد يئستُ منها لما قد استولى عليّ من النسيان، واحتوى على قلبي من الهموم والأحزان. وإلى الله الشكوى لا منه، وليس يحسن أن أشكو من يرحمني إلى من لا يرحمني، وليس بحكيم من شكا رحيماً إلى غير رحيم. ١،١٠

وكان أبو بكر الشِبلي يقول: ليس غير الله غيرٌ، ولا عند غير الله خيرٌ. وقال

١ في كل الطبعات: (ظريف).

noble soul and the burnisher of subtle minds. I used to write fifty folios each day and study two hundred; but now I write but one single folio and my eyes smart in pain and when I study five folios my eyes grow weary.

Then I was compelled to survive long enough to witness times in which no one desires knowledge or erudition; rather they want silver and gold! Though I may have been Iyās, I have become Bāqil.[139] I put a book down on my right and then look for it on my left. In spite of my weakness I try to make a living with a back that does not back me up but is broken and wounded, with a spinal column no longer firm. If I sit down it is like having a boil; if I walk I am all boils! All I have left is a trifle, a scant remainder of what was once a huge amount. If I could find a reliable person I would give it to him in return for something with which I could ease my body with not having to move, and my heart by not being preoccupied. I have, in fact, found someone to give it to, but it remains for him to render me his service.

A man gave a slave girl to a friend, entrusting her to his keeping while he went on a journey. After a few days the latter said to someone with whom he was on intimate terms and whom he trusted, "My friend, one can no longer trust people these days! A friend has entrusted a slave girl to me, thinking that she was a virgin. But I tried her myself and she wasn't a virgin!"[140] 9.3

Another curious[141] story is that my sister's daughter stole eighty-three dinars from me. When the ruler—may God prolong his life, extend his term, and perpetuate his loftiness and his elevation!—threatened her and she produced some of them to him, she said, "By God, if I had known that matters would end up thus I would have killed him!"—"Be amazed about my *harīsah* and my customer!"[142]

By God, were it not that I am too weak and feeble to travel I would go and visit the Sheikh, to be honored by sitting with him and talking to him. As for a learned discussion with him, I despair of this on account of the forgetfulness that has come over me and the worries and sorrows that have enveloped my heart. To God, not about Him, I complain; it would not be proper if I complained about Someone who has mercy upon me to someone who has no mercy upon me. One who complains about a Merciful One to someone who is unmerciful is not wise. 10.1

Abū Bakr al-Shiblī used to say, "Other than God there is no other, and there is no good but with God." He said one day, "O Generous One!" Then he

يوماً: يا جواد! ثم أمسك مُفكرًا ورفع رأسه ثم قال: ما أوقحني! أقول لك يا جواد، وقد قيل في بعض عبيدك:

ولو لم يكنْ في كفّه غيرُ نفسِه لجاد بها فليتّقِ اللهَ سائلُهْ

وقد قيل في آخر:

تراه إذا ما جئتَه مُتهلّلا كأنك مُعطيه الذي أنتَ سائلُهْ

ثم قال: بلى، أقول: ياجواداً فاق كل جواد، وبجوده جاد من جاد.

٢،١٠ ودخل ابن السَّمّاك على الرشيد فقال له: عِظْني – وفي يد الرشيد كوز ماء. فقال: مهلاً يا أمير المؤمنين، أرأيتَ إن أقدرَ الله عليك مُقدّرًا فقال: لن أمكّنك من شربة إلا بنصف مُلكِك، أكُنت فاعلاً ذلك؟ قال: نعم. قال: اشرب، هنّاك الله. فلما شرب قال: أرأيت يا أمير المؤمنين، أن لو أُسِفتَّ نفس هذا المقدّر عليك فقال: لن أمكّنك من إخراج هذا الكوز إلا بأن استبدّ بملكك دونك، أكُنت فاعلاً ذلك؟ قال: نعم. قال: فاتقِ الله في مُلكٍ لا يساوي إلا بَولةً.

١،١١ وكيف أشكو من قاتني وعالني نيفاً وسبعين سنة: كان قميصي ذراعين، فوكل بي والدَين حدبين مُشفقيْن، يتناهيان في دقته ورقته وطيبه، فلما صار اثني عشر ذراعاً توَلاه هو وطعامي، فما أجاعني قط ولا أعراني: ﴿وَالَّذِي هُوَ يُطْعِمُنِي وَيَسْقِينِ﴾ خاطب ربّه بالأدب فقال: ﴿وَإِذَا مَرِضْتُ فَهُوَ يَشْفِينِ﴾ فنسب المرض إلى نفسه، لأنها تنفر من الأعراض والأمراض. وكلّ شيء يطرأ على الإنسان لا يقدر على دفعه، مثل النوم واليقظة والضحك والبكاء والغم والسرور والخصب والجدب والغنى والفقر، فهو منه تقدّست أسماؤه. ألا ترى أنه لا يتوعّد على فعله، ولا

stood still, thinking. He raised his head; then he said, "How impudent am I! I say to Thee, 'O Generous One!' whereas someone has said about one of Thy servants:

And if in his hand he held only his soul,
he would give it away; let who asks him beware![143]

"And on someone else the following was said:

You see him, when you come to him, exulting,
as if you had just given what you ask from him."[144]

Then he said, "But of course, I'll say 'O Generous One, who surpasses every generous one, and through whose generosity every one who is generous can be generous!'"

Ibn al-Sammāk[145] entered into the presence of al-Rashīd, who said to him: 10.2
"Preach to me!" The caliph held a beaker containing water in his hand. "Wait, O Commander of the believers!" said Ibn al-Sammāk, "What do you think: if God made a divine decree about you and said, 'I shall only let you drink in return for half your empire,' would you do it?" The caliph replied, "Yes, I would." "Drink," said Ibn al-Sammāk, "May God let you enjoy it!" When he had drunk, the preacher said, "What do you think: if the same divine decree was applied to you[146] and God said, 'I shall only let you pass the water of this beaker from your body if I rob you of your empire,' would you accept?" The caliph answered, "Yes, I would." "Then fear God," said Ibn al-Sammāk, "and reflect upon an empire that is worth only a piss."

How could I complain about Him who fed me and sustained me for more 11.1
than seventy years? When my shirt was two cubits long(?)[147] He appointed for me two loving and caring parents, who spared no effort to make it fine and soft and pleasant. When it was twelve cubits long He took care of it and of my sustenance. He never let me go starving or naked. «And He who gives me food and drink»;[148] the speaker addressed his Lord tactfully and said, «And when I am ill He cures me»,[149] attributing the illness to himself, because one shuns mishaps and illnesses, though everything that befalls a person and which he is unable to prevent, such as sleep and wakefulness, laughter and weeping, sorrow and joy, fecundity and drought, wealth and poverty—all this comes from Him, sanctified be His names. Do you not see

يعاقب عليه؟ وما يقدر على دفعه فهو منه، مثل أن يريد الكتابة فلا يقع منه البناء، ويريد البناء فلا تقع منه الكتابة. ومن به الرعشة لا يقدر على إمساك يدٍ، ومن ليست به يقدر على إمساكها.

٢،١١ كنت بِتِنّيسَ وبين يديّ إنسان يقرأ ويُحزِن: ﴿يُوفُونَ بِالنَّذْرِ وَيَخَافُونَ﴾ ويبكي، فخطر لي خاطر فقلت: أنا بضدّ هؤلاء القوم صلوات الله عليهم، أنا لا أنذر ولا أفي، ولا أخاف شقاء ولا عناء، ولوكنت أخاف ما أصحبت[1] محموماً، وكنته.

وحدّثني مَن أثق به ولا أتّهمه، عن أبيه – وكان زاهداً – قال: كنت مع أبي بكر الشبلي ببغداد، في الجانب الشرقي بباب الطاق، فرأينا شاوياً قد أخرج حملاً من التنّور كأنه بُسْرة نضجاً، وإلى جانبه قد عمل حَلاوِيٌّ فالوذجا. فوقف ينظر إليهما وهو ساهٍ يُفكِّر، فقلت: يا مولاي دعني آخُذ من هذا وهذا ورِقاقاً وخبزاً، ومنزلي قريب، تُشَرِّفني بأن تجعل راحتك اليوم عندي. فقال: يا هذا، أظننتَ أني قد اشتهيتُهما؟ وإنما فكري في أن الحيوان كله لا يدخل النار إلا بعد الموت، ونحن ندخلها أحياء:

يا ربِّ عفوَكَ عن ذي شيبَة وَجِلٍ   كأنَّه من حذارِ النارِ مجنونُ
قد كان قدّم[2] أفعالاً مُذمَّمَةً   أيامَ ليس له عقلٌ ولا دينُ

١٢ تمّت الرسالة والحمد لله ذي الإفضال،[3] وصلواته على محمد وخيرة الآل.

ما فرغتُ من السوداء حتى ثارت بي السوداءُ، وأنا أعتذر من خَطَل فيها أو زلل، فإن الخطأ مع الاعتذار والاجتهاد والتحرّي، موضوعٌ عن المخطئ:

---

١ بياض في الأصل، والسياق يقتضي زيادة (إلا)، كما في ب. ٢ ب: (ذمم). ٣ في كل الطبعات ما خلا كع: الأفضال.

that He neither threatens[150] nor punishes for doing these things? Whereas anything a human being is able to prevent is his own doing, for instance when one wants to write something, and thus it happens that one does not build anything; or when one wants to build something, and thus it happens that one does not write. But someone who suffers from tremors is unable to steady his hand whereas someone who does not is able to hold it steady.

When I was in Tinnīs there was someone who was reciting the Qur'an with a 11.2
plaintive voice:[151] «They fulfill their vows and fear», and he wept. A thought occurred to me and I said to myself, "I am the opposite of those people, God's blessings be upon them. I neither make nor fulfill vows and do not fear misery and suffering. If I were fearful I would not be anything but[152] feverish"—And then I was!

An unimpeachable and trustworthy acquaintance told me the following story on the authority of his father, an ascetic, who had said, "I was with Abū Bakr al-Shiblī in Baghdad, in East Side in Bāb al-Ṭāq, when we saw a seller of roasted meat who took a lamb from the oven, which was as tender as a fresh, ripe date. Next to him was a pastry cook who was making *fālūdhaj*. Abū Bakr stopped and looked at them, lost in thought. 'My master,' I said to him, 'let me get some of both, along with some thin cakes and bread! My house is nearby; will you honor me by relaxing at my place today?' But he said, 'Really, do you think I have an appetite for these things? I was merely thinking that all other living beings enter the fire only after they have died, whereas we enter it alive!'"

O Lord, forgive a gray-haired, fearful man,
who's like a madman, fearful of the Fire!
He has committed, in the past, blameworthy deeds,
during the days he had no sense and no religion.[153]

The epistle is finished, praise be to God, giver of graceful gifts, and His bless- 12
ings be on Muḥammad and the elect of his family.

I had hardly finished a draft when I was stirred by a bout of melancholy.[154] I apologize for the rambling or any error in this letter; for someone who makes a mistake is forgiven if it is accompanied by apology, effort, and careful scrutiny.

ومَن ذا الذي يؤتى الكمالَ فيكملُ

قال عمر بن الخطّاب: رحم الله امرأً أهدى إليّ عيوبي.

وأسأله - أدام الله عزّه - تشريفي بالجواب عنها، فإن هذه الرسالة - على ما بها - قد استُحْسِنَت وكُتِبَت عني وسُمِعَت مني، وشرّفتُها باسمه، وطرّزتُها بذكره. والرسالة التي كتبها الزَهْرَجي إليّ، كانت أكبر الأسباب في دخولي إلى حلب. وإذا جاء جواب هذه، سيّرْتُها بحلب وغيرها إن شاء الله، وبه الثقة، وصلّى الله على سيّدنا محمّد وعلى آله وسلّم.

But who will be given perfection, then, and be perfect?[155]

ʻUmar ibn al-Khaṭṭāb said, "God have mercy on any man who points out my defects to me!"

And I ask the Sheikh—may God give him lasting power!—to honor me by answering my letter, for in spite of its imperfections it has been appreciated, taken down from my dictation, and received from me through lectures; I have honored it with the Sheikh's name and adorned it by mentioning him. The letter that al-Zahrajī wrote to me was the main reason why I came to Aleppo. If its answer comes I shall make it go round Aleppo and elsewhere, God willing. In Him is our trust, and God bless and preserve our lord Muḥammad and his family.

رسالة الغفران

المجلّد الأوّل

The Epistle of Forgiveness

Volume One

بسم الله الرحمن الرحيم

اللهم يسّر وأعن

قد علِم الجَبْرُ الذي نُسب إليه جبرئيل، وهو في كلّ الخيْرات سبيل، أن في مَسْكَني حَماطةً ما كانت قطّ أفانِيَة، ولا النَاكزةُ بها غانِيَة، تُثْمِر من مودّة مولاي الشيخ الجليل، كبت الله عَدُوّه، وأدام رَواحَه إلى الفضل وغُدوّه، ما لو حملته العالية من الشجر، لدَنَتْ إلى الأرض غصونُها، وأُذيلَ من تلك الثمرة مَصونُها. ١٠١

والحَماطة ضربٌ من الشجر يقال لها إذا كانت رطْبة: أفانية، فإذا يبِست فهي حماطة. قال الشاعر:

إذا أمّ الوُليّد لم تطِعْني حنوتُ لها يدي بعصا حَماطِ
وقلتُ لها عليكِ بني أُقيْشٍ فإنّكِ غيرُ مُعجبة الشّطاطِ

وتوصَف الحماطةُ بإلفِ الحيّات لها، قال الشاعر:

أُتيحَ لها وكان أخا عِيالٍ شُجاعٌ في الحماطة مستكِنٌّ

وأن الحماطة التي في مَقرّي لتَجِد من الشوق حماطةً، ليست بالمصادَفة إماطة. والحماطة حُرقة القلب، قال الشاعر:

وهَمٍّ تُملأُ الأحشاءُ منه

فأما الحماطة المبدوء بها فهي حَبّة القلب، قال الشاعر:

Preamble

In name of God, the Merciful, the Compassionate

O God, give ease and help

The Mighty One (*al-Jabr*), from whom comes the name of Gabriel—He is the Way to all good things—knows that there is a tree (*ḥamāṭah*)[156] within me, one that never was an *afāniyah* tree, and on which there lived no stinging snake,[157] one that produces fruit for the love of my lord the venerable Sheikh[158]—may God subdue his enemy, and always, evening and morning, lead him to superiority![159] If a lofty tree were to bear these fruits its branches would sink to earth and all this fruit, once well-protected, would be trampled underfoot. 1.1

Ḥamāṭah is a kind of tree, which is called *afāniyah* when tender and *ḥamāṭah* when dry. A poet says:

> When Umm al-Wulayyid[160] does not obey me,
> I bend my hand around a stick of *ḥamāṭ* wood for her
> And I say to her, "Get the Banū Uqaysh![161]
> For you haven't got a nice figure!"

A characteristic of the *ḥamāṭah* is that it is a familiar haunt of snakes. A poet says:

> Destined for her was—one from a numerous brood—
> a bold male snake that hid in the *ḥamāṭah* tree.

He knows that the tree (*ḥamāṭah*) found in me feels a burning (*ḥamāṭah*) of great yearning which, as it happens, is not to be removed (*imāṭah*).[162]

Ḥamāṭah also means "heartburn." A poet says: "Many a worry that fills one's inside . . . ."[163] At the beginning of the Preamble, *ḥamāṭah* means "core of the heart." A poet says:

رمتْ حماطةَ قلبٍ غيرِ منصرفٍ عنها بأسهُمِ لحظٍ لم تكن غَرَبا

وأنّ في طِمرّي لِحضْباً وُكّل بأذاتي، لو نطق لَذكرشَذاتي، ما هو بساكن في الشّقاب، ولا بمتشرف على النِّقاب، ما ظهر في شتاء ولا صيْف، ولا مرّ بجبل ولا خيْف، يُضْمِر من محبّة مولاي الشيخ الجليل، ثبت الله أركان العلم بحياته، ما لا تُضمِره للولد أمّ، أكان سمّها يُدّكر أم فُقد عندها السّم. وليس هذا الحضب مجانساً للذي عناه الراجز في قوله:

وقد تطوّيتُ انطواءَ الحِضْبِ

وقد علم، أدام الله جمالَ البَراعة بسلامته، أن الحِضْب ضرب من الحيات، وأنه يقال لحبّة القلب حضب. وأنّ في منزلي لأسْود، هوأعزُّعليّ من عَنْترَة على زَبيبة، وأكرم عندي من السُّليْك عند السُّلكة، وأحقُّ بإيْثاري من خُفاف السُّلَميّ بخبايا نَدْبةَ وهو أبداً محجوب، لا تُجاب عنه الأغْطِيةُ ولا يجوب، لو قدر لسافر إلى أن يلقاه، ولم يحْذ عن ذلك لشقاءٍ يَشْقاه. ٢.١

وإنه إذ يُذكَر، ليؤنّث في المنطق ويذكّر، وما يُعلم أنه حقيقيُّ التذكير، ولا تأنيثُه المعتمد بنكير.

لا أفتأُ دائباً فيما رَضي، على أنه لا مدفع لما قُضي. أُعظِمه أكثرَ من إعظام لَخْمٍ الأسْودَ بن المُنْذِر وكِنْدةَ الأسْودَ بن مَعْدِ يكَرِب، وبني نَهْشَل بن دارم الأسْود بن يَعْفرذا المقال المُطرب. ولا يَبْرح مُولَعاً بذكره كإيلاع سُحَيْم بعُمَيْرَة في مَحْضَره ومَبْداه، ونُصيْب مولى أُميّةَ بسُعْداه.

وقد كان مِثلُه مع الأسْود بن زَمْعة، والأسْود بن عبد يَغوث والأسودين اللذيْن ذكرهما اليَشكُري في قوله: ٣.١

فهداهم بالأسودَينِ وأمرُ الله بَلْغٌ يَشْقى به الأشقياءُ

She shot at the core (*ḥamāṭah*) of my heart, unswervingly,
with arrows from her glance, the shooter unknown.

And God knows that in my two ragged robes[164] there is a "male snake (*ḥiḍb*)"[165] charged with harming me; if it could speak it would mention my misery. It does not live in a rocky crack or nook; down on to narrow mountain passes it does not look. It appears neither in winter nor in summer time; it passes neither by mountain nor by incline. It harbors for my lord, the venerable Sheikh—may God make the cornerstones of scholarship firm by giving him long life!—such a love as a mother cannot harbor for her son, no matter whether she is considered venomous or not.[166] This "snake" is no kin of the one meant by the *rajaz* poet[167] who said,

I curled up like a *ḥiḍb*.

The Sheikh—may God perpetuate beautiful performance by keeping him well!— knows that a *ḥiḍb* is a kind of snake, and that it is also used for the "bottom of the heart." He knows that this "black thing,"[168] which is dearer to me than ʿAntarah was to Zabībah, more precious to me than al-Sulayk was to al-Sulakah, and more entitled to my affection than Khufāf al-Sulamī was entitled to the innermost feelings of Nadbah, is always concealed, its coverings never removed and it never moves far afield. If it could travel it would, so that the Sheikh and it could meet; no mishap befalling it could make it retreat. 1.2

When mentioned in speech, it can be feminine and also masculine.[169] It is not known if it is really masculine; using it as a feminine is not rejected.

To please it, incessantly I take pains, although one cannot avert what God ordains. I esteem it more than Lakhm esteemed al-Aswad ("Black")[170] ibn al-Mundhir, more than Kindah esteemed al-Aswad ibn Maʿdīkarib, and more than the Banū Nahshal ibn Dārim esteemed al-Aswad ibn Yaʿfur, who composed such ravishing poetry. At the same time it never ceases to be as fond of mentioning the Sheikh as Suḥaym, be he in town or desert, was fond of his ʿUmayrah, or as Suʿdā was loved by Nuṣayb, the client of Umayyah.

Just such a thing[171] was found with al-Aswad ibn Zamʿah, al-Aswad ibn ʿAbd Yaghūth, the two men called al-Aswad mentioned in al-Yashkurī's[172] verse: 1.3

He guided them with the two Aswads; [173] God's command
strikes home: with it the wretched are made wretched

ومع أسوَدان الذي هو نَبْهان بن عمرو بن الغوْث بن طَيء، ومع أبي الأسود الذي ذكره امرؤ القيس في قوله:

وذلكَ من خبرٍ جاءني ونُبّئته عن أبي الأسْوَدِ

وما فارَقه أبو الأسْود الدؤلي في عمره طَرْفةَ عين، في حال الراحة ولا الأين، وقارن سُويْد بن أبي كاهل يَرِدُ به على المَناهل. وحالَفَ سُويد بن الصامت، ما بين المبتهج والشامت. وساعَفَ سُويد بن صُمَيْع، في أيّام الرّتَب والرّبَع. وسُويد هذا الذي يقول:

إذا طلبوا مني اليمين منحتُهم يميناً كبُرْد الأتْحَميّ الممزّقِ
وإن أحلفوني بالطّلاق أتيتُها على خيرِ ما كُنّا، ولم نتفرقِ
وإن أحلفوني بالعِتاق فقد درى عُبيْدٌ غُلامي أنه غيرُ مُعْتَقِ

وكان يألف فِراش سَودةَ بنت زَمْعة بن قيس امرأة النبيّ صلى الله عليه وسلم، ٤،١
ويعرف مكانه الرسولُ، ولا ينحرف عنه السُّول، ودخل الجَدَث مع سَوادة بن عَديّ، وما ذلك بزوْل بديّ، وحضر في نادٍ حَضَرَه الأسْودان اللذان هما الهَنَم والماء، والحَرّة الغابرة والظّلْماء. وإنه ليَنْفِر عن الأبيضيْن، إذا كانا في الرّهج معرّضيْن، الأبيضان اللذان ينفر منهما: سيفان، أو سيف وسِنان، ويصبِر عليهما إذا وجدهما، قال الراجز:

الأبيضانِ أبردا عِظامي الماءُ والفَثُّ[1] بلا إدامِ

ويرتاح إليهما في قول الآخر:

ولكنه يمضي لِيَ الحَوْلُ كلُّه وما لِيَ إلاّ الأبيضيْن شرابُ

---

[1] ب٤، إف، ق: (والفَتُّ).

and with Aswadān, viz. Nabhān ibn ʿAmr ibn al-Ghawth ibn Ṭayyiʾ, and with Abū l-Aswad, mentioned by Imruʾ al-Qays[174] in his verse:

And that is because of what I have heard,
something that I was told about Abū l-Aswad.

Abū l-Aswad al-Duʾalī never parted from it in his lifetime for one second, whether during easy relaxation or tiring occupation. With Suwayd ibn Abī Kāhil it enjoyed a close link whenever he went to wells to drink. With Ibn al-Ṣāmit, another Suwayd, it was always closely allied, be he rejoicing gladly or gloating badly. It helped Suwayd ibn Ṣumayʿ as an ally, in days of poverty and prosperity. He was the one who said:[175]

When they demand from me an oath, I'll swear for them
an oath that's like a torn and tattered robe with yellow stripes!
And if they make me swear upon my wife's divorce, I'll come to her
as happily as ever, and we shall not part.
And if they make me swear upon the freeing of my slave,
ʿUbayd, my slave, knows well he won't be freed!

It was familiar with Sawdah bint Zamʿah ibn Qays's bed, when to the Prophet (God bless and preserve him) she was wed. God's messenger knew its force, and in good grace did not resort to divorce.[176] It entered the grave with Sawādah ibn ʿAdī, which is not a strange oddity. It is found in any congregation where the "two black things" are found, viz. water and dates, or maybe they are darkness and dusty volcanic ground. It flees from the "two things white" when these are exposed to a dustcloud raised by a fight—the "two things white" from which it flees are either two swords, or a sword and a spearhead. Yet it will bear with them both when it finds them,[177] as the *rajaz* poet says, 1.4

The "two white things" have cooled my bones:
Water and millet bread, no added condiments.[178]

And it will delight in two other "white things," as in the following verse:[179]

But a whole year has passed for me
without a drink of anything except the two white things.

فأمّا الأبيضان اللذان هما شحمٌ وشَباب، فإنّما تفرح بهما الرَّباب، وقد يبتهج بهما عند غيري، فأمّا أنا فيئسا من خيري. وكذلك الأحامرة والأحمران، يجب لهما أسْودُ رانٍ، فيتبعه حليفُ سِترٍ، ما نزل به حادثُ هِترٍ.

As for the two white things that are youthfulness and fat, these are the things that al-Rabāb rejoices at,[180] and what perhaps other people are delighted to see. But they despair of getting anything out of *me*! It is the same with "the three, or two, red things"[181] that gratify the black (i.e. pupil) of a beholder's eye, which is then followed by something hidden away[182], as long as it has not yet been struck with mental decay.

وقد وصلت الرسالة التي بحرُها بالحِكَم مسجور، ومن قرأها مأجور، إذ كانت تأمر ٢
بتقبُّل الشرع، وتَعيب من ترك أصلاً إلى فرع. وغرِقتُ في أمواج بِدَعها الزاخرة، وعجِبتُ من اتّساق عقودها الفاخرة، ومثلها شَفَع ونَفَع، وقرّب عند الله ورفع. وألفيتُها مفتتحةً بتمجيدٍ، صدَر عن بليغٍ مُجيد، وفي قدرة ربّنا، جلّت عَظَمته، أن يجعل كلّ حرف منها شَبَحَ نور، لا يمتزج بمقال الزُّور؛ يستغفر لمن أنشأها إلى يوم الدين، ويذكُره ذِكْرَ محبٍّ خدين. ولعلّه، سبحانه، قد نصب لسطورها المُنجية من اللَّهب، معارِيجَ من الفِضّة أو الذَّهب، تعرُج بها الملائكة من الأرض الراكدة إلى السماء، وتكشِف سجوفَ الظلماء، بدليل الآية: ﴿إِلَيْهِ يَصْعَدُ الْكَلِمُ الطَّيِّبُ وَالْعَمَلُ الصَّالِحُ يَرْفَعُهُ﴾. وهذه الكلمة الطيّبة كأنها المَعْنيّة بقوله: ﴿أَلَمْ تَرَ كَيْفَ ضَرَبَ اللَّهُ مَثَلًا كَلِمَةً طَيِّبَةً كَشَجَرَةٍ طَيِّبَةٍ أَصْلُهَا ثَابِتٌ وَفَرْعُهَا فِي السَّمَاءِ، تُؤْتِي أُكُلَهَا كُلَّ حِينٍ بِإِذْنِ رَبِّهَا﴾. وفي تلك السطور كَلِمٌ كثير، كلّه عند الباري، تقدّس، أثير.

I have received your letter, which is a sea with words of wisdom brimming, rewarding any reading or skimming, because it enjoins one to accept God's laws and to condemn holding the branches instead of the trunk. I drowned in the billows of its abundant ideas and its originality, amazed by these well-arranged jewels of great quality. Such a letter helps to intercede, and nearer to God's favor it will lead. I found its opening praise of our Lord's magnificence to be by a master of eloquence. It is in the power of God (great is His might) to turn its every letter into a body of light, not mixed with falsehood's blight, which will ask for forgiveness for its writer until Judgment Day at the world's end, and which will remind him like a loving friend. Perhaps God has already made for its written lines, which will deliver from the Fire, silver or golden ladders going higher and higher, on which the angels from stagnant earth to heaven are ascending, and the veils of darkness rending, according to the Qur'anic verse,[183] «To Him ascend good words and a righteous deed He raises». Such «good words» seem to be meant also by God's word:[184] «Have you not seen how God has coined a comparison: a good word is like a good tree, its trunk stands firm and its branches are in the sky.[185] It brings its fruit every season, by its Lord's leave». In these lines there is many a word, all of which by the most Holy Creator to be favorably heard. 2

al-Maʿarrī's description of Ibn al-Qāriḥ's letter

١،٣ فقد غُرِسَ لمولاي الشيخ الجليل، إن شاء الله، بذلك الثناء، شجرٌ في الجنة لذيذُ اجتناء، كلُّ شجرةٍ منه تأخذ ما بين المشرق إلى المغرب بظِلٍّ غاطٍ، ليست في الأَعْيُن كذاتِ أنواطٍ. وذات أنواطٍ، كما يَعلم، شجرةٌ كانوا يعظّمونها في الجاهلية. وقد روي أن بعض الناس قال: يا رسول الله، اجعَلْ لنا ذاتَ أنواطٍ كما لهم ذات أنواطٍ، وقال بعض الشعراء:

لنـا المُهيـمِن يكْفيـنا أعـادِيَنا   كمـا رفضْنا إليـه ذاتَ أنواطِ

والوِلدان المخلَّدون في ظِلال تلك الشجر قِيام وقُعود، وبالمغْفِرة نِيلت السُّعود؛ يقولون، والله القادر على كلِّ عزيز: نحن وهذه الشجر صِلَةٌ من الله لعليّ بن منصور، نُخبَأُ له إلى نفخ الصُّور. وتجري في أصول ذلك الشجر أنهارٌ تختلِج من ماء الحيوان، والكوثر يمُدُّها في كلّ أَوان؛ من شرب منها النُّغبة فلا موت، قد أمِنَ هنالك الفوْت. وسُعُدٌ من اللبن متخرّقات، لا تُغيَّرُ بأن تطول الأَوقات. وجَعافِرُ من الرحيق المختوم، عزَّ المقتدر على كلّ محتوم. تلك الراح الدائمة، لا الذميمة ولا الذائمة، بل هي كما قال عَلْقَمة مفترِياً، ولم يكن لعفْوٍ مقترِياً:

تشفي الصُّداعَ ولا يؤذيه صالبُها   ولا يخـالط منها الرأسَ تدويـمُ

٢،٣ ويعمِد إليها المغترف بكؤوس من العَسْجَد، وأباريقَ خُلقت من الزَّبَرْجَد، ينظر منها الناظر إلى بَديّ، ما حلم به أبو الهِنديّ، رحمه الله، فلقد آثَرَ شرابَ الفانية، ورغِب في الدّنية الدّانية. ولا ريبَ أنه يروي ديوانَه، وهو القائل:

Paradise (I)

On account of this praise, if God wills, for the venerable Sheikh trees will have been planted and their delicious fruit to him granted. Each tree provides shade from the East to the West extending, not at all like the "Tree of Suspending."—As you know, this was a tree that was venerated in pre-Islamic times.[186] It is said that someone asked the Messenger of God: "Make for us a Tree of Suspending like they have!" A poet said, 3.1

Description of Paradise

> We have the Guardian who protects us from our enemies,
> and we refused to have a Tree of Suspension.

Ever-living youths in the shade of those trees stand or sit and rest; with forgiveness truly one's life is forever blessed. They say—God is powerful over every difficulty—"We along with the trees are God's gifts to ʿAlī ibn Manṣūr, hidden for him alone, until the day the Last Trumpet is blown." Rivers drawn from the Water of Life flow at the roots of every tree; the river Kawthar (Abundance) feeds them incessantly. Whosoever drinks from one of those, will never die or suffer fortune's blows. Rivers overflowing with milk that will not sour but last, no matter how much time has passed. Rivulets of choice, pure wine that was sealed when retained—mighty is He with power over all things ordained. This is the wine eternal, not the wine vile and infernal. Rather, it is as ʿAlqamah[187] said (though he lied and never for forgiveness applied):

> It cures a headache, its heat will not harm;
> it does not befuddle the brain.

One scoops from it with cups of gold and jugs formed from peridot: the onlooker sees something novel, undreamt of even by Abū l-Hindī,[188] the poet (God rest his soul) who did not know it. The vile, available wine of the world he did cherish, though it was sure to perish. The Sheikh will no doubt have memorized and transmitted his collected verse; he is the one who said, 3.2

سيُغني أبا الهِنديّ عن وَطْبِ سالِمٍ　　أباريقُ لم يَعْلَقْ بها وَضَرُ الزُّبْدِ
مفدَّمةٌ قَزّاً كأنّ رِقابَها　　رِقابُ بناتِ الماء أفزعها الرَّعْدُ

هكذا يُنْشَد على الإقواء وبعضهم ينشد:

رقابُ بناتِ الماءِ رِيعت من الرعدِ

والرواية الأولى إنشادُ النحويين. وأبو الهندي إسلاميّ، واسمه عبد المؤمن بن عبد القدُّوس، وهذان اسمان شرعيان، وما استُشهد بهذا البيت إلا وقائلُه عند المستشهِد فصيح، فإن كان أبو الهنديّ ممن كتب وعرف حروفَ المعجم فقد أساء في الإقواء، وإن كان بنى الأبياتَ على السكون، فقد صحَّ قول سعيد بن مَسْعَدة في أن الطويل من الشِّعر له أربعةُ أضرُب.

ولو رأى تلك الأباريقَ أبو زُبَيْد لعلم أنه كالعبد الماهن أو العُبَيْد، وأنه ما تشبّب بخيرٍ، ورضي بقليل المَيْر وهَرِئ بقوله: ٣،٣

وأباريقُ مِثْلُ أعناقِ طيرِ الـ　　ـماءِ قد جِيبَ فوقَهنّ خنيفُ

هيهات! هذه أباريقَ، تحمِلها أباريق، كأنها في الحُسن الأباريق.

فالأُولى هي الأباريق المعروفة، والثانية من قولهم: جاريةٌ إبريقٌ، إذا كانت تبرق من حُسنها: قال الشاعر:

وغيداءَ إبريقٍ كأنّ رُضابَها　　جَنى النحلِ ممزوجاً بصَهْباءِ تاجرِ

والثالثة من قولهم: سيفٌ إبريقٌ، مأخوذ من البريق. قال ابن أحمر:

تقلدتَ إبريقاً وعلّقتَ جَعْبةً　　لتُهلِكَ حيّاً ذا زُهاءٍ وجاملِ

Abū l-Hindī does not need a perfect skin of milk:
he is content with jugs to which there sticks no greasy muck;
Provided with a strainer made of silk,
their necks like those of waterfowl, when thunderstruck.

Thus it is recited, with the rhyme defect called *iqwāʾ* in the rhyme words *zubdī* and *raʿdū*. Others read it as *mina l-raʿdī*,

their necks like those of waterfowl, frightened by thunder,

but the former reading is that of the grammarians.[189] Abū l-Hindī is a poet of the Islamic period; his proper name is ʿAbd al-Muʾmin ibn ʿAbd al-Quddūs. Both these names are Islamic. The verse is only quoted as evidence by people who think the poet uses correct Arabic. If Abū l-Hindī is a poet who could write and knew the letters of the alphabet he made a bad mistake with this rhyme defect. If he intended the verses to end with an unvowelled consonant, then Saʿīd ibn Masʿadah is correct in saying that the poetic meter called *ṭawīl* has four variants.[190]

If Abū Zubayd had seen those jugs he would have known that he was as good as a lowly knave, a mere little slave, that the subject of his lyrical verse was worth very little, and that he was content with scanty victual. He would have laughed at his verse: 3.3

Jugs with spouts like the necks of waterfowl, clothed with a linen cover.[191]

Far from the mark! These *abārīq*, carried by *abārīq*, are brilliant like *abārīq*![192]

The first *abārīq* refer to the well-known "jugs." The second is from the expression *jāriyah ibrīq*, "radiant maiden," when she "shines" (*tabruqu*) with her beauty, as in the verse:

A radiant (*ibrīq*), graceful girl; it is as if her saliva
is nectar harvested by bees, mixed with the merchant's reddish wine.

The third is from the expression *sayf ibrīq*, "a shining sword," derived from *barīq* ("glitter"). Ibn Aḥmar said,

You girded yourself with a shining (*ibrīq*; viz. sword) and slung on a quiver,
to wipe out a populous tribe with a herd of their camels.

ولو نظر إليها علقمةُ لبرق وفرق، وظنَّ أنه قد طُرق، وأين يراها المسكينُ علقمةُ، ولعله في نار لا تَغير، ماؤها للشارب وَغِيرٌ. ما ابن عَبَدةَ وما فريقُه؟ خُسِر وكُسِر إبريقُه! أليس هو القائل:

كأنَّ إبريقهم ظبيٌ برابيةٍ مجلّلٌ بسبا الكتّان مفدومُ
أبيضُ أبرزه للضِّحّ راقبُه مقلّدٌ قُضُبَ الرّيحان مفغومُ

نظرةٌ إلى تلك الأباريق، خيرٌ من بنت الكَرْمة العاجلية ومن كل رِيقٍ، ضِمْنتْه هذه الدارُ الخادعة، التي هي لكلّ شَمَمٍ جادعةٌ.

ولو بصر بها عَديّ بن زيد، لشغل عن المُدام والصَّيد، واعترف بأن أباريق مُدامه، وما أدرك من شَرْب الحِيرة ونِدامه، أمرُهنَّ لا يُعدَل بنابتٍ من حَمَصيص، أو ما حَقُر من خَرْبَصيص.

وكنت بمدينة السّلام فشاهدتُ بعض الورّاقين يسأل عن قافيّة عَديّ بن زيد التي أوّلها: ٤،٣

بَكَرَ العاذلاتُ في غَلَس الصُّبح يعاتبنه أما تستفيقُ
ودعا بالصَّبوح فجرًا فجاءت قينةٌ في يمينها إبريقُ

وزعم الورّاق أن ابن حاجب النعمان سأل عن هذه القصيدة وطُلبت في نُسَخ من ديوان عديّ فلم توجد. ثمّ سمعتُ بعد ذلك رجلًا من أهل أستراباذ يقرأ هذه القافيّة في ديوان العِباديّ، ولم تكن في النسخة التي في دار العلم.

فأمّا الأُقيشر الأسديّ فإنه مُني بقاشر، وشقي إلى يومٍ حاشر، قال ولعله سيندم، إذا تفرّى الأَدَم: ٥،٣

أفنى تِلادي وما جمّعتُ من نَشَبٍ قرعُ القواقيزِ أفواهَ الأباريقِ

And if ʿAlqamah looked at them, he would be bedazzled and afraid, thinking he had lost his wits.—But how could poor ʿAlqamah see them? He may well be in a Fire that scorches the soil, where the drinking water will always boil. What has become of ʿAlqamah ibn ʿAbadah and his clan? His jug is broken and lost. But did he not say,

Their jug resembled a gazelle upon a hill,
  wrapped in a cloth, and with a linen veil,
Adorned with necklace of sweet-scented herb sprigs, white,
  brought by its keeper out into the light.

One look at these jugs is better than all the wine, daughter of the vine, of the world that passes, better than the saliva-sipping kisses[193] of sweet lasses one finds in the deceptive world, in which all pride is downward hurled. And if seen by ʿAdī ibn Zayd, from hunting and wine he would have been preoccupied, and would acknowledge that his wine jugs and all his drinking companions and friends in al-Ḥīrah were but a trifling thing: less than a blade of grass on sandy soil is its worth, less than a pebble lying on the earth.

When I was in Baghdad I saw a bookseller looking for the poem by ʿAdī ibn Zayd that begins with: 3.4

The women reproached him when morning
  dawned: "Hey, aren't you sober yet?"
But he called for a morning drink of wine;
  a songstress came, holding in her hand a jug.

The bookseller declared that Ibn Ḥājib al-Nuʿmān had asked for this poem; they searched for it in the copies of ʿAdī's collected poetry but did not find it. Afterward I heard a man from Astarabad recite this poem from the collected poetry of ʿAdī; but it was not contained in the copy in the library.

Take al-Uqayshir al-Asadī, he placed his bet on a bad horse in the event! 3.5
Wretched until Judgement Day he may still repent when his skin is rent. He said,

My wealth, inherited or earned, has been consumed
  by clinking cups on mouths of jugs.

ما هو وما شرابه؟ تقضّت في الخائنة آرابُه. لو عاين تلك الأباريقَ لأيقن أنه فُتن بالغرور، وسُرَّ بغيرِ مُوجِب للسرور. وكذلك إياس بن الأرتّ، إن كان عجب لأباريق كإوَزّ الطَّف، فإن الحوادث بسطتْ له أقبضَ كفّ. فكأنه ما قال:

كأنَّ أباريقَ المُدامـة بيـنهم إوزٌّ بأعلى الطَّفّ عُوجُ الحناجرِ

ورحم الله العجّاج، فإنه خلط في رجزه العُلَبِط والسَّجاج، أين إبريقه الذي ذكر فقال:

قطّفَ من أعنابها ما قطّفا فغمّها حولين ثمّ استودفا
صهباءَ خُرطومًا عُقارًا قرقفا فسَنَّ في الإبـريق منها نُزَفا
من رَصَفٍ نازَعَ سيلًا رَصَفا

وكم على تلك الأنهار من آنيةِ زَبَرجَدٍ محفور، وياقوتٍ خُلق على خلق الفُور، من أصفر ٦،٣
وأحمر وأزرق، يُخال إن لُمس أحرق، كما قال الصنوبريّ:

تخيّـلُه سـاطعًا وهجُـه فتأبى الدُّنوّ إلى وهجِهِ

وفي تلك الأنهار أوانٍ على هيئة الطير السابحة، والغانية عن الماء السائحة، فمنها ما هو على صور الكَراكيّ، وأُخَر تُشاكل المكاكيّ، وعلى خلق طواويس وبَطّ. فبعضٌ في الجارية وبعضٌ في الشّطّ، ينبُع من أفواهها شرابٌ، كأنه من الرِقّة سَرابٌ، لو جرع جُرعةً منه الحَكَميّ لحكم أنه الفوز القدَميّ. وشهد له كلُّ وُصّاف الخمر، من مُحْدَثٍ في الزمن وعتيق الأمر، أنّ أصناف الأشربة المنسوبة إلى الدار الفانية، كخمر عانة وأذرِعات، وهي مَظِنّةٌ للنُّعّات؛ وغزّةَ وبيت راس والفِلَسطية ذوات الأحراس؛ وما جُلب من بُصرى في الوسوق، تُبغى به المرابحة عند سوق، وما ذخره ابن بُجرَةَ بوَجّ، واعتمد به أوقاتَ الحجّ، قبل أن تُحرّم على الناس القهوات، وتُحظَر لخوف الله الشهوات. قال أبو ذؤيب:

What has happened to him and his wine? All his desires, without exception, have come to nought in the world of deception. If he beheld these jugs, he would know for certain that it was an illusion which seduced him, and that it was no joyful thing that to joy induced him. Likewise Iyās ibn al-Aratt, however pleased he was with jugs "like geese on a river bank," his fate played him a nasty prank. It is as if he never said,

The jugs of wine between them look like geese
  high on the river bank, with their crooked necks.

And God have mercy on al-ʿAjjāj, whose *rajaz* verse is a hodgepodge: where is the jug that he mentioned when he said,

He picked a quantity of grapes,
He stored it for two years; then he examined it:
A red and potent wine that makes you shudder.
And this he poured into the jug in little spurts,
Like torrent-water over mountain ledge.

How many vessels are there at those rivers, made of engraved peridot, and of 3.6
ruby, jacinth, or sapphire, carved like gazelles, of various hue: red, yellow, and blue; their sparkle is such that they burn to the touch, as al-Ṣanawbarī said,

You would think it ablaze
  and refuse to come close to its blaze.

In these rivers are vessels shaped like waterfowl that swim, or others that do not need the flowing stream. Some are formed like cranes, others resemble songbirds, or are shaped like peacocks and ducks. Some are in the water, others on the riverbank. From their spouts flows wine, like a mirage so clear and fine. If al-Ḥakamī Abū Nuwās had sipped it from a glass, he would have deemed it a cordial he had desired from times primordial. All those poets, both the moderns and the ancients,[194] who have described wine would testify in its favor, above all other kinds of wine that belong to the Perishable World, such as the old wine from ʿĀnah, Adhriʿāt, Gaza, Bayt Raʾs, or Palestine; the wine imported from Bostra on camelback, with which one hopes to make a profit on the market; the wine stored by Ibn Bujrah in Wajj,[195] on which he relied at the time of the Hajj, before alcoholic drinks were prohibited and base desires, for fear of God, were limited—Abū Dhuʾayb said:

ولو أنَّ ما عند ابن بُجرة عندها   من الخمر لم تبلُل لَهاتي بناطلِ

وما اعتُصر بصَرْخَد أو أرض شِبام لكلّ ملكٍ غير عَبام، وما تردّد ذكره من كُميتِ بابل وصريفين واتُّخذ للأشراف المُنيفين، وما عُمل من أجناس المسكرات، مفوّقاتٍ للشارب وموكّرات، كالجِعة والبِتْع والمِزر والسُّكُرْكة ذات الوِزر، وما وُلد من النخيل، لكريم يُعترف أو بخيل، وما صُنع في أيّام آدم وشِيثٍ، إلى يوم المبعث من معجّلٍ أو مكيث، إذ كانت تلك النُّطفة ملِكةً، لا تصلح أن تكون برعاياها مشتبكة.

٧،٣ ويعارض تلك المدامة أنهارٌ من عسلٍ مصفًّى ماكسبته النحل الغادية إلى الأنوار، ولا هو في مُومٍ متوارٍ، ولكن قال له العزيز القادر: كُنْ فكان، وبكرمه أعطي الإمكان. واهاً لذلك عسلاً، لم يكن بالنار مُبَسّلا، لو جعله الشارب المحرور غذاءه طول الأبد ما قُدر له عارضُ مُوم، ولا لبس ثوب المحموم؛ وذلك كلُّه بدليل قوله: ﴿مَثَلُ الجَنَّةِ الَّتِي وُعِدَ الْمُتَّقُونَ فِيهَا أَنْهَارٌ مِن مَّاءٍ غَيْرِ آسِنٍ وَأَنْهَارٌ مِن لَّبَنٍ لَّمْ يَتَغَيَّرْ طَعْمُهُ وَأَنْهَارٌ مِّنْ خَمْرٍ لَّذَّةٍ لِّلشَّارِبِينَ وَأَنْهَارٌ مِّنْ عَسَلٍ مُّصَفًّى وَلَهُمْ فِيهَا مِن كُلِّ الثَّمَرَاتِ﴾ فليت شعري عن النَّمِر بن تَوْلَبٍ العُكْليّ، هل يقدر له أن يذوق ذلك الأَرْي، فيعلم أن شُهْد الفانيةِ إذا قيس إليه وُجد يشاكِهُ الشَّرْي؛ وهو لمّا وصف أمّ حِصْن، وما رُزقته في الدّعة والأمن، ذكر حُوّارَى بسَمْن، وعسلٍ مصفًّى؛ فرحمه الخالق متوفًّى، فقد كان أسلم وروي حديثاً منفرداً، وحسبنا به للكلم مسرِّداً. قال المسكين النمر:

ألمّ بصُحبتي وهُمُ هجوعُ   خيالٌ طارقٌ من أمّ حِصْنِ
لها ما تشتهي عسلاً مصفًّى   إذا شاءت وحُوّارَى بسَمْنِ

١،٨،٣ وهو، أدام الله تمكينه، يعرف حكاية خَلَف الأحمر مع أصحابه في هذين البيتين،

Even if she had as much wine as Ibn Bujrah
she would not wet my palate with a sip

—or the wine pressed in Ṣarkhad or in the region of Shibām for any wise king, or the famed red wine of Ṣarīfīn and Babel made for all who are noble; or any type of intoxicating drink that makes the heavy drinker drink his fill, such as barley beer and wheat beer, mead made of honey, Abyssinian millet wine, and wine sired by date palms, made for both the miser and the generous man asked for alms; wines made from the days of Adam and Seth until Resurrection Day, for ready consumption or after long delay: they would testify that this drop of Paradise is a queen, who should never mixed up with her subjects be seen.

Opposite this wine are rivers of purified honey that has not been gathered by bees that in the morning hours swarm out to flowers and not hidden in waxen bowers. Rather, the Almighty said "Be!" and it was; by His generosity it was granted the possibility to be. Such honey! It is not spoiled by fire; if some overheated drinker made it his morning drink forever, he would never be afflicted with pleurisy and he would never don the cloak of fever. All this is according to God's word:[196] «The likeness of the Garden that has been promised to the God-fearing: in it are rivers of water that is not stale, and rivers of milk whose taste will not go sour, and rivers of wine, a delight to the drinkers, and rivers of purified honey; and in it they have some of all kinds of fruit». I wish I knew if al-Namir ibn Tawlab al-ʿUklī was permitted to taste this honey! Then he would know that compared with it the honey of the Perishable World would resemble bitter colocynth. When he described Umm Ḥiṣn and the life of luxury and security that she led, he mentioned white bread, with butter clarified, as well as honey purified. God have mercy with him now that he has died! For he converted to Islam and transmitted a single saying of the Prophet. To have transmitted it correctly is for us sufficient profit. Poor al-Namir said, 3.7

To my companions,[197] when they all were sleeping tight,
there came a phantom of Umm Ḥiṣn in the night.[198]
She has what she desires: honey purified
whenever she wants, white bread with butter clarified.

The Sheikh knows (may God always empower him!) the story of Khalaf al-Aḥmar with his companions in connection with these verses. He asked 3.8.1

ومعناها أنه قال لهم: لوكان موضعَ أمّ حِصْن أمُّ حَفْص، ماكان يقول في البيت الثاني؟ فسكتوا، فقال: حوّارى بلَمص، يعني الفالُوذ. ويفرّع على هذه الحكاية فيقال: لوكان مكانَ أمّ حصن أمّ جُزْء وآخره همزةٌ، ماكان يقول في القافية الثانية؟ فإنّه يحتمل أن يقول: وحوارى بكَشْء، من قولهم: كشأت اللحم إذا شويته حتى ييبَس، ويقال: كشأ الشواء إذا أكله. أو يقول بوَزْء، من قولهم: وزأت اللحم إذا شويته. ولو قال: حوّارى بنَسْء،لجاز وأحسن ما يُتأوّل فيه، أن يكون من نسأ اللهُ في أجله، أي لها خبزٌ مع طول حياة، وهذا أحسن من أن يُحمَل على أن النسء اللبنُ الكثير الماء، وقد قيل: إن النسء الخمر، وفسّروا بيت عُروة بن الوَرْد على الوجهين:

سقوني النّسءَ ثم تكنّفوني عُداةُ الله من كذبٍ وزُورِ

ولو حُمل حوّارى بنسء على اللبن أو الخمر لجاز، لأنها تأكل الحوّارى بذلك، أي لها الحوّارى مع الخمر، وقد حدّث محدّثٌ أنه رأى بَسيلَ[1] ملك الروم وهو يغمِس خبزًا في خمرٍ ويصيب منه.

ولو قيل: حوّارى بلَزْء، من قولهم: لزأ إذا أكل، لما بعُد، [وتكون الباء في بلزء بمعنى في].[2]

ولا يمكن أن يكون رويُّ هذا البيت ألفًا، لأنها لا تكون إلاّ ساكنة، وما قبل الرويّ هاهنا ساكنٌ، فلا يجوز ذلك.

فإن خرج إلى الباء فقال: من أمّ حرْب، جاز أن يقول: وحوّارى بصَرْب، وهو اللبن الحامض، ويجوز بإِرْب، أي بعُضوٍ من شواءٍ أو قديد، ويجوز بكَشْب وهو أكل الشواء. ٢،٨،٣

فإذا قال: من أمّ صَمْت، جاز أن يقول: وحواري بكَمْت، يعني جمع تمرةٍ كُميت، وذلك من صفات التمر، وينشَد للأسود بن يعفُر:

١ راجع ب عن اختلاف النسخ: (بسيل)، (بسبيل)، (بسل)، (أبسئل) وكلها تحريفات.

٢ هذه العبارة موجودة بهامش بعض النسخ وترجّحت بنت الشاطئ أن العبارة من أصل النصّ.

them what the poet would have said in the second verse if the first had not rhymed in "Umm Ḥiṣn" but in "Umm Ḥafṣ." They did not come up with an answer; so he said: "white bread with *lamṣ*," which means a kind of sweatmeat.[199] One could expand this story[200] and ask: if the first verse had ended in "Umm Jazʾ," rhyming on the *hamzah*[201], what would he have said in the second? It would have been possible to say "white bread with *kashʾ*," from the expression *kashaʾa l-laḥm*, "to roast meat until it is dry," or *kashaʾa l-shuwāʾ*, "to eat meat that has been roasted until dry." Or he could have said "white bread with *wazʾ*," from the expression *wazaʾa l-laḥm*, "to roast meat." Possible, too, is "white bread with *nasʾ*." The best interpretation of this is that it is derived from the expression *nasaʾa Allāhu fī ajalih*, "May God postpone his end," and here meaning "she will have bread with a long life." This is better than explaining *nasʾ* as "milk mixed with a lot of water." It has also been said that *nasʾ* means "wine." Two interpretations have been given of the verse by ʿUrwah ibn al-Ward:[202]

> They gave me *nasʾ* to drink; and then those enemies of God
> surrounded me with lies and falsehood.

It would also be possible to interpret "white bread with *nasʾ*" as "with milk" or "with wine," because white bread is eaten with these things; i.e., "she has white bread with wine." Someone recounted how he saw Basīl, the king of the Byzantines, dipping bread in wine and eating it.

And if one would say "white bread with *lazʾ*," from the expression *lazaʾa*, "to satiate," it would not be too far-fetched; the preposition "with" would then mean "while (being satiated)" here.[203]

The rhyme letter of the verse could not be *alif*, since this *alif* is always unvowelled; the preceding consonant is unvowelled here, which is not possible with this rhyme.[204]

But if the poet were to turn to the letter *b*, and said "of Umm Ḥarb," 3.8.2
he could rhyme the next verse with "white bread with *ṣarb*," which means "sour milk"; or "with *irb*," i.e. with a joint of roast meat or sliced dried meat; or "with *kashb*," meaning "eating roast meat greedily."

If he says "of Umm Ṣamt," he can continue with "white bread with *kumt*," i.e. the plural of *kumayt* (reddish-brown) dates, one of the ways to characterize dates. The following verse by al-Aswad ibn Yaʿfur is recited:

وكنتُ إذا ما قُرِّب الزاد مُولَعًا   بكلّ كُميتٍ جَلْدةٍ لم توَسَّفِ

وقال الآخر:

ولستُ أُبالي بعدما أكْتَّ مِرْبَدي   من التمر أن لا يُمطر الأرضَ كوكبُ

ويجوز وحُوّارى بِحُمّت، من قولهم: تمرٌ حمتٌّ، أي شديد الحلاوة.

فإن أخرجه إلى الثاء فقال: من أمّ شَثّ، قال: وحوّارى ببَثّ، والبثُّ: تمرٌ لم يُجَدْ كنْزُه فهو متفرق.

فإن أخرجه إلى الجيم فقال: أمّ لُجّ، جاز أن يقول: وحوّارى بدُجّ، والدُّجُّ: الفرّوج، ٣،٨،٣
جاء به العُمانيُّ في رجزه.

فإن خرج إلى الحاء، فقال: من أمّ شُحّ، جاز أن يقول: وحوارى بمُحّ، وبجُحّ، وبرُحّ، وبجُحّ، وبسُحّ. فالمحُّ: مُحّ البيضة، وبحٌّ: جمع أبحّ، من قولهم: كِسرٌ أبحُّ، أي كثير الدّسَم، وقال:

وعــاذلةٍ هــبّت عليّ تلومني   وفي كفّها كِسْرٌ أبحُّ رذومُ

ويجوز أن يُعنى بالبحّ القِداح، أي هذه المرأة أهلها أيسار، كما قال السُّلَميُّ:

قروْا أضيافَهم رِبحًا ببُحّ   يعيش بفضلهنّ الحيُّ سُمْرِ

ورُحٌّ: جمع أرحّ، وهو من صفات بقر الوحش، أي يصاد لهذه المرأة، ويقال لأظلاف البقر: رُحٌّ، قال الشاعر الأعشى:

ورحٌّ بالزّمـاع مردّفـاتٌ   بها تنضو الوغى وبها تـرودُ

Whenever the food was brought near I was fond
of all those reddish-brown firm unpeeled dates.

Another poet said,

I do not mind, now that my drying store is full of red-brown
dates, if stars do not cause rain to fall on earth.[205]

Possible, too, is "white bread with *ḥamt*," as one says "*ḥamt* dates," i.e. intensely sweet ones.

If the poet turns to the letter *th* and says "of Umm Shathth," he could continue with "white bread with *baththth*." *Bathth* are dates that have not been well packed together, and are found loose.

If he moved on to the letter *j*, saying "of Umm Lujj," it is possible to rhyme 3.8.3
it with "white bread with *dujj*." *Dujj* means "chicken"; al-ʿUmānī used it in his *rajaz* poetry.

If he moved on to the letter *ḥ*, saying "of Umm Shuḥḥ," he could have said "white bread with *muḥḥ*" or "with *buḥḥ*," or "with *ruḥḥ*," or "with *juḥḥ*," or "with *suḥḥ*." *Muḥḥ* is "the yolk of an egg," *buḥḥ* is the plural of *abaḥḥ*, as in the expression "an *abaḥḥ* bone covered with meat," meaning one with lots of fat. A poet said,

Many a reproaching woman got up to blame me,
holding in her hand a bone that drips with fat.

Buḥḥ could also mean "arrows," i.e., this woman's kinsmen play the *maysir* game,[206] as al-Sulamī said:

They regaled their guests on meat gained at play with arrow shafts,
brown ones, and thanks to them the tribe lives comfortably.

Ruḥḥ is the plural of *araḥḥ*, "with broad hoofs," which is one of the characteristics of wild oryx bulls, i.e.,these are hunted for that woman. Or the word is used for the cloven hoofs themselves, as the poet al-Aʿshā said:

And (he has) broad hoofs with hair behind the fetlocks, firmly planted,
with which he outstrips all in fighting, and with which he scouts
about the land.

والسُحّ: تمرٌ صغار يابس. والجُحُّ: صغار البطيخ قبل أن ينضج. ٤،٨،٣

فإن قال: أمّ دُخ، قال: حوّارى بجُخّ، ونحو ذلك.

فإن قال: أمّ سَعْد، قال: حوّارى بثَعْد، وهو الرُّطَب الذي لان كلّه.

فإن قال: أمّ وَقْذ، قال: حوّارى بِشقْذ، وهي فراخ الحَجَل.

فإن قال: أمّ عمرو، فإنّ أشبه ما يقول: حوّارى بتمر.

فإن قال: أمّ كُرْز، فإن أشبه ما يقول: وحوّارى بأُرْز، وفيه لغات ستّ: أَرُزٌّ على وزن أَشُدّ، وأُرُزّ على وزن صُمُلّ، وأُرُزٌ على وزن شُغُل، وأُرْزٌ في وزن قُفْل، ورُزّ مثل جُدٍّ، ورُنْز، بنونٍ وهي رديئة.

فإن قال: أمّ ضِبْس، قال: وحوّارى بدِبْس. والعرب تسمّي العسل دبساً. وكذلك فسّروا قول أبي زُبيد:

فنهزةٌ من لقُوا حسبتُهُمُ   أشهى إليه من بارد الدِّبِسْ[1]

حرّك للضرورة.

فإن قال: من أمّ قَرْشٍ، جاز أن يقول: حوّارى بورْش، والورش: ضربٌ من الجُبن، ويجوز أن يكون مولّداً، وبه سمّي ورشٌ الذي يروي عن نافع واسمه عثمان بن سعيد.

والصاد قد مضت. ٥،٨،٣

فإن قال: أمّ غَرْض، جاز أن يقول: حوّارى بفَرْض، والفرض: ضربٌ من التمر، قال الراجز:

إذا أكلتُ لبناً وفَرْضا   ذهبتُ طولاً وذهبتُ عَرْضا

وفي نَصبِ طُول وعَرض اختلافٌ بين المبرّد وسيبويه.

فإن قال: من أمّ لَقْط، جاز أن يقول: حوّارى بأَقْط، يريد أَقِط على اللغة الربَعية.

---

١ في البيت غموض ولعله محرّف.

Suḥḥ means "small dry dates." *Juḥḥ* means "small watermelons," before they are ripe. And if he said "of Umm Dukhkh," he could rhyme it with "white bread with *mukhkh*," i.e., "marrow," or something like it. 3.8.4

If he said, "of Umm Saʿd," he could say "white bread with *thaʿd*," which means ripe dates that are wholly soft.[207]

If he said, "of Umm Waqdh," he could say "white bread with *shiqdh*," viz. partridge chicks.

If he said, "of Umm ʿAmr," the closest match is "white bread with *tamr*," i.e., dates.

If he said, "of Umm Kurz," the closest match is "white bread with *urz*," i.e., rice; there are six variants of this word: *aruzz*, of the pattern ʾaC_1uC_2C_3, *uruzz* (pattern C_1uC_2uC_3C_3), *uruz* (C_1uC_2uC_3), *urz* (C_1uC_2C_3), *ruzz* (C_1uC_2C_3), and *runz*, with an *n*— but this is a bad form.

If he said, "of Umm Ḍibs," he could say "white bread with *dibs*" (i.e., honey); the Bedouin Arabs call *ʿasal* ("honey") *dibs*. Thus they explain the verse of Abū Zubayd:

An opportunity, indeed: I thought that those they met
were more delicious to him than cool *dibis*.[208]

The poet has inserted the extra vowel (in *dibis*) out of metrical necessity, as a poetic license.

If he said, "of Umm Qarsh," he could say "white bread with *warsh*," which is a kind of cheese. It may be a "post-classical" word.[209] Warsh, who transmitted a Qurʾanic reading on the authority of Nāfiʿ, was called after it; his proper name was ʿUthmān ibn Saʿd.[210]

The letter *ṣ* has already been dealt with. If he said, "of Umm Gharḍ," he could say "white bread with *farḍ*," which is another kind of date, as in the verses by the *rajaz* poet:[211] 3.8.5

When I eat milk with with *farḍ* dates
I grow in length and I grow in breadth.

Al-Mubarrad and Sībawayh[212] differ on the precise function of the accusative in "length" and "breadth."

And if he said, "of Umm Laqṭ," he could say "white bread with *aqṭ*," a variant found in the dialect of the tribal group of Rabīʿah for *aqiṭ*, which means "sour cheese."

فإن قال: من أمّ حظّ، فإن الأطعمة تقلّ فيها الظاء، كقلّتها في غيرها، لأن الظاء قليلةٌ جدّاً، ويجوز أن يقول: حوّارى بكَظّ، أي يكظّها الشِّبَع، أو نحو ذلك من الأشياء التي تدخل على معنى الاحتيال.

٦،٨،٣ فإن قال: أمّ طَلْع، جاز أن يقول: حوّارى بخَلْع، والخلع: هو اللحم الذي كان يُطبخ ويحملونه في القروف وهي أوْعِيةٌ من أدَم، ويُنشَد:

كُلي اللحم الغريض فإنّ زادي لِمن خَلْعٍ تضمّنَه القُروفُ

فإن قال: أمّ فَزْع، جاز أن يقول: حوّارى بضَرْع، لأن الضروع تُطبخ، وربّما تطرب إلى أكلها الملوكُ.

فإن قال: أمّ مُبْغ، قال: حوّارى بصِبْغ، والصبغ ما تُغمس فيه اللقمة من مَرَقٍ أو زيت أو خلٍّ.

فإن قال: أمّ نَخْف، قال: حوّارى برَخْف، والرخف زُبْدٌ رقيق، والواحدة رخفة، قال الشاعر:

لنا غَنَمٌ يُرضِي النزيلَ حليبُها ورَخْفٌ يغاديه لها وذبيحُ

فإن قال: أمّ فَرْق، قال: حوّارى بعَرْقٍ، والعرق: عظمٌ عليه لحمٌ من شواءٍ أو قديد.

فإن قال: أمّ سَبْك، جاز أن يقول: حوّارى برَبْك، أو بلَبْك، من قولهم: ربكت الطعامَ أو لبكته، إذا خلطته، وكان ذلك ممّا فيه رطوبةٌ، مثل أن يخالطه لبنٌ أو سمنٌ، أو نحو ذلك، ولا يقال: ربكت الشعيرَ بالحنطة، إلاّ أن يستعار.

٧،٨،٣ فإن قال: أمّ نَخْل، قال: حوّارى برَخْل، يريد الأنثى من أولاد الضأن، وفيه أربع لغات: رَخِل ورَخْل ورِخْل ورِخِل.

فإن قال: أمّ صِرْم، قال: حوارى بطِرْم، والطرم: العسل، وقد يسمّى السمن طِرماً.

وقد مضت النون في أمّ حِصْن.

If he said, "of Umm Ḥaẓẓ," then there are few edibles ending in *ẓ*, which is infrequent anyway, for it is a letter that is very rare. He could say, "white bread with *kaẓẓ*," i.e., "eating a surfeit", or some such contrived expressions that could be used.

If he said, "of Umm Ṭalʿ," he could say "white bread with *khalʿ*," i.e., with boiled meat carried in leather containers called *qurūf*. The following verse is recited: 3.8.6

Eat the tender meat! My food, for sure, is meat well-seasoned (*khalʿ*),
contained in leather vessels (*qurūf*).

If he said, "of Umm Farʿ," he could say "white bread with *ḍarʿ*," i.e., "udder," for udders are cooked. Kings sometimes love to eat them.

If he said, "of Umm Mubghī,"[213] he could say "white bread with *ṣibgh*," which is a seasoning made of gravy, olive oil, or vinegar, in which one dips a morsel.

If he said, "of Umm Nakhf," he could say "white bread with *rakhf*," which is soft butter, a lump of which is called *rakhfah*. A poet says:

We have sheep that give fresh milk that pleases lodging guests,
and we've soft butter for a morning meal, and slaughtered meat.

If he said, "of Umm Farq," he could say "white bread with *ʿarq*," i.e., a bone with meat on it, either roasted or boiled in a cauldron.

If he said, "of Umm Sabk," it would be possible to say "white bread with *rabk*," or " . . . with *labk*," (i.e., "with a mixture"), from the expression *rabaka* or *labaka l-ṭaʿām*, "to mix food with something;" that is, with things that are moist, for instance mixing it with milk, clarified butter, or similar things. One cannot use the verbs for mixing barley with wheat, except by way of metaphor.

If he said, "Of Umm Nakhl," he could say "white bread with *rakhl*," meaning a female lamb. There are four dialect variants: *rakhil*, *rakhl*, *rikhl*, and *rikhil*. 3.8.7

If he said, "Of Umm Ṣirm," he could say "white bread with *ṭirm*," i.e., honey. Clarified butter is also sometimes called *ṭirm*.

The letter *n* has already been dealt with, in "Umm Ḥiṣn."

فإن قال: أمّ دَوّ، قال: حوارى بحَوّ، والحوُّ: الجدْي، فيما حكى بعض أهل اللغة في قولهم: ما يعرف حَوًّا من لَوٍّ، أي جَدْيًا من عَناقٍ.

فإن قال: أمّ كُرْه، قال: حوّارى بُورْه، يريد جمع أوْرَه، من قولهم: كبشٌ أوره، أي سمين.

فإن قال: أمّ شَرْي، قال: حوارى بأَرْي، أي عسل.

وهذا فصل يتّسع، وإنما عرض في قولٍ نامٍ، كخيال طرق في المنام.

ولو خالط مَنًا من عسل الجنان، وما خلقه الله، سبحانه، في هذه الدار الخادعة، كالصاب والمقِر والسَّلَع والجَعْدة والشِّيح والهَبيد، لعاد ذلك كلُّه، وغيره من المُعْقِيات، يُعَدُّ من اللذائذ المرتقيات، فآض ماكُره من الصَّاب، كأنه المعتصَر من المُصاب، والمصاب: قصب السكّر، وأمسى الحَدَج وكأنه المتّخذ بالأهواز، إلّا يكُن السُّكَّ، فإنه موازٍ؛ ولصارت الراعية في الإبل، إذا وجدت الحنظلة أتحفتْ بها السيدةَ المُحَظَّلة، وهي التي تعظُم عليها الغَيْرة، من قولهم: حظل نساءه، إذا أفرط في الغيرة عليهنَّ، قال الراجز: ١،٩،٣

ولا تـرى بعـلاً ولا حـلائلا   كَهُ ولا كَهُنَّ إلا حاظِـلا

وانقطعت معايشُ أرباب القصب في ساحل البحر، وصُنع من المرّ الفالوذ المُحكم بلا سِحرٍ، أي بلا خَدْع.

ولو أن الحارث بن كَلَدة طعِم من ذلك الطِّرْيَم لعلم أن الذي وصفه يجري من هذا المنعوت، مجرى الدِّفْلى الشّاقة من الرِّعديد، ومَدوف ما يُكره من القنديد، وذكرتُ الحارث بقوله: ٢،٩،٣

فما عَسَلٌ ببـاردِ مـاءِ مُـزنٍ   على ظَـمَإٍ لشاربه يُشابُ
بأشهى من لُقِيّكُمُ إلينا   فكيف لنا به ومتى الإيابُ

If he said, "of Umm Daww," he could say "white bread with *ḥaww*," i.e. "kid," according to the Arabic expression quoted by a lexicographer: "He does not know a *ḥaww* from a *laww*," meaning "a male kid from a she-kid."[214]

If he said, "of Umm Kurh," he could say "white bread with *wurh*," which is the plural of *awrah*, "fat," as in the expression "*kabsh awrah* (a fat ram)."

And if he said, "of Umm Shary," he could say "white bread with *ary*," i.e. "honey."

This is a chapter that could be expanded[215]—such things happen in discourse that grows from such a theme, like an apparition that visits in a dream.

If a mere two pounds of Paradise honey were mixed with all the bitter things God created in this Treacherous World, such as colocynth, aloes, *Soelanthus*, *jaʿdah*, wormwood, and *habīd*, then they would be deemed delicious and superb, along with every other bitter herb. Then hateful colocynth would again taste like sugar pressed from cane; unripe colocynth would seem to have been made in al-Ahwāz, being sugar's equal. A woman herding camels, finding a colocynth,[216] would present it as a gift to her mistress who is *muḥẓalah*, which means a woman who is very jealously guarded; this is derived from the expression *ḥaẓala nisāʾahū*, "to guard one's women with excessive jealousy." A *rajaz* poet says: 3.9.1

You will not see a husband with his wives
like he and they but he will guard them jealously (*ḥāẓil*).[217]

For the owners of the plantations of sugarcane on the coast, their livelihood would be lost, and from bitter myrrh, without any wizardry, i.e. trickery, one would make *fālūdh*, honey-sweet and smooth.

If al-Ḥārith ibn Kaladah had tasted this honey he would have known that his description stands in relation to what is described here as bitingly bitter oleander[218] stands in relation to sweet jelly, or as an abhorrent medicinal concoction to sugar wine. I have in my mind the verses by al-Ḥārith: 3.9.2

Honey, to a thirsty drinker, with cold water
    from a raincloud mixed,
Is not more delicious than your meeting us:
    so when will it be and when will it return?

وكذلك السَّلْوى التي ذكرها الهُذَلي هي عند عسل الجنّة كأنها قارٌ رَمْليّ، والقار: شجرٌ مُرّ ينبُت بالرّمل، قال بشرٌ:

يُرَجُّون الصِّلاحَ[1] بذات كهفٍ ... وما فيها لهم سَلَعٌ وقارُ

وعنيتُ قول القائل:

فقاسمَها بالله جهداً لأنتُمُ ... ألذُّ من السَّلوى إذا ما نَشورُها

١٠،٣ وإذا منّ الله تبارك اسمه بورود تلك الأنهار، صاد فيها الواردُ سمكَ حلاوةٍ، لم يُرَ مثله في مُلاوة، لو بصُر به أحمد بن الحسين لاحتقر الهديّة التي أُهديت إليه فقال فيها:

أقلُّ ما في أقلّها سَمَكٌ ... يلعب في بِركةٍ من العَسَلِ

فأمّا الأنهار الخمريّة، فتلعب فيها أسماكٌ هي على صُوَر السَّمك بحريّةٌ ونهريّة، وما يسكن منه في العيون النّبْعية، ويظفَر بضروب النَّبت المرعيّة، إلا أنه من الذَّهب والفضّة وصنوف الجواهر، المقابَلة بالنُور الباهر. فإذا مدّ المؤمن يده إلى واحدةٍ من ذلك السَّمك، شرب من فيها عذباً لو وقعت الجرعة منه في البحر الذي لا يستطيع ماءه الشاربُ، لحَلَتْ منه أسافلُ وغوارب؛ ولصار الصَّمر كأنه رائحة خُزامى سهلٍ، طلّته الداجنة بدَهْل، والدَّهل: الطائفة من اللّيل، أو نشرُ مدامٍ خَوّارةٍ، سَيّارةٍ في القُلَل سَوّارة.

---

[1] ب، إف، ي: (الصَّلاح).

Likewise, the honey that is mentioned by the poet of the tribe of Hudhayl is, compared with the honey of Paradise, like the bitter *qār* tree—this is a tree that grows in the sand; Bishr says:

> They're hoping to make peace in Dhāt Kahf,[219]
> but what is in it for them: bitter aloe trees and *qār*.

The verse by the poet of Hudhayl[220] I meant is:

> He swore to them by God a forceful oath: "You are
> more sweet to me than honey when we gather it!"

When God—blessed be His name—grants someone the right to approach these rivers he can land sweet fish, not to be found on any dish. If Aḥmad ibn al-Ḥusayn[221] had seen them he would have despised the present he was given, on which he said: 3.10

> The least of the least of this gift is a fish
> that plays in a pond of honey.

As for the rivers of wine, in them too fishes of all shapes are playing: sea fish, river fish, in water salty or fresh, those that live in springs that gush and feed where plants are lush—but these are fishes made of gold, silver, jewels, and all things precious, a sight like dazzling light. When a believer stretches out his hand to one of these fish, he drinks from its mouth a drink so sweet that if a mouthful of it dropped into the salty undrinkable sea, its lowest depths and the crests of its waves would turn as sweet as could be. The briny stench would be found to smell as lavender on soft ground, where at night the dew will abound; or like the odor of an old, mild[222] wine that moves in small jugs but overpowers the brain.

١٠٤ وكأني به، أدام الله الجمال ببقائه، إذا استحقّ تلك الرُّتبة، بيقين التوبة، وقد اصطفى له نُدامى من أُدباء الفردوس: كأخي ثُمالةَ، وأخي دوْسٍ، ويونس بن حبيب الضَّبّيّ، وابن مَسْعَدةَ المُجاشعيّ، فهم كما جاء في الكتاب العزيز: ﴿وَنَزَعْنَا مَا فِي صُدُورِهِم مِّنْ غِلٍّ إِخْوَانًا عَلَىٰ سُرُرٍ مُّتَقَابِلِينَ، لَا يَمَسُّهُمْ فِيهَا نَصَبٌ وَمَا هُم مِّنْهَا بِمُخْرَجِينَ﴾ فصدر أحمد بن يحيى هنالك قد غُسل من الحِقْد على محمد بن يزيد، فصارا يتصافَيان ويتوافَيان، كأنها نَدْمانا جَذيمةَ: مالكٌ وعَقيل، جمعها مَبيتٌ ومَقيل.

وأبو بِشْر عمرو بن عثمان سيبويه، قد رُحضت سُويْداء قلبه من الضِّغْن على علي بن حَمزةَ الكِسائي وأصحابه، لما فعلوا به في مجلس البرامكة. وأبو عُبيدة صافي الطويّة لعبد الملك بن قُريب، قد ارتفعت خُلّتهما عن الرِّيَب، فهُما كأربدَ ولَبيد أَخَوانِ، أو ابني نُويْرةَ فيما سبق من الأوان، أو صَخْرٍ ومُعاويةَ ولديْ عمرو، وقد أخمدا من الإحَن كلّ جَمْر. ﴿وَالْمَلَائِكَةُ يَدْخُلُونَ عَلَيْهِم مِّن كُلِّ بَابٍ، سَلَامٌ عَلَيْكُم بِمَا صَبَرْتُمْ فَنِعْمَ عُقْبَى الدَّارِ﴾ وهو أيّدَ الله العلم بحياته، معهم كما قال البَكريُّ:

نازعتُهُم قُضُبَ الرّيحان مرتفِقاً ... وقَهوةً مُزّةً راووقُها خَضِلُ
لا يستفيقون منها وهْي راهنةٌ ... إلا بِهاتِ وإن عَلُّوا وإن نهلوا
يَسعى بها ذو زُجاجات له نُطَفٌ ... مقلِّصٌ أسفلَ السربال معتمِلُ
ومستجيبٌ لصوت الصَّنْجِ يَسمعه ... إذا تُرجّع فيه القينةُ الفُضُلُ

وأبو عُبيدة يذاكرهم بوقائع العرب ومَقاتل الفُرسان، والأصمعيُّ ينشدهم من الشعر ما أحسن قائلُه كلَّ الإحسان.

I imagine our Sheikh (may God make beauty perpetual by letting him live forever!), having gained a high rank, deserving entrance through true repentance. He has chosen fellow carousers from among the literate and erudite in Paradise, such as the man of the tribe of Thumālah, the man of the tribe of Daws, Yūnus ibn Ḥabīb al-Ḍabbī, and Ibn Masʿadah al-Mujāshiʿī.[223] They are as it is said in the Glorious Book:[224] «We have taken away the rancor that was in their breasts, as brothers, sitting on couches facing one another. No fatigue will touch them there and they will not be expelled from there». Thus the breast of Aḥmad ibn Yaḥyā has been cleansed there of its hatred of Muḥammad ibn Yazīd.[225] Now they are devoted and loyal friends, like Jadhīmah's two drinking companions, Mālik and ʿAqīl, who were never apart during the siesta and at night.[226] 4.1 *A drinking scene*

Abū Bishr ʿAmr ibn ʿUthmān Sībawayh is there too. His innermost heart has been washed clean of any grudge against ʿAlī ibn Ḥamzah al-Kisāʾī and his followers, for what they did to him during a gathering at the Barmakids.[227] Abū ʿUbaydah only harbors thoughts of pure devotion toward ʿAbd al-Malik ibn Qurayb, their friendship now without any doubt beyond diatribe. They are now like the two brothers Arbad and Labīd, or Nuwayrah's two sons in the past, or like ʿAmr's two sons Ṣakhr and Muʿāwiyah in their amity:[228] they have extinguished the embers of enmity. «And the angels go in to them from every gate, saying "Peace be upon you, because you were patient. How excellent, the Ultimate Abode!"»[229] ʿAlī ibn Manṣūr (may God support knowledge through our Sheikh's life!) is there with them, just as al-Bakrī says,[230]

> I took from friends the fragrant basil sprigs
> and a strong-tasting wine, its strainer always moist.
> They do not sober up from it (it lasts!) except to shout
> for "More!"—no matter if it is their first or second time.
> A page with pearls adorned with glasses serves them,
> his hose tucked up, a nimble page.
> A lute responds—you'd think the harp can hear it,
> whenever the singer in her negligée plays the refrain.

Abū ʿUbaydah mentions to them the battles of the ancient Arabs and the fights of hero knights, while excellent poetry is what al-Aṣmaʿī recites. They delight in playing, so they throw their cups into the rivers of wine; filled by

وتهَشّ نفوسُهم للّعِب فيقذِفون تلك الآنية في أنهار الرحيق، ويصفّقها الماذيُّ المعترض أيّ تصفيق، وتقترع تلك الآنية فيُسمَع لها أصواتٌ، تُبْعَث بمثلها الأموات.

٢٠٤ فيقول الشيخ، حسّن الله الأيّام بطول عمره: آه لمَصْرَع الأعشى ميمْون وكم أعملَ من مَطيّةٍ أَمون! ولقد وددتُ أنه ما صدّته قُرَيْشٌ لمّا توجّه إلى النبي صلى الله عليه وسلم وإنّما ذكرتُه الساعة لمّا تقارعتْ هذه الآنية بقوله في الحائيّة:

وشَمولٍ تحسب العينُ إذا صُفِّقتْ جُنْدُعَها نَوْرَ الذُّبَحْ
مثلَ ريحِ المسْك ذاكٍ ريحُها صبّها الساقي إذا قيل: توَحْ
من زِقاق التَّجْر في باطِيَةٍ جَوْنةٍ حاريّةٍ ذاتِ رَوَحْ
ذاتِ غَوْرٍ، ما تبالي يومَها غَرَفَ الإبريقُ منها والقَدَحْ
وإذا ما الراح فيها أزبدتْ أَفَلَ الإزبادُ عنها فمَصَحْ
وإذا مَكّوكُها صادمَه جانباها كَرَّ فيها فسَبَحْ
فترامتْ بزُجاجٍ مُعْمَلٍ يُخْلِف النّازحَ منها ما نَزَحْ
وإذا غاضتْ رفعْنا زِقَّنا طُلُقَ الأوداج فيها فانسفَحْ

ولو أنه أسلم لجاز أن يكون بيننا في هذا المجلس، فينشدنا غريبَ الأوزان، ممّا نظم في دار الأحزان، ويحدّثنا حديثَه مع هَوْذة بن عليّ، وعامر بن الطُّفيل، ويزيد بن مُسْهِر وعلقمة بن عُلاثة، وسَلامة بن ذي فائش، وغيرهم ممّن مدحه أو هجاه، وخافه في الزمن أو رجاه.

the liquid that offers itself, of taste divine. These cups clink and tunes are heard, by which even the dead would be stirred.

The Sheikh (may God adorn Time by prolonging his life!) says, "Alas for the fall of al-Aʿshā Maymūn! How many a reliable mount has he urged on! I wish that Quraysh[231] had not obstructed him when he turned to the Prophet (God bless and preserve him). I am reminded of him this moment by the clinking cups, on account of his verses: 4.2

Cool wine: when poured, the eye would think
  its bubbles are wild carrot blossom, red;
Its odor is like fragrant musk. The cupbearer
  pours it when people say 'Be quick!'
It comes from wineskins of the merchants, then
  in a black, ample pitcher from al-Ḥīrah,
A deep one; on that day not minding being scooped from
  by a jug and by a cup.
And when the wine produces foam in them,
  the bubbles disappear from it and fade;
But when they hit the two sides of the cup
  they reappear and swim upon the wine.
The wine is handed out, in well-used glasses, and
  what has been depleted is topped-up.[232]
When all has gone we lift our wineskin, when
  its strings are loose, and wine pours out!

"If he had embraced Islam he might have been sitting together with us, reciting many a rare-metered ode, which he composed in the Sad Abode, and tell us his stories with Hawdhah ibn ʿAlī, ʿĀmir ibn al-Ṭufayl, Yazīd ibn Mus'hir, ʿAlqamah ibn ʿUlāthah, Salāmah ibn Dhī Fā'ish,[233] and others on whom he composed eulogies or lampoons, those he feared at the time or from whom he expected boons."

ثمّ إنه، أدام الله تمكينه، يخطِر له حديثُ شيءٍ كان يسمّى النُّزهة في الدار الفانية، ١٫٥
فيركب نجيباً من نُجُب الجنّة خُلق من ياقوتٍ ودُرٍّ، في سَجْسَجٍ بعُد عن الحرّ والقرّ، ومعه إناءُ فهْجٍ، فيسير في الجنّة على غير منهجٍ، ومعه شيءٌ من طعام الخلود، ذُخر لوالد سعِدَ أو مولود، فإذا رأى نجيبه يَمْلَع بين كُثبان العنبر، وضَيْمُرانٍ وُصِل بصَعْبَرٍ، رفع صوتَه متمثّلاً بقول البكريّ:

ليت شِعْري متى تخُبُّ بنا النا   قةُ نحو العُذيب فالصيّبونِ
مُحْقِباً زُكرةً وخُبزَ رُقاقٍ   وحِباقاً وقطعةً من نُونِ

يعني بالحباق جُرزة البَقل.

فيهتِف هاتفٌ: أتشعر أيّها العبد المغفور له لمن هذا الشّعر؟ فيقول الشيخ: نعم، ٢٫٥
حدّثنا أهل ثِقتنا عن أهل ثقتهم، يتوارثون ذلك كابرًا عن كابر، حتى يصِلوه بأبي عمرو بن العَلاء، فيرويه لهم عن أشياخ العرب، حَرَشَةِ الضِّباب في البلاد الكَلَدات، وجُناةِ الكَمْأة في مَغاني البُداة، الذين لم يأكلوا شِيراز الألبان، ولم يجعلوا الثمر في الثِبان، أنّ هذا الشعر لميمون بن قيس بن جَنْدَلٍ أخي بني ربيعةَ بن ضُبيعة بن قيس بن ثَعْلَبة بن عُكابة بن صَعْب بن عليّ بن بكر بن وائلٍ. فيقول الهاتف: أنا ذلك الرّجل، منّ الله عليَّ بعدما صِرتُ من جهنّم على شفير، ويئستُ من المغفرة والتكفير.

فيلتفت إليه الشيخ هَشّاً بَشّاً مرتاحاً، فإذا هو بشابٍّ غُرانِق غَبَرَ في النعيم المُفانق، وقد صار عَشاه حَوَرًا معروفاً، وانحناءُ ظهره قَواماً موصوفاً، فيقول: أخبِرْني كيف كان خلاصُك من النار، وسلامتك من قبيح الشِنار؟ فيقول:

سحبتني الزبانِيَةُ إلى سَقَر، فرأيت رجلاً في عَرَصات القيامة يتلألأ وجهه تلألؤ القمر، والناس يهتِفون به من كلّ أوْبٍ: يا محمّدُ يا محمّد، الشّفاعةَ الشّفاعةَ! نمُتُّ

Then it occurs to him (may God give him lasting power!) to think of something called "excursion" in the Perishable World. He mounts one of the noble camels in Paradise, created of rubies and pearls. It is a mild day, neither hot nor cold. He takes a flagon with wine with him, and sets out in Paradise at random, on a whim. He brings along some of the food of eternity taken from a hoard for a happy father or son stored. When he sees how his mount speeds between the hills of ambergris, through fragrant *ḍaymurān* trees and then lotus trees, he raises his voice and recites two verses by the Bakrite: [234] 5.1 *The Sheikh's excursion*

I wish I knew if my camel will ever trot with us
toward al-ʿUdhayb and al-Ṣaybūn,
With behind my saddle a skin of wine, a loaf of bread,
with some sweet-smelling basil, and fillet of fish!

By "sweet-smelling basil" he means sprigs of any herbs.

Then a voice[235] calls, "Do you know, servant of God who has been forgiven, who composed this poem?" The Sheikh replies, "Yes, we have been told by scholars whom we trust and who have relied on trusted predecessors who have transmitted it from generation upon generation, all the way back to Abū ʿAmr ibn al-ʿAlāʾ, who transmitted it on the authority of Bedouin elders, hunters of the lizard in rough terrain and truffle-gatherers in desert and plain, those who have not eaten curds and whey, nor put fruit into their pocket to take away[236]—that this poem is by Maymūn ibn Qays ibn Jandal, of the clan of Rabīʿah ibn Ḍubayʿah ibn Qays ibn Thaʿlabah ibn ʿUkābah ibn Ṣaʿb ibn ʿAlī ibn Bakr ibn Wāʾil."[237] 5.2 *The conversation with al-Aʿshā Maymūn*

The voice answers, "I am that man! God showed me His mercy after I was already on the brink of Hell's damnation, and despaired of forgiveness and expiation."

The Sheikh turns to him, happy, smiling, and glad. He sees a young man with a skin fair and light, who lives a life of blissful cornucopia. He now has beautiful black eyes after his former nyctalopia. His once crooked spine is straight and fine. The Sheikh asks him, "Tell me how you escaped from Hell's fire and flame and how you were saved from horrible disgrace and shame!" Al-Aʿshā says:

"Hell's angels dragged me to the Fire, but then I saw a man standing on the Courtyards of Resurrection. His face shone like the moon; people were calling to him from every direction: 'Muḥammad, O Muḥammad, intercede

بكذا ونمتُ بكذا. فصرختُ في أيدي الزبانية: يا محمد أغِثْني فإنّ لي بك حُرمةً! فقال: يا عليّ بادرْه فانظُرْ ما حرمته. فجاءني عليّ بن أبي طالبٍ، صلوات الله عليه، وأنا أُعتَل كي أُلقى في الدَّرْك الأسفل من النار، فزجرهم عني، وقال: ما حرمتك؟ فقلت: أنا القائل:

ألا أيهذا السائلي أين يمّمتْ ... فإنّ لها في أهل يثْرِبَ موْعدا
فآليتُ لا أرثي لها من كَلالة ... ولا من حَفًى حتى تلاقي محمّدا
متى ما تُناخي عند باب ابن هاشمٍ ... تُراحي وتَلْقَيْ من فواضله نَدا
أَجِدّكَ لم تسمعْ وَصاةَ محمّدٍ ... نبيّ الإله حين أوْصى وأشهدا
إذا أنت لم ترحَلْ بزادٍ من التُّقى ... وأبصرتَ بعد الموت من قد تزوّدا
ندِمتَ على أن لا تكون كمثْله ... وأنك لمْ تُرْصِدْ لما كان أرصدا
فإيّاك والميْتاتِ لا تقربنّها ... ولا تأخُذَنْ سهمًا حديدًا لتقصدا
ولا تقربَنّ جارةً إنّ سِرّها ... عليك حرامٌ فانكِحَنْ أو تأبّدا
نبيٌّ يرى ما لا يرَوْن وذكرُه ... أغار لَعَمْري في البلاد وأنجدا

٣،٥ وهو، أكمل الله زِينة المحافل بحضوره، يعرف الأقوال في هذا البيت، وإنّما أذكُرها لأنه قد يجوز أن يقرأ هذا الهذَيان ناشئٌ لم يبلُغه: حكى الفرّاء وحدَه أغار في معنى غار، إذا أتى الغوْر، وإذا صحّ هذا البيت للأعشى فلم يُرِدْ بالإغارة إلا ضدّ الإنجاد. ورُوي عن الأصمعيّ روايتان: إحداهما أنّ أغار في معنى عَدا عَدْوًا شديدًا، وأنشد في كتاب الأجناس:

for us, intercede for us![238] We have such-and-such a connection!' So I also shouted, still held by the hands of Hell's angels, 'Muḥammad, save me, for I deserve to be spared by you!' He ordered, ''Alī, go to him quickly and find out why he should be spared!' Then 'Alī ibn Abī Ṭālib (God's blessings be upon him) came to me, as I was forcibly dragged away to be cast into the lowest reaches of Hellfire. But he drove them away and asked, 'On what grounds should you be spared?' I said, 'I am the one who has said:[239]

You there who ask me where my camels have been going:
they're due to meet some persons down in Yathrib.
I swore an oath: I will not pity them if they get tired
or suffer from sore feet, until I reach Muḥammad.
As soon as you[240] will halt at Hāshim's grandson's door
you will have rest and you'll experience his bounty.
Really, have you[241] not heard the counsel of Muḥammad,
God's prophet, when he counselled, when he testified?
If you don't travel with provisions of God-fearing,
and then see, after your death, someone who has,
Then you'll regret that you are not like him
and did not prepare yourself just as he did.
Beware all carrion, don't touch it![242]
Don't stab a camel with an iron arrow, bleeding it![243]
And don't approach a woman: her hidden, private parts
are not allowed to you; so marry or abstain!
He is a prophet who can see what you can't see; his fame
has reached—upon my life!—the lowlands and the hills.'"

The Sheikh—may God perfect the adornment of gatherings with his presence!—knows the various interpretations of this last verse. I only mention them because it is possible that some young person who has not heard it before may read this nonsense. Al-Farrā' is the only one to report the verb *aghāra* in the sense of *ghāra*, i.e. "to penetrate into the lowlands." If this verse is really by al-A'shā then he merely meant by it the opposite of *anjada*, "to travel to the hills." Two views are transmitted on the authority of al-Aṣma'ī:[244] one is that *aghāra* means "to run fast"; in his *Book of Related Words* he quotes this verse: 5.3

فعدِّ طِلابَهَا وتَسَلَّ عنه   بناجيةٍ إذا زُجِرتْ تُغيرُ

والأخرى أنه كان يقدّم ويؤخّر فيقول: لعمري غار في البلاد وأنجدا، فيجيء به على الزِّحاف. وكان سعيد بن مَسْعَدة يقول: غار لعمري في البلاد وأنجدا، فيخرمه في النصف الثاني.

٤،٥ ويقول الأعشى: قلت لعلّي: وقدكنت أُومن بالله وبالحساب وأصدّق بالبعث وأنا في الجاهليّة الجَهْلاء، فمن ذلك قولي:

فما أَيْبُليٌّ على هيْكلٍ   بناه وصلّب فيه وصارا
يراوح من صلوات المليـ   ـكِ طوْرًا سجودًا وطوْرًا جؤارا
بأعْظمَ منك تُقًى في الحسابِ   إذا النَّسَماتُ نفضْن الغُبارا

فذهب عليٌّ إلى النبي صلى الله عليه وسلم، فقال: يا رسول الله، هذا أعشى قيسٍ قد رُوي مدحُه فيك، وشهِد أنك نبيٌّ مُرْسَلٌ. فقال: هلّا جاءني في الدار السابقة؟ فقال عليٌّ: قد جاء، ولكن صدّته قريشٌ وحبُّه للخمر. فشفع لي، فأُدخلتُ الجنّة على أن لا أشرب فيها خمرًا؛ فقرّت عيناي بذلك، وإنّ لي مَنادحَ في العسل وماء الحيوان. وكذلك من لم يتُبْ من الخمر في الدار الساخرة، لم يُسْقَها في الآخرة.

١،٥،٥ وينظر الشيخ في رياض الجنّة فيرى قصرين مُنيفيْن، فيقول في نفسه: لأبلغنَّ هذين القصرين فأسأل لمن هما. فإذا قرُب إليهما رأى على أحدهما مكتوبًا: هذا القصر لزُهير بن أبي سُلْمى المُزَني وعلى الآخر: هذا القصر لعَبيد بن الأبرص الأسديّ فيعجب من ذلك ويقول: هذان ماتا في الجاهليّة، ولكنّ رحمة ربّنا وسِعت كلَّ شيء؛

Give up your quest of her; console yourself
with a fleet camel that, when it's spurred on, runs fast.[245]

The other is that the poet in fact used a different word order and said "—upon my life!—it has penetrated deeply (*ghāra*) into the lowlands and the hills," with a metrical shortening.[246] Sa'īd ibn Mas'adah, however, reads *ghāra* for *aghāra*, leaving out the first syllable at the beginning of the second hemistich.[247]

Al-A'shā continues, "I said to 'Alī, 'I already believed in God and the final Reckoning and I believed in the truth of the Resurrection when I still lived in the pre-Islamic times of Ignorance. Hence my verses:[248] 5.4

No bell-ringing monk at a church
he has built, and in which he has crossed himself,
Who has prayed to the King of the World,
now lying prostrate, now wailingly praying,
Is more pious than you at the Reckoning, when
the people, revived, resurrected, will shake off the dust.'

"Then 'Alī went to the Prophet (God bless and preserve both of them) and said to him, 'Messenger of God! This is al-A'shā of the tribe of Qays, whose poem in your praise has been transmitted. He has testified that you are a prophet sent with a message to the world.' The Prophet replied, 'But why did he not come to me in the previous world?' 'Alī answered, 'He did come, but he was prevented by Quraysh and his love of wine.' Then the Prophet interceded for me and I was allowed to enter Paradise on condition that I should not drink any wine there. I was happy with that, for I have ample compensation with all the honey and the Water of Life. But whoever does not renounce drinking wine in the False World will not be given to drink it in the hereafter."

The Sheikh gazes out upon the meadows of Paradise. He sees two lofty castles and says to himself, "I'll go to these castles and ask to whom they belong." When he is close to them he sees on one of them an inscription that reads: "This castle belongs to Zuhayr ibn Abī Sulmā al-Muzanī" and one on the other that says: "This castle belongs to 'Abīd ibn al-Abraṣ al-Asadī." He is amazed and says, "Both died in the time of Ignorance, but the mercy of 5.5.1

وسوف ألتمس لقاء هذين الرجلين فأسألهما بم غُفر لهما.

فيبتدئ بزهير فيجده شاباً كالزَّهْرة الجنيّة، قد وُهب له قصرٌ من ونيّة، كأنه ما لبس جِلباب هَرَمٍ، ولا تأفّف من البَرَم. وكأنه لم يقل في الميميّة: ٢،٥،٥

سئمتُ تكاليفَ الحياةِ ومن يعِشْ   ثمانين حولاً لا أبا لكَ يسأمِ

ولم يقل في الأخرى:

ألم ترني عُمّرتُ تسعين حِجّةً   وعَشراً تِباعاً عشتُها وثمانيا

فيقول: جيْرِ جيْر! أنت أبو كعب وبُجير؟ فيقول: نعم. فيقول، أدام الله عزّه: بم غُفر لك وقد كنتَ في زمان الفَترة والنّاس هَمَلٌ، لا يحسُن منهم العمل؟ فيقول: كانت نفسي من الباطل نَفوراً، فصادفتُ مَلِكاً غفوراً، وكنت مؤمناً بالله العظيم، ورأيت فيما يرى النائم حبلاً نزل من السّماء، فمن تعلّق به من سُكّان الأرض سلِم، فعلمت أنه أمرٌ من أمر الله، فأوصيتُ بَنيَّ وقلت لهم عند الموت: إن قام قائمٌ يدعوكم إلى عبادة الله فأطيعوه. ولو أدركتُ محمّداً لكنت أوّلَ المؤمنين. وقلت في الميميّة، والجاهليّة على السّكِنة والسَّفَه ضاربٌ بالجِران:

فلا تكتُمُنّ اللهَ ما في نفوسكمْ   ليَخفى ومهما يُكتَمِ اللهُ يَعلمِ
يؤخَّرْ فيوضَعْ في كتابٍ فيُدَّخرْ   ليومِ الحساب أو يعجَّلْ فينْقَمِ

فيقول: ألست القائل:

وقد أغدو على ثُبةٍ كِرامٍ   نَشاوى واجدين لما نشاءُ
يجُرّون البرودَ وقد تمشّتْ   حُميّا الكأس فيهمْ والغِناءُ

our Lord embraces everything.[249] I will seek to meet these two men and ask them how it is they were forgiven."

5.5.2 *The conversation with Zuhayr*

He begins with Zuhayr and finds him to be a young man like a flower freshly collected, who has been given a castle of pearls erected. It is as if he has never donned the cloak of decrepitude, nor ever sighed from lassitude. It is as if he never said, in his poem rhyming on *-mī*:[250]

I'm weary of life's burdens. Mind you, he who lives
for eighty years—alas!—gets weary!

or as if he never said, in another poem:

Have you not seen that I have lived for ninety years,
followed by ten I've lived, plus eight?[251]

The Sheikh exclaims, "Rather, rather! You are Kaʿb and Bujayr's father!" Zuhayr says, "Yes, I am." Then the Sheikh (may God keep him strong forever!) asks him, "How is it that you have been forgiven? For you lived in the interval without revelation,[252] when people were like cattle left to their own devices, practising only their vices!" Zuhayr replied, "I shunned falsehood as long as I was living, and I found a Lord who was forgiving. I believed in God Almighty. Once I dreamed and saw a rope that came down from heaven. The people on earth who held fast on to it of were saved.[253] Then I knew that it was a command from God, so I admonished my two sons and said to them, when I was on my deathbed: 'If someone stands up and calls upon you all to serve God, obey him then!' If I had lived to see Muḥammad I would have been the first believer! When Ignorance was still reigning and foolishness still firmly established, I said in my poem rhyming in *-mī*:

Hide not from God what is in your souls, as if
to conceal it! Whatever one hides, God knows!
It's postponed, it is kept in a book and stored
for the Day of Reckoning; or it is quickly avenged."

"But," says the Sheikh, "Did you not also say:

Oft I went out in the morn, at the head of troop of nobles,
intoxicated, finding whatever we wanted to find.
They trailed behind them their mantles, after the strength
of the wine in the cups and the singing had crept into them.

أفأُطلقتْ لك الخمرُ كغيرك من أصحاب الخلود؟ أم حُرّمتْ عليك مثلما حُرّمت على أعشى قيسٍ؟ فيقول زهيرٌ: إن أخا بَكرٍ أدرك محمّدًا فوجبت عليه الحُجّة، لأنه بُعث بتحريم الخمر، وحظرِ ما قَبُح من أمرٍ؛ وهلكتُ أنا والخمرُ كغيرها من الأشياء، يشربها أتباع الأنبياء، فلا حجّة عليّ.

فيدعوه الشيخ إلى المنادمة، فيجده من ظِراف النُّدَماء، فيسأله عن أخبار القُدَماء. ومع المِنْصَف باطِيَةٌ من الزُّمُرُّد، فيها من الرَّحيق المختوم شيءٌ يُمزج بزَنْجَبيل، والماء أُخذ من سَلْسَبيل. فيقول، زاد الله في أنفاسه: أين هذه الباطية من التي ذكرها السَّرَويُّ في قوله: ٣،٥،٥

ولنا باطيةٌ مملوءةٌ جَونةٌ يتْبعها بِرْزِينُها[1]
فإذا ما حاردتْ أو بكأتْ فُتَّ عن خاتَمِ أُخرى طينُها

[1] ب، إف، ق: (بَرْذِينُها) تحريف.

"Are you allowed to drink wine, like all others who have eternal life? Or are you forbidden to drink it just as al-Aʿshā of the tribe of Qays?" "That Bakrite," said Zuhayr, "lived in the time of Muḥammad, so he had to conform to the explicit command, because Muḥammad's message included the prohibition of alcoholic drinks and forbidding all ugly things. I died when wine was like any other thing and was drunk by the followers of former prophets. So the command did not concern me."

The Sheikh invites him for a drink and finds him to be a charming drinking 5.5.3
companion. He asks him for stories about people from the past. The servant has a pitcher of emerald which contains some wine that has been kept under seal. It is mixed with ginger and water from Paradise's well-spring Salsabīl.[254] The Sheikh says (may God increase the number of his breaths!), "How can this pitcher be compared with the one that al-Sarawī mentions! He said:[255]

We have a pitcher, full,
  a black one, followed by its mug;
Whenever the pitcher yields us less, when it falls dry,
  the clay is broken from another pitcher's seal."

ثم ينصرف إلى عَبيد فإذا هو قد أُعطي بقاءَ التأبيد،[1] فيقول: السلام عليك يا أخا بني أسدٍ. فيقول: وعليك السلام، وأهل الجنّة أذكياء، لا يخالطهم الأغبياء، لعلّك تريد أن تسألني بم غُفر لي؟ فيقول: أجل، وإنّ في ذلك لَعجبًا! أألفيتَ حُكمًا للمغفرة مُوجِبًا، ولم يكن عن الرّحمة مُحتجبًا؟ فيقول عبيدٌ: أُخبرك أني دخلت الهاوية، وكنت قلت في أيّام الحياة: ١،٦

من يسـألِ النـاس يَحْـرِموه   وسـائـلُ الله لا يخـيـبُ

وسارهذا البيت في آفاق البلاد، فلم يزل يُنشَد ويخِفُّ عني العَذاب حتى أُطلقتُ من القيود والأصفاد، ثم كُرِّر إلى أن شملتْني الرحمة ببركة ذلك البيت، ﴿وَإِنَّ رَبَّنَا لَغَفُورٌ رَحِيمٌ﴾.

فإذا سمع الشيخ، ثبّت الله وطأته، ما قال ذانِك الرّجلان، طمِع في سلامةٍ كثير من أصناف الشعراء.

فيقول لعبيدٍ: ألك علمٌ بعَديّ بن زيدٍ العِباديّ؟ فيقول: هذا منزلُه قريبًا منك. فيقف عليه فيقول: كيف كانت سلامتُك على الصِّراط ومَخلَصك من بعد الإفراط؟ فيقول: إنّي كنت على دين المسيح ومن كان من أتباع الأنبياء قبل أن يُبعَث محمد فلا بأس عليه، وإنّما التَّبِعة على مَن سجد للأصنام، وعُدّ في الجَهَلة من الأنام. فيقول الشيخ: يا أبا سَوادة، ألا تُنشدني الصاديّة، فإنها بديعة من أشعار العرب. فينبعث منشدًا: ١،٢،٦

أبلغ خليـلي عـبدَ هِـنْدٍ فـلا   زِلْتَ قريبًا من سَواد الخُصوصْ ١،٢،٢،٦
مُوازِيـي الفُورة أو دونهـا   غيرَ بعيـدٍ من غُمـير اللّصوصْ
تُجْنَى لك الكَمْـأةُ رِبْعـيّة   بالخَبِّ تَنْدَى في أُصول القَصيصْ
تَقْنِصك الخيلُ وتصطادك الـ   طّيرُ ولا تُنْكَع لهوَ القنيصْ
تأكل مـا شئتَ وتعـتلُها   حمراءَ مِلْحُصّ كلون الفُصوصْ

[1] ب٤، إف، ق: (التأييد) وهو تحريف.

Then he turns to ʿAbīd. He, too, has been granted a life of eternity to lead.[256] "Greetings, friend of the tribe of Asad!" says the Sheikh. ʿAbīd replies, "Greetings to you too! Perhaps you want to ask me why I have been forgiven?" (Anyone who lives in the Garden has a clever mind; stupid people you will never find!) "Indeed I do," answers the Sheikh. "It is rather odd. Did you find a compelling reason for being forgiven and not being excluded from the mercy of God?" "I'll tell you," says ʿAbīd, "I had already entered Hell's abyss. But when I was alive on earth I had said, 6.1

The conversation with ʿAbīd ibn al-Abraṣ

He who asks of people will be denied;
but he who asks of God will not be disappointed.[257]

"This verse traveled to the ends of the earth; it kept being recited, while I was gradually relieved of my pains and freed of my fetters and chains. It was repeated until God's mercy enveloped me through the blessing of this verse. «Our Lord is truly forgiving and merciful»."[258]

When the Sheikh (may God steady his steps!) hears what these two men have to say, he hopes that many different poets have obtained salvation.

He asks ʿAbīd, "Do you know about ʿAdī ibn Zayd al-ʿIbādī?" "Yes," he replies, "He lives nearby, over there!" The Sheikh stops at his place and asks, "How did you cross the Bridging Path[259] and reach salvation, rescued after your life of immoderation?"[260] ʿAdī replies, "I adhered to the religion of Christ. Those who follow the prophets before Muḥammad's mission will come to no harm; but retribution shall come to those who prostrated themselves before idols and who are counted among the ignorant heathens." The Sheikh asks him, "Abū Sawādah, please recite for me your poem rhyming on the letter *ṣ*,[261] for it is one of the extraordinary poems of the Arabs!" Then ʿAdī begins to recite: 6.2.1

The conversation with ʿAdī ibn Zayd

Inform ʿAbd Hind, my friend:[262] may you stay close 6.2.2.1
to the black, fertile land of al-Khuṣūṣ,
Facing al-Fūrah, or this side of it,
not distant from Ghumayr al-Luṣūṣ,
Where truffles will be gathered for you in the spring,
in the soft earth, so succulent, between the stems of the *qaṣīṣ*;
Where horses hunt for you and birds as well:
you will not be deprived of some distraction, hunting!
You'll eat what you desire, and drink
wine from al-Ḥuṣṣ, red, colored like gemstones.

٦،٢،٢،٢ غُيّبتَ عنّي عبدُ في ساعة ال شَّرّ وجُنِّبتَ أوانَ العويص
لا تنسَيَنْ ذِكْريَ على لذّة ال كأس وطوْفٍ بالخَذوف النَّحوص
إنّك ذو عهدٍ وذو مَصْدَقٍ مُخالفًا هَدْيَ الكَذوب اللَّموص
يا عبدُ هل تذكُرني ساعةً في موكبٍ أو رائدًا للقنيص
يومًا مع الرّكْب إذا أوفضوا نَرفع فيهمْ من نَجاء القَلوص
قد يُدْرك المبْطئُ من حظّه والخيرُ قد يسْبِق جهْدَ الحريص
فلا يزلْ صدرُك في ريبَةٍ يذكر مِنّي تَلَفي أو خُلوص
يا نفسِ أبْقِي واتَّقي شتْمَ ذي ال أعراض إنّ الحِلْم ما إن ينوص
٦،٢،٢،٣ يا ليت شِعْري وانَ ذو عَجّةٍ متى أرى شَرْبًا حَوالَيْ أصيص
بيتِ جلوفٍ باردٍ ظلُّه فيه ظِباء ودواخيلُ خوص
والرّبْرب المكفوف أردانُه يمشي رُويدًا كتَوَقّي الرَّهيص
ينفَح من أردانه المِسْكُ وال عَنْبر والغَلْوى ولُبْنى قَفوص
والمُشْرَف المشمول نُسقَى به أخضرَ مطموثًا بماء الخَريص
ذلك خيرٌ من فُيوجٍ على ال سباب وقَيْدَيْن وغُلٍّ قَروص
أو مرتقى نِيقٍ على نِقْنِقٍ أدْبَرَ عَوْدٍ ذي إكافٍ قَموص
لا يُشْمِن البيعَ ولا يَحْمِل ال رِّدْفَ ولا يُعْطى به قلبُ خوص
أو من نسورٍ حول موْتَى معًا يأكلن لحمًا من طريّ الفريص

May you be far from me, ʿAbd, when times 6.2.2.2
are bad, and kept away when times are difficult!
Do not forget to think of me during the pleasure of
a cup of wine, or when you hunt a fat and bulky she-ass!
You are a man who keeps his pledge, reliable,
refusing to be led by lying, cunning folk.
O ʿAbd, do you remember me a little while,
when riding in procession or when scouting on a hunt,
One day, together with the riders when they hastened,
while we, among them, raised our young she-camel's speed?
A slow man may attain his lucky share,
whereas good things sometimes escape the effort of the keen.
But in your breast you always harbored doubt,
thinking of me, how I might perish or escape.
My soul, spare me! Beware, do not revile the honor of
good people. Wise restraint will not abandon you.
I wish I knew—and I say it loud— 6.2.2.3
when shall I see again the drinkers round a wine vat's base
In a house that's built of broken earthy jugs: cool is its shade;
"gazelles"[263] are there, and palm leaf bins for dates,
And more "gazelles," their sleeves hemmed with brocade,
dragging their steps, the wary walk of one whose sole is hurt.[264]
Musk wafts from their sleeve cuffs, and ambergris,
and *ghalwā* perfume, and sweet storax from Qafūṣ.
A wind-chilled cup of vintage wine is poured for us,
dark, mixed with water of a pool.[265]
Much better that, than guardsmen at the door,
a pair of fetters, and a painful chain around the neck;[266]
Or being raised on top[267] of a male "ostrich,"
ulcered, restive, with a saddle[268]
(It will not fetch a high price at a sale,[269] nor will it
carry a second rider; it is not fed with choicest palm-tree leaves);
Or vultures gathered round the dead,
that eat the flesh, still fresh, between the shoulders and the ribs.

فيقول الشيخ: أحسنتَ والله أحسنت، لوكنتَ الماء الراكد لما أسنْت. وقد عمل أديبٌ ٣٠٦
من أدباء الإسلام قصيدة على هذا الوزن، وهو المعروف بأبي بكر بن دُريدٍ، قال:

يسعَد ذو الجَدِّ ويشقى الحريصْ   ليس لخلْقٍ عن قضاءٍ محيصْ

ويقول فيها:

أين ملوك الأرض من حِميَرٍ   أكْرَمُ مَن نُصَّت إليهم قلوصْ
جيفَرٌ الوهّاب أوْدى به   دهرٌ على هدم المَعالي حريصْ

إلا أنك يا أبا سَوادة أحرزت فضيلة السَّبق.

وماكنت أختار لك أن تقول: يا ليت شعري وانَ ذو عَجّةٍ، لأنك لا تخلو من أحد أمرَيْن: إمّا أن تكون قد وصلتَ همزةَ القطع وذلك رديء، على أنهم قد أنشدوا:

إن لم أقاتلْ فألبِسوني بُرقُعًا   وفَتَخاتٍ في اليدينِ أربعا

ويزيد ما فعلتَ من إسقاط الهمزة بُعدًا أنك حذفتَ الألف التي بعد النون، فإذا حُذفت الهمزةُ من أوّل الكلمة بقيتْ على حرفٍ واحدٍ، وذلك بها إخلال. وإمّا أن تكون حقّقتَ الهمزة فجعلتها بيْنَ بيْنَ، ثم اجترأت على تصييرها ألفًا خالصةً، وحسْبُك بهذا نقضًا للعادة، ومثل ذلك قول القائل:

يقولون: مهلاً ليس للشيخ عيِّلٌ   فها أنا قد أعيَلْتُ وانَ رَقوبُ

ولو قلت: يا ليت شعري أنا ذو عجّةٍ، فحذفتَ الواو، لكان عندي أحسن وأشبه.

فيقول عديُّ بن زيد: إنّما قلت كما سمعتُ أهل زمني يقولون، وحدثَتْ لكم في الإسلام أشياءُ ليس لنا بها علم. فيقول الشيخ: لا أراك تفهم ما أريده من الأغراض، ولقد هممت أن أسألك عن بيتك الذي استشهد به سيبويه، وهو قولك:

The Sheikh says, "Well done, by God, well done! That's what I think: if you were stagnant water you would never turn stale or stink! There is an erudite man of the Islamic period who has composed a poem in this meter;[270] he is known as Abū Bakr Ibn Durayd. He said: 6.3

The fortunate are happy; wretched is the greedy one.
No creature can escape his fate.

"In this poem he says,

Where are on earth the kings of Ḥimyar,
the noblest men to whom a she-camel was ever urged?
Jayfar the Spender: destroyed by Time,
forever eager to demolish lofty things.

"But you, Abū Sawādah, are better since you were the first. However, I wish you had not said in your poem 'I wish I knew—and I (*wa-na*, or *wāna*, instead of *wa-ʾana*) say it loud,' because you are doing one of two things. Either you omit the glottal stop of *ʾana*, which is ugly, even though they recite the following verse:

If I don't fight, then dress me (*fa-lbisūnī*, instead of *fa-ʾalbisūnī*) with a woman's veil
and put four rings on both my hands!

"And you went further than merely dropping the glottal stop, by shortening the vowel after the letter *n*, for if you elide the glottal stop at the beginning of the word, it consists of only one remaining letter, which makes it defective.[271] Or you realize the glottal stop, making it intermediate, but then you dare turn it into a pure long vowel![272] This is enough to violate normal practice. It is the same in the following verse:

They say: 'Gently! This old man has no dependents.'
But look at me, I had dependents, but I'm (*wāna*) childless now.

"If you had said, 'I wish I knew—I say it loud,' without 'and,' it would have been better in my opinion, and more normal." ʿAdī ibn Zayd replies, "I merely said what I have heard the people in my time say. All sorts of new things happened in Islam that we don't know of!" The Sheikh says, "I see you do not understand my purpose. But I was about to ask you about a line of yours that is quoted as linguistic evidence by Sībawayh. It is when you say:

أَرَواحٌ مودِّعٌ أمْ بُكورُ   أنتَ فانظرْ لأيِّ حالٍ تصيرُ

فإنه يزعم أنّ أنت يجوز أن يرتفع بفعلٍ مُضْمَرٍ يفسّره قولك: فانظر، وأنا استبعد هذا المذهب ولا أظنُّك أردتَه. فيقول عديّ بن زيدٍ: دعْني من هذه الأباطيل، ولكني كنت في الدار الفانية صاحب قَنَص.

ولعلّه قد بلغك قولي: ١،٤،٦

ولقد أغدو بطِرْفٍ زانَه   وجهُ منزوفٍ وخدٌّ كالمِسَنّ
ذي تليلٍ مُشْنِقٍ قائدَه   يَسَرٍ في الكفِّ نَهْدٍ ذي غُسَنْ
مُدْمَجٍ كالقِدْحِ لا عيبَ به   فيُرى فيه ولا صَدْعٌ أُبَنْ
رمَّه الباري فسوّى دَرْأَه   غَمْزُ كفَّيه وتخليقُ السَّفَنْ
أيُّ ثغرٍ ما يُخَفْ يُنْدَبْ له   ومتى يُخْلَ من القَوْدِ يُصَنْ
كربيب البيت يَفْري جُلَّه   طاعةُ العُضِّ وتسحيرُ اللَّبَنْ
فبلغنا صنعَه حتى شتا   ناعمَ البالِ لَجوجاً في السَّنَنْ
فإذا جال حمارٌ مُوحِشٌ   ونَعامٌ نافرٌ بعد عَنَنْ
شاءنا ذو ميعةٍ يُبْطِرُنا   خَمَرَ الأرضِ وتقديمَ الجُنَنْ
يرأب الشدَّ بسيحٍ مُرسَلٍ   كاحتفال الغيث بالمرّ اليَفَنْ
أنسلَ الذِّرعانَ غربٌ خذِمٌ   وعلا الرَّبربَ أزمٌ لم يُدَنْ
فالذي يُمسكه يحمده   تَئِقٌ كالسِّيد ممتدُّ الرَّسَنْ
وإذا نحن لدينا أربعٌ   يهتدي السائلُ عنّا بالدَّخَنْ

A farewell in the evening or a morning one?
You—see where you are going!

"Sībawayh claims that 'you' could be taken as a nominative, on account of an implied verb, which is explained by the following word, 'see!' But I think this explanation is far-fetched and not, I think, what you intended."[273] 'Adī exclaims, "O spare me all that nonsense! Actually, I was a great hunter in the Perishable World.

"You may have heard this poem of mine: 6.4.1

Oft I went out in the morning, riding a noble steed, adorned
with a face drained of blood[274] and a cheek like a whetstone,
With the length of his neck raised high,
easily led with the rein in the hand, strong and large, with locks of hair,
Smooth and slim like the shaft of an arrow that has no faults in it
to be seen, and no blemishing cracks:
He who trimmed it has shaped it, the touch of his hands
and the adze's planing have straightened its crookedness.
Whenever a dangerous spot in a fight is feared, it is charged to be there,
and when it is left without being led it is still guarded well,
As if brought up at home; its saddle blanket is torn
by obediently eating its wheat and drinking its milk.
We looked after it until, in the winter, it was in a happy mood,
stubbornly pacing and prancing.
Whenever a wild ass would roam,
or an ostrich, that fled at its first appearance,
A horse at the start of its run that amazed us would take us
so fast that we don't have to hide and seek cover in bushes.[275]
It combines a fast running, let loose like a downpour,
like a rainfall amassed, with a rapid pace(?)[276]
A brisk, fast horse that overtakes the young calves;
while biting its bridle it reaches the herd, not weakened.[277]
He who holds it will praise it,
an excitable, noble horse, like a lion, its halter stretched.
And when we have caught four beasts
a beggar for food will be guided by smoke from our fire.

٢،٤،٦ وقولي في القافيّة:

وَمَجُودٍ قد اسْجهرَّ تناوِ رَ كلون العهون في الأعلاقِ
عن خريف سقاه نوءٌ من الدَّلْـ وِ تدَلّى ولم توارَ العراقي
لم يَعِبْه إلا الأداحي فقدْ وبَّـ رَ بعضُ الرِّئال في الأفلاقِ
وإرانُ الثّيران حول نِعاجٍ مُطْفلاتٍ يَحْمين بالأرواقِ
وتراهن كالأعِزّة في المَحْـ ـفِل أو حين نَعمةٍ وارتفاقِ
قد تبطّنَتُه بكفِّيَّ خرّا جُ من الخيل فاضلٌ في السّباقِ
يَسَرٌ في القياد نهْدٌ ذفيف الـ ـعَدْو عبْلُ الشَّوى أمين العُراقِ
لم يقيّل حرَّ المَقيظ ولم يُدْ ـجَمْ لطوفٍ ولا فسادِ نِزاقِ
غيرَ تيسيره لرغباءَ إن كا نت وحربٍ إن قلَّصتْ عن ساقِ
وله النّجعة المَريُّ تجاهَ الـ ـرَّكْب عِدْلاً بالنابئ المِخْراقِ
والخِذبُّ العاري الزّوائد مِلْحَفّـ ـانِ دا في الدّماغ للآماقِ

٥،٦ فهل لك أن نركب فرَسيْن من خيل الجنّة فنبعثهما على صِيرانها، وخِيطان نَعامها، وأسراب ظِبائها، وعانات حُمُرها؟ فإن للقنيص لذّة قد تنغضتُ[١] لك بها. فيقول الشيخ: إنّما أنا صاحب قلم وسَلَم، ولم أكن صاحب خيل، ولا ممّن يسحب طويل الذيل، وزرتُك إلى منزلك مهنئًا بسلامتك من الجحيم، وتنعُّمك بعفو الرحيم. وما يؤْمنني إذا ركبتُ طِرفًا زَعِلاً رتَعَ في رياض الجنّة فآض من الأَشَر مستسعلاً، وأنا كما قال القائل:

لم يركبوا الخيل إلّا بعْدما كبروا فهمْ ثِقالٌ على أكتافها عُنُفُ

---

١ في النسخ : (تنغصت) كما في إف، ق، ي و(تنقصت).

"Or this poem, rhyming in *-āqī*: 6.4.2

A meadow, well rained-upon, that has blazed
into blossom, like the color of tufts of wool in sacks,
After an autumn season with rain from Aquarius, which
descended in buckets; the 'bucket handles' did not remain hidden.[278]
The only blemishes there:[279] the places of ostriches' eggs, in which
some chicks sprouted down, between the cracked shells,
And the energy of the wild bulls around the cows
with their calves, defending themselves with their horns.
You can see them, like mighty men in a meeting,
or when they recline, at ease.
In that meadow I would ramble, with under my hands
a horse that often rides out, which excels in a race,
A tractable horse, a strong, large one, quick
in running, robust in his legs, and firm in his bones,
One not ridden during the midday heat,
not bridled for idle strolls or frivolous, trivial things,
But led only to any desirable aim, whenever it occurs,
or to war, when it tucks up its skirt.
It catches a milk-rich oryx cow in front
of the riders, a match for a far-roaming bull,
And an ostrich, big, with bare extra toes,[280] a young one,
its brain being close to its tearducts.

"Now, would you like us to mount two horses of Paradise and to drive them toward herds of wild cows, strings of ostriches, flocks of gazelles, and droves of onagers? For hunting is a pleasure for which I surely have raised your appetite!" But the Sheikh says, "I am a man of pen and peace, not a horse-riding type! I am not a man for ostentation and all that hype. I have come to visit you at your place to congratulate you on having been saved from Hell, you who, through the Merciful One's pardon, are now blessed and well! I do not want to take the risk of mounting a noble steed that is brisk, who has fed on pastures paradisiacal and has turned wild and demoniacal! I am like the one who said,[281] 6.5

They never rode horses until they were old;
now they sit heavily, clumsily on their steeds' flanks.

أن يَلحقني ما لحِق جَلَماً صاحب المتجرّدة لمّا حُمل على اليحموم، والتّعرض لما لم تسبق به العادةُ من المُوم، وقد بلغك ما لقِي ولد زُهيرٍ، لمّا وُقص عن العتِد ذي الميْر، فسلك في طريقٍ وَعْبٍ، وما انتفع ببُكاء كَعْب؛ وكذلك ولدك عَلْقمة، حلّت في العاجلة به النّقِمة، لمّا ركب للصّيد، فأصبح لجَدِّه زيد، وقلت فيه:

انعَمْ صَباحاً علقمَ بن عديّ   أثويتَ اليومَ لم ترحَلِ

وإنّي لأَحارُ يا مَعاشرَ العرب في هذه الأوزان التي نقلها عنكم الثقات، وتداولتها الطبقات؛ ومن كلمتك التي على الراء، وأوّلها:

قد آن أن تصْحوَ أو تُقْصِرْ   وقد أتى لِما عهِدتَ عُصُرْ
عن مُبرَقات بالبُرِينَ وتَبْـ   ـدو بالأَكُفّ اللامعات سُوُرْ
بيضٌ عليهنَّ الدِمَقْس وبالـ   أعناق من تحتِ الأكِفّة دُرّْ

ويجوز أن يقذفني السابح على صخور زُمُرّدٍ فيكسِر لي عَضُداً أو ساقاً، فأصيرَ ضُحكةً في أهل الجنان.

فيتبسّم عديّ ويقول: ويحك! أما علمتَ أنّ الجنة لا يُرهَب لديها السَّقَم،ولا تنزل بسُكّانها النِّقَم؟ فيركبان سابحَيْن من خيل الجنة، مَرْكَبُ كلِّ واحدٍ منهما لو عُدل بممالك العاجلة الكائنة من أوّلها إلى آخرها لرجح بها، وزاد في القِيمة عليها. فإذا نظر إلى صِوار ترتَع في دَقاري الفردوس، والدَّقاريُّ: الرياض، صوّب مولاي الشيخُ المِطْرَد، وهو الرُّمح القصير، لأخنس ذَيّال، قد رتع هناك طويلَ أيام وليال؛ فإذا لم يبق بين السِّنان وبينه إلا قيدُ ظُفرٍ، قال: أمسِكْ، رحمك الله، فإني لست من وحْش الجنّة التي أنشأها الله سبحانه ولم تكن في الدار الزائلة، ولكني كنت في محلة الغرور أرُود في بعض القِفار، فمرّ بي ركْبٌ مؤمنون قد كرِيَ زادُهم، فصرعوني واستعانوا ٦،٦

"I might suffer the same that befell Jalam, the friend of al-Mutajarridah,[282] when he was made to ride al-Yaḥmūm: doing what one is not wont to do leads to one's doom. You have heard what happened to the son of Zuhayr, who broke his neck when he fell from the courser Dhū l-Mayr. He rode out on a high road, but it did not avail him that his brother Kaʿb lamented him in an ode. Likewise your own son, ʿAlqamah, who came to grief in the Fleeting World when, hunting he went for a ride, and became like his grandfather Zayd.[283] You said of him:

> Good morning to you, ʿAlqamah, the son of ʿAdī!
> Have you stayed at home today and not departed?[284]

"I am bewildered, all you Arabs, about what reliable informants have transmitted about all these metrical variations, used by subsequent generations; and about your poem that rhymes in *-r*:[285]

> Now it is time to sober up or else you'll be remiss;
> ages have passed since those old times you spent
> With girls with sparkling rings, with bracelets that
> appeared upon their flashing wrists,
> White-skinned, in silken clothes, and at their necks,
> below the earlobes, pearls.

"The swiftly running horse may throw me on to the emerald rocks, breaking my arm or leg! I would be the laughingstock to the people of the Garden."

ʿAdī smiles. "Come now! Don't you know that of accidents in Paradise 6.6
one need have no fear, and that mishaps never happen to those that dwell here!" So they mount two fleet coursers from among the horses of Paradise. If either were compared with all the empires of the Fleeting World, from the first to the last, it would outweigh them and be more valuable. When our Sheikh sees a herd that grazes on the leas of Paradise (and "leas" means "meadows") he aims his javelin (which is a short spear) toward a flat-nosed, long-tailed oryx bull, who there did graze for long nights and days. When there is but a mere nail's length between it and the spear point, the bull says, "Stop! God have mercy upon you! I am not one of the wild beasts created by God, praised be He, those that never existed in the Transitory World. But I lived in the abode of delusion; while I was searching pasture grounds in some wasteland or other, a caravan of believers came past. Their provisions

بي على السَّفَر، فعوّضني الله، جلّت كلمته، بأن أسكنني في الخلود. فيكُفُّ عنه مولاي الشيخ الجليل.

ويعمِد لِعِلْجٍ وحشيٍّ، ما التّلَفُ عنده بمخشيّ، فإذا صار الخِرصُ منه بقدْر أُنمُلة قال: أمسِكْ يا عبد الله، فإن الله أنعم عليَّ ورفع عني البؤس، وذلك أني صادني صائد بمِخْلَب، وكان إهابي له كالسَّلَب، فباعه في بعض الأمصار، وصراه للسَّانية صارٍ، فاتُّخذ منه غربٌ، شُفي بمائه الكَرْب، وتطهّر بنزيعه الصالحون، فشملتني بركةُ من أولئك، فدخلتُ الجنّة أُرزَقُ فيها بغير حساب.

فيقول الشيخ: فينبغي أن تميّزن، فما كان منكنّ دخل الفانية فما يجب أن يختلط بوحوش الجنّة. فيقول ذلك الوحشيُّ: لقد نصحتَنا نُصْح الشفيق، وسوف نمتثل ما أمرتَ.

had run out, so they killed me. They survived their journey because of me, and therefore God (exalted be His word) gave me compensation by making me dwell in Eternity." Thus our lord, the venerable Sheikh, spares him.

He then at a wild ass aims his spear, from which he has nothing to fear. However, when the tip of the spear is no more than a fingertip away from it, the ass says, "Stop, servant of God! For God has blessed me and saved me from harm. That was because once a hunter hunted me with a scythe; it was my skin that he was keen to make his prize. He sold it in a certain town, where somebody cut the skin down, to make a bucket for a waterwheel, which many an ailing person with its water did heal. With it, pious people performed their ablutions. So the blessings of all these encompassed me and I entered the Garden, where I subsist without any reckoning."

The Sheikh says, "You ought to distinguish yourself, for those of you that have lived in the Perishable World ought not to mix with the beasts of the Garden." The wild ass replies, "You have given us good advice, like a kind friend. We shall do as you tell us."

١،٧ وينصرف مولاي الشيخ الجليل وصاحبه عديّ فإذا هما برجلٍ يحتلب ناقةً في إناءٍ من ذهب، فيقولان: من الرّجل؟ فيقول: أبو ذؤيب الهُذَليُّ. فيقولان: حُيّيت وسعِدتَ، لا شقِيتَ في عيشك ولا بعدت، أتحتلب مع أنهار لبن؟ كأنّ ذلك من الغَبَن. فيقول: لا بأس! إنما خطر لي ذلك مثلما خطر لكما القنيص، وإني ذكرت قولي في الدهر الأول:

وإنّ حديثًا منكِ لو تعلمينه   جَنى النّحل في ألبان عُوذٍ مَطافلِ
مطافيلَ أبكارٍ حديثٍ نتاجُها   تُشاب بماءٍ مثلِ ماء المفاصلِ

فقيَّض الله بقُدرته لي هذه النّاقة عائذًا مطفلاً، وكان بالنِّعَم متكفّلاً، فقمت أحتلب على العادة، وأريد أن أشوب ذلك بضَرْب نحلٍ، تبْعَن في الجنّة طريقة النّحل.

فإذا امتلأ إناؤه من الرِّسل، كوّن الباري، جلّت عظمته، خليّةً من الجوهر، رتع ثَوْلُها في الزّهَر، فاجتنى ذلك أبو ذؤيب، ومزج حليبه بلا ريب، فيقول: ألا تشربان؟ فيجرَعان من ذلك المِحلَب جُرعًا، لو فُرّقت على أهل سَقَر لفازوا بالخُلد شَرعًا. فيقول عديٌّ: ﴿ الْحَمْدُ لِلَّهِ الَّذِي هَدَانَا لِهَٰذَا وَمَا كُنَّا لِنَهْتَدِيَ لَوْلَا أَنْ هَدَانَا اللَّهُ ۖ لَقَدْ جَاءَتْ رُسُلُ رَبِّنَا بِالْحَقِّ ۖ وَنُودُوا أَنْ تِلْكُمُ الْجَنَّةُ أُورِثْتُمُوهَا بِمَا كُنْتُمْ تَعْمَلُونَ ﴾

٢،٧ ويقول، أدام الله تمكينه، لعديّ: جئت بشيئين في شعرك ودِدتُ أنك لم تأت بهما، أحدهما قولك:

فصافَ يُفرّي جُلّه عن سَراته   يَبُذُّ الرِّهانَ فارهًا متشابعا

والآخر قولك:

7.1 Our lord, the venerable Sheikh and his companion, ʿAdī, proceed. They see a man who is milking a camel in a pail of gold. "Who is this man?" they ask, and he answers, "Abū Dhuʾayb, of the tribe of Hudhayl." They say, "Long life and joy! May you never be unhappy in your life and never die!—But are you milking, with all these rivers of milk around? That does not seem sound!" "That is all right," he replies, "It occurred to me, just as it occurred to you to go hunting. I was thinking of the verses I composed on the olden times:

The conversation with Abū Dhuʾayb al-Hudhalī

Words from you—if only you knew—are honey
of bees in milk of suckling camels,
Mothers of calves firstborn and newly born,
and mixed with water found in mountain streams.

"Then this she-camel that has given birth to her first young was for me by the Omnipotent God decreed, Whose blessings are guaranteed. So I got up and milked as usual. And now I want to mix it with the honey of bees that in the Garden followed their king bee."[286]

As soon as his pail is filled with milk, by the Creator (exalted is His glory) a beehive made of precious stones is formed, of which the pasturing bees over flowers have swarmed. Abū Dhuʾayb gathers the honey and mixes it with the milk. "Will you not drink?" he asks them. They drink from his pail a few mouthfuls so nice—had it been distributed among the inhabitants of Hell, they would have been as if in Paradise. ʿAdī says, "«Praise be to God Who has guided us to this! We would not have been guided to it if God had not guided us. The messengers of our Lord came with the Truth. It is proclaimed to them: This is the Garden that you have been given as inheritance for what you used to do.»"[287]

7.2 The Sheikh (may God make his abilities last!) says to ʿAdī: "There are two things in your poetry that I wish you had not said! One is your verse

In the summer it rends the covering on its back;
it humiliates the horses in the racecourse; brisk, and
well-proportioned.[288]

"The other is your verse:

فـليْتَ دفعتَ الهـمَّ عنِّيَ ساعـةً   فنُمْسي على مـا خيّـلتْ ناعـمَيْ بالِ

فيقول عديّ بعَباديته: يا مكبور، لقد رُزقتَ ما يَكِبُ أن يشغلك عن القريض، إنما ينبغي أن تكون كما قيل لك: ﴿كُلُوا وَاشْرَبُوا هَنِيئًا بِمَا كُنتُمْ تَعْمَلُونَ﴾. قوله يا مكبور، يريد: يا مجبور، فجعل الجيم كافًا، وهي لغةٌ رديئةٌ يستعملها أهل اليمن. وجاء في بعض الأحاديث أن الحارث بن هانئ بن أبي شَمِر بن جَبَلة الكِنْدي استُلِم يومَ ساباطَ فنادى: يا حُكْر يا حُكْر، يريد: يا حُجْر بن عديّ الأدبر. فعطف عليه فاستنقذه. ويَكِب في معنى يَجِب. فيقول، زاد الله في أنفاسه: إنّي سألتُ ربّي عزّ سلطانه، ألا يحرمني في الجنّة تلذُّذًا بأدبي الذي كنت أتلذّذ به في عاجلتي، فأجابني إلى ذلك، ﴿وَلَهُ الْحَمْدُ فِي السَّمَاوَاتِ وَالْأَرْضِ وَعَشِيًّا وَحِينَ تُظْهِرُونَ﴾.

٣،٧ ويمضي في نُزْهته تلك بشابّيْن يتحادثان، كلُّ واحدٍ منهما على باب قصرٍ من دُرٍّ، قد أُعفي من البؤس والضُّرّ. فيسلّم عليهما ويقول: من أنتما رحمكما الله، وقد فعل؟ فيقولان: نحن النابغتان، نابغةُ بني جَعْدةَ ونابغةُ بني ذُبيان. فيقول، ثبّت الله وطأته: أمّا نابغةُ بني جعدة فقد أستوجب ما هو فيه بالحنيفيّة، وأمّا أنت يا أبا أُمامةَ فما أدري ما هَيّانُك،[1] أي ما جِهَتك. فيقول الذُّبياني: إني كنت مُقِرًّا بالله، وحججت البيت في الجاهليّة، ألم تسمع قولي:

فـلا لَعَمْـرُ الذي قـد زرتُـه حِججًا   وما هُريقَ على الأنصاب من جَسَدِ
والمؤمنِ العـائذات الطيـرِ تمسحـها   رُكبانُ مكّة بين الغيـل والسَّنَدِ

ووقولي

١ في النسخ : هياتك، هيئتك، هيئاتك.

Would that you had dispelled my worries for a while!
For then, in spite of what one could imagine, both of us would have been happy."[289]

ʿAdī replies in his ʿIbādī dialect,[290] "Got help you! You have been blesst with somesing zat ought to distract you from poetry. You ought to behafe as it is sait: «Eat and drink with relish, for what you used to do.»"[291] He said "*magbūr*," i.e., *majbūr*, turning the *j* into a *g*, which is a bad dialect pronunciation, used by the people in Yemen.[292] It is said in some tradition that al-Ḥārith ibn Hāniʾ ibn Abī Shamir ibn Jabalah al-Kindī, in the midst of the fray at the battle of Sābāṭ, exclaimed "Ḥugr, hey, Ḥugr!", meaning Ḥujr ibn ʿAdī al-Adbar, who turned to him and rescued him. ʿAdī also said *yagibu*, i.e., *yajibu*.

The Sheikh says (may God increase the number of his breaths!), "I have asked my Lord the Almighty not to deprive me in the Garden of the pleasure I have in my literary erudition, from which I derived such pleasure in my ephemeral life; and He has answered my prayer. «Praise be to Him in heaven and on earth, in the evening and at noontide»."[293]

Continuing his excursion the Sheikh meets two young men who are talking together. They stand each at a palace with a pearly door free of any damage or flaw. He greets them and says, "Who are you? May God have mercy upon you!—but He has done so already!" They answer, "We are the two Nābighahs, al-Nābighah of the tribe of Jaʿdah and al-Nābighah of the tribe of Dhubyān."[294] The Sheikh says (may God steady his steps!), "Al-Nābighah of Jaʿdah has deserved his present state by his adherence to the true religion. But what's with thee, Abū Umāmah?" (He means: "What about you?"). Al-Dhubyānī replies, "I used to profess belief in God and I have been on pilgrimage to the Kaaba before the coming of Islam. Surely you have heard my verses: 7.3

The conversation with the two Nābighahs, al-Dhubyānī and al-Jaʿdī

No, by the life of Him whom I visited in pilgrimages,
by the blood that was shed on the sacrificial stones,
And by Him who protects the shelter-seeking birds, where the stones
of the Kaaba are stroked by Mecca's riders between al-Ghayl and al-Sanad![295]

"I also said:

حلفْتُ فلم أترك لنفسكَ ريبةً   وهل يأْثَمَنْ ذو إمّـةٍ وهْو طائعُ
بمصطحِباتٍ من لَصافٍ وثَبْرةٍ   يزُرن إلالًا سَيْرُهنّ تدافُعُ

ولم أُدرك النّبيَّ صلى الله عليه وسلم، فتقومَ الحُجّة عليّ بخلافه. وإنَّ الله تقدّست أسماؤه، عزَّ مَلِكًا وجلَّ، يغفر ما عظُم بما قلَّ.

١،٤،٧ فيقول، لا زال قوله عاليًا: يا أبا سَوادة، ويا أبا أُمامة، ويا أبا ليلى، اجعلوها ساعةَ منادَمةٍ، فإنّ من قول شيخنا العِباديّ:

أيّها القلب تعلَّلْ بددَنْ   إنّ همّي في سماعٍ وأَذَنْ
وشرابٍ خُسْروانيٍّ إذا   ذاقه الشيخُ تغنّى وارجحَنْ

وقال:

وسماعٍ يأذَن الشيخُ له   وحديثٍ مثل ماذيٍّ مُشارْ

فكيف لنا بأبي بَصير؟ فلا تتمّ الكلمة إلا وأبو بصيرٍ قد خَمَسَهم، فيسبّحون الله ويقدّسونه ويحمدونه على أن جمع بينهم، ويتلو، جمّل الله بقائه، هذه الآية: ﴿هُوَ عَلَىٰ جَمْعِهِمْ إِذَا يَشَاءُ قَدِيرٌ﴾.

٢،٤،٧ فإذا أكلوا من طيّبات الجنّة، وشربوا من شرابها الذي خزنه الله لعباده المتّقين قال، كبّ الله أنفَ مُبْغِضه: يا أبا أمامة إنك لحصيف الرأي لبيبٌ، فكيف حسّن لك لبُّك أن تقول للنُّعمان بن المُنْذر:

زعم الهُمامُ بأنّ فاها باردٌ   عذبٌ إذا ما ذُقْتَه قلتَ ازدَدِ
زعم الهُمامُ ولم أذُقْه بأنه   يُشفى ببَرد لثاتها العطِشُ الصَّدي

I swear, not leaving any doubt within your mind
(Can any pious man obedient to God commit a sin?),
By camels drinking in the morning at Laṣāf and Thabrah
coming to Ilāl, while struggling keeping up the pace.

"I have not lived long enough to meet the Prophet (God bless and preserve him) so I cannot be accused of having acted against his commands. God, whose names be sanctified, mighty and glorious King, forgives great sins for the sake of a little thing."

The Sheikh (may his speech always be lofty!) says, "Abū Sawādah, Abū Umāmah, and Abū Laylā,[296] let us have a drink together! Our worthy ʿIbādī poet has said, 7.4.1

My heart, divert yourself with pleasure:
I long for music and for listening,
And for imperial Persian wine:[297] when tasted by
an old man he will sing and swing his body!

"He also said,

Music, appreciated even by old men,
and conversation sweet like honey gathered from the hive.

"But we want Abū Baṣīr, how do we get him here?"[298] He has not finished speaking, when who does appear but Abū Baṣīr! He is the fifth of the company. They praise and sanctify God, thanking Him for bringing them all together. The Sheikh (may God spread beauty through his longevity!) recites this Qurʾanic verse: «He is able to gather them whenever He wishes».[299]

While they are eating from the good things of the Garden and drinking its wine, which God has stored for His God-fearing servants, he says (may God subdue the noses of those that snub him!), "Abū Umāmah, you have a sound judgement and you are intelligent, so how could you find it proper to say to al-Nuʿmān ibn al-Mundhir:[300] 7.4.2

The great man stated that her mouth is cool
and sweet; whenever you taste it, you say: more!
The great man stated (I've not tasted it myself):
a parched man will recover through the coolness of her gums.

ثمّ استمرّ بك القول حتى أُكرِه عليك خاصّةٌ وعامّةٌ.

فيقول النابغة بذكاءٍ وفهم: لقد ظلمني من عاب عليّ، ولو أنصف لعلم أنني احترزتُ أشدَّ احترازٍ. وذلك أنّ النعمان كان مستهتراً بتلك المرأة، فأمرني أن أذكرها في شعري، فأدرتُ ذلك في خَلَدي فقلت: إن وصفتُها وصفاً مُطلَقاً، جاز أن يكون بغيرها معلَّقاً. وخشيت أن أذكر اسمها في النَّظم، فلا يكون ذلك مُوافقاً للملك، لأنّ الملوك يأنفون من تسمية نسائهم، فرأيت أن أُسنِد الصّفةَ إليه فأقول: زعم الهمامُ، إذ كنتُ لو تركتُ ذكره لظنَّ السّامع أن صفتي على المشاهَدة، والأبيات التي جاءت بعدُ داخلةٌ في وصف الهمام، فمن تأمّل المعنى وجده غير مختلٍّ. وكيف ينشدون:

وإذا نظرْتَ رأيْتَ أقمَرَ مُشرِقًا

وما بعده؟ فيقول، أرغم الله أنفَ شانئه: نُنشد: وإذا نظرتَ، وإذا لمستَ، وإذا طعنتَ، وإذا نزعتَ، على الخِطاب. فيقول النابغة: قد يسوغ هذا، ولكنّ الأجود أن تجعلوه إخباراً عن المكلّمِ، لأنّ قولي: زعم الهمامُ يؤدّي معنى قولنا: قال الهمام، فهذا أسلمُ، إذ كان الملك إنما يحكي عن نفسه. وإذا جعلتموه على الخطاب قبُح: إن نسبتموه إليّ فهو مُنْديةٌ، وإن نسبتموه إلى النّعمان فهو إزراءٌ وتنقُّص.

فيقول: أيّدَ الله الفضل بزيادة مُدّته: الله دَرُّك يا كوكب بني مُرّةَ. ولقد صحّف عليك أهلُ العلم من الرُّواة، وكيف لي بأبويْ عمرو: المازنيّ والشّيبانيّ، وأبي عُبيدة، وعبد الملك، وغيرهم من النَّقَلة لأسألهم: كيف يروون، وأنت شاهدٌ، لتعلم أني غير المتخرّص ولا الولاّغ؟

فلا يقِرُّ هذا القول في حُذُنّة أبي أُمامةَ إلاّ والرواةُ أجمعون قد أحضرهم الله ٣،٤،٧ القادر، من غير مَشقّةٍ نالتهم، ولا كُلفةٍ في ذلك أصابتْهم، فيسلّمون بلطفٍ ورفقٍ. فيقول، أعلى الله قوله: مَن هذه الشّخوص الفردوسيّة؟ فيقولون: نحن

"And then you went on to say things such that everyone, high and low, condemned you!"[301]

Al-Nābighah, sensibly and intelligently, replies: "Those who found fault with me have wronged me. If they were fair they would understand that I had been extremely careful. Al-Nuʿmān was besotted with that woman and he told me to describe her in my verse. I turned it over in my mind and said to myself: If I depict her in terms that are general, they could be applied not merely to her but to several. However, I was afraid to mention her name in verse, because the king would not agree, for kings do not like their women to be mentioned. So I thought I would put her description into his mouth and say 'The great man stated,' for if I had omitted to mention him the listener would think that my description was based on personal observation. The verses that follow still belong to the description by the 'great man.' Therefore, if one considers the sense one will find it to be not incorrect. But how do people recite my verse,

When I look I see a shining moon[302]

"and what follows?"

The Sheikh (may God humble his haters!) says, "We recite it as 'when you look,' 'when you touch,' 'when you stab,' and 'when you withdraw,' all in the second person singular." "That is a possibility," admits al-Nābighah, "but it is better to put it in the first person singular, as direct speech in quotation, because when I say 'the great man stated' it means 'the great man said.' That is safer; for then the king himself is the speaker. But when you read it in the second person it is improper: if you attribute the words to me it would be an affront to him, and if you attribute them to al-Nuʿmān it would be shameful and lacking in respect."

"Bravo, star of the tribe of Murrah!" says the Sheikh (May God lend assistance to virtue through prolonging his term!), "but the learned transmitters of your verse have corrupted it. I wish they were all here, Abū ʿAmr al-Māzinī, Abū ʿAmr al-Shaybānī, Abū ʿUbaydah, ʿAbd al-Malik,[303] and the other transmitters of poetry, that I could ask them in your presence how they read the lines, and you could know I neither falsely accuse you nor put a slur on you."

No sooner has he impressed these words on Abū Umāmah's audile organs 7.4.3
than all the transmitters of poetry are made to appear at God Almighty's

الرُّواة الذين شئتَ إحضارهم آنفاً. فيقول: لا إله إلا الله مكوّناً مدوّناً، وسبحان الله باعثاً وارثاً، وتبارك الله قادراً لا غادراً! كيف تروون أيها المرحومون قولَ النابغة في الداليّة: وإذا نظرتَ، وإذا لمستَ، وإذا طعنتَ، وإذا نزعتَ، أبفتح التاء أم بضمّها؟ فيقولون: بفتحها. فيقول: هذا شيخنا أبو أمامة يختار الضَّمّ، ويخبر أنه حكاه عن النُّعمان. فيقولون: هو كما جاء في الكتاب الكريم: ﴿وَالْأَمْرُ إِلَيْكِ فَانْظُرِي مَاذَا تَأْمُرِينَ﴾

٥،٧ فيقول، ثبّت الله كلمتَه على التوفيق: مضى الكلام في هذا يا أبا أمامة، فأنشِدْنا كلمتك التي أوّلها:

أَلِمّا على المطمورة المتأبِّدَهْ   أقامت بها في المَرْبَعِ المتجرِّدَهْ
مضمَّخَةً بالمسك مخضوبةَ الشَّوى   بدُرٍّ وياقوتٍ لها متقلِّدَهْ
كأنّ ثناياها وما ذُقتُ طعمَها   مُجاجةُ نحلٍ في كُمَيْتٍ مبرَّدَهْ
لِيَقْرَرْ بها النُّعمانُ عيناً فإنّها   له نِعمةٌ في كلّ يومٍ مجدَّدَهْ

فيقول أبو أمامة: ما أذكر أني سلكتُ هذا القَرِيَّ قطّ. فيقول مولاي الشيخ، زيّنَ الله أيّامه ببقائه: إن ذلك لعَجَبٌ، فمَن الذي تطوّع فنسبها إليك؟ فيقول: إنها لم تُنسَب إليّ على سبيل التَّطوّع، ولكن على معنى الغَلَط والتَّوهّم، ولعلّها لرجل من بني ثَعْلبة بن سعد.

فيقول نابغة بني جَعْدة: صحبني شابٌّ في الجاهليّة ونحن نريد الحِيرة، فأنشدني هذه القصيدة لنفسه، وذكر أنه من ثعلبة بن عُكابة، وصادف قدومُه شَكاةً من

call, without any trouble or effort to them at all. They greet politely and gracefully. The Sheikh (may God raise the prestige of his words!) asks them, "Who are these paradisial persons?" "We are the transmitters," they reply, "those whose presence you have just now requested!" "There is no god but God," exclaims the Sheikh, "He who forms and records everything, praise be to God who resurrects and inherits,[304] blessed be God who is almighty and does not betray! How do you read, O deceased gentlemen—God rest your souls—the verses by al-Nābighah in his poem rhyming on *d*: 'when you (or I) look,' 'when you (or I) touch,' 'when you (or I) stab,' and 'when you (or I) withdraw:' do you read them as second or first person singular?" "As second person singular," they answer. The Sheikh continues, "Here is our master poet, Abū Umāmah, and he prefers the first person singular. He informs me that it is direct speech put into the mouth of al-Nuʿmān." The transmitters say, "That is as it is said in the Holy Book: «The matter rests with you, so consider what you will command.»"[305]

The Sheikh says (may God grant him success in whatever he says!), "Enough said about this, Abū Umāmah. But recite for us your poem that begins: 7.5

Alight, you two,[306] on the rain-soaked desolate meadow,
  where once, in springtime, al-Mutajarridah stayed!
Anointed with musk she is, with hennaed hands and feet,
  while pearls and rubies are hanging around her neck.
Her teeth—but I never tasted them—seem
  like honey of bees mixed with chilled wine:
May al-Nuʿmān be happy with her! She's a blessing
  to him, renewed from day to day!"

"I don't remember ever to have walked that path," replies Abū Umāmah.[307] Then our master, the Sheikh (may God adorn his days by making him live forever!) says, "Amazing! Who is it then who has knowingly attributed them to you?" "It was not done knowingly," says al-Nābighah, "but it was a mistake, a false assumption. Perhaps the verses are by a man of the tribe of Thaʿlabah ibn Saʿd."[308]

Then the other al-Nābighah, of the tribe of Jaʿdah, joins in and says, "Once, in the days before the coming of Islam, a young man accompanied me; we were going to al-Ḥīrah. He recited this poem, as his own composition.

النُّعمان فلم يصلْ إليه. فيول نابغة بني ذُبيان: ما أجدرَ ذلك أن يكون!

ويقول الشيخ، كتب الله له مَثوبة المتقين، لنابغة بني جعدة: يا أبا ليلى، أنشِدْنا كلمتك ١،٦،٧
التي على الشين التي تقول فيها:

ولقد أغدو بشَرْبٍ أُنُفٍ قبل أن يظهَرَ في الأرض رَبَشْ
معنا زِقٌّ إلى سُمَّهَةٍ[١] تَسِقُ الآكالَ من رَطْبٍ وهَشّ
فنزلنا بمَليعٍ مُقْفِرٍ مسّه طَلٌّ من الدَّجْن ورَشّ
ولدينا قَيْنةٌ مُسْمِعةٌ ضَخْمةُ الأرداف من غير نَفَشْ
وإذا نحن بإجْلٍ نافرٍ ونَعامٍ خِيطُه مثلُ الحَبَشْ
فحملنا ماهنًا ينصِفنا فوق يَعْبوبٍ من الخيل أَجَشّ
ثمّ قلنا: دونَك الصَّيدَ به تُدرك المحبوبَ منّا وتَعِشْ
فأتانا بشَبوبٍ ناشطٍ وظليمٍ معه أمُّ خُشَشْ
فاشتوينا من غريضٍ طيّبٍ غيرِ ممنونٍ وأُبْنا بغَبَشْ

فيقول نابغة بني جعدة: ما جعلت الشّين قطّ رويًّا، وفي هذا الشعر ألفاظٌ لم أسمع بها قطّ: رَبَش وسُمَّهَة وخُشَش.

فيقول مولاي الشيخ الأديب المُغْرَم بالعلم: يا أبا ليلى، لقد طال عهدك بألفاظ الفُصحاء، وشَغَلَك شرابٌ ما جاءتك بمثله بابلُ ولا أذرِعات، وثنتك لحومُ الطَّير الراتعة في رياض الجنّة، فنسيتَ ما كنت عرفت، ولا مَلامةَ إذا نسيتَ ذلك، ﴿إِنَّ أَصْحَابَ الْجَنَّةِ الْيَوْمَ فِي شُغُلٍ فَاكِهُونَ، هُمْ وَأَزْوَاجُهُمْ فِي ظِلَالٍ عَلَى الْأَرَائِكِ مُتَّكِئُونَ، لَهُمْ فِيهَا فَاكِهَةٌ وَلَهُمْ مَا يَدَّعُونَ﴾

١ في النسخ: (سمه)، (سهمه)، وفي ي : (سُهَّمَةٍ).

He told me that he belonged to the tribe of Thaʿlabah ibn ʿUkābah.[309] But when he arrived, King al-Nuʿmān was ill and he was not granted access to him." Al-Nābighah al-Dhubyānī remarks, "In all probability that is what happened."

The Sheikh (may God write down for him the recompense of the god-fearing!) says to al-Nābighah of the Banū Jaʿdah, "Abū Laylā, recite to us your poem on the rhyme letter *sh*,[310] in which you say: 7.6.1

I often went out in the morning with drinking companions
  proud, before the grass's verdancy was seen.
A wineskin with us, to a trencher of palm fronds, laid
  with dishes both fresh and dried.
We dismounted on a wide and deserted plain,
  that was touched by dew, by rain and by drizzle.
With us was a singing girl, chanting to us,
  her ample behind not in need of a woollen bustle.
And then we suddenly saw a herd of fleeing oryxes,
  and a string of ostriches, black like Ethiopians.
We brought with us a servant who helped us,
  riding a fast and loudly neighing horse.
We said to him, 'Go, catch the quarry with it! Then you
  will win, through us, your loved one and live happily!'
He brought us a sprightly oryx bull
  and a male ostrich with a dam of a fawn.
We roasted the tender, tasty meat,
  «a reward unfailing»,[311] and returned at dusk."

But al-Nābighah of the Banū Jaʿdah replies, "I have never composed any poetry on this rhyme letter! And there are words in this poem that I have never heard myself: 'verdancy,' 'trencher,' 'dam of fawns,' indeed!"

Our master, the erudite, learning-loving Sheikh says, "Abū Laylā, You were familiar with the diction of the eloquent for so long! But you have been too busy drinking wine—a wine not found in Babel nor in Adhriʿāt[312]—and you have been diverted by the meat of birds that feed on the meadows of Paradise, and now you have forgotten all you knew. However, you cannot be blamed if you have forgotten it: «The people of the Garden are busy today, rejoicing, they and their spouses on couches, reclining. There they have fruit and all for which they are calling.»

أمّا رَبَش، فمن قولهم: أرضٌ رَبْشاء إذا ظهرت فيها قِطَعٌ من النَّبات وكأنها مقلوبةٌ عن بَرْشاء، وأمَّا السُّمّهة فشبيهةٌ بالسُّفرة تتَّخذ من الخُوص، وأمّا خُشَش فإنّ عمرو الشَّيبانيّ ذكر في كتاب الخاء أن الخُشَش ولد الظَّبية.

٢،٦،٧ فكيف تنشد قولك:

وليس بمعروف لنا أن نَرُدّها صِحاحاً ولا مستنكَرًا أن تعقَّرا

أتقول: ولا مستنكرًا، أم مستنكرٍ؟ فيقول الجعديُّ: بل مستنكرًا. فيقول الشيخ: فإن أنشد منشدٌ: مستنكرٍ، ما تصنع به؟ فيقول: أزجُره وأزبُره، نطق بأمرٍ لا يخبُره.

فيقول الشيخ، طوّل الله له أَمَد البقاء: إنّا لله وإنّا إليه راجعون، ما أرى سيبويه إلا وَهِم في هذا البيت، لأنّ أبا ليلى أدرك جاهليةً وإسلاماً، وغُذِيَ بالفصاحة غلاماً.

٧،٧ وينثني إلى أعشى قيس فيقول: يا أبا بصير أنشِدْنا قولك:

أمِنْ قَتْلَةَ بالأنقا ءِ دارٌ غيرُ محلولَهْ
كأن لم تصحبِ الحيَّ بها بيضاءُ عُطبولَهْ
أناةٌ يُنْزِلُ القوسِيَّ منها منظرٌ هُولَهْ
وما صهباءُ من عانَةَ في الذارع محمولَهْ
تولَّى كَرْمَها أصهبُ يَسْقيه ويغدو لَهْ
ثوتْ في الخَرْسِ أعواماً وجاءت وهْيَ مقتولَهْ

"As for the word *rabash* ('verdancy'), it is derived from the expression *arḍ rabshāʾ* ('verdant land'), when vegetation is visible on it; it seems to be an inversion of *barshāʾ* ('verdant'). A *summahah* ('trencher, or mat of palm fronds') is like a *sufrah* ('traveler's provision bag') made of palm leaves. Finally, *khushash* ('fawn'), as mentioned by Abū ʿAmr al-Shaybānī in his lexicon, means 'young of a gazelle.'

"And how do you recite your verse: 7.6.2

It would not be proper for us to bring them back
in sound condition, nor reprehensible to have them slaughtered.[313]

"Do you read *mustankaran* ('reprehensible') in the accusative, or *mustankarin*, with a genitive?"

Al-Jaʿdī replies, "In the accusative." "But what will you do," continues the Sheikh, "if someone recites it in the genitive?" "I would chide and reprimand him for speaking of things he does not understand!" The Sheikh says to himself (may God lengthen the extent of his life!), "«We belong to God and to Him we return!» [314] Sībawayh must have been mistaken about this verse, I think, because Abū Laylā al-Jaʿdī lived both before and after the coming of Islam. Hence, as a young lad he was fed and bred on a diet of pure diction and eloquence."

The Sheikh turns to al-Aʿshā of Qays and says to him, "Abū Baṣīr, recite to us your poem: 7.7

Is there a dwelling place, now uninhabited,
of Qatlah midst the sand dunes?
It is as if this plump and white-skinned woman
never walked there with her tribe!
Languid she was; a look at her would make
a monk prostrate himself in awe.
A reddish wine from ʿĀnah,
carried in a wineskin,
(its vine was tended by a ruddy man,
who watered it each morning),
Stored in its cask for many years,
but now brought out and 'killed'

بمـاء المُـزْنـة الغـرّا ءِ راحت وهْيَ مشمولَهْ
بأَشْهى مـنكِ للظّمْآ نِ لو أنكــ مبـذولَهْ

فيقول أعشى قيس: ما هذه مما صدر عني، وإنك منذ اليوم لَمُولَعٌ بالمنحولات.

With water from a rain cloud bright,
  cooled by the northern wind:
Such wine is to a thirsty man not more delicious
  than you are—if only you could be available!"

Al-Aʿshā of Qays says, "This does not come from me! You seem to have developed a taste for spurious poems today!"

ويمُرُّ رِفٌّ من إوَزّ الجنّة، فلا يلبث أن ينزل على تلك الرّوضة ويقف وقوفَ ١،٨
منتظرٍ لأمرٍ، ومن شأن طير الجنّة أن يتكلّمَ، فيقول: ما شأنكنّ؟ فيقلن: أُلهِمْنا أن نسقُطَ في هذه الرّوضة فنغنّي لمن فيها من شَربٍ. فيقول: على بركة الله القدير. فينتفضن، فيصرن جوارِيَ كواعبَ يرفُلن في وشْي الجنّة، وبأيديهنّ المَزاهر وأنواع ما يُلتمس به المَلاهي. فيعجَب، وحُقّ له العجب، وليس ذلك ببديعٍ من قدرة الله جلّت عَظَمته، وعزّت كلمته، وسبَغَت على العالَم نعمته، ووسِعت كلَّ شيءٍ رحمته، ووقعت بالكافر نِقمته.

فيقول لإحداهنّ على سبيل الامتحان: اعمَلي قول أبي أُمامة، وهو هذا القاعد: ٢،٨

أمِنَ آلِ مَيّةَ رائحٌ أو مغتدِ عَجْلانَ ذا زادٍ وغيرَ مزوَّدِ؟

ثقيلاً أوّل. فتصنَعه، فتجيء به مُطْرِبًا، وفي أعضاء السامع متسرّبًا. ولو نُحِت صَنَمٌ من أحجار، أو دَفٌّ أُشرعند النّجّار، ثمّ سمع ذلك الصوت لَرَقَص، وإن كان متعاليًا هَبَط ولم يراعِ أن يُوقَص. فيرد عليه، أو رد الله قلبه المحابّ، زولٌ، تعجز عنه الحِيَل والحوْل، فيقول: هلُمّ خفيف الثقيل الأوّل! فتنبعث فيه بنَغَمٍ لو سمعه الغريض، لأقرَّ أنّ ما ترنّم به مَريضٌ. فإذا أجادته، وأعطته المِهرة وزادته، قال: عليكِ بالثقيل الثاني، ما بين مَثالثك والمَثاني؛ فتأتي به على قَرِيٍّ لو سمعه عبد الله بن جعفرلَقرن أغانيّ بُديحٍ إلى هديرِ ذي المِشفَر. فإذا رأى ذلك قال: سبحان الله! كلّما كُشِفت القدرة بدتْ لها عجائب، لا تثبت لها النجائب؛ فصيري إلى خفيف الثقيل الثاني، فإنّك لَجُيدةٌ مُحسنة، تُطرِد بغنائك السِنةُ. فإذا فعلتْ ما أمر به، أتت بالبُرَحين، وقالت للأنفُس: ألا تمرَحين؟ ثمّ يقترح عليها: الرَّمَل وخفيفه، وأخاه الهزَج وذفيفه؛ وهذه الألحان الثمانية، للأُذن تَمنّيها المانِيَة.

A gaggle of heavenly geese goes by. Immediately they descend on that meadow and stand as if awaiting a command. Since the birds in the Garden are able to speak, the Sheikh asks them, "What do you want?" They reply, "We have been inspired to alight in this meadow in order to sing to those that are drinking there." "With God Almighty's blessing!" says the Sheikh. They shake off their plumage and turn into full-breasted girls, who strut in the garden, an embroidery of flowers. They carry lutes and instruments for musical entertainment. The Sheikh is amazed, and with reason; but it is in fact not so wonderful, coming as it does from the omnipotence of God the Glorious, whose Word is mighty, whose blessings flow abundantly on the world, whose mercy encompasses every thing, and whose vengeance falls on the unbeliever. 8.1 *The geese of Paradise*

The Sheikh says to one of them, to test them, "Sing for us, in the 'first heavy' rhythmical mode, the verse by Abū Umāmah, that man who is sitting over there: 8.2

Will someone come from Mayyah's clan, in the evening or morning,
in a hurry, with provisions or without any food?"[315]

The girl does this. With her music she enraptures; the listener, in whose limbs it creeps, it captures. An idol, carved from stone, or a tambourine sawn by a carpenter, if, by any chance, they heard that song would dance. If they stood on high they would fall, and if they broke their necks they would not mind at all. The Sheikh (may God send all kinds of lovely things into his heart!) is faced with marvellous scenes that cannot be resisted by any means. "Come on," he says, "let's now have it in the 'light first heavy' mode!" The girl starts to sing, with a melody such that if heard by al-Gharīḍ he would have to concede that by comparison his own singing was feeble indeed. When the girl, to general admiration, has exceeded expectation, he says, "And now let the 'second heavy' mode follow suit, between the second and third strings of your lute!" She proceeds in a manner such that if ʿAbd Allāh ibn Jaʿfar had heard it, he would have to declare that the songs of Budayḥ could only compare to a camel's blare. When the Sheikh realizes this he exclaims, "God be praised! Whenever His omnipotence is made clear, unsurpassable marvels appear. And now turn to the 'light second heavy'! For you are doing a truly excellent thing; you banish slumber when you sing!" When she does what he has told her to do, she produces things that are fearfully good,[316] and says

فإذا تيقّن لها حَذاقةً، وعرف منها بالعُود لَباقةً، هلّل وكبّر، وأطال حمد ربّه واعتبر. وقال: وِيحكِ! ألم تكوني الساعة إوَزّةً طائرة، والله خلقك مَهْديّة لا حائرة؟ فمن أين لك هذا العلم، كأنك لِجَذَل النفس خِلْمٌ؟ لو نشأتِ بين مَعْبَدٍ وابن سُريج، لما هِجْتِ السامع بهذا الهيج، فكيف نفضتِ بَلَهَ إوزّ، وهززتِ إلى الطَّرَب أشدَّ الهزّ؟ فتقول: وما الذي رأيتَ من قدرة بارئك؟ إنّك على سِيفِ بحرٍ، لا يُدرَك له عِبْرٌ، سبحان ﴿مَن يُحۡيِ ٱلۡعِظَٰمَ وَهِيَ رَمِيمٞ﴾.

فبينا هم كذلك، إذ مرّ شابٌّ في يده مِحْجَنُ ياقوت، ملكه بالحُكم الموقوت، فيسلّم عليهم ١٠،٣،٨
فيقولون: من أنت؟ فيقول: أنا لَبيد بن رَبيعة بن كِلاب. فيقولون: أُكرمتَ أُكرمت! لو قلت: لبيدٌ وسكتّ، لَشُهرتَ باسمك وإن صمتَّ. فما بالك في مغفرة ربّك؟ فيقول: أنا بحمد الله في عيشٍ قصّر أن يصِفه الواصفون، ولديَّ نواصف وناصفون، لا هَرَم ولا بَرَم. فيقول الشيخ: تبارك الملك القدّوس، ومن لا تُدرِك يقينَه الحُدوس، كأنك لم تقل في الدار الفانية:

ولقد سئمتُ من الحياة وطولها وسؤالِ هذا الناس: كيف لبيدُ؟

ولم تَفُهْ بقولك:

فمتى أهْلِكْ فلا أحفِلُه بَجَلِي الآن من العيْش بَجَلْ
من حياةٍ قد مللنا طولَها وجديرٌ طولُ عيشٍ أن يُمَلّ

to the people, "Are you not in a cheerful mood?" Then he suggests that she should use the *ramal* mode and its "light" variety, and its brother the *hazaj* with its fast modality. All these eight modes to the ears she does impart, a master in her art.

When the Sheikh knows how well she can execute, and is aware of her skill with the lute, he proceeds to state that there is no god but God, that God is great, and that his Lord be praised, for he is truly amazed. "Mind you," he says to her, "weren't you a goose just now, that was flying? Then God turned you into a rightly guided being, no longer straying! So how did you acquire this skill? You seem to be an intimate friend of the soul's thrill. Even if you had grown up between Maʿbad and Ibn Surayj, with such exciting songs you would not have been able to oblige! How could you shed the goose's stupidity and excite your listeners with such rapidity?" She answers, "What have you seen then of your Creator's omnipotence? You are on the beach of a sea so wide that one cannot reach the other side. Praised be He «who revives the bones when they are decayed»!"[317]

8.3.1 *The first conversation with Labīd*

While they are talking like this, a young man passes by. In his hand he holds a ruby crook, which through a divine decree he took. He greets them and they ask, "Who are you?" "I am Labīd ibn Rabīʿah ibn Kilāb," he replies. "Noble man! Noble man!" they say, "Why did you not merely say 'Labīd'? For more there is no need: your first name has sufficient fame. How did you obtain the forgiveness of your Lord?" Labīd says, "I live here, God be praised, a life of which every description would fail. I have servants, female and male. Youth that does not fade, a life that does not jade!" The Sheikh says, "Blessed be the Holy King, whose certainty cannot be guessed by any intuiting! It is as if you never said in the Perishable World:

> Tired I am of life and of its length,
> of people asking, 'How's Labīd?'

"Or as if you never uttered these words:

> Whenever I may die—I do not care.
> Enough, this life of mine now, enough!
> A life so long we're tired of it;
> A lengthy life is apt to be found tiresome.

فأنشدنا ميميّتك المعلّقة. فيقول: هيهات! إنّي تركت الشعر في الدار الخادعة، ولن أعود إليه في الدار الآخرة، وقد عُوّضت ما هو خيرٌ وأبرّ.

فيقول: أخبِرْني عن قولك: ٢،٣،٨

تَرّاكُ أمكنةٍ إذا لم أرْضَها أو يرتبِطْ بعضَ النُّفوس حِمامُها

هل أردتَ ببعض معنى كلٍّ؟ فيقول لبيد: كلا، إنّما أردت نفسي، وهذا كما تقول للرَّجل: إذا ذهب مالُك أعطاك بعضُ الناس مالاً، وأنت تعني نفسك في الحقيقة، وظاهر الكلام واقعٌ على كلّ إنسان، وعلى كلّ فِرقة تكون بعضاً للناس. فيقول، لا فتئ خصمُه مُفْحَماً: أخبِرْني عن قولك: أو يرتبِطْ، هل مَقصِدك: إذا لم أرضها أو يرتبط، فيكون: لم يرتبط؟ أم غرضُك: أترك المنازلَ إذا لم أرضها، فيكون[1] يرتبط كالمحمول على قولك: ترّاك أمكنةٍ؟ فيقول لبيد: الوجه الأوّل أردتُ

فيقول، أعظم الله حظّه في الثواب: فما مَغزاك في قولك:

وصَبوحِ صافيةٍ وجَذْبِ كرينةٍ بموتَّرٍ تأْتالُهُ إبهامُها

فإن الناس يروون هذا البيت على وجهيْن: منهم من ينشده تأْتالُه، يجعله تفتعله من آلَ الشيءَ يؤوله إذا ساسَه، ومنهم من ينشد: تأْتا لَهُ من الإتيان. فيقول لبيد: كِلا الوجهيْن يحتمله البيتُ، فيقول، أرغم الله حاسَده: إنّ أبا عليّ الفارسيّ كان يدّعي في هذا البيت أنه مثلُ قولهم: استحى يستحي، على مذهب الخليل وسيبويه لأنهما يريان أنّ قولهم: استحَيْتُ إنما جاء على قولهم استحايَ، كما أن استقَمْتُ على استقام، وهذا مذهبٌ طريفٌ، لأنه يعتقد أنّ تأْتَى مأخوذة من أوى، كأنه بُنِيَ منها افتعل، فقيل: ائتايَ، فأُعِلّت الواو كما تُعَلُّ في قولنا: اعتان من العوْن، واقتال من القول. ثمّ قيل: ائتيْتُ، فحُذفت الألف، كما يقال: اقتلْتُ. ثمّ قيل في المستقبل

[1] هذه العبارة مضافة من هامش نسخة الأصل والأرجح أنها من النصّ الأصليّ.

"Please recite to us your poem rhyming in *m*, the *Muʿallaqah*!" But Labīd replies, "Out of the question! I gave up poetry in the Treacherous World[318] and I shall not return to it in the Hereafter, now that I have been given something in return that is better and more righteous."

"Tell me then," says the Sheikh, "about your verse: 8.3.2

> Abandoning places when I don't like them
> or when some soul is bound to its death

"when you say 'some soul,' do you mean 'any soul'?" "No," answers Labīd, "I meant my own soul. It is just as when you say to a man, 'If your money is gone someone will give you money,' meaning in fact you yourself even though the literal meaning is 'any person,' or 'any group that is part of mankind.'"

The Sheikh says (may his opponent always be silenced), "Tell me about your words 'or when . . . is bound (*aw yartabiṭ*)': do you mean 'when I don't like them or when . . . is not bound,' where the verb is dependent on *lam* ('not'), or do you intend 'abandoning places when I don't like them,' so that *aw yartabiṭ* ('unless . . . is bound') is to be connected with 'abandoning places?'" Labīd replies, "I intended the former."[319]

Then the Sheikh (may God enlarge his share of reward!) asks, "What do you mean with your words:

> A morning drink of clear wine, and a lute-playing girl who plays upon
> a stringed instrument, adjusted by her thumb (*taʾtāluhū ibhāmuhā*)

"For people have read this verse in two ways. Some read it as *taʾtāluhū* ('adjusting it'), deriving the form from the verb *āla*, 'to lead, conduct (something).'[320] Others read it as *taʾtā lahū* ('to which [the thumb] comes'), from the verb *atā* 'to come.'"[321] Labīd answers, "Both readings are possible." The Sheikh says (may God spite those who envy him!), "Abū ʿAlī al-Fārisī[322] used to claim that the form *taʾtā* is like saying *istaḥā, yastaḥī* ('to be ashamed'),[323] in the opinion of al-Khalīl and Sībawayh, because they think that *istaḥaytu* ('I was ashamed') is formed on the analogy of *istaḥāya*,[324] just as *istaqamtu* ('I was upright') is based on *istaqāma* ('he was upright'). This is a curious view; he believes that *taʾtā* is derived from the verb *awā* ('to seek refuge'), as if it were from form VIII of it: the verb would them be *iʾtāya*, in which the *W* is made weak, as it is when we say: *iʿtāna* ('to help one another'), from the word *ʿawn* ('help'),[325] or *iqtāla* ('to choose') from the word *qawl* ('word, speech'). Then one says *iʾtaytu* ('I sought refuge'), in which the long vowel is shortened,

بالحذف، كما قيل: يستحي. فيقول لبيد: معترِضٌ لعَنَنٍ لم يَعْنِه، الأمرُ أيسرُ ممّا ظنّ هذا المتكلّف.

٤،٨ ويقول لبيد: سبحان الله يا أبا بصير، بعد إقرارك بما تعلم، غُفر لك وحصلتَ في جنّة عَدْن؟ فيقول مولاي الشيخ متكلّماً عن الأعشى: كأنك يا أبا عَقيلٍ تعني قوله:

وأشربُ بالرّيف حتى يقا ... لَ قد طال بالريف ما قد رَجَنْ
صَريفيّةً طيّباً طعمُها ... تصفّقُ ما بين كوبٍ ودَنّ
وأقررتُ عيني من الغانيا ... تِ إمّا نِكاحاً وإمّا أُزَنّ

وقولَه:

فبتُّ الخليفةَ من بَعْلها ... وسيِّدَ تيّا ومُستادِها

وقولَه:

فظلِلتُ أَرعاها وظلّ يحوطُها ... حتى دنوتُ إذ الظّلامُ دنا لَها
فرميتُ غَفْلةَ عينِه عن شاتِه ... فأصبتُ حبّةَ قلبِها وطِحالَها

ونحوَ ذلك ممّا رُوي عنه؛ فلا يخلو من أحد أمرين: إمّا أن يكون قاله تحسيناً للكلام على مذهب الشُّعراء، وإمّا أن يكون فعَله فغُفر له. ﴿قُلْ يا عِبادِيَ الّذِينَ أَسْرَفُوا عَلَى أَنْفُسِهِمْ لا تَقْنَطُوا مِنْ رَحْمَةِ اللهِ، إِنَّ اللهَ يَغْفِرُ الذُّنوبَ جَمِيعًا، إِنَّهُ هُوَ الْغَفُورُ الرَّحِيمُ﴾. ﴿إِنَّ اللهَ لا يَغْفِرُ أَنْ يُشْرَكَ بِهِ وَيَغْفِرُ ما دُونَ ذَلِكَ لِمَنْ يَشاءُ، وَمَنْ يُشْرِكْ بِاللهِ فَقَدْ ضَلَّ ضَلالاً بَعِيداً﴾.

just as *iqtāla* becomes *iqtaltu* ('I chose'), and then, in the future tense,[326] it is pronounced with elision, just as one says *yastaḥī*."[327]

Labīd answered, "Someone who objects to a phenomenon that does not concern him! The matter is easier than this fussy pedant thinks."

Labīd turns to al-Aʿshā and says, "God be praised, Abū Baṣīr! Having confessed to you-know-what, have you been forgiven and are you now in the Garden of Eden?" Our master the Sheikh speaks on behalf of al-Aʿshā, "You seem to refer, Abū ʿAqīl, to al-Aʿshā's verses: 8.4

I'm drinking in the countryside—so that they say:
He has been staying in the country for some time!—
A wine from Ṣarīfūn that is delicious,
poured out 'twixt cup and jug.
And I amused myself with pretty girls,
either through marriage or by whoring.

"And his verse:

I spent the night being her husband's substitute,
and of that woman's master too, and hers as well!

"And his verses:

I kept an eye on her, while he kept guarding her,
until, the darkness closing in, I too came close,
And, aiming for the moment that his eyes were heedless of his sheep,
I struck her in the depths of heart and spleen.

"There are more such verses of his that have been transmitted. Now there are two possibilities: either al-Aʿshā said all this merely to compose good poetry, according to the conventions of the poets, or he did actually do these things and he has been forgiven. «Say: O my servants, who have been profligate against themselves, do not despair of God's mercy! God forgives sins altogether. He is the Forgiving, the Compassionate.»[328] and «God does not forgive anything being associated with Him, but He forgives what is less than that to whomsoever He wishes. Whoever associates anything with God has gone far astray»."[329]

ويقول، رفع الله صوته، لنابغة بني جَعْدة: يا أبا ليلى، إنّي لأستحسنُ قولك: ٨،٥،١

طـيّبةُ النَّشْرِ والبُـداهة والـ ـعِلات عند الرُّقـاد والنَّسَمِ
كأنّ فـاها إذا تُنبّـهُ من طِـيب مَشَمٍّ وحُسنِ مبتسَمِ
يُسَنُّ بالضِّـرْو من بَـراقِشَ أو هيْـلانَ أو ضـامرٍ من العُتُـمِ
رُكِّزَ فـي السام والزَّبيب أقـا حِيُّ كثيبٍ تُعَلُّ بالرِّهَـمِ
بمـاء مُزْنٍ من مـاء دَوْمـةَ قد جُـرِّد فـي ليلِ شَمْألٍ شَبِمِ
شُجَّتْ به قَرْقَفٌ من الراح إسْـ ـفَـنْطُ عُـقارٍ قليلـةُ النَّـدَمِ
أُلْقِيَ فيـها فِلجانِ من مِسْكِ دا رِينَ وفِـلْجٌ من فُـلفُلٍ ضَـرِمِ
رُدَّتْ إلى أكْلَفِ المَناكبِ مَرْ سومٍ مُقيمٍ في الطّين محتدِمِ
جوْنٍ كجوْزِ الحمار جرَّده الـ بيْطـارُ لا ناقسٍ ولا هَـزِمِ
تهـدِرُ فـيه وسـاورتُه كمـا رُجِّع هَدْرٌ من مُصْعَبٍ قَطِمِ

أين طِيب هذه الموصوفة من طيبٍ من تُشاهده من الأتراب العُرُب؟ كلّا والله! ٨،٥،٢ أين الأهل من الغُرُب؟ وأين فوها المذكَّر من أفواهٍ ما وَلَب إليها المُنكَر؟ إنها لَتفضُل على تلك فضلَ الدُّرّة المختزَنة على الحَصاة المُلْقاة، والخيراتِ الملتمَسة على الأعراض المتّقاة. ما سامُك أيّها الرَّجل وزبيبك؟ ما حسُن في العاجلة حبيبُك. وإنَّ ثغرًا يفتقر إلى قضيب البَشام لَيُحْشِمُ حليفَه بعضَ الإحشام! لولا أنه ضَرِيَ بالحَبَر ما افتقر إلى ضِرْوٍ مطلوب، أو غُصنٍ من العُتْم مجلوب. وما الماء الذي وصفته من دَوْمة، وغيرُه ينافي اللَّومة؟ أليس هو إن أقام أَجَنَ، ولا يدوم للماكث إذا دَجَنَ؟ وإن فقد بَرْدَ الشَّمْأَل، رجع كغيره من السَّمَل. تُلْقِي الغَسَر فيه الهابة، وتُشبِّه الغَرّاءُ

The Sheikh (may God make his voice sound loudly!) continues, addressing al-Nābighah al-Jaʿdī: "Abū Laylā, I like these verses of yours: 8.5.1

Lovely she smells, even when you see her without warning,
in every situation, when she sleeps or when she breathes on you.
It is as if her mouth, when she is woken,
with her sweet nose and her fine teeth,
Has been cleaned with aromatic wood[330]
from Haylān or Barāqish or a slender stick of the wild olive tree:
Camomile flowers on a dune, set in
a vein of silver ore and raisin wine, by light rain watered,[331]
With rain-cloud water from the well in Dawmah, which
was poured down[332] on a cold night when the north wind blew,
Mixed with an old and potent,
wormwood-flavored wine[333] that one has little cause to rue,
To which two doses have been added: one of Dārīn musk,
and one of burning pepper,
Sent to the tawny-shouldered amphora, which is then sealed
stored in the clay, and where the wine ferments,
Black like a donkey's back,[334] stripped by
the farrier; not acid, and not whirring(?).[335]
In it, raging against it, the wine rumbles, like
the repeated roaring of an agitated stallion.

"How could the sweet smell of the woman described in these lines be compared with the fragrance of these «loving, well-matched women»[336] that you see here? Impossible, by God! How can the familiar be compared with the novel and strange? How would her mouth, of which we have heard, compare with those mouths never sullied by a base word? The damsels surpass that girl just as a cast-away pebble is surpassed by a safely kept pearl, or as blessings to be won are superior to accidental matters one should shun. I say, what is this 'vein of silver ore' of yours, and your 'raisin wine'? Your loved one in the Fleeting World is not so fine! A mouth that requires regular cleaning with twigs of the balsam tree[337] is to its owner quite a bit of a liability! If its teeth were not covered with plaque and filth, there would be no need for twigs of terebinth, much sought, or of branches of the wild olive tree from afar to these parts brought. And what makes this water from Dawmah that you describe 8.5.2

الشابَّة. والغَرّاء: الهاجرة ذات السَّراب. وما قَرْقَفك هذه المشجوجة، ولو أنها للشَّرَبة مجوبة؟ قُرْبَتَ من حاجتك فلا تَنُط، لا كانت الفيهجُ ولا الإسفَنْط: طالما ثمِلتَ في رُفْقتك فندِمتَ، وأنفقتَ ما تملِك فعدِمتَ. ما عقارك وما فِلْجاك؟ زالت عن مُقْلتك دُجاك! ولو دخل مِسكُ دارينَ، جنةَ ربّنا الموهوبة لغير المُمارين، لعُدَّ في ترابها الذَّفِر كصِيق المقتول، أو دَنَسِ قَدَم مبتول.

زعمتَ أنها تُطَيَّب بالفُلفُل، وشبّهها غيرك بنسيم القَرَنْفُل! إنّ في هذه المنزلة لنشرًا، لا يزيد على نشر الفانية عشرًا، ولكن يشِفُّ بعَددٍ لا يُدرَك، ليس وراءه مُتَّرَك. نزاهةً لهذه القهوة أن تُدَّخر في أكلَفِ مَناكب، مَن حفِظه عُدَّ النّاكب! أصبح بطينها مرسومًا،[1] وضع فيه المتربصُ وُسومًا، فهو جوْن كجوْز الحمار، لا سلِم ذُخرًا للخَمّار! ليس بناقسٍ ولكن منقوس، ذمّه المتحنّف ومَن فِناؤه القُوس، تهدِر فيه الصهباء المعتصَرة وهي في قُرب نِتاج، كالسِّقاب الموضوعة بغير إخداج. فإذا وصلتْ سنَّ البازل بَطَل الهديرُ، وأدارها في الكأس مُدير.

---

١ ب: (مَوسُومًا).

excel, whereas there is nothing wrong with water from any other well? Does it not, if left standing, turn stale, to the drinker of no avail, if he tarries for a while? If the north wind stops making it cool, it becomes like the water in any stagnant pool, into which the wind blows dirt and what not, and which the shimmering afternoon heat makes piping hot. And what is this 'mixed potent wine,' even if the drinkers like pilgrims to it incline? May your wishes always be favored—but spare us your claret 'wormwood-flavored'! How often did you, with your friends get drunk and then repent, all your wealth having been spent! What is this 'old wine' of yours and your 'two doses?' May darkness be removed from your sight! If the musk of Dārīn were to enter the Garden of our Lord, given to those who do not stubbornly doubt, it would on its soil with its pleasant flavor be deemed the filth scraped off a foot or the stink of a cadaver! You said that the wine was spiced with pepper as a condiment, whereas another poet compared it to a whiff of carnation scent. But this place here where we dwell does so sweetly smell that it will excel, not tenfold but many, many times impossible to tell, the smell of the Perishable World. But let's hope this wine of yours will not be stored in a 'tawny-shouldered amphora'! He who keeps it must be deemed misguided. Then it came to be 'marked[338] in its clay'; he who was watching it put marks on it. Then it became 'black like a donkey's back': may it not be kept in good order for the wine-merchant, its hoarder! It is not 'acid' but it is bad, condemned by any pious Muslim as well as one who sits in the courtyard of a monk's cell. The ruddy, pressed must 'rumbles' in it, close to giving birth, surely, like camel calves, not born prematurely! When it has reached the age it cuts its first teeth, it ceases its rumbling sound, and someone will make the cup go round."

١،٩ وبخطِر له، جعل الله الإحسان إليه مربوبًا، ووَدّه في الأفئدة مشبوبًا، غِناءُ القِيان بالفُسطاط ومدينة السلام. ويذكر ترجيعهنّ بميميّة المخبَّل السَّعْدي فتندفع تلك الجواري التي نقلتهنّ القدرة من خِلَق الطَّير اللاقطة، إلى خِلَق حُورٍ غير متساقطة، تلحّن قول المخبَّل السَّعدي:

ذَكَرَ الرِّبَابَ وذِكْرُها سُقْمُ ... وصَبا وليس لمن صبا عزْمُ
وإذا ألمَّ خَيالها طَرفتْ ... عيني فماءُ شؤونها سَجْمُ
كاللؤلؤ المسجور توبِعَ في ... سِلك النِّظام فخانه النَّظْمُ

فلا يمرُّ حرف ولا حركة، إلا ويوقِع مَسَرَّةً لو عُدلت بمسرّات أهل العاجلة، منذ خلق الله آدم إلى أن طوى ذُرّيّته من الأرض، لكانت الزائدة على ذلك زيادةَ اللُّجِّ المتموج على دمعة الطِّفل، والهَضْب الشامخ على الهَباءة المنتفضة من الكِفْل.

ويقول لنُدمائه: ألا تسمعون إلى قول السعديّ:

وتقول عاذِلتي وليس لها ... بغدٍ ولا ما بعده عِلْمُ
إنَّ الثَّراءَ[1] هو الخلودُ وإنَّ ... المرء يكرب يومَه العُدْمُ
ولئن بنيتَ ليَ المشقَّرَ في ... عَنْقاءَ تقصُر دونها العُصُمُ
لَتُنقِّبَنْ عنِّي المَنيَّة إنَّ ... الله ليس كحُكمه حُكْمُ

٢،٩ فيقول إنه المسكين، قال هذه الأبيات وبنو آدم في دار المِحَن والبَلاء، يقبضون من الشدائد على السُّلاء؛ والوالدة تخاف المنيّة على الولد، ولا يزال رُعبها في الخَلَد؛ والفقر يُرْهَب ويُتّقى، والمال يُطلب ويُستبَق؛ والسَّغب موجود والظَّماء، والكَمَه معروف والكُماء؛ ولم يُكفَف للغير عِنان، ولا سُكِّنت بالعفو الجنان. ﴿فَالْحَمْدُ لِلَّهِ الَّذِي أَذْهَبَ عَنَّا الْحَزَنَ إِنَّ رَبَّنَا لَغَفُورٌ شَكُورٌ. الَّذِي أَحَلَّنَا دَارَ الْمُقَامَةِ مِنْ فَضْلِهِ، لا

١ في كل النسخ (الثواء) والصحيح ما في المراجع كالمفضّليات.

The Sheikh (may God cause all manner of benefaction to him and kindle all hearts with affection for him!) thinks of the singing girls in Fustat and the "City of Well-being," Baghdad. He remembers how they performed the poem rhyming on *m* by al-Mukhabbal al-Saʿdī.[339] Spontaneously those girls—those who by God's omnipotence were changed from the shape of pecking birds into shapely black-eyed girls—burst out intoning al-Mukhabbal's verses: 9.1

The singing of the damsels

He thought of al-Rabāb—the thought of her was misery;
he longed for her, but he who longs lacks a firm will.[340]
Whenever her nightly phantom visits me
my eyes are hurt, my tear ducts overflow,
With tears like pearls let loose—strung on a string,
but now the string has let them down.

Any consonant, any vowel that passes gives delight such that if it was matched with all the delights of the people of the Fleeting World since God created Adam until the time He folded up his descendants on earth, it would exceed them just as the billows of the deep sea exceed a toddler's tear, or as a lofty mountain exceeds a speck of dust that one flicks off one's saddle blanket. He says to his drinking companions, "Listen to al-Mukhabbal al-Saʿdī's verses:

She who blames me says (she does not know
about tomorrow and of what comes after it):
'Wealth is the life eternal! Poverty
will bring a man near to his death.'[341]
But even if you built for me the fort of al-Mushaqqar, on
a mountaintop unscalable to ibex goat,
My doom would seek me out and find me there:
there's no decree like God's decree.

"Poor man! He composed these verses while mankind lived in the abode of tribulations, careworn, their hands gripping afflictions' thorn. A mother feared for the life of her child, always grieving, terror in her heart never leaving. Poverty was feared and kept at bay; wealth sought and made to stay. Famine was found there, and burning thirst, and people blind from birth; feet chapped like truffles, rough. Jealousy reigned unbridled, and no one dwelled in a garden, pardoned and forgiven. «Praise be to God who removed from us all sorrow. Our Lord is truly forgiving and thankful; 9.2

يَمَسُّنا فيها نَصَبٌ وَلا يَمَسُّنا فيها لُغُوبٌ﴾. فتبارك الله القُدُّوس! نقل هؤلاء المُسْمِعاتِ من زيِّ ربّات الأَجْنحة، إلى زيِّ ربّات الأكفال المترجّحة؛ ثمّ ألهمهنّ بالحكمة حِفظَ أشعارٍ لم تمرُر قبلُ بمَسامعهنّ، فجئن بها مُتْقَنةً، محمولة على الطَّرائق ملحَّنة، مُصيبةً في لحن الغِناء، منزَّهةً عن لحن الهِجَاء. ولقد كانت الجارية في الدار العاجلة، إذا تفُرِّسَتْ فيها النَّجابة، وأُحضرت لها الملحِّنة لتُلقي إليها ما تعرف من ثقيلٍ وخفيف، وتأخذها بمأخذٍ غير ذفيف؛ تقيم معها الشهر كَرِيتاً، قبل أن تلقَّن كذباً حَنبَريتاً: بيتاً من الغَزَل أو بيتَيْن، ثم تُعْطى المائةَ أو المائتين. فسبحان القادر على كل عزيز، والمميِّز بفضله كلَّ مَزِيز.

ويقول نابغة بني جعدة، وهو جالس يستمع: يا أبا بصير أهذه الرَّباب التي ذكرها السعديُّ هي رَبابك التي ذكرتَها في قولك: ١،٣،٩

بِعاصي العواذلِ طَلْق اليديـ ـنِ يُعْطي الجزيلَ ويُرْخي الإزارا
فما نطق الدِّيكُ حتّى ملأ تُ كوب الرَّباب له فاستدارا
إذا انكبَّ أزهرُ بين السُّقاةِ تراموْا به غَرَباً أو نُضارا

فيقول أبو بصير: قد طال عمرك يا أبا ليلى، وأحسبك أصابك الفَنَد، فبقيت على فندك إلى اليوم! أما علمتَ أنّ اللواتي يُسمَّيْن بالرَّباب أكثر من أن يُحْصَيْن؟ أفتظنّ أنّ الرَّباب هذه هي التي ذكرها القائل:

ما بالُ قومكِ يا ربابُ خُزْراً كأنهم غِضابُ
غاروا عليكِ وكيف ذا كِ ودونكِ الخَرْقُ اليَبابُ

أو التي ذكرها امرؤ القيس في قوله:

who, of His bounty, has made us dwell in the Lasting Abode, where no weariness touches us and where no fatigue touches us».[342] Blessed be God the Holy One! He has changed each girl who sings from a creature with wings into a woman with a bum that swings! Then He, with His wisdom, inspired them with the knowledge of poems they had never heard before, which they performed with perfection, with various tunes for every section, with musical melodies, free from vulgar linguistic and grammatical maladies. When in the Fleeting World a girl was perceived to be gifted and was given a teacher who taught her the rhythmical modes, the 'heavy' and the 'light,' her instruction being 'heavy' rather than 'light,' she would spend a full month with her before the girl could perform even one or two verses of love poetry (pure lies, all untrue!), and then she is taught at most a hundred or two! Praised, therefore, be He who is able to do anything that is arduous, and who by His grace distinguishes anything that is virtuous!"

Al-Nābighah of the Jaʿdah tribe, who has been sitting and listening, asks al-Aʿshā, "Abū Baṣīr, this Rabāb who is mentioned by al-Mukhabbal al-Saʿdī, and the Rabāb that you mention in your poem, 9.3.1

An altercation in Paradise

He[343] disobeys reproaching women and bestows
with open hands and generously gives, proud and relaxed.
No sooner crows the cock than I have filled
the cup of al-Rabāb for him,[344] and it goes round.
Whenever a radiant wine is poured amidst the servants,
is what they hand to one another silver or gold?

"Are they the same woman?"

Al-Aʿshā replies, "You have lived for too long, Abū Laylā! I think you have become old and dotty, and have remained thus until today.[345] Don't you know that there are innumerable women called al-Rabāb? Do you really think that this Rabāb is the same as the one in these verses:

Why is it, Rabāb, that your people are looking
askance, narrow-eyed, as if they were angry?
They have guarded you jealously. Why?
For around you lies nothing but desolate desert.

". . . or the same as the one mentioned by Imruʾ al-Qays:

دارٌ لهندٍ والرَّبابِ وفَرْتَنَى ولميسَ قبلَ حوادثِ الأيامِ

ولعلّ أمّها أمُّ الرَّباب المذكورة في قوله:

وجارتِها أمِّ الرَّبابِ بمأْسَلِ

فيقول نابغة بني جعدة: أتكلّمني بمثل هذا الكلام يا خليع بني ضُبيعة، وقد مُتَّ كافرًا، وأقررتَ على نفسك بالفاحشة، وأنا لقيت النبيَّ، صلى الله عليه وسلّم، فأنشدته كلمتي التي أقول فيها: ٢،٣،٩

بلغْنا السماءَ مَجدُنا وسَناؤنا وإنّا لَنبغي فوقَ ذلك مَظْهرا

فقال: إلى أين يا أبا ليلى؟ فقلت: إلى الجنّة بك يا رسول الله! فقال: لا يفضُض الله فاك. أغرّك أن عَدّك بعض الجُهّال رابعَ الشُّعراء الأربعة؟ وكذب مفضِّلك، وإنّي لأطول منك نَفَساً وأكثر تصرُّفًا. ولقد بلغتُ بعدد البيوت ما لم يبلغه أحد من العرب قبلي، وأنت لاهٍ بعَفارتك، تفتري على كرائم قومك. وإن صدقتَ فخزيًا لك ولمُقارِك! ولقد وُفّقت الهِزّانيّةُ في تخليتك: عاشرتْ منك النابحَ، عشيَ فطاف الأخوِيَة على العظام المنتبَذة، وحرص على انتباث الأجداث المنفردة.

فيغضَب أبو بصير فيقول: أتقول هذا وإنّ بيتاً ممّا بنيتُ لَيُعدَل بمائةٍ من بنائك؟ وإن أسهبتَ في مَنطقك، فإنّ المُسهِب كحاطب الليل. وإنّي لفي الجرثومة من ربيعة الفَرَس، وإنك لمن بني جعدة، وهل جعدةُ إلاّ رائدةُ ظليم نَفور؟ أتعيّرني في مدح الملوك؟ ولو قدرتَ يا جاهل على ذلك لَهجرتَ إليه أهلَك وولدَك، ولكنّك خُلقت جبانًا هِدانًا، لا تُدلج في الظلماء الدّاجية، ولا تهجّر في الوديقة الصاخدة. وذكرت لي طلاق الهِزّانية ولعلّها بانت عني مُسِرّةَ الكَمَد، والطلاق ليس بمنكرٍ للسُّوَق ولا للملوك.

٣،٣،٩ فيقول الجعديّ: اسكتْ يا ضُلَّ بن ضُلّ، فأُقسم أنّ دخولك الجنّة من المنكَرات، ولكنّ الأقضية جرت كما شاء الله! لحقُّك أن تكون في الدَّرَك الأسفل من النار،

An abode of Hind and al-Rabāb and Fartanā,
and of Lamīs, before Time struck with all its vagaries.

"... or perhaps her mother is Umm al-Rabāb in another verse by Imruʾ al-Qays:[346]

And her neighbor, Umm al-Rabāb, in Maʾsal."

Al-Nābighah al-Jaʿdī replies, "How dare you talk to me like that, you bastard of Ḍubayʿah![347] You died as an unbeliever and you have confessed to immoralities; whereas I have met the Prophet (God bless and preserve him) and I have recited a poem to him, in which I say: 9.3.2

We, with our glory and splendor, have reached the sky;
but we desire a state that is still higher yet.

"The Prophet then asked, 'Where would you go, Abū Laylā?' And I answered, 'To Paradise, with you, Messenger of God!' Then the Prophet said, 'Well spoken, God bless you!'[348] Has it gone to your head that you have been ranked by some ignoramus as the fourth of the great poets?[349] In preferring you he has lied: I am more prolific than you, and more versatile too! I have composed more verses than any Arab before me; you merely amuse yourself with malicious stuff, slandering the women of your own tribe. Or, if you spoke the truth, shame on you and those who are with you! That woman from the tribe of Hizzān was fortunate that you got rid of her, having lived with a barking night-blind dog that prowled among the tribal tents seeking discarded bones and looking to dig up graves in lonely spots!"[350]

"How dare you say that!" says al-Aʿshā angrily. "But one verse composed by me is worth one hundred of yours. You may have been prolix, but a prolix poet is like someone who gathers firewood at night.[351] I am rooted in the tribe of Rabīʿat al-Faras whereas you are from Jaʿdah; and what is Jaʿdah but a party of ostrich hunters? Are you upbraiding me for eulogizing kings? If you had been capable of doing that, you fool, you would have left your wife and children for it. But you are a natural coward and a weakling. You are not one to set out in the dark night, you will not travel in the scorching midday heat. You mentioned my divorce from the woman of Hizzān; but she was sorry to part from me. And divorce is not shameful, neither to common people nor to kings."

"Shut up!" says al-Jaʿdī, "you nobody, son of nobody! I swear, your entry into the Garden is an abominable thing. But divine decisions happen as God 9.3.3

ولقد صلي بها من هو خير منك، ولو جاز الغلطُ على ربِّ العزّة لقلت: إنّك غُلط بك! ألست القائل:

فدخلتُ إذ نام الرقيـ بُ فبتُّ دون ثيابِـها
حتى إذا ما استرسلتْ للنوم بعد لِعابِها
قسَّمتُها نِصفَيْن كلُّ مسوَّدٍ يُرمى بِها
فثنيتُ جِيدَ غريرةٍ ولمستُ بطنَ حِقابها
كالحُقّة الصفراء صا لَ عبيرُها بملابِها
وإذا لها تامورةٌ مرفوعة لشَرابِها

واستقللتَ ببني جعدة، ولَيومٌ من أيّامهم يرجَح بمَساعي قومك. وزعمتَني جبانًا وكذبت! لأنا أشجعُ منك ومن أبيك، وأصبرُ على إدلاج المُظلمة ذات الأريز، وأشدُّ إيغالاً في الهاجرة أمّ الصَّخدان.

٤،٣،٩ ويثب نابغة بني جعدة على أبي بصير فيضربه بكُوز من ذهب. فيقول: أصلح الله به وعلى يديه: لا عَربدةَ في الجنان، إنّما يُعرف ذلك في الدار الفانية بين السَّفِلة والهَجاج، وإنك يا أبا ليلى لمتنزّع. وقد رُوي في الحديث أنّ رجلاً صاح بالبصرة: يا آل قيسٍ! فجاء النابغة الجعديُّ بعُصَيّةٍ له، فأخذه شُرَطُ أبي موسى الأشعريّ فجلده لأنّ النبيَّ صلّى الله عليه وسلّم قال: من تَعزّى بعزاء الجاهليّة فليس منّا. ولو لا أنّ في الكتاب الكريم: ﴿لا يُصَدَّعونَ عَنها ولا يُنزِفُونَ﴾ لظنتّاك أصابك نَزْفٌ في عقلك. فأمّا أبو بصيرٍ فما شرب إلّا اللّبن والعسل، وإنّه لَوقور في المجلس، لا يخِفُّ عند حلِّ الحُبْوة. وإنّما مَثَلُه معنا مَثَلُ أبي نواسٍ في قوله:

wills. You deserve to be in the lowest reach of the Fire, where better people than you now roast. If it were possible to think that the Lord of Might had made a mistake, I would say that a mistake was made in your case. Did you not say:

I entered when the watchman slept, and spent
the night, while no clothes were between us.
When, finally, she gave herself to sleep,
after her playfulness,
I turned my mind to her two halves,
each one desirable!
I bent a neck like that of an innocent creature[352]
and touched what was inside her underclothes:
Just like a scent box, pale,
its fragrance mixed with liquid perfume.
And see! she had a cup
raised to receive the wine![353]

"You despise the Banū Jaʿdah; yet one of their battle-days alone outweighs all the efforts of your tribe! You have asserted that I am a coward: you lied! I am braver than you and your father, I can better endure traveling on a freezing night, and I go further into the scorching midday heat."

Al-Nābighah al-Jaʿdī pounces upon Abū Baṣīr al-Aʿshā and strikes him with a golden beaker. The Sheikh (may God give peace through him, at his hands!) says, "No quarreling in Paradise! That is only known in the Perishable World, among the lower classes and the ignorant. You, Abū Laylā, are a hothead. There is a story about you: a man in Basra shouted 'Men of Qays!' whereupon you, al-Nābighah al-Jaʿdī, came with a little stick. You were apprehended by the constables of the governor, Abū Mūsā al-Ashʿarī, who had you flogged, because the Prophet (God bless and preserve him) has said, 'He who is patient in the manner of the pre-Islamic period is not one of ours!' Had it not been said in the Holy Book[354] about the wine in Paradise that «they will not suffer headache from it and not be intoxicated», we would have thought that you were out of your mind. As for Abū Baṣīr, he has drunk only milk and honey here.[355] He is dignified when he sits in a gathering; he is not unseemly quick when he unwraps, getting up.[356] His behavior with us is like that of Abū Nuwās, when he says: 9.3.4

أيها العاذلان في الراح لوما لا أذوق المُدام إلا شميما
نالني بالعِتاب فيها إمامٌ لا أرى لي خِلافَه مستقيما
إنّ حظّي منها إذا هي دارت أن أراها وأن أشُمَّ النسيما
فاصرِفاها إلى سِواي فإنّي لستُ إلا على الحديث نديما
فكأنّي وما أحسِّن منها قَعَديٌّ يحسِّن التحكيما
لم يُطِق حملَه السِّلاحَ إلى الحرْ بِ فأوصى المُطيقَ ألا يقيما

فيقول نابغة بني جعدة: قد كان الناس في أيّام الخادعة يظهر عنهم السَّفَهُ بشُرب اللبن، لا سيَّما إذا كانوا أرِقَّاء لئاماً، كما قال الراجز:

يا ابنَ هشام أهلكَ الناسَ اللَّبَنْ فكلُّهم يغدو بسيفٍ وقَرَنْ

وقال آخر:

ما دهرُ ضَبّةَ فاعلمْ نَحتُ أَثْلَتِنا وإنّما هاج من جُهّالها اللَّبَنُ

وقيل لبعضهم: متى يُخاف شرُّ بني فلانٍ؟ قال: إذا ألبنوا.

فيريد، بلّغه الله إرادته، أن يُصلِح بين النُّدماء، فيقول: يجب أن يُحْذَر من ملَكٍ ٥،٣،٩ يعبُر فيرى هذا المجلس، فيرفع حديثَه إلى الجبّار الأعظم، فلا يجُرُّ ذلك إلا ما تكرَهان. واستغنى ربُّنا أن تُرفَع الأخبار إليه، ولكنْ جرى مَجْرى الحَفَظة في الدار العاجلة، أما علمتُما أنّ آدم خرج من الجنّة بذنبٍ حقير، فغيرُ آمنٍ مَن ولدَ أن يُقْدَر له مثلُ ذلك.

فسألتك يا أبا بصير بالله هل يهجِس لك تَمنّي المُدام؟ فيقول: كلا، واللهِ إنها عندي لَمِثلُ المَقِر لا يخطِر ذكرُها بالخَلَد. فالحمد لله الذي سقاني عنها السُّلوانة، فما

You two, who censure me for drinking wine, go blame me!
I taste the wine by merely smelling it.
A caliph[357] has reproached me on account of it:
I do not think it right to disobey.
My share of it, when it goes round,
is only seeing it and smelling its bouquet.
Turn it away from me then, to another: I
shall only be a conversation partner.
I am in praising it, it seems, a Khārijite abstainer,
who speaks in favor of the arbitration:[358]
Incapable of carrying arms to war,
he orders others not to sit and stay behind."

Al-Nābighah al-Jaʿdī replies, "In the days of the Deceptive World people often behaved foolishly when drinking milk, especially if they were lowly slaves. A *rajaz* poet said:

Ibn Hishām, milk has destroyed the people!
They all come in the morning with a sword and with a quiver.

"And another said:

What do the men of Ḍabbah want? Know this: it is defaming us!
Some stupid men among them got excited, drinking milk.

"Someone was asked, 'When should one be most afraid of the Banū So-and-So?' He answered, 'When they have plenty of milk.'"

The Sheikh (may God make him attain what he wants!) means to spread 9.3.5
peace among the carousers and says, "One must beware of an angel who might pass by, see this gathering, and then report to the Omnipotent, the Almighty, which may bring about unpleasant consequences for you both. In fact, our Lord does not need reports to be brought to Him, but it happens just as it does with the recording angels in the Fleeting World.[359] Don't you know that Adam had to leave Paradise for a trivial sin? Those born later cannot be sure that a like fate will not be theirs. I ask you, Abū Baṣīr, by God, do you not secretly long for wine?"

"Certainly not, by God!" replies al-Aʿshā. "To me it is like bitter aloes: even the thought of it never occurs to me. Praise be to God, who quenched

أحفِل بأمّ زَنْبَقٍ أخرى الدهر.

٤،٩ وينهض نابغة بني جعدة مُغْضَباً، فيكره، جنّبه الله المكاره، انصرافَه على تلك الحال، فيقول: يا أبا ليلى، إنّ الله، جلّت قدرته، منّ علينا بهؤلاء الحُور العِين اللواتي حوّلهنّ عن خَلق الإِوَزّ، فاخترْ لك واحدةً منهنّ فلتذهبْ معك إلى منزلك، تُلاحنك أرقَّ اللِّحان، وتُسمعك ضروبَ الألحان.

فيقول لبيد بن ربيعة: إن أخذ أبو ليلى قينةً، وأخذ غيرُه مثلها، أليس ينتشر خبرُها في الجنّة، فلا يؤْمَن أن يُسمّىَ فاعلو ذلك أزواجَ الإوزّ؟ فتُضرب الجماعةُ عن اقتسام أولئك القيان.

my thirst with the oblivion of wine! I no longer care for another sip of 'Mother Iris.'[360]"

Al-Nābighah al-Jaʿdī, angry, stands up. The Sheikh (may God keep unpleasant things far from him!) does not want him to leave in this manner. "Abū Laylā," he says, "God, the Almighty, has granted us these black-eyed damsels, whom He transformed from geese. Choose one of them for yourself and take her home with you, where she will speak to you with the subtlest intimations and sing to you all kinds of intonations." 9.4

Then Labīd ibn Rabīʿah says, "If Abū Laylā takes a singing girl, and someone else takes another, will the news not spread throughout Paradise? Then these people will run the risk of being nicknamed 'goose spouses'!" So the whole company abstains from dividing the girls among themselves.

١،١٠ ويمرُّ حسّان بن ثابت فيقولون: أهلاً أبا عبد الرحمن، ألا تحدّثُ معنا ساعة؟ فإذا جلس إليهم قالوا: أين هذه المشروبة من سبيئتك التي ذكرتها في قولك:

كأنَّ سبيئةً من بيتِ رأسٍ   يكون مِزاجَها عَسَلٌ وماءُ
علىٰ أنيابها أو طعمَ غَضٍّ   من التُّفَّاح هصَّره اجتناءُ
علىٰ فيها إذا ما الليلُ قلَّتْ   كواكبُه ومال بها الغطاءُ
إذا ما الأشرباتُ ذُكرنَ يومًا   فهنَّ لطيِّبِ الراحِ الفِداءُ

ويحك! ما استحييت أن تذكر مثلَ هذا في مِدْحتك رسول الله، صلى الله عليه وسلم؟ فيقول: إنّه كان أسجحَ خُلُقاً ممّا تظنُّون، ولم أقل إلا خيراً، لم أذكر أني شربت خمراً، ولا ركبت ممّا حُظر أمراً، وإنّما وصفتُ رِيق امرأةٍ يجوز أن يكون حلاًّ لي، ويمكن أن أقوله على الظَّنِّ. وقد شفع صلى الله عليه في أبي بصيرٍ بعد ما تهكَّم في مَواطن كثيرة، وزعم أنه مُستَتِرٌ، مفترياً أو ليس بمفترٍ. وما سُمع بأكرم منه صلى الله عليه: لقد أفكتُ فجلدني مع مِسْطَحٍ ثم وهب لي أختَ ماريةَ فولدتْ لي عبد الرحمن، وهي خالة ولده إبراهيم.

٢،١٠ وهو، زيّن الله الآداب ببقائه، يخطر في ضميره أشياءُ، يريد أن يذكرها لحسّان وغيره، ثم يخاف أن يكونوا لما طلب غير محسنين، فيضرب عنها إكراماً للجليس، مثلُ قول حسّان:

يكون مزاجَها عسلٌ وماءُ

يَعرض له أن يقول: كيف قلتَ يا أبا عبد الرحمن: أيكون مزاجَها عسلٌ وماءُ، أم مزاجُها عسلاً وماءُ، أم مزاجُها عسلٌ وماءُ على الابتداء والخبر؟

Ḥassān ibn Thābit passes by.[361] "Welcome, Abū ʿAbd al-Raḥmān!" they all say, "Won't you talk with us for a while?" He sits down and they ask him, "How does this wine compare with the wine you bought and described in your verses: 10.1

The conversation with Ḥassān ibn Thābit

It is as if a wine imported from Bayt Raʾs,
its mixture being honey and water,
Surrounds her teeth; as if the taste
of apples freshly harvested
Were in her mouth, when fewer stars are visible
at night, when darkness' cover takes the stars along.[362]
If ever all the wines on earth were listed, they
would sacrifice themselves for that fine wine!

"Woe betide you! Are you not ashamed to mention this in your eulogy on the Messenger of God (God bless and preserve him)?"

"He was more tolerant than you think," replies Ḥassān, "I have said nothing but good things, I did not say that I drank wine, and I have not committed anything forbidden. I merely described the saliva of a woman who might have been my own wife after all;[363] I could also have said it by way of hypothesis. The Prophet (God bless him[364]) has interceded for Abū Baṣīr al-Aʿshā even after he boasted in his verse on many occasions and asserted that he traveled at night, either lying or being right. One has never heard of a more magnanimous man than the Prophet (God bless and preserve him). After I had lied and he had me flogged together with Misṭaḥ, he gave me the sister of Māriyah.[365] She bore my son ʿAbd al-Raḥmān. She is the aunt of the Prophet's son Ibrāhīm."[366]

The Sheikh (may God adorn belles lettres by granting him long life!) can think of many things he wants to ask Ḥassān and the others; but he is afraid they may be unable to give the right answers, so he refrains from asking, out of respect of his companions. 10.2

For instance, Ḥassān's verse "its mixture being honey and water": it occurs to him to ask, "What would you say, Abū ʿAbd al-Raḥmān, *mizājahā* ('its mixture,' accusative) *ʿasalun* ('honey,' nominative) *wa-māʾū* ('and water,' nominative)? Or *mizājuhā* (nominative) *ʿasalan* (accusative) *wa-māʾū* ('and water,' nominative)? Or rather *mizājuhā ʿasalun wa-māʾū* (all nominatives), assuming that this is a nominal sentence?"[367]

وقوله:

فمن يهجو رسولَ الله منكمْ ويمدحه وينصُره سَواءُ

يذهب بعضهم إلى أنّ مَنْ محذوفة من قولك: ويمدحه وينصره، على أن ما بعدها صِلة لها. وقال قوم: حُذفت على أنها نَكِرة، وجُعل ما بعدها وصفاً لها، فأُقيمت الصفة مقامَ الموصوف.

ويقول قائل من القوم: كيف جُبْنك يا أبا عبد الرحمن؟ فيقول: أَلي يقال هذا وقومي أشجع العرب؟ أراد ستّة منهم أن يميلوا على أهل الموْسم بأسيافهم، وأجاروا النبيَّ على أن يحاربوا معه كلّ عَنودٍ؛ فرمتْهم ربيعةُ ومُضَرُ وجميع العرب عن قوْس العَداوة، وأضمروا لهم ضِغْن الشَّنآن. وإن ظهر منّي تحرُّزٌ في بعض المواطن، فإنّما ذلك على طريقة الحزم، كما جاء في الكتاب الكريم: ﴿وَمَن يُوَلِّهِمْ يَوْمَئِذٍ دُبُرَهُ إِلَّا مُتَحَرِّفًا لِّقِتَالٍ أَوْ مُتَحَيِّزًا إِلَىٰ فِئَةٍ فَقَدْ بَاءَ بِغَضَبٍ مِّنَ اللَّهِ وَمَأْوَاهُ جَهَنَّمُ وَبِئْسَ الْمَصِيرُ﴾.

ويفترق أهل ذلك المجلس بعد أن أقاموا فيه كعُمر الدُّنيا أضعافاً كثيرةً، فبينا هو يطوف في رياض الجنّة، لقيه خمسة نفرٍ على خمس أَيْنُق، فيقول: ما رأيت أحسن من عيونكم في أهل الجنان! فمن أنتم خَلَدَ عليكم النعيم؟ فيقولون: نحن عُورانُ قيسٍ: تميم بن مُقْبِلٍ العَجْلانيّ وعمرو بن أحمر الباهليُ والشَّمّاخ مَعْقِل بن ضِرار، أحد بني ثَعْلَبة بن سعد بن ذُبيان، وراعي الإبل عُبيد بن الحُصين النُّميريّ، وحُميد بن ثوْر الهِلاليّ. فيقول للشَّمّاخ بن ضرار: لقد كان في نفسي أشياء من قصيدتك التي على الزاي، وكلمتك التي على الجيم، فأنشدْنيهما لا زلتَ مخلَّداً كريماً. ١٠،٣،١٠

فيقول: لقد شغلني عنهما النَّعيم الدائم فما أذكر منهما بيتاً واحداً. فيقول لفرط حُبّه الأدبَ وإيثارِه تشييدَ الفضل: لقد غفلْتَ أيها المؤمن وأضعْتَ! أما علمتَ أنّ كلمتيك، أنفع لك من ابنتيك؟ ذُكرتَ بهما في المواطن، وشُهرتَ عند راكب

Or his verse:

He of you who lampoons the messenger of God
  and praises him and helps him, are they equal then?[368]

Some believe that the word "who" is elided before "praises" and "helps," and that what follows it is a syndetic relative clause serving as an adjunct. Others say, however, that "who" is elided because it has an indefinite sense, in which case what follows it is a description of it, so that the asyndetic attributive relative clause takes the place of the thing that is described.[369]

One of those present asks Ḥassān: "What about this cowardice of yours, Abū ʿAbd al-Raḥmān?" Ḥassān replies, "Are you saying this to me, when my tribe is the bravest of all Arab tribes?[370] Six men of my tribe wanted to attack the heathen pilgrims with their swords and they protected the Prophet, agreeing to fight with him against any opponent. Then the tribes of Rabīʿah, Muḍar, and all the Arabs plunged their knives into our people and harbored hatred against them. If I have appeared to act with caution on some occasions, then it was merely a matter of being prudent. It is said in the Holy Book:[371] «He who turns his back to them on that day—unless withdrawing to fight again, or siding with another group—he will have to bear God's anger and his refuge will be Hell: an evil destiny!»"

The company disperses, having spent a time equivalent to many earthly lifetimes. While he wanders through the meadows of Paradise, the Sheikh meets five men riding five she-camels. He says, "I have never seen people in Paradise with eyes as beautiful as yours! Who are you? May God give you eternal bliss!" They answer, "We five were the one-eyed men of the tribe of Qays: Tamīm ibn Muqbil al-ʿAjlānī, ʿAmr ibn Aḥmar al-Bāhilī, al-Shammākh ibn Ḍirār of the Banū Thaʿlabah ibn Saʿd ibn Dhubyān, ʿUbayd ibn al-Ḥuṣayn al-Numayrī nicknamed the Camel-herd, and Ḥumayd ibn Thawr al-Hilālī."[372] 10.3.1

The five one-eyed men of Qays

The Sheikh addresses al-Shammākh: "I should like to ask you about a few things in your poem that rhymes in *-zū* and another poem rhyming in *-jī*; please recite them for me, may you be noble-hearted forever!" But al-Shammākh replies, "The perpetual bliss has made me forget these poems; I cannot remember a single verse from them." The Sheikh, with his exceeding love of literature and his eagerness to attribute virtue where it is due, says, "You have been neglectful, you true believer, and you have lost something precious! Don't you know that your two poems were more useful to

السَّفر والقاطن؛ وإنّ القصيدة من قصائد النابغة لأنفعُ له من ابنته عَقْرَب، ولعل تلك شانتُه، وما زانتْه، وأصابها في الجاهلية سِباء، وما وَفَر لأجْلها الحِباء. وإن شئت أن أنشدك قصيدتيك، فإن ذلك ليس بمتعذرٍ عليّ. فيقول: أنشدْني، ضَفَتْ عليك نعمةُ الله، فينشده:

عفا من سُليمى بطنُ قوٍّ فعالِزُ   فذاتُ الغَضا فالمُشْرِفاتُ النَّواشِزُ

۲،۳،۱۰ فيجده بها غيرَ عليم. ويسأله عن أشياء منها، فيصادفه بها غير بصير، فيقول: شغلتني لذائذ الخلود عن تعهُّد هذه المُنْكَرات: ﴿ إِنَّ الْمُتَّقِينَ فِي ظِلَالٍ وَعُيُونٍ، وَفَوَاكِهَ مِمَّا يَشْتَهُونَ، كُلُوا وَاشْرَبُوا هَنِيئًا بِمَا كُنتُمْ تَعْمَلُونَ ﴾، إنّما كنت أَسِقُ هذه الأمور، وأنا آمُل أن أُفْقَرَ بها ناقةً، أو أُعطَى كيْلَ عِيالي سنةً، كما قال الراجز:

لو شاكَ من رأسك عَظْمٌ يابسُ   آلَـــ منك جَمَلٌ حُمارِسُ
سوّى عليك الكيلَ شيخٌ بائسُ   مثلَ الحَصى يعجب منه اللامسُ

وأنا الآن في تفضُّل الله، أغترف في مَرافد العَسْجَد من أنهار اللَّبَن: فتارةً ألبان الإبل، وتارةً ألبان البقر، وإن شئت لبن الضأن فإنه كثيرٌ جَمٌّ، وكذلك لبن المَعِيز، وإن أحببت وِرْدًا من رِسْل الأراويّ، فرُبّ نهرٍ منه كأنه دِجلةُ أو الفُرات. ولقد أراني في دار الشِّقوة أَجْهَدُ أخلافَ شِياهٍ لَجِباتٍ، لا يمتلئ منهنّ القَعْب.

۱،٤،۱۰ فيقول، لا زال مِقْوَلاً للخير: فأين عمرو بن أحمر؟ فيقول عمروٌ: ها أنا ذا. فيقول: أنشدْني قولك:

you than your two daughters? By virtue of these poems you are mentioned in every place by name; travelers and those staying at home know your fame! Likewise, one of al-Nābighah al-Dhubyānī's poems was more useful to him than his daughter ʿAqrab, who may have brought him shame whereas the poem brought him fame; she could, in those heathen times, have been abducted and abused and her bride-price would have been greatly reduced! If you want me to recite your two poems to you, I could do so without difficulty." Al-Shammākh replies, "Recite them, may God's favors to you be plentiful!" The Sheikh recites:[373]

No trace of Sulaymā is found in the valley of Qaww,
nor in ʿĀliz, or Dhāt al-Ghaḍā, or the peaks of the highlands.

He finds that the poet is not knowledgeable about his own verse; he asks him about various things but he realizes that al-Shammākh does not understand them. "The delights of the eternal life," he explains, "have distracted me from being aware of these objectionable matters. «The god-fearing are amidst shade and springs, and such fruits as they desire: 'Eat and drink with relish, in return for what you did!'»[374] I accumulated my store of good deeds[375] merely in the hope of someone lending me a she-camel, or being given a year's ration of wheat for my family, as the *rajaz* poet says: 10.3.2

If a dry bone stuck out from your head,
A sturdy camel would come back from you;[376]
A wretched old man would dole out for you a measure
Of wheat like pebbles, amazing to him who touches it.[377]

"But now I am living in God's grace, scooping from the rivers of milk with golden mugs: camel's milk, cow's milk, or sheep's milk if I wish, all are abundant here; and goat's milk too. And if I feel like having a draught of ibex milk, there's many a river full, like the Tigris or the Euphrates. But often I saw[378] myself in the world of misery, milking dry the udders of sheep with little yield, without filling even a small pail."

Then the Sheikh (may he always speak for the sake of the good!) asks, "Where is ʿAmr ibn Aḥmar?" "Here I am," replies ʿAmr. "Recite for us," continues the Sheikh, "your poem that begins with 10.4.1

بان الشّبابُ وأخلفَ العَمْرُ وتغيّرَ الإخوانُ والدّهْرُ

وقد اختلف الناس في تفسير العَمْرِ، فقيل: إنّك أردت البَقاء، وقيل: إنّك أردت الواحد من عمور الأسنان، وهو اللّحم الذي بينها. فيقول عمرو متمثلاً:

خُذا وجهَ هَرْشَى أو قَفاها[١] فإنّه كِلا جانبيْ هَرْشَى لهُنّ طريقُ

ولم تترك فيّ أهوال القيامة غُبَّرًا للإنشاد، أما سمعت الآية: ﴿يَوْمَ تَرَوْنَهَا تَذْهَلُ كُلُّ مُرْضِعَةٍ عَمَّآ أَرْضَعَتْ، وَتَضَعُ كُلُّ ذَاتِ حَمْلٍ حَمْلَهَا، وَتَرَى النَّاسَ سُكَـٰرَىٰ وَمَا هُم بِسُكَـٰرَىٰ وَلَـٰكِنَّ عَذَابَ اللَّهِ شَدِيدٌ﴾ وقد شهدتَ الموْقف، فالعَجَب لك إذ بقي معك شيء من روايتك! فيقول الشيخ: إنّي كنت أُخلِص الدُّعاء في أعقاب الصلوات، قبل أن أنتقل من تلك الدار، أن يُمتِعني الله بأدبي في الدُّنيا والآخرة، فأجابني إلى ما سألتُ وهو الحميد المجيد.

ولقد يُعجِبني قولك: ٢،٤،١٠

ولقد غدوتُ وما يفزّعني خوفٌ أُحاذره ولا ذُعْرُ
رؤْدَ الشّباب كأنني غُصُنٌ بحرامِ مكّةَ ناعمٌ نَضِرُ
كشرابِ قيلٍ عن مَطيتّهِ ولكلِّ أمرٍ واقعٍ قَدَرُ
مُدَّ النّهارُ له وطال عليْـ ـه الليلُ واستنعتْ به الخمْرُ
ومُسِفّةٌ دَهْماءُ داجنةٌ ركدتْ وأُسبِل دونها السِّتْرُ
وجرادتانِ تغنّيانهمُ وتلألأ المَرجانُ والشّذْرُ
ومجلجلٌ دانٍ زَبرجدُهُ حَدِبٌ كما يتحدّب الدّبْرُ
ونأيٌ حنّانان بينهما وتَرٌ أجشُّ غِناؤه زَمْرُ

١ في نسخة الأصل: '(كلاها) والصواب ما أثبتت بنت الشاطئ.

Youth has gone and *'amr* has failed us,
Friends and times have changed;

"for people have different opinions on the meaning of *'amr*. Some say you meant 'long life' but others say that you intended 'gums', the flesh between the teeth." 'Amr replies with a proverb in verse:

"Take the road to Harshā or the other way:
Either side of Harshā is the road to go.[379]

"The horrors of the Resurrection have not left any place for reciting poetry. You must have heard the Qur'anic verse: [380] «On the day that you see it,[381] every suckling mother will be numb and forget the child she suckles, every pregnant woman will deliver what she carries, and you will think people drunk, yet they are not drunk. But God's torment is severe». You have been at the Standing Place;[382] it is a miracle that you can still recite poems!" The Sheikh explains: "Before I moved from that abode, I always prayed after the ritual devotions, imploring God to make me enjoy my literary erudition not only in this world but also in the Hereafter; and He has granted what I asked, praised be He!

"I like your poem: **10.4.2**

I set out in the morning, not being afraid,
with nothing to fear or to dread,
In the prime of my youth; like a fresh, tender branch,
in the sacrosanct precinct of Mecca,
For a wine[383] like the wine of a *qayl*,[384] who has turned his mind
away from his mount[385] (everything has its time and its measure).
His day was drawn out and his night has been long
and he had been longing for wine all the time.
There was also a low-lying, dark, gloomy one[386]
that was hanging, unmoving, a curtain let down this side of it,
And two locusts were singing to them,
while coral and gold beads were glittering;
And something made to resound, its peridot near to us,
its back with a hump like the back of a bee,
And two cymbals, their sound full of longing; between them
a string, sounding stridently, shawm-like its sound.

وَبَعيرُهم ساجٍ بجَرَّته　　لم يؤذه غَرَثٌ ولا نَفَرُ
فإذا تجرّرَ شَقّ بازلُهُ　　وإذا أصاخ فإنّه بَكَرُ
خَلُّوا طريقَ الديدَبون فقد　　وَلّى الصِّبا وتفاوتَ النَّجَرُ

فما أردت بقولك: كشراب قَيلٍ: الواحد من الأقيال أم قيل ابن عِترٍ من عاد؟ فيقول عمرو: إن الوجهين ليُتصوّران. فيقول الشيخ، بلّغه الله الأمانيّ: ممّا يدل على أنّ المراد قيل بن عتر، قولك: وجَرادتان تغنيّانهم، لأن الجرادتين، فيما قيل، مغنِّيَتان غنّتا لوفدِ عادٍ عند الجُرْهُميّ بمكة، فشُغلوا عن الطواف بالبيت وسؤال الله، سبحانه وتعالى، فيما قصدوا له فهلكتْ عاد وهُمْ سامدون. ولقد وجدتُ في بعض كُتُب الأغاني صوتاً يقال غنَّته الجرادتان، فتفكّرْتُ لذلك، والصوت: ٣،٤،١٠

أَقْفرَ من أهله المَصيفُ　　فبَطْنُ عَرْدَةَ فالغَريفُ
هل تبلّغنِي ديارَ قومي　　مَهْرِيّةٌ سَيرُها تلقيفُ
يا أمَّ عُثمانَ نوّليني　　هل ينفع النائلُ الطّفيفُ

وهذا شعر على رَوِيّ:

أقفرَ مِن أهله ملحوبُ

ومَن الذي نقل إلى المغنّين في عصر هارون وبعده أنّ هذا الشعر غنَّته الجرادتان؟ إنّ ذلك لَبعيد في المعقول، وما أجدرَه أن يكون مكذوباً. وقولك: ومُسِفّة دهماءُ داجنة، ما أردت به؟

وقولك: ومجلجَل دانٍ زبرجدُه؟ فيقول ابن أحمر: أمّا ذكر الجرادتين فلا يدُلّ على أني خصصتُ قيل بن عترٍ وإن كان في الوفد الذي غنَّته الجرادتان، لأن العرب

And their camel is quietly chewing the cud,
neither hunger nor fright has disturbed it;
When it is chewing the cud its firm teeth show,
when it listens to me it looks young like a calf.[387]
Abandon the way of fooling around, for the days
of your youth are now gone and you yourself have changed.

"What did you mean when you said 'the wine of a *qayl*'? Does it mean 'pre-Islamic king from Yemen'? Or does it refer to Qayl ibn 'Itr of the people of 'Ād?" 'Amr replies: "Both interpretations are conceivable."[388] The Sheikh continues (may God fulfill his wishes!), "An indication that Qayl ibn 'Itr is meant is where you say 'Two locusts were singing to them,' because the 'Two Locusts,' it is said, were two singing girls who sang for the deputation of 'Ād, in the presence of al-Jurhumī in Mecca. Thereby they were distracted from performing the circumambulation around the Kaaba and from asking God, praised and exalted be He, for rain, which is why they had come. Thus perished 'Ād, while they 'made merry'![389] I found, to my surprise, in some manuscript of the *Book of Songs*[390] a song text said to have been sung by the 'Two Locusts': 10.4.3

The summer resort is empty of people,
as is 'Ardah's valley and al-Gharīf.
Will I be brought to my people's dwellings
by a fast dromedary, stretching widely its legs?
O Umm 'Uthmān, let me obtain your favor!
—But what is the use of a trifling favor?

"This is an imitation of

Malḥūb is empty of people[391]

"—But who could possibly have transmitted to the singers in the time of Hārūn al-Rashīd or even later the information that this song was performed by the 'Two Locusts'? That is clearly preposterous; it must be a lie! As for your words 'a low-lying, dark, gloomy one,' what do you mean by them? And your words 'something made to resound, its peridot near to us'?"

Ibn Aḥmar replies, "That I mentioned the 'two locusts' does not prove that I especially meant Qayl ibn 'Itr, even though he was part of the deputation for whom the Two Locusts sang, for the Arabs came to call every

صارت تسمّي كلَّ قينةٍ جرادةً، حملاً على أنّ قينة في الدهر الأول كانت تُدعى الجرادة. قال الشاعر:

تُغنِّينا الجَرادُ ونحنُ شَرْبٌ نُعَلُّ الراحَ خالَطها المَشُورُ

وأمّا المِسفّة الدَّهماء فإنّها القِدْر. وأمّا المجلجل الداني زبرجده، فهو العُود، وزبرجدُه ما حُسّن منه، أما تسمع القائل يسمّي ما تلوّن من السحاب زِبْرِجاً؟ ومن روى: مجلجِل، بكسر الجيم، أراد السحاب.

فيعجب الشيخ من هذه المقالة ويقول: كأنك أيها الرجل وأنت عربي صميم ١٠،٤،٤
يُستشهد بألفاظك وقريضك، تزعُم أن الزَّبَرجَد من الزِّبرِج، فهذا يقوّي ما ادّعاه صاحب العينْ من أنّ الدال زائدة في قولهم: صَلَخدم، وأهل البصرة ينفِرون من ذلك.

فيُلْهم الله القادر ابنَ أحمر عِلمَ التصريف، ليري الشيخ بُرهان القدرة، فيقول ابن أحمر: وماذا الذي أنكرتَ أن يكون الزبرج من لفظ الزَّبَرجَد؟ كأنّ فعلاً صُرّف من الزبرجد، فلم يمكن أن يُجاء بحروفه كلّها، إذا كانت الأفعال لا يكون فيها خمسةُ أحرُفٍ من الأصول، فقيل: يُزَبْرِج، ثم بُني من ذلك الفعل اسمٌ فقيل: زِبرِج، ألا ترى أنهم إذا صغَّروا فَرَزْدَقاً قالوا: فُرَيْزِد، وإذا جمعوه قالوا: فَرازِد؟ وليس ذلك بدليل على أن القاف زائدة.

فيقول، خلّد الله ألفاظه في ديوان الأدب: كأنك زعمت أنّ فعلاً أُخذ من الزَّبَرجد، ثم بُني منه الزِّبرِج، فقد لزِمك على هذا أن تكون الأفعال قبل الأسماء. فيقول ابن أحمر: لا يلزَمني ذلك، لأني جعلتُ زبرجداً أصلاً، فيجوز أن يحدُث منه فروعٌ ليس حُكمها لحكم الأصول. ألا ترى أنهم يقولون: إنّ الفعل مشتقٌّ من المصدر؟ فهذا أصل، ثم يقولون: الصِّفة الجارية على الفعل، يعنون: الضارب والكريم وماكان نحوهما، فليس قولهم هذه المقالة بدليلٍ على أنّ الصفة مشتقّة من الفعل، إذاكانت اسماً، وحقُّ الأسماء أن تكون قبل الأفعال، وإنّما يراد أنه يُنْطَق

singing girl 'locust,' because that term was used for a singing girl in ancient times. A poet has said:

Locusts sing to us while we are drinking,
and drinking once again, the wine with honey mixed.

"As for 'a low-lying, dark, gloomy one,' that is a cooking pot; and 'something made to resound, its peridot near to us,' that is a lute, 'its peridot' being the decorated part of it. And haven't you heard that one calls the various colors of a multicolored cloud *zibrij*, which is like *zabarjad*, peridot? [392] But if one reads 'resounding,' *mujaljil* instead of 'made to resound,' *mujaljal*, it refers to a thundercloud."

The Sheikh is amazed by these words. "It seems to me," he says, "that you, a true Arab whose expressions and verses are quoted as authoritative, assert that the word *zabarjad* is derived from *zibrij*! This supports what the author of *al-'Ayn* claims: that the letter *d* is secondary in the word *ṣalakhdam* ('strong camel'). But the Basran grammarians do not like this explanation."[393] 10.4.4

At this point God Almighty inspires Ibn Aḥmar with the knowledge of morphology, in order to prove to the Sheikh His omnipotence. "Why do you find it odd," replies Ibn Aḥmar, "that *zibrij* should be derived from the word *zabarjad*? It is as if a verb was derived from the noun *zabarjad*, in which not all its consonants could be used, for verbs cannot have roots of five consonants.[394] So one makes a verbal form '*yuzabriju*' and then one builds from this verb a noun: *zibrij*. Don't you see that when they make a diminutive of *farazdaq* ('piece of bread')[395] they say *furayzid*, and when they make a plural of it they say *farāzid*? This does not prove that the letter *q* is secondary."

The Sheikh (may God immortalize his utterances in the Register of Literature!) says, "You seem to assert that a verb can be derived from *zabarjad*, and that subsequently the noun *zibrij* is built on this. By this argument you are forced to maintain that verbs are prior to nouns!" Ibn Aḥmar replies, "I am not forced to say that, because I made *zabarjad* the original stem; it is possible that new branches are formed from it that should not be taken to be original stems. Don't you see that they say: a verb is derived from a verbal noun,[396] which is the stem. Furthermore, they speak of 'an attribute that is analogous to the verb,' meaning words such as 'striking' or 'noble' and the like.[397] But the fact that they make these statements does not prove that an attribute is derived from a verb, since it is a noun, and nouns deserve to be prior to verbs. Rather, what is intended is that many nouns can

بالفعل منها كثيرًا. ولمدّعٍ أن يقول: الفعل مشتقٌّ من المصدر فهو فرعٌ عليه، والصِّفة فرع آخر، فيجوز أن يتقدّم أحد الفرعين على صاحبه.

ثمّ يذكُر له أشياءَ من شعره، فيجده عن الجواب مستعجِمًا، إن نطق نطق مجَمْجِمًا.

٥،١٠ فيقول: أيكم تميم بن أُبيّ فيقول رجل منهم: ها أنا ذا. فيقول أخبرْني عن قولك:

يا دارَ سَلمى خَلاءً لا أُكلِّفها إلا المَرانةَ حتى تَسأمَ الدِّينا

ما أردت بالمرانة؟ فقد قيل: إنّك أردت اسم امرأة، وقيل: هي اسم ناقةٍ، وقيل: العادة. فيقول تميم: والله ما دخلتُ من باب الفردوس ومعي كلمة من الشعر ولا الرَّجز، وذلك أني حوسبتُ حسابًا شديدًا، وقيل لي: كنتَ فيمن قاتل عليَّ بن أبي طالب. وانبرى لي النّجاشيّ الحارثيّ، فما أفلتُّ من اللّهب حتى سفعني سَفَعاتٍ. وإن حِفظك لَمُبقٍ عليك، كأنك لم تشهد أهوالَ الحساب، ومُنادي الحشر يقول: أين فلان بن فلان؟ والشُّوس الجبابرة من الملوك تجذِبهم الزّبانيةُ إلى الجحيم، والنِّسوة ذوات التِّيجان يُصَرْن بألسِنةٍ من الوَقود، فتأخذ في فروعهنّ وأجسادهنّ، فيصِحْنَ: هل من فِداء؟ هل من عُذرٍ يقام؟ والشباب من أولاد الأكاسرة يتضاغَوْن في سلاسل النار ويقولون: نحن أصحاب الكنوز، نحن أرباب الفانية، ولقد كانت لنا إلى الناس صنائعُ وأيادٍ فلا فادِيَ ولا مُعين!

فهتف داعٍ من قِبَل العرْش: ﴿أَوَلَمْ نُعَمِّرْكُم مَّا يَتَذَكَّرُ فِيهِ مَن تَذَكَّرَ وَجَاءَكُمُ النَّذِيرُ فَذُوقُوا فَمَا لِلظَّالِمِينَ مِن نَّصِيرٍ﴾ لقد جاءتكم الرُّسُل في زمانٍ بعد زمانٍ، وبذلت ما وُكِّد من الأمان،[1] وقيل لكم في الكتاب: ﴿وَاتَّقُوا يَوْمًا تُرْجَعُونَ فِيهِ إِلَى اللَّهِ ثُمَّ تُوَفَّىٰ كُلُّ نَفْسٍ مَّا كَسَبَتْ وَهُمْ لَا يُظْلَمُونَ﴾ فكنتم في لذّات الساخرة واغلين، وعن أعمال الآخرة متشاغلين، فالآنَ ظهر النبأ، لا ظُلْمَ اليومَ إنّ الله قد حكم بين العِباد.

١ ب؛ : (الأيمان) كما في بعض النسخ وفي ي، إف، ق؛ وفي ب : (الأمان) كما في نسخة الأصل.

be spoken of in terms of a verb.[398] One could claim that a verb is derived from a verbal noun and thus a branch of it, while an attribute is another branch. Thus either branch could be prior to the other."

The Sheikh asks the poet some more questions about his poetry, but he finds him unable to answer them and unpersuasive; if he speaks he is evasive.

"Which one of you is Tamīm ibn Ubayy?" asks the Sheikh. "That's me," says one of them. The Sheikh says, "Tell me about your verse: 10.5

The story of Tamīm ibn Ubayy ibn Muqbil

> O Salmā's abode! I'll not charge anybody with seeking that lonely place,
> save al-Marānah, until she is bored with the custom.[399]

"What did you mean by al-Marānah? Some have said that it is a woman's name, others say it is the name of a camel. Yet others say it is a noun meaning 'habit.'"

Tamīm replies, "By God, from the moment I entered the gate of Paradise I cannot remember a line of verse, whether proper poetry or *rajaz*. That is because I have been severely taken to account. They said to me, 'You were among those who fought against 'Alī ibn Abī Ṭālib!'[400] Then al-Najāshī al-Ḥārithī came forward to speak against me, and I only escaped the flames of Hell after it had already scorched me a few times. Truly, your memory is still intact! It is as if you have not witnessed the horrors of the Reckoning, where the Herald of the Resurrection says, 'Where is So-and-so, son of So-and-so?' And then proud and mighty potentates are dragged to the Inferno by Hell's angels; women wearing crowns are pulled aside by means of tongues of ignited fuel that take them by their hair and their bodies, while they cry: 'Can't we buy ourselves out? Isn't there a good excuse?' Young sons of emperors are whimpering in their fetters of fire, saying, 'We have treasures, we are the lords of the Perishable World! We have performed good deeds and bestowed favors on the people! Will no one ransom us or help us?' But then a voice cried from the direction of God's Throne:[401] «Did We not give you a lifetime to reflect, for those who reflect, when the warner had come to you? Now taste! The wrong-doers have no helper.» Time after time have messengers come to you, who gave the security[402] that had been confirmed. It is said in the Holy Book:[403] «Beware of a day on which you will be returned to God. Then every soul will be paid in full what it has earned and they will not be wronged.» You were far gone in the pleasures of the world of mockery indeed, and to the works of the hereafter you paid no heed! Now the tiding is manifest. There is no injustice today; God has judged among the people."

فيقول، أنطقه الله بكل فضل، إن شاء ربُّه أن يقول: ١،١١

أنا أقُصّ عليك قِصّتي: لما نهضتُ أنتفض من الرَّيم، وحضرتُ حَرَصاتِ القيامة، والحرصات مثل العَرَصات، أُبدلت الحاء بالعين، ذكرتُ الآية: ﴿ تَعْرُجُ الْمَلَائِكَةُ وَالرُّوحُ إِلَيْهِ فِي يَوْمٍ كَانَ مِقْدَارُهُ خَمْسِينَ أَلْفَ سَنَةٍ، فَاصْبِرْ صَبْرًا جَمِيلًا ﴾ فطال علي الأَمَد، واشتدّ الظمأ والوَمَد، والومد: شدّة الحرّ وسكوت الريح، كما قال أخوكم النُّميري:

كأنّ بيْضَ نَعامٍ في مَلاحفها   جَلاه طَلٌّ وقَيْظٌ ليلُه وَمِدُ

وأنا رجل مِهْيافٌ، أي سريع العَطَش، فافتكرت فرأيت أمرًا لا قِوام لمثلي به. ولقيني المَلَكُ الحفيظ بما زُبِر من فعل الخير، فوجدتُ حَسَناتي قليلةً كالنُّفا في العام الأرمل، والنُّفأ الرياض، والأرمل قليل المطر. إلا أن التوبة في آخرها كأنها مصباح أبيلٍ، رُفع لسالك السبيل.

فلمّا أقمت في الموقف زُهاءَ شهر أو شهرين، وخِفتُ في العرق من الغرق، زيّنت ١،٢،١١ لي النفس الكاذبة أن أنظِم أبياتًا في رِضْوان، خازن الجنان، عملتها في وزن:

قِفا نَبْكِ مِنْ ذِكْرَى حَبيبٍ وعِرْفانِ

ووسمتُها برضوان. ثمّ ضانكتُ الناس حتى وقفتُ منه بحيث يسمع ويرى، فما حفل بي، ولا أظنّه أَبِهَ لما أقول. فغبرتُ بُرهة، نحو عشرة أيام من أيّام الفانية، ثم عملتُ أبياتًا في وزن:

The Sheikh's Story of his Resurrection, the Day of Judgement, and his Entry into Paradise

Then the Sheikh says (may God make him speak meritoriously when he says something, if his Lord will him to say something!): 11.1

The Sheikh's conversation with Riḍwān and Zufar, guards of the Garden

I'll tell you my own story. After I got up and rose from my grave and had arrived at the Plane of Resurrection ("plane" being like "plain," with a different spelling),[404] I thought of the Qur'anic verse, «To Him the angels and the Spirit ascend in a day the length of which is fifty thousand years. So be patient in a decent manner».[405] It did seem a long time to me; I got parched and torrid (meaning "very hot, without a puff of wind"), as your friend al-Numayrī says:

> The girls, in their wraps, are like ostrich eggs
> exposed by drizzle and the heat of a sultry night.

I am easily desiccated (that is, "quick to thirst"), so I thought about my situation, which I found quite unbearable for someone like me. There came an angel to me, the one that had recorded all the good deeds I had performed. I found that my good deeds were few, as few as tussocks of grass in a year of destitution (a tussock being a tuft of vegetation, destitution being a drought). But my repentance at the end shone like a light, bright like a lamp for travelers at night.

When I had stood there for one or two months, fearing I would drown in my sweat, I persuaded myself that I should compose a few lines for Riḍwān, Paradise's Porter Angel. I composed them on the meter and rhyme pattern of 11.2.1

> Stop, you two, for the memory of a beloved, and the recognition . . .[406]

In them I incorporated the name of Riḍwān. Then I jostled my way through the people until I stood where he could hear and see me, but he took no notice of me and I don't think he paid attention to what I said. I waited for a short while, perhaps ten days in earthly reckoning, and then I composed some lines on the pattern of

بانَ الخليطُ ولو طُووِعْتُ ما بانا ‌ ‌ ‌ ‌ وقطّعوا من حِبال الوصْل أقْرانا

ووسمتُها برضوان، ثمّ دنوتُ منه ففعلت كفعلي الأوّل، فكأني أحرّك ثبيرًا، وألتمس من الغَضْرِم[1] عبيرًا، والغَضْرِم: ترابٌ يُشْبه الجِصّ، فلم أزل أتتبع الأوزان التي يمكن أن يُوسَم بها رضوان حتى أفنيْتُها، وأنا لا أجد عنده مَغوثةً، ولا ظننته فَهِمَ ما أقول، فلمّا استقصيتُ الغَرَض فما أنجحتُ، دعوتُ بأعلى صوتي: يا رضوان، يا أمين الجبّار الأعظم على الفراديس، ألم تسمع ندائي بك واستغاثتي إليك؟

٢،٢،١١ فقال: لقد سمعتُك تذكر رضوان وما علمتُ ما مَقْصِدُك، فما الذي تطلب أيها المسكين؟ فأقول: أنا رجل لا صبر لي على اللُّوَاب، أي العَطَش، وقد استطلتُ مُدّة الحساب، ومعي صَكٌّ بالتوبة، وهي للذنوب كلّها ماحِيَة، وقد مدحتُك بأشعارٍ كثيرة ووسمتُها باسمك.

فقال: وما الأشعار؟ فإني لم أسمع بهذه الكلمة قطّ إلا الساعة. فقلت: الأشعار جمع شِعْرٍ، والشعر كلام موزون تقبله الغريزة على شرائط، إن زاد أو نقص أبانه الحِسُّ، وكان أهل العاجلة يتقرّبون به إلى الملوك والسادات، فجئت بشيء منه إليك لعلك تأذن لي بالدُّخول إلى الجنة في هذا الباب، فقد استطلتُ ما الناس فيه، وأنا ضعيف مَنِين؛ ولا رَيب أنّي ممن يرجو المغفرة، وتصحُّ له بمشيئة الله تعالى. فقال: إنك لَغبين الرأي! أتأمل أن آذَن لك بغير إذن من ربّ العزة؟ هيْهات هيْهات! ﴿وَأَنَّىٰ لَهُمُ ٱلتَّنَاوُشُ مِن مَّكَانٍۭ بَعِيدٍ﴾.

٣،١١ فتركتُه وانصرفت بأَمَلي إلى خازن آخَر يقال له زُفَر، فعملت كلمةً ووسمتها باسمه في وزن قول لبيد:

تَمَنّى ابنتايَ أن يعيشَ أبوهما ‌ ‌ ‌ ‌ وهل أنا إلا من ربيعةَ أو مُضَرْ

وقَرُبتُ منه فأنشدتها، فكأني إنّما أخاطب رَكودًا صمّاء، لأستنزل أَبودًا عَصْماء.

---

[1] في كل النسخ (العضرم) وهو تصحيف.

The gathered clans have parted. If I'd had my way,
they wouldn't have. They severed bonds of loving union.[407]

Again I mentioned Riḍwān in it; I approached him and did as before. But he did not appear to hear: it was as if I tried to move Mount Thabīr, or attempted to extract scent from cement ("cement" being a mixture of limestone and clay). Then I continued with all other metrical patterns that could accommodate "Riḍwān" until I had exhausted them; but still he did not help me and I don't think he even understood what I said. When I had tried everything without success I cried out as loud as I could, "Riḍwān, who are trusted by the Omnipotent Almighty, charged with guarding Paradise! Can't you hear me calling on you for help?"

He replied, "I heard you mention Riḍwān, but I had no idea that you meant me. What do you want, poor wretch?" I said, "I am a man who cannot endure to be dehydrated (that is, 'thirsty'); it is for the Reckoning that I have waited and waited. I've got my Document of Repentance, which cancels all my sins. I have composed numerous poems in praise of you, mentioning you by name!" 11.2.2

Riḍwān asked, "Poems, what's that? This is the first time I have heard that word." I replied: "'Poems' is the plural of 'poem', which is speech that is metrical and, on certain conditions, sounds pleasant. If the meter is defective, either by an excess or a shortfall, one notices it. People in the Temporal World used to ingratiate themselves with kings and lords by means of poems. So I composed some for you, hoping that you might let me enter Paradise by this gate. I think people have waited long enough now. I am only a weak, feeble person. Surely I am someone who may hope for forgiveness, and righly so, if God the Exalted wills." But Riḍwān said, "Do you expect me to allow you to enter without permission from the Lord of Glory, you dimwit? Forget it! Forget it! «How could they attain it from a remote place?»"[408]

So I left him and, expectantly, turned to a guard who was called Zufar. For him I composed a poem, mentioning him by name, on the meter of Labīd's line: 11.3

My two daughters hope their father will live;
but don't I belong to Rabīʿah or Muḍar?[409]

I approached him and recited the poem; but it was as if I was speaking to a mute and solid rock in the end, trying to get a wild ibex to descend.[410] I composed poems using the name Zufar in every possible meter and rhyme, but to no avail each time. I said, "God have mercy on you! In the Past World

ولم أترك وزنًا مقيّدًا ولا مُطلَقًا يجوز أن يُوسَم بزُفَر إلا وسمتُه به، فما نجع ولا غيّر. فقلت: رحمك الله! كنّا في الدار الذاهبة نتقرّب إلى الرئيس والملك بالبيتين أو الثلاثة، فنجد عنده ما نحبّ، وقد نظمتُ فيك ما لو جُمع لكان ديوانًا، وكأنك ما سمعتَ لي زَجْمةً، أي كلمة. فقال: لا أشعر بالذي حممتَ، أي قصدتَ، وأحسب هذا الذي تجيئني به قرآنُ إبليس المارد، ولا ينفُق على الملائكة، إنّما هو للجانّ وعلّموه ولدَ آدم، فما بُغْيتك؟ فذكرت له ما أريد، فقال: والله ما أقدرُ لك على نفع، ولا أملِك لخلقٍ من شفع، فمن أيّ الأمم أنت؟ فقلت: من أُمّة محمّد بن عبد الله بن عبد المطّلب. فقال: صدقتَ، ذلك نبيّ العرب، ومن تلك الجهة أتيتني بالقريض، لأنّ إبليسَ اللعين نفثه في إقليم العرب فتعلّمه نساءٌ ورجالٌ. وقد وجب عليّ نُصحُك، فعليك بصاحبك لعلّه يتوصّل إلى ما ابتغيتَ.

فيئستُ ممّا عنده، فجعلت أتخلل العالَم، فإذا أنا برجل عليه نور يتلألأ، وحواليْه رجال تأتلق منهم أنوار. فقلت: من هذا الرجل؟ فقيل: هذا حَمزة بن عبد المطّلب صريع وَحْشيٍّ، وهؤلاء الذين حوله من استُشهد من المسلمين في أُحدٍ. فقلت لنفسي الكذوب: الشعر عند هذا أنفقُ منه عند خازن الجنان، لأنه شاعر، وإخوته شُعَراء، وكذلك أبوه وجدُّه، ولعلّه ليس بينه وبين مَعَدّ بن عَدْنان إلا من قد نظم شيئًا من موزون، فعملتُ أبياتًا على مَنْهج أبيات كَعْب بن مالكٍ التي رثى بها حمزة، وأوّلها: ٤،١١

صَفِيّةُ قُومِي ولا تعْجَزِي وبَكِّي النِّساءَ على حَمْزةِ

وجئت حتى ولِيتُ منه فناديتُ: يا سيّد الشهداء، يا عمّ رسول الله صلّى الله عليه، يا ابن عبد المطّلب! فلمّا أقبل عليّ بوجهه أنشدتُه الأبيات. فقال: ويحك! أفي مثل هذا المَوْطِن تجيئني بالمديح؟ أما سمعت الآية: ﴿لِكُلِّ امْرِئٍ مِنْهُمْ يَوْمَئِذٍ شَأْنٌ يُغْنِيهِ﴾ فقلت: بلى قد سمعتُها، وسمعت ما بعدها: ﴿وُجُوهٌ يَوْمَئِذٍ مُسْفِرَةٌ، ضَاحِكَةٌ مُسْتَبْشِرَةٌ، وَوُجُوهٌ يَوْمَئِذٍ عَلَيْهَا غَبَرَةٌ، تَرْهَقُهَا قَتَرَةٌ، أُولَئِكَ هُمُ الْكَفَرَةُ الْفَجَرَةُ﴾. فقال: إنّي لا أقدِر على ما تطلُب. ولكني أُنفذ معك تَوْرًا، أي رسولًا، إلى ابن أخي عليّ

we would seek the favor of leaders and kings with two or three lines of verse and our wishes would be fulfilled; but for you I have composed enough to fill a tome of Collected Poems and still you don't seem to have heard one susurrus, i.e., a whisper!"

He replied, "I have no idea what you are expostulating (i.e., 'talking about'). I suppose all that jabbering of yours is the Qur'an of the Devil, that rebel! But the angels won't buy it! It belongs to the Jinn, who have taught it to Adam's children. Now what do you want?"

I explained what I wanted. He said, "By God, I can't help you in what you need; for humans I cannot intercede. What community are you from?" "The community of Muḥammad ibn ʿAbd Allāh ibn ʿAbd al-Muṭṭalib," I answered. "Ah, yes," he said, "the prophet of the Arabs. So that is why you have come to me with that poetry, because the accursed Devil spat it out in the lands of the Arabs, where women and children learned it. I'll give you some good advice: look for your friend and perhaps he will be able to let you have your way."

Thus I despaired of him. I worked my way through the multitude. Then I saw 11.4
a man bathed in a glimmering of light, surrounded by others who shone with bright light. I asked, "Who is that man?" They said, "That is Ḥamzah ibn ʿAbd al-Muṭṭalib, the one who was killed by Waḥshī; those around him are those Muslims who died as martyrs at Uḥud." Inspired with false hope I said to myself: poetry will work better with Ḥamzah than with the Porter of Paradise, because Ḥamzah is a poet, as were his brothers and his father and his grandfather. It could well be that each and every one of his forefathers from Maʿadd ibn ʿAdnān on have composed verses. So I composed some lines after the model of Kaʿb ibn Mālik's elegy[411] on Ḥamzah, which opens with

Ṣafiyyah, get up, don't be weak!
  Let the women weep for Ḥamzah!

I approached him and called out: "Lord of martyrs, uncle of God's messenger! Son of ʿAbd al-Muṭṭalib!" When he turned to me I recited the verses. But he said, "Shame upon you! Must you eulogize me here, of all places? Haven't you heard this Qur'anic verse: [412] «Every man of them that day will have enough to preoccupy him?»" "Yes," I said, "I've heard it; and I've also heard what follows: «Some faces that day will be bright, laughing and expecting delight; other faces that day will be glum, by gloom overcome: these are the unbelievers, the sinners»!" He replied, "I can't do what you ask, but I will

بن أبي طالبٍ، ليخاطب النبيَّ، صلّى الله عليه، في أمرك.

١٠٥،١١ فبعث معي رجلاً، فلمّا قصَّ قصّتي على أمير المؤمنين، قال: أين بَيِّنَتُك؟ يعني صحيفة حَسَناتي. وكنتُ قد رأيت في المحشر شيخًا لنا كان يدرِّس النحو في الدار العاجلة، يُعرَف بأبي عليّ الفارسيّ، وقد امترس به قومٌ يطالبونه، ويقولون: تأوَّلتَ علينا وظلمتَنا. فلمّا رآني أشار إليّ بيده، فجئته فإذا عنده طَبَقَةٌ، منهم يزيد بن الحَكَم الكِلابيُّ، وهو يقول: ويحك، أنشدتَ عني هذا البيت برفع الماء، يعني قوله:

فـليتَ كَفافـًا كان شـرُّك كلُّهُ   وخيرُك عني ما ارتوى الماءُ مُرتَوي

ولم أقل إلّا الماءَ. وكذلك زعمتَ أني فتحت الميم في قولي:

تبَدَّلْ خليلاً بي كشَكْلِكَ شَكْلُهُ   فإنّي خليلاً صالحًا بك مَـقْتَوي

وإنّما قلتُ: مُقْتَوي بضمّ الميم.

وإذا هناك راجزٌ يقول: تأوّلتَ عليّ أني قلت:

يا إبلي مـا ذنبُـه فتـأبيَهْ؟   ماءٌ رَواءٌ ونـصِيٌّ حوليَـهْ

فحرّكت الياء في تأبيَه ووالله ما فعلتُ ولا غيري من العرب وإذا رجلٌ آخَر يقول: ادّعيتَ عليَّ أن الهاء راجعةٌ على الدّرس في قولي:

هـذا سُراقةُ للقـرآن يدرُسُهُ   والمرءُ عند الرّشا إن يلقَها ذِيبُ

أفمجنونٌ أنا حتّى أعتقدَ ذلك؟

send a nuncio (meaning a 'messenger') along with you to my nephew 'Alī ibn Abī Ṭālib, who can speak to the Prophet, God bless him, on your behalf."

He sent a man with me. When he had told my story to the Commander of the Believers,[413] the latter asked, "Where is your evidence?" He meant the document with my good deeds.[414] 11.5.1

The conversation with 'Alī ibn Abī Ṭālib

At the assembling place I had seen an elderly man who used to teach us grammar in the Fleeting World. He was called Abū 'Alī al-Fārisī. Some people had thrown themselves upon him to call him to account, saying "You have misinterpreted us and wronged us!" When he saw me he beckoned me with his hand, so I went over to him. There was a whole group with him, including Yazīd ibn al-Ḥakam al-Kilābī, who was saying, "Shame on you, you recited the following verse by me on my authority, the word 'water' (*al-mā'*) in the nominative!"—He meant his verse

If only all your evil and your good deeds
were kept from me, for as long as a drinker drinks water to quench his thirst

—"But I put 'water' in the accusative![415] Likewise, you asserted that I said *maqtawī* in my verse:

Take another friend instead of me, someone who looks like you,
for I shall get myself a good and decent friend in your place!

"for I said *muqtawī*, with *u*!"[416]

There was a *rajaz* poet,[417] who said, "You have foisted on me a wrong reading of my verse:

Camels of mine, what is his crime that you should scorn him?
There is fresh water and tender thistles around him!

"for you read *ta'bayah*[418] instead of *ta'bayh* ('you scorn him'). By God, I have never said that, nor has any other Arab!"

There came another man, who said, "You have charged me with thinking that the pronoun 'it' refers to an implied 'studying' in my verse:

Here's this Surāqah: the Qur'an, he studies it,
whereas the man, with bribes if he can get them, is a wolf.

"Would I be so mad as to believe that?"[419]

وإذا جماعةٌ من هذا الجنس كلُّهم يلومونه على تأويله. فقلت: يا قوم، إن هذه أمورٌ هيِّنةٌ، فلا تُعنِتوا هذا الشيخ، فإنّه يمُتُّ بكتابه في القرآن المعروف بكتاب الحُجّة، وإنه ما سفك لكم دماً، ولا احتجن عنكم مالاً، فتفرّقوا عنه.

وشُغلتُ بخطابهم والنَّظر في حَوِيرهم، فسقط منّي الكتاب الذي فيه ذكر التَّوبة، ٢،٥،١١
فرجعتُ أطلبه فما وجدته.

فأظهرتُ الوَلَه والجزَع، فقال أمير المؤمنين: لا عليك، ألك شاهدٌ بالتَّوبة؟ فقلت: نعم، قاضي حَلَبَ وعُدولُها. فقال: بمن يُعرف ذلك الرجل؟ فأقول: بعبد المنعم بن عبد الكريم قاضي حلب، حرسها الله، في أيّام شِبل الدَّولة.

فأقام هاتفاً يهتِف في الموقف: يا عبد المنعم بن عبد الكريم قاضي حلب في زمان شبل الدَّولة، هل معك علمٌ من توبة عليّ بن منصور بن طالب الحلبيّ الأديب؟

فلم يُجبْه أحد. فأخذني الهلَع والقِلُّ، أي الرِّعدة، ثم هتف الثانيةَ، فلم يجبه مجيب، فلِيحَ بي عند ذلك، أي صُرعتُ إلى الأرض، ثمّ نادى الثالثةَ، فأجابه قائلٌ يقول: نعم، قد شهدتُ توبة عليّ بن منصور، وذلك بأَخَرةٍ من الوقت، وحضرتْ مَتابه عندي جماعةٌ من العدول، وأنا يومئذٍ قاضي حلب وأعمالها، والله المستعان.

فعندها نهضتُ وقد أخذتُ الرَّمَق، فذكرت لأمير المؤمنين، عليه السَّلام، ما ألتمس، فأعرض عنّي وقال: إنّك لَتَرومُ حَدَداً[1] ممتنعاً، ولك أُسْوةٌ بولد أبيك آدم.

وهممتُ بالحوض، فكِدت لا أصِل إليه، ثمّ نغبتُ منه نُغَباتٍ لا ظمأ بعدها؛ وإذا ١،٦،١١
الكفَرة يحملون أنفسهم على الوِرد، فتذودهم الزَّبانية بعِصيّ تضطرم ناراً، فيرجع أحدهم وقد احترق وجهُه أو يدُه وهو يدعو بويلٍ وثبور. فطُفتُ على العِترة المنتجَبين فقلت: إنّي كنت في الدار الذاهبة إذا كتبتُ كتاباً وفرغت منه قلت في آخره: وصلّى الله على سيّدنا محمّد خاتَم النَّبيّين، وعلى عِترته الأخيار الطَّيّبين.

[1] رواية الأصل (جددا).

A throng of such people came, all of whom blamed him for his interpretations; but I said: "People, these are trivial things! Don't be so hard on this learned old man. At least he can boast of being the author of his book on the Qur'an, *The Proof*.[420] It is not as if he has shed your blood or stolen your money!"

Then they left him and went their various ways.

Now while I was busy addressing them and discussing their complaints, I had dropped the writing that mentioned my repentance. I went back to look for it but could not find it! 11.5.2

I displayed much confusion and distress. But the Commander of the Believers said, "Don't worry. Did anybody witness your repentance?"[421] "Yes," I replied, "the qadi of Aleppo and his notaries." "What's his name?" "'Abd al-Mun'im ibn 'Abd al-Karīm, the qadi of Aleppo (may God guard it!) in the days of Shibl al-Dawlah."

He got a crier to stand up and call out: "'Abd al-Mun'im ibn 'Abd al-Karīm, qadi of Aleppo in Shibl al-Dawlah's time! Have you any knowledge of the repentance of 'Alī ibn Manṣūr ibn Ṭālib (ibn al-Qāriḥ), the Aleppine man of letters?"

But no one answered. I was dismayed and began to tremulate, i.e., to tremble. The man cried out a second time, and again nobody answered. I fell into a swoon, i.e., I fainted. Then he cried a third time, and someone spoke up: "Yes, I have witnessed the repentance of 'Alī ibn Manṣūr, in the nick of time![422] And a number of notaries were present at my place when he repented. I was then the qadi of Aleppo and adjacent districts. It is God whom we ask for succor!"

At that I got up and was able to breathe again. I told the Commander of the Believers (peace be upon him) what I wanted, but he turned away, saying, "You want something impossible. Follow the example of the other children of your forefather Adam!"

11.6.1 *The conversation with Fāṭimah, the Prophet's daughter*

I wanted to get to the Basin[423] but had real trouble getting there. I drank a few gulps after which there would never be any thirst. The unbelievers also tried to reach the water, but the Angels of Hell drove them away with sticks that burned like fire, so that they retreated, with scorched faces or hands, wailing and squealing. I walked to the Chosen Progeny[424] and said, "In the Past World I always wrote at the end of any book of mine: 'God bless our lord Muḥammad, the Seal of Prophets, and his excellent and good descendants,'[425] to show my respect and hoping for a favor." They said, "What can we do for you?" I replied, "Our lady Fāṭimah (peace be upon her) entered

وهذه حُرمةٌ لي ووسيلةٌ. فقالوا:ما نصنع بك؟ فقلت: إنّ مولاتَنا فاطمة، عليها السلام، قد دخلت الجنّة مذ دهرٍ، وإنّها تخرج في كلِّ حينٍ مقدارُه أربعٌ وعشرون ساعةً من الدُّنيا الفانية فتُسلّم على أبيها، وهو قائمٌ لشهادة القضاء، ثمّ تعود إلى مستقَرّها من الجنان، فإذا هي خرجت كالعادة، فاسألوا في أمري بأجمعكم، فلعلّها تسأل أباها فيّ.

فلمّا حان خروجها ونادى الهاتفُ أن غُضّوا أبصارَكم يا أهل الموقف حتى تعبُر فاطمةُ بنت محمد، صلّى الله عليه، اجتمع من آل أبي طالبٍ خلقٌ كثيرٌ من ذكورٍ وإناثٍ، ممّن لم يشرب خمرًا، ولا عرف قطُّ مُنكرًا. فلقُوها في بعض السبيل، فلمّا رأتهم قالت: ما بالُ هذه الزّرافة؟ ألكم حالٌ تُذكر؟ فقالوا: نحن بخيرٍ، إنّا نلتذّ بتُحَف أهل الجنّة، غير أنّا محبوسون للكلمة السابقة، ولا نريد أن نتسرّع إلى الجنّة من قبل الميقات، إذ كنّا آمنين ناعمين بدليل قوله: ﴿ إِنَّ الَّذِينَ سَبَقَتْ لَهُمْ مِنَّا الْحُسْنَى أُولَئِكَ عَنْهَا مُبْعَدُونَ. لا يَسْمَعُونَ حَسِيسَهَا وَهُمْ فِيمَا اشْتَهَتْ أَنْفُسُهُمْ خَالِدُونَ. لا يَحْزُنُهُمُ الْفَزَعُ الأَكْبَرُ، وَتَتَلَقَّاهُمُ الْمَلائِكَةُ: هَذَا يَوْمُكُمُ الَّذِي كُنْتُمْ تُوعَدُونَ ﴾ ٢،٦،١١

وكان فيهم عليُّ بن الحسين وابناه محمّدٌ وزيدٌ، وغيرهم من الأبرار الصالحين. ومع فاطمة، عليها السلام، امرأة أخرى تجري مجراها في الشرف والجلالة، فقيل: من هذه؟ فقيل: خديجة ابنة خُويلد بن أسد بن عبد العُزّى.

ومعها شبابٌ على أفراسٍ من نُورٍ. فقيل: عبد الله والقاسم والطّيب والطاهر وإبراهيم: بنو محمدٍ، صلّى الله عليه. فقالت تلك الجماعة التي سألتُ: هذا وليٌّ من أوليائنا، قد صحّت توبته، ولا ريبَ أنه من أهل الجنّة، وقد توسّل بنا إليكِ، صلّى الله عليك، في أن يُراح من أهوال الموقف، ويصير إلى الجنّة فيتعجل الفوزَ.

فقالت لأخيها إبراهيم، صلّى الله عليه: دونَك الرجلَ. فقال لي: تعلّقْ بركابي. وجعلت تلك الخيلُ تخلّلُ الناسَ وتنكشف لها الأُمم والأجيال، فلما عظُم الزِّحام

Paradise ages ago. But from time to time she leaves it for twenty-four hours, by the reckoning of the Transitory World, to greet her father who is busy testifying for God's Judgment. Then she returns to her place in Paradise. Now when she appears as usual, please could you all ask her on my behalf? Perhaps she will ask her father to help me."

When the time had come for her to emerge a crier called out: "Lower your eyes, people that stand here, until Fāṭimah, the daughter of Muḥammad (God bless him) has passed." A large number of men and women of Abū Ṭālib's family gathered, people who had never drunk wine or done evil things, and they came to meet her on her way. When she saw them she asked, "What is this crowd? Is anything the matter?" They answered, "We are fine; we enjoy the presents from those that dwell in Paradise. But we are being kept here because of the «word that preceded»;[426] we do not want to enter Paradise precipitously, before our time. We are safe and having a good time, on account of God's word:[427] «Those who have already been given the finest thing that came from Us, they shall be kept far from it, nor shall they hear any sound of it but they shall forever be in what their souls desire, the greatest distress shall not grieve them and the angels shall receive them: this is your day, that you have been promised!»" 11.6.2

ʿAlī ibn al-Ḥusayn and his two sons, Muḥammad and Zayd, were among them, with other pious and righteous persons. Next to Fāṭimah (peace be upon her) stood another woman, who resembled her in nobility and majesty. People asked, "Who is she?" The answer was: "That is Khadījah, daughter of Khuwaylid ibn Asad ibn ʿAbd al-ʿUzzā."

With her were some young men, riding horses of light. People asked, "Who are they?" They were told: "They are ʿAbd Allāh, al-Qāsim, al-Ṭayyib, al-Ṭāhir, and Ibrāhīm, the sons of Muḥammad (God bless him)."[428] Then those whom I had asked said, "This man is one of our followers. His repentance is genuine and there can be no doubt that he will be among those in Paradise. He turns to you in supplication, God bless you, that he may be relieved from the terrors of this Place of Judgment, that he may enter Paradise and hasten to attain the triumph."

Thereupon Fāṭimah said to her brother Ibrāhīm (God bless him), "You look after this man!" He said to me, "Hold on to my stirrup." The horses then passed through the throng, whole nations and peoples making way for us. Where the

طارت في الهواء، وأنا متعلّق بالرِّكاب، فوقفتْ عند محمّدٍ، صلّى الله عليه وسلّم.

٧،١١ فقال: مَن هذا الأتاويُّ؟ أي الغريب، فقالت له: هذا رجلٌ سأل فلانٌ وفلانٌ، وسمّتْ جماعةً من الأئمة الطاهرين، فقال: حتّى يُنْظَر في عمله. فسأل عن عملي فوُجد في الدّيوان الأعظم وقد خُتم بالتوبة، فشفع لي، فأُذِن لي في الدُّخول. ولمّا انصرفت الزَّهراء، عليها السلام، تعلّقْتُ بركاب إبراهيم، صلّى الله عليه.

١،٨،١١ فلمّا خلصتُ من تلك الطُّموش، قيل لي: هذا الصِّراطُ فاعبرْ عليه. فوجدتُه خالياً لا عَريبَ عنده فبلوتُ نفسي في العبور، فوجدتُني لا أستمسك. فقالت الزَّهراء، صلّى الله عليها، لجاريةٍ من جواريها: يا فلانة أجيزيه. فجعلتْ تُمارسني وأنا أتساقط عن يمينٍ وشمالٍ، فقلت: يا هذه، إن أردتِ سلامتي فاستعملي معي قول القائل في الدار العاجلة:

سِتِّ إن أعياكِ أمري فاحْمِليني زَقَفُونَهْ

فقالت: وما زَقَفُونَة؟ قلت: أن يطرَح الإنسانُ يديه على كَتِفَي الآخَر، ويُمسك الحاملُ بيديه، ويحمله وبطنُه إلى ظهره، أما سمعتِ قول الجَحْجَلول من أهل كَفَرْطاب:

صلحتْ حالتي إلى الخَلْف حتى صِرْتُ أمشِي إلى الوَرى زَقَفُونَهْ

فقالت: ما سمعتُ بزقفونة، ولا الجحجلول، ولا كفرطاب، إلّا الساعةَ. فتحملني وتجوز كالبرق الخاطف. فلمّا جُزتُ، قالت الزَّهراء، عليها السلام: قد وهبْنا لك هذه الجارية فخُذها كي تخدمك في الجنان.

٢،٨،١١ فلمّا صرتُ إلى باب الجنّة، قال لي رضوانُ: هل معك من جوازٍ؟ فقلت: لا. فقال لا سبيل لك إلى الدخول إلا به فبَعِلتُ بالأمر، وعلى باب الجنّة من داخلٍ شجرةُ صَفْصافٍ، فقلت: أعطِني ورقةً من هذه الصَّفصافة حتى أرجع إلى الموْقف

crowd was too dense they flew up in the air, while I was holding on to the stirrup. They halted at Muḥammad (God bless him and give him peace).

11.7 *The Prophet's intercession*

The Prophet asked, "Who is this alien?" (meaning "stranger"). Fāṭimah replied, "This is a man for whom So-and-so and So-and-so have interceded." She named some of the Pure Imams.[429] He said, "First one must look at his works." He inquired about them and they were found in the Grand Register, sealed with Repentance. Then he interceded for me and I was permitted entrance. When Fāṭimah, the Resplendent (peace be upon her), returned I grabbed the stirrup of Ibrāhīm (God bless him).

11.8.1 *The crossing of the Bridging Path*

Having thus left the multitudes behind me I was told: "This is the Bridging Path, now cross it!"[430] I noticed it was empty, not one soul on it. I braced myself to cross but I found that I could not control myself. Fāṭimah, the Resplendent (God bless her), said to a servant girl of hers, "Girl, help him cross!" The girl began to push and pull me while I was tottering to the right and the left. "Girl," I said, "if you want me to arrive safely, then do with me as the poet put it in the Temporary World:

> Madam, if I'm tiring you,
> then let me ride you piggyback."

"Piggyback," she asked, "what is that?" " That is when you put your hands on someone's shoulders, who holds your hands and carries you, belly-to-back. Haven't you heard the line by al-Jaḥjalūl from Kafr Ṭāb,[431] when he says:

> My state improved backward
> until I began to move piggybackward."[432]

She replied, "I've never heard of piggyback, or al-Jaḥjalūl, or Kafr Ṭāb before!"

She picked me up and crossed like a bolt of lightning. When I reached the other side Fāṭimah, the Resplendent (peace be upon her), said, "I am giving you this girl. Take her and she will serve you in Paradise."

11.8.2 *The second conversation with Riḍwān; the entry into Paradise*

When I arrived at the gate of Paradise, Riḍwān asked, "Have you got your permit?" "No," I said. "Then you can't enter." I was desperate. I saw at the gate, just inside Paradise, a willow tree. I asked, "Can I have a leaf of that willow tree, so that I can go back to the Place of Judgment and get a permit, written on that leaf?" "I won't let anything leave Paradise without permission from the Most High, sanctified and blessed be He." I was at my wits' end

فآخذَ عليها جوازًا، فقال: لا أُخرِج شيئًا من الجنّة إلا بإذنٍ من العليّ الأعلى، تقدَّس وتبارك. فلمّا دَجِرتُ بالنازلة، قلت: إنّا لله وإنّا إليه راجعون! لوأن للأمير أبي المُرَجّى خازنًا مثلك، ما وصلتُ أنا ولا غيري إلى قُرقوفٍ من خِزانته. والقرقوف: الدِّرهم.

والتفت إبراهيم، صلّى الله عليه، فرآني وقد تخلفتُ عنه، فرجع إليّ فجذبني جَذْبةً حصَّلني بها في الجنة. وكان مُقامي في الموقف مُدّةَ ستّة أشهُرٍ من شهور العاجلة، فلذلك بقي عليّ حِفظي ما نزفته الأهوال، ولا نهكه تدقيقُ الحساب.

at this new blow and said, "We belong to God and to Him we shall return! If Abū l-Murajjā, the Emir, had had a treasurer like you we would never have received a groat from his coffers." (A groat is a silver coin worth fourpence).

But then Ibrāhīm (God bless him) turned around! He saw me—I had stayed behind. Now he came back and he dragged me along with him and brought me into Paradise. I had spent six months, earthly reckoning, at the Place of Judgment. That is why my memory is still intact: the horrors have not depleted it, nor has the detailed Reckoning weakened it.

فأيكم راعي الإبل؟ فيقولون: هذا. فيسلّم عليه الشيخ ويقول: أرجو أن لا أجِدك مثل أصحابك صِفرًا من حِفْظك وعربيّتك. فيقول: أرجو ذلك، فاسألني ولا تُطيلنّ. فيقول: أحقٌّ ما روى عنك سيبويه في قصيدتك اللاميّة التي تمدَح بها عبد الملك بن مَروان من أنك تنصِب الجماعة في قولك: ١،١٢

أيَّامَ قَوْمِي والجماعةَ كالذي ... لزِمَ الرِّحالةَ أن تَميلَ مَميلا

فيقول: حقٌّ ذلك.

وينصرف عنه رشيدًا إلى حُميد بن ثوْر فيقول: إيه يا حميد! لقد أحسنت في قولك: ١،٢،١٢

أرى بَصَري قد رابني بعد صِحّةٍ ... وحسْبُك داءً أن تصِحّ وتَسْلَما
ولن يلبَثَ العَصْرانِ يومٌ وليلةٌ ... إذا طلبا أن يُدرِكا ما تَيَمّما

فكيف بصرك اليوم؟ فيقول: إني لأكونُ في مَغارب الجنّة، فألمح الصَّديق من أصدقائي وهو بمَشارقها، وبيني وبينه مَسيرة ألوف أعوامٍ للشمس التي عرفتَ سُرعة مسيرها في العاجلة! فتعالى الله القادر على كلّ بديع.

فيقول: لقد أحسنت في الداليّة التي أوّلها: ٢،٢،١٢

جُلُبّانةٌ وَرْهاءُ تَخْصي حِمارَها ... بِفي مَن بغى خيرًا لديها الجلامدُ
إزاءُ مَعاشٍ لا يَزال نِطاقُها ... شديدًا وفيها سَوْرةٌ وهْي قاعدُ

Paradise (II)

12.1 "So which one of you" (continues the Sheikh, addressing the five one-eyed poets) "is the Camel-herd?" "This is he," they answer. The Sheikh greets him and says, "I hope I shall not find you like your friends, without any recollection or having lost your knowledge of the Arabic language!" The Camel-herd replies, "I hope so too. Ask me, but be brief!" The Sheikh asks him, "Is it true, as Sībawayh[433] says about you, that in your poem rhyming in *-lā*, in which you praise the caliph ʿAbd al-Malik ibn Marwān, you put the word 'people' in the accusative, in the verse:

The conversation with "the Camel-herd" and Ḥumayd ibn Thawr

In the days when my tribe and the people were like
one sitting firmly in the saddle, not letting it slip aside."[434]

"It is true," he answers.

12.2.1 The Sheikh turns from him straight to Ḥumayd ibn Thawr. "I say, Ḥumayd," he says, "you composed some good poetry with your verses:

I see that my eyes, once healthy, are troubling me;
being healthy and sound is sufficient disease![435]
Before long the two times, day and night,
will have reached what they want and set out to achieve.

"How is your eyesight now?" Ḥumayd replies, "I could be in the western regions of the Garden and yet notice one of my friends in the eastern parts, with a traveling distance of thousands of solar years between us—you know how fast the sun moved in the Fleeting World! God, the Exalted One, is able to create any wonderful thing."

12.2.2 The Sheikh continues: "You also said well in your poem rhyming in *-dū*, that begins:

A noisy, clumsy female, who castrates her donkey[436]—
if one expects some good from her, one bites on stones!
She works, provides a living; girdle always tightly bound;
some youthful strength is left to her, but she is past childbearing.

تتابعَ أعوامٌ عليها هزَلْنَها وأقبل عامٌ يَنعَش النّاسَ واحدُ

فيقول حميدٌ: لقد ذهلتُ عن كلّ ميمٍ ودال، وشُغلتُ بملاعَبة حُورٍ خِدال. فيقول: أمِثْلُ هذه الداليّة تُرْفَض وفيها:

عَضَمّرةٌ فيها بقاءٌ وشِدّةٌ ووالٍ لها بادي النصيحة جاهدُ
إذا ما دعا أَجْيادَ جاءت خناجرٌ لهاميمُ لا يمشي إليهنّ قائدُ
فجاءت بمعيوف الشريعة مُكْلَعٍ أرشّتْ عليه بالأكُفّ السواعدُ

وفيها الصفة التي ظننت القُطاميَّ أخذها منك، وقد يجوز أن يكون سبقك لأنكما في عصرٍ واحد، وذلك قولك: ٣،٢،١٢

تأوّبها في ليلِ نَحْسٍ وقِرّةٍ خليلي أبو الخَشْخاش والليلُ باردُ
فقام يصاديها فقالت تُريدني على الزاد؟ شَكْلٌ بيننا متباعدُ
إذا قال مهلاً أَسْجِحي لمحتْ له بزرقاءَ لم تدخُلْ عليها المراودُ
كأنّ حِجاجيْ رأسها في ملثّمٍ من الصخرِ جونٍ أخلقته المواردُ

هذه الصِّفة نحوٌ من قول القُطاميّ:

تلفّعتُ في طَلٍّ وريحٍ تلُفُّني وفي طِرْمساءَ غيرِ ذاتِ كواكبِ
إلى حيزَبونٍ توُقد النارَ بعدما تصوّبتِ الجوْزاءُ قَصْدَ المَغاربِ
فما راعها إلا بُغامُ مَطيّةٍ تروح بمحسورٍ من الصوت لاغبِ
وجُنّت جُنونًا من دِلاثٍ مُناخةٍ ومن رَجُلٍ عاري الأشاجع شاحبِ
تقول وقد قرّبتُ كُوري وناقتي إليك فلا تَذْعَرْ عليّ رِكائبي

Years upon years went by, emaciating her;
then came one year of plenty that reinvigorated people."

But Ḥumayd says, "I have become quite oblivious of any rhyme letter, whether *d* or *m*. I am too busy dallying with the black-eyed plump-legged damsels!" "Can one then renounce," says the Sheikh, "this poem, in which you also say:

An ill-tempered woman, who has still some strength;
her master is a man of diligence and good advice.
Whenever he calls: 'O noble creatures!' milk-rich camels come
without a driver leading them.
And then she brought a vessel to a filthy 'watering place,'
and her hands made the udder's milk ducts sprinkle into it.[437]

"In this poem there is a scene that al-Quṭāmī, I think, has taken over from you; or possibly he got to it before you, because you and he were contemporaries.[438] It is where you say: **12.2.3**

Upon an evil, chilly night she had a visit from
my friend Abū l-Khashkhāsh. The night was cold.
When he tried to inveigle her, she said, 'Is it with food
you want to buy my favors? Ah, there's little chance of that!'[439]
When he said, 'Gently, please be kind to me!', she ogled him
with a blue eye,[440] to which no kohl-stick ever had been applied.
Her eyebrow bones were set as if in a black boulder,
made jagged by the steps of treading camels.

"This description is similar to the one by al-Quṭāmī:

I wrapped myself in dew and wind that coiled around me
in a dark night when no stars shone,
And went to an old crone who lit a fire
after Orion had begun to sink.
All of a sudden she perceived the groaning of a camel,
its sound exhausted and fatigued.
Then she went raving mad about a swift-paced camel, made
to kneel down, and a haggard man with fleshless fingers.
When I approached her with my saddle and my camel,
she said, 'Go away! Don't frighten my own animals!'

والأبيات معروفةٌ. وقلتَ في هذه القصيدة: ٤،٢،١٢

فجـاء بذيـي أَوْنَيْنِ أُعبِرَ شأنُـه وعُـمِّرحتى قيـل هـل هو خـالدُ
فـعـزّاه حـتى أسـنداه كأنّـه على القَرْوِ عُلفوفٌ من التُّرْكِ ساندُ

وفيها ذكر الزُّبدة:

فلمّا تجلّى الليلُ عنها وأسفرتْ وفي غَلَس الصُّبح الشُّخوصُ الأباعدُ
رمى عينَه منها بصفراءَ جَعْدةٍ عليها تُعانيه وعنها تُراوِدُ

فيقول حميدٌ: لقد شُغلتُ عن زُبدٍ، وطَرْدِ النافرة من الرُّبد، بما وهب ربّي الكريم، ولا خوفَ عليَّ ولا حَزَن. ولقدكان الرجل منا يُعْمِل فكرَه السَّنة أو الأشهُر، في الرَّجل قدآتاه الله الشَّرف والمال، فربّما رجع بالخيْبة، وإن أعطى فعَطاءٌ زهيدٌ، ولكنّ النظم فضيلة العرب.

٣،١٢ ويعرض لهم لبيد بن رَبيعة فيدعوهم إلى منزله بالقيسيّة، ويُقْسِم عليهم لَيذهبُنّ معه، فيمشوْن قليلاً، فإذا هم بأبياتٍ ثلاثةٍ ليس في الجنّة نظيرُها بَهاءً وحُسناً، فيقول لبيدٌ: أتعرف أيها الأديب الحلبيّ هذه الأبيات؟ فيقول: لا والذي حجّت القبائلُ كعبتَه! فيقول: أمّا الأول فقولي:

إنّ تقْوى ربّنا خيرُ نفَلْ وبإذن الله ريْثي وعَجَلْ

وأمّا الثاني فهو قولي:

أحـمَدُ اللهَ فـلا نِـدَّ له بيديْه الخيرُ ما شاء فَعَلْ

وأمّا الثالث فقولي:

"These verses are well known. You, in your own poem, also said: 12.2.4

He came with something with two bags, made of an unshorn sheep,[441]
so ancient that they said, 'Has it life everlasting then?'
They seized it until they made it lean; it looked
like an old Turk that leaned over the trough.

"And butter is mentioned in it:

When night was cleared away, and distant shapes
were visible in morning's twilight,
His eye fell on a compact, yellow thing,
for which she suffered him and which seduced her."[442]

But Ḥumayd replies, "I am no longer concerned with butter, or with the hunting of shy ash-colored ostriches, because of the gifts from my Lord, the Generous One; I have no more fear nor grief.[443] People such as I used to rack their brain for a year or at least several months,[444] on behalf of some other man whom God had given honor and wealth, yet often meeting with total disappointment; and if the man gave something, it would be a paltry gift. But poetry happens to be that in which the Arabs excel."

Labīd ibn Rabīʿah passes by them and invites them to his dwelling in the Qaysite quarter.[445] He adjures them to come with him. They walk a short distance and then find themselves at three houses that have no match in Paradise in their splendor and beauty. "Do you know, my erudite Aleppine friend, what these houses are?" asks Labīd.[446] "I don't know," replies the Sheikh, "by Him to whose Kaaba the tribes went on pilgrimage!" Labīd explains: "The first is my verse: 12.3

The second conversation with Labīd

Fear of our Lord is the best spoil;
with God's permission is my tarrying and haste.

"The second is my verse:

I praise God; He has no equal.
His hands hold good things; what He wills He does.

"And the third is this verse of mine:

مَن هداه سُبُلَ الخير اهتدى ناعمَ البالِ ومن شاء أَضَل

صيرَّها ربِّي اللطيف الخبير أبياتًا في الجنة، أسكُنها أُخرى الأبد، وأنعَمُ نعيمَ المخلَّد. فيعجب هو وأولئك القوم ويقولون: إنَّ الله قديرٌ على ما أراد.

He whom He guides on the paths of the good is guided well
and is happy; but He leads astray whosoever He wills.

"My Lord, the Benevolent and Knowing One, has turned these verses into houses in Paradise, in which I shall dwell forever, enjoying eternal bliss."[447]

The Sheikh and all the others are amazed and say, "God is able to do what He wants!"

وبدو له، أيّد الله مجدَه بالتأييد، أن يصنع مأدُبةً في الجنان، يجمع فيها من أمكن من شُعراء الخَضْرَمة والإسلام، والذين أصّلوا كلام العرب، وجعلوه محفوظًا في الكتب، وغيرهم ممن يتأنس بقليل الأدب. فيخطِر له أن تكون كآدب الدار العاجلة، إذ كان البارئ، جلّت عَظَمته، لا يُعجزه أن يأتيهم بجميع الأغراض من غير كُلفة ولا إبطاء. ١٣،١،١

فتُنشأ أرحاءٌ على الكوثَر، تجَعْجع لطَحْن بُرٍّ من بُرّ الجنّة، وإنه لأفضلُ من برِّ الهُذَليّ الذي قال فيه:

لا دَرَّ دَرّيَ إن أطعمتُ رائدَهم قِرْفَ الحتيّ وعندي البرُّ مكنوزُ

بمقدارٍ تفضُل به السموات الأرَضِين.

فيقترح، أمضى القادر له اقتراحه، أن تحضر بين يديه جوارٍ من الحُور العِين، يعتملن بأرحاء اليد: فرَحًى من دُرٍّ ورحًى من عَسْجَدٍ، وأرحاءٌ لم ير أهل العاجلة شيئًا من شكل جواهرهنّ. فإذا نظر إليهنّ، حمد الله سبحانه على ما منح، وذكر قول الراجز: ١٣،١،٢

أعددتُ للضّيْف وللجيرانِ حَرَيّتَيْنِ تتعاورانِ
لا ترأمان وهُما ظئرانِ

يصف رحى اليد.

ويبتسم إليهنّ ويقول: اطْحَنّ شَزْرًا وبتًّا. فيقلن: ما شزْرٌ وما بتّ؟ فيقول: الشَّزر على أيمانكنّ، والبتُّ على شمائلكنّ، أما سمعتنّ قول القائل:

ونُصبِح بالغداة أتَرَّ شيءٍ ونُمسي بالعشيّ طَلَنْفَحِينا
ونَطحَن بالرّحى شَزْرًا وبَتًّا ولو نُعْطى المَغازِلَ ما عَيِينا

ويقال: إن هذا الشعر لرجل أُسِرَ فكتب إلى قومه بذلك.

ويجِسُ في صدره، عمّره الله بالسُّرور، أرحاءٌ تدور فيها البهائم، فيمثُل بين يديه ما

It occurs to the Sheikh (may God buttress his fame!) that he should give a banquet in Paradise, to be attended by as many poets as possible, those born in the pre-Islamic period who died as Muslims, or those born in Islam: those who consolidated the speech of the Arabs such as it is now preserved in books; in addition to some others with a measure of erudition who might be good company. He thinks it should be like a banquet of the Fleeting World; after all, the Creator (sublime is His glory) is not incapable of bringing them everything needed, without effort or delay. 13.1.1

A banquet in Paradise

Thus, mills are erected at the Kawthar stream, which noisily grind heavenly wheat, as superior to the wheat described by the poet of the Hudhayl tribe, who said:

May I not thrive if I regale their visitor
on crusts and peelings while I have a store of wheat[448]

as Heaven is superior to earth.

He suggests (may the Omnipotent fulfill his suggestions!) that some girls with black, lustrous eyes[449] come before him, to work the hand mills: one millstone is made of pearl, another of gold, others from precious stones never yet seen by dwellers in the Fleeting World. When he looks at the girls he praises God for His gift and is reminded of the words of the *rajaz* poet who describes a hand mill: 13.1.2

For guests and neighbors I've prepared
Two girls, hard-working, who cooperate,
Without compassion, though they feed us.[450]

He smiles to them and says, "Grind along! Sideways and contrary!" They ask him, "What are sideways and contrary?" " Sideways is to the right and contrary is to the left. Haven't you heard the words of the poet:

In the morning, having breakfast, we are fattest,
but at dinner in the evening we are hollow-bellied.
We grind with hand mills, sideways and contrary;
and if they gave us spindles we would not tire.

"They say these verses were written by a prisoner-of-war to his people."

In his mind the Sheikh (may God let him live long and joyously!) sees millstones being turned by animals. Before him appear all kinds of buildings,

شاء الله من البيوت، فيها أحجارٌ من جواهر الجنّة، تدير بعضَها جِمالٌ تسوم في عِضاه الفردوس، وأينُقٌ لا تعطِف على الحِيران، وصنوفٌ من البِغال والبقر وبنات صَعْدة.

فإذا اجتمع من الطّحن ما يظنُّ أنه كافٍ للمأدُبة، تفرّق خدمُه من الوِلدان المخلَّدين فجاؤوا بالعماريس، وهي الجِداء، وضروب الطير التي جرت العادة بأكلها، كأبجاج العَكارم، وجوازل الطواويس، والسَّمين من دَجاج الرَّحمة وفراريج الخُلد. وسيقت البقر والغنم والإبل لتُعتبَط؛ فارتفع رُغاء العَكَر ويُعار المِعز وثؤاج الضأن وصياح الدِّيَكة لعِيان المُدية. وذلك كلُّه، بحمد الله، لا ألَمَ فيه، وإنما هو جِدٌّ مثلُ اللَّعِب، فلا إله إلّا الله الذي ابتدع خَلقَه من غير رويّةٍ، وصوّره بلا مِثال. ٣،١،١٣

فإذا حصلت النُّحوضُ فوق الأوفاض، والأوفاض مثل الأوضام بلغة طَيّئ، قال، زاد الله أمره من النَّفاذ: أحضِروا من في الجنّة من الطُّهاة الساكنين بحَلَب على ممرّ الأزمان.

فتحضُر جماعةٌ كثيرةٌ، فيأمرهم باتّخاذ الأطعمة، وتلك لذّةٌ يَهَبها الله، عزّ سلطانه، بدليل قوله: ﴿ فِيهَا مَا تَشْتَهِيهِ الْأَنفُسُ وَتَلَذُّ الْأَعْيُنُ وَأَنتُمْ فِيهَا خَالِدُونَ. وَتِلْكَ الْجَنَّةُ الَّتِي أُورِثْتُمُوهَا بِمَا كُنتُمْ تَعْمَلُونَ. لَكُمْ فِيهَا فَاكِهَةٌ كَثِيرَةٌ مِّنْهَا تَأْكُلُونَ ﴾. فإذا أتت الأطعمة، افترق غِلمانه الذين ﴿ كَأَنَّهُمْ اللُّؤْلُؤُ الْمَكْنُونُ ﴾، لإحضار المدعُوّين، فلا يتركون في الجنّة شاعرًا إسلامياً ولا مخضرَماً ولا عالمًا بشيءٍ من أصناف العلوم ولا متأدّبًا، إلا أحضروه. فيجتمع بجُدٍّ عظيمٍ، والبجد: الخَلق الكثير، قال الشاعر:

تطوف البجودُ بأبوابه ... من الضُّر في أزَمات السّنينا

فتوضَع الخُون من الذهب، والفواثير من اللُّجَين، ويجلس عليها الآكلون، وتُنقَل إليهم الصِّحاف، فتُقيم الصّحفة لديهم وهم يُصيبون ممّا ضُمِّنته كعُمر كُوَيّ وسُرَيٍّ وهما النَّسْرانِ من النجوم. فإذا قضَوُا الأرَب من الطّعام، جاءت السُّقاة بأصناف الأشربة، والمُسْمِعات بالأصوات المُطرِبة.

containing precious stones of Paradise. Some mills are turned by camels that graze on the paradisical thorn-bushes, she-camels that do not bend over their calves, and various kinds of mules, cattle, and wild asses.

When he thinks enough flour has been milled for the banquet his servants, 13.1.3
the youths who live forever, disperse and return with yearlings, that is kids, various kinds of edible birds such as pigeon chicks, pea chicks, fat chickens of Mercy, and pullets of Eternity. Cows, sheep, and camels are driven to be slaughtered. There rises a loud camel-groaning, a goat-whickering, a sheep-bleating, and a cock-crowing, when they see the knife. Yet, God be praised, none suffers any pain: it is in earnest but like play.[451] There is no god but God, who creates marvelously out of nothing, without having to think about it, and shapes it without having a model.

Now when the chunks of meat lie on the meat planks, as they say in the dialect of Ṭayyi' instead of "blocks," he says (may God increase the efficacy of his intentions!), "Let the cooks of Paradise come, all those who have worked in Aleppo through the ages!"

A large crowd comes forward. He orders them to take the food: a delicious treat from God, sublime is His might, in accordance with His word: [452] «In it is what the souls desire and the eyes delight in; you shall dwell therein forever. That is Paradise, which you have inherited as a reward for what you used to do. Therein you shall have fruits in plenty of which you may eat.» When the dishes arrive his servant boys, who are like «well-kept pearls»,[453] disperse to collect the invited guests. Not one poet from the Islamic period did they leave behind, nor any of those who straddled the pre-Islamic and the Islamic periods, nor any scholar learned in various disciplines, nor any erudite person: they fetched them all. Thus a large throng, or many people, gathered.

(The word "throng" is used by a poet:[454]

> Throngs flock at his doors
>   from distress in years of famine.)

Golden tables are erected and silver trays are put down. The dinner guests sit down. Bowls are brought; and a bowl remains with them while they eat its contents for a time as long as the lifetimes of Kuwayy and Surayy, the two "vultures" among the stars.[455] When all have eaten their fill the cupbearers come with various potations and singing girls who produce sweet-sounding intonations.

ويقول، لا فتئ ناطقاً بالصواب: عليّ بمن في الجنة من المغنّين والمغنّيات ممن كان ١،٢،١٣
في الدار العاجلة، فقُضيتْ له التّوبة. فتحضر جماعةٌ كثيرةٌ من رجال ونساء، فيهم
الغَريض ومَعْبَدٌ وابن مِسْجَحَ وابن سُريج، إلى أن يحضر إبراهيم المَوْصِليّ وابنه إسحاق.
فيقول قائلٌ من الجماعة، وقد رأى أسراب قِيانٍ قد حضرن، مثل بَصْبَص[1] ودنانير
وعِنان: من العجب أن الجَرادتيْن في أقاصي الجنّة. فإذا سمع ذلك، لا برح سمعُه
مطروقاً بما يُبْهجه، قال: لا بُدّ من حضورهما. فيركب بعض الخدم ناقةً من نُوق
الجنّة، ويذهب إليهما على بُعد مكانهما.

فتُقْبِلان على نجيبين أسرع من البرق اللامع. فإذا حصلتا في المجلس، حيّاهما
وبشَّ بهما وقال: كيف خلصتما إلى دار الرحمة بعدما خبطتُما في الضلال؟
فتقولان: قُدرتْ لنا التّوبة ومُتْنا على دين الأنبياء المرسَلين. فيقول: أحسن الله
إليكما، أسمِعانا شيئاً من القصيدة الحائية التي تُروى لعَبيد مرةً ولأَوْس أخرى، وما
سَمِعَتا قطّ بعبيد ولا أوس، فتُلْهمان أن تُغنيا بالمطلوب.

فتلحّنان: ٢،٢،١٣

وَدِّعْ لَمِيسَ وَداعَ الوامقِ اللاحي قد فنَكتْ في فَسادٍ بعد إصلاحِ
إذ تستبيكَ بمصقولٍ عوارضُه حَمْشِ اللّثاتِ عِذابٍ غيرِ مِمْلاحِ
كأنّ رِيقتَها بعد الكَرى اغتبقتْ من ماءِ أدكنَ في الحانوت نَضّاحِ
ومن مُشَعْشَعةٍ ورَهاءَ نشْوتُها ومن أنابيبِ رُمّانٍ وتُفّاحِ
هبّتْ تلوم وليست ساعةَ اللاحي هلاّ انتظرتِ بهذا اللّوم إصباحي!
قاتَلها الله تَلْحاني وقد علمتْ أني لنفسِيَ إفسادي وإصلاحي
إن أشرَبِ الخمرَ أو أُرزأْ لها ثمنًا فلا مَحالةَ يومًا أنّني صاحِ
ولا مَحالةَ من قبرٍ بمحْنِيةٍ أو في مَليعٍ كظَهْر التُّرْس وضّاحِ

[1] في نسخة الأصل وفي ي: (بصيص).

The Sheikh (may he always say the right thing!) says, "Bring me all the singers, male and female, in Paradise, those who lived in the Fleeting World and for whom repentance was decreed!" A large crowd of men and women appears, among them al-Gharīḍ, Maʿbad, Ibn Misjaḥ, and Ibn Surayj, until finally Ibrāhīm al-Mawṣilī and his son Isḥāq arrive.[456] Someone among the crowd says, having seen the flocks of singing girls that have come, such as Baṣbaṣ, Danānīr, and ʿInān:[457] "It is strange that 'the two Locusts' are still in the most remote parts of Paradise." When the Sheikh hears this (may his ears always be struck by what delights him!) he says, "They must come too!" One of the servants mounts a she-camel of Paradise and goes to them, however far away they are. **13.2.1**

The conversation with the two "Locusts"

They approach on two noble steeds, faster than flashing lightning. When they have arrived at the company the Sheikh greets them and gives them a friendly welcome. He asks them, "How did you manage to enter the Abode of Mercy, after having stumbled blindly in error?"[458] They answer, "Repentance was decreed for us and we died in the religion of the prophets sent by God." "God has been good to you both!", says the Sheikh. "Please recite for us some verses of the poem rhyming in *-āḥī*, that is sometimes attributed to ʿAbīd and by others to Aws!"[459] They have never heard of either ʿAbīd or Aws, but they are divinely inspired to sing what is requested.

They intone the following lines: **13.2.2**

Bid Lamīs farewell, as a reproaching tender lover!
  She obstinately wronged me, though she was good before,
When captivating you with polished teeth,
  thin gums, sweet to the taste, and not unpleasant;
After her slumber her saliva tastes as if it had an evening draught
  of a liquid from a dark skin in the tavern, richly flowing,
And of a strong, inebriating wine with water mixed;
  or from the tubes of pomegranates and apples.[460]
She woke, full of reproach—it is no time for blame!
  Why couldn't you have waited with reproach until I'd woken up?
God curse her! She rebukes me, though she knows
  that it is up to me to waste or keep my wealth!
If I drink wine or buy it at a price,
  one day I shall be sober, certainly, again.
We'll not escape a grave set in a winding wadi, or
  a wasteland wide and flat like a shield's surface.

فتُطْرِبان مَن سمع، وتستفزّان الأفئدة بالسُّرور، ويكثر حمدُ الله، سبحانه، كما أنعم على المؤمنين والتائبين، وخلّصهم من دار الشِّقوة إلى محلّ النعيم.

٣،١٣ ويعرِض له، أدام الله الجمال ببقائه، الشَّوقُ إلى نظر سَحابٍ كالسحاب الذي وصفه قائل هذه القصيدة في قوله:

إنّي أرِقتُ ولم تأرَقْ معي صاحِ ... لمستكِفٍّ بُعيد النَّوم لَمّاحِ
قد نِمتَ عنّي وبات البرقُ يُسْهِرني ... كما استضاء يهوديٌّ بمصباحِ
تَهْدي الجنوبُ بأُولاه وناء به ... أعجازُ مُزْنٍ يسوق الماءَ دلاّحِ
كأنّ ريّقَه لمّا علا شَطِبًا ... أقرابُ أبلقَ ينفي الخيلَ رَمّاحِ
كأنّ فيه عِشارًا جِلّةً شُرُفًا ... عُوذًا مطافيلَ قد همّت بإرشاحِ
دانٍ مُسِفٌّ فُويق الأرض هيْدَبُهُ ... يكاد يدفعه مَن قام بالراحِ
فمَن بنَجْوته كمن بعَقْوته ... والمستكِنُّ كمن يمشي بِقِرواحِ
وأصبح الروضُ والقِيعانُ مُمْرِعةً ... ما بين منفتقٍ منه ومُنصاحِ

فينشئ الله، تعالت آلاؤه، سحابةً كأحسنِ ما يكون من السُّحب، من نظر إليها شهِد أنه لم ير قَطّ شيئًا أحسن منها، محلّاةً بالبرق في وَسَطها وأطرافها، تُمطر بماء وَرْد الجنّة من طَلٍّ وطَشٍّ، وتنثُر حَصى الكافور كأنه صِغار البَرَد. فعزّ إلهنا القديم الذي لا يُعجزه تصويرُ الأمانيّ وتكوين الهواجس من الظُّنون.

٤،١٣ ويلتفت فإذا هو بجِران العَوْد النُّميريّ، فيُحيّيه ويرحّب به، ويقول لبعض القِيان: أسمِعينا قول هذا المُحسِن:

The girls enrapture those who hear them, stirring the hearts with joy. There is much thanking of God (praised be He) for the blessings He bestowed on those who believe and repent, saving them from the Abode of Misery and bringing them to the Place of Bliss.

13.3 There occurs to the Sheikh (may God make beauty perpetual by letting him live forever!) a longing to see a cloud such as was described by the poet in the same ode:

> Sleepless I lay (you, my friend, were not lying awake!),
> having spied a round cloud, very soon after falling asleep, which flashed,
> You were asleep, but the lightning kept me awake all night,
> like a Jew with a lamp, lucubrating.
> The south wind is driving its front, while its hindermost parts,
> bringing water, are tottering, heavily laden with rain.
> Its opening rain, when it falls on Mount Shaṭib,
> resemble the flanks of a back-kicking piebald horse, chasing horses.
> It is as if she-camels, large and full-grown, are rumbling inside it—
> recently they've given birth; they are gently nudging their calves with their heads.
> Close down, with its fringe hanging only a little above the earth—
> standing up, you could almost drive it back with your hand!
> Those on the high ground and those on the low are alike;
> he who seeks shelter at home is like he who walks on the bare plain.
> In the morning the meadows and plains are verdant with herbage,
> in all cracks and crevices, nooks and crannies.

Then God (exalted are His gifts) forms a cloud as beautiful as a cloud can be. Whoever looks at it will testify that he has never seen a more beautiful one, adorned as it is with lightning in the middle and at its extremities; it rains rosewater from Paradise, made with dew and drizzle, and it scatters pebbles of camphor like small hailstones. Mighty is our God, the Pre-existent, who is not incapable of giving shape to any wish and bringing into existence any surmised suggestion.

13.4 *The conversation with Jirān al-ʿAwd*

The Sheikh turns around and sees Jirān al-ʿAwd al-Numayrī.[461] He greets him and welcomes him. "Let us hear some verses of this master," he says to a singing girl, "such as these:

حملْن جِرانَ العوْدِ حتى وضعنه   بعَلْياءَ في أرجائها الجِنُّ تعْزِفُ
وأحرزْن منا كلَّ حُجزةِ مئزرٍ   لهنَّ وطاح النَّوْفَليُّ المزَخْرَفُ
وقُلْن تمتّعْ ليلةَ النّأي هذه   فإنّك مرجومٌ غداً أو مسيَّفُ

وهذا البيت يُروى لسُحَيم. فتُصيب تلك القَيْنة وتجيد. فإذا عَجِبت الجماعةُ من إحسانها وإصابتها قالت: أتدرون من أنا؟ فيقولون: لا والله المحمود! فتقول: أنا أمُّ عمرٍو التي[١] يقول فيها القائل:

تصُدُّ الكأسَ عنّا أمَّ عمرٍو   وكان الكأسُ مَجراها اليمينا
وما شرُّ الثلاثة أمَّ عمرٍو   بصاحبكِ الذي لا تَصْبَحينا

فيزدادون بها عَجَباً ولها إكراماً، ويقولون: لمن هذا الشعر؟ ألعمرو بن عديّ اللَّخْمي أم لعمرو بن كلثوم التَّغْلبيّ؟ فتقول: أنا شهدت نَدْمانَيْ جَذيمةَ: مالكاً وعَقيلاً، وصَبَحتُهما الخمرَ المشعشَعة لمّا وجدا عمرو بن عديٍّ، فكنت أصرف الكأس عنه، فقال هذين البيتين، فلعلَّ عمرو بن كلثومٍ حسَّن بهما كلامَه واستزادهما في أبياته.

٥،١٣ ويذكر، أذكره الله بالصالحات، الأبياتَ التي تُنسَب إلى الخليل بن أحمد. والخليل يومئذٍ في الجماعة، وأنها تصلحُ لأن يُرقَص عليها، فيُنْشئ الله، القادر بلُطف حكمته، شجرةً من عفَز، والعفزُ الجوْز، فتونِع لوقتها، ثمّ تنفُض عَدَداً لا يُحصيه إلا الله سبحانه، وتنشقُّ كلُّ واحدةٍ منه عن أربع جوارٍ يرُقْن الرائين، ممّن قرُب والنائين، يرقُصن على الأبيات المنسوبة إلى الخليل، وأوّلها:

إنَّ الخليط تَصَدَّعْ   فطِرْ بدائكَ أو قَعْ
لولا جَوارٍ حِسانٌ   مثلُ الجآذر أربَعْ

١ في كل النسخ: (الذي).

The women carried Jirān al-ʿAwd and laid him down
 on a high spot, around which the jinn were humming.[462]
They guarded from me all those places where they wore
 their underclothes, while their embroidered veils had fallen.
'Enjoy this night,' they said, 'before we part,
 because tomorrow you'll be stoned or killed with swords!'"

(This last verse has also been attributed to Suḥaym).[463] The singing girl performs with complete mastery. When the company, amazed, admires her virtuosity, she says, "Do you know who I am?" They all say, "No, by God, praise Him!" She says, "I am Umm ʿAmr, of whom the poet says:

Umm ʿAmr withholds the cup from us;
 but the cup should move to the right.
Your friend, Umm ʿAmr, whom you deny
 a morning drink, is not the worst of us three!"

They grow yet more amazed about her and honor her. "Who composed this poem," they ask, "is it ʿAmr ibn ʿAdī al-Lakhmī or ʿAmr ibn Kulthūm al-Taghlibī?"[464] "I have known the two drinking companions of Jadhīmah, Mālik and ʿAqīl. I gave them a morning drink of wine mixed with water. When they noticed ʿAmr ibn ʿAdī and I withheld the wine from him, ʿAmr said these two verses. Perhaps ʿAmr ibn Kulthūm wanted to adorn his poem with them and added them to his verses."

13.5 *The dance of the damsels*

The Sheikh (may God always remind him of good deeds!) is reminded of the verses that are ascribed to al-Khalīl ibn Aḥmad, who was among the company. It occurs to him that these verses are fit to be danced to. God, the Omnipotent, by the grace of His wisdom, makes a *Juglans regia* grow, i.e., a walnut tree,[465] which bears fruit immediately: it sheds a number of walnuts that can only be counted by God, praised be He. Each single walnut splits into four parts, disclosing four girls who delight the onlookers, nearby and far. They dance to the verses attributed to al-Khalīl, beginning:[466]

The gathered clans have split asunder:
 Fly up or fall with your love sickness!
If there were no pretty maidens,
 four, like oryx calves,

أمُّ الرِّبابِ وأسماءُ والبَغومُ وبَوْزَعْ
لقلتُ للظاعنِ: اظعَنْ إذا بدا لكَ أو دَعْ!

فتهتزّ أرجاءُ الجنّة، ويقول، لا زال مُنطَقاً بالسَّدَد[1]: لمن هذه الأبيات يا أبا عبد الرحمن؟ فيقول الخليل: لا أعلم. فيقول: إنّا كنّا في الدار العاجلة نروي هذه الأبيات لك. فيقول الخليل: لا أذكر شيئاً من ذلك، ويجوز أن يكون ما قيل حقّاً. فيقول: أفنسِيتَ يا أبا عبد الرحمن وأنت أذكَرُ[2] العرب في عصرك؟ فيقول الخليل: إنّ عبور الصِّراط ينفُض الخَلَد ممّا استُودع.

٦،١٣ ويخطِر له ذكرُ الفُقّاع الذي كان يُعمَل في الدار الخادعة، فيُجري الله بقُدرته أنهاراً من فُقّاع، الجُرعة منها لو عُدلت بلذّات الفانية، منذ خلقَ اللهُ السمواتِ والأرضَ إلى يومِ تَطْوي الأُمَمَ الآخرةُ، لكانت أفضلَ وأشفَّ. فيقول في نفسه: قد علمتُ أنّ الله قديرٌ، والذي أريد نحوُ ما كنتُ أراه مع الطّوّافين في الدار الذاهبة. فلا تكمُل هذه المقالة حتى يجمع الله كلَّ فقّاعيٍّ في الجنّة من أهل العراق والشام وغيرهما من البلاد، بين أيديهم الوِلْدانُ المخلَّدون يحملون السِّلال إلى أهل ذلك المجلس.

فيقول، حفِظ الله على أهل الأدب حوْباءه، لمن حضره من أهل العلم: ما تُسمّى هذه السِّلال بالعربيّة؟ فيُرِمُّون، أي يسكُتون، ويقول بعضهم: هذه تُسمّى البواسن، واحدتها باسنةٌ. فيقول قائلٌ من الحاضرين: من ذكر هذا من أهل اللغة؟ فيقول، لا انفكّت الفوائد واصلةً منه إلى الجُلساء: قد ذكرها ابن دُرُستَوَيْه، وهو يومئذٍ في الحضرة. فيقول له الخليل: من أين جئت بهذا الحرف؟ فيقول ابن درستويه: وجدتُه في كتب النَّضر بن شُميل. فيقول الخليل: أتحُقُّ هذا يا نضر، فأنت عندنا الثقة؟ فيقول النَّضر: قد التبس عليَّ الأمر، ولم يحكِ الرجل إن شاء الله، إلا حقّاً.

٧،١٣ ويعبُر بين تلك الأكراس، أي الجماعات، طاووسٌ من طواويس الجنّة يروق من

١ ب٤، ق، إف: (بالسداد). وفي ب: (بالسدد) كما في نسخة الأصل.
٢ في كل النسخ: (أذكى) والأرجح أن الصواب (أذكر) كما ظنّ نيكلسون، وتبعته بنت الشاطئ.

Umm al-Rabāb, Asmā',
  al-Baghūm, and Bawza',
I'd tell the man who leads away the women in their litters:
  "Lead them, if you must, or leave them here!"

All regions of the Garden shake. The Sheikh (may he always be inspired to say the right thing!) asks al-Khalīl, "Whose verses are these, Abū 'Abd al-Raḥmān?" "I don't know," replies al-Khalīl. "But in the Fleeting World we used to transmit them as yours." "I don't remember anything of that," answers al-Khalīl. "But it may be true what they say!" The Sheikh exclaims, "Have you then forgotten, Abū 'Abd al-Raḥmān? You had the best memory of all Arabs in your time!" Al-Khalīl replies, "Crossing the Bridging Path has shaken out all that was stored in the mind."

The Sheikh happens to think of beer, the kind that used to be made in the Deceptive World. Instantly God, in His omnipotence, lets rivers of it flow; one draught of it is nicer and more refreshing than all the delights of the Perishing World from God's creation of heaven and earth until the day that the last nations are wrapped up. He says to himself, "I know that God is omnipotent, but really I wanted the kind I used to see with the beer sellers in the Fleeting World!" No sooner has he said that than God gathers all beer sellers in Paradise, Iraqis, Syrians, and from other regions, preceded by the immortal youths,[467] who carry baskets to the company. 13.6

Beer, marinated peacock, and roast goose

The Sheikh (may God preserve him for all lettered people!) asks the scholars that are present, "What are these baskets called in correct Arabic?" They are taciturn, i.e., silent. One of them says, "They are called 'hampers,' in the singular 'hamper.'" One of the others says, "And which lexicographer says that?" The Sheikh replies (may his learning never fail to reach his companions!), "It is mentioned by Ibn Durustawayh." He happens to be present. Al-Khalīl asks him, "Where did you find that word?" "In the writings of al-Naḍr ibn Shumayl," answers Ibn Durustawayh. Al-Khalīl asks, "Is that correct, Naḍr? You are a reliable source in my view." "I can't remember precisely," replies Naḍr, "but I think the fellow is quoting accurately, if God wills."

At that moment there comes along, past the throng, i.e., the assembled people, a paradisical peacock, a veritable feast for the eye. Abū 'Ubaydah would like to eat it marinated. Instantly it is like that, on a golden plate.[468] When he has had his fill the bones reassemble and become a peacock as 13.7

رآه حُسناً، فيشتهيه أبو عُبيدة مَصوصاً، فيتكوّن كذلك في صَحفةٍ من الذَّهب. فإذا قُضي منه الوَطَر، انضمّت عظامُه بعضها إلى بعضٍ، ثمّ تصير طاووساً كما بدأ. فتقول الجماعة: سبحان ﴿مَن يُحْيِي ٱلْعِظَامَ وَهِيَ رَمِيمٌ﴾. هذا كما جاء في الكتاب الكريم: ﴿وَإِذْ قَالَ إِبْرَٰهِـۧمُ رَبِّ أَرِنِي كَيْفَ تُحْيِ ٱلْمَوْتَىٰ قَالَ أَوَلَمْ تُؤْمِن قَالَ بَلَىٰ وَلَٰكِن لِّيَطْمَئِنَّ قَلْبِي قَالَ فَخُذْ أَرْبَعَةً مِّنَ ٱلطَّيْرِ فَصُرْهُنَّ إِلَيْكَ ثُمَّ ٱجْعَلْ عَلَىٰ كُلِّ جَبَلٍ مِّنْهُنَّ جُزْءًا ثُمَّ ٱدْعُهُنَّ يَأْتِينَكَ سَعْيًا وَٱعْلَمْ أَنَّ ٱللَّهَ عَزِيزٌ حَكِيمٌ﴾.

ويقول هو، آنس الله بحياته، لمن حضر: ما موضع يطمئنّ؟ فيقولون: نَصْبٌ بلامِ كَيْ. فيقول: هل يجوز غير ذلك؟ [فيقولون:][١] لا يحضُرنا شيءٌ. فيقول: يجوز أن يكون في موضع جَزْمٍ بلام الأمر، ويكون مخرَجُ الكلام مخرَج الدُّعاء، كما يقال: يا ربِّ اغْفِرْ لي، وأمّا قوله الحكايةَ عن عازَر: ﴿قَالَ أَعْلَمُ أَنَّ ٱللَّهَ عَلَىٰ كُلِّ شَيْءٍ قَدِيرٌ﴾ فقد قُرِئَ برفْع الميم وسكونها، فالرفع على الخبر والسكون على أنه أمرٌ من الله، جلّ سلطانه. وأجاز أبو عليّ الفارسيُّ أن يكون اعلمْ مُخاطَبةً من عازر لنفسه، لأن مثل هذا معروفٌ. يقول القائل، وهو يعني نفسَه: ويحك ما فعلتَ وما صنعتَ! ومنه قول الحادرة الذُّبيانيّ:

بكرتْ سُميّـةُ غُدْوةً فتمتّعِ   وغدتْ غُدُوَّ مُفـارِقٍ لم يَرْبَعِ

وتمرُّ إوَزّةٌ مثل البُخْتيّة، فيتمنّاها بعض القوم شِواءً، فتمثّل على خِوانٍ من الزُّمُرُّد، فإذا ٨،١٣
قُضيت منها الحاجةُ، عادت بإذن الله إلى هيئة ذوات الجَناح، ويختارها بعض الحاضرين كَرْدَناجاً، وبعضهم معمولةً بسُمّاقٍ، وبعضهم معمولةً بلبنٍ وخَلٍّ، وغير ذلك، وهي تكون على ما يريدون. فإذا تكرّرت بينهم قال أبو عثمان المازنيّ لعبد الملك بن قُريب الأصمعيّ: يا أبا سعيدٍ، ما وزن إوَزّة؟ فيقول الأصمعيّ: ألي تُعَرِّض بهذا يا فُصَعُل، وطال ما جئتَ مجلسي بالبصرة وأنت لا يُرفَع بك رأسٌ؟ وزن إوزّة في الموجود إفَعْلةٌ، ووزنُها في الأصل إفْعَلةٌ. فيقول المازنيّ: ما الدليل على أنّ الهمزة

---

١ أضافتها بنت الشاطئ، إذ يقتضيها السياق.

before. They all exclaim, "Glory to Him «who revives the bones after they have decayed»! It is just as it says in the Qur'an: «When Ibrāhīm said, 'My Lord, show me how Thou revivest the dead!' He said, 'Don't you believe me, then?' 'Yes, I do,' he said, 'but just so that my heart be reassured.' 'Then,' He said, 'Take four birds and cut them up, then put a piece of them on each hill, then call them and they will come running toward you! Know that God is all-mighty and all-wise!'»"

Then the Sheikh (may God delight mankind with his life!) asks, "What is the mood of 'be reassured'?" They reply, "Subjunctive, because it is dependent on the conjunction 'so that' in the sense of purpose." "Could there be another interpretation?" asks the Sheikh. (They answer,)[469] "We cannot think of anything." "It is possible," continues the Sheikh, "that it is a jussive, after the particle *li-* that denotes a command,[470] which here could express a prayer, as when one says, 'O Lord, forgive me!' As for 'Āzar's words that are quoted,[471] these have been recited either as «He said: I know (*aʿlamu*) that God is powerful over everything» or «He said: know (*iʿlam*) . . . !», the former as a statement and the latter as a command from God, mighty is His power. Abū 'Alī al-Fārisī thinks that 'know!' can be taken as addressed by 'Āzar to himself, because this is a well-known phenomenon. Someone will say, 'Woe unto you! What have you done?' meaning himself. Al-Ḥādirah al-Dhubyānī says:[472]

Sumayyah rose early this morning. Enjoy!
But she came in the morning like someone departing, not staying."

Then a goose comes along, big like a Bactrian camel.[473] One person wants it roasted, and thus it appears, on a table of emerald. As soon as he has had his fill, it returns, with God's permission, to its former winged state. Another prefers it as kebab, someone else wants it spiced with sumac, yet another with milk and vinegar, and so on, while the goose turns into whatever is desired. This process repeats itself for some time. 13.8

Then Abū 'Uthmān al-Māzinī says to 'Abd al-Malik ibn Qurayb al-Aṣmaʿī, "I say, Abū Saʿīd, what is the morphological pattern of *iwazzah*, 'goose'?" Al-Aṣmaʿī replies, "Are you insinuating something, you scorpion? You were in my class in Basra for so long when nobody paid any attention to you. The pattern is factually *ifaʿlah* ('iC_1aC_2C_3ah) but originally *ifʿalah* ('iC_1C_2aC_3ah)."[474] Al-Māzinī asks, "What is your proof that the glottal stop ' is

فيها زائدة، وأنها ليست بأصليّة ووزنها ليس فِعَلّةً؟ فيقول الأصمعيّ: أمّا زيادة الهمزة في أوّلها فيدلُّ عليه قولهم وَزٌّ. فيقول أبو عثمان: ليس ذلك بدليلٍ على أنّ الهمزة زائدة، لأنهم قد قالوا ناسٌ، وأصلُه أُناس، ومِيهةٌ لجُدَريّ الغَنَم، وإنّما هو أَمِيهةٌ. فيقول الأصمعيُّ: أليس أصحابك من أهل القِياس يزعُمون أنها إفْعَلةٌ، وإذا بنَوْا من أوى اسماً على وزن إوزّة قالوا: إيّاهٌ ولو أنها فِعَلّةٌ قالوا: إوَيّةٌ، ولو جاؤوا بها على إفْعَلةٍ، بسكون العين، قالوا: إيِيَةٌ، والياء التي بعد الهمزة، وهي همزة أوى، جُعلت ياءً لاجتماع الهمزتين، ولأنّ قبلها مكسوراً وهي مفتوحةٌ. وإذا خفّفتَ همزة مِئْزَرٍ، جعلتَها ياءً خالصةً. فيقول المازنيُّ: تأوُّلُ من أصحابنا وادّعاءٌ، لأنّ إوَزّة لم يثبُت أنّ الهمزة فيها زائدةٌ. فيقول الأصمعيُّ:

رَيَّشتْ جُرْهُمُ نَبْلاً فرمى   جُرْهُماً منهنَّ فُوقٌ وغِرارُ[1]

تبِعتَهم مستفيداً، ثمّ طعنتَ فيما قالوه مُعيداً، ما مَثَلُك ومَثَلهم إلّا كما قال الأوّل:

أُعلّمُه الرِّمايةَ كلَّ يومٍ   فلمّا اشتدّ ساعدُه رماني

وينهَض كالمُغْضَب، ويفترق أهل ذلك المجلس وهم ناعمون.

---

١ ب، ي: (غرارُ) والقافية مطلقة غير مقيّدة.

secondary and not an original root consonant, the pattern then being *fiʿallah* ($C_1iC_2aC_3C_3ah$)?" Al-Aṣmaʿī answers, "That the glottal stop is secondary is proved by the fact that people also say *wazz*." "But that does not prove that the glottal stop is secondary," counters Abū ʿUthmān, "for people say *nās* ('people'), the original form of which is *ʾunās*, and *mīhah*, for 'sheep pox,' which is in fact *ʾamīha*." Al-Aṣmaʿī says, "Don't you and your friends, the 'Analogists,'[475] assert that the pattern is *ʾifʿalah* ('$iC_1C_2aC_3ah$)? If they then build a noun from the root *ʾ-W-Y* ('to seek refuge') on the pattern of *ʾiwazzah*, they would say *ʾiyyāh*![476] And if the pattern were *fiʿallah* ($C_1iC_2aC_3C_3ah$), they would say *ʾiwayyah*; if it were *ʾifaʿlah* ('$iC_1aC_2C_3ah$), the *ʿayn* having no vowel, they would say *ʾiyayyah*, in which the *y* that follows the glottal stop—which is the original glottal stop of the root *ʾ-W-Y*—has been changed into a *y* because two glottal stops coincide here, and because a short *i* precedes it, while it has itself been vowelled with a short *a*. If you soften the glottal stop in *miʾzar* ('loin-cloth, wrap') you say *mīzar*, with a pure, long *ī*." Al-Māzinī says, "This is merely an arbitrary interpretation and claim of our colleagues, for it has not been established conclusively that the glottal stop in *ʾiwazzah* is secondary". Al-Aṣmaʿī says,

"The tribe of Jurhum feathered arrows; Jurhum then
was shot by notches and by tips of their own arrows![477]

"You followed them, deriving much benefit; then you came back and attacked what they said! You and they are like the ancient poet who said,

I taught him shooting, every day;
and when his arm was steady he shot me."[478]

Angrily, he gets up; the people of that session go their separate ways, having a blissful time.

ويخلو، لا أخلاه الله من الإحسان، بحُوريّتين له من الحور العِين، فإذا بهره ما يراه ١،١٤
من الجمال قال: أعْزِزْ عليَّ بهلاك الكِنْديّ، إنّي لأذكُرُ بكما قوله:

كدأبكَ من أُمِّ الحويْرث قبلَها   وجارتِها أُمِّ الرَّباب بمأسَلِ
إذا قامتا تَضوَّعَ المِسكُ منهما   نسيمَ الصَّبا جاءت بِريّا القرنفُلِ

وقوله:

كعاطفتيْن من نِعاجِ تَبالةٍ   على جؤذَرَين أو كبعض دُمى هَكِرْ
إذا قامتا تَضوَّعَ المسكُ منهما   وأصْوِرةٌ من اللّطيمة والقُطُرْ

وأين صاحبتاه منكما لا كرامةَ لهما ولا نُعمة عينٍ؟ لَجَلسةٌ معكما بمقدار دقيقةٍ من دقائق ساعات الدُّنيا خيرٌ من مُلك بني آكل المُرار وبني نَصْر بالحِيرة وآل جَفْنة ملوك الشام.

ويُقبّل على كلّ واحدةٍ منهما يترشّف رُضابها ويقول: إنّ امرأ القيس لَمسكينٌ مسكينٌ! تحترق عِظامُه في السّعير وأنا أتمثّل بقوله:

كأنّ المُدامَ وصوْبَ الغَمام   وريحَ الخُزامى ونَشْرَ القُطُرْ
يُعَلُّ به بَرْدُ أنيابها   إذا غرّدَ الطائرُ المستحِرْ

وقوله:

أيّامَ فُوها كُلّما نَبّهتَها   كالمسْك بات وظلَّ في الفَدّامِ
أُنُفٌ كلوْنِ دم الغَزال معتّقٌ   من خمرِ عانةَ أو كرومِ شِبامِ

فتستغرب إحداهما ضَحِكاً. فيقول: ممّ تضحكين؟ فتقول: فَرَحاً بتفضّل الله الذي ٢،١٤
وهب نعيماً، وكان بالمغفرة زعيماً، أتدري من أنا يا عليَّ بن منصور؟ فيقول: أنت

Thereupon he is alone (may God's beneficence never leave him alone!) with two black-eyed damsels of Paradise. Dazzled by their beauty he exclaims, "Alas, the poor Kindite, who perished![479] You remind me of his verses: 14.1

The conversation with the two damsels

As was your wont before her, with Umm al-Ḥuwayrith,
and her neighbor friend, Umm al-Rabāb, in Maʾsal:
When they rose the scent of musk would waft from them,
like the eastern breeze, bringing the smell of cloves.

"and his verses:

Just like two oryxes, ewes from Tabālah, bending tenderly
toward their calves; or like some Hakir statues:
When they rose the scent of musk would waft from them,
of perfume from a flask, and odoriferous aloe wood.

"But his girlfriends are no match for you, no nobility, no treat for the eye! Sitting in your company for even one minute, of earthly reckoning, is better than the realm of Ākil al-Murār and his kin, or that of the Naṣrids in al-Ḥīrah, or the Jafnids, kings of Syria."

He turns to the two girls, sipping their sweet saliva, and says, "Imruʾ al-Qays is a poor, poor soul! His bones are burning in hellfire, while here I am quoting his verse:

It seems the coolness of her teeth,
when birds at dawn are warbling, is
infused with wine, with rain, the smell
of lavender, the scent of aloe wood.

"or his verses:

Days when her mouth, as I roused her from her sleep,
would smell like musk, kept in its filter overnight,
Wine the color of gazelle's blood, kept for years,
vintage from ʿĀnah or the vineyards of Shibām."

One of the girls begins to laugh uncontrollably. The Sheikh asks, "Why are you laughing?" "For joy," she replies, "because of the favor that God has bestowed on me, and the forgiveness that he showed to me! Do you know who I am, ʿAlī ibn Manṣūr?" "You are one of the black-eyed damsels whom 14.2

من حُور الجنان اللواتي خلقكنّ الله جزاءً للمتّقين، وقال فيكنّ: ﴿ كَأَنَّهُنَّ الْيَاقُوتُ وَالْمَرْجَانُ ﴾ فتقول: أنا كذلك بإنعام الله العظيم، على أني كنت في الدار العاجلة أُعْرَف بحمدونة، وأسكُن في باب العراق بحَلَب وأبي صاحبُ رَحىً، وتزوّجني رجلٌ يبيع السَّقَط فطلّقني لرائحةٍ كَرِهَها من فيَّ، وكنت من أقبح نساء حلب، فلمّا عرفتُ ذلك زهِدتُ في الدنيا الغرّارة، وتوفّرتُ على العبادة، وأكلتُ من مِغزَلي ومِرْدَني، فصيّرني ذلك إلى ما ترى.

وتقول الأخرى: أتدري من أنا يا عليَّ بن منصور؟ أنا توفيق السَّوْداء التي كانت تخدُم في دار العلم ببغداد على زمان أبي منصورٍ محمّد بن عليٍّ الخازن وكنت أُخرِج الكتب إلى النُّسّاخ.

فيقول: لا إله إلا الله، لقد كنتِ سوداءَ فصِرتِ أنصعَ من الكافور، وإن شئت القافور. فتقول: أتعجَب من هذا، والشاعر يقول لبعض المخلوقين:

لو أنّ من نُورِه مِثقالَ خَرْدلةٍ   في السُّود كلِّهِمُ لابيَضَّتِ السُّودُ

ويمرُّ مَلَكٌ من الملائكة، فيقول: يا عبد الله، أخبرْني عن الحور العين، أليس في الكتاب ٣،١٤
الكريم: ﴿ إِنَّا أَنْشَأْنَاهُنَّ إِنْشَاءً فَجَعَلْنَاهُنَّ أَبْكَارًا عُرُبًا أَتْرَابًا لِأَصْحَابِ الْيَمِينِ ﴾. فيقول الملك: هنَّ على ضربَين: ضربٌ خلقه اللهُ في الجنّة لم يعرِفْ غيرها، وضربٌ نقله الله من الدار العاجلة لمّا عمِل الأعمالَ الصالحة.

فيقول، وقد هَكِر ممّا سمع، أيْ عَجِبَ: فأين اللواتي لم يكُنَّ في الدار الفانية؟ وكيف يتميّزْن من غيرهنَّ؟ فيقول الملك: اقفُ أثَري لترى البديءَ من قدرة الله.

فيَتبَعه، فيجيءُ به إلى حدائقَ لا يعرف كُنهَها إلا الله، فيقول الملك: خُذْ ثمرةً من هذا الثمر فاكسِرْها فإنّ هذا الشجر يُعرَف بشجر الحور.

فيأخذ سَفَرجلةً أو رُمّانةً أو تُفّاحةً أو ما شاء الله من الثِّمار فيكسِرها، فتخرج منها جاريةٌ حوراءُ عيناءُ تبرَق لحُسنها حوريّاتُ الجنان، فتقول: من أنت يا عبد الله؟

God has created as a reward for the god-fearing. He said of you: «It is as if they are rubies and pearls».”[480] She says, “Yes, I am indeed, through God Almighty’s kindness. But in the Fleeting World I was known as Ḥamdūnah and I used to live in Iraq Gate in Aleppo, where my father worked a mill. A rag-and-bone dealer married me, but he divorced me because of my bad breath. I was one of the ugliest women in Aleppo. When I realized that I became pious and renounced this Delusive World. I devoted myself to religious worship and earned a living from my spindle. This made me what you see now.”

The other one says, “And do you know who I am, ʿAlī ibn Manṣūr? I am Black Tawfīq, who used to work in the House of Learning in Baghdad in the time of Abū Manṣūr Muḥammad ibn ʿAlī al-Khāzin. I used to fetch the manuscripts for the copyists.”

He exclaims, “There is no god but God! You were black and now you are more dazzlingly white than camphor, or camphire[481] if you like.” “Do you find that odd?” replies the girl, “After all, the poet says of some mortal being:

One mustard-seed of light from him, with all
black people mixed, would whiten all the blacks.”[482]

14.3 *The tree of damsels*

At that instant an angel comes along. The Sheikh asks him, “Servant of God, tell me about the damsels with black, lustrous eyes: doesn’t it say in the Holy Book: [483] «We have raised them and made them virgins and loving companions for the people in the right»?” The angel replies, “There are two kinds. One kind has been created by God in Paradise and they have never known otherwise, and there is another kind that God has transferred from the Temporary World because they have done pious deeds.”

The Sheikh is stupefied, i.e., amazed by what he has heard. “Where are the ones that have never been in the Transitory World?” he asks, “And how do they differ from the others?” The angel answers, “Just follow me and you will see a wondrous example of God’s omnipotence.”

He follows the angel, who takes him to gardens the true nature of which only God knows. The angel says, “Take one of these fruits and break it open. This tree is known as the tree of the black-eyed damsels.”[484]

The Sheikh takes a quince, or a pomegranate, or an apple, or whatever God wills, and breaks it open. A girl with black, lustrous eyes emerges whose beauty dazzles the other damsels of the Paradisical gardens. She says,

فيقول: أنا فُلان بن فلانٍ. فتقول: إني أُمَنَّى بلقائك قبل أن يخلق الله الدُّنيا بأربعة آلاف سنة. فعند ذلك يسجُد إعظاماً لله القدير ويقول: هذا كما جاء في الحديث: أعددتُ لِعبادي المؤمنين ما لا عينٌ رأت ولا أُذُنٌ سمعت، بَلْهَ ما أطلعتُهم عليه، وبَلْهَ في معنى: دعْ وكيفَ.

٤،١٤ ويخطِر في نفسه وهو ساجدٌ أنّ تلك الجارية على حُسنها ضاوِيَةٌ، فيرفع رأسه من السُّجود وقد صار من ورائها رِدْفٌ يضاهي كُثْبانَ عالِج وأنقاءَ الدَّهْناء وأرْمِلةَ يَبْرِينَ وبني سَعْدٍ، فيُهال من قدرة الله اللطيف الخبير ويقول: يا رازقَ المُشْرِقة سَناها، ومُبلِغ السائلة مُناها، والذي فعل ما أَعْجز وهال، ودعا إلى الحِلم الجُهّال، أسألك أن تقصُر بُوصَ هذه الحوريّة على مِيلٍ في مِيل، فقد جاز بها قدرُك حدَّ التأميل. فيقال له: أنت مخيّر في تكوين هذه الجارية كما تشاء. فيقتصر من ذلك على الإرادة.

"Who are you, servant of God?" He gives his name. She says, "I was promised I would meet you four thousand years before God created the world!" At that the Sheikh prostrates himself to magnify the omnipotent God and says, "Thus it says in the Hadith: 'I have prepared for my believing servants things no eye has seen nor any ear has heard—let alone that I should have told them about it!'"[485] ("let alone" is used in the sense of "don't think about it and why").

It occurs to him, while he is still prostrate, that the girl, though beautiful, is rather skinny. He raises his head and instantly she has a behind that rivals the hills of ʿĀlij, the dunes of al-Dahnāʾ, and the sands of Yabrīn and the Banū Saʿd.[486] Awed by the omnipotence of the Kind and Knowing God, he says, "Thou who givest rays to the shining sun, Thou who fulfillest the desires of everyone, Thou whose awe-inspiring deeds make us feel impotent, and summon to wisdom the ignorant: I ask Thee to reduce the bum of this damsel to one square mile, for Thou hast surpassed my expectations with Thy measure!" An answer is heard: "You may choose: the shape of this girl will be as you wish." And the desired reduction is effected. 14.4

١٥،١ ويبدو له أن يطّلع إلى أهل النار فينظرَ إلى ما هم فيه ليعظُم شُكرُه على النعم، بدليل قوله تعالى: ﴿قالَ قائِلٌ مِنهُم: إني كانَ لي قَرينٌ يَقولُ أئنَّكَ لَمِنَ المُصَدِّقينَ، أئذا مِتنا وَكُنّا تُرابًا وَعِظامًا أئنّا لَمَدينونَ. قالَ هَلْ أنتُم مُطَّلِعونَ. فاطَّلَعَ فَرَآهُ في سَواءِ الجَحيمِ، قالَ: تَاللهِ إنْ كِدتَ لَتُرْدينِ، وَلَوْلا نِعمَةُ رَبّي لَكُنتُ مِنَ المُحضَرينَ﴾.

١٥،٢،١ فيركب بعضَ دوابِّ الجنّة ويسيرُ، فإذا هو بمدائنَ ليست كمدائن الجنّة، ولا عليها النور الشَّعْشعانيّ، وهي ذات أدحالٍ وغماليل. فيقول لبعض الملائكة: ما هذه يا عبد الله؟ فيقول: هذه جنّة العفاريت الذين آمنوا بمحمّد، صلّى الله عليه، وذُكروا في الأحقاف، وفي سورة الجنّ، وهم عددٌ كثيرٌ. فيقول: لأعْدِلَنَّ إلى هؤلاء فلن أخلُوَ لديهم من أُعجوبة. فيعُوج عليهم، فإذا هو بشيخٍ جالسٍ على باب مَغارة، فيسلِّم عليه فيُحسن الرّدَّ ويقول: ما جاء بك يا إنسيّ؟ إنّك بخيرٍ لعَسيّ، ما لك من القوم سِيّ! فيقول: سمعتُ أنكم جنٌّ مؤمنون فجئتُ ألتمس عندكم أخبار الجِنّان، وما لعلّه لديكم من أشعار المَرَدة.

فيقول ذلك الشيخ: لقد أصبتَ العالم بجَدّة الأمر، ومن هو منه كالقمر من الهالة، أنا كالحاقن من الإهالة،[١] فسَلْ عمّا بدا لك.

فيقول: ما اسمك أيّها الشيخ؟ فيقول: أنا الخَيْتَعُور[٢] أحدُ بني الشَّيْصَبان، ولسنا من ولد إبليس ولكنّا من الجنّ الذين كانوا يسكُنون الأرض قبل ولد آدم، صلّى الله عليه.

---

١ رواية الأصل وكل الطبعات: (لاكالحاقن من الإهالة) ولعل الصواب ما أثبتناه؛ راجع التعليق على الترجمة الإنكليزية.

٢ في كل النسخ (الخيثعور) بالثاء والمشهور (الخيتعور) كما في ب.

Between Paradise and Hell

Then it occurs to him that he would like to see the people in Hell and how things are with them, that his gratitude for his blessings be magnified. For God says,[487] «One of them said: I had a companion who would say, "Are you really one of those who believe that if we die and have turned to dust and bones we will be judged?" He said, "Won't you look down?" So he looked down and saw him in the midst of blazing Hell. He said, "By God, you had nearly let me perish; but for my Lord's blessing I would have been one of those brought there!"» 15.1

15.2.1 *The Paradise of the demons*

The Sheikh mounts one of the animals of Paradise and goes forth. He sees some towns unlike the towns of Paradise, without the glittering light; there are caves and dark, wooded valleys. He asks one of the angels, "What are they, servant of God?" He replies, "This is the Paradise of those demons[488] who believed in Muḥammad (God bless him), those that are mentioned in the Surah of the Sand Dunes and the Surah of the Jinnees.[489] There are lots of them." "I should like to pay them a visit," says the Sheikh, "I am bound to hear some wonderful stories from them!"

He turns toward them and sees an old person who is sitting at the mouth of a cave. He greets him and the other answers the greeting politely, asking, "What brings you to this place, human? You would deserve a better one; like you there is none!" The Sheikh replies, "I heard that you are the believing jinnees, so I've come to ask for some stories about the jinnees, and perhaps to hear some poems by the rebellious jinnees."[490]

The old jinnee says, "You've hit the bull's eye; you've found me like the moon in its halo in the sky, like someone who waits before pouring away the hot fat:[491] here am I! Ask whatever you like." The Sheikh asks, "What is your name, old man?" "I am al-Khaytaʿūr, one of the sons of al-Shayṣabān.[492] We are not descended from the devil: we belong to the jinnees that lived on earth before the children of Adam (God bless him)."

فيقول: أخبرْني عن أشعار الجنّ، فقد جمع منها المعروف بالمَرْزُبانيّ قطعةً صالحة. ٢،٢،١٥
فيقول ذلك الشيخ: إنّما ذلك هَذَيانٌ لا مُعتمَد عليه، وهل يعرف البَشَر من النظيم إلّا كما تعرف البقر من علم الهيئة ومِساحة الأرض؟ وإنّما لهم خمسة عشر جنساً من الموزون قلَّ ما يَعْدوها القائلون، وإنّ لنا لآلافَ أوزانٍ ما سمع بها الإنس. وإنّما كانت تخطِر بهم أُطَيفالٌ منّا عارمون فتَنفِث إليهم مقدار الضُّوارة من أَراكِ نُعمانَ. ولقد نظمتُ الرَّجَز والقصيد قبل أن يخلق الله آدمَ بكَوْرٍ أو كوريْن. وقد بلغني أنكم مَعْشَرَ الإنس تلهجون بقصيدة امرئ القيس: قِفا نَبكِ من ذِكرى حبيبٍ ومَنزِلِ، تحفّظونها الحَزاورة في المكاتب، وإن شئت أمليتُك ألف كلمةٍ على هذا الوزن على مثل: مَنزِلِ وحَوْمَلِ، وألفاً على ذلك القَريّ يجيء على مَنزِلُ وحَوْمَلُ، وألفاً على مَنزِلا وحَوْمَلا، وألفاً على مَنزِلَهْ وحَوْمَلَهْ، وألفاً على مَنزِلُهْ وحَوْمَلُهْ، وألفاً على مَنزِلِهْ وحَوْمَلِهْ. وكلُّ ذلك لشاعرٍ منّا هلك وهو كافرٌ، وهو الآن يشتعل[١] في أطباق الجحيم.

فيقول، وَصَلَ الله أوقاتَه بالسعادة: أيها الشيخ، لقد بقي عليك حِفظك! فيقول: لسنا مثلكم يا بني آدم يغلِب علينا النِّسيان والرُّطوبة، لأنكم خُلِقتم ﴿مِنْ حَمَإٍ مَسْنُونٍ﴾، وخُلِقْنا ﴿مِن مَّارِجٍ مِّن نَّارٍ﴾.

فتحمله الرَّغبةُ في الأدب أن يقول لذلك الشيخ: أَفَتُمِلُّ عليَّ شيئاً من تلك الأشعار؟ فيقول الشيخ: فإذا شئتَ أمللتُك ما لا تَسِقُه الرِّكاب، ولا تَسَعُه صُحُف دنياك.

فيهُمُّ الشيخ، لا زالت هِمّته عاليةً، بأن يكتب منه، ثمّ يقول: لقد شَقِيتُ في الدار العاجلة بجمع الأدب، ولم أَحظَ منه بطائلٍ، وإنّما كنت أتقرّب به إلى الرؤساء، فأحتلب منهم دَرَّ بَكِيءٍ وأَجهَد أخلافَ مَصورٍ، ولستُ بموفَّقٍ إن تركتُ لَذّاتِ الجنّة وأقبلتُ أتنسخ آداب الجنّ ومعي من الأدب ما هو كان لاسِيّما وقد شاع النسيانُ في أهل أدب الجنة، فصِرتُ مِن أكثرهم روايةً وأوسعهم حفظاً، ولله الحمد.

١ ب: (يشتغل) واخترنا رواية ب٤ والطبعات الأخرى.

15.2.2 *The poetry of the demons*

The Sheikh says, "Tell me about the poems of the jinnees! Someone called al-Marzubānī has collected a fair number of them." The old man replies, "But that is all rubbish, wholly unreliable. Do humans know more about poetry than cattle know about astronomy and geodesy? They have fifteen different meters, and rarely transcend them;[493] whereas we have thousands of meters that humans have never heard of. Some naughty toddlers of ours happened to pass by some humans and spat some poetry at them, a trifle like a splinter from an arak tree of al-Naʿmān.[494] I myself have composed informal *rajaz* and formal *qaṣīd* poetry an eon or two before God created Adam. I have heard that you, race of humans, are rapturous about Imru' al-Qays's poem, 'Stop, let us weep for the remembrance of a loved one and a dwelling place,'[495] and make your kids learn it by heart at school. But if you wish I could dictate to you a thousand poems with the same meter and the same rhyme, *-lī*, a thousand such poems rhyming in *-lū*, a thousand in *-lā*, a thousand in *-lah*, a thousand in *-luh*, and a thousand in *-lih*, all composed by one of our poets, an unbeliever now burning in the depths of Hell."

The Sheikh (may God make him happy continually!) says, "You have got a good memory, old man!" The jinnee replies, "We are not like you, children of Adam, overcome by forgetfulness and moistness, for you have been created from «moulded mud»[496] but we have been created from «a fiery flame»."[497]

The Sheikh is moved by a desire for erudition and literature to ask the old man, "Will you dictate some of these poems to me?" "If you like," says the jinnee, "I will dictate to you loads more than camels can carry and all the pages of your world can contain."

The Sheikh has a mind (may his mind ever be lofty!) to take some dictation from him. But then he says to himself: in the Transitory World I was always wretched when I collected literature; I never profited from it. I tried to curry the favor of leading persons but I was milking the udder of a bad milk camel and was exerting myself with the teats of a slow cow. I'll never be a success if I give up the pleasures of Paradise in order to copy the literature of the jinn. I've got enough erudition as it is, all the more so because forgetfulness is rife among the dwellers in Paradise, so that I have turned out to be one of those with the greatest erudition and the largest memory, thanks be to God!

٣،٢،١٥ ويقول لذلك الشيخ: ما كُنيتك لأُكرمك بالتكنية؟ فيقول: أبو هَدْرَش، أولدتُ من الأولاد ما شاء الله، فهم قبائل بعضهم في النار المُوقَدة وبعضهم في الجنان. فيقول: يا أبا هدرش، مالي أراك أشيَبَ وأهل الجنّة شبابٌ؟ فيقول: إنّ الإنس أُكرموا بذلك وأُحرمناه، لأنا أُعطينا الحُولةَ في الدار الماضية، فكان أحدنا إن شاء صار حيّةً رَقْشاءَ، وإن شاء صار عصفوراً، وإن شاء صار حَمامة، فمُنعنا التصوُّر في الدار الآخرة، وتُركنا على خَلْقنا لا نتغيّر، وعُوّض بنو آدم كونَهم فيما حَسُن من الصُّوَر. وكان قائل الإنس يقول في الدار الذاهبة: أُعطينا الحِيلةَ، وأُعطِيَ الجنُّ الحُولة.

٤،٢،١٥ ولقد لقيتُ من بني آدم شرّاً، ولقُوا منّي كذلك، دخلت مرّةً دار أناسٍ أريد أن أصرَع فتاةً لهم، فتصوّرتُ في صورة عَضَلٍ، أي جُرَذٍ، فدعوا لي الضّياون، فلمّا أرهقتني تحوّلتُ صِلّاً أرقَمَ ودخلتُ في قطيلٍ هناك، فلمّا علموا ذلك كشفوه عني، فلمّا خِفتُ القتل صرت رِيحاً هفّافةً فلحقتُ بالرّوافد ونقضوا تلك الخُشُب والأجذال فلم يروْا شيئاً. فجعلوا يتفكّنون ويقولون: ليس هاهنا مكانٌ يمكن أن يستتر فيه. فبينا هم يتذاكرون ذلك عمدتُ لكَعابهم في الكِلّة، فلمّا رأتني أصابها الصَّرع، واجتمع أهلها من كلّ أوبٍ، وجمعوا لها الرُّقاة، وجاؤوا بالأطِبّة وبذلوا المُنفِسات، فما ترك راقٍ رُقْيةً إلا عرضها عليَّ وأنا لا أُجيب، وغَبَرَت الأُساةُ تسقيها الأشْفِيَةَ وأنا سَدِكٌ بها لا أزول، فلمّا أصابها الحِمام طلبتُ لي سِواها صاحبةً، ثمّ كذلك حتى رزق الله الإنابة وأثاب الجزيل، فلا أفتأ له من الحامدين:

٥،٢،١٥ حَمِدتُ مَن حطّ أوزاري ومزّقها ... عنّي فأصبح ذَنْبي اليومَ مغفورا
وكنتُ آلَفُ مِن أتراب قُرْطُبةٍ ... خُوداً وبالصّين أُخرى بنتَ يَغبورا
أزورُ تلك وهذي غير مكترثٍ ... في ليلةٍ قبل أن أستوضح النُّورا
ولا أمُرُّ بوحْشيٍّ ولا بَشَرٍ ... إلا وغادرتُهُ وَلْهانَ مذعورا

He asks the old man, "How should I address you respectfully?"[498] He answers, "As Abū Hadrash. I have fathered God knows how many children, whole tribes of them, some in the burning Fire, others in Paradise." The Sheikh asks him, "Abū Hadrash, how come you are gray-haired? I thought those who dwell in Paradise would be young."[499] He replies, "Humans have been given that privilege, but we have been denied it, because we could change shape in the Past World. Anyone of us could be a speckled snake if he so wished, or a sparrow if he wanted, or a pigeon. But in the Hereafter we are forbidden to change shape. We are left as we were created originally. The children of Adam have been given a beautiful appearance by way of compensation. As some human said in the World that Was: 'We have been given make-shift, and the jinn have been given shape-shift.'" 15.2.3

Abū Hadrash al-Khayta'ūr's heroic deeds

The jinnee continues, "I have met evil at the hands of humans, but they have met the like from me! Once I entered the house of some persons, wanting to strike a girl with fits.[500] I took on the shape of a *Rattus rattus*, i.e. a rat; they called the cats, and when I was hard pressed by these I changed myself into a speckled viper and hid in a hollow tree trunk. When they found out they uncovered me. Afraid that they would kill me, I became a whizzing wind and clung to the rafters. They tore down the wooden beams but could not see anything. Then they were puzzled and said, 'There is no place here where it could be hiding!' While they were deliberating I went for the full-bosomed maiden in her mosquito net. When she saw me she had a fit. Her family came from all sides; they gathered exorcists and brought doctors and spent large sums. Every exorcist left no spell untried on me, but I did not react. The physicians kept giving her potions but I stayed put and did not budge. When death overtook her I looked for another girl, and so on, until God granted me repentance and rewarded me richly! I shall always be one of those who praise Him![501] 15.2.4

I praise Him who took my sinful burdens and destroyed them 15.2.5
for me! My crime has been forgiven now.
I had a close affair once with a pretty girl
from Cordova; and then, in China, with the daughter of an emperor.
I visited now one and then another, unconcerned,
at night, before I could discern the light of dawn.
And any animal or human I encountered
I would leave distraught and terrified.

أُرَوِّعُ الزَّنجَ إلمامًا بِنسْوتها   والرُّومَ والتُّركَ والسِّقلابَ والغورا
وأَرْكَبُ الهَيْقَ في الظَّلْماءِ معتسِفًا   أو لا فذَبَّ رِيادٍ باتَ مقرورا
وأحضُرُ الشَّرْبَ أغْروهمْ بآبدةٍ   يُزْجون عُودًا ومِزْمارًا وطُنْبورا
فلا أُفارِقهم حتَّى يكونَ لهم   فعلٌ يَظَلُّ به إبليسُ مسرورا
وأصْرِفُ العَدْلَ خَتْلاً عن أمانته   حتى يخونَ وحتى يشهدَ الزُّورا
وكم صرعتُ عَوانًا في لَظَى لَهَبٍ   قامت تُمارس للأطفال مسجورا
وذادني المرءُ نُوحٌ عن سفينته   ضربًا إلى أن غدا الظُّنبوبُ مكسورا
وطِرتُ في زَمَنِ الطُّوفان معتليا   في الجوِّ حتى رأيتُ الماء محسورا
وقد عرضتُ لموسى في تفرُّده   بالشاء ينتجُ عُمْروسًا وفُرفورا
لم أُخْلِه من حديثٍ مّا ووَسْوَسةٍ   إذ دلَّك ربّك في تكليمه الطُّورا
أضللتُ رأْيَ أبي ساسانَ عن رَشَدٍ   وسِرتُ مستخفيًا في جيشِ سابورا
وسادَ بَهْرامُ جُورٍ وهْو لي تَبَعٌ   أيّام يبْني على عِلاّته جورا
فتارةً أنا صِلٌّ في نَكارته   وربّما أبصرتْني العينُ عصفورا
تلوح لي الإنس عُورًا أو ذوي حَوَلاً   ولم تكنْ قطّ لا حُولاً ولا عورا
ثمّ اتّعظتُ وصارت توْبتي مَثَلاً   من بعدِ ما عِشْتُ بالعِصْيان مشهورا
حتى إذا انفضَّت الدُّنيا ونُودِيَ إس   رافيلُ ويْحَك هلاّ تنفخُ الصُّورا
أماتني اللهُ شيئًا ثمّ أيقظني   لمَبْعَثي فرُزِقتُ الخُلْدَ مبرورا

I frightened Blacks, by visiting their womenfolk,
and Byzantines, and Turks, and Slavs, and Afghān Ghūr![502]
I'd ride an ostrich in the dark, haphazardly
or not; then a wild bull, who spent the night in freezing cold.
I'd be with drinkers, to afflict them with mishap perpetual,
while they played on their lute, their shawm, and their sitar.[503]
I would not part from them before they had performed
a deed that would make Satan glad.
I'd cheat a notary, make him betray the trust
they had in him, and give false testimony.
Many a woman middle-aged I cast into a blazing fire,
when she was working at a heated oven for her children.
And that man, Noah, drove me off his Ark
and beat me till my shin bone broke.
I flew up high into the sky during the Flood,
until I saw the waters in retreat.
I bothered Moses, when he had withdrawn alone
with sheep and goat that bore him lamb and kid,
And I kept talking to him with insinuating whispers,
until your Lord, who spoke to him, crumbled the mountain.[504]
I led the father of Sāsān astray, away from the right path,
and hid myself, marching in Shapur's army.
Bahrām then reigned, being my follower,
the days at least when he built Gūr.[505]
At times I am a viper with its wicked wiles,
at other times the eye will spy me as a bird.
Humans, because of me, will turn one-eyed or squint,
though they were never one-eyed or cross-eyed.
But then I took a warning; my repentance was exemplary,
after I'd lived a life notorious for disobedience.
And finally the world came to an end. A call was heard:
'Why don't you blow the trumpet, Isrāfīl?'[506]
God made me die for a short while and then He woke me up
and resurrected me. Then I was given life eternal, blessed!"

فيقول: لله دَرُّك يا أبا هدرش لقد كنتَ تُمارس أوابدَ ومُنْدياتٍ، فكيف ألسِنتُكم؟ ٦،٢،١٥ أيكون فيكم عربٌ لا يفهمون عن الروم، وروم لا يفهمون عن العرب، كما نجد في أجيال الإنس؟ فيقول: هيْهاتَ أيّها المرحوم! إنّا أهل ذكاء وفِطَنٍ، ولا بدّ لأحدنا أن يكون عارفًا بجميع الألسن الإنسيّة، ولنا بعد ذلك لسانٌ لا يعرفه الأنيس. وانا الذي أنذرتُ الجنَّ بالكتاب المُنْزَل: أدلجتُ في رُفقةٍ من الخابل نريد اليمن، مررنا بيَثْرِب في زمان المَعْو، أي الرُّطَب ف ﴿سَمِعۡنَا قُرۡءَانًا عَجَبٗا يَهۡدِيٓ إِلَى ٱلرُّشۡدِ فَـَٔامَنَّا بِهِۦۖ وَلَن نُّشۡرِكَ بِرَبِّنَآ أَحَدٗا﴾ وعُدتُ إلى قومي فذكرتُ لهم ذلك، فتسرّعتْ منهم طوائف إلى الإيمان، وحثّهم على ما فعلوه أنهم رُجموا عن استراق السَّمع بكواكب مُحْرِقاتٍ.

٧،٢،١٥ فيقول: يا أبا هدرش، أخبِرْني، وأنت الخبير، هل كان رَجْمُ النُّجوم في الجاهليّة؟ فإنّ بعض الناس يقول إنّه حدث في الإسلام. فيقول: هيهات! أما سمعتَ قول الأَوْديّ:

كشِهاب القَذْف يَرْميكم به   فارسٌ في كفّه للحرب نارُ

وقول ابن حَجَر:

فانصاعَ كالدُّرّيِّ يَتْبعه   نَقْعٌ يثور تخالُه طُنُبا

ولكنّ الرّجم زاد في أوان المبعث، وإن التخرُّص لكثيرٌ في الإنس والجنّ، وإنّ الصِّدق قليلٌ،[١] وهنيئًا في العاقبة للصادقين. وفي قصّة الرَّجم أقول:

١،٨،٢،١٥ مكّةُ أَقْوَتْ من بني الدَّرْدبيسْ   فما لجنّيٍّ بها من حسيسْ
وكُسِّرت أصنامُها عَنْوةً   فكلُّ جِبْتٍ بنصيلٍ رديسْ
وقام في الصَّفوة من هاشمٍ   أزهرُ لا يغفِل حقَّ الجليسْ

١ في ي، إف، ق: (وإن الصدق لمعوز قليل).

The Sheikh exclaims, "Wonderful, Abū Hadrash! And that after you practiced all these wicked and calamitous things!—But tell me about your languages: are there among you Arabs who do not understand the Byzantines, and Byzantines who do not understand the Arabs, as we find among the human nations?" The jinnee answers, "Far from it, may God have mercy on you! We are clever and intelligent people. Everyone of us must have knowledge of all the human languages, and besides that we have a language unknown to humans. I am the one who warned the jinn that the Holy Book was being revealed.[507] One night I was traveling with some jinnee friends, on our way to Yemen. When we came past Yathrib (it was the time of fresh dates) «we heard a wondrous Recitation which leads to the right course; so we believed in it and we shall not associate anyone with our Lord.»[508] Then I returned to my people and told them about it. Some of them hastened to believe; they were moved to do this all the more because they had been pelted with scorching stars when they were eavesdropping."[509] 15.2.6

The Sheikh says, "Abū Hadrash, inform me (for you are well-informed): this pelting with stars, did it happen in the pre-Islamic period? For some people say that it happened in Islamic times." "That is wholly wrong," replies Abū Hadrash. "Have you not heard the verse by al-Afwah al-Awdī: 15.2.7

[An arrow(?)] like a shooting star thrown at you
by a horseman, with fire in his hand for the battle.

"And the verse by Aws ibn Ḥajar:[510]

Then it darted away, like a scintillating star, with in its wake
a dust cloud which one could imagine was a tent.[511]

"However, this pelting increased at the time of the Prophet's mission. There was a lot of lying among humans and jinn, and truthfulness was scarce. Good health, in the end, to those who have spoken the truth! Regarding the story of the pelting with shooting stars I composed the following poem:[512]

Mecca has been abandoned by the Banū l-Dardabīs: 15.2.8.1
no demon's sound is heard there now.
Its idol statues have been smashed to bits with force,
each idol, with an axe destroyed.
Among Hāshim's elite a brilliant man stood up,[513]
one never to neglect the rights of his companion.

يسمع ما أُنزِلَ من ربّه الـ | قدُّوس وَحيًا مثلَ قرعِ الطَّسيسْ
يجلد في الخمر ويشتدُّ في الـ | أمرِ ولا يُطلِق شُربَ الكسيسْ
ويرجُم الزانيَ ذا العِرس لا | يقبَل فيه سؤلةً من رئيسْ
وكم عروسٍ بات حُرّاسُها | لجُرهُمٍ في عِزّها أو جديسْ ٢،٨،٢،١٥
زُفَّت إلى زوجٍ لها سيّدٍ | ما هو بالنِّكس ولا بالضبيسْ
غِرتُ عليها فتخلَّجتُها | بواشك الصَّرعة قبل المسيسْ
وأسلكُ الغادةَ محجوبةً | في الخِدر أو بين جوارٍ تميسْ
لا أنتهي عن غرَضي بالرُّقى | إذا انتهى الضَّيغمُ دون الفريسْ
وأُدلجُ الظَّلماءَ في فِتيةٍ | مِلجِنّ فوق الماحل العَرَبسيسْ
في طاسمٍ تعزف جِنّانُهُ | أقفرَ إلا من عفاريتَ لِيسْ
بيضٍ بهاليلَ ثِقالٍ يَعا | لِيلَ كرامٍ ينطِقون الهسيسْ
تحمِلنا في الجُنح خيلٌ لها | أجنحةٌ ليست كخيل الأنيسْ
وأيْنُقٌ تسبقُ أبصارَكم | مخلوقةٌ بين نَعامٍ وعِيسْ
تقطعُ من عَلْوةَ في ليلها | إلى قُرى شاسٍ[1] بسيرٍ هميسْ
لا نُسُكٌ في أيّامنا عندنا | بل نُكِسَ الدِّينُ فما إن نكيسْ ٣،٨،٢،١٥
فالأحَدُ الأعظم والسّبتُ كالـ | إثنين والجُمعةُ مثلُ الخميسْ
لا مُجُسٌ نحن ولا هُوَّدٌ | ولا نصارى يبتغون الكنيسْ
نُمزِّق التّوراةَ من هُونها | ونحطِم الصُّلبانَ حطمَ اليبيسْ

---

١ ٢٨ رواية بعض النسخ: (شاش).

He heard the revelation by his Holy Lord sent down,
sounding like metal basins being struck.
He flogged severely those who would drink wine,
and even drinking date wine he would not allow.
He stoned the married fornicator, not accepting
intercession from a tribal chief.[514]
Many a bride, guarded at night by guards 15.2.8.2
as strong as Jurhum or Jadīs,
Escorted to a tribal leader as his spouse
—no weakling or a dastard he—
I jealously assaulted, snatching her with a swift fit,
before her husband even touched her.
And I would go to a young girl, secluded in
her bower, or walking proudly 'midst her servant girls.
A lion might be stopped before he has his prey:
not even spells could stop me from attaining what I wanted.
I would set out in a dark night among
some jinnee friends, over a bare flat plain,
A trackless desert where the demons hum,
a wasteland, only by the bravest jinn inhabited,
White, mighty, heavy, like white clouds,
yet noble, speaking with a whispering.
At night horses with wings would carry us,
unlike the horses of mankind,
And female camels, faster than your eyes could see,
created from a cross of ostrich and of camel,
Which in one night would pace from ʿAlwah
to the hamlets of Tashkent, with only muffled sounds.[515]
There was no piety among us in those days: 15.2.8.3
religion suffered a relapse and we were not astute.
Sunday and Saturday were just like any Monday,
and Friday was like any Thursday.
We were no Zoroastrians, nor Jews,
nor Christians who go to church.
The Torah we would tear apart in scorn
and we would shatter crosses like dry wood.

نحاربُ اللهَ جنودًا لإبْ   لِيسَ أخي الرأي الغبين النَّجيسْ
نسلِّم الحُكمَ إليه إذا   قاسَ فنرضى بالضَّلال المَقيسْ
نزِينُ للشارخ والشيخ أن   يُفْرِغَ كِيسًا في الخَنا بعد كِيسْ
ونقتري جِنَّ سُليمانَ كيْ   نُطْلِقَ منها كلَّ غاوٍ حبيسْ
صُيِّرَ في قارورةٍ رُصِّصت   فلم تغادر منه غيرَ النَّسيسْ
ونُخرج الحسناءَ مطرودةً   من بيتها عن سُوء ظنٍّ حديسْ ١٥،٢،٨،٤
نقول لا تقنَعْ بتطليقةٍ   واقْبَلْ نصيحًا لم يكُن بالدَّسيسْ
حتى إذا صارت إلى غيره   عادَ من الوجد بجَدٍّ تَعيسْ
نُذْكِره منها وقد زُوِّجت   ثغرًا كدُرٍّ في مُدامٍ غريسْ
ونخدَع القِسّيسَ في فِصْحه   من بعدِ ما مُلِّئ بالأنقَليسْ
أصبح مشتاقًا إلى لذّةٍ   معلَّلًا بالصِّرف أو بالخفيسْ
أُقْسم لا يشرب إلّا دُوَيْ   نَ السُّكر والبازلُ تالي السديس
قُلنا له ازْدَدْ قَدَحًا واحدًا   ما أنت أن تزداده بالوكيسْ
يُحِمك في هذا الشفيف الذي   يُطْفِئ بالقُرِّ الْتهابَ الحميسْ
فعَبَّ فيها فوَهَى لُبُّه   وعُدَّ من آل اللعين الرجيسْ
حتّى يَفيضَ الفمُ منه على   نُمْرُقتيْه بالشَّراب القليسْ
ونُسْخِط المَلْكَ على المُشْفِق الْ   مُفْرِط في النُّصْح إذا المُلْكُ سِيسْ
وأُعجِلُ السِّعلاةَ عن قُوتها   في يدها كَشْحُ مَهاةٍ نهيسْ

We battled against God as troops of Satan, friend
of swindling, impure views.
To him we left the judgment when he weighed decisions
and we consented to the error when it was decided.
Both young and old men we inveigled into emptying
purse after purse for lecherous behavior.
The jinn of Solomon we followed, to set free
those wicked ones that were detained,
Put into bottles sealed with lead,
which left them with a mere last gasp.[516]
We let a pretty wife be driven from her house 15.2.8.4
because of a suspicion, a mere guess,
'Don't be content with a revocable divorce,'[517] we tell
the husband, 'do take our advice, it is no trick!'
Then, when she has become another's wife,
his former passion, with a vengeance, will return to him,
While we remind him, though she's married to another, of
her pearly teeth that bathe in wine.[518]
We used to cheat the priest at Easter, after he
had filled himself with eel;
He had already drunk and drunk again, pure wine or mixed,
but in the morning yearned for more delight.
He swore he would not drink to drunkenness,
but 'teeth will follow after milk teeth!'
We said to him, 'Come on, just one more cup!
That wouldn't do you any harm!
'T will warm you in this weather
in which the oven's fire will be extinguished by the cold!'
And thus he gulped it down. His mind gave way
and he was counted 'mongst the cursed and the disgraced;
And in the end his mouth spilled the regurgitated wine
on his two pillows.
We would infuriate the king against his councillor,
so kind and full of good advice, whenever the realm was ruled.
And I would snatch an ogress's repast when she
held in her hands the sirloin of a skinny antelope.

لا أتَّقي البَرَّ لأهواله وأركَبُ البحرَ أوانَ القريسْ
نادمتُ قابيلَ وشِيثاً وها بيلَ على العاتقة الخَنْدَريسْ
وصاحبي لَمْكٍ لدى المِزْهَرا لمُعْمَلِ لم يَعْيَ بزيرٍ جسيسْ
ورَهْطَ لُقْمانَ وأيْسارَه عاشرتُ من بعدِ الشَّباب اللّبيسْ
ثُمَّتَ آمنتُ ومَن يُرزَقِ الـ إيمانَ يظفَرْ بالخطير النفيسْ ٥،٨،٢،١٥
جاهدتُ في بَدْرٍ وحاميتُ في أُحْدٍ وفي الخَنْدَق رُعْتُ الرئيسْ
وراءَ جِبريلَ ومِيكالَ نَخْـ لي الهامَ في الكَبّة خَلْيَ اللّسيسْ
حينَ جيوشُ النصْر في الجوِّ والـ طاغوتُ كالزَّرْع تَناهى فديسْ
عليهِمُ في هَبَوات الوَغى عمائمٌ صُفْرٌ كلونِ الوريسْ
صهيلُ حيْزومَ إلى الآنَ في سَمْعِيَ أكْرِمْ بالحِصان الرغيسْ
لا يَتْبعِ الصَّيْدَ ولا يألَفِ الـ قَيْدَ ولا يشكو الوَجى والدَّخيسْ
فلم تَهَبْني حُرَّةٌ عانسٌ ولا كَعابٌ ذاتُ حُسنٍ رسيسْ
وأيقنتْ زَيْنَبُ منّيَ التُّقى ولم تَخَفْ من سَطَواتي لَميسْ
وقلتُ للجنِّ ألا يا اسْجُدوا لله وانْقادوا انقيادَ الخسيسْ ٦،٨،٢،١٥
فإنّ دنياكُمْ لها مُدّةٌ غادرةٌ بالسَّمْح أو بالشكيسْ
بِلْقيسُ أوْدتْ ومضى مُلكُها عنها فما في الأُذْن من هَلْبَسيسْ
وأُسرةُ المُنْذِر حاروا عن الـ حِيرةِ كلٌّ في تُرابٍ رميسْ
إنّا لمَسْنا بعدكم فاعْلموا بِرْقِعَ فاهْتاجتْ بشَرٍّ بئيسْ

I did not fear the terrors of the land
    or traveling by sea when it was freezing cold.
I drank with Cain and Seth and Abel
    an ancient vintage wine,
And the two friends of Lamech, while the lute
    was played with touch unfaltering on the highest string.[519]
I was familiar with Luqmān and with his gambling friends[520]
    having worn out the cloak of youth.
But subsequently I believed.[521] To whom belief is given 15.2.8.5
    will gain what matters and is precious!
I fought at Badr for the Faith; at Uḥud I defended; and
    I terrorized the foe's commander at the Ditch,[522]
Behind the angels Gabriel and Michael, in the thick of battle, we
    would sever heads as blades of grass are cut.[523]
When the victorious hosts flew in the sky
    and Satan's forces were undone and trampled down like plants,
Their heads were wearing, in the battle's dust clouds,
    yellow turbans, as if dyed with *wars*.[524]
Even now I hear the neighing of Ḥayzūm still ringing in
    my ears: ah, such a noble, blessed stallion![525]
He follows not the hunt, he knows no fetters, nor
    does he complain of injuries or ulcers of his hooves.
No free-born woman, whether old or young and beautiful,
    has given me a taste of love since my conversion.
Now Zaynab could be certain of my piety;
    Lamīs would have no fear of my assaulting her.[526]
I told the jinn: 'Come on, prostrate yourselves 15.2.8.6
    for God, and let yourselves be humbly led!
Your world has, for so long, been treacherous
    both in its tolerance and in its harshness.
Bilqīs has died, her realm has gone from her,
    and not a whisper in the ear is left of it.[527]
Al-Mundhir's dynasty in Ḥīrah: neither here nor there;[528]
    each one of them is buried in the earth.
Know that we tried, like you before us, to attain
    the highest heaven, but it was astir with evil things:[529]

تَرْمي الشياطينَ بنيرانها   حتى تُرى مثلَ الرّماد الدريسْ
فطاوعتْني أُمّةٌ منهمُ   فازت وأُخرى لحِقتْ بالركيسْ
وطار في اليَرْموك بي سابحٌ   والقوم في ضَرْبٍ وطعْنٍ خليسْ ٧،٨،٢،١٥
حتّى تجلَّتْ عنِّيَ الحربُ كالـ   ـجَمْرةِ في وَقْدة ذاك الوطيسْ
والجمَلُ الأنكدُ شاهَدتُه   بئسَ نتيجُ الناقةِ العَنْتَريسْ
بين بني ضَبّةَ مستقدِمًا   والجهلُ في العالَم داءٌ نجيسْ
وزُرْتُ صِفّينَ على شَطْبةٍ   جَرداءَ ما سائسُها بالأَريسْ
مجدِّلًا بالسيف أبطالَها   وقاذفًا بالصَّخرة المَرْمَريسْ
وسِرْتُ قُدّامَ عليٍّ غَداةَ   النَّهرحتى فُلَّ غَرْبُ الخميسْ
صادَفَ منّيَ واعظٌ توبةً   فكانت اللَّقوةُ عند القبيسْ

فيعجب، لا زال في الغِبطة والسُّرور، لِما سمعه من ذلك الجنّيّ، ويكره الإطالةَ عنده فيودّعه.

It shoots the devils with its fires until
 they look like ashes strewn about.'
A group of them obeyed me then, and gained salvation;
 another party of them joined the overthrown.
At the Yarmūk a fleet horse flew with me,[530] 15.2.8.7
 where men outwitted one another, striking, stabbing,
Until the war revealed me as
 a burning ember in the battle's blaze.
And I have seen that wretched camel [531]
 (ill-fated offspring of sturdy dam!),
While bravely I advanced among the Banū Ḍabbah;[532]
 ignorance is a fatal illness in the world!
I visited Ṣiffīn,[533] riding a sleek and short-haired horse,
 never by a peasant groomed,
Felling its heroes with my sword
 and hurtling at them hard, smooth rocks.
I marched in front of ʿAlī on the morning of
 the battle of al-Nahrawān until the army's edge was blunted.[534]
Someone admonished me and found in me repentance:
 'The fertile mare met with a virile male!'"[535]

The Sheikh is amazed (may he always be joyous and glad!) about what he has heard from the jinnee. He does not want to stay too long with him, so he bids him farewell.

ويمرُّ فإذا هو بأسدٍ يفترس من صِيران الجنّة وحسيلها فلا تكفيه هُنيدةٌ ولا هِنْدٌ، ١،١٦
أيْ مائة، ولا مائتان، فيقول في نفسه: لقد كان الأسد يفترس الشاة العَجفاء، فيُقيم عليها الأيّامَ لا يطعَم سِواها شيئاً.

فيُلهِم اللهُ الأسدَ أن يتكلّمَ، وقد عرف ما في نفسه، فيقول: يا عبد الله، أليس أحدكم في الجنّة تُقدَّم له الصَّحفةُ وفيها البَهَطُ والطِّرِيَم مع النَّهيدة، فيأكل منها مثل عُمر السموات والأرض، يلتذّ بما أصاب فلا هو مكتفٍ، ولا هي الفانية؟ وكذلك أنا أفترس ما شاء الله، فلا تأذى الفريسةُ بظُفرٍ ولا نابٍ، ولكن تَجِد من اللّذّة كما أَجِدُ بلُطف ربِّها العزيز. أتدري من أنا أيُّها البزيع؟ أنا أسد القاصرة التي كانت في طريق مِصر، فلمّا سافر عُتبَة بن أبي لَهَبٍ يريد تلك الجهة، وقال النبيُّ صلى الله عليه: اللّهُمَّ سلِّط عليه كلباً من كلابك، أُلهِمْتُ أن أتجوّع له أيّاماً، وجئت وهو نائمٌ بين الرُّفقة فتخلَّلتُ الجماعةَ إليه، وأُدخلتُ الجنّةَ بما فعلت.

ويمرُّ بذئبٍ يقتنص ظِباءً فيُفني السُّربة بعد السُّربة، وكلّما فرغ من ظبيٍ أو ظبية، عادت ٢،١٦
بالقدرة إلى الحال المعهودة، فيعلم أنّ خَطْبه لخطب الأسد، فيقول: ما خبرك يا عبد الله؟ فيقول: أنا الذئب الذي كلّمَ الأَسلَميَّ على عهد النبيّ صلى الله عليه وسلم. كنت أُقيم عشر ليالٍ أو أكثر لا أقدرُ على العِكرِشة ولا القُواع، وكنت إذا هممتُ بعجيّ المَعيز، آسَدَ الراعي عليَّ الكلاب، فرجعتُ إلى الصاحبة مخرّق الإهاب، فتقول: لقد خطئتَ في أفكارك، ما خِيرَ لك في ابتكارك. وربّما رُميتُ بالسِّروة فنشبتْ في الأقراب، فأبيتُ ليلتي لما بي، حتى تنتزعها السِّلقةُ وأنا بآخِر النسيس، فلحقتني بَركة محمّد صلى الله عليه وسلم.

He urges on his mount. Suddenly he faces a lion, who is busy devouring cows and calves from the animal herds of Paradise—he is not content with scoring a century or two, i.e., one hundred or even two hundred animals. The Sheikh says to himself, this lion may have been used to devouring a skinny sheep, living on it for days on end without tasting anything else! 16.1

Animals in Paradise

Thereupon God inspires the lion (who has understood the Sheikh's inner thoughts) with speech. "Servant of God!" says the lion, "Has nobody of you been presented, in Paradise, with a bowl of rice pudding with honey and fresh butter? And eaten it for as long the heavens and the earth last, enjoying what he consumes without ever being satiated, and the bowl never being exhausted? In the same way I devour God knows how many animals, yet without the prey being harmed by claw or tooth. Rather, they enjoy it just as much as I do, through the kindness of their almighty Lord. Do you know, handsome and amiable young man, who I am? I am the lion from al-Qāṣirah, a wadi on the way to Egypt! When ʿUtbah ibn Abī Lahab[536] was traveling in that region, after the Prophet (God bless him) had said, 'O God, let one of Your dogs get him!' I was inspired to go hungry for his sake for several days. I came upon him when he was sleeping among some companions. I crept through the company toward him; and I was allowed entry into Paradise because of what I had done."

Then the Sheikh comes past a wolf who is busy catching gazelles. He consumes herd after herd, but whenever he has finished a buck or a doe it returns, by God's might, to its former state. The Sheikh understands that it is the same with the wolf as with the lion. He asks, "What is your story, servant of God?" and the wolf replies, "I am the wolf who spoke to al-Aslamī[537] in the time of the Prophet (God bless and preserve him). For ten days or more I had not been able to catch even a hare, whether buck or doe. Whenever I set my eyes on a motherless kid the goatherd would set his dogs on me who attacked me madly, and I would get back to the wife with my hide torn badly. She would say, 'You were wrong in your guess! Going out in the morning was not a success!' Sometimes my flank was shot at with an arrow that stuck in me, and I spent the night in agony, until my bitch pulled it out, while I was on my last legs. But then the blessing of Muḥammad reached me, God bless and preserve him!" 16.2

فيذهب، عرّفه الله الغِبْطةَ في كلّ سبيل، فإذا هو ببيتٍ في أقصى الجنة، كأنه ٣،١٦
حِفْش أَمَةٍ راعيةٍ، وفيه رجلٌ ليس عليه نور سُكّان الجنّة، وعنده شجرةٌ قَمِيئةٌ ثمرها ليس بزاكٍ. فيقول: يا عبد الله، لقد رضيتَ بحقيرٍ شَقِنٍ. فيقول: والله ما وصلتُ إليه إلا بعد هِياطٍ ومِياطٍ وعَرَقٍ من شَقاءٍ، وشَفاعةٍ من قُرَيشٍ ودِدتُ أنها لم تكن. فيقول: من أنت؟ فيقول أنا الحُطيئة العَبْسي فيقول: بم وصلتَ إلى الشفاعة؟ فيقول بالصِدق. فيقول: في أيّ شيء؟ فيقول: في قولي:

أبتْ شَفَتايَ اليومَ إلا تكلُّمًا   بهُجرٍ فما أدري لمن أنا قائلُهْ
أرى لِيَ وجْهًا شوّهَ اللهُ خَلْقَه   فقُبِّحَ من وجهٍ وقُبِّحَ حامِلُهْ

فيقول: ما بال قولك:

من يفعلِ الخيرَ لا يَعْدَمْ جوازِيَهُ   لا يذهبُ العُرْفُ بين الله والناسِ

لم يُغْفَر لك به؟ فيقول: سبقني إلى معناه الصالحون، ونظمتُه ولم أعمَل به، فحُرِمتُ الأجْرَ عليه. فيقول: ما شأن الزِبْرِقان بن بدرٍ؟ فيقول الحُطيئة: هو رئيسٌ في الدُّنيا والآخرة، انتفع بهجائي ولم ينتفع غيرُه بمديحي.

فيخلّفه ويمضي، فإذا هو بامرأة في أقصى الجنّة، قريبةٍ من المطّلَع إلى النار. فيقول: ٤،١٦
من أنتِ؟ فتقول: أنا الخنْساء السُّلَميّة، أحببتُ أن أنظُر إلى صَخْرٍ فاطلَّعتُ فرأيته كالجبل الشامخ والنار تضطرم في رأسه، فقال لي لقد صحَّ مَزْعَمُكِ فِيَّ، يعني قولي:

وإنّ صَخْرًا لَتأتمُّ الهُداةُ به   كأنه عَلَمٌ في رأسه نارُ

16.3 The Sheikh moves on (may God acquaint him with joy on every path!). He sees, in the furthest part of the Garden, a dwelling that resembles the hut of a shepherd girl. In it is a man on whom the light of the dwellers of Paradise does not shine. Near him stands a stunted tree with poor fruit. "You, servant of God," he says, "are content with paltry things!" The man replies, "By God, I arrived here only after much hustle and bustle, a lot of sweat and tears, and the intercession of the tribe of Quraysh, which I wish had not happened!" "Who are you?" asks the Sheikh. The man answers, "I am al-Ḥuṭay'ah al-ʿAbsī." "How did you manage to receive intercession?" "Because of my truthfulness." "In which matter?" " Because I said:

In the furthest reaches of Paradise; a conversation with al-Ḥuṭay'ah

> Today my lips refuse to utter anything but
> indecency—but I don't know to whom I'll speak.
> I see I have a face that is malformed by God's creation:
> shame on that ugly face and on its carrier!"

Then the Sheikh asks him, "What about your verse:

> He that does good will not lack his reward:
> kind deeds will not be lost between mankind and God.

"Why wasn't it this verse for which you were granted repentance?" Al-Ḥuṭay'ah replies, "Because pious people before me had already said the same. I may have composed it but I did not act accordingly; therefore I was denied a reward for it." The Sheikh asks, "And what about al-Zibriqān ibn Badr?"[538] "He was a leader in the former world and is one now in the Hereafter," answered al-Ḥuṭay'ah, "He benefited from my lampoons, whereas others did not benefit from my eulogies."

16.4 The Sheikh leaves al-Ḥuṭay'ah and goes on. He sees a woman in the furthest part of Paradise, close to the place from where one can look down into Hell. "Who are you?" he asks. She replies, "I am al-Khansāʾ, of the tribe of Sulaym. I wanted to see my brother Ṣakhr, so I had a look and I saw him, like a lofty mountain, with a fire burning on his head. He said to me, 'What you said about me has come true!' He meant my verse:

The conversation with al-Khansāʾ

> Truly, leaders follow Ṣakhr's example;
> he's like a marker mountain with a fire on top."[539]

فيطلّع فيرى إبليسَ، لعنه الله، وهو يضطرب في الأغلال والسلاسل ومَقامع الحديد تأخذه من أيدي الزَّبانِيَة. فيقول: الحمد لله الذي أمكن منك يا عدوَّ الله وعدوَّ أوليائه! لقد أهلكتَ من بني آدم طوائفَ لا يعلم عددَها إلّا الله. فيقول: مَن الرجل؟ فيقول: أنا فُلان بن فلانٍ من أهل حلب، كانت صناعتي الأدب، أتقرّب به إلى الملوك. فيقول: بئسَ الصناعة! إنها تَهَبُ غُفّةً من العيش، لا يتّسع بها العِيال، وإنها لَمَزَلّةٌ بالقَدَم وكم أهلكتْ مثلَك! فهنيئاً لك إذ نجوتَ. ﴿فَأَوْلَى لَكَ ثُمَّ أَوْلَى﴾! وإنّ لي إليك لَحاجةً، فإنْ قضيتَها شكرتُك يدَ المَنون. ١٠،١٧

فيقول: إنّي لا أقدِر لك على نفعٍ، فإن الآيةَ سبقتْ في أهل النار، أعني قوله تعالى: ﴿وَنَادَى أَصْحَابُ النَّارِ أَصْحَابَ الْجَنَّةِ أَنْ أَفِيضُوا عَلَيْنَا مِنَ الْمَاءِ أَوْ مِمَّا رَزَقَكُمُ اللهُ، قَالُوا إِنَّ اللهَ حَرَّمَهُمَا عَلَى الْكَافِرِينَ﴾.

فيقول: إنّي لا أسألك في شيء من ذلك، ولكن أسألك عن خبرٍ تُخبرنيه: إنّ الخمر حُرِّمت عليكم في الدُّنيا وأُحلّت لكم في الآخرة، فهل يفعل أهل الجنّة بالوِلْدان المخلَّدين فِعْلَ أهل القَريات؟ فيقول: عليك البَهْلة! أما شَغَلَك ما أنت فيه؟ أما سمعت قوله تعالى: ﴿وَلَهُمْ فِيهَا أَزْوَاجٌ مُطَهَّرَةٌ وَهُمْ فِيهِ خَالِدُونَ﴾؟

فيقول: وإنّ في الجنّة لأشْرِبةً كثيرةً غير الخمر. فما فعل بشّار بن بُرْد؟ فإنّ له عندي يداً ليست لغيره من ولد آدم: كان يفضّلني دون الشعراء، وهو القائل:

إبليسُ أفضلُ من أبيكم آدمٍ   فتبيّنوا يا معشرَ الأشرارِ
النارُ عُنصرُه وآدمُ طِينةٌ   والطِّين لا يسمو سُمُوَّ النارِ

Hell

17.1 *The conversation with Satan*

The Sheikh looks down and sees Satan[540] (God curse him!), writhing in fetters and chains, while Hell's angels have a go at him with iron cudgels. The Sheikh says, "Thanks be to God, who has got the better of you, enemy of God and of His friends! How many generations of Adam's children you have destroyed innumerable, only God can count." The devil asks, "Who is this man?" "I am ʿAlī ibn Manṣūr ibn al-Qāriḥ, from Aleppo," replies the Sheikh. "I was a man of letters by profession, by which I tried to win the favor of rulers." "A bad profession indeed!" says Satan. "You'll live on a minimum income, hardly enough to keep your family. It's a slippery business; many like you have gone to perdition because of it. Congratulations on being saved! «So beware, and again, beware!»[541] But I'd like you to do something for me. If you do I will be much obliged."

"I cannot possibly do anything to help you," replies the Sheikh, "for there is a Qur'anic verse already about those in Hell; I mean the words of the Exalted,[542] «Those in Hell will call to those in Paradise, 'Pour us some water or whatever God has given you!' They will reply, 'God has forbidden these things to the unbelievers!'»"

"I am asking you none of that," says Satan. "I am asking you to tell me something: wine is forbidden to you in the Temporal World but permitted in the Hereafter; now, do the people in Paradise do with the immortal youths what the people of Sodom and Gomorra did?" The Sheikh exclaims, "Damn you, haven't you got enough to distract you? Haven't you heard what the Exalted says:[543] «There they will have pure spouses and they will live there forever»?"

Satan says, "In Paradise there are many drinks apart from wine . . . ![544]—But tell me, what happened to Bashshār ibn Burd? I owe him something that I do not owe any other son of Adam: he, unlike all other poets, preferred me to Adam, for he said:

Satan is better than your father, Adam;
  you wicked people, understand this well!
His element is fire, and Adam is of mud:
  mud will never rise as high as fire!

لقد قال الحقَّ، ولم يزل قائله من الممقوتين.

١،٢،١٧ فلا يسكُت من كلامه إلا ورجلٌ في أصناف العذاب يغمِّض عينيه حتى لا ينظر إلى ما نزل به من النِّقَم، فيفتحهما الزَّبانيةُ بكلاليبَ من نارٍ، وإذا هو بشّار بن بُرد قد أُعطي عينين بعد الكَمَه، لينظر إلى ما نزل به من النَّكال.

فيقول له، أعلى الله درجتَه: يا أبا مُعاذٍ، لقد أحسنتَ في مقالك، وأسأت في معتقَدك، ولقد كنتُ في الدار العاجلة أذكُر بعضَ قولك فأترحّم عليك، ظنّاً أنَّ التوبة ستلحَقك، مثلَ قولك:

ارْجِعْ إلى سَكَنٍ تعيشُ به ذهبَ الزّمانُ وأنت منفرِدُ
ترجو غداً وغدٌ لحاملةٍ في الحيِّ لا يدرون ما تَلِدُ

وقولك:

واهاً لأسماءَ ابنةِ الأشدِّ قامت تَراءى إذ رأتني وحْدي
كالشمس بين الزِّبْرِج المنقدِّ ضنَّت بخَدٍّ، وجلَتْ عن خدِّ
ثمَّ انثنتْ كالنَّفَس المرتدِّ وصاحبٍ كالدُّمَّل المُمِدِّ
أرقُبُ منه مثلَ حُمَّى الوِرْدِ حملتُه في رُقعةٍ من جِلْدي
الحرُّ يُلحَى والعصا للعبدِ وليس لِلمُلْحِف مثلُ الرَّدِّ

٢،٢،١٧ الآن وقع منك اليأس! وقلتَ في هذه القصيدة: السُّبْد، في بعض قوافيها، فإن كنتَ أردت جمع سُبَدٍ، وهو طائرٌ، فإنّ فُعَلاً لا يُجمَع على ذلك؛ وإن كنتَ سكّنت الباء فقد أسأت، لأنّ تسكين الفتحة غير معروفٍ، ولا حُجّةَ لك في قول الأخطل:

وما كلُّ مغبونٍ إذا سَلْفَ صَفقةً براجعِ ما قد فاتَه برَدادِ

"He spoke the truth; but those who speak the truth will always be hated!"

No sooner does Satan fall silent than a man appears, plagued with various kinds of torment. He closes his eyes so as not to have to see the punishment that has come upon him; but then the Angels of Hell open them again with pincers of fire. This is Bashshār ibn Burd, who has been given eyes after having been blind from birth, to make him see the chastisement that has come over him. 17.2.1

The conversation with Bashshār ibn Burd

The Sheikh (may God raise his rank!) says to him, "Abū Muʿādh, you were excellent as a poet but bad in your beliefs! In the Fleeting World I would often think of some of your verses and ask God's mercy for you, assuming that repentance might still come to you. I mean, for instance, these verses:

Return to an abode where you can live in comfort;
The time has passed and now you are alone.
You hope for a tomorrow; but tomorrow is like a pregnant woman
in the tribe: one does not know what she will bear.

"Or these:[545]

Woe for Asmāʾ, the daughter of al-Ashadd!
She stood up to be seen and saw me, all alone.
She's like the sun that breaks through the thin clouds.
She was stingy with one cheek but revealed the other.
And then she turned away, just like a breath sighed inwardly.
—Many a 'friend' was like a suppurating boil,
(I feared his coming like a fit of fever),
A boil I had to carry on a patch of skin. . .
A free-born, noble man may be rebuked; sticks are for slaves.
There's nothing for the importune except rebuff.

"But now your situation is desperate!—Actually, in one rhyme of this poem you use the word *subd*.[546] Now, if you meant the plural of *subad*, which is a kind of bird,[547] you are mistaken because a word of this pattern cannot have such a plural. Or, if you simply left out the second vowel of *subad*, you have made a bad verse, because omitting the vowel *a* is not a recognized poetic license. You cannot use the argument that al-Akhṭal said: 17.2.2

Not everyone who is duped, when he's concluded (*salfa*, for *salafa*) a sale,
can return to rescind and get back what he lost;

ولا في قول الآخر:

وقـالوا تُرابيٌّ فـقلتُ صدقتُمُ   أبي من تُرابٍ خَلَقَـهُ اللهُ آدمـا

لأنّ هذه شَواذٌّ. فأمّا قول جَميل:

وصـاحَ ببينٍ من بُثَينـةَ والنَّوى   جميعٌ بذات الرَّضْم صَرْدٌ مُجَحَّلُ

فإنّ مَن أنشده بضمّ الصّاد مخطئ، لأنه يذهب إلى أنه أراد الصُّرَد فسكّن الراء، وإنّما هو صَرْدٌ، أي خالصٌ، من قولهم: أُحبّك حُبّاً صَرْداً، أي خالصاً، يعني غُراباً أسْود ليس فيه بياضٌ، وقوله: مُجَحَّلٌ، أي مقيّد، لأنّ حَلْقة القيد تُسمّى حِجْلاً. قال عَديُّ بن زيد:

أعاذلَ قد لاقيْتُ ما يَزَعُ الفتـى   وطابقتُ في الحِجْلَيْن مشْيَ المقيّدِ

والغراب يوصف بالتقييد لِقصَرِ نَساه، قال الشاعر:

ومـقيّدٍ بين الدّيارِ كأنـه   حَبَشيٌّ داجنةٍ يخرُّ ويعتلي

فيقول بشّار: يا هذا! دعْني من أباطيلك فإنّي لمشغولٌ عنك.

ويسأل عن امرئ القيس بن حُجْر، فيقال: ها هو ذا بحيث يسمعك. فيقول: يا أبا ١٠٣،١٧
هِنْد إنّ رُواة البغداديين يُنشدون في قِفا نَبْكِ، هذه الأبيات بزيادة الواو في أوّلها، أعني قولك:

وكأنّ ذُرى رأسِ المُجَيمِرِ غُدْوةً

وكذلك:

وكأنّ مَكاكِيَّ الجِواءِ

"nor that someone else said:

They said: 'You dusty one!' I said, 'You're right!
My father is from dust, since God created (*khalqahu*, for *khalaqahu*)
him an Adam.'

"For these are irregular forms. As for the verse by Jamīl:

There cried of parting from Buthaynah—the aim is a gathered tribe
at Dhāt al-Raḍm—a pure black (*ṣard*, for *ṣarad*), 'fettered' crow.[548]

"Those who recite it with *ṣurd*, meaning *ṣurad* ('shrike'?)[549] and then deleting the second vowel, are wrong, for correct is *ṣard*, i.e., 'pure,' as in the expression 'I love you with a *ṣard* (pure) love,' here meaning a black crow in which there is no white. The word *muḥajjal* ('fettered') is derived from *ḥijl*, an ankle-ring used as a fetter. ʿAdī ibn Zayd says:

You, woman, you who blame me: I've encountered what holds back a man
and I've been hopping with two ankle-rings, like a shackled man.

"A crow is described as being 'shackled' on account of the shortness of its heel tendons.[550] A poet says:

Many a 'shackled one' that hopped between the dwellings, like
an Ethiopian under a deep-black cloud, now falling, now rising."[551]

But Bashshār replies, "Hey man, spare me your trivialities! I am busy with other concerns and have no time for you!"

17.3.1 *The conversation with Imru' al-Qays*

The Sheikh asks where he might find Imru' al-Qays ibn Ḥujr. "There he is, within hearing distance!" is the answer. He says to him, "Abū Hind, the transmitters in Baghdad recite, from your poem 'Stop, you two and let us weep,'[552] a few of the lines with the addition of an extra-metrical 'and' at the beginning. I mean these verses:[553]

And the peaks at al-Mujaymir's crest, the morning after,
[with debris from the flood, looked like a spindle's whorl.]

"Likewise:

And the songbirds of the valley, in the morning, [seemed
to have been made to drink a fine and spicy wine.]

وكأنّ السِّباع فيه غَرْقَى

فيقول: أبْعَدَ الله أولئك! لقد أساؤوا الرواية، وإذا فعلوا ذلك فأيُّ فرقٍ يقع بين النظم والنثر؟ وإنما ذلك شيءٌ فعله من لا غريزة له في معرفة وزن القريض، فظنَّه المتأخِّرون أصلاً في المنظوم، وهيهات هيهات!

فيقول: أخبِرْني عن قولك:

كبِكْرِ المُقاناةِ البَياضِ بصُفْرةٍ

ماذا أردتَ بالبِكر؟ فقد اختلف المتأوِّلون في ذلك فقالوا: البيْضة، وقالوا: الدُّرَّة، وقالوا: الرَّوْضة، وقالوا الزَّهرة، وقالوا: البَرْديّة.

وكيف تنشد: البياضِ، أم البياضَ، أم البياضُ؟ فيقول: كلُّ ذلك حسنٌ، وأختار البياضِ، بالكسر.

فيقول، فرّغ الله ذِهنه للآداب: لو شرحتُ لك ما قال النحويّون في ذلك لعجبتَ. وبعض المعلِّمين ينشد قولك:

من السيْلِ والغُثّاءِ فَلْكةُ مِغْزَلِ

فيشدِّد الثاء. فيقول: إنّ هذا لجهولٌ. وهو نقيض الذين زادوا الواو في أوائل الأبيات: أولئك أرادوا النَّسَق، فأفسدوا الوزن، وهذا البائس أراد أن يصحِّح الزِّنة فأفسد اللفظ. وكذلك قولي:

فجِئتُ وقد نضَّتْ لنوْمٍ ثيابَها

منهم من يشدِّد الضاد، ومنهم من ينشد بالتخفيف، والوجهان من قولك: نضوت الثوب. إلا أنك إذا شدّدتَ الضاد، أشْبهَ الفعلَ من النضيض، يقال: هذه نضيضةٌ من المَطَر، أي قليلٌ، والتخفيف أحبُّ إليَّ، وإنما حملهم على التشديد كراهةُ الزِّحاف، وليس عندنا بمكروه.

And the wild beasts in the evening, lying drowned [in all
its furthest reaches, looked like wild uprooted onion bulbs.]"

Imru' al-Qays replies, "May God do away with those people! They have spoiled the transmitted text. If they do such things, then what difference is there between poetry and prose? This is something done only by people without any instinct for knowing about poetic prosody. And as a result later critics assume that this is allowed in principle in verse.[554] Wrong! Wrong!"

The Sheikh continues: "Tell me about your verse,

She's like the first-born one, the whiteness mixed with yellow
[nourished with pure water that has not been sullied].[555]

"What did you mean by 'first-born'? The commentators have different opinions. Some say it is an egg; others say it is a pearl; or a meadow; or a flower; or a papyrus plant. And is the word 'whiteness' a nominative, a genitive, or an accusative?"

Imru' al-Qays answers, "All these are good, but I prefer to read it as a genitive." The Sheikh says (may God free his mind so that he can devote himself to literature!) says, "You would be surprised if I explained to you what the grammarians had said about it! Now as for your verse:

. . . with debris from the flood, looked like a spindle's whorl,

"some scholar recites the word 'debris' as *ghuththā'*, with geminated *th*."[556] "That man is really ignorant!" replies Imru' al-Qays, "It is the opposite of what those do who add the word 'and' at the beginning of lines, for they wanted the text to cohere but spoiled the meter, and this wretch wanted to correct the meter but corrupts the word. Likewise, in my verse

I came when she had shed (*naḍat*), for sleep, her clothes,

"some read it with doubled *ḍ* (as *naḍḍat*), others recited it with a single one (as *naḍat*). Both mean 'to shed one's clothes,'[557] but if you double the *ḍ*, the verb looks as if it is from *naḍīḍ* ('small quantity'),[558] as when one says 'this is small quantity of rain (*naḍīḍah min al-maṭar*),' meaning 'light rain.' I prefer to read it with a single *ḍ*, but people have been moved to read it with double *ḍ* because they do not like the metrical shortening. But I do not dislike it myself."[559]

فيقول: لا برح مِنطقياً بالحِكَم: فأخبِرْني عن كلمتك الصاديّة والضاديّة والنُّونيّة التي أوّلها: ٢،٣،١٧

لمن طَلَلٌ أبصرتُه فشجاني كخطِّ زَبورٍ في عَسيبِ يمانِ

لقد جئت فيها بأشياء يُنكرها السّمع، كقولك:

فإن أمسِ مكروباً فيا رُبَّ غارةٍ شهِدتُ على أقبَّ رِخْوِ اللَّبانِ

وكذلك قولك في الكلمة الصاديّة:

على نِقْنِقٍ هيقٍ له ولِعِرسه بمنقطع الوَعْساء بيْضٌ رَصيصُ

وقولك:

فأُسْقي به أختي ضَعيفةَ إذ نأتْ وإذ بَعُد المُزدارُ غيرَ القريضِ

في أشباهٍ لذلك، هل كانت غرائزكم لا تُحِسُّ بهذه الزِّيادة؟ أم كنتم مطبوعين على إتيان مَغامض الكلام وأنتم عالمون بما يقع فيه؟ كما أنه لا ريب أنّ زُهيراً كان يعرف مكان الزِّحاف في قوله:

يطلُب شأْوَ امرأين قَدّما حَسَباً نالا الملوكَ وبذّا هذه السُّوقا

فإنّ الغرائز تُحسُّ بهذه المواضع، فتبارك الله أحسن الخالقين.

فيقول امرؤ القيس: أدركنا الأوّلين من العرب لا يحفِلون بمجيء ذلك، ولا أدري ما شجن عنه، فأمّا أنا وطبقتي فكنّا نمُرُّ في البيت حتى نأتي إلى آخره، فإذا فني وقارب تبيّن أمره للسامع.

فيقول، ثبّت الله تعالى الإحسان عليه: أخبِرْني عن قولك: ٣،٣،١٧

ألا رُبَّ يومٍ لك منهنّ صالحٍ ولا سيّما يومٌ بدارة جُلْجُلِ

The Sheikh says (may he never cease to utter wise words), "Tell me about your poems that rhyme in *-ānī*, in *-īṣū* and *-īḍī*. The first begins with: 17.3.2

To whom do these remains belong that I can see, which made me sad:
like lines of script upon a palm leaf from the Yemen?[560]

"In this poem you say several things that are rejected by the ear, such as:

Though I may be grieving in the evening, yet at many raids
I have been present, on a lean, soft-chested horse.[561]

"It is the same with the poem on *-īṣū*:

. . . On a tall ostrich male, which with its spouse has,
at the sand dune's ridge, some heaped-up eggs.[562]

"And also your verse:

I pray this rain may fall upon my sister, far away Ḍaʿīfah:
too far to visit her myself, except in verse.

"There are more like these. Did you and the others not instinctively notice these irregularities? Or did these recondite ways of speech come to you naturally, while you were fully aware of its possibilities? There can surely be no doubt that Zuhayr knew the metrical irregularity he committed, when he said,[563]

He seeks to surpass two men, who, before him, were of noble descent,
who reached the status of kings and excelled above subjects.

"for one perceives it through one's inborn instinct; God be blessed, the best of creators!"

Imruʾ al-Qays answers, "As far as we know, the early Arabs did not mind at all about coming up with such things, and I do not know what stopped them. My contemporaries and I would just compose a verse from beginning to end, and when it failed, or almost,[564] then its quality would be clear to whoever heard it."

The Sheikh continues (may God steadily give him His beneficence!), "Tell me about your verse[565] 17.3.3

O yes, so many splendid days you had with them,
one day (*yawm-*) at Dārat Juljul in particular!

أتنشده: لك منهنّ صالِح فتُراحِف الكَفّ؟ أم تنشده على الرواية الأخرى؟ فأمّا يومٌ، فيجوز فيه النصب والخفض والرفع. فأمّا النصب فعلى ما يجب للمفعول من الظُّروف، والعامل في الظَّرف هاهنا فِعلٌ مُضْمَرٌ، وأمّا الرفع فعلى أن تجعل ما كافّةً، وما الكافّةُ عند بعض البصريّين نَكِرةٌ، وإذا كان الأمر كذلك فهو بعدها مضمرةٌ، وإذا خفض يومٌ، فما من الزيادات. ويُشدَّد سِيَّ ويخفَّف: فأمّا التشديد فهو اللغة العالية، وبعض الناس يخفّف، ويقال: إنّ الفرزدق مرَّ وهو سَكرانُ على كلابٍ مجتمعةٍ فسلَّم عليها فلمّا لم يسمع الجوابَ أنشأ يقول:

فما ردَّ السّلامَ شيوخُ قومٍ مررتُ بهم على سِكَكِ البريدِ
ولا سِيما الذي كانت عليه قَطيفةُ أُرجُوانٍ في القعودِ

فيقول امرؤ القيس: أمّا أنا فما قلت في الجاهليّة إلا بزحافٍ: لك منهنّ صالِح. وأمّا المعلّمون في الإسلام فغيّروه على حَسَب ما يريدون، ولا بأس بالوجه الذي اختاروه. والوجوه في يوم متقاربةٌ، وسِيَّ تشديدها أحسنُ وأعرف. فيقول: أَجَلْ، إذا خُفّفَتْ صارت على حرفين أحدهما حرف عِلّة.

ويقول: أخبرْني عن التَّسميط المنسوب إليك، أصحيحٌ هو عنك؟ وينشده الذي ١٧،٣،٤
يرويه بعض الناس:

يا صَحْبَنا عرِّجوا تقِفْ بكم أُسُجُ
مَهْرِيّةٌ دُلُجُ في سيرِها مُعُجُ
طالت بها الرِّحَلُ
فعرَّجوا كلُّهمْ والهمُّ يَشغَلهمْ
والعِيس تحملهمْ ليست تُعلّلهمْ
وعاجت الرُّمُلُ

"Do you read *laka* ('you had') with a shortened syllable at the end of the second foot, or do you recite it in the other transmitted version?[566] As for the word *yawm* ('day') in the second hemistich, it is possible to have it in the accusative, the genitive, and the nominative. The accusative, because this is required for adverbial adjuncts; the operator is here an implied verb. The nominative, if one takes the *-mā* in *siyyamā* to be the 'preventing' *mā*, which according to some Basran scholars is indefinite; if this is the case, then the pronoun *huwa* ('he, it') is implied after it.[567] Finally, if one reads *yawm* in the genitive, then *mā* is considered to be one of the 'redundant additions.'[568] Instead of *lā siyyamā* ('in particular') one can also read *lā siyamā*, with a single *y*. The former is standard, but some people use the lightened form, al-Farazdaq for instance.[569] It is said that he, being drunk, came past a pack of dogs. He greeted them and, not hearing an answer, he said:

The leaders of the tribe did not return my salutation
  when I came past at Postal Service Street,
and in partic'lar (*lā siyamā*) one who wore
  a purple woollen garment, sitting there."

"As for the metrical irregularity in 'so many splendid days you had,'" says Imru' al-Qays, "that is what I said in those pre-Islamic days. But the school-teachers in the Islamic period changed it according to their taste, and there is no harm in their preference. The various opinions on the case of *yawm* ('day') are equally plausible. But *siyya-*, with doubled *y*, is better and more usual than *siya-*." "Certainly;" replies the Sheikh, "if you use the lightened form it would contain merely two consonants, one of which is a weak one.[570]

"But tell me about the stanzaic poem that is attributed to you: is it genu- 17.3.4
ine?" He recites to him what some people have transmitted in his name:[571]

My friends, turn off the track and halt!
Then will the swift she-camels halt,
The Mahrī dromedaries, travelers at night,
Fast-footed in their march,
  And used to lengthy journeying.
They all turned off the track and stopped,
Preoccupied with worrying,
Still carried by the ruddy mounts,
But not consoled by them;
  The parties turned aside and stopped.

يا قوم إنّ الهوى إذا أصاب الفتى
في القلب ثمّ ارتقى فهدَّ بعضَ القُوى
فقد هَوى الرّجلُ

فيقول: لا والله ما سمعتُ هذا قطُّ، وإنه لَقَريٌّ لم أسلُكه، وإنّ الكذب لكثير، وأحسب هذا لبعض شعراء الإسلام، ولقد ظلمني وأساء إليّ! أبعد كلمتي التي أوّلها:

ألا انعَمْ صباحًا أيها الطَّلَلُ البالي وهل يَنْعَمَنْ من كان في العُصُرِ الخالي؟

وقولي:

خليليَّ مُرّا بي على أمّ جُنْدُبِ لأقضيَ حاجاتِ الفؤادِ المعذَّبِ

يقال لي مثلُ ذلك؟ والرَّجَز من أضعف الشعر، وهذا الوزن من أضعف الرَّجز.
فيعجَب، ملأ الله فؤاده بالسُّرور، لما سمعه من امرئ القيس ويقول: كيف تُنْشد: ١٧،٣،٥

جالت لتصرَعَني فقلت لها: اقْصِري إنّي امرؤٌ صَرعي عليكِ حَرام

أتقول: حرامُ، فتُقْوي؟ أم تقول: حرامِ، فتُخْرِجه مُخْرَج حَذامِ وقَطامِ؟ وقد كان بعض علماء الدَّولة الثانية يجعلك لا يجوز الإقواءُ عليك. فيقول امرؤ القيس: لا نَكِرة عندنا في الإقواء، أما سمعتَ البيت في هذه القصيدة:

فكأنّ بَدْرًا واصلٌ بكُتَيْفةٍ وكأنّما من عاقلٍ إرمامُ

فيقول: لقد صدقتَ يا أبا هِند، لأنّ إرمامًا هاهنا ليس واقعًا موقع الصِّفة فيُحمَلَ على المجاوَرة، لأنه محمول على كأنما، وإضافته إلى ياء النَّفس تضعِّف الغرض. وقد ذهب

My fellow tribesmen! When
Love hits a youthful man
First in his heart, then rises up,
And wrecks his strength—
That man has fallen deeply down.

Imru' al-Qays exclaims, "No, I swear by God I have never heard this! It is a style I have never attempted. Truly, a lot of lies are being told. I think it must be by some poet in Islamic times. He has wronged me and done me a bad turn! After my poem that begins:

A happy morning to you, O decaying traces!
—But can be happy he who lived in bygone times?

"And my poem

Two friends of mine, let's pay a visit to Umm Jundub,
so that I can fulfill a need for my tormented heart!

"is it conceivable that such things are attributed to me? *Rajaz*[572] is among the weakest kinds of poetry and this meter is one of the weakest kinds of *rajaz*!"

17.3.5 The Sheikh (may God fill his heart with joy!) is amazed by what he hears from Imru' al-Qays. "How do you recite," he asks, "this verse:

She swayed,[573] to throw me off. 'Hold it!', I said to her,
'You are forbidden to throw down a man such as I am!'

"Do you say *ḥarāmu* ('forbidden,' nominative), making an imperfect rhyme, or do your say *ḥarāmi*, making it like Ḥadhām(i) or Qaṭām(i)?[574] For some scholars of the Second Dynasty[575] think so much of you that they think you could not have committed such a fault."

Imru' al-Qays answers, "In our view there is nothing amiss with this imperfect rhyme. Have you not heard this verse from the same poem:

It is as if Badr were adjacent to Kutayfah,
and as if Irmām were part of 'Āqil."[576]

The Sheikh says, "You are right, Abū Hind, because 'Irmām' is not an attribute here, so that it could take the genitive by adjacency,[577] since it is dependent on the word *ka-annamā* ('it is as if'). Adding the possessive pronominal

بعض الناس إلى الإضافة في قول الفرزدق:

فَما تـدري إذا قعـدتْ عـليه أَسَـعْدُ اللهِ أكثَـرُ أمْ جُـذامِ

فقالوا: أضاف كما قال جريرٌ:

تِلْكُمْ قُرَيشِيَ والأنصارُ أنـصاري

وكذلك قوله:

وإذا غضِبْتُ رمَتْ وراِئيَ مازنٌ أولادُ جَـنْدَلتي كخَيـرِ الجَـنْدَلِ

وبعضهم يروي: أولادُ جندلةٍ كخَيْرِ الجندلِ، وجندلةُ هذه هي أمُّ مازن بن مالك بن عمرو بن تميم وهي من نساء قريش.

وإنّا لَنروي لك بيتاً ما هو في كلّ الرِّوايات، وأظُنّه مصنوعاً لأنّ فيه ما لم تجرِ عادتُك بمثله، وهو قولك: ٦،٣،١٧

وعمرُو بن دَرْماءَ الهُمامُ إذا غدا بِصـارمِهِ يمشي كمِشْـيةِ قَسْوَرا

فيقول: أبعد اللهُ الآخَر، لقد اخترص، فما اتَّرَص! وإنّ نسبةَ مثلِ هذا إليَّ لأعُدُّه إحدى الوَصَمات، فإن كان من فعله جاهلياً، فهو من الذين وُجدوا في النار صلياً، وإن كان من أهل الإسلام، فقد خبط في ظلام.

وإنما أُنكِرُ[1] حذفَ الهاء من قَسْوَرة، لأنه ليس بموضع الحذف، وقلَّ ما يُصاب في أشعار العرب مثلُ ذلك. فأمّا قول القائل:

إنّ ابنَ حارثَ إنْ أَشْـتَقْ لرؤيته أو أمتـدِحْه فإنّ الناس قد عَلِموا

فليس من هذا النحو، إذ كان التغيير إلى الأسماء الموضوعة أسرعَ منه إلى الأسماء التي هي نَكِراتٌ، إذ كانت النَّكرة أصلاً في الباب.

١ ب، ي، إف: (أُنْكَرَ)؛ راجع التعليق على الترجمة الإنكليزية.

suffix of the first person would weaken the intended effect.[578] Some people believe that such a possessive is found in the verse by al-Farazdaq:

> And you don't know, when she sits upon it,
> 'if Saʿd Allāh is more numerous or (my?) Judhām.'[579]

"They say that he used a possessive pronoun (*Judhāmī*, 'My Judhām'), as did Jarīr when he said:

> These are my Quraysh (*Qurayshiya*) and the Helpers are my helpers.'[580]

"And similarly when he said:

> And when I am angry the tribe of Māzin will be behind me, throwing,
> and the sons of my Jandalah ('Rock') are as the best of rocks.[581]

"Some recite it as 'the sons of Jandalah (*Jandalatin*) are as the best of rocks.' This Jandalah is the mother of Māzin ibn Mālik ibn ʿAmr ibn Tamīm; she is one of the women of Quraysh.

"We also transmit a verse of yours that is not found in all recensions, and 17.3.6
I suspect it is spurious, since it contains things that do not conform to your practice; it is this verse of yours:

> When in the morning ʿAmr ibn Darmā', the hero, comes
> with his cutting sword, he walks like a lion."

Imru' al-Qays says, "God blast the wretch! He has forged a lie and did not rectify. To attribute something like this to me, I consider it a scandal! If he who did this lived in pre-Islamic times, he is one of those found roasting in the flames;[582] if he was a Muslim, he was stumbling in the dark." The Sheikh says,[583] " I disapprove of the elision of the ending *-ah* of *qaswarah* ('lion'), for it cannot be elided here. This happens very rarely in the poetry of the Arabs. As for the verse by a certain poet:[584]

> Ibn Ḥārith,[585] whether I long to see him
> or aim to praise him—people know!

"—this is different, for changing the form of personal names occurs more readily than changing indefinite nouns, for the indefinite noun is the original in this respect."[586]

وينظر فإذا عَنْتَرة العَبْسيُّ متلدّدٌ في السعير، فيقول: ما لك يا أخا عَبْسٍ؟ كأنك لم تنطِق بقولك: ١٠٤،١٧

ولقـد شـرِبْتُ من المُـدامة بعدمـا ركد الهواجـرُ بالمَشُوفِ المُعْـلَمِ
بـزُجاجةٍ صـفراءَ ذاتِ أَسِـرَّةٍ قُـرِنتْ بأزهـرَ في الشِّمال مفـدَّمِ

وإنِّي إذا ذكرتُ قولك:

هل غادَرَ الشُّعَراءُ من متـردَّمِ

لأقولُ: إنّما قيل ذلك وديوان الشِّعر قليلٌ محفوظٌ. فأمّا الآنَ وقد كثُرت على الصائد ضِباب[١]، وعرفتَ مكانَ الجهل الرّبَاب. ولو سمعتَ ما قيل بعد مبعث النّبي، صلى الله عليه وسلّم، لعتبتَ نفسَك على ما قلتَ، وعلمتَ أنّ الأمر كما قال حبيب بن أوسٍ:

فلو كان يَفْنى الشِّعرُ أفناه ما قَرتْ حِياضُك منه في العصور الذواهبِ
ولكنّه صوْبُ العقول إذا انجلتْ سحائبُ منه أُعقِبتْ بسحائبِ

فيقول: وما حبيبكم هذا؟ فيقول: شاعرٌ ظهر في الإسلام. وينشده شيئاً من نظمه فيقول: أمّا الأصل فعربيٌّ، وأمّا الفرع فنطق به غبيٌّ، وليس هذا المذهب على ما تعرف قبائلُ العرب. فيقول، وهو ضاحكٌ مستبشرٌ: إنّما يُنكَر عليه المستعار، وقد جاءت العارية في أشعار كثيرٍ من المتقدّمين، إلا أنها لا تجتمع كاجتماعها فيما نظمه حبيبُ بن أوس.

فما أردتَ بالمَشوف المُعْلَمِ؟ الدينار أم الرِّداء؟ فيقول: أيَّ الوجهين أردتَ، فهو حسنٌ ولا ينتقض.

فيقول، جعل الله سمعه مستودَعاً كلَّ الصالحات: لقد شقّ عليَّ دخولُ مثلك إلى الجحيم، وكأنّ أُذني مُصْغيةٌ إلى قَيْنات الفُسطاط وهي تغرِّد بقولك:

---

١ كذا في ب، وفي ي، إف، ق: (الضباب) ولعله الصواب.

17.4.1 *The conversation with 'Antarah*

The Sheikh looks and sees 'Antarah al-'Absī,[587] wholly bewildered, in Hellfire. "What is wrong with you, my friend from 'Abs?" asks the Sheikh, "It is as if you never composed your lines:

And I have drunk, after the midday heat slowed down,
 some good old wine *bi-l-mashūfi l-mu'lam*,[588]
From a striped, yellow glass, paired, in my left
 hand, with a gleaming pitcher fitted with a strainer.

"When I think of your line:

Have poets still left anything to patch?[589]

"then I say: this was said when the total amount of recorded poetry was still small and committed to memory. But now that 'for the hunter there are too many lizards' and 'ten thousand people have become wizards,'[590] if you heard all the poetry that was composed after the mission of the Prophet (God bless and preserve him), then you would blame yourself for what you said and you would realize that it is rather as Ḥabīb ibn Aws said:

If poetry could be exhausted, then it would already have been so
 by the collected water in your cisterns, in past times.[591]
Rather, it is the rainfall of the mind: some clouds
 may vanish, only to be followed by more clouds."

"Who is this 'darling' (*ḥabīb*) of yours?" asks 'Antarah. "He is poet who appeared in the Islamic period," answers the Sheikh; he recites some of his verse. "The root is Arabic," says 'Antarah, "as for this branch of it, it is uttered by a dunce! This is not the style known to the Arab tribes." The Sheikh laughs, amused. "True, he was criticized for all these metaphors. Yet there are metaphorical expressions in many poems of the ancients; only they are not heaped together as in the poetry of Ḥabīb ibn Aws.

"But what did you mean by *bi-l-mashūf al-mu'lam*? A dinar or a garment?" 'Antarah replies, "Whichever way you prefer. Both are good and unobjectionable." Then the Sheikh (may God make his ears the repository of all pious deeds!) says, "I find it hard to bear that someone like you has entered Hell. It is as if my ears still listen to the singing girls in al-Fusṭāṭ, warbling your verses:[592]

أمِنْ سُمَيَّةَ دمعُ العين تذريفُ؟   لوأنَّ ذا منكِ قبلَ اليومِ معروفُ

تجلَّلتْني إذا أهوى العصا قِبَلي   كأنها رشأٌ في البيت مطروفُ

العبدُ عبدُكُمُ والمالُ مالُكُمُ   فهل عذابُكِ عنّي اليومَ مصروفُ

٢،٤،١٧

وإني لأتمثّلُ بقولك:

ولقد نزلتِ فلا تظنّي غيرَهُ   منّي بمنزلة المُحَبِّ المُكْرَمِ

ولقد وُفِّقْتَ في قولك: المُحَبِّ، لأنك جئت باللفظ على ما يجب في أحْبَبْتُ، وعامّة الشُّعراء يقولون: أحْبَبْتُ، فإذا صاروا إلى المفعول قالوا: محبوبٌ. قال زُهيرُ بن مسعودٍ الضَّبّيّ:

واضحةُ الغُرّةِ محبوبةٌ   والفَرَسُ الصالحُ محبوبُ

وقال بعض العلماء: لم يُسمَع بمُحَبٍّ إلا في بيت عنترة. وإنّ الذي قال: أحْبَبْتُ، لَيَجِب عليه أن يقول: مُحَبٌّ، إلا أنّ العرب اختارت: أحَبَّ في الفعل، وقالت في المفعول: محبوب. وكان سيبويه ينشد هذا البيت بكسر الهمزة:

إحِبُّ لحبِّها السُّودانَ حتى   إحِبَّ لحبِّها سُودَ الكِلابِ

فهذا على رأي من قال: مِغيرة، فكسر الميم على معنى الإتباع، وليس هو عنده على: حَبَبْتُ أحِبُّ.

وقد جاء حَبَبْتُ، قال الشاعر:

ووالله لولا تَمرُهُ ما حَبَبْتُه   ولا كان أدنى من عُبيدٍ ومُرْشِقِ

ويقال: إن أبا رَجاءٍ العُطارديّ قرأ: ﴿فاتَّبِعوني يَحبِبْكُمُ اللهُ﴾ بفتح الياء. والباب فيما

These tears, are they Sumayyah's, dripping from the eyes?
If only I had been aware of this from you before today!
She threw herself upon me when the stick fell down on me:
as if a young gazelle were in the tent, with tearful eyes.
This slave is *your* slave and this wealth is yours!
Your torment, will it be dispelled from me today?[593]

"I also like to quote this verse of yours:[594] 17.4.2

You have become to me—don't think it otherwise—
someone much loved and honored.

"You did right in using the word *muḥabb* ('loved'), for it is the word that is required by the form *aḥbabtu* ('I loved'), which is the form generally used by poets; but when they use a passive participle they turn to the form *maḥbūb*.[595] Zuhayr ibn Masʿūd al-Ḍabbī says:

With a bright white blaze, much loved (*maḥbūbah*):
a decent horse is loved indeed.

"Some scholar or other said that the word *muḥabb* is never heard, except in ʿAntarah's verse. Someone who says *aḥbabtu* ('I loved') must also say *muḥabb*; however, the Arabs chose to use *aḥabba* for the verb but they use *maḥbūb* for the passive participle. Sībawayh quotes this verse with the form *iḥibbu* ('I love'), with initial *i*:[596]

Because I love her I love black people: I even
love, for the love of her, black dogs.

"This is according to the view of those who say 'Mighīrah,'[597] with *i* after the *m*, for the sake of vowel harmony. But in his view this form is not from the verb *ḥababtu* - *aḥibbu* ('I loved - I love').[598] The form *ḥababtu* does in fact occur; a poet said:[599]

By God, but for his dates I would not love him (*mā ḥababtuhū*)
and he would not be beneath ʿUbayd and Murshaq.[600]

"It is said that Abū Rajāʾ al-ʿUṭāridī recited:[601] «So follow me and God will love you (*yaḥbibkumu*)». As a general rule verbs of geminate roots with a transitive meaning have *u* as vowel of the imperfect tense, as in *ʿadadtu* - *aʿuddu* ('I counted - I count') and *radadtu* - *aruddu* ('I sent back - I send back');

كان مضاعَفاً متعدّياً أن يجيء بالضَّمّ، كقولك: عَدَدْتُ أعُدُّ، ورَدَدْتُ أرُدُّ، وقد جاءت أشياءُ نوادرُ كقولهم: شَدَدْتُ الحبلَ أَشُدُّ وأَشِدُّ، ونَمَمْتُ الحديثَ أنُمّ وأنِمّ، وعَلَلْتُ القولَ أعُلُّ وأعِلُّ. وإذا كان غير متعدٍ فالباب الكسر، كقولهم: حلَّ عليه الدَّين يحِلُّ، وجلَّ الأمرُ يجِلُّ. والضمّ في غير المتعديّ أكثرُ من الكسر فيما كان متعدّياً، كقولهم: شَحَّ يَشُحُّ وَيشِحُّ، وشَبَّ الفَرَسُ يَشُبُّ ويَشِبُّ، وصحَّ الأمرُ يَصِحُّ ويَصُحُّ، وفحّتِ الحيّةُ تفِحُّ وتفُحُّ، وجَمَّ الماءُ يجِمُّ ويجُمُّ، وجدَّ في الأمر يجِدُّ ويجُدُّ في حروفٍ كثيرةٍ.

وينظر فإذا علْقَمة بن عَبَدَةَ فيقول: أَعزِزْ عليَّ بمكانك! ما أغنى عنك سِمطا لؤلؤك، ١٧،٥،١
يعني قصيدته التي على الباء:

طحا بك قلبٌ في الحِسان طَروبُ

والتي على الميم:

هل ما علِمتَ وما استُودِعتَ مكتومُ

فبالذي يقدِر على تخليصك، ما أردتَ بقولك:

فلا تَعْدِلي بيني وبين مُغمَّرٍ　　سقتْكِ روايا المُزْنِ حين تصُوبُ
وما القلب أمْ ما ذكْرُها رَبَعيَّةً　　يُخَطُّ لها من ثَرْمَداءَ قَليبُ

أعَنيْتَ بالقليب هذا الذي يُورَد أم القبر؟ ولكلٍ وجهٌ حسنٌ.

فيقول علقمة: إنّك لَتستضحك عابساً، وتُريد أن تجني[١] الثَّمَر يابساً، فعليك شُغْلَك أيها السليم!

---

١ في ب: (تَجْنِيَ) كما في نسخة الأصل وفي ي، إف، ق (تجني).

but there are some rare irregular cases, such as *shadadtu l-ḥabl* ('I fastened the rope'), with imperfect tense both *ashuddu* and *ashiddu*, *namamtu l-ḥadīth* ('I reported slanderous talk'), imperfect tense *anummu* or *animmu*, and *ʿalaltu l-qawl* ('I repeated the words'), imperfect tense *aʿullu* and *aʿillu*. If such a verb is intransitive it has *i* as the vowel of the imperfect as a general rule, as in *ḥalla ʿalayhi l-dayn* ('the debt became due for him'), imperfect *yaḥillu*, or *jalla l-amr* ('the matter became important'), imperfect *yajillu*. The imperfect vowel *u* occurs more often in intransitive verbs than the vowel *i* occurs in transitive verbs; for example in *shaḥḥa* ('to be stingy'), imperfect *yashuḥḥu* or *yashiḥḥu*, *shabba l-faras* ('the horse pranced'), imperfect *yashubbu* or *yashibbu*, *ṣaḥḥa l-amr* ('the matter was correct'), imperfect *yaṣiḥḥu* or *yaṣuḥḥu*, *faḥḥat al-ḥayyah* ('the snake hissed'), imperfect *tafiḥḥu* or *tafuḥḥu*, *jamma l-māʾ* ('the water gathered'), imperfect *yajimmu* or *yajummu*, *jadda fī l-amr* ('he was serious about the matter'), imperfect *yajiddu* or *yajuddu*, and many other verbs."

The Sheikh looks up and sees ʿAlqamah ibn ʿAbadah. "How painful to see you in this place!" he exclaims. "Of no avail to you now are your two 'strings of pearl'!"[602] (He means his poem rhyming in *-ūbū*: 17.5.1

The conversation with ʿAlqamah

A heart by pretty girls enraptured carried you away,

and the other rhyming in *-ūmū*:

Is what you know, what you have been entrusted with, concealed?[603])

"By Him who is able to release you, what did you mean by:

Do not equate me then, girl, with a callow youth—
may rain-filled clouds pour down their loads on you!
—But why's your heart still thinking of her, that Rabīʿah girl,
for whom a well is being dug in Tharmadāʾ?[604]

"By 'well' did you mean a well one goes to for water, or is it a grave? Both interpretations make good sense." ʿAlqamah replies, "You try to make laugh someone who would rather cry;[605] you want to pluck fruit when it is dry! Mind your own business, you who are saved!"

فيقول: لو شفعتْ لأحدٍ أبياتٌ صادقةٌ ليس فيها ذكر الله، سبحانه، لشفعتْ لك أبياتُك في وصف النساء، أعني قولك: ٢،٥،١٧

فإن تسألوني بالنساء فإنني بصيرٌ بأدواء النساء طبيبُ
إذا شاب رأسُ المرء أو قلّ مالُهُ فليس له في ودّهنّ نصيبُ
يُرِدْن ثَراءَ المال حيث علِمنَه وشَرْخُ الشَّباب عندهنّ عجيبُ

ولو صادفتُ منك راحةً لسألتُك عن قولك:

وفي كلِّ حيٍّ قد خَبَطَ بنعمةٍ فحُقَّ لشاسٍ من نَداكَ ذَنوبُ

أهكذا نطقتَ بها طاءً مشدّدةً، أم قالها كذلك عربيٌّ سواك؟ فقد يجوز أن يقول الشاعر الكلمة، فيغيّرها عن تلك الحال الرُّواة.

وإنّ في نفسي لحاجةً من قولك:

كأسُ عزيزٍ من الأعناب عتّقها لبعض أربابها حانيّةٌ حُومُ

فقد اختلف الناس في قولك حُومُ، فقيل: أراد حُمًّا، أي سُودًا، فأبدل من إحدى الميمَيْن واوًا. وقيل: أراد حَوْمًا، أي كثيرًا، فضمّ الحاء للضَّرورة، وقيل: حُومٌ يُحام بها على الشَّرب، أي يُطاف.

وكذلك قولك:

يَهْذي بها أكلَفُ الخدَّين مختَبَرٌ من الجِمال كثيرُ اللحم عيثُومُ

فرُوِي: يهدي، بالدال غير مُعجَمةٍ، ويهذي بذالٍ معجمةٍ. وقيل: مختَبَرٌ، من اختبار الحوائل من اللواقح، وقيل: هو من الخبير، أي الزَّبَد، وقيل: الخبير اللحم، وقيل: هو الوَبَر.

The Sheikh says, "If truthful verses could intercede for you, even though God, praised be He, is not mentioned in them, then your verses on women could; I mean your lines: 17.5.2

You ask me about women? I'm a specialist,
a doctor, knowing about women's ailments all![606]
When a man's hair turns gray, or when his wealth is scarce,
he has no share of their affection.
What women want is wealth, wherever they know it is;
men's bloom of youth is wonderful to them.

"If I found you in more comfortable circumstances I would ask you about your verse:

On every tribe you have conferred (*khabaṭṭa*) a benefit:
so Sha's, too, is entitled to a bucketful of boon.[607]

"Did you really pronounce it as *khabaṭṭa*, with doubled *ṭ*?[608] Or did some other Arab say it like that? After all, it is possible for a poet to say one thing in a poem after which the transmitters change it.—I also want to ask about your verse:

A cup of grape-wine of a powerful man, that was kept for ages
for some of its owners; it came from the wine shop, in plenty
(*ḥūm*).[609]

"People have different views about your word *ḥūm*. Some say: he means *ḥumm*, i.e. 'black,' with one *m* changed into *w*;[610] but others say: he means *ḥawm*, meaning 'plenty,' with the *a* changed into *u*, as required by the rhyme. Yet others say that *ḥūm* means 'circulated (*yuḥām bihā*) for the drinkers,' i.e. 'passed round.' Likewise, your verse:

One with reddish-brown cheeks leads them, experienced (*mukhtabar*),
a camel stallion, thickly fleshed, bulky.

"This has been transmitted with *yahdī* ('he leads'), with *d*, and with *yahdhī*, with *dh*.[611] As for the word *mukhtabar*, it is said that it refers to finding out the difference between non-pregnant camels and those that have been impregnated; others say that it comes from *khabīr*, meaning 'foam at the mouth,' or, according to others, 'flesh,' or 'camel hair.'"

١،٦،١٧ فليتَ شِعْري ما فعل عمرو بن كلثوم، فيقال: ها هوذا من تحتِك، إن شئت أن تحاوره فحاوِرْه. فيقول: كيف أنت أيها المصطبِح بصحن الغانية، والمغتبِق من الدُّنيا الفانية؟ لَوَدِدتُ أنك لم تساند في قولك:

كأنّ مُتونهنّ متونُ غُدْرٍ تصفِّقها الرِّياحُ إذا جرَيْنا

فيقول عمروٌ: إنك لَقرير العين لا تشعُر بما نحن فيه، فاشْغَلْ نفسَك بتمجيد الله واترُكْ ما ذهب فإنه لا يعود. وأمّا ذكرُك سِنادي، فإنّ الإخوةَ لَيكونون ثلاثةً أو أربعةً، ويكون فيهم الأعرج أو الأبخق فلا يُعابون بذلك، فكيف إذا بلغوا المائة في العدد، ورُهاقَها في المُدَد؟ فيقول: أَعْزِزْ عليَّ بأنك قُصرتَ على شُربِ حميم، وأُخذتَ بعملك الذميم، من بعدِ ماكانت تُسْبأُ لك القهوةُ من خُصٍّ أو غير خُصّ، تقابلك بلون الحُصّ.

وقالوا في قولك سَخينا قولين: أحدهما أنه فَعِلْنا من السَّخاء والنون نونُ المتكلمين، والآخر أنه من الماء السخين لأنّ الأندَرِين وقاصِرِين كانتا في ذلك الزمن للرُّوم، ومن شأنهم أن يشربوا الخمر بالماء السخين في صيف وشتاء.

٢،٦،١٧ ولقد سُئل بعض الأدباء بمدينة السلام عن قولك:

فما وجدتْ كوجْدي أمُّ سَقْبٍ أَضلّتْه فرجّعتِ الحنينا
ولا شَمْطاءُ لم يترُكْ شَقاها لها من تِسْعةٍ إلّا جنينا

هل يجوز نصبُ شَمْطاء؟ فلم يُجِبْ بشيء، وذلك يجوز عندي من وجهين: أحدُهما على إضمار فعلٍ دلَّ عليه السامعَ معرفتُه به، كأنك قلت: ولا أذكرُ شمطاءَ، أي أنّ حنينها شديدٌ، ويجوز أن يكون على قولك: ولا تَنْسَ شمطاءَ، أو نحو ذلك من الأفعال، وهذا كقولك: إنّ كعب بن مامة جَوادٌ ولا حاتماً، أي ولا أذكر حاتماً، أي أنه جوادٌ عظيم الجُود، قد استغنيتُ عن ذكره باشتهاره.

The Sheikh muses, "I wonder what ʿAmr ibn Kulthūm is doing." He is told, "There he is, below you! If you wish you can have a chat with him." The Sheikh asks him, "How are you, 'drinker in the morning' from the bowl of the pretty woman, and 'drinker in the evening' in the Perishable World?[612] I wish you had not made a faulty rhyme in your verse: 17.6.1

The conversation with ʿAmr ibn Kulthūm

Their coats of mail were like the surfaces
of ponds, when struck by skimming winds."[613]

ʿAmr replies, "You are happy and unaware of our misery! Rather keep yourself busy with glorifying God and let alone what is past, for it will never return. As for that rhyming defect of mine that you mention, well, it happens that among three or four brothers there is one who is lame or one-eyed, but they are not blamed for that. Let alone when their number reaches five score, or even more!"[614] "I am very sorry" says the Sheikh, "that now you drink nothing but water boiling hot,[615] because you sinned such a lot; and that after you used to purchase vintage wine from Khuṣṣ or elsewhere, standing before you, like saffron its hue![616]—They have two explanations of the word *sakhīnā*: one is that it is from *sakhāʾ*, 'generosity,' i.e., 'we were generous (with the wine),' and the other is that it derives from 'hot water' (*al-māʾ al-sakhīn*),[617] because al-Andarīn and Qāṣirīn[618] belonged to the Byzantines at that time, and they used to drink wine mixed with hot water, in summer or winter.

"Some lettered person in Baghdad was once asked about your verses: 17.6.2

Such grief as mine has not been suffered by a camel mother who
has lost her calf and lets resound her yearning moans,
Nor by a gray-haired woman whose misfortune left to her
of nine sons none who are not buried.

"Is it possible to read *shamṭāʾ* ('gray-haired woman') in the accusative? The man did not answer, but in my opinion this is possible on two grounds. One is that a verb is implied, to which the listener's knowledge guides him, as when one says, 'nor *shall I mention* a gray-haired woman,' namely that her yearning is strong. It is also possible that it is as when one says, 'And *do not forget* a gray-haired woman,' or some other verb.[619] This is like saying 'Kaʿb ibn Māmah is generous, and not (*wa-lā*) Ḥātim,' that is, 'I shall not mention Ḥātim,' meaning 'he is extremely generous and I need not mention him since he is so famous.'[620]

والآخَر، أن يكون مِنْ وَلاه المَطَرُ إذا سقاه السَّقْيَةَ الثانية، أي هذا الحنين اتَّفق مع حنيني، فكأنه قد صار له وليّاً، ويحتمل أن يكون من وَلِيَ يَلي، وقَلْبَ الياءَ على اللغة الطائيّة.

وينظر فإذا الحارث اليَشْكُري فيقول: لقد أتعبْتَ الرُّواة في تفسير قولك: ١،٧،١٧

زعموا أنّ كلَّ مَنْ ضَرَبَ العَيْـ ـرَ مُوالٍ لنا وأنّا الوَلاءُ

وما أحسَبُك أردتَ إلا العيْرَ الحمار.

ولقد شنَّعتَ هذه الكلمة بالإقواء في ذلك البيت، ويجوز أن تكون لُغتُكَ أن تقف على آخر البيت ساكناً، وإذا فعلتَ ذلك اشتبه المُطْلَق بالمقيّد، وصارت هذه القصيدة مضافةً إلى قول الراجز:

دارٌ لظَمْيا وأين ظَمْيا أَهَلَكَتْ أمْ هي بين الأحْيا

وبعض الناس ينشد قولك:

فِعشَنْ بخيرٍ لا يَضِرْ كَ النُّوكُ ما أُعطيتَ جَدّا

فيجمع بين تحريك الشِّين وحذف الياء، من عاش يعيش، وذلك قليل رديءٌ. ومنه قول الآخَر:

متى تَشَئِي يا أمَّ عثمانَ تَصرِمي وأُوذِنْكِ إيذانَ الخليطِ المُزايِلِ

وإنّما الكلام: متى تَشائي، لأنّ هذا الساكن إذا حُرِّك عاد الساكنُ المحذوف. ولقد أحسنتَ في قولك:

لا تَكْسَعِ الشَّوْلَ بأغبارِها إنّكَ لا تدري مَنِ الناتِجُ

"The other ground is that *walā* can be derived from *walāhu l-maṭar*, 'the rain irrigated it a second time'; meaning that this yearning concurs with my yearning, so it has become, as it were, its associate (*waliyy*). It is also conceivable that it is from the verb *waliya – yalī* ('to be near, to follow'), which has been changed into *walā*, according to the dialect of the tribe of Ṭayyi'."

The Sheikh has another look and sees al-Ḥārith al-Yashkurī.[621] He says to him, "You have given much trouble to the transmitters, with the explanation of your verse: 17.7.1

al-Ḥārith ibn Ḥillizah

They claim that everybody who has 'beaten the wild ass'
is a vassal unto us and that we are their protectors.

"I think you must have meant a real wild ass.[622] And you made a bad mistake in the rhyme in that poem.[623] Perhaps in your dialect you do not pronounce the final vowel at the end of a verse; but when you do that rhymes ending in a vowel and rhymes ending on a consonant will get confused, and this ode of yours would be on a par with these verses of a *rajaz* poet:

An abode that belonged to Ẓamyā—but where is Ẓamyā?
Has she died or is she still among the living?[624]

"Some people recite this verse of yours:

So live (*fa-ʿishan*) in good health; may foolishness not harm
you, as long as you will be granted good fortune,

"with a vowel after the *sh* of *ʿishan* together with a shortening of the long *ī*, from the verb *ʿāsha - yaʿīshu* ('to live'); and this is rare and ugly.[625] It is the same in the verse by another poet:

Whenever you wish (*tasha'ī*), O Umm ʿUthmān, sever the bond,
and I shall inform you like a parting friend.

"In normal speech one would say *tashā'ī*, for when *tasha'* is followed by a vowel, the vowel length is restored.[626] But this verse of yours is good:[627]

Don't stop the milk flow of your camels, leaving them with milk:
you don't know who may help them to give birth!

وقد كانوا في الجاهليّة يَعْكِسون ناقةَ الميّت على قبره، ويزعُمون أنه إذا نهض لحَشْره ١٧،٧،٢
وجدها قد بُعثت له فيركبُها فليتَه لا يَهِضُ بثقله مَنْكِبها. وهيهات! بل حُشروا عُراةً حُفاةً بُهْماً، أي غُرْلاً، وتلك البليّة التي ذكرتَ في قولك:

أتلهّى بها الهواجرَ إذ كُـ   ـلُّ ابنِ هَمٍّ بليّـةٌ عـمْيـاءُ

ويعمد لسؤال طَرَفة بن العبد فيقول: يا ابن أخي يا طرفة خفّف الله عنك، أتذكر قولك: ١٧،٨،١

كريمٌ يُرَوِّي نفسَه في حياته   ستعلمُ إن مُتْنا غداً أيُّنا الصَّدي

وقولك:

أرى قبرَ نحّامٍ بخيلٍ بمالِهِ   كقبرِ غويٍّ في البَطالة مُفْسِدِ

وقولك:

متى تأتِني أَصْبِحْكَ كأساً رَوِيّةً   وإن كنتَ عنها غانيًا فاغْنَ وازْدَدِ

فكيف صَبوحك الآن وغَبوقك؟ إنّي لأحسَبهما حميماً، لا يفتأ مَنْ شرِبهما ذميماً.

وهذا البيت يُتنازَع فيه: فيَنْسُبه إليك قومٌ وينسبه آخرون إلى عَديّ بن زيدٍ، ١٧،٨،٢
وهو بكلامك أشبهُ، والبيت:

وأصْفَرَ مضبوحٍ نظرتُ حَويرَهُ   على النار واستودعتُه كفَّ مُجْمِدِ

وشدَّ ما اختلف النُّحاة في قولك:

ألا أيهاذا الزاجري أَحْضُرَ الوغى   وأن أشهَدَ اللّذّاتِ هل أنت مُخْلِدي؟

وأمّا سيبويه فيكرَه نَصْبَ أحضرَ، لأنه يعتقد أنّ عوامل الأفعال لا تُضمَر. وكان

"In pre-Islamic days they used to tether a she-camel, its head turned, to the grave of its deceased owner, claiming that when the man was resurrected he would find it revived for him, so that he could mount it straight.[628] O, may he never break her shoulder with his weight! But they are wrong! Rather, people will be resurrected naked, barefoot, uncircumcised.[629]—This camel left to die is mentioned in your verse: 17.7.2

My mount is my pleasure on hot afternoons, when
each worrying man is a blind beast-of-death!"

The Sheikh turns to Ṭarafah ibn al-ʿAbd[630] and asks him, "Ṭarafah, my friend,[631] may God lighten your suffering! Do you remember your verse: 17.8.1

The conversation with Ṭarafah

I am a noble man who drinks his fill as long as he's alive;
when we have died you'll know who is the thirsty one of us!

"and

I see no difference between a grumbling miser's grave
and that of one who frivolously, rashly spends his wealth.

"and

Whenever you come to me I'll let you have a quenching morning drink;
and if you've had enough, then be content and more content!

"But how are your morning drink and evening drink now? Both consist of 'water boiling hot,' I think; forever condemned are those who take this drink!

"There is some dispute about the following verse: some people ascribe it to you and others attribute it to ʿAdī ibn Zayd; but it resembles more your style: 17.8.2

From many a yellow, fire-scorched arrow I awaited a reply,
beside the fire, having entrusted it to an unlucky hand.[632]

"The grammarians strongly differ in their views on your verse:

O you who are rebuking me I'm present at the battle's din,
and that I attend pleasures: can you let me live forever?

"Sībawayh dislikes the subjunctive *aḥḍura* ('[that] I'm present'), because he believes that the particles that govern the modes cannot be hidden.[633]

الكوفيّون يَنْصِبون أحضُر بالحرف المقدَّر، ويقوّي ذلك: وأن أشهدَ اللّذّات، فجئت بأنْ، وليس هذا بأبعد من قوله:

مَشائيمُ ليسوا مُصْلِحين قَبيلةً ولا ناعبٍ إلا ببَيْنٍ غُرابُها

وقد حكى المازنيُّ عن عليّ بن قُطْرُبٍ أنه سمع أباه قطرباً يحكي عن بعض العرب نصْبَ أحضُر.

ولقد جئتَ بأعجوبةٍ في قولك:

لو كان في أملاكنا ملِكٌ يَعصِر فينا كالذي تَعصِرْ
لاجتبْتُ صَحْنَيِ العراقِ على حَرْفٍ أمونٍ دَفُّها أَزْوَرْ
متَّعني يومَ الرحيل بها فَرْعٌ تنقّاه القِداحُ يَسَرْ

ولكنّك سلكتَ مَسالك العرب، فجئت بقريِّ كلمة المرقّش:

هل بالديار أن تُجيبَ صَمَمْ؟ لو كان حيّاً ناطقاً كلَّمْ

وقول الأعشى:

أَقْصِرْ فكلُّ طالبٍ سيَمَلّ

على أنَّ مرقّشاً خلط في كلمته فقال:

ماذا علينا أن غزا ملِكٌ من آل جَفْنةَ ظالمٌ مُرْغِمْ

وهذا خروجٌ عمّا ذهب إليه الخليل.

ولقد كثُرت في أمرك أقاويلُ الناس: فمنهم من يزعُم أنك في مُلك النُّعمان اعتُقلتَ، وقال قومٌ: بل الذي فعل به ما فعل عمرو بن هندٍ. ولو لم يكن لك أثرٌ في العاجلة إلا قصيدتك التي على الدال، لكنتَ قد أبقيت أثراً حسناً. ٣،٨،١٧

فيقول طرفة: ودِدتُ أني لم أنطِق مِصراعاً، وعَدِمتُ في الدار الزائلة إمراعاً،

The Kūfan grammarians, however, read it as a subjunctive on account of the implied particle. This is corroborated by its presence in 'that I attend pleasures,' where you have 'that.' This is not more unusual than in the verse:

Ill-omened people, who do not make a tribe prosper,
and whose crow is croaking of naught but ill omen.[634]

"Al-Māzinī relates from 'Alī ibn Quṭrub that the latter had heard his father Quṭrub quote some Bedouin Arab who read *aḥḍura*, with a subjunctive.— You made a marvellous piece when you said:

If among us there were kings who bestow
upon us like what you are bestowing on us,
I would cross the two plains of Iraq[635] on a lean,
trusty she-camel, with flanks sloping down.
On the day of departure I was given pleasure with her,
by a branch selected by the arrow shafts . . . (?)[636]

"But you followed the ways of the Bedouin Arabs, doing what al-Muraqqish did in his poem beginning:

The abodes, are they deaf, since they do not reply?
If only they lived and had speech, they would speak!

"Or al-A'shā when he says:

Leave off! For everyone will become weary of what once he sought.

"But Muraqqish mixed meters[637] in his poem when he said:

Why should we be blamed if a raid has been made
by a king of the Jafnids, an unjust oppressor?

"This goes against the system of al-Khalīl.[638]

"Much has been speculated," continues the Sheikh, "about what happened to you. Some people assert that you were imprisoned during the rule of al-Nu'mān, others say that it was 'Amr ibn Hind who did these things to you. But if you had left no other trace in the Fleeting World than your ode rhyming on *-dī*,[639] you would have left your mark splendidly." 17.8.3

"I wish," replies Ṭarafah, "I had not uttered one single hemistich and I had not found, in the Transitory World, any rich pasturing ground, but instead

ودخلت الجنّة مع الهَمَج والطَّغام، ولم يُعْمَد لِمَرْسِني بالإرغام، وكيف لي بهَدْءٍ وسُكون، أركَنُ إليه بعض الركون؟ ﴿وَأَمَّا ٱلْقَاسِطُونَ فَكَانُوا لِجَهَنَّمَ حَطَبًا﴾ .

ويلفِت عُنقَه يتأمّل، فإذا هو بأوْس بن حَجَر، فيقول: يا أوس، إنّ أصحابك لا يجيبون ١٠،٩،١٧
السائل فهل لي عندك من جوابٍ؟ فإنّي أريد أن أسألك عن هذا البيت:

وقارفتْ وهْيَ لم تَجْرَب وباع لها ... من الفَصافص بالنُّمِّيّ سِفْسيرُ

فإنّه في قصيدتك التي أوّلها:

هل عاجلٌ من مَتاع الحيِّ منظورُ ... أم بيتُ دَوْمةَ بعد الوصل مهجورُ

ويُروى في قصيدة النابغة التي أوّلها:

ودِّعْ أُمامةَ والتوديعُ تعذيرُ ... وما وَداعُك مَنْ قفَّتْ به العِيرُ

وكذلك البيت الذي قبله:

قد عُرِّيَتْ نِصفَ حَوْلٍ أَشْهُرًا جُدُدًا ... تَسفي على رَحْلها في الحِيرة المُورُ

وكذلك قوله:

إنّ الرحيل إلى قومٍ وإن بعُدوا ... أمسوْا ومِن دونِهم ثَهْلانُ فالنِّيرُ

وكِلاكُما[1] معدود في الفحول، فعلى أيِّ شيءٍ يُحَمَل ذلك؟ فلم تزل تعجبني لاميّتُك التي ذكرتَ فيها الجُرْجة، وهي الخريطة من الأَدَم فقلتَ لمّا وصفتَ القوس:

فجئتُ ببيْعي مُوليًا لا أَزيدُهُ ... عليه بها حتى يؤوبَ المنخَّلُ
ثلاثةُ أبرادٍ جِيادٍ وجُرْجةٌ ... وأدكَنُ من أَرْيِ الدَّبورِ معسَّلُ

---

١ في النسخ: (كلاهما) والسياق يقتضي الخطاب.

had entered Paradise with the mob and the vulgar herd at least, without having been led forcibly with a halter like a beast. How could I get some quiet and some peace, whereby I find at least some release? «But those who are unjust are firewood for Hell».”[640]

The Sheikh turns his head in order to have a good look. There he sees Aws ibn Ḥajar. He says, “Aws! Your companions do not answer my questions. Will you give me an answer? For I want to ask you about your verse:[641] **17.9.1** *The conversation with Aws ibn Ḥajar*

She did not get the mange, but nearly did; a groom
has bought for her fresh clover for some coins.

“It is from your ode that begins:

Can any of the tribe’s belongings still be seen,
or is, after our union, Dawmah’s dwelling now deserted?

“But it has also been transmitted as a line in al-Nābighah’s[642] ode that begins:

Say farewell to Umāmah—but saying farewell is so hard!
How can you bid farewell to one who is taken away by the caravan?

“It is the same with the line that precedes it:

For half a year, month after month, she was not ridden,
dust being blown upon her saddle in al-Ḥīrah by the wind.

“And also his verse:

The departure is to a tribe, though they are far,
who are now beyond Mount Thahlān and al-Nīr.

“Now both of you are counted among the great poets. So how can this confusion be explained?—Actually, I have always admired your poem rhyming in *-lū*, in which your mention a *jurjah*, which is a leather saddlebag. You said, after having described a bow:

Then I came back with what I’d bought; I’ll give no more
for it (I shall, when pigs will fly!)[643]
Than three good cloaks, a saddle-bag,
and a dark skin filled with bees’ honey.”

فيقول أوس: قد بلغني أنّ نابغة بني ذُبيان في الجنّة، فاسأله عمّا بدا لك فلعلّه يُخبرك، ٢،٩،١٧
فإنّه أجدرُ بأن يعي هذه الأشياء، فأمّا أنا فقد ذهلتُ: نارٌ تُوقَد، وبَنانٌ يُعقَد؛ إذا غلب عليّ الظَّمأ، رُفع لي شيءٌ كالنهر، فإذا اغترفتُ منه لأشرَب، وجدتُه سعيرًا مضطرِماً، فليتني أصبحتُ دَرِماً، وهو الذي يقال فيه: أوْدى دَرِمٌ. وهو من بني دُبّ بن مُرّة بن ذُهْل بن شيْبان ولقد دخل الجنّة من هو شرٌّ منّي، ولكنّ المغفرة أرزاقٌ، كأنها النَّشَب في الدار العاجلة.

٣،٩،١٧ فيقول، صار وليُّه من المتبوعين، وشانئُه بالسَّفَه من المسبوعين: إنّما أردتُ أن آخذَ عنك هذه الألفاظ، فأُتحِف بها أهلَ الجنّة فأقول: قال لي أوسٌ، وأخبرني أبو شُريح.

وكان في عَزْمي أن أسألك عمّا حكاه سيبويه في قولك:

تُواهِقُ رِجلاها يداه ورأسُه لها قَتَبٌ خلْفَ الحقيبة رادفُ

فإني لا أختار أن تُرفَع الرِّجلان واليدان، ولم تدعُ إلى ذلك ضرورةٌ، لأنك لو قلت: تواهق رجليها يداه لم يَزِغ الوزنُ؛ ولعلّك، إن صحّ قولك لذلك، أن تكون طلبتَ المشاكَهة، وهذا المذهب يَقوى إذا رُوِي: يداها بالإضافة إلى المؤنَّث، فأمّا في حال الإضافة إلى ضمير المذكَّر فلا قُوّة له.

وإنّي لكارهٌ قولك:

والخيلُ خارجةٌ من القَسْطالِ

أخرجتَ الاسمَ إلى مثالٍ قليلٍ، لأنّ فَعْلالاً لم يجئ في غير المُضاعَف، وقد حُكي: ناقةٌ بها خَزْعالٌ، أي بها ظَلَعٌ.

١٠،١٧ ويرى رجلاً في النار لا يميّزه من غيره، فيقول: من أنت أيها الشَّقيّ؟ فيقول: أنا أبو كبيرٍ الهُذَلي، عامر بن الحُلَيس، فيقول: إنّك لَمِن أعلام هُذيلٍ، ولكني لم أوثِر قولك:

Aws replies, "I heard that al-Nābighah of the Banū Dhubyān is in Paradise! Ask him whatever occurs to you and he may tell you. He is more likely to pay attention to these things than me. As for me, I have become oblivious of all that. A fire has been kindled, fingers have been crossed.[644] When I am overcome with thirst, something looking like a river is raised for me, but when I scoop up some of it to drink I find it to be a blazing fire. I wish I were Darim!—He is the one of whom it is said, 'Darim has perished'; one of the Banū Dubb ibn Murrah ibn Dhuhl ibn Shaybān.[645]—Some worse people than I have entered Paradise! But it is not everybody's fortune to be granted forgiveness, it is like wealth in the Fleeting World." 17.9.2

The Sheikh replies (may his friends be obeyed and those fools who hate him be made afraid!), "I should like to quote these words of yours and present them to those who live in Paradise, saying, 'Aws said to me, Abū Shurayḥ told me!'—I intended to ask you about what Sībawayh says about your verse: 17.9.3

Her hind legs (*rijlāhā*) keep pace with his forelegs (*yadāhu*); his head
appears like a pack saddle mounted behind the saddle bag.[646]

"I do not think it is proper to put both 'hind legs' and 'forelegs' in the nominative; there is no metrical necessity that calls for this, because if you had said 'his forelegs (*yadāhu*, nominative) keep pace with her hind legs (*rijlayhā*, accusative),' the meter would not be impaired. Perhaps—if you really said it like this—you strove to achieve assonance; this would have a stronger effect if one read *yadāhā* ('her forelegs'), with a feminine suffix; but in this case, with a masculine suffix, it has no effect. And I really dislike this verse of yours:

The horses emerge from the dust cloud (*qasṭāl*),

"where you changed the noun into a rare pattern, for CaCCāC is found only for reduplicate roots,[647] even though the expression 'a she-camel with *khazʿāl*,' i.e., 'with a limp' has been recorded."

17.10

The conversations with the Hudhalī poets Abū Kabīr and Ṣakhr al-Ghayy

The Sheikh sees a man in the Fire; he is unable to discern his identity. "Who are you, poor soul?" he asks. "I am Abū Kabīr al-Hudhalī ʿĀmir ibn al-Ḥulays," replies the man. The Sheikh says, "You are one of the leading poets of Hudhayl! However, I do not like your words:

أَزُهيرُ هل عن شيْبَةٍ من مَعْدَلِ ‏ أم لا سبيلَ إلى الشَّباب الأوّلِ

وقلتَ في الأخرى:

أَزُهيرُ هل عن شيْبَةٍ من مَصْرِفِ ‏ أم لا خلودَ لعاجزٍ متكلِّفِ

وقلتَ في الثالثة:

أَزُهيرُ هل عن شيْبَةٍ من مَعْكِمِ

أي من مَحْبَس. فهذا يدُلُّ على ضِيقِ عَطَنك بالقريض، فهلا ابتدأتَ كلَّ قصيدة بفَنّ؟ والأصمعيُّ لم يَرْوِ لك إلا هذه القصائد الثلاث، وقد حُكي أنه يُروى عنك الرائية التي أوّلها:

أَزُهيرُ هل عن شيْبَةٍ من مَقْصَرِ

وأَحْسِنْ بقولك:

ولقد وردتُ الماءَ لم يشرَبْ به ‏ بين الشتاء إلى شهور الصَّيِّفِ
إلا عواسلُ كالمِراط مُعيدةً ‏ بالليل مَوْرِدَ أيِّمٍ متغضِّفِ
زَقَبٌ يظلُّ الذِّئبُ يتْبع ظِلَّهُ ‏ فيه فيستنُّ استنانَ الأخلفِ
فصددتُ عنه ظامئًا وتركتُه ‏ يهتزُّ غَلْفَقُه كأن لم يُكْشَفِ

فيقول أبو كبير الهذليّ: كيف لي أن أقضِم على جَمَراتٍ مُحْرِقاتٍ، لأَرِدَ عِذابًا غَدِقاتٍ؟ وإنّما كلامُ أهلِ سَقَرَ ويلٌ وعويلٌ، ليس لهم إلا ذلك حَويلٌ، فاذهبْ لِطيّتك، واحذَرْ أن تُشغَل عن مَطِيَّتك.

فيقول، بلّغه الله أقاصِيَ الأمل: كيف لا أَجْذَل وقد ضُمنتْ لي الرَّحمة الدائمة، ضَمِنَها من يصدُق ضَمانُه، ويَعمُّ أهلَ الخِيفة أمانُه؟

Zuhayr! Is there no way to keep gray hair away?
    Is there no going back to one's first youth?[648]

"For in another poem you said:

Zuhayr! Is there no way to turn gray hair away?
    Is there no staying for a weak, much-burdened man?

"And in a third you said:

Zuhayr! Is there no way to keep gray hair at bay?

"—meaning 'to restrain.'—This shows the limitation of your poetic talents. Why did you not begin each poem in a different manner? Al-Aṣmaʿī transmitted only these poems of yours; it is said that a fourth poem is transmitted in your name, one rhyming in *-rī*, which begins:

Zuhayr! Is there no way to hold gray hair away?

"But these verses are very fine:

And I came to the well, where none had drunk
    between the winter and the months of spring,
Except fast-moving wolves like unfletched arrows,
    back at the well at night, where a lone coiling viper drinks,
A narrow path, on which the wolf keeps following his shadow,
    keeping his body at an angle as he goes.
I turned away from it, still thirsty, and I left it, while
    the duckweed rippled, as if it had not been cleared before."

Abū Kabīr al-Hudhalī replied, "How can I gnaw my way through heaps of burning coal, to arrive at a sweet-streaming water hole? The speech of the inhabitants of Hell is Woe and Wail, they have naught else that will avail! Go away, on your intended course, and take care you are not distracted from your horse!"

The Sheikh (may God make him reach the utmost of his hopes!) says, "How can I not be merry, since I have been guaranteed eternal mercy, by Him whose guarantee is true, and whose safeguard encompasses all those who fear Him, too?"

١١،١٧ فيقول: ما فعل صَخرُ الغَيِّ؟ فيقال: هاهو حيث تراه. فيقول: يا صخر الغيّ ما فعلت دَهْماؤك؟ لا أرضُك لها ولا سماؤك! كانت في عهدك وشبابها رؤدٌ، يأخذك من حِبابها الزؤد، فلذلك قلتَ:

إنّي بدَهْماءَ عزّ ما أجِدُ   يعتادُني من حِبابها زُؤُدُ

وأين حصل تَليدُك؟ شَغَلَك عنه تخليدُك، وحُقّ لك أن تنساه، كما ذهل وَحْشيٌّ دَمِيَ نَساه.

١،١٢،١٧ وإذا هو برجلٍ يتضوّر، فيقول: مَن هذا؟ فيقال: الأخطل التَّغْلِبيّ، فيقول له: ما زالت صِفتُك للخمر حتى غادرتك أُكُلاً للجَمْر، كم طرِبَت السادات على قولك:

أناخوا فجرّوا شاصياتٍ كأنها   رجالٌ من السُّودان لم يتسربلوا
فقلت: اصْبَحوني لا أبا لأبيكُمُ   وما وضعوا الأثقالَ إلا ليفعلوا
فصبُّوا عُقارًا في الإناء كأنها   إذا لَمحوها جَذْوةٌ تتأكّلُ
وجاؤوا ببَيْسانيّةٍ هي بعدما   يُعَلُّ بها الساقي ألذُّ وأسهلُ
تمُرُّ بها الأيدي سنيحًا وبارحًا   وتوضَع باللّهُمّ حَيِّ وتُحمَلُ
فتُوقَف أحيانًا فيَفْصِل بيننا   غِناءُ مُغَنٍّ أو شِواءٌ مُرَعْبَلُ
فلذّتْ لمرتاحٍ وطابت لشاربٍ   وراجَعَني منها مِراحٌ وأخْيَلُ
فما لَبّثَتْنا نَشْوةٌ لحِقتْ بنا   توابِعُها ممّا نُعَلّ ونُنْهَلُ
تَدِبُّ دبيبًا في العِظام كأنه   دبيبُ نِمالٍ في نَقًا يتهيّلُ
رَبَتْ ورَبا في كَرْمِها ابنُ مَدينةٍ   مُكِبٌّ على مِسْحاته يتركّلُ

Then the Sheikh asks, "How is Ṣakhr al-Ghayy doing?" "You can see him there!" is the answer. The Sheikh asks him, "Where is your Dahmā' now, Ṣakhr al-Ghayy? You are not on the same earth or under the same sky! Once, in your time, her youth was blooming and bright, but then the love of her caused you a fright. That is why you said: 17.11

I suffer so badly because of Dahmā':
since I love her so much I have frequent visits of fright.

"And what has become of your son Talīd? Your eternal damnation has distracted you from him indeed! And you are justified in forgetting him, just as a wild animal pays no heed, if his heel tendon should bleed."[649]

Then he spots a man who is writhing with pain. "Who is this?" he asks. 17.12.1

The conversation with al-Akhṭal

The answer is, "al-Akhṭal, of Taghlib." He says to him, "You always used to describe wine, but as a result you are doomed by hot embers to be consumed! How the lords were enraptured by your poem:[650]

They let their camels kneel and dragged skins full of wine,
the skins with stumps protruding, just like breechless blacks.
I said, 'Give me my morning drink, I say!'
and in no time they did so, having taken down their loads.
And then they poured into the jug a wine that, when they glanced
at it, was like an ember being consumed by fire.
They came with a Baysānī wine that, when the pourer poured
a second time, was even more delicious and more smooth.
Hands passed it round to right and left;
it was put down with 'Cheers!'[651] and taken up again.
At times the cups were stopped and we were interrupted by
the singing of a singer or by slices of roast meat.
Delightful was that wine for a relaxing man, delicious for a drinker; I
was tossed by it between hilarity and arrogance.
But instantly inebriation overcame us
from drinking in succession once and twice.
It crept into our bones like ants
that creep upon a dune of fine loose sand.
The vine grew where an expert vintner in the vineyard grew up too,
who sedulously plied his feet upon his spade.

إذا خاف من نَجْمٍ عليها ظَماءةً   أدبَّ إليها جَدْوَلاً يتسلسلُ
فقلتُ: اقْتلوها عنكمُ بِمزاجها   وحُبَّ بها مقتولةً حين تُقْتَلُ

فقال التَّغلبيّ: إنّي جررتُ الذارع، ولقيتُ الدارع، وهجرتُ الآبدة، ورجوتُ أن تُدْعى النَّفسُ العابدة، ولكن أبَتِ الأقْضِيَة.

فيقول، أحلَّ اللهُ الهَلَكَةَ بمُبْغِضيه: أخطأتَ في أمرين، جاء الإسلام فجزتَ أن تدخل فيه، ولزِمتَ أخلاقَ سفيه؛ وعاشرتَ يزيدَ بن مُعاوية، وأطعتَ نفسَك الغاوية؛ وآثرتَ ما فنِيَ على باقٍ، فكيف لك بالإباق؟ ٢،١٢،١٧

فيَزفِر الأخطل زَفْرةً تعجب لها الزَّبانية، ويقول: آه على أيّام يزيدَ أَسُوفُ عنده عَنْبَرا، ولا أعدَمُ لديه سِيسَنْبَرا؛ وأمزَحُ معه مَزْحَ خليل، فيحتملني احتمالَ الجليل؛ وكم ألبسني من مَوْشيّ، أسحبُه في البُكرة أو العَشيّ، وكأني بالقِيان الصادحة بين يديه تُغنّيه بقوله:

ولها بالماطِرونِ إذا   أنفدَ النَّمْلُ الذي جَمَعا
خِلْفةٌ حتى إذا ظَهرتْ   سكنتْ من جِلِّقٍ بِيَعا
في قِبابٍ حوْلَ دَسْكَرَةٍ   حولَها الزَّيتونُ قد يَنَعا
وقفتْ للبدرِ ترقُبه   فإذا بالبدرِ قد طَلَعا

ولقد فاكهتُه في بعض الأيّام وأنا سَكرانُ مُلْتَخٌّ فقلت:

اِسْلَمْ سَلِمتَ أبا خالدٍ   وحيّاك ربُّك بالعَنْقَزِ
أكلتَ الدَّجاجَ فأفنيتَها   فهل في الخنانيص من مَغْمَزِ

فما زادني عن ابتسام، واهتزَّ للصِّلة كاهتزاز الحُسام.

Whenever he feared a thirst caused by a failing star[652]
he'd let a trickling channel flow to it.
I said, 'Kill her, that wine, by mixing her!
How loveable she is when killed!'"[653]

The Taghlibite says, "Yes, many a wineskin did I trail, and I met many a man armored in mail! I avoided any great sin, and I had hoped that my God-serving soul would be called in. But the divine decrees decided otherwise."

The Sheikh says (may God let perdition come over those who hate him!): "You erred in two things: you failed to embrace Islam when it came; and you were close to a man who behaved without shame: you were an intimate friend of Muʿāwiyah's son Yazīd and you obeyed your soul that misleads! You preferred that which perishes to that which will always be, so how could you hope to flee and be free?" 17.12.2

Al-Akhṭal utters a sigh that makes Hell's angels marvel. "Ah, those days with Yazīd!" he says, "With him I would smell ambergris; the supply of mint would never cease. I would jest with him as one jests with a friend; he tolerated me just as a noble man would condescend. So often would he dress me in robes embroidered with brocade, in which mornings and evenings I, trailing it, would parade! I can still see the singing girls when they played before him and sang his verses:

In Māṭirūn, when ants consume
what they have hoarded,
She gathers autumn fruits, but when at last
she comes, she dwells in churches near Damascus,[654]
Or in pavilions round a tavern,[655] with
around it olive trees with ripened fruit.
She stops to watch the rising of the moon;
but see! Already the full moon—she—has appeared!

"I was joking with him one day, being drunk and befuddled, and I said,

Be hale and healthy, Abū Khālid!
And may your Lord with fragrant mint revive you!
You've eaten chicken and consumed it all;
and what is wrong with eating piglets?

"But he only smiled and gave me an award, as fast as the quivering of a sword."

٣،١٢،١٧ فيقول، أدام الله تمكينه: من ثَمّ أُتيتَ! أما علمتَ أنّ ذلك الرجل عاندٌ، وفي جبال المَعْصِيَة ساندٌ؟ فعَلامَ اطّلعتَ من مذهبه: أكان مُوَحّدًا، أم وجدتَه في النُّسك مُلْحِدًا؟ فيقول الأخطل: كانت تُعجبه هذه الأبيات:

أخالدَ هاتي خَبِّريني وأَعْلِني حديثَكِ إنّي لا أُسِرُّ التناجيا
حديثَ أبي سُفْيانَ لمّا سما بها إلى أُحُدٍ حتى أقام البواكيا
وكيف بغى أمرًا عليٌّ ففاتَهُ وأَوْرَثَه الجَدُّ السعيد مُعاويا
وقُومي فعُلّيني على ذاكِ قَهْوةً تَحَلَّبها العِيسِيُّ كَرْمًا شآميا
إذا ما نظرْنا في أمورٍ قديمةٍ وجدنا حلالاً شُربَها المتواليا
فلا خُلْفَ بين النّاس أنّ محمّدًا تَبَوّأ رَمْسًا في المدينة ثاويا

فيقول، جعل الله أوقاتَه كلَّها سعيدةً: عليك البَهْلة! قد ذهلت الشعراءُ من أهل الجنّة والنار عن المدح والنسيب، وما شُدهتَ عن كُفْرك ولا إساءتك.

٤،١٢،١٧ وإبليسُ يسمع ذلك الخطاب كلّه فيقول للزّبانية: ما رأيتُ أعجزَ منكم إخوانَ مالكٍ! فيقولون: كيف زعمتَ ذلك يا أبا مُرّة؟ فيقول: ألا تسمعون هذا المتكلِّمَ بما لا يعنيه؟ قد شغلكم وشغل غيرَكم عمّا هو فيه! فلو أنّ فيكم صاحبَ نحيزةٍ قويّةٍ، لَوَثب وثبةً حتى يلحق به فيجذبه إلى سَقَر. فيقولون: لم تصنع شيئًا يا أبا زَوْبعة! ليس لنا على أهل الجنّة سبيلٌ.

فإذا سمع، أسمعه الله مَحابَّه، ما يقول إبليس، أخذ في شَتْمه ولَعْنه وإظهار الشَّماتة به. فيقول، عليه اللّعنة: ألم تُنْهَوا عن الشَّمات يا بني آدم؟ ولكنّكم، بحمد الله، ما زُجرتم عن شيءٍ إلّا وركبتُموه. فيقول، واصَلَ الله الإحسانَ إليه: أنت بدأتَ آدمَ بالشَّماتة،

The Sheikh (may God empower him!) says, "That is why you were given what you deserve! Did you not know all that this obstinate man persisted in, who scaled the mountains of sin! What did you find out about his belief: was he a monotheist, or did you find him to be an apostate?" Al-Akhṭal replies, "He liked these verses: 17.12.3

O Khālidah, come here and tell me, let me know
your story (I shall not reveal[656] a confidential talk):
The story of Abū Sufyān, when he went up
to Uḥud, leaving wailing women standing![657]
And how ʿAlī sought power, but he failed,
and fortune favored then Muʿāwiyah and gave it him.[658]
Stand up, pour me another cup of wine
pressed by a Christian from a Syrian vine!
When we consider things in bygone ages
we find that drinking it continually is allowed.
There's no dispute among mankind: Muḥammad, in
Medina, has been laid to rest forever in a grave!"

The Sheikh says (may God make all his moments happy!), "A curse upon you! The poets in Heaven and Hellfire have forgotten their panegyrics and love lyrics, but you have not been confused to the extent of being distracted from your unbelief and misdeeds!"

Satan, who has heard all this speech, says to his angels of Hell, "I have never seen creatures more impotent than you, brothers of Mālik!" "How can you say that, Father Bitterness?"[659] they answer. He continues, "Can't you hear this man speaking about things that do not concern him? He has distracted you and the others from your job! If there was anybody with guts among you he would jump up, seize him, and drag him to Hellfire!" They reply, "You can't do anything, Father Whirlwind! We have no power over those who dwell in Paradise." 17.12.4

When the Sheikh (may God make him hear the things he loves!) hears what Satan says he begins to scold and curse him, openly gloating. Satan (a curse be upon him!) replies, "Have you not been forbidden to gloat, children of Adam? But— God be praised!—whenever you were told not to do something you always did it!" The Sheikh (may God continue to favor him!) says, "You are the one who first gloated at Adam's misery; and he who starts

والبادئُ أظلمُ. ثمّ يعود إلى كلام الأخطل فيقول: أأنت القائل هذه الأبيات:

ولستُ بصائمٍ رمضانَ طوعًا ولستُ بآكلٍ لحمَ الأضاحي
ولستُ بقائمٍ كالعيرِ أدعو قُبيلَ الصبحِ حيَّ على الفلاحِ
ولكنّي سأشربُها شمولاً وأسجُدُ عند منبلجِ الصباحِ

فيقول: أَجَلْ، وإني لَنادمٌ سادمٌ، وهل أغنتِ النّدامةُ عن أخي كُسَعٍ؟

is the more unjust one!" He turns to address al-Akhṭal again. "Is it you who said these verses:

I shan't obediently fast in Ramadan
nor eat the sacrificial meat![660]
I shan't stand up like a wild ass and cry,
just before dawn, 'Come to salvation!'[661]
Rather, I'll drink it, a chilled wine;
I shall prostrate myself when dawn is breaking."

"Yes," says al-Akhṭal, "I am sorry and full of worry! But did repentance avail the man of the tribe of Kusaʿ?"[662]

ويملُّ من خطاب أهل النار، فينصرف إلى قصره المَشِيد، فإذا صار على مِيلٍ أو ميلَيْن، ذكر أنه ما سأل عن مهَلْهِل التَّغلبيّ ولا عن المُرقِّشَيْن وأنه أغفل الشَّنفَرى وتأبَّط شَرّاً، فيرجع على أدراجه، فيقف بذلك الموقف ينادي: أين عَديّ بن رَبيعة؟ فيقال: زِدْ في البيان. فيقول: الذي يستشهد النَّحويُّون بقوله: ١٠١،١٨

ضربتْ صدرَها إليّ وقالت: يا عَديّاً لقد وَقَتْك الأَواقي

وقد استشهدوا له بأشياءَ كقوله:

ولقد خبطْن بيوتَ يَشْكُرَ خَبْطةً أخوالَنا وهُمُ بنو الأعمامِ

وقوله:

ما أُرجّي بالعيْش بعد ندامى كلّهمْ قد سُقُوا بكأسِ حَلاقِ

فيقال: إنك لَتُعرّف صاحبَك بأمرٍ لا معرفةَ عندنا به، ما النّحويّون؟ وما الاستشهاد؟ وما هذا الهَذَيان؟ نحن خَزَنة النار، فبيِّنْ غرضَك تُجَبْ إليه.

فيقول: أريد المعروف بمهَلْهِل التَّغلبيّ، أخي كُليْبٍ وائلٍ الذي كان يُضرَب به المَثَل.

فيقال: ها هو ذا يسمع حِوارك، فقل ما تشاء.

فيقول: يا عديّ بن ربيعة، أَعْزِزْ عليّ بوُلوجك هذا المَوْلج! لو لم آسَف عليك إلا لأجْل قصيدتك التي أوّلها: ٢،١،١٨

أليْلتَنا بذي حُسَمٍ أَنيري إذا أنتِ انقضيتِ فلا تحُوري

لكانت جديرةً أن تُطيل الأَسَفَ عليك، وقد كنتُ إذا أنشدتُ أبياتك في ابنتك المزوّجة في جَنْب تَغرْوَرِق من الحُزن عيناي، فأخبِرْني لِمَ سُمّيتَ مهلِهلاً؟ فقد قيل: إنك سُمّيت بذلك لأنك أوّل من هلهل الشعْرَ، أي رقّقه.

The Sheikh is bored with talking to the inhabitants of Hell. He turns toward his lofty castle again. Having gone for a mile or two it occurs to him that he has not asked about Muhalhil al-Taghlibī, nor about the two called Muraqqish. He has also neglected al-Shanfarā and Ta'abbaṭa Sharrā. So he retraces his steps and stops at that same place. "Where is ʿAdī ibn Rabīʿah?" he calls. They reply, "Be more specific!" He says, "The one whose verse is quoted as linguistic evidence by the grammarians: 18.1.1

The conversation with Muhalhil

She struck her breast and said to me:
ʿAdī, you have had strong protectors![663]

"And also this verse:

(The horses) struck down Yashkur's tents,
our uncles matrilineal, the sons of uncles patrilineal.[664]

"And his verse:

What can I hope for in my life, now that my friends
have all been given to drink the cup of Death?"

The answer is, "You describe your friend with things of which we have no knowledge. What are 'grammarians'? What is 'linguistic evidence'? What is all this drivel? We are the Guards of Hell. Say clearly what you want, and you may get a reply!"

The Sheikh says, "I want him who is known as Muhalhil al-Taghlibī, the brother of Kulayb of the tribe of Wā'il, who has become proverbial." They reply, "There he is, listening to your speech. Say what you want."

The Sheikh says, "ʿAdī ibn Rabīʿah! I am grieved that you have entered 18.1.2
this place! If I were sorry for you only on account of your ode that begins:

O, night of ours in Dhū Ḥusam, be bright!
When you are past, do not return![665]

"then this poem alone were worthy of causing lengthy grief for your sake. And whenever I recited your verses about your daughter, who married into the tribe of Janb, my eyes would brim over with tears. Now tell me, why were you called Muhalhil? It is said that this is because you were the first who 'finely wove' (*yuhalhil*) poetry."

فيقول: إنّ الكذب لكثيرٌ، وإنّما كان لي أخٌ يقال له امرؤ القيس فأغار علينا زُهير بن جَنابٍ الكَلْبيُّ، فتبعه أخي في زَرافةٍ من قومه، فقال في ذلك:

لما توَقَّلَ في الكُراعِ هجينُهمْ هلهلتُ أثأرُ مالكًا أو صِنْبِلا
وكأنه بازٌ عَلَتْه كَبْرةٌ يَهدي بِشكّته الرَّعيلَ الأوّلا

هلهلتُ: أي قاربتُ، ويقال: توقّفتُ، يعني بالهجين زُهير بن جَنابٍ. فسُمّيَ مهلهلاً، فلمّا هلك شُبّهتُ به فقيل لي: مهلهل. فيقول: الآن شفيتَ صدري بحقيقة اليقين.

فأخبرْني عن هذا البيت الذي يُروى لك: ٣،١،١٨

أرْعَدوا ساعةَ الهِياج وأبرَقْـ ـنا كما تُوعِد الفُحولُ الفحولا

فإنّ الأصمعيّ كان يُنكره ويقول: إنه مولَّدٌ، وكان أبو زيدٍ يستشهد به ويُثبته.

فيقول: طال الأَبَد على لُبَدٍ! لقد نسيتُ ما قلتُ في الدار الفانية، فما الذي أنكر منه؟ فيقول: زعم الأصمعيّ أنه لا يقال أرعد وأبرق في الوعيد ولا في السحاب.

فيقول: إنّ ذلك لَخطأٌ من القول، وإنّ هذا البيت لم يقُلْه إلا رجلٌ من جِذْم الفصاحة، إمّا أنا وإمّا سِواي، فخُذ به وأَعْرِضْ عن قول السُّفَهاء.

٢،١٨ ويسأل عن المرقّش الأكبر، فإذا هو به في أطباق العذاب، فيقول: خفّف الله عنك أيها الشابّ المغتصَب، فلم أزل في الدار العاجلة حزينًا لما أصابك به الرجلُ الغُفَليُّ، أحد بني غُفيلةَ بن قاسطٍ، فعليه بَهْلة الله! وإنّ قومًا من أهل الإسلام كانوا يستَزْرون بقصيدتك الميميّة التي أوّلها:

هل بالديار أن تُجيب صَمَمْ لو كان حيًّا ناطقًا كلَّمْ

وإنها عندي لَمِن المُفْردات، وكان بعض الأدباء يرى أنها والميميّة التي قالها المرقّش

"There are many lies that go round," says Muhalhil, "I had a brother called Imru' al-Qays. Zuhayr ibn Janāb al-Kalbī raided us; my brother followed him with some of his people. He composed verses on this:

When their half-bred climbed up the summit of the road I was within
an inch (*halhaltu*) of vengeance for the deaths of Mālik and of Ṣinbil.
He's like a goshawk of great age,
leading the vanguard with his weapons.

"The word *halhaltu* means: 'I almost did'; it is also said that it means 'I stopped.' By the 'half-bred' he meant Zuhayr ibn Janāb. Then he was nicknamed Muhalhil.[666] But when he died I was confused with him and I was called Muhalhil." The Sheikh replied, "Now at last I have stilled my thirst for knowledge with truth of certainty!

"But tell me about this verse that is attributed to you: 18.1.3

They thundered in the hour of turmoil and we flashed like lightning,
like stallions threatening stallions.

"Al-Aṣmaʿī thought it spurious and said it was not early Arabic, but Abū Zayd used it as linguistic evidence, declaring it to be authentic. " "Lubad lived a long life!" [667] says Mulhalhil, "I have forgotten what I said in the Perishable World. Why did he think it was spurious?" The Sheikh replies, "Al-Aṣmaʿī claimed that the verbs 'thunder' and 'flash' are not used for threats or for clouds." "That is an error," says Muhalhil, "This verse was said by a man who was rooted in the purity of language—whether it was me or someone else! So stick to that and pay no heed to the words of fools."

The Sheikh asks about al-Muraqqish the Elder; he spots him in the echelons of Hell's torment. "May God lighten your pain, you wronged young man," says the Sheikh, "for I always grieved, in the Fleeting World, because of what that man of the tribe Ghufaylah did to you, one of the Banū Ghufaylah ibn Qāsiṭ, God's curse be upon him![668]—Some people in Islamic times would scorn your ode rhyming in *-m*, which begins 18.2

The conversation with the two poets called Muraqqish

The abodes, are they deaf, since they do not reply?
If only they lived and had speech, they would speak!

"I myself think it is a singularly good poem. Some literate person thought that this poem and the other poem rhyming in *m* by Muraqqish the Younger fall

الأصغر ناقصتان عن القصائد المُفَضّليّات، ولقد وَهَمَ صاحب هذه المقالة. وبعض الناس يروي هذا الشعر لك:

تخـيّرتُ من نَعْمـانَ عُودَ أَراكةٍ   لهنْـدٍ ولكنْ مَن يبلّغـه هِـنْدا؟
خليلـيَّ جُورا باركَ اللهُ فيكمـا   وإن لم تكن هندٌ لأرضكما قَصْدا
وقُولا لها: ليس الضلالُ أجارَنا   ولكـنّنا جُرْنا لنَـلْقاكِمُ عَمْدا

ولم أَجِدْها في ديوانك، فهل ما حُكي صحيحٌ عنك؟

فيقول: لقد قلتُ أشياءَ كثيرةً، منها ما نُقل إليكم ومنها ما لم يُنقَل، وقد يجوز أن أكون قلتُ هذه الأبيات[1] ولكني سرِقْتُها لطُول الأبد، ولعلّك تُنكر أنها في هندٍ، وأنّ صاحبتي أسماءُ، فلا تَنْفِر من ذلك، فقد ينتقل المُشبِّب من الاسم إلى الاسم، ويكون في بعض عُمره مُستهترًا بشخصٍ من الناس، ثمّ ينصرف إلى شخصٍ آخَر، ألا تسمع إلى قولي:

سَفَـهٌ تـذكُّره خُويلةَ بعـدما   حـالت ذُرا نَجْرانَ دونَ لقائها

ويَنعطف إلى المُرَقّش الأصغر فيسأله عن شأنه مع بنت المُنذِر وبنت عَجْلانَ فيجده ٣،١٨
غير خبيرٍ، قد نسي لترادف الأحقاب فيقول: ألا تذكرُ ما صنع بك جنابٌ الذي تقول فيه:

فآلى جنـابٌ حِلْفةً فـأطعتَهُ   فنفسَكَ وَلِّ اللَّوْمَ إن كنتَ لائما

فيقول: وما صنع جناب؟ لقد لقيتُ الأَقْوَرِين، وسُقيتُ الأَمَرَّيْن، وكيف لي بعذاب الدار العاجلة!

١ العبارة (منها ما نُقل . . . هذه الأبيات) ساقطة من بعض النسخ.

short of the quality of the other odes in the *Mufaḍḍaliyyāt*.[669] But whoever said so was wrong!—Someone has attributed the following verses to you:

In Naʿmān I selected a piece of *arāk* wood[670]
for Hind—but who will be able to take it to Hind?
My two friends (may God bless you!), leave the road, visit Hind, even if
it is not on your way to your land!
And then tell her: We lost not our way when we swerved,
but we turned from the road for the purpose of meeting with you!

"But I do not find them in your collected verse. Is the attribution to you correct?"

"I have said so many things," replies Muraqqish. "Some of it has been transmitted to you and other things have not. It is possible that I have composed these verses, but I have forgotten them because of the eternally long time. Perhaps you find it odd that they are about Hind, whereas my girl was Asmā'. But do not disapprove of this, for someone who composes love poetry may move from one name to another. At one stage of his life he may rave about one person and then he may turn to another. Haven't you heard this verse of mine:

Stupid it is to remember Khuwaylah, now that the tops
of Najrān's mountains stand in the way of a meeting with her!"

The Sheikh turns to Muraqqish the Younger and asks him about his affair 18.3
with the daughter of al-Mundhir and the daughter of ʿAjlān,[671] but he does not find him very knowledgeable: he has forgotten the affair because of the epochs that have succeeded one another. "Don't you remember," he asks, "what Janāb did to you, the one of whom you say;

Janāb swore an oath; I obeyed him.
So blame yourself, if you must blame someone!"[672]

"What did he do?" asks Muraqqish. "I have encountered calamitous things and have been given to drink bitter drinks![673] I wish I could have the torment of the Fleeting World instead!"

٤،١٨ فإذا لم يجد عنده طائلاً تركه وسأل عن الشَّنفَرى الأَزديّ فألفاه قليلَ التشكّي والتألُّم لما هو فيه. فيقول: إنّي لا أراك قَلِقاً مثل قَلَق أصحابك. فيقول: أَجَل، إنّي قلت بيتاً في الدار الخادعة فأنا أتأدّب به حِيرِيَّ الدهرِ. وذلك قولي:

غَوى فغَوَتْ، ثمّ ارعوى بَعْدُ وارْعَوَتْ   وللصبرُ إن لم ينفع الشَّكْوُ أجملُ

٥،١٨ وإذا هو قرينٌ مع تأبّط شرّاً، كما كان في الدار الغرّارة.

فيقول، أسنى الله حظّه من المغفِرة، لتأبّط شرّاً: أحقٌّ ما رُوي عنك من نكاح الغِيلان؟ فيقول: لقد كنّا في الجاهليّة نتقوّل ونتخرّص، فما جاءك عنّا ممّا يُنكره المعقول فإنّه من الأكاذيب، والزّمن كلّه على سجيّةٍ واحدةٍ، فالذي شاهده مَعَدُّ بن عَدْنانَ كالذي شاهد نُضاضةُ ولد آدم. والنُّضاضة آخِر ولد الرّجل.

فيقول، أجزل الله عطاءه من الغفران: نُقلتْ إلينا أبياتٌ تنْسَب إليك:

أنا الذي نكحَ الغِيلانَ في بلدٍ   ما طَلَّ فيه سِماكيٌّ ولا جادا
في حيثُ لا يعْمِتُ الغادي عَمايتَه   ولا الظّليمُ به يبْغي تَهَبّادا
وقد لهوْتُ بمصقولٍ عوارضُها   بكرٍ تُنازعني كأساً وعِنقادا
ثمّ انقضى عَصرُها عنّي وأعقبَه   عَصرُ المَشيب فقُلْ في صالحٍ بادا

فاستدللتُ على أنها لك لمّا قلتَ: تِهِبّادا، مصدر تهبّد الظليمُ إذا أكل الهبيد، فقلتُ: هذا مثلُ قوله في القافيَة:

طيفُ ابنةِ الحُرِّ إذ كُنّا نُواصلها   ثمّ اجتُنِنْتُ بها بعد التّفِرّاقِ

18.4 Since the Sheikh does not find with him any useful information he leaves him. He asks about al-Shanfarā al-Azdī[674] and finds him to be someone who complains little about his sufferings. "I see you are not as troubled as your companions," says the Sheikh. "True," replies al-Shanfarā, "I made a verse in the Deceptive World and I intend to live up to it for all eternity. It is this:

The conversation with the two brigand poets, al-Shanfarā and Ta'abbaṭa Sharrā

He erred, they erred; but then he refrained, they refrained.
    Forbearance, when complaining is of no avail, is best."[675]

18.5 And there he is joined by Ta'abbaṭa Sharrā, as he was in the Deluding World. The Sheikh (may God raise his share of forgiveness!) asks Ta'abbaṭa Sharrā, "Is it true what they tell about you, that you married female ghouls?" "In the pre-Islamic times of Ignorance," he replies, "we would spread all kinds of false reports and rumors. Common sense rejects those things that have reached you; they are all lies. It is the same with all history. What Ma'add ibn 'Adnān has witnessed is like what the youngest of Adam's descendants has witnessed."

The Sheikh says (may God give him abundant forgiveness!), "Some verses have been quoted to us that were attributed to you:

I'm he who married ghouls in a country
    where no autumnal rain[676] gives dew or downpour,
Where no lion, hunting in the morning, overcomes his blindness (?)[677]
    and where no ostrich is a-seeking bitter colocynths.
I've sported with a girl with polished teeth,
    a virgin who tried to pinch my cup and bunch of dates.
My time with her is past and gone; and on its heels there came
    the time of graying hairs. Of all good things, say: Gone!

"I have found indications that this poem is by you, for you speak of an ostrich 'a-seeking' colocynths, using the verbal noun *tihibbād*, so I said to myself, this is like when he says, using a similar word pattern in rhyme:

The apparition of the noble man's daughter—when we were together;
    but then I went mad because of her, when a-drifting asunder (*tifirrāq*).

مصدر تفرَّقوا تِفرّاقاً، وهذا مطَّرِدٌ في تفعَّل، وإن كان قليلاً في الشعر، كما قال أبو زُبيدٍ:

فثار الزاجرون فزادَ منهم تِقِرّاباً وصادَفه ضَبيسُ

فلا يجيبه تأبَّط شرّاً بطائلٍ.

"The verbal noun pattern *tifirrāq* can be derived regularly from the verb *tafarraqa* ('to separate'), even though it is rare in poetry. Likewise, Abū Zubayd says:

The scolders raged; then he came ever more
  a-nearing (*tiqirrāb*), and a wicked man met him."

But Ta'abbaṭa Sharrā gave no useful reply.

فإذا رأى قِلّة الفوائد لديهم، تركهم في الشَّقاء السَّرْمَد، وعمد لمحلّه في الجنان، فيلقى ١٠،١،١٩
آدم، عليه السلام، في الطريق فيقول: يا أبانا، صلّى الله عليك، قد رُوي لنا عنك شعرٌ منه قولك:

نحنُ بنو الأرض وسُكّانُها مِنها خُلِقنا وإليها نَعودْ
والسَّعدُ لا يَبقى لأصحابه والنَّحسُ تمحوه ليالي السُّعودْ

فيقول: إنّ هذا القول حقّ، وما نطقه إلا بعضُ الحكماء، ولكنّي لم أسمع به حتّى الساعة.

فيقول: وفّر الله قِسمه في الثّواب: فلعلّك يا أبانا قُلته ثمّ نسيت، فقد علمتَ أنّ النِّسيان متسرّعٌ إليك، وحَسْبُك شهيداً على ذلك الآيةُ المتلوّة في فُرقان محمّد، صلّى الله عليه وسلّم: ﴿وَلَقَدْ عَهِدْنَا إِلَىٰ آدَمَ مِن قَبْلُ فَنَسِيَ وَلَمْ نَجِدْ لَهُ عَزْمًا﴾ وقد زعم بعض العلماء أنك إنّما سُمّيت إنساناً لنسيانك، واحتجّ على ذلك بقولهم في التصغير: أُنَيْسِيان، وفي الجمع: أَناسيّ، وقد رُوي أنّ الإنسان من النِّسيان عن ابن عبّاس، وقال الطائيّ:

لا تَنْسَيَنْ تلك العهودَ وإنّما سُمِّيتَ إنساناً لأنك ناسِ

وقرأ بعضهم: ﴿ثُمَّ أَفِيضُوا مِنْ حَيْثُ أَفَاضَ النَّاسِ﴾ بكسر السِّين، يريد النّاسي، فحذف الياء، كما حُذفت في قوله: ﴿سَوَاءً الْعَاكِفُ فِيهِ وَالْبَادِ﴾. فأمّا البصريّون فيعتقدون أنّ الإنسان من الأُنس، وأنّ قولهم في التصغير: أُنَيْسِيان، شاذّ، وقولهم في الجمع:

Return to Paradise

Having found few pearls of wisdom with them, the Sheikh leaves them in their neverending misery. He sets out for his dwelling in Paradise. On the way he meets Adam (peace be upon him). "Our father," he says, "May God bless you! There is some poetry that has been transmitted as being by you, such as this: **19.1.1** *A meeting with Adam*

> We are the sons of the earth and those who dwell on it:
> from it we've been created, and to it we shall return.
> Good fortune will not stay with those who have it, and
> bad fortune is obliterated by good fortune's nights."

"True words," says Adam, "They must have been uttered by some sage. But I have never heard them until this moment." The Sheikh says (may God given him an ample portion of reward!), "Perhaps, father, you composed these verses and then forgot about them. For you know that you were prone to forgetting quickly, which is sufficiently proved by the verse recited in the Revelation[678] of Muḥammad (God bless and preserve him): «We made a covenant with Adam before, but he forgot and We did not find constancy in him». Some scholar asserted that you were called *insān*, 'human being,' because of your forgetfulness, *nisyān*. The proof, he argued, is that the diminutive form, 'little man,' is *unaysiyān* and the plural, 'men' is *anāsīy*.[679] That 'human being' is derived from 'forgetfulness' is also transmitted on the authority of Ibn ʿAbbās, and the poet from the tribe of Ṭayyi'[680] said:

> Do not forget those pledges! You are called *insān* ('a man')
> because you are a *nāsī* ('someone who forgets').

"Someone read the Qur'anic verse «Then move on from where the people (*al-nāsu*) move on»,[681] reading *al-nāsi*, meaning *al-nāsī* ('he who forgets'), shortening the *ī*, as it is shortened in «equally for him who stays in it and him who comes to it (*al-bādi*)».[682] The Basrian scholars, however, believe that *insān* ('human being') is derived from *uns* ('sociability') and that the

أَناسيٌّ، أصله أَناسِينُ، فأُبدلت الياء من النون. والقول الأوّل أحسن.

فيقول آدم، صلّى الله عليه: أبيْتُم إلا عقوقًا وأذيّةً، إنّما كنتُ أتكلّمُ بالعربيّة وأنا في ١٩،١،٢
الجنّة، فلمّا هبطتُ إلى الأرض نُقل لساني إلى السُّريانيّة، فلم أنطِق بغيرها إلى أن هلكتُ، فلمّا ردّني الله، سبحانه وتعالى، عادت عليَّ العربيّة، فأيَّ حينٍ نظمتُ هذا الشعر: في العاجلة أم الآجلة؟ والذي قال ذلك يجب أن يكون قاله وهو في الدار الماكرة، ألا ترى قوله: منها خُلِقْنا وإليها نَعودُ فكيف أقول هذا المقال ولساني سُريانيّ؟ وأمّا الجنّة قبل أن أخرُج منها فلم أكُن أدري بالموت فيها، وأنه ممّا حُكم على العِباد، صُيِّر كأطواق حَمام، وما رعى لأحدٍ من ذِمامٍ، وأمّا بعد رجوعي إليها، فلا معنى لقولي: وإليها نَعودُ، لأنه كذبٌ لا مَحالة، ونحن مَعاشرَ أهلِ الجنّة خالدون مخلّدون.

فيقول، قُضي له بالسَّعد المؤرَّب: إن بعض أهل السِّيَر يزعُم أنّ هذا الشعر وجده يَعرُبُ في متقدم الصُّحُف بالسُّريانيّة، فنقله إلى لسانه، وهذا لا يمتنع أن يكون.

وكذلك يروون لك، صلّى الله عليك، لمّا قتل قابيلُ هابيلَ: ١٩،١،٣

تغيّرتِ البلادُ ومَن عليها   فوجهُ الأرض مُغبَرٌّ قبيحُ
وأَوْدى رَبعُ أهلها فبانوا   وغودر في الثّرى الوجهُ المليحُ

وبعضهم ينشد:

وزال بَشاشةُ الوجهِ المليحِ

على الإقواء. وفي حكايةٍ، معناها على ما أذكُر أنّ رجلاً من بعض ولدك يُعرَف بابن دُريد أنشد هذا الشعر، وكانت روايته:

وزال بشاشةُ الوجهِ المليحِ

فقال أوّلَ ما قال: أَقْوى. وكان في المجلس أبوسعيد السِّيرافيُّ فقال: يجوز أن يكون قال:

وزال بشاشةَ الوجهُ المليحُ

diminutive form *unaysiyān* is irregular.[683] The plural form *anāsīy* was originally *anāsīn*, the *n* having been changed into *y*. But the former opinion is better."

Adam (God bless him) replies, "Must you always be insolent and hurtful? I spoke Arabic when I was in the Garden. When I fell down to earth my language changed into Syriac and I never spoke any other tongue until I died. But when God, praised and exalted be He, returned me to the Garden, I spoke Arabic again. So when am I supposed to have composed these verses, in the Fleeting World or the Latter World? The man who made them must have done so in the Deluding World. Look at his words: 'from it we've been created, and to it we shall return.' How could I have said this when my language was Syriac? And before I left the Garden I did not know about death, or that it was to be decreed for all men, made like a dove's neck ring,[684] not respecting anybody or anything! As for the time after my return, the words 'to it we shall return' would not make sense then, because it would be a plain untruth. We, dwellers in the Garden, are here forever, as immortals." 19.1.2

The Sheikh says (may he be destined for ultimate happiness!), "A certain historian asserts that Ya'rub found the verses in some ancient folios, in Syriac, and then translated them into his language. This is not impossible.

"Likewise they transmit verses by you (God bless you), composed after Cain killed Abel:[685] 19.1.3

The lands have changed, their inhabitants too;
    the face of the earth is dust-colored and ugly.
The abode of its people has fallen into ruin. They've gone,
    and the handsome face[686] was left in earth.

"Some people recite the last half-verse as

and gone is the cheer of the handsome face,

"with a rhyme defect.[687] There is a story, which I summarize here, that a man, a descendant of yours known as Ibn Durayd, recited this poem, with the version

and gone is the cheer of the handsome face.

"The first thing he said was, 'He has made a faulty rhyme!' Among those present was Abū Sa'īd al-Sīrāfī, who said, 'But it is possible to read it as

and gone is, in cheerfulness, the handsome face,

بنصب بشاشة على التمييز، وبحذف التنوين لإلتقاء الساكنَيْن، كما قال:

عمرُو الذي هَشَمَ الثَّرِيدَ لقومه ورجالُ مكّةَ مُسْنِتون عِجافُ

قلت أنا: هذا الوجه الذي قاله أبو سعيدٍ شرٌّ من إقواءِ عشرِ مرّاتٍ في القصيدة الواحدة.

فيقول آدم، صلّى الله عليه: أَعْزِزْ عليّ بكم مَعْشرَ أُبَيْنِيَّ! إنّكم في الضّلالة متهوّكون! آليتُ ما نطقتُ هذا النظيم، ولا نُطِقَ في عصري، وإنّما نظمه بعضُ الفارغين، فلا حوْل ولا قوّة إلا بالله! كذبتم على خالقكم وربّكم، ثمّ على آدم أبيكم، ثمّ على حوّاءَ أمّكم، وكذب بعضكم على بعض، ومآلكم في ذلك الأرض.

١،٢،١٩ ثمّ يضرب سائرًا في الفردوس فإذا هو بروضةٍ مؤنقةٍ، وإذا هو بحيّاتٍ يلعبن ويتماقلن، يتخاففن ويتثاقلن، فيقول: لا إله إلا الله! وما تصنع حيّةٌ في الجنّة؟ فيُنْطِقها الله، جلّتْ عَظَمتُه، بعدما ألهمها المعرفةَ بهاجس الخَلَد فتقول: أما سمعتَ في عمرك بذات الصَّفاء، الوافية لصاحبٍ ما وفى؟ كانت تنزل بوادٍ خصيب، ما زمنُها في العيشة بقصيب، وكانت تصنع إليه الجميل في وِرْد الظاهرة والغِبّ، وليس مَن كفر للمؤمن بِسِبٍّ، فلمّا ثمّر بودّها ماله، وأمّل أن يجتذب آماله، ذكرعندها ثاره، وأراد أن يقتفر آثاره، وأكبّ على فأسٍ مُعْمَلةٍ، يحُدّ غُرابها للآملة، ووقف للساعية على صخرةٍ، وهمّ أن ينتقم منها بأَخْرةٍ، وكان أخوه ممّن قتلته، جاهرته في الحادثة أو قيل ختلته، فضربها ضَرْبةً، وأَهْوَنْ بالمَقرشَرْبةً، إذا الرجل أحسّ التَّلَف، وفقد من الأنيس الخَلَف! فلمّا وُقيتْ ضربةَ فأسِه، والحِقدُ يُمْسك بأنفاسه، نَدِم على ما صنع أشدَّ النَّدَم، ومن له في الجِدة بالعَدَم؟ فقال للحيّة مُخادعًا، ولم يكن بما كتم صادعًا: هل لكِ أن نكون خِلَّيْن، ونحفظ العهدَ إلَّيْن؟ ودعاها بالسَّفَه إلى حِلف، وقد سُقي

"'with "cheerfulness" in the accusative of specification, with the indefinite ending shortened to avoid a cluster of three consonants,[688] just as in

> ʿAmr, who made bread pudding for his people
> when the men of Mecca were starving and skinny.'[689]

"But I say, Abū Saʿīd's suggestion is worse than ten cases of faulty rhyme in one poem!"

Adam says (God bless him), "I am sorry for you, all you dear children of mine! You are truly sunken deep into error. I swear, I have not composed this poem and it was not uttered in my lifetime. Some idle layabout must have made it. There is neither might nor power but through God! You have uttered lies first about your Creator and Lord,[690] then about Adam, your father, then about Eve, your mother; and finally amongst yourselves you would lie—but in the end it is in the earth that you will lie!"[691]

19.2.1 *The snakes of Paradise*

The Sheikh moves on apace through Paradise. Suddenly he sees a pretty meadow. He spots snakes in the water, playing and plunging, now lightly, then heavily lunging, "There is no god but God!" he exclaims. "What is a snake doing in the Garden?" Then God (great is His might) gives it speech, after having inspired it with knowledge of what was in the Sheikh's mind. "Haven't you heard in your lifetime," it says, "of She of the Rock, who was true to another as long as he was true? She lived in the fertile river valley, on the water of which she would thrive as long as she was alive. Her human partner she would decently pay whenever she went to drink at noon every other day[692]—someone who is ungrateful is not entitled to abuse a benefactor.[693] But when, through her affection, he made his wealth grow abundantly, and he hoped to perform what he had hoped to do, he thought again about avenging his brother's murder, and he was bent on taking the matter further. He reached for an axe, well-made, and sharpened for the unsuspecting one its blade. He stood himself next to a rock waiting for her to come along fast, and to wreak vengeance upon her at long last: for his brother was among those she had killed, either openly meeting him, or, as some said, from an ambush cheating him. So he hit her—it is easy to drink the cup of death, so bitter! But soon he felt his deed had gone to waste: he had lost a friend that could not be replaced. However, the axe's blow had not resulted in the snake's death, since his hatred had impeded his breath. He repented as strongly as anybody can repent—but who can undo such an event? He

من الغدر بخِلْف. فقالت: لا أفعلُ وإن طال الدهر، وكم قُصِم بالغِيَر ظَهرٌ! إنّي أَجِدُك فاجرًا مسحورًا، لم تأْلُ في خُلّتك حُورًا؛ تأبى لي صَكّةٌ فوق الرأس، مارستُها أبأسَ مِراسٍ، ويمنعك من أَرَبك قبرٌ محفور، والأعمال الصالحة لها وُفور.

وقد وصف ذلك نابغةُ بني ذُبيان فقال: ٢،٢،١٩

وإنّي لألْقى من ذَوي الضِّغْن منهمُ ... وما أصبحتْ تشكو من البثّ ساهِرَهْ
كما لقِيَتْ ذاتُ الصَّفا من خليلها ... وكانت تَديه المالَ غِبًّا وظاهِرَهْ
فلمّا رأى أنْ ثمّرَ اللهُ مالَه ... فأصبح مسرورًا وسَدَّ مَفاقِرَهْ
أكَبَّ على فأسٍ يُحِدُّ غُرابَها ... مذكَّرةٍ من المَعاول باتِرَهْ
وقام على جُحْرٍ لها فوقَ صَخرةٍ ... ليقتلَها، أو تُخطئَ الكفُّ بادِرَهْ
فلمّا وقاها اللهُ ضَربةَ فأسِه ... وللبرِّ عينٌ لا تُغمِّض ناظِرَهْ
فقال تعالَيْ نجعلِ اللهَ بيننا ... على مالِنا أو تُنجِزي ليَ آخِرَهْ
فقالت: مَعاذَ اللهِ أفعلُ إنني ... رأيتُك مسحورًا يمينُك فاجِرَهْ
أبى ليَ قبرٌ لا يزال مُقابِلي ... وضربةُ فأسٍ فوق رأسيَ فاقِرَهْ

وتقول حيّةٌ أخرى: إنّي كنت أسكُن في دار الحَسَن البصريّ فيتلو القرآنَ ليلًا، ٣،٢،١٩
فتلقّيتُ منه الكتابَ من أوّله إلى آخره.

فيقول، لا زال الرُّشد قرينًا لمحلّه: فكيف سمعتَه يقرأ: ﴿فالِقُ الإِصْباحِ﴾؟ فإنّه يُروى عنه بفتح الهمزة كأنه جَمْعُ صُبحٍ، وكذلك: ﴿بِالْعَشِيِّ وَالْإِبْكَارِ﴾ كأنه جمعُ

said to the snake, deceitfully concealing what he was really feeling, 'Shall we be friends again, ending our estrangement, and both swear to keep our former arrangement?' He invited her to a pact with foolish trickery, having drunk from the milk of treachery. But she replied, 'However long it may be, in all eternity, I shall never again be your mate! How many a back has been broken by fickle Fate! I have found you to be a sinner badly deluded, who in your "friendship" on my ruin has always brooded. I cannot be friends again, because I had to cope with a blow on my head that caused me great pain! A grave that has been dug [694] lies between your aim and me; but of good works there is an abundant quantity.'

"Al-Nābighah of the Banū Dhubyān described this and said, **19.2.2**

From those who hold a grudge against me I shall meet
—no sleepless woman suffers in the morning such a worry—
Like what 'She of the Rock' encountered from her ally, though
she paid to him the wergild every other day at noon.
But when he saw that God increased his wealth
and he was happy now, God having stopped his poverty,
He then reached for an axe, the blade of which he sharpened,
a cutting implement of steel.
He stood upon a rock, above her hole,
to kill her; yet his hand, though quick, just failed to hit.
When God had saved her from the axe's blow—
the Kind One[695] has a watchful eye that never blinks—
He said, 'Come on, let's make a pact to God
about our money, till you've paid the sum in full!'
But she replied, 'No, God forbid that I should do this!
For I have seen you are deluded and your oath is false.
I am prevented by a grave that has been dug, always confronting me,
also a neck bone-breaking axe's blow upon my head!'"

Another snake says, "I used to live in the house of al-Ḥasan al-Baṣrī. He would recite the Qur'an at night and thus I learned the Holy Book from him, from beginning to end." The Sheikh asks (may right guidance always be with him wherever he is!), "How did you hear him recite «He who splits the sky in the morning (*fāliqu l-iṣbāḥ*)»?[696] For some have transmitted that he read it with *a* instead of *i*, as if it were a plural: 'mornings (*aṣbāḥ*).' Likewise with **19.2.3**

بَكرٍ، من قولهم: لِقيتُه بَكَرًا، وإذا قلنا: إنّ أَنعُمًا وأَشُدًّا جمعُ نِعمة وشِدّة على طَرح الهاء، فيجوز أن تكون الأبكار جمعَ بُكْرةٍ، فتكون على قولنا: بُكُرٌ وأبكارٌ، كما يقال جُنُدٌ وأجناد. فتقول: لقد سمعتُه يقرأ هذه القراءةَ، وكنتُ عليها بُرهةً من الدهر، فلمّا تُوُفِّيَ، رحمه الله، انتقلتُ إلى جِدارٍ في دار أبي عمرو بن العَلاء، فسمعتُه يقرأ، فرغبتُ عن حروفٍ من قراءة الحسن كهذين الحرفين، وكقوله: الأَنجيل، بفتح الهمزة. فلمّا تُوفّي أبو عمرو كرِهتُ المُقام، فانتقلتُ إلى الكوفة، فأقمتُ في جِوار حَمْزةَ بن حبيبٍ، فسمعتُه يقرأ بأشياءَ يُنكره عليه أصحابُ العربيّة، كخفض الأرحام في قوله تعالى: ﴿وَاتَّقُوا اللَّهَ الَّذِي تَسَاءَلُونَ بِهِ وَالْأَرْحَامِ﴾ وكسر الياء في قوله تعالى: ﴿وَمَا أَنتُم بِمُصْرِخِيِّ﴾ وكذلك سكون الهمزة في قوله تعالى: ﴿اسْتِكْبَارًا فِي الْأَرْضِ وَمَكْرَ السَّيِّئْ﴾ وهذا إغلاقٌ لباب العربيّة، لأنّ الفُرقان ليس بموضِع ضَرورةٍ.

وإنّما حُكي مثلُ هذا في المنظوم. وقد رُوي أنّ امرأ القيس قال: ٤،٢،١٩

فاليومَ أَشرَبْ غيرَ مستحقِبٍ ... إثمًا من الله ولا واغلِ

وبعضهم يروي: فاليومَ أُسْقى، وإذا رُوي: فاليومَ أَشرَبْ، فيجوز أن يكون ثَمَّ إشارةٌ إلى الضّمّ لا حُكمَ لها في الوزن، فقد زعم سيبويه أنهم يفعلون ذلك في قول الراجز:

متى أنامُ لا يؤرِّقْني الكَرى ... ليلاً ولا أسمعُ أصواتَ المَطي

وهذا يدلّ على أنهم لم يكونوا يحفِلون بطرح الإعراب، فأمّا قول الراجز:

إذا اعوجَجْن قلتُ صاحِبْ قوِّمِ ... في الدَّوِّ أمثالَ السَّفينِ العُوَّمِ

«at evening and morn (*wa-l-ibkār*)»,[697] reading «morns (*abkār*)», as if it were a plural of *bakr*—one says, 'I met him in the morn (*bakaran*).' And if we argue that *anʿum* and *ashudd* are plurals of *niʿmah* and *shiddah*, and ignore the feminine ending, then it is also possible to think that *abkār* is the plural of *bukrah*, just as *ajnād* (troops) is the plural of *jund*."

The snake replies, "I have indeed heard him recite it like this. I followed him for a while; but when he died (God have mercy on him) I moved to a wall in the house of Abū ʿAmr ibn al-ʿAlāʾ[698] and I heard him recite the Qurʾan. Then I turned away from the variant readings of al-Ḥasan, such as these two, or his reading 'godspell' (*anjīl*) instead of 'gospel' (*injīl*).[699] When Abū ʿAmr died I did not want to stay there and I moved to Kufa, where I became the neighbor of Ḥamzah ibn Ḥabīb. I heard him recite many readings that are rejected by experts in the Arabic language, such as the reading *arḥāmi* ('bonds of kinship'), in the genitive instead of the accusative (*arḥāma*), in God's word[700] «Fear God, through whom you make requests of one another, and bonds of kinship», or reading *muṣrikhiyyi* instead of *muṣrikhiyya* in «neither can you aid me»,[701] or reading *sayyiʾ* instead of *sayyiʾi* in «waxing proud in the land and plotting evil».[702] This means locking the door of Arabic, because in the Revelation there is no need for poetic license!

"Such things occur in verse, as has been transmitted from Imruʾ al-Qays, who said: 19.2.4

> Today I'll drink (*ashrab*, instead of *ashrabu*) without incurring
> sin with God, nor as an uninvited guest.[703]

"Some people read it as 'Today I'll be given a drink (*usqā*).' If one reads 'Today I'll drink (*ashrab*),' it is possible to have a hint of the elided *u*, which has no metrical value,[704] for Sībawayh asserts that they do this in the verse by the *rajaz* poet:

> When shall I sleep and not be kept awake (*yuʾarriqᵘnī*) by the donkey man
> At night, not hearing the sounds of the beasts?

"This proves that they did not mind the omission of case endings. As for the following verse by another *rajaz* poet:[705]

> Whenever the camels swerved I said, 'My frien' (*ṣāḥib*, for *ṣāḥibī*),
> straighten them up!
> There in the desert, just like ships that swim!'

فإنّه من عجيب ما جاء، وقد بَلِهَ قائلُه عن أن يقول: صاحِ قَوِّم، فلا يكون بالوزن إخلالٌ، ولكنّ الذين يحتجُّون له يزعمون أنه أراد أن يعادل بين الجزئين، لأنّ قوله: حِبْ قَوِمِ، في وزن قوله: نِلْ عُوَّمِ، وهذا يُشبه ما ادَّعوْه في قول الهُذَلي:

أَبِيتُ على مَعارِيَ فاخراتٍ   بهنّ ملوَّبٌ كدَمِ العِباطِ

يزعُم النّحويُّون أنّ قوله: معاريَ، بفتح الياء، حمله عليه كَراهةُ الزِّحاف، وهذا قولٌ ينتقض، لأنّ في هذه الطائيّة أبياتاً كثيرةً لا تخلو من زحافٍ، وكلُّ قصيدةٍ للعرب غيرِها على هذا القريّ. وكذلك قوله:

عرفتُ بأَجْدُثٍ فنِعافِ عِرْقٍ   عَلاماتٍ كتَحبيرِ النِّماطِ

فيه زِحافان من هذا الجنس، ثمّ يجيء في كلّ الأبيات إلا أن يندُرَ شيءٌ. وقد رُوي عن الأصمعيّ أنه لم يسمع العربَ تنشد إلا: أَبِيتُ على مَعارٍ، بالتنوين، وهذا لا ينقُض مذهبَ أصحاب القياس، إذا كانوا يروون عن أهل الفصاحة خِلافَه.

ويَهكِر، أزلفه الله مع الأبرار المتّقين، لما سمع من تلك الحيّة، فتقول هي: ألا تُقيم عندنا بُرهةً من الدهر؟ فإنّي إذا شئتُ انتفضتُ من إهابي فصرتُ مثل أحسنِ غَواني الجنّة، لو ترشَّفتَ رُضابي لَعلمتَ أنه أفضلُ من الدِّرياقة التي ذكرها ابن مُقبِل في قوله: ٥،٢،١٩

سقتْني بصهباءَ دِرْياقةٍ   متى ما تُلَيِّنْ عِظامي تَلِنْ

ولو تنفَّستُ في وجهك لأعلمتُك أنّ صاحبة عَنْترة تَفِلةٌ صَدوفٌ، والصَّدوف: الكريهة رائحةِ الفم، وإنّما تعني قوله:

وكأنّ فارةَ تاجرٍ بقسيمةٍ   سبقتْ عوارضَها إليكَ من الفَمِ

"—this is very strange; the poet was too stupid to say *ṣāḥi*,[706] which would not affect the meter! But those who defend him assert that he wished to balance the meter of the two hemistichs, so that the meter of *-ḥib qawwimī* ('-n straighten') would be identical to *-ni l-ʿuwwamī* ('-ps that swim').[707] This resembles what they claim for the verse of the poet of the tribe of Hudhayl:[708]

I spent the night enjoying their luxurious naked bits;
covered with saffroned perfume, red as sacrificial blood.

"The grammarians assert that the poet said *maʿāriya* ('naked bits'), instead of *maʿārin*, because he disliked the metrical shortening.[709] However, this view is refuted by the fact that in the same poem rhyming in *-āṭī* there are many verses with such shortening, and it is the same with any long poem of the Arabs. Similarly, in his verse:

I recognized, in Ajduth and Niʿāf ʿIrq,
marks like patterns woven on carpets

"there are two shortenings of this kind;[710] and the same happens in all but a few of its verses. It has been transmitted that al-Aṣmaʿī heard the Arabs recite only *maʿārin* ('naked bits'); but this does not refute the view of the Partisans of Analogy, when they transmit the other version from people that are experts in the pure Arabic tongue."

The Sheikh is astounded (may God bring him near the pious and the god-fearing!) by what he has heard from this snake. She says, "Won't you stay awhile with us? If you wish I could shed my skin and take the form of the most beautiful of the girls in Paradise. If you sipped my saliva you would realize that it is more excellent than the elixir that is mentioned by Ibn Muqbil: 19.2.5

She gave me to drink a red wine, an elixir;
whenever it softened my bones, it[711] too would soften.

"Were I to breathe in your face you would know that ʿAntarah's girl friend[712] suffers from bad breath and halitosis (which means 'foul odor of the mouth') compared with me."—She meant ʿAntarah's verse:

It was as if a whiff of musk, straight from a merchant's pouch,
came from her mouth to you, before her teeth.

ولو أدنيتَ وِسادَكَ إلى وِسادي، لفضّلتَني على التي يقول فيها الأوّل:

باتت رَقودًا وسار الرَّكْبُ مُدَّلِجًا   وما الأوانسُ في فِكْرٍ لِسارينا
كأنّ رِيقتَها مِسْكٌ على ضَرَبٍ   شِيبتْ بأصهبَ من بيْع الشآمينا
يا ربِّ لا تسْلُبَنّي حُبَّها أبدًا   ويرحمُ اللهُ عبدًا قال آمينا

فيُذْعَرُ منها، جعل الله أمْنَه متَّصِلًا، والطالبَ شأْوَه من تقصيرٍ منتصِلًا، ويذهب ٦،٢،١٩
مُهَرْوِلًا في الجنّة ويقول في نفسه: كيف يُرْكَن إلى حيّةٍ شَرَفُها السُّمُّ، ولها بالفَتْكة هَمٌّ؟ فتُناديه: هلمَّ إن شئتَ اللّذّة، فإنّي لأفضلُ من حَيّةَ ابنةِ مالكٍ التي ذكرها العَبْسيُّ في قوله:

ما ولدتْني حَيّةُ ابنةُ مالكٍ   سِفاحًا ولا قوّلي أحاديثُ كاذبِ

وأحمدُ عِشارًا من حيّةَ ابنةِ أزهرَ التي يقول فيها القائل:

إذا ما شربْنا ماءَ مُزْنٍ بقهوةٍ   ذكرنا عليها حيّةَ ابنةَ أزهرا

ولو أقمتَ عندنا إلى أن تَخْبُر ودَّنا وإنصافنا، لَندِمتَ إن كنتَ في الدار العاجلة قتلتَ حيّةً أو عُثمانًا.

فيقول وهو يسمع خطابها الرائق: لقد ضيّق اللهُ عليَّ مَراشفَ الحُور الحِسان، إن رضِيتُ بترشُّف هذه الحيّة.

"And if I brought your pillow near to my pillow you would rather have me than the woman described in the words of the early poet:[713]

She slept all night; the caravan set off at nightfall.
But the women in our thoughts don't truly travel.
Her sweet saliva is like musk with honey, mixed
with a red wine bought from the Syrians.
Lord, never rob me of her love!
God will have mercy on His servant when he says Amen!"

The Sheikh is frightened of her (continually safe may God make him, and may He thwart him who attempts to overtake him!). He scuttles off hurriedly through Paradise, saying to himself, "How can one trust a snake whose poison is her pride and glory, and whose concern is a murderous foray?" She calls after him, "Come to me if you want to have pleasure! I am better than that Ḥayyah ('Snake'), Mālik's daughter, who is mentioned by the man of the tribe of 'Abs[714] when he says: 19.2.6

Ḥayyah, Mālik's daughter, has not out of wedlock given birth to me,
nor do I speak the tales of one who lies.

"And I am better company than Ḥayyah, Azhar's daughter, of whom a poet says:

When we have drunk clouds' water mixed with wine,
we thereby think of Ḥayyah, Azhar's daughter.

"If you stayed with us long enough to find out how affectionate and fair we are, you would be sorry you had ever killed, in the Fleeting World, a snake or a young viper!"[715]

But the Sheikh, hearing her enticing words, says, "May God close the lips of the fair black-eyed damsels for me if I bring myself to suck the lips of this snake!"

١،٢٠ فإذا ضرب في غِيطان الجنّة، لقيتْه الجارية التي خرجتْ من تلك الثَّمَرة فتقول: إنّي لأنتظرُك منذ حينٍ فما الذي شجَنَك عن المَزار؟ ما طالت الإقامةُ معك فأُمِلَّ بالمحاوَرة مَسْمَعَك، قد كان يحُقّ لي أن أُوثَر لديك على حَسَب ما تنفرد به العَروسُ، يخُصُّها الرجل بشيءٍ دون الأزواج.

فيقول: كانت في نفسي مآربُ من مخاطَبة أهلِ النار، فلمّا قضيتُ من ذلك وَطَرًا عُدتُ إليكِ، فاتّبعيني بين كُثُبِ العنبر وأنقاء المِسْك.

فيتخلّل بها أهاضيبَ الفردوس ورِمال الجنان؛ فتقول: أيّها العبد المرحوم، أظنُّك تحتذي بي فعال الكِنْديّ في قوله:

فقُمْتُ بها أمشي تجُرُّ وراءنا ... على إثْرنا أذيالَ مِرْطٍ مرحّلِ
فلمّا أجَزْنا ساحةَ الحيّ وانتحى ... بنا بَطْنُ خَبْتٍ ذي قِفافٍ عَقَنْقَلِ
هصَرتُ بفَوْدَيْ رأسِها فتمايلتْ ... عليَّ هضيمَ الكَشْحِ ريّا المخلخَلِ

فيقول: العجَب لقدرة الله! لقد أصبتِ ما خطر في السُّوَيداء، فمن أين لكِ علمٌ بالكنديّ وإنّما نشأتِ في ثَمَرةٍ تُبْعدكِ من جنٍّ وأنيس؟ فتقول: إنّ الله على كلّ شيءٍ قديرٌ.

ويعرض له حديثُ امرئ القيس في دارةِ جُلْجُلٍ، فينشئ الله، جلّتْ عَظَمته، حورًا عينًا يتماقلن في نهرٍ من أنهار الجنّة، وفيهنّ مَن تفضُلهنّ كصاحبة امرئ القيس، فيترامين بالتُّرْمُد، وإنّما هو كأَجَلِّ طِيب الجنّة، ويَعقِر لهنّ الراحلة، فيأكل ويأكلن من بضيعها ما ليس تقع الصِّفةُ عليه من إمتاع ولَذاذة.

٢،٢٠ ويمُرُّ بأبيات ليس لها سُموقُ أبيات الجنّة، فيسأل عنها فيقال: هذه جنّة الرُّجَز، يكون فيها أغلبُ بني عِجْلٍ والعجّاجُ ورؤبةُ وأبو النّجْمِ وحُمَيْدٌ الأرقط وعُذافِر بن أوْسٍ وأبو نُخَيْلةَ وكلُّ مَن غُفر له من [الرُّجّاز، فيقول:] تبارك العزيزُ الوهّاب! لقد صدق الحديث المرويّ إنّ الله يحُبُّ مَعاليَ الأمور ويكرَه سَفْسافَها؛ وإنّ الرَّجَز

20.1 *The Sheikh's return to his paradisical damsel*

Passing through the fields of Paradise he meets the girl that had come out of the fruit. She says, "I have been waiting for you for some time. What has kept you from visiting me? Surely I have not been with you long enough yet to bore your ears with my conversation! I am entitled to preferential treatment from you like any newly wedded wife! A husband has to give her special attention, more than his other wives."

The Sheikh replies, "I felt like having a chat with the people in Hell and when I had done what I wanted I came back to you. Now follow me, between the Ambergris Hills and the Musk Dunes!"

They cross the hills of Heaven and the sands of Paradise, and she says, "Dear departed servant of God, I think you are imitating the deeds of the Kindite with me,[716] when he says:

> Then I got up, taking her with me, as she trailed
> over our tracks the train of an embroidered gown.
> When we had crossed the clan's enclosure, turning to
> a sandy coomb with twisting slopes,
> I drew her temple-locks toward me and she leaned
> to me, slender her waist but plump her calves."

The Sheihk replies, "God's omnipotence is truly marvellous! You have said precisely what I was thinking, too, in my heart of hearts. But how do you know about Imru' al-Qays? I thought you had grown up in a fruit, far from jinnees and humans?" She answers, "God is able to do everything."

He remembers the story of Imru' al-Qays at Dārat Juljul.[717] Instantly God, the Almighty, creates girls with black, lustrous eyes, who contend with one another in plunging into one of the rivers of Paradise, playing together. In their midst is one prettier than all the others, like Imru' al-Qays's girlfriend. They throw bitter, acid weeds to one another,[718] but they smell like the costliest perfume of Paradise. He slaughters for them his riding animal; he eats and they eat some of it, which is indescribably delicious and delectable.

20.2 *In the Paradise of the rajaz poets*

He passes by some houses that are not as lofty as the other houses in Paradise. He asks about them and is told that this is the Garden of the *Rajaz* poets, the dwelling place of al-Aghlab al-ʿIjlī, al-ʿAjjāj, Ru'bah, Abū l-Najm, Ḥumayd al-Arqaṭ, ʿUdhāfir ibn Aws, and Abū Nukhaylah,[719] and all the others who received forgiveness.[720] [The Sheikh says,] "Blessed be the Almighty Giver! The tradition that has come down to us has come true: 'God loves that which

لمن سفساف القريض، قصّرتم أيّها النَّفر فقصّر بكم.

ويعرِض له رؤبةُ فيقول: يا أبا الجحّاف، ما أَكْلَفَكَ بقوافٍ ليست بالمُعْجِبة! تصنَعُ رجزًا على الغيْن ورجزًا على الطاء وعلى الظاء وعلى غير ذلك من الحروف النافرة، ولم تكن صاحبَ مَثَلٍ مذكورٍ، ولا لفظٍ يُستحسن عَذْبٍ.

فيغضَب رؤبةُ ويقول: أَلِي تقول هذا وعنّي أخذ الخليلُ، وكذلك أبو عمرو بن العَلاء، وقد غبرتَ في الدار السالفة تفتخر باللَّفظة تقع إليك ممّا نَقَلَه أولئك عنّي وعن أشباهي؟

فإذا رأى، لا زال خصمُه مغلّبًا، ما في رؤبةَ من الانتخاء[1] قال: لو سُبك رجزُك ورجزُ أبيك، لم تخرُج منه قصيدةٌ مستحسَنةٌ، ولقد بلغني أنّ أبا مُسلم كلّمك بكلامٍ فيه ابن ثأداءَ، فلم تعرِفْها حتى سألتَ عنها بالحيّ، ولقد كنت تأخذ جوائزَ الملوك بغير استحقاق، وإنّ غيرَك أَولى بالأَعْطِيَة والصِّلات.

فيقول رؤبة: أليس رئيسُكم في القديم، والذي ضهلت إليه المقاييسُ، كان يستشهد بقولي ويجعلني له كالإمام؟ فيقول، وهو بالقول مُنْطَقٌ: لا فخْر لك أن استُشهِد بكلامك، فقد وجدْناهم يستشهدون بكلام أَمَةٍ وَكْعاءَ تحمل القُطَلَ إلى النار المُوقَدة في السَّبْرة التي نفض عليها الشَّبَمُ رِيشَه، وهدم لها الشيخُ عرشَه، تأخُذ خَشَبةً للوَقود، كيما يَصِلُ إلى الرُّقود، وأجَلُّ أيّامها أن تجْنِيَ عَساقِلَ ومغرودًا، وتتلو نَعَمًا مطرودًا، وإنّ بَعْلها في المِهْنة لَسَيّءُ العذير، غَلُظ عن الفَطَن والتحذير؛ وكم روى النُّحاةُ عن طِفْلٍ، ما له في الأدب من كِفْلٍ، وعن امرأة، لم تَعْدُ يومًا في الدَّرَأة.

فيقول رؤبة: أجئتَ لخِصامنا في هذا المنزل؟ فامضِ لطِيّتك، فقد أخذتَ بكلامنا ما شاء الله. فيقول، أَسكت اللهُ مُجادِلَه: أُقسمتُ ما يصلُح كلامكم للثَّناء، ولا يفضُل عن الهِناء، تصُكُّون مَسامعَ الممتدَح بالجَنْدَل، وإنّما يُطرَب إلى المَنْدَل، ومتى خرجتم عن صفةِ جَمَلٍ، تَرْثُون له من طُول العَمَل، إلى صفةِ فَرَسٍ سابحٍ، أو كلبٍ للقَنَص نابحٍ، فإنّكم غيرُ الراشدين. فيقول رؤبة: إنّ الله سبحانه

[1] في النسخ: (الانتحاء) وما أُثبت في ب وسائر الطبعات أنسب للسياق.

is lofty and dislikes that which is lowly.'[721] *Rajaz* is really a lowly sort of poetry: you, people, have fallen short so you have been given short measure."

Ru'bah appears on the scene. The Sheikh says to him, "Abū l-Jaḥḥāf! You were rather fond of unpleasant rhyme letters. You composed poetry on the letter *gh*, on *ṭ*, on *ẓ*, and other intractable consonants! And you have produced not even a single memorable saying nor a single sweet expression."

Ru'bah says angrily, "Do you say this to me, though I am quoted by al-Khalīl and Abū 'Amr ibn al-'Alā'! And, in the Past World, you yourself used to flaunt your knowledge of words that those scholars have taken from me and my colleagues!"

Seeing Ru'bah's sense of his own self-importance, the Sheikh (may his opponent ever be defeated!) replies, "If your *rajaz* verse and that of your father were melted down you wouldn't get one single decent *qaṣīdah* out of it. I have heard that Abū Muslim was talking to you and spoke of the son of a 'slattern' and you did not know the word, so that you had to ask about it in your tribe! You have received rewards from kings without deserving them; others would have been more entitled to them."

Ru'bah answers, "But surely your leader, in the past, whose views were accepted as normative,[722] used to quote my verses as evidence, making me a kind of authority!" The Sheikh, quick at repartee, says, "Being quoted is nothing to boast about.[723] For we find that they also quote any sluttish slave girl who brings brushwood to fan a fire that blazes on a cold morning when frost has shaken out its feathers and a hoary-headed man fashions firewood from his humble hut, flinging it into the flames so that he can huddle in its heat; to pick mushrooms and fungi is her most glorious day, or to follow a camel driven away. Her master is a brute who is stupid and doesn't care a hoot. And how often do grammarians quote any tiny tot, who knows of letters not a jot? Or any person of the female gender, in need of men to defend her?"

Ru'bah replies, "Have you come to my place only to quarrel with me? In that case, please be on your way! You criticize everything I say!" The Sheikh says (may God silence his opponent!), "I swear that your verses are not suitable for praising those that hear them:[724] they are no better than tar with which you besmear them! You hit your patrons' ears with verses like boulders; one would rather be pleased with the scent of mandal wood when it smoulders. When you pass on from describing the need of a long-suffering camel to describing a galloping steed, or barking hounds at full speed, then you are lost indeed!"

قال: ﴿يَتَنَازَعُونَ فِيهَا كَأْسًا لَا لَغْوٌ فِيهَا وَلَا تَأْثِيمٌ﴾، وإنّ كلامك لمن اللّغو، ما أنت إلى النَّصَفة بذي صَغْو.

فإذا طالت المخاطَبة بينه وبين رؤبة، سمع العجّاجُ فجاء يسأل المحاجَزة.

ويذكر، أذكره الله بالصالحات، ما كان يلحق أخا النِّدام، من فُتور في الجَسَد من المُدام، فيختار أن يعرض له ذلك من غير أن يُنْزَف له لُبٌّ، ولا يتغيّر عليه خُبٌّ، فإذا هو يَخال في العِظام الناعمة دبيبَ نَمْل، أَسْرى في المُقْمِرة على رَمْل، فيترنّم بقول إياس بن الأَرَتّ: ٣،٢٠

أعاذلَ لو شرِبتِ الخمرَ حتى … يظلَّ لكلِّ أُنْمُلةٍ دبيبُ
إذاً لعَذَرْتِني وعلمتِ أنّي … لِما أتلفتُ من مالي مُصيبُ

ويتّكئ على مَفْرَش من السُّنْدُس، ويأمر الحُورَ العِينَ أن يحملن ذلك المفرش فيضعنه على سرير من سُرُر أهل الجنّة، وإنّما هو زَبَرْجَدٌ أو عَسْجَدٌ، ويكون البارئُ فيه حَلَقاً من الذَّهب تُطيف به من كلِّ الأشراء حتى يأخذ كلُّ واحدٍ من الغِلْمان، وكلُّ واحدةٍ من الجواري المشبَّهة بالجُمان، واحدةً من تلك الحَلَق، فيُحمَل على تلك الحال إلى مَحَلِّه المُشيَّد بدار الخلود، فكلّما مرَّ بشجرةٍ نَضَحَتْه أغصانُها بماء الوَرْد قد خُلط بماء الكافور، وبمسكٍ ما جُني من دِماء الفُور، بل هو بتقدير الله الكريم.

وتُناديه الثَّمَراتُ من كلِّ أَوْبٍ وهو مستلقٍ على الظَّهر: هل لك يا أبا الحسن، هل لك؟ فإذا أراد عُنقوداً من العِنَب أو غيره انقضب من الشجرة بمشيئة الله، وحملته القدرة إلى فيه، وأهل الجنّة يَلْقَوْنه بأصناف التحيّة ﴿وَآخِرُ دَعْوَاهُمْ أَنِ الْحَمْدُ لِلَّهِ رَبِّ الْعَالَمِينَ﴾ لا يزال كذلك أبداً سَرْمَداً، ناعماً في الوقت المتطاول منعَّماً، لا تجد الغِيَرُ فيه مَرْغَماً.

***

وقد أطَلْتُ في هذا الفصل، ونعود الآن إلى الإجابة عن الرسالة.

Ru'bah replies, "God, praised be He, has said,[725] «They hand one another cups; neither drivel is there nor recrimination». But what you say is complete drivel; it is neither fair nor civil!" After this lengthy exchange between him and Ru'bah, al-ʿAjjāj hears of it and approaches to separate the two.

The Sheikh is reminded (may God remind him of pious deeds!) that those who drink old wine will reposefully recline. This is what he now chooses, but with a mind unbefuddled and a foot unstumbling.[726] And behold, he imagines the wine seeping through his relaxed limbs like ants creeping on a dune in the light of the moon. He hums the verse of Iyās ibn al-Aratt: 20.3

The joys of Paradise

If you, fault-finding woman, would drink wine
till all your fingers tingled,
You would forgive me, knowing I was right
to squander all my money.

He reclines on a silk mat, telling the damsels with their black, lustrous eyes to lift the mat and put it on one of the couches of the dwellers in Paradise. It is made of peridot, or of gold. The Creator has formed rings of gold, fixed on all its sides, that the immortal youths and the girls, who have been compared to pearls,[727] can take hold of a ring each. In this manner Ibn al-Qāriḥ is carried to the dwelling place that has been erected for him in the Eternal Abode. Whenever he passes a tree, its twigs sprinkle him with rose water mixed with camphor, and with musk though not from a musk rat's blood obtained, but by God the Almighty ordained.

The fruits call at him from every side, as he lies on his back, "Would you like me, Abū l-Ḥasan, would you like me?" Thus, if he wants a bunch of grapes, for instance, it is plucked from its branch by God's will and carried to his mouth by His omnipotence, while the people of Paradise shower him with various greetings: «Their final call will be: Praise be to God, Lord of all Beings!».[728] Thus he is employed, for aye and ever, blessed in length of time delectable, not to change susceptible.

***

I have been long-winded in this part. Now we shall turn to reply to the letter.[729]

Notes

1 The English-language synopses have been supplied by the editor-translators and are not part of the original Arabic text.

2 Reading (with Kurd ʿAlī and Dechico) *qibalahu* instead of Bint al-Shāṭiʾ's *qablahu*.

3 The author uses, in what seems a rather unscientific fashion, four technical terms: *ustuquṣṣāt* (derived from Greek στοιχεῖα), *ʿanāṣir*, *arkān*, and *jawāhir*. Professor Hans-Hinrich Biesterfeld (Bochum), in a private communication to the translators, characterized this passage as "*terminologisches Geklingel*" ("terminological jingling").

4 Reading *aḥmada* (with Kurd ʿAlī and Dechico) instead of Bint al-Shāṭiʾ's *uḥmida*.

5 A play on words: *ṭabʿ* means both "imprint, seal" and "natural talent."

6 This and the following two poetic quotations are printed as prose in all editions and translations; it is a hemistich (minus the first word) by al-Mutanabbī; see *Dīwān*, p. 253.

7 Another hemistich by al-Mutanabbī; *Dīwān*, p. 494.

8 A verse by al-Ṣanawbarī (d. 334/945); *Dīwān*, p. 414.

9 Literally, "from his (own) skull, or brain."

10 The sense is not wholly clear and the translation uncertain.

11 Q Qamar 54:29, on the man from the people of ʿĀd who killed the God-sent camel.

12 Or "who wallows in the dust."

13 From a famous poem by the pre-Islamic poet al-Aʿshā.

14 Ample hips and buttocks are regularly compared to a sand dune. The syntax is not wholly clear.

15 Reading *murratan* (Dechico), "bitter," instead of *marratan*, is less likely, despite the parallel with *taṭību*.

16 There is a lacuna in the text here, found in all manuscripts, and al-Maʿarrī received the epistle with the same lacuna, for in the second part of *Risālat al-Ghufrān* he notes that "in the section where he mentions al-Khalīl the name of the extolled person—me—

is lacking." Apparently, Ibn al-Qāriḥ arrives at a gathering where someone speaks; the subject of "and [someone] said" is unknown.

17 *Taṣḥīf*, a common kind of mistake in Arabic, is to err in assigning the proper dots that distinguish different consonants (such as *r*/*z*, *ḥ*/*j*/*kh*, *b*/*n*/*t*/*th*/*y*); for two examples, see below, Ibn al-Qāriḥ §3.6.1.

18 Bint al-Shāṭi' thinks that something may be missing here, because the connection with the following is somewhat tenuous. Ibn al-Qāriḥ picks up the theme of "belittling" (*taṣghīr*) again, a term also used for the diminutive.

19 For the hemistich see his *Dīwān*, p. 298.

20 Echoing the saying of the pious ʿUbayd Allāh ibn ʿAbd Allāh (d. 97/716), when blamed for making verse: "He who suffers from phthisis must needs expectorate" (see, e.g., al-Jāḥiẓ, *Bayān*, i, 357, ii, 97, iv, 46; see also below, *IQ* §3.13).

21 Q Nisā' 4:143. The odd phrase «between this» is explained as "between belief and unbelief."

22 Identified by Bint al-Shāṭi' as Abū l-Ḥasan Aḥmad ibn ʿAbd Allāh al-Quṭrabbulī, mentioned in Ibn al-Nadīm, *al-Fihrist*, which was composed in 377/987–88.

23 Abū Bakr Muḥammad ibn Aḥmad Ibn Abī l-Azhar (d. after 313/925), also mentioned in *al-Fihrist*. Nothing is known about a book written by him and al-Quṭrabbulī.

24 The sources do not confirm the historicity of the following encounter. See Heinrichs, "The Meaning of *Mutanabbī*."

25 Since the names Aḥmad and Muḥammad are similar in sense ("most praiseworthy"), and the Prophet Muḥammad is sometimes called Aḥmad, al-Mutanabbī, saying this, seems to identify himself with the Prophet.

26 The Prophet Muḥammad is said to have had a mark (called "the seal of prophethood") between his shoulder blades.

27 i.e., the reproachful reminder of gifts.

28 The poet complains to Sayf al-Dawlah, reproaching him for being angry after his former generosity.

29 *Zanādiqah*, pl. of *zindīq*: someone professing Islam but having heretical (often Manichaean) beliefs.

30 *Mulḥidīn*, a somewhat vague term for heretics, atheists, and all those who deviate from orthodoxy (the technical term for an apostate from Islam is *murtadd*).

31 A hemistich by Abū Nuwās, see Abū Nuwās, *Dīwān*, i, 210 and v, 463.

32 He is Bashshār's rival, the poet Ḥammād ʿAjrad (d. between 155/772 and 168/784), who was also accused of Manichaeism.

33 Poet unidentified.

34 He is known as al-Muqannaʿ ("the veiled one"); his real name is not known. His rebellion, which began around 160/777, was suppressed after a siege in 166/783. Reports on his doctrine are somewhat vague; it seems to have been inspired by Mazdakism. See *EI2*, vii, 500 ("al-Muḳannaʿ").

35 The report is obviously exaggerated.

36 Reading *yudkhilu l-rijāla ʿalayhinna* (with Qumayḥah and al-Iskandarānī/Fawwāl); Dechico has *yadkhulu l-rijālu*, Bint al-Shāṭiʾ has *yudkhilu ʿalayhinna*.

37 The verses are not found in the collected verse published by Francesco Gabrieli, "Al-Walīd ibn Yazīd: il califfo e il poeta." With "tales of Ṭasm" he refers to the legends about the pre-Islamic Arab tribe of Ṭasm. Nothing is known about Umm al-Ḥunaykil ("mother of the little dwarf").

38 With a variation on the traditional exclamation pilgrims utter when entering the sacred area of the Hajj.

39 Bint al-Shāṭiʾ reads *bunābijah* (earlier editions *bunāyijah*), an unknown word. One could think of a corruption of Persian *piyālah* ("cup, goblet"), with middle Persian ending *-ag* or even the diminutive ending *-čah* (a suggestion by Professor Ludwig Paul, Hamburg).

40 It is not clear who is speaking. The word *ʿilj*, here translated as "lout," is sometimes applied to non-Muslims or non-Arabs, but also to uncouth persons in general.

41 cf. the version in al-al-Zamakhsharī, *Rabīʿ al-abrār*, iv, 81.

42 Al-Walīd uses the Persian word *haftajah*.

43 "Stinkmouth," on account of a malodorous lake in the neighborhood (thus, rather than "al-Baḥrā," as in Bint al-Shāṭiʾ's edition). Instead of being "in the environs of Damascus," it was located south of Palmyra; see H. Kennedy in *EI2*, xi, 128a, and Hamilton, *Al-Walīd and his Friends*, p. 154.

44 Reading *jamal*, with Bint al-Shāṭiʾ, ninth edition and Dechico, instead of *ḥml*.

45 i.e., the "Black Stone;" the "place of attachment" (*al-multazam*) is the part of the Kaaba between its door and the corner that contains the stone, so called because the pilgrims press themselves against it.

46 A waterspout mounted on top of the Kaaba, also called "the spout of mercy."

47 The speaker cannot be Ibn al-Qāriḥ.

48 An example of *taṣḥīf* (see above, §2.6.1): Rakhamah (which means "vulture") and Raḥmah ("mercy") differ only by one diacritical dot. The tradition is likely to have been one with eschatological content.

49 The words *rīḥ* ("wind") and *zanj*, when written, differ only in their diacritical dots. The Zanj were blacks originally from East Africa; widely exploited as slaves on plantations in southern Iraq, they revolted several times, most dangerously between 255/869

and 270/883, when they defeated several caliphal armies and sacked Basra. Their leader was, or called himself, ʿAlī ibn Muḥammad; he claimed descent from ʿAlī ibn Abī Ṭālib.

50 Unidentified; Warzanīn, a place near al-Rayy (close to present-day Tehran in Iran), is where the leader of the Zanj is said to have been born.

51 Perhaps ʿAlī ibn Abī Ṭālib is meant.

52 In fact a Qur'anic quotation (Q Āl ʿImrān 3:97), and thus by Muslim standards not a saying of the Prophet.

53 This seems to be the sense, but it is not clear which religious duty is meant.

54 Q Baqarah 2:228, continuing «for three monthly periods», i.e., before remarrying.

55 Taking *ḥill* as the opposite of *al-ḥaram*; it could also be "a non-sacred state" (*iḥlāl*, opposite of the *iḥrām* of the pilgrim).

56 Q ʿAnkabūt 29:67.

57 Surely a synecdoche, meaning "I."

58 Al-Ḥallāj "followed the ways of the Sufis in his mad speech and often spoke of the 'glittering light'" (al-Tanūkhī, *Nishwār al-muḥāḍarah*, i, 169). Ibn al-ʿArabī explains this "glittering light" as the light that takes vision away when God reveals Himself, cf. Louis Massignon, *Essay on the Origins of the Technical Language of Islamic Mysticism*, pp. 29–30. See also §15.2.1.

59 There is a lacuna in the text.

60 Adopting Bint al-Shāṭiʾ's emendation: *khashyatahū*. The manuscript readings *khashabah* and *khashabatahū* ("[his] piece of wood") could refer to the gibbet, gallows, or crucifixion cross on which al-Ḥallāj was executed, but the lacuna makes it impossible to decide and the translation is conjectural.

61 This seems to refer to a theory of vision, going back to Empedocles, according to which both object and eyes emit rays.

62 Unidentified.

63 It was the caliph al-Muqtadir, who (after initial reluctance) eventually signed the death warrant.

64 He was executed in Baghdad in 322/934.

65 In Shi'ite theology a prophet has a legatee (*waṣī*) who must uphold the law given by the prophet.

66 Quoting al-Khalīl ibn Aḥmad's verdict on Ibn al-Muqaffaʿ (who said the reverse of the former); see, e.g., Ibn Khallikān, *Wafayāt*, ii, 151.

67 Muḥammad ibn Yasīr al-Riyāshī (d. early third/ninth century).

68 *Al-Dāmigh* could also be rendered as *The Refutation*; graphic titles of invective poems or polemic treatises are not uncommon (cf. al-Ḥātimī's treatise of poetry criticism *al-Mūḍiḥah, Laying Bare the Bone*).

69 When al-Maʿarrī discusses this passage in Part Two of *Risālat al-Ghufrān* another work is listed: *al-Farīd* (*The Unique One*), said to be an attack on the Prophet. The editions by Kaylānī and Kurd ʿAlī (followed by Dechico) have "*al-Farīd, fī l-ṭaʿn ʿalā l-nabiyy ʿalayhi l-ṣalāh wa-l-salām.*"

70 In view of the somewhat abrupt transition to the following there may be a lacuna in the text.

71 Unlike the preceding etymologies, this one is wholly fanciful. The connection made next, between *shimāl* and *shuʾm*, has some support in historical linguistics.

72 The original connects it with *siyāq*, "agony."

73 Ibn al-Rūmī, *Dīwān*, p. 1889.

74 For the following anecdote see al-Masʿūdī, *Murūj al-dhahab*, v, 367 and compare al-Ṣūlī, *Akhbār Abī Tammām*, p. 172.

75 cf. Q Ghāfir 40:39.

76 This expression occurs in several sources that relate this episode; in one of them it is explained as "Zoroastrianism" (*al-Majūsiyyah*); see al-Dhahabī, *Tārīkh al-Islām, Ḥawādith* 221–30, p. 18. "White" may have been chosen in opposition to black, the official color of the Abbasid Dynasty.

77 From a famous poem by Abū Tammām, composed only a few years before, on al-Muʿtaṣim's victory over the Byzantines at Amorium in 223/838. In other sources it is Māzyār who tries to save his life with his wealth, see, e.g., al-Masʿūdī, *Murūj*, iv, 360.

78 Much in this passage is very unclear and the text seems corrupt. Bint al-Shāṭiʾ has the ungrammatical *ithnayn qatalū* (changed to *qatalā* in the editions of Qumayḥah and al-Iskandarānī/Fawwāl). The "two (men)" could be Bābak and Māzyār (if *ithnayn* is a corruption of Afshīn, one misses the article that it normally has). "Three million and five hundred" may be either a mistake for "two and a half million" or for the rather more plausible "three thousand five hundred." It is unclear what *dhabbāḥ* (lit. "slaughterer") means here.

79 A proverb (usually with *jarā* instead of *atā*).

80 The text is lacunose.

81 Apparently Jaʿfar, called al-Ṣādiq, the sixth imam of the Twelver Shīʿah (whose father was in fact called Muḥammad).

82 The sense is not clear. Perhaps: "I would be sent to prison, because I would have to incriminate powerful people (all of them heretics!)." See the verse quoted above, §3.2.

83 Lines by Abū Ḥamzah al-Mukhtār ibn ʿAwf, a Khārijite rebel (d. 130/748).

84 Not identified.

85 See his criticism of al-Mutanabbī, above, §2.7.1.

86 Ibn al-Rūmī, *Dīwān*, p. 1506.

87 A line by Ibn al-Rūmī (*Dīwān*, p. 1419); the interpretation follows Ibn Rashīq, *ʿUmdah*, i, 323.

88 Quoted anonymously in several sources (which have, more appropriately, "flew up" instead of "was agitated"); the vulture and crow stand for white and black hairs, respectively, the two nests are probably hair and beard; see Ibn Abī l-Iṣbaʿ, *Taḥrīr*, p. 274; Ibn Ḥijjah, *Khizānah*, iv, 86, first hemistich in *Lisān al-ʿArab*. s.v. *Gh-R-B*.

89 The verses are nos. 3, 26, 27, and 24 of a vaunting ode, which explains the incoherence of the quotation (*Dīwān*, pp. 590, 593). "Its days:" viz. of youth; in the second verse "they" refers to the poet's fellow tribesmen of Ṭayyiʾ.

90 There is an untranslatable play on words: *ḥaddatha* "to talk to" and *ḥādatha* "to furbish (a sword)."

91 The Hejaz, part of the traditional territory of Ṭayyiʾ (the poet himself grew up in Syria).

92 The words *mā khalā* cannot mean "except" here; "to say nothing of" is apparently to be taken in the sense of "especially."

93 The profusion of third person singular pronouns causes the usual confusion; it is somewhat unclear whether it is Abū l-ʿAbbās or Abū l-ʿAlāʾ who is doing the praising.

94 Bilāl, born as a slave, was the first black Muslim and on account of his powerful voice became the first muezzin; ʿAmmār ibn Yāsir was the son of a freedman; Ṣuhayb ibn Sinān was called al-Rūmī, "the Byzantine," because he had been taken captive by the Byzantines as a child. A freedman (*mawlā*) was associated with a tribe without having a proper tribal descent.

95 All were leading figures in Quraysh, ancestors of the Prophet, except ʿAbd Shams, an ancestor of the Umayyads.

96 *Al-Jāhiliyyah*, literally "ignorance," is the normal term for the pre-Islamic period.

97 Abū Ṭālib died without converting to Islam but protected his nephew during the difficult early stages of his preaching. See Ibn Hishām, *Sīrah*, i, 266, trans. Guillaume, p. 119.

98 Literally, "for a few *qīrāṭ*," a *qīrāṭ* ("carat") being the twenty-fourth part of a dinar.

99 The campaign to the Byzantine outpost at Tabūk, in northwestern Arabia, in 9/630 achieved rather little.

100 i.e., motionless (the expression is found in early poetry).

101 Reading *mūbiq*, "pernicious, noxious," instead of *mūniq* as in the various editions.

102 The editions by Kurd ʿAlī and Dechico add "and its joy having mixed with my mirth, my spirit, and my friends."

103 Verses by Abū l-ʿAtāhiyah; see *Dīwān*, p. 117.

104 The same verse as above, §4.2.

105 Poet unidentified.

106 Boiling down wine to reduce or eliminate its alcohol content made it permissible to drink it according to some jurists.

107 In the following rambling passage it is not always clear who is speaking, nor is it clear where the passage ends.

108 Quoting Ibn al-Sammāk; see Ibn Qutaybah, *ʿUyūn al-akhbār*, ii, 368.

109 Translation tentative, reading *alā mutaʿalliq bi-adhyāl dalīlihī* (cf., e.g., Ibn Abī Yaʿlā, *Ṭabaqāt al-Ḥanābilah*, ii, 160: *alā mutaʿalliqun bi-adhyāli ayimmatih*; al-Ḥātimī, *al-Risālah al-Mūḍiḥah*, p. 142: *mutaʿalliqan bi-adhyāli l-adab*). The editions of Qumayḥah and al-Iskandarānī & Fawwāl both have *alā mutaʿalliqun wa-l-adhyālu adhyālu dalīlihī*, which does not seem better.

110 viz. Ibrāhīm/Abraham; cf. Q Nisāʾ 4:125 «God took Abraham as a friend».

111 Or "when you remember them"?

112 Q Baqarah 2:186.

113 Q Isrāʾ 17:83 and Fuṣṣilat 41:51.

114 cf. Q Infiṭār 82:6 («What has deceived you about your generous Lord?»).

115 The meaning is not quite clear.

116 From a poem by Abū ʿUyaynah ibn Muḥammad ibn Abī ʿUyaynah (d. during the reign of Hārūn al-Rashīd). In line 3, "world of mine (*dunyāya*)" could also be translated "my Dunyā" (the name given to his beloved, who was in fact called Fāṭimah); see, e.g., al-Mubarrad, *al-Kāmil*, ii, 62; al-Iṣfahānī, *al-Aghānī*, xx, 87–88.

117 The Pharaoh who oppressed Mūsā (Moses) and the Israelites, and who was drowned; see Q Ṭā Hā 20:78; Gabriel (Jibrīl) is the archangel.

118 ". . . but through God," a very common phrase.

119 The sentence puns on several grammatical terms: *taʿrīf* "making acquainted/making definite," *tankīr* "making unknown/making indefinite," *khafḍ* "lowering/genitive," *rafʿ* "raising/nominative," *furādā* "single/singular forms," *jamʿ* "gathering/plural."

120 Printed as prose in previous editions, it is in fact a proverb in *rajaz* verse, found with many variants in several sources, see, e.g., al-ʿAskarī, *Jamharah*, ii, 219; Ibn ʿAbd Rabbih, *al-ʿIqd al-farīd*, iii, 77; al-Tanūkhī, *Nishwār al-muḥāḍarah*, iii, 135; al-Maydānī, *Majmaʿ al-amthāl*, ii, 359; Abū ʿUbayd, *Faṣl al-maqāl*, p. 461.

121 i.e., 397/1007.

122 In present-day Lebanon.

123 Khawlah is called "*al-māyisṭiriyyah*."

124 A proverb (al-Maydānī, *Majmaʿ*, ii, 495; al-ʿAskarī, *Jamharah*, ii, 337).

125 Quoted, anonymously, by al-Jāḥiẓ, *al-Ḥayawān*, iii, 109 and vi, 243.

126 The Arabic word for mad, *majnūn*, literally means "possessed by jinn."

127 i.e., by a mangy camel. This and the following expression are used for a person on whom one can rely.

128 *Ṭārimah* can be the cabin on a boat.

129 *Al-farqadān*: the two major stars of the Little Bear (α and β Ursae Minoris), including the Pole Star.

130 In popular psycho-physiology the liver was thought to be the seat of passions and emotions.

131 Taking *ʿawd* as a synonym of *ʿāʾidah*; alternatively, "one does not hope to see him again."

132 The tortuous style, here and elsewhere in the epistle, reflects that of the original (which is, admittedly, less verbose).

133 Not, as Bint al-Shāṭiʾ says, a verse from the famous poem attributed to al-Shanfarā called *Lāmiyyat al-ʿArab* ("the poem of the Arabs rhyming in L;" cf. its third verse, which resembles it). The verse is in fact by Maʿn ibn Aws (born in the pre-Islamic period, d. 64/684 or some years later) and is found in the celebrated anthology by Abū Tammām, *al-Ḥamāsah* (see al-Marzūqī's commentary, *Sharḥ Dīwān al-Ḥamāsah*, p. 1129).

134 i.e., he does not feather arrows nor trim wood for them, an expression meaning "he is neither useful nor harmful."

135 With this money he financed an unsuccessful rebellion against the Fatimids, in the name of a Meccan *sharīf* set up as a counter-caliph.

136 The words *maʿānīhi wa-mabānīhi* have been taken to refer to the content and style of al-Maʿarrī's works (cf. Ḥāzim al-Qarṭājannī's work on poetics, *Minhāj al-bulaghāʾ*, where the major sections are entitled *al-mabānī* and *al-maʿānī*).

137 Not identified.

138 Both are lexicographical works, the former (*al-Faṣīḥ*) by Thaʿlab (d. 291/904) and the latter (*Iṣlāḥ al-manṭiq*) by Ibn al-Sikkīt (d. ca. 244/857).

139 Iyās ibn Muʿāwiyah, judge in Basra under Caliph ʿUmar ibn ʿAbd al-ʿAzīz (r. 99–101/717–20), proverbial for his sagacity; Bāqil, an obscure figure said to have been a member of the tribe of Iyād, proverbial for his inarticulateness.

140 In joke collections the unreliable keeper is a muezzin (al-Ābī, *Nathr al-durr*, vii, 311; al-Ibshīhī, *al-Mustaṭraf*, Cairo, 1952, ii, 273).

141 Reading *ṭarīf* instead of *ẓarīf*.

142 Apparently a proverb; it scans as a hemistich in *khafīf* meter. On *harīsah* see above, §6.5. In a note in the edition by al-Iskandarānī and Fawwāl the word *zabūn* is taken to mean "(she-camel) who kicks a lot," and the saying is interpreted as "Be amazed at the one that I feed and that kicks me with her foot or kills me." But feeding a camel with *harīsah* seems unlikely.

143 This verse has been attributed (in al-Baghdādī, *Khizānat al-adab*, ii, 265) to ʿAbd Allāh ibn al-Zabīr al-Asadī (second/eighth century), in praise of the poet Asmāʾ ibn Khārijah (d. 66/686 or some years later); but it is also found in the *Dīwān* of Abū Tammām in praise of Caliph al-Muʿtaṣim (*Dīwān*, iii, 29).

144 From a poem by the pre-Islamic poet Zuhayr ibn Abī Sulmā in praise of Ḥiṣn ibn Ḥudhayfah, a leader of the Fazārah tribe.

145 For the anecdote, compare Ibn ʿAbd Rabbih, *al-ʿIqd al-farīd*, iii, 164.

146 *Usfitta* does not really make sense; it is not about "drinking a lot without quenching one's thirst" but about not being able to urinate (one would expect a form of the verb *ḥaqana*); the version in *al-ʿIqd* is clearer: *fa-law ḥubisa ʿanka khurūjuhā*.

147 The "shirt" is apparently used figuratively for his material circumstances; but the measures given here, if taken literally, are odd: "two cubits" seems rather too long for a newborn child. In the following, "twelve cubits" is also too long (and would still be even if one assumes that the author confuses *dhirāʿ* with *shibr*, "span of the hand").

148 Q Shuʿarāʾ 26:79; the following "he" is Ibrāhīm/Abraham.

149 Q Shuʿarāʾ 26:80.

150 One would expect, e.g., "promise a reward," but *tawaʿʿada* normally has a negative sense. The acts listed are involuntary or automatic and thus beyond our control, and so we cannot be punished for them.

151 Q Insān 76:7; its continuation is «. . . a day whose evil will fly up».

152 Emendation suggested by Bint al-Shāṭiʾ.

153 By ʿUbayd ibn Ayyūb al-ʿAnbarī, a "brigand poet" from the Umayyad period (see al-Jāḥiẓ, *al-Bayān wa-l-tabyīn*, iv, 62), adopting the reading *qaddama* instead of *dhammama* as in Bint al-Shāṭiʾ's edition.

154 Untranslatable play on two meanings of the word *al-sawdāʾ* ("the black one"), the former apparently used for *musawwadah* ("draft, rough copy"), the latter short for *al-mirrah al-sawdāʾ*, "melancholy." Abū l-ʿAlāʾ picks up the theme of "blackness" in the beginning of his epistle.

155 Anonymous in al-Farrāʾ, *Maʿānī l-Qurʾān*, i, 262; al-Baghdādī, *Khizānat al-adab*, viii, 486 and 514.

156 *Ḥamāṭah* is (a) a tree, or (b) its fruit, said to resemble the wild fig or a peach. Other meanings are (c) "heartburn" (the sensation of acridity in throat or chest) and (d) "blackness or bottom of the heart" (which "dwells" in the writer and which is his intended meaning here). The whole preamble is an exercise in such double entendre (*tawriyah* in Arabic).

157 Snakes are said to live on the *afāniyah* tree on which the *ḥamāṭah* fruits grow.

158 Ibn al-Qāriḥ.

159 In Arabic usage a day of twenty-four hours begins at sunset.

160 Either "the mother of the little babe," or "the mother of little al-Walīd;" probably referring to the poet's wife.

161 A tribe; the reference is unclear.

162 Translation uncertain.

163 The rest of the verse, with the crucial word, is lacking.

164 It is likely that with the "two robes" the author means his body and his real clothes.

165 Another double entendre: *ḥiḍb* is said to mean a kind of snake; it also means "the sound made by a bow," and, as the author will explain, "heart."

166 i.e., whether she is a snake or human.

167 Ru'bah ibn al-ʿAjjāj.

168 *Aswad*, "black (thing)," here standing for the "black bottom" of the heart, also means "large snake."

169 The masculine word *aswad* (literally, "black") and its feminine equivalent *sawdāʾ* both can mean "bottom of the heart," as does the diminutive of the latter, *suwaydāʾ*.

170 In the following many personal names (Aswad, Suwayd, Sawdah, Sawādah, Suḥaym) refer to "blackness."

171 viz. a "black thing" or "heart." In the following, "it" always means "the heart."

172 The verse is from his most famous poem, one of the seven celebrated long pre-Islamic poems called *Muʿallaqāt*.

173 *Bi-l-aswadayn* is ambiguous; some commentators believe, with al-Maʿarrī, that two men called al-Aswad are meant, but most think it means "the two black things," here standing either for "dates and water" or "night and day" (in Arabic a dual is sometimes used for complementary pairs, such as "the two fathers" for "parents"). A variant has *bi-l-abyaḍayn* "with the two white things," also variously explained.

174 The identity of this Abū l-Aswad is not known; he may be his cousin Abū l-Aswad Yazīd mentioned in the Glossary s.v. Aswad ibn Maʿdīkarib.

175 Elsewhere the lines are attributed to al-Akhyal ibn Mālik al-Kilābī (*Ḥamāsat al-Buḥturī*) or Muzarrid (al-Nushshābī al-Irbilī, *Mudhākarah*).

176 Literally, "(his) desire did not turn away from it;" probably referring to the fact that she dissuaded him from divorcing her (Q Nisāʾ 4:127 alludes to this).

177 "The two white things (*al-abyaḍān*)" also stand for water and flour.

178 Another version of these lines (Ibn Qutaybah, *Maʿānī*, p. 425) has "two black things," explaining that *fathth* is an inferior grain from which "black" bread is made.

179 The poet is Hudhayl ibn ʿAbd Allāh al-Ashjaʿī; here "the two white things" are water and milk.

180 The common female name Rabāb stands for any woman who, as so often in poetry, will only love a healthy young man (see also below, the passage on the various Rabābs, §9.3.1).

181 Wine, meat, and gold, or a kind of perfume made with saffron, according to the lexicographers. There are other interpretations.

182 The eye is followed by the heart.

183 Q Fāṭir 35:10.

184 Q Ibrāhīm 14:24–25.

185 The Arabic for "sky" used here is the same as that for "heaven."

186 Weapons were suspended from it.

187 He will appear later in the text.

188 The following lines are found in al-Iṣfahānī, *al-Aghānī*, xx, 330.

189 This verse is quoted in the famous grammar by Sībawayh, where it is attributed to Abū ʿAṭāʾ al-Sindī.

190 Traditionally only three variants are recognized (ending in SLLL, SLSL, and SLL, where S stands for a short and L for a long syllable); if Abū l-Hindī's verses end on a consonant (*-zubd*, *-raʿd*), the fourth variant would end in SLO, where O stands for an overlong syllable.

191 Again, the strainer is described (see Ibn Manẓūr, *Lisān al-ʿarab*, s.v. *Kh-N-F*; in the entry *B-R-Q* the verse is ascribed to ʿAdī ibn Zayd).

192 With untranslatable play on obscure additional meanings of *abārīq* ("jugs").

193 The expression "sipping (the beloved's) saliva," which sounds somewhat odd in modern English, is a recurrent motif in classical Arabic love poetry; cf. below, §§10.1, 13.2.2, 14.1, 19.2.5.

194 "Modern" refers to the Abbasid period, from the middle of the second/eighth century.

195 Said to be a wine merchant in al-Ṭāʾif in Arabia, only known from the following line by the first/seventh-century poet Abū Dhuʾayb.

196 Q Muḥammad 47:15.

197 The poet means: "to me;" he is imagining or dreaming of his beloved.

198 The "nightly phantom" (*khayāl*) of the beloved, either her image in a dream or a fantasy, is an extremely common motif in Arabic poetry.

199 The rare word *lamṣ* is explained with the common word *fālūdh,* the same as *fālūdhaj,* a sweet made of flour and honey.

200 This is indeed what the author does, at some length, suggesting alternative rhyme words with all the other letters of the alphabet in their proper order. Not content with this, he ensures that most of the following rhymes are "rich rhymes," involving two consonants instead of one, just as he did in his extensive collection of verse called *Luzūm mā lā yalzām* (loosely translated as *The Self-Imposed Constraint*).

201 The glottal stop (').

202 In Sībawayh's grammar the verse is quoted with *al-khamr* ("wine") instead of *al-nash'*.

203 The last sentence, found as a marginal addition, may have been part of the main text.

204 In other words, a rhyme in *-ā* (called *alif maqṣūrah,* spelled with either *alif* or *yā',* the only rhyme that is not based on a "true" consonant) hides an unvoweled "virtual consonant" ($\bar{a} = a^0$); it cannot immediately follow an unvoweled consonant, though the meter requires this here.

205 The Bedouins had a kind of popular meteorology based on the stars; some stars and constellations were associated with rain.

206 In the pre-Islamic gambling game called *maysir*, forbidden in Islam (cf. Q Baqarah 2:219, Mā'idah 5:90–91), portions of a slaughtered camel were divided by shuffling marked arrow shafts. The implication is that her family is wealthy.

207 *Alladhī qāla lāna kulluh*: the word *qāla* ("he said") is either a mistaken insertion or refers to an unnamed lexicographer.

208 The verse is possibly corrupt and rather unclear. Bint al-Shāṭi''s suggestion of reading *mimman laqū* instead of *man laqū,* is unmetrical. Al-Iṣfahānī, *Aghānī* xii, 136 has *fa-Bahratun* (for *fa-Bahrā'u,* a tribe); rejected by the editor of Ibn Sallām, *Ṭabaqāt*, p. 513, who emends to *muntahizan man laqū* and gives a lengthy explanation.

209 *Muwallad,* here meaning "not found in the 'pure' Arabic of pre- and early Islamic Arabs."

210 On the seven readings of the Qur'anic text generally recognized as "canonical," see below, notes 420 and 696.

211 They are quoted in Sībawayh's grammar, attributed to "a man from Oman;" elsewhere they are attributed to al-'Umānī.

212 The issue is whether the accusatives of *ṭūlan* and *'arḍan* are to be explained as adverbial qualifications of place or adverbial specifications ("qua length and breadth").

213 All rhymes in this digression end in *-ī*, the pausal genitive ending, which has been left out in the translations, where the normal prose forms are given; but Mubghī cannot be shortened in the same manner.

214 This explanation is not given by most sources, which say that *ḥaww* and *laww* in this expression mean "truth" and "falsehood," respectively, or "yes" and "no" (see e.g. *Lisān al-ʿArab*, *Ḥ-W-W/Y*; al-ʿAskarī, *Jamharat al-Amthāl*; *WKAS* II, iv, 1901, 1903; Lane, *Lexicon*, p. 681b). Al-Maʿarrī's source is unknown.

215 Or: that has become (too) longwinded (the use of the imperfect tense, in that case, is unusual but not impossible: see Reckendorf, *Arabische Syntax*, p. 12, par. 8, 2a).

216 After using various near synonyms (*ṣāb*, *habīd*, *ḥadaj*) the more usual word, *ḥanẓal(ah)* is used here.

217 The poet is Ru'bah ibn al-ʿAjjāj. The verse is quoted by Sībawayh and other grammarians because of the unusual *kahū* and *kahunna*, here imitated in the translation.

218 *Diflā*; poisonous, used to kill or repel vermin.

219 Bint al-Shāṭi''s edition has *ṣalāḥ*, but according to the grammarians and lexicographers the correct reading is *ṣilāḥ*, alternative of *muṣālaḥah* (hence the feminine suffix of *fīhā*); see, e.g., *Lisān. al-ʿArab* s.v. *Ṣ-L-Ḥ*, al-Akhfash, *al-Ikhtiyārayn*, p. 601.

220 Khālid ibn Zuhayr al-Hudhalī (a contemporary of the Prophet), in response to a poem by his uncle Abū Dhu'ayb. The verse is not by Abū Dhu'ayb himself as Bint al-Shāṭi' says (see al-Sukkarī, *Sharḥ ashʿār al-Hudhaliyyīn*, pp. 212, 215).

221 The quoted line, on a gift including a fish made of sugar and almonds "swimming" in honey, is uncharacteristic of the poet, who despised trifles and who excelled in sonorous and rhetorical eulogy, vaunting, and invective.

222 The meaning of *khawwārah* is not clear ("mild, weak" seems incompatible with what follows).

223 The famous grammarian al-Mubarrad (d. 285/898) belonged to Thumālah; the lexicographer Ibn Durayd (d. 321/933) belonged to Daws.

224 Q Ḥijr 15:47.

225 The former is better known as Thaʿlab (d. 291/904), grammarian from Kufa, bitter rival of al-Mubarrad of Basra (here called Muḥammad ibn Yazīd).

226 Jadhīmah, a legendary pre-Islamic king of Iraq, killed his two inseparable friends while drunk, bitterly repenting afterward; later killed by Queen al-Zabbā' of Palmyra, who may be (partially) identified as Zenobia.

227 Al-Kisā'ī, who was the tutor of Hārūn al-Rashīd's sons, and Sībawayh discussed a point of grammar in a session arranged by Yaḥyā al-Barmakī; al-Kisā'ī apparently instructed Bedouin Arabs to support his (incorrect) view, thus defeating Sībawayh.

228 Labīd, famous pre- and early Islamic poet, lamented his brother's death in several elegies. Al-Maʿarrī's protagonist Ibn al-Qāriḥ will meet the poet in Paradise (see §8.3.1). Mutammim ibn Nuwayrah and his brother Mālik were both poets of the pre- and early Islamic periods; Mutammim composed elegies on his brother after his death in 13/634. Ṣakhr and Muʿāwiyah are lamented in numerous poems by their famous sister, al-Khansāʾ (d. ca. 23/644); Ibn al-Qāriḥ meets her later (§16.4).

229 Q Raʿd 13:23–24.

230 Maymūn ibn Qays, known as al-Aʿshā. Ibn al-Qāriḥ will meet him soon (below, §5.2).

231 Quraysh, the Prophet's tribe but still opposed to him when al-Aʿshā sought to visit him, bribed the poet into changing his mind, thus preventing his conversion to Islam, even though he had already composed an ode on the Prophet (see below). But according to another version, told by Ibn Qutaybah (d. 276/889), al-Aʿshā, on his way to convert, had second thoughts when he was told that the Prophet forbade drinking wine and committing adultery. He decided to enjoy himself for one more year, but died before the year was over.

232 According to Nicholson (p. 654), "And the wine bowl conveyed from hand to hand long-used cups of glass (i.e., the drinkers filled their cups from it in turn, by means of the *ibrīq*), while those who drew therefrom mixed their draught with water)", adding, "This seems to be the sense if the reading is correct."

233 These five persons were tribal leaders on whom al-Aʿshā composed panegyric odes. ʿĀmir ibn al-Ṭufayl, a bitter enemy of the Prophet, was himself a poet.

234 i.e., al-Aʿshā; the verses are not found in his *Dīwān*. Yāqūt, in his geographical dictionary, lists al-Ṣaybūn, merely saying that "it is mentioned in al-Aʿshā's verse" and quoting the two lines.

235 The word *hātif* (lit., "shouting, calling") is often used for an invisible being such as a demon (*jinnī*) inspiring a poet or a mysterious prophetic voice bringing messages.

236 One cannot help thinking that with this mocking description of the Arab nomads (not unusual in refined urban circles) the author is also casting some doubt on the process of transmission and the reliability of the chain of authorities (*isnād*), a method ubiquitous in Islamic disciplines. Curdled milk and dates are part of the normal Bedouin diet; here they are described as too poor and destitute even for this.

237 The genealogy in al-Iṣfahānī's *al-Aghānī* (ix, 108) is almost identical and traces it even further back, to Nizār, the legendary ancestor of the "North Arabs."

238 Muslims believe that the Prophet Muḥammad will intercede on behalf of his community on Judgment Day. According to popular belief his cousin and son-in-law ʿAlī (who became the fourth Caliph) will assist him there.

239 For another English translation of these verses (a longer version of the poem) see A. Guillaume's translation of *Sīrat Rasūl Allāh*, the second/eighth-century biography of the Prophet (Ibn Isḥāq, *The Life of Muhammad*, pp. 724–25), where the story is told in the additions by Ibn Hishām (third/ninth century).

240 He addresses his camel. Hāshim was in fact the Prophet's great-grandfather.

241 Here, of course, the poet addresses his audience (a few lines have been omitted by Abū l-ʿAlāʾ).

242 Muslims may eat only ritually slaughtered animals (with some exceptions in connection with hunting and shooting).

243 This refers to the practice of bleeding cattle to drink the blood or prepare dishes from it such as *majdūḥ* (a kind of black pudding); Muslims are forbidden to consume blood. The translation combines the readings *li-tuqṣidā*, "to stab it" (found in all MSS) and *li-tufṣidā* "to bleed it" (found in the *Dīwān* and many other sources).

244 The book mentioned here is lost; it is mentioned in the early treatise on figures of speech by Ibn al-Muʿtazz (d. 296/908) when he speaks of *tajnīs* (paronomasia).

245 Or: "that, even when held back, runs fast." The verb *zajara* ("to hold back"), when applied to camels, can mean "to spur on."

246 Here the second foot, normally SLLL, is SLSL, which is not uncommon in early poetry but very rare in later periods.

247 i.e., LL instead of SLL here, a feature called *kharm* and only found in early poetry at the beginning of a whole verse (and in fact only in the first line of a poem).

248 From an ode in praise of Qays ibn Maʿdīkarib, a famous tribal leader.

249 A nearly literal quotation of Q Ghāfir 40:7: «Our Lord, Thou embracest everything in mercy and knowledge».

250 This is from his most famous poem, one of the seven celebrated pre-Islamic odes called *al-Muʿallaqāt*.

251 Not found in the ode of the same meter and rhyme in his *Dīwān*, but ascribed to Zuhayr in *al-Muʿammarūn* (*Long-lived People*) by Abū Ḥātim al-Sijistānī (d. 254/868).

252 Between the two prophets Jesus and Muḥammad.

253 See Q Āl ʿImrān 3:103 («Hold fast to the rope of God, all together») and cf. 112.

254 See Q Insān 76:17–18 («And they are given to drink a cup whose admixture is ginger; a spring therein called Salsabīl»).

255 The verses are found elsewhere ascribed to the pre-Islamic poet ʿAdī ibn Zayd; the designation al-Sarawī (probably referring to the Arabian mountain range called al-Sarāh) is not clear.

256 Reading *taʾbīd* (as in Bint al-Shāṭiʾ's ninth edition) instead of *taʾyīd*, found in other editions.

257 The verse is sometimes found in ʿAbīd's most famous poem, but it is lacking from many versions, and its authenticity is therefore rather suspect.

258 Q Fāṭir 35:34.

259 The path (*al-ṣirāṭ*, from Latin *strata*, via Greek and Syriac) that bridges Hell toward Paradise is not mentioned in the Qur'an but found in the Hadith. It can only be crossed by the believers; in due course (see below, §11.8.1) the Sheikh will tell how he crossed it.

260 ʿAdī was famous for his descriptions of wine.

261 All lines of a classical Arabic poem have the same rhyme; the basis of the rhyme is a consonant, very often (but not here) followed by a long vowel. The letter *ṣ* is a very rare rhyme consonant.

262 Identified by the editor as ʿAbd Hind ibn Lakhm, a mistake for ibn Lujam (see al-Kalbi / Caskel, *Ǧamharat an-nasab*, Tab. 175, Register p. 124).

263 Either wineskins made of gazelle hides (thus the dictionary *Lisān al-ʿArab*) or large pitchers (thus Ibn Qutaybah, *al-Maʿānī*, p. 449).

264 Attractive women are often described as moving slowly, because of their plumpness.

265 Another interpretation of this verse is: "On a high spot, chilled by the wind, for us is poured | a dark wine mixed with water from a cloud."

266 A victim of intrigues at the court of King al-Nuʿmān in al-Ḥīrah, the poet was imprisoned and later put to death.

267 According to Bint al-Shāṭi' *nīq* ("mountain top") could mean "a wooden plank on which a person subjected to torture is carried"; we were unable to verify this. The "ostrich" is a metaphor (instead of the more usual simile) for a camel.

268 This line is difficult to understand; a more comprehensible version is found in Ibn Qutaybah, *al-Shiʿr*, p. 239: *au murtaqā nīqin ʿalā markabin | adfara ʿawdin* ("Or being raised on top of an old animal [i.e., mule or donkey], stinking... ").

269 Perhaps the reading in Ibn Qutaybah's *al-Shiʿr* (*lā yuḥsinu l-mashya*, "It cannot walk well") is to be preferred.

270 Not only in the same meter (*sarīʿ*, not uncommon) but also with the same, very unusual rhyme (*-ī/ūṣ*).

271 The word *anā* ("I") very often scans as *ana*, with a short second syllable (here it is necessary because of the meter). If, however, the first syllable is elided, only *na* would remain, in which case it can no longer count as a true word according to Arabic grammarians.

272 i.e., turning *wa-ana* (with a "half-realized" glottal stop) into *wāna*.

273 The verse is discussed in Sībawayh's *Kitāb*, i, 70–71 and many subsequent works on grammar. In *al-Aghānī* (ii, 152) a variant without the puzzling "you" is quoted

and paraphrased as "Shall we say goodbye to you in the evening or in the morning? Which do you want?"

274 Several interpretations are supplied in Ibn Manẓūr, *Lisān al-ʿArab* (on a similar verse by Qays ibn al-Khaṭīm): the animal has been ridden to exhaustion, or it has fine features.

275 The translation of this verse is based on the paraphrase in Ibn Qutaybah, *al-Maʿānī*, p. 70.

276 The last word, *yafan*, is explained as "rapid pace" in a marginal gloss; the dictionaries only give "old man." Ibn Qutaybah has a different interpretation: "It makes a good run, with rapidity, let loose like a downpour, just as a mature cloud (reading *muzn* instead of *marr*) is filled with rain."

277 Interpretation based on Ibn Qutaybah.

278 On the "rain stars" see above, §3.8.2. The Arabic for Aquarius *al-Dalw*, means "bucket"; the "bucket handles" are rain stars associated with Aquarius.

279 This is meant ironically, praise in the form of blame, according to Ibn Qutaybah, *Maʿānī*, p. 360.

280 The meaning of *zawāʾid* ("additions") is unclear; cf. Ibn Qutaybah, *Maʿānī*, p. 339: "perhaps they are on its feet, like people with extra fingers, or the *zawāʾid* of a lion."

281 From a poem by Kaʿb ibn Maʿdān al-Ashqarī (d. ca. 95/714); see, e.g., al-Iṣfahānī, *al-Aghānī*, xiv, 299.

282 The wife of the pre-Islamic King al-Nuʿmān ibn al-Mundhir, subject of stories and poems. Al-Mutajarridah is a nickname and means "she who stripped [herself], the denuded woman." The king's horse was called al-Yaḥmūm ("Black Smoke"). Jalam is mentioned in al-Zabīdī's dictionary *Tāj al-ʿarūs* as Jalam ibn ʿAmr, where it is said "there is a story about him with al-Nuʿmān ibn al-Mundhir," but the story itself is not found.

283 See al-Iṣfahānī, *Aghānī*, ii, 154.

284 *Aghānī*, ii, 153.

285 The preceding line and the following piece are in *sarīʿ* meter, but the fact that the opening hemistich of the first line and all hemistichs of the second piece end in SSL rather than LSL makes them unusual.

286 The Arabs assumed, with Aristotle, that the head of a bee colony could only be male.

287 Q Aʿrāf 7:43.

288 The word "brisk" (*fāriḥ*) is appropriate for donkeys and packhorses but not for a noble horse.

289 The particle *layta* ("if only, would that") should be followed by a noun or pronoun, not by a verb.

290 The ʿIbād (lit., "servants") is the name of the Christian Arabs that lived in al-Ḥīrah in the pre-Islamic period. The philologists had reservations about their language (including the poetry of ʿAdī) because they were sedentary and exposed to Persian influence.

291 Q Ṭūr 52:19, Mursalāt 77:43.

292 The pronunciation of *j* as [g] is mentioned by the early grammarians (they, like Abū l-ʿAlāʾ here, spell it with *k*, since standard Arabic has no letter for [g]).

293 Q Rūm 30:18.

294 The nickname al-Nābighah ("the copious genius") was given to at least eight early poets, the two most famous being al-Nābighah al-Dhubyānī (sixth century AD) and al-Nābighah al-Jaʿdī (d. ca. 63/683).

295 Birds may not be killed in Mecca, which was already a sanctuary and a holy place before Islam.

296 He addresses ʿAdī ibn Zayd and the two Nābighahs. With the "ʿIbādī poet" he means ʿAdī.

297 Literally "Chosroan wine," after Chosroes/Khusraw, the name of several Sasanian emperors in the pre-Islamic period.

298 He refers to al-Aʿshā, whom he has met before.

299 Q Shūrā 42:29.

300 Al-Nābighah's poem from which the following lines (on the king's spouse al-Mutajarridah) are quoted lost him the king's favor; he fled and composed a number of famous apologetic odes, eventually becoming reconciled to the king.

301 This refers to some verses in the same meter and rhyme that describe, in hardly veiled terms, the queen's private parts engaged in sexual intercourse, not quoted by Abū l-ʿAlāʾ but found in several sources (e.g. Ibn Qutaybah, *al-Shiʿr*, p. 166, Ahlwardt, *The Divans of the six ancient Arabian poets*, p. 11). Their attribution to al-Nābighah may well be spurious.

302 In unvoweled Arabic script *naẓartu* and *raʾaytu* etc. (first person singular) could also be read as *naẓarta* and *raʾayta* (second person singular), which is in fact how the lines are usually read. The following lines, not quoted, are already so improper, irrespective of the grammatical person being used, as to make the poet's (or rather al-Maʿarrī's) defense rather feeble.

303 ʿAbd al-Malik is normally known as al-Aṣmaʿī.

304 See for instance Q Maryam 19:40, where God says «We shall inherit the earth and all those who are on it».

305 Q Naml 27:33; the Queen of Sheba is addressed by her counselors.

306 The dual refers to the traditional motif, very often found at the beginning of odes, of the "two companions"; they are supposed to accompany the poet-persona on his desert journey, stopping with him when he wants to reminisce at an abandoned site.

307 i.e., I did not compose this poem.

308 The verses are not found in al-Nābighah's collected poems.

309 Thaʿlabah ibn ʿUkābah was a tribe associated with al-Ḥīrah in the sixth century AD. There are several clans called Thaʿlabah ibn Saʿd, but they are unimportant and it is likely a mistake, put into al-Dhubyānī's mouth, who subsequently seems to admit this.

310 The letter *Sh* is another very rare rhyme consonant.

311 A Qur'anic quotation (see Q Fuṣṣilat 41:8, Qalam 68:3, Inshiqāq 84:25, Tīn 95:6).

312 Babel and Adhriʿāt are often mentioned for their wine.

313 The poet refers to horses who have suffered in battle (see the complete poem in al-Qurashī, *Jamharat ashʿār al-ʿarab*).

314 Q Baqarah 2:156.

315 The opening line of the poem in which he describes al-Mutajarridah, mentioned above. On the various rhythmical modes (not to be confused with the poetical meters), see, e.g., O. Wright, "Music," pp. 450–59.

316 *Buraḥīn*: explained by the dictionaries as "calamities," but here obviously meaning "terribly good things."

317 Q Yā Sīn 36:78.

318 There is a report, probably spurious, that Labīd did not compose any poetry after his conversion to Islam.

319 The problem is the jussive of *yartabiṭ*: does it still depend on *lam*, or is it a poetic license for *yartabiṭa*, subjunctive after *aw*, with the force of "unless"? See, e.g., Alan Jones, *Early Arabic Poetry*, ii, 188, who prefers a third interpretation, making the verb dependent on *idhā* ("when") but not on *lam* ("not"): "and if [I feel that their] fate may attach itself to a certain soul." This and the following line are from the *Muʿallaqah* and have therefore often been the subject of grammatical analysis.

320 Arabic grammarians normally derive forms from a verb in the base stem (I) or from a noun (as below), whereas a more modern way would be to derive them from an abstract consonantal root (here *ʾ-W-L*). No doubt the grammarians are right in terms of historical linguistics: the roots are themselves derived from concrete words.

321 The former reading should be connected with the word *ālah* "instrument"; the latter assumes that *ta'tā* is an irregular shortening of *ta'attā*, itself a normal shortening of *tata'attā*; the meaning would be "which her thumb handled easily."

322 Al-Fārisī was known to the "Sheikh," ʿAlī ibn Manṣūr Ibn al-Qāriḥ.

323 Common but irregular variants of *istaḥyā* and *yastaḥyī* (root *Ḥ-Y-W/Y*).

324 A reconstructed form, not attested, in which the root is treated as a "hollow root" (i.e., a root with *W* or *Y* as middle root consonant) rather than as a geminate root (where the

second and third consonants are identical); something similar applies to the following **i'tāya*, in which the *W* is "weakened," instead of the normal *i'tawā* (root *'-W-Y*).

325 Oddly, form VIII of the root *ʿ-W-N* is in fact the irregular *iʿtawana*, rather than the "normal" *iʿtāna*.

326 Normally called "present" or "imperfect" tense (*al-muḍāriʿ*).

327 The reasoning is as follows: form VIII of the root *'-W-Y*, if treated (irregularly) as a "hollow root," is **i'tāya*; the imperfect third person feminine would be **ta'tāyu* and elision of the final root consonant would give *ta'tā*, as in the poem.

328 Q Zumar 39:53.

329 Q Nisā' 4:116.

330 The syntax and the sense of the passage are somewhat problematic.

331 According to a commentator (Abū ʿUbayd al-Bakrī, *Simṭ al-la'ālī*, p. 432) her teeth are compared to white camomile, her dark gums to silver ore, and her saliva with wine made from raisins.

332 The interpretation of *jurrida* ("was despatched"?) is not wholly clear and here it has been taken as a possible mistake for *juwwida*, cf. *jāda jawdan* "to be copious (rain)."

333 *Qarqaf*, as a word for wine, is usually explained as "making the drinker shiver," apparently a recommendation; "potent" will do. *Isfanṭ* is derived from "absinthe," i.e., wormwood.

334 This verse is rather obscure; cf. Lyall, *The Mufaḍḍalīyat*, ii, 98, 100, on line 75 of an ode by ʿAbdah ibn al-Ṭabīb, ("the flagon was a mixing bowl, like the middle of a wild ass"), where it is suggested that "the bowl is compared to the belly of a wild ass because it is constantly being refilled," the animal having to drink frequently. Perhaps the color is what is meant: the amphora is coated with black pitch.

335 The meaning of the word *hazim* is unclear; it seems to denote a kind of sound; the noise of the fermenting wine is often described in Arabic wine poetry, as it is in the following line. In that case it apparently is a different kind of noise to that in the next line. It is also somewhat odd that the words *nāqis* and *hazim* are masculine, whereas wine is usually feminine in Arabic, as in the rest of the passage.

336 Q Wāqiʿah 56:37.

337 Arabs traditionally clean the teeth and the gums with brushes made of twigs of aromatic wood.

338 Bint al-Shāṭi''s edition has *mawsūman*; we read *marsūman*, as in the poem.

339 The poem is found in the celebrated second/eighth century anthology *al-Mufaḍḍaliyyāt* (see Lyall's translation and commentary, pp. 73–78).

340 Al-Rabāb is a woman's name often found in early Arabic love poetry. The poet speaks about himself, shifting to the first person singular in the next line.

341 The female reproacher, a stock figure in many poems, represents the voice of reason, warning the poet-hero against reckless spending or engaging in hazardous ventures.

342 Q Fāṭir 35:34–35.

343 The poet seems to be speaking about himself here (perhaps quoting someone else). There is a confusing shift of pronouns in the complete poem.

344 Presumably his guest, implied in the first line.

345 According to Islamic belief, those in Paradise are restored to the prime of their life physically and mentally.

346 The verse is from the most celebrated of the *Muʿallaqah* odes.

347 The word *khalīʿ*, in al-Maʿarrī's time, normally meant "shameless, profligate, depraved," but here its older sense of "repudiated (e.g., a son by his father)" is certainly relevant.

348 Literally, "May God not break your mouth!"

349 The early critic Ibn Sallām al-Jumaḥī (d. ca. 232/846), in his *Ṭabaqāt fuḥūl al-shuʿarāʾ* (*The Categories of the Master Poets*) lists in his first class Imruʾ al-Qays, al-Nābighah al-Dhubyānī, Zuhayr, and al-Aʿshā.

350 Al-Aʿshā, "the night blind," married this woman but did not like her and divorced her. His parting poem addresses her as a chaste and blameless woman (see al-Iṣfahānī, *Aghānī*, ix, 121–22).

351 A common idiom for someone who indiscriminately produces or accepts good and bad.

352 Perhaps the word *gharīrah* "innocent, inexperienced" implies a comparison of the girl to a gazelle or oryx cow.

353 The sense is possibly obscene: her pale belly is like a scent box (possibly made of ivory) and he is about to (re)fill her "cup."

354 Q Wāqiʿah 56:19.

355 Compare above, §5.4 (al-Aʿshā was allowed to enter Paradise on condition that he would not drink any wine there).

356 This refers to the way a Bedouin Arab sits, with legs drawn up and wrapped in his garment.

357 The caliph al-Amīn (r. 193–8/809–13).

358 The "arbitration," a key moment in Islamic history, was between ʿAlī ibn Abī Ṭālib, the fourth caliph, and his opponent Muʿāwiyah (who became the first Umayyad caliph). The Khārijites ("Seceders"), fervent partisans of ʿAlī at first, became fierce opponents because he consented to the arbitration; but some abstained from fighting.

359 Just as in the Christian tradition, Islam has its recording angels, who keep account of good and bad deeds (see Q Anʿām 6:61). As the Sheikh says, God, being Omniscient, does not really need them (and this being so, there is no reason why they should especially fear a passing angel. Is the author mocking orthodox belief?).

360 One of the many appellations of wine, perhaps because of its fragrance or its color.

361 The following lines are from the "amatory introduction" of a poem that satirizes Abū Sufyān, the leading Meccan adversary of the Prophet.

362 Interpretation uncertain: is *al-ghiṭā'* the "covering" of the woman or the darkness of the night? Does the suffix *-hā* refer to the woman or the stars?

363 The masculine form of the verb (*yakūnu*) is odd; but it could refer to "saliva" rather than the woman.

364 Here and on several other occasions Bint al-Shāṭi' has completed the customary formula after a mention of the Prophet by adding *wa-sallama* ("and give [him] peace"). We have given the original text.

365 Ḥassān and others had accused ʿĀ'ishah, the Prophet's young wife, of improper behavior with a young man who had picked her up after she had inadvertently been left behind by the caravan with which she was traveling. The Prophet's initial doubts were repelled by a revelation from God and the accusers were flogged. Māriyah and her sister Sīrīn were Coptic slaves, given to Muḥammad by the Byzantine governor of Egypt; Muḥammad took Māriyah as his concubine and gave Sīrīn to Ḥassān.

366 Ibrāhīm died before he was two years old.

367 The verse is discussed by Sībawayh and later grammarians. The predicate after *yakūnu* ("is") should take the accusative; since the nominative ending of *mā'ū* ("water") is secured by the rhyme, this must be the subject (with *ʿasalun*, "honey"), and *mizājahā* must be the predicate, taking the accusative. It is unusual to have an indefinite subject and a definite predicate like this, and a poetic license is assumed. In the second version a rather contrived explanation for the odd nominative *mā'ū* has been given: it is a shortening of a sentence such as "and water (is also mixed with it)." It has also been argued that *yakūnu* is "superfluous" here, in which case "its mixture being honey and water" is a nominal, verbless sentence in which all nouns have the nominative.

368 The verse (from the same poem) is cast as a statement, but a rhetorical question is surely intended (as is found in other sources that have *a-man* instead of *fa-man*).

369 Arabic grammar distinguishes between two kinds of relative clause: one attached to a definite antecedent, in which case a relative pronoun is needed, and another attached to an indefinite antecedent, in which case a relative pronoun is not used (as in English "a man I know"). The problem is whether the relative pronoun *man* should be interpreted as "he who" (definite) or "one who" (indefinite).

370 He belonged to Khazraj, one of the two leading tribes settled in Medina. He was accused of cowardice during the "Battle of the Ditch" at Medina and the subsequent raid against

the Banū Qurayẓah (5/627) when the Meccans attacked the Muslims (see, e.g., *al-Aghānī*, iv, 164–66 and Ibn Isḥāq, *The Life of Muhammad*, trans. A. Guillaume, p. 458).

371 Q Anfāl 8:16,

372 All were poets. The "Camel-herd" died ca. 96/714; the others were born in the pre-Islamic period and died after the coming of Islam.

373 The beginning of the poem rhyming in *-zū* (a rare rhyme), famous for its description of a bow. The poem opens with the customary motif of the deserted places where the poet reminisces about his meeting with the beloved and her tribe.

374 Q Mursalāt 77:41–43.

375 Literally, "things." Perhaps he refers to his poetry, made for the sake of gain.

376 Meaning unclear.

377 The sense of these lines is obscure.

378 Or "I see."

379 Harshā is a mountain pass near Mecca. The sense is "either way leads to Mecca" or, in English, "All roads lead to Rome"; Ibn Aḥmar means that both interpretations are valid. The line is by ʿAqīl ibn ʿUllafah, a younger contemporary of Ibn Aḥmar.

380 Q Ḥajj 22:2.

381 viz. the "earthquake of the Hour" at the Resurrection.

382 The place where mankind will be gathered after the Resurrection (see below, §11.1).

383 The words "For a wine" have been added; it seems that something is missing; or perhaps the wine (with its effects) serves as another *secundum comparationis* for "the prime of youth."

384 This word and subsequent enigmatic descriptions in the poem will be discussed later.

385 We follow the interpretation of this line by Ibn Qutaybah, *Maʿānī*, p. 463: *anā fī sukri shabābī ka-dhālika idh lahā ʿan maṭiyyatih.*

386 The poem seems to describe a rain cloud (but see the poet's explanation, below). Such metonyms, instead of straightforward nouns, are extremely common in early Arabic poetry.

387 Bint al-Shāṭiʾ has another interpretation: "When its tongue is split (to prevent it from sucking), it is a *bāzil* (camel whose first teeth have come through)." Here the interpretation of early commentators has been followed. Another interpretation is given by Ibn Qutaybah, *Maʿānī*, p. 463: "when it is chewing the cud its eye-teeth appear"; it means the animal looks healthy and young.

388 Another possible interpretation of *sharāb qayl* in line 3 is "a drink (of wine) at midday." That the poet does not mention it is understandable, in view of his diminished memory; but one would have expected the Sheikh to do so.

389 See Q Najm 53:61: «while you make merry».

390 The great *Kitāb al-Aghānī* by Abū l-Faraj al-Iṣfahānī (d. ca. 363/972), devoted to singers, musicians, and especially poets. For the verses, with some variants, see viii, 326. There, the "two locusts of ʿĀd" are said to belong to ʿAbd Allāh ibn Judʿān, who lived shortly before the coming of Islam; they cannot have been identical with the two singers from ancient times and "locust" was obviously a general nickname for singers, as ʿAmr will explain.

391 The opening of a famous poem by the pre-Islamic poet ʿAbīd ibn al-Abraṣ.

392 The poet makes a spurious connection between *zabarjad* (peridot, or chrysolite) and *zibrij* ("ornamentation"); the words are not related (*zabarjad* is to be connected with *zumurrud*, Targumic Hebrew *zᵉmargad*, Greek *smaragdos*, English "emerald," ultimately probably from Sanskrit).

393 The author of *al-ʿAyn* is said to be al-Khalīl ibn Aḥmad. He will appear later in the text. The word *ṣalakhdam* ("strong camel") is connected here with *ṣalkham* ("big and strong").

394 There are nouns, such as *zabarjad*, that have five consonants, but verbal roots always have either three or four. In the present example the last consonant of *zabarjad* is ignored in *yuzabriju* (which can be translated as "he peridots"). The same happens with the formation of so-called "broken" plurals.

395 A word taken from Persian, it is also the name under which a famous and very Arab poet is known (see below, §17.3.3).

396 The Arabic term, *maṣdar*, literally means "place from which something proceeds, place of origin."

397 The corresponding verbs are *ḍaraba* ("to strike") and *karuma* ("to be noble"). Thus, e.g., *al-rajulu ḍāribun* ("the man is striking") = *yaḍribu l-rajulu* ("the man strikes"), *al-rajulu karīmun* ("the man is noble") = *yakrumu l-rajulu*.

398 Translation uncertain.

399 One wonders if Abū l-ʿAlāʾ chose this line because the words *ḥattā tasʾama l-dīnā* could also be interpreted (wrongly) as "until she is bored with religion." The known versions of this famous poem (e.g., in the anthologies *Jamharat ashʿār al-ʿarab* and *Muntahā l-ṭalab*) have *taʿrifa* ("she knows") instead of *tasʾama* ("she is bored with").

400 Nothing is known about Ibn Muqbil's active participation in the conflicts between ʿAlī ibn Abī Ṭālib and his various opponents.

401 Q Fāṭir 35:37.

402 Reading *al-amān*, as in Bint al-Shāṭiʾ's ninth edition (earlier editions had *al-aymān*).

403 Q Baqarah 2:281.

404 The Sheikh (or rather the author) has an irritating habit of using unusual words and explaining them himself; it has been imitated in the translation.

405 Q Maʿārij 70:4–5. For eloquent descriptions of the arid plain where the waiting humans, naked and barefoot, crowding together, are tormented by heat and thirst, see, e.g., al-Ghazālī (d. 505/1111), *Iḥyāʾ ʿulūm al-dīn*, iv, 512–15: "the place of assembling and its people," "the sweating," "the length of the Day of Resurrection," all of it supported with relevant quotations from Qurʾan and Hadith.

406 The beginning of a *qaṣīdah* by the pre-Islamic poet Imruʾ al-Qays; not his famous *Muʿallaqah* but another, with a near-identical opening line. The rhyme is *-ānī*, which accommodates the name Riḍwān in the genitive.

407 The opening of a poem by the famous poet Jarīr (d. 111/729), rhyming in *-ānā*, which suits the name Riḍwān in the accusative.

408 Q Sabaʾ 34:2.

409 Rabīʿah and Muḍar are two ancient ancestors of the Arabs, giving their names to large tribal confederations. Labīd's father was also called Rabīʿah.

410 A common image for something impossible.

411 For this and other elegies on Ḥamzah, see Guillaume's translation of Ibn Isḥāq's *al-Sīrah al-nabawiyyah*, *The Life of the Prophet*, p. 420 (with several other elegies composed after the battle, pp. 404–26).

412 Q ʿAbasa 80:37, on the Day of Judgment.

413 Customary phrase for addressing or speaking of caliphs, in particular ʿAlī.

414 cf., e.g., Q Ḥāqqah 69:18–23, «On that day you will be exposed, not one secret of yours will be concealed. Then as for him who is given his writ in his right hand, he will say, "Here it is, read my writ! I thought that I should meet my reckoning." He will be in a pleasing life, in a lofty Garden, its clusters within reach».

415 The syntax of this verse has been discussed extensively by the grammarians (see, e.g., ʿAbd al-Qādir al-Baghdādī, *Khizānat al-adab*, x, 472–84). It is not clear why *al-māʾ* could be nominative.

416 *Muqtawī* is derived from the root *Q-W-Y* (form VIII: "to appropriate"); there is some confusion with the root *Q-T-W*, giving *muqtawī* "taking as a servant" and *maqtawiyy* "servant."

417 Al-Zafayān al-Saʿdī (fl. ca. 80/700).

418 Or *taʾbiyah*; see e.g. Ibn Manẓūr, *Lisān al-ʿArab* s.v. *ʾ-B-Y*.

419 The verse is quoted anonymously in Sībawayh's grammar on account of the word order (normal would be *al-marʾu dhiʾbun in yalqa l-rushā* or *al-marʾu ʿinda l-rushā in yalqahā fa-huwa dhīb*); later grammarians argue that the suffix in *yadrusuhū* "he studies it" cannot refer to *qurʾān*, because it is not compatible with the preposition *li-* in *lil-qurʾān*, which already has the function of defining the direct object, and therefore the suffix

must refer to an implied verbal noun *darsan* "studying." Al-Maʿarrī clearly thinks this reasoning is faulty.

420 In full: *The Proof Concerning the Seven Variant Readings (of the Qur'an)*. The consonants of the Qur'anic text can be read in several ways; seven versions are recognized as equally valid and canonical. See also below, n. 696.

421 In Islamic law written documents are considered valid and legally binding only when two or more witnesses can testify to their validity.

422 Some Islamic scholars are of the view that repentance shortly before one's death will not save one from Hell.

423 The place where the believers will meet the Prophet on the Day of Judgment; see, e.g., A. J. Wensinck, entry "Ḥawḍ" in *EI2*, III, 286.

424 The Prophet's descendants.

425 This is a customary formula written by copyists at the end of a manuscript.

426 See, e.g., Q Yūnus 10:19, Hūd 11:110, Fuṣṣilat 41:45: «but for a word that preceded from your Lord» (to postpone Judgment).

427 Q Anbiyā' 21:101–03; "it" refers to Hell.

428 They all died young, without issue.

429 The word "imam" has several meanings; here it refers to ʿAlī and his male descendants mentioned before.

430 See above, n. 259.

431 Al-Jaḥjalūl (if he is a real person at all) has not been identified.

432 The sense is rather obscure. The words *ilā l-warā* are (possibly intentionally) ambiguous: "toward people" and "backward" (as a poetic license for *ilā l-warāʾ*).

433 In his famous book, the first and most authoritative Arabic grammar.

434 i.e., in the days when things were all right. One would expect "the people" to be in the nominative, but the particle *wa-*, usually meaning "and," sometimes means "together with," in which case it is followed by the accusative.

435 Since man is mortal and subject to decay, even being healthy implies sickness.

436 i.e., she is shameless and does not mind doing unpleasant things.

437 i.e., she took a pail to an udder decked with muck.

438 Visiting women at night is an extremely common theme in Arabic poetry; but visiting old women is a rarity.

439 A variant (Ibn Qutaybah, *al-Shiʿr*, p. 393) has *zubd* ("butter") instead of *zād* ("food"). Buttermaking is described in the poem (see below); the precise meaning of some verses is rather obscure.

440 Traditionally blue eyes are considered inauspicious.

441 He is carrying a pair of skins filled with milk, presumably on a yoke.

442 As is made clear by additional verses in another source (Ibn Qutaybah, *Maʿānī*, pp. 599–600), the woman tastes the milk approvingly and then churns it to make butter. This seems to be the meaning; but several things remain unclear. Ibn Qutaybah has *fa-ghuṣṣat tarāqīhī bi-ṣafrā'a jaʿdatin | fa-ʿanhā tuṣādīhī wa-ʿanhā turāwidū*. In *ʿalayhā tuʿānīhī, ʿalā* may have the same function as in the earlier phrase *turīdunī ʿalā l-zādi/zubdi*: "for the sake of it (the butter) she (the woman) suffered (or: kept herself busy with) him (the man)."

443 An allusion to the common Qur'anic expression, on the people in Paradise: «there is no fear upon them, nor will they grieve», e.g. Q Baqarah 2:35, 62, 112, Āl ʿImrān 3:170.

444 Making a panegyric poem.

445 Apparently the Arabs in Paradise live according to their tribal affiliations. Labīd's tribe, ʿĀmir ibn Ṣaʿṣaʿah, is part of the large federation called Qays, a major branch of the "North Arabs."

446 The passage exploits an untranslatable play on words: the Arabic word *bayt* means not only "tent" or "house" but also "line of verse."

447 The verses seem to demonstrate that the Lord is more concerned with piety than with good poetry.

448 The verse is by al-Mutanakhkhil.

449 *Al-ḥūr al-ʿīn*: the paradisial damsels or "houris" (see Q Dukhān 44:54, Ṭūr 52:20, Wāqiʿah 56:22).

450 The two merciless "girls" are the two grinding millstones.

451 Abū l-ʿAlā', exceptionally in Islam, was a vegan who preached abstinence from meat, fish, eggs, milk, and honey, in order not to harm animals.

452 Q Zukhruf 43:71–73.

453 Q Ṭūr 52:24.

454 Kaʿb ibn Mālik, a contemporary of the Prophet, in a boasting poem (the original has "our shelters" instead of "his doors").

455 A vulture (*nasr*) is proverbial in Arabic for its longevity. Surayy has not been identified; on Kuwayy see *WKAS* I, 582b; it is called "one of the rain stars" in the dictionary *Lisān al-ʿArab*. *Nasr* is also the name of two stars: *al-nasr al-ṭā'ir* (Altair, or alpha *Aquilae*) and *al-nasr al-wāqiʿ* (alpha *Lyrae*). Perhaps these two stars are called Kuwayy and Surayy, and here used for longevity because they are both "vultures." In al-Maʿarrī, *al-Fuṣūl wa-l-ghāyāt*, p. 148, Kuwayy is also used to denote longevity.

456 All of them famous male singers.

457 Famous female singers from the early Abbasid period. They started their careers as highly trained and educated slave girls, bought for large sums by caliphs, viziers, and

others. Several of them, such as ʿInān (for a time a girl friend of the poet Abū Nuwās) were also poets.

458 i.e., lived in the pre-Islamic period of "ignorance" (*jāhiliyyah*).

459 The Sheikh will see Aws in Hell (below, §17.9.1). There is much confusion in the sources not only about the ascription but also concerning the text of this poem. For an English translation of one version, see Lyall, *The Dīwāns of ʿAbīd ibn al-Abraṣ of Asad, and ʿĀmir ibn aṭ-Ṭufail, of ʿĀmir ibn Ṣaʿṣaʿah*, pp. 59–60.

460 The "tubes" or "pipes" (*anābīb*) puzzled the critics. The use of the word is criticized in al-ʿAskarī, *Ṣināʿatayn*, p. 79. He suggests that "it could mean the ducts in the pomegranate;" al-Zamakhsharī, *Asās al-balāghah* (s.v. *N-B-B*) says that *anābīb* is "figurative (*majāz*)" here.

461 Jirān al-ʿAwd is a nickname, meaning "leather whip made from an old camel stallion," an expression he used in a poem in which he threatens his two wives with a whipping. He refers to himself by this nickname in the present poem, in which he describes a nocturnal adventure.

462 Poets often mention the "humming of the jinn," apparently the "singing sands," a well known phenomenon of desert lands. It has been shown that the sound of "the singing dunes," when it is real and not caused by one's imagination in the stillness of the desert, may be the result, under particular circumstances, of the friction of sand grains against one another. See Hogan, "Dunes Alive with the Sand of Music"; Merali, "Dune Tune: The Greatest Hits."

463 This verse is not found in the poem of the same meter and rhyme in his *Dīwān*.

464 ʿAmr ibn ʿAdī, pre-Islamic king of al-Ḥīrah, is connected with the famous ancient legend about Jadhīmah, "the Leprous" and al-Zabbāʾ, the Arabian queen in whom memories of Queen Zenobia survive. Jadhīmah had two drinking companions, Mālik and ʿAqīl. ʿAmr ibn Kulthūm (sixth century AD) was also connected with al-Ḥīrah. The lines are from his only famous poem, one of the seven *Muʿallaqāt* but are not found in all versions.

465 The author again uses a very rare word and immediately explains it.

466 Ibn Qutaybah, in his book on poetry and poets, condemns these lines as "obviously constrained and badly composed." It is perhaps the meter (with its eight syllables per hemistich, much shorter than average) that makes it suitable for dancing.

467 See Q Wāqiʿah 56:17 and Insān 76:19.

468 Compare hadiths quoted by al-Ghazālī, *Iḥyāʾ ʿulūm al-dīn*, iv, 540: "Ibn Masʿūd said, The messenger of God, God bless and preserve him, said: Truly, you will merely look at a bird in Paradise and desire it, and it will fall before you, roasted." "Ḥudhayfah said, The messenger of God, God bless and preserve him, said: There are birds in Paradise

like Bactrian camels. Abū Bakr, may God be pleased with him, asked: Are they nice, messenger of God? He answered: Nicer than they are those who eat them, and you, Abū Bakr, will be among those who eat them!" The following Qur'anic quotations are Q Yā Sīn 36:78 and Baqarah 2:260.

469 The parenthesis is an editorial addition.

470 The conjunction *li-*, when followed by a subjunctive, means "so that, in order that"; when followed by a jussive (which in this case has the same form as the subjunctive) it expresses an order or invitation ("let my heart be reassured"). Since God cannot be commanded, it functions as a prayer.

471 Q Baqarah 2:259; according to most commentators the speaker (not named in the Qur'an) is ʿUzayr (sometimes identified as Ezra) or the "Green Man", al-Khaḍir. God made him die for a hundred years and then brought him back to life; ʿĀzar is one of the Arabic names for Lazarus (cf. John 11:1–46).

472 The verse is from a poem in the famous collection *al-Mufaḍḍaliyyāt*.

473 The Central Asian, "Bactrian" camel has two humps and is bigger than the Arabian, one-humped camel.

474 Morphological patterns in Arabic are expressed by means of the "dummy" root *F-ʿ-L* (of the verb *faʿala* "to do"); prosodists do the same for metrical feet (e.g., *faʿūlun* is short-long-long). Here the three root consonants are given, alternatively, as C_1, C_2, C_3. The pattern of *iwazzah* is discussed, e.g., by Ibn Jinnī (d. 392/1002), *al-Khaṣāʾiṣ*, iii, 6–7.

475 The grammatical "school" of Basra (to which al-Māzinī belongs) traditionally accords a greater role to analogy in formulating grammatical rules than the rival "school" of Kufa, which is more tolerant of irregularities sanctioned by actual usage.

476 ʾiC_1C_2aC_3ah would give **ʾiʾwayah*; Arabic phonotactic rules would automatically change *ʾiʾ* into *ʾiy*, the sequence *yw* into *yy*, and *aya* into *ā*, giving *ʾiyyāh*.

477 A verse from a famous poem by al-Afwah al-Awdī; the authenticity of the poem is dubious (see al-Jāḥiẓ, *Ḥayawān*, vi, 275, 280).

478 A verse often quoted as a proverb, attributed to several poets (Maʿn ibn Aws, Mālik ibn Fahm al-Azdī, or ʿAqīl ibn ʿUllafah), on being shot by one's own son.

479 The great poet Imru' al-Qays (first half of sixth century AD). The first quotation is from his *Muʿallaqah*; the poet (addressing himself) reminisces about his amorous adventures.

480 Q Raḥmān 55:58.

481 The Sheikh uses two Arabic forms of the word, the usual *kāfūr* and the rare *qāfūr*.

482 By al-Ḥusayn ibn Muṭayr (d. ca. 179/786), on the Abbasid caliph al-Mahdī.

483 Q Wāqiʿah 56:35–38.

484 The English word "houri," now no longer well known, goes back, via Persian, Turkish and French, to Arabic *ḥūr* (plural of *ḥawrāʾ*), the word used in the Qurʾan and here for the "black-eyed damsels" in Paradise.

485 Compare 1 Cor. 2:9 (which is not about damsels).

486 Heavy posteriors are part of the ideal beauty in classical Arabic love poetry, whether on women or boys; the standard poetic simile is that of the sand hill or dune.

487 Q Ṣāffāt 37:51–57.

488 *ʿAfārīt*, plural of *ʿifrīt* ("afreet, afrit"), a demon of the more malicious kind; the general word for demons is *jinn* (singular *jinnī*, "jinnee, djinnee, genie").

489 See Q Aḥqāf 46:29–32 and Jinn 72:1–16, respectively.

490 The *maradah* (sg. *mārid*), a particularly evil kind of jinn, who rebelled with Satan against God.

491 All editions have *lā ka-l-ḥāqin min al-ihālah*; the negative particle *lā* is problematical, because without it the idiom refers to a person with skill and experience: "someone who retains the melted fat (waiting to pour it until it cools down, so as not to burn the vessel)"; see the identical explanations in Abū ʿUbayd al-Bakrī, *Faṣl al-maqāl*, 298; al-ʿAskarī, *Jamharat al-amthāl*, ii, 135; al-Maydānī, *Majmaʿ al-amthāl*, i, 76. Apparently, the word *lā* is a mistake, perhaps a misreading of *anā* "I am," on the part of the author or a scribe. However, an interpretation that retains the word *lā* has been proposed by Gregor Schoeler and Tilman Seidensticker: "(You have found) someone who (in relation to the question, or the questioner) is like the moon to the halo, not like someone who suffers from strangury and cannot pass urine" (meaning that the jinnee's knowledge pours forth freely).

492 Thus, instead of "al-Khaythaʿūr" as found in the manuscripts. *Khaytaʿūr* is an unusual word for "mirage" or "fata morgana"; *shayṣabān* is said to mean "male ant" or perhaps "termite mound."

493 This refers, of course, to Arabic. Al-Khalīl ibn Aḥmad was the first to describe and systematize the meters (some of which are hardly ever found but were constructed for the sake of his system).

494 Twigs of the *arāk* tree were used as toothbrushes or toothpicks.

495 The first half of the opening line of the *Muʿallaqah* by Imruʾ al-Qays, probably the most famous verse in Arabic.

496 Q Ḥijr 15:26, 15, 33.

497 Q Raḥmān 55:15.

498 He asks for the *kunyah*, a name beginning with Abū/Umm ("father/mother of"), usually followed by the name of the eldest son.

499 It is said in the Hadith (see, e.g., al-Zamakhsharī, *Kashshāf*, ad Q Wāqiʿah 56:37) that everyone in Paradise will always be thirty-three years old.

500 It was believed that epilepsy was caused by a jinnee entering the body.

501 The following poem (obviously by al-Maʿarrī himself) is a parody of a vaunting poem, in which a poet boasts of the virtues and heroic exploits of himself and his tribe; it is the most important poetic genre of pre- and early Islamic poetry. See Bürgel, "Les deux poèmes autobiographiques du démon Khaytaʿūr."

502 Ghūr, here used for the people living in the region of that name, a mountainous territory in present day Afghanistan.

503 The Arabic *ṭunbūr* is a long-necked stringed instrument. The word entered Europe as "pandore," "pandora," or "bandora"; "sitar" was chosen because it will be more familiar to most readers than "pandore."

504 A reference to Q Aʿrāf 7:143, where Mūsā (Moses) at Mt. Sinai expresses a desire to see God, which a human being cannot aspire to.

505 References to the Persian Sassanids, who ruled from AD 224 until they were overthrown by the early Muslim conquests. Sāsān was the eponymous founder of the dynasty. Shapur (Shāhpur in Middle Persian, Sābūr in Arabic) was the name of several Sassanian kings; the reference could be to Shapur II, who led punitive actions against the Arabs in the fourth century AD, acquiring the nickname "Shoulder-man" (Dhū l-aktāf) because of his habit of dislocating or piercing the shoulders of captives. Bahrām V (Middle Persian Vahrām, r. 420–38) was called Bahrām Gūr "the Onager" (Jūr in Arabic) on account of his vigor. In the poem Gūr/Jūr is mistaken for the Persian town of that name.

506 Isrāfīl, one of the archangels, will blow the trumpet on the Last Day. The blast on the trumpet is often referred to in the Qur'an (without Isrāfīl being mentioned).

507 See Q 72, Sūrat al-Jinn (the "Surah of the Jinn").

508 Abū Hadrash literally quotes the Qur'anic text (Q Jinn 72:1–2); the Arabic for "recitation" is *qur'ān*.

509 As is told in the Qur'an and the relevant exegesis (Q Ḥijr 15:18, Jinn 72:8–9), some jinn were eavesdropping on God's High Council, whereupon they were pelted by angels with meteors or shooting stars.

510 The line describes an oryx bull.

511 This follows James Montgomery's interpretation (*The Vagaries of the Qaṣīdah*, pp. 120, 123–24, with several parallels); *ṭunub* ("tent-rope") should therefore be taken as *pars pro toto*, standing for a tent.

512 This long poem is again a parody with self-praise as its main theme. It alludes to numerous common motifs, such as the abandoned abodes at the beginning. It contains some rather abrupt transitions, wholly in the style of early poetry.

513 The Prophet belonged to Hāshim, the leading clan of the tribe of Quraysh.

514 The stoning of married fornicators is not mentioned in the Qur'an but mentioned in the Hadith.

515 The text has Shās, said to be a road near Mecca. Other manuscripts have Shāsh, i.e., the town better known as Tashkent, which is better suited to the hyperbolical vaunting (compare the broad geography in the preceding poem). It is slightly odd, however, that it should be linked with the obscure ʿAlwah instead of, e.g., Mecca.

516 Sulaymān (Solomon) is the master of demons in Islamic lore; the motif of the jinnee in a bottle is familiar from the *Thousand and One Nights.*

517 Literally "a single divorce," which is easily revoked, unlike a triple divorce, after which the husband can only remarry the same woman after she has been married to someone else first.

518 In Arabic poetry the mouth of the beloved is often said to taste like wine.

519 According to Arabic lore the lute (*al-ʿūd*) was invented by Lamak (Lamech), a few generations after Cain; there is a grisly story that the construction was inspired by the decomposing body parts of a young son of his. The two companions are presumably Lamak's son Tūbal (cf. Biblical Jubal or Tubal), the inventor of the drum and tambourine, and his daughter Ḍilāl (cf. Biblical Zillah, who is Lamech's wife), who invented stringed instruments. Compare Gen. 4:21–22.

520 Legendary long-lived pre-Islamic sage, associated with ʿĀd; he is mentioned in the Qur'an (Q Luqmān 31:12 ff.) in the Sura that bears his name. Many maxims and fables were later attributed to him. Other sources, including a verse by the pre-Islamic poet Ṭarafah, mention Luqmān (the same?) as a famous player of *maysir*, an ancient Arab gambling game.

521 A reference to the motif often found in early Arabic poems in which the poet renounces his youthful follies once he is old.

522 The three main battles between the unbelieving Meccans and the Muslims led by the Prophet, which took place in 2/624, 3/625, and 5/627, respectively.

523 According to Muslim tradition angels fought on the Muslim side at the battle of Badr.

524 This refers to a well-known tradition according to which the angels who intervened in the battle of Badr wore yellow turbans.

525 Ḥayzūm is said to be the horse of Jibrīl (Gabriel).

526 Zaynab and Lamīs are typical women's names found in early Arabic poetry; see above, §9.3.1.

527 Bilqīs is the Arabic name of the Queen of Sheba.

528 Al-Mundhir's dynasty is the Lakhmid Dynasty.

529 A reference to the jinn who had listened to God's high council (see above, §15.2.6). Abū Hadrash had apparently done the same, from his lowly place in Paradise.

530 In a crucial battle the Muslims defeated a Byzantine force at the river al-Yarmūk, south of Damascus, in 15/636.

531 At the "Battle of the Camel" (36/656) ʿAlī, the fourth caliph, defeated his rivals al-Zubayr and Ṭalḥah, who were supported by Muḥammad's widow, ʿĀʾishah; she witnessed the fight seated on a camel.

532 The Banū Ḍabbah were a tribe that fought on the losing side at the Battle of the Camel.

533 The protracted Battle of Ṣiffīn (37/657), on the upper Euphrates, between the caliph ʿAlī and his rival Muʿāwiyah (who was to be the first Umayyad caliph a few years later), ended in stalemate.

534 On the heels of the Battle of Ṣiffīn, ʿAlī had to fight his former partisans who had been disappointed about his assent to arbitration and had become fierce opponents. He defeated them at al-Nahrawān (here shortened to al-Nahr, "the river") in Iraq in 38/658.

535 A proverb; i.e., with a similar metaphor, the admonition fell on fertile ground.

536 ʿUtbah ibn Abī Lahab married Ruqayyah, a daughter of the Prophet, before the latter's mission, but divorced her when Muḥammad began to preach Islam. In spite of ʿUtbah's later conversion to Islam, the curse seems to have worked. His father Abū Lahab, an uncle of Muḥammad, is the object of a curse in Q 111, Sūrat al-Masad.

537 Uhbān ibn al-Akwaʿ (or ibn Aws), nicknamed Mukallim al-Dhiʾb ("Spoke with Wolf"). One day, while Uhbān is herding his sheep, a wolf grabs one of them. Uhbān goes after the wolf, who stops and speaks: "Why do you want to rob me of the livelihood God has given me?" Uhbān is amazed that the wolf can speak, but the wolf replies, "Yet more amazing is that God's messenger is preaching in Mecca!" Then Uhbān converts to Islam.

538 He and al-Ḥuṭayʾah exchanged a series of lampoons; a complaint by al-Zibriqān to the caliph ʿUmar led to al-Ḥuṭayʾah's imprisonment in Medina.

539 The word here rendered as "marker mountain," *ʿalam*, is any sign, a post or natural feature such as a hill or mountain, that may serve as a road marker. The word *raʾs* ("head") can also mean "mountaintop." Unfortunately for Ṣakhr, the metaphor has been taken literally in Hell.

540 In English, "Satan" is the devil's name; Arabic reverses this, for al-Shayṭān ("the Satan," or the devil) is the more general designation, whereas his name (used here) is Iblīs (possibly derived from Greek *diabolos* and cognate with "devil").

541 Q Qiyāmah 75:35; the interpretation of the verse is uncertain. It could also mean "nearer to you and nearer."

542 Q A'rāf 7:50.

543 Q Baqarah 2:25.

544 Possibly he suggests that in addition to the "pure spouses" (i.e., wives) the "immortal youths" would also be available to the male believers. The question whether homosexual intercourse with them would be possible in the hereafter was seriously discussed by the theologians; for arguments pro and contra, see, e.g., al-Ṣafadī, *al-Wāfī*, ii, 84–85.

545 The following lines are discontinuous fragments from a lengthy ode on a governor, composed in *rajaz* meter (hence the shorter lines).

546 "On a morning before the *subd* were up."

547 The dictionaries identify it, not very convincingly, as "wild swallow," "a bird like the eagle," and "a bird with water-repellent feathers" (apparently a water fowl). The editor of Bashshār's poetry, Muḥammad al-Ṭāhir ibn 'Āshūr, explains *subd* as the plural of *asbad*, "long-haired," referring to oryxes, but this is not confirmed by other attestations.

548 The crow, bird of ill omen, is often described as announcing the separation of lovers.

549 Identification uncertain: *ṣurad* has been translated as "shrike" (*EI2*, vii, 906b, 951b s.v. "naḥl" and "naml"), "magpie" (*EI2*, iii, 307a, s.v. "ḥayawān"), "sparrow hawk" and "green woodpecker" (both in Hava, *al-Farāʾid al-durriyyah*).

550 A strange explanation of the hopping of crows, perhaps forgivable in a blind man.

551 The translation follows that of Ullmann, *Der Neger*, p. 50: "einen, der . . . einem Abessinier im Dauerregen gleicht." The verse is not found elsewhere.

552 See above, *Gh* §§15.2.2 and 14.1 and below, §20.1.

553 The Arabic text only gives the beginnings of the lines, which have here been given in full.

554 Writers on poetic metrics mention such extra-metrical irregularities in early poetry; but they would never allow it in later verse.

555 This line, describing a beautiful woman, has received much commentary. One notes that the poet fails to settle the question, unless the answer is subsumed in his words "all these are good."

556 This reading would make the meter more regular.

557 Root *N-Ḍ-W*, forms II and I, respectively.

558 Root *N-Ḍ-Ḍ*.

559 In early poetry the second and sixth feet of *ṭawīl* are sometimes SLSL (as in *wa-qad naḍat*) instead of SLLL (as in *wa-qad naḍḍat*); in later, urban poetry this is extremely rare.

560 According to the commentators the Yemenis used to write deeds and covenants on palm leaves.

561 The sixth foot of this verse is again SLSL instead of SLLL; moreover, the penultimate foot is SLL, which is highly unusual in this shortened form of *ṭawīl*, which almost always ends with SLS SLL. The two following lines have the same irregularity.

562 The poet, riding his dromedary, compares it to sitting on an ostrich.

563 The metrical irregularity is found in the third foot (SLSL instead of LLSL, extremely unusual in the *basīṭ* meter). The "two men" are father and grandfather of the addressee, Harim ibn Sinān.

564 A tentative translation of the somewhat obscure *idhā faniya wa-qāraba*.

565 From the famous *Muʿallaqah*; for the story connected with this verse, see below, §20.1.

566 As quoted, *alā rubba yawmin laka minhunna ṣāliḥin*, has a second foot SLLS, instead of SLLL, which is extremely rare. An alternative version, *alā rubba yawmin ṣālihin laka minhumā* (with a pronominal suffix referring to only two women instead of more), is probably an attempt by a transmitter to remedy the fault.

567 The particle *mā* has many functions; sometimes it is considered *zāʾidah*, "redundant," in which case it may be "preventing" (*kāffah*) the influence of a preceding particle. Thus one finds *innamā huwa* (nominative), even though the particle *inna* normally governs the accusative.

568 If *mā* is *zāʾidah* but not *kāffah*, it has no influence at all, and in this case *yawm* would take the same genitive case as the word *yawm* in the first hemistich.

569 In the quoted line, the lightened form *siyamā* ("partic'lar") is the only possible reading, whereas both forms scan correctly in Imruʾ al-Qays's line.

570 The consonants *w* and *y* are considered "weak" because in various circumstances they change into the long vowels *ū* and *ī*, or disappear altogether.

571 The great majority of classical Arabic poems have monorhyme (*aaaaaa*. . .). Stanzaic or strophic forms (with rhyme schemes such as here: *aaaab ccccb ddddb*) do not occur until later in Islamic times, notably in the Hispano-Arabic *muwashshaḥ* ("girdle poem") and *zajal*, with their hotly debated similarity to the Provençal poetry of the troubadours. It is utterly unlikely that Imruʾ al-Qays should have composed the present poem.

572 The Sheikh will later meet some *rajaz* specialists in a less posh part of Paradise, see below, §20.2.

573 The poet's camel.

574 The poem rhymes in *-āmī*, so that *ḥarāmū* would not give a proper rhyme. Ḥadhām and Qaṭām are women's names; they are among a number of names and nouns of the pattern $C_1aC_2\bar{a}C_3$ that are indeclinable and end in *-i* (omitted in pausal forms in prose but in poetry usually lengthened to *-ī*). In a list of all these forms (al-Suyūṭī, *Muzhir*, ii, 131–34) the form *ḥarāmi* does not occur.

575 The Abbasids (from 132/750).

576 The poet says that his camel is so fast that that there seemed to be hardly any distance between places remote from one another. The verse ends in *irmāmū*, again with the rhyme defect called *iqwāʾ*.

577 "Adjacency" (linguists would speak of "attraction") happens in Arabic when an adjective receives an improper case ending "attracted" from an immediately preceding word, rather than from the word it qualifies; a well-known example from Imruʾ al-Qays's *Muʿallaqah* is *kabīru unāsin fī bijādin muzammalī* ("an elder tribesman wrapped in a striped cloth"), where *muzammal* ("wrapped") has attracted the genitive case of *bijād* ("cloth") although it qualifies *kabīr* ("elder tribesman"), nominative.

578 *Irmāmī*, "my Irmām," would rhyme perfectly but sound strange.

579 A verse from an obscene passage in a longer poem; the sense is not wholly clear. Saʿd Allāh and Judhām are names of tribes; the words are a proverb. The syntax would require a nominative *Judhāmū* but the rhyme demands *Judhāmī*, either genitive or, oddly, "my Judhām."

580 The Helpers (*al-Anṣār*) are those Medinans who supported the Prophet after the Hijra.

581 A play on words: *jandal* means "rock, stone."

582 A near-quotation of Q Maryam 19:70; one must assume that the pre-Islamic Imruʾ al-Qays has heard some Qurʾan in Hell.

583 The words "The Sheikh says," have been added, for it is unlikely that the poet is still speaking: not only is what follows more characteristic of the Sheikh than of the poet, it is also difficult to explain how the sixth-century AD poet could know a verse by a poet who lived much later (see the next note). Instead of *ankara* "he disapproved" (Bint al-Shāṭiʾ's edition) we read *unkiru*.

584 al-Mughīrah ibn Ḥabnāʾ (d. 91/710); the verse is quoted in Sībawayh's grammar.

585 Instead of Ḥārithah.

586 Personal names, even if indefinite in form, are syntactically definite; personal names are normally derived from (indefinite) nouns, which are therefore original; e.g., *muḥammadun*: "a much-praised person," *ḥārithatun*: "someone who cultivates much land," giving the personal names Muḥammad(un), Ḥāritha(tu).

587 The following two quotations have been taken from his *Muʿallaqah*.

588 The meaning of these words (literally, "a marked, bright thing") is uncertain; the commentators generally seem to prefer to interpret them as "(wine I bought) for minted cash" but also give "(which I drunk) from a polished cup," "(bought) for a camel treated with tar (i.e., protected against mange)," and "in a decorated garment" as possible meanings. Below, the poet shows his indifference to the matter.

589 The opening hemistich of the *Muʿallaqah*.

590 The reading and interpretation of the last sentence is rather obscure and the editor gives several possibilities.

591 The lines are from a eulogy on Abū Dulaf, a general and patron of literature. The meaning is that the patron's noble ancestors would already have "exhausted" panegyric poetry; there may also be an allusion to the fact that Abū Dulaf was himself an able poet.

592 It is said that ʿAntarah composed this poem when still a slave. His father had beaten him when Sumayyah, his wife, had claimed that ʿAntarah had tried to seduce her; but then she pitied her stepson, shedding tears.

593 It is assumed that in the first half of this line the father is addressed. If, in the second half, one reads *ʿadhābuki*, as given by the editor, the poet addresses Sumayyah (whose "torment," is to see ʿAntarah as a beaten slave); if one reads *ʿadhābuka* (as, e.g., in al-Baṭalyawsī, *Sharḥ al-ashʿār al-sittah al-jāhiliyyah* and Ahlwardt's *The Divans*) the whole verse is addressed to the father, in which case *ʿadhābuka* means "the punishment coming from you."

594 From the *Muʿallaqah*; the poet addresses his beloved, ʿAblah.

595 The normal verb for "to love" uses form IV of the root *Ḥ-B-B*, the passive participle of which is *muḥabb*; nevertheless, the common word for "loved," *maḥbūb*, is derived from the base stem (I) of the verb even though this is seldom used.

596 The form *iḥibbu*, for *uḥibbu*, is irregular; the prefix vowel *i* (instead of *u*) is found in some ancient forms, remains of old Arabic dialect forms (and common in modern Arabic dialects). *Pace* the author, the verse is not quoted in Sībawayh's grammar; it is found, anonymously, in various other sources, e.g., Ibn Qutaybah, *ʿUyūn*, iv, 43; Ibn Yaʿīsh, *Sharḥ al-Mufaṣṣal*, ix, 47; al-Baghdādī, *Khizānat al-adab*, vii, 273, xi, 459.

597 Instead of Mughīrah, a common man's name.

598 In other words, the form *iḥibbu* in the quoted verse is a variant of *uḥibbu* (form IV), not of a non-existent **aḥibbu* (form I).

599 The verse has been attributed to Ghaylān ibn Shujāʿ al-Nahshalī.

600 Or "nearer than ʿUbayd and Marshaq;" the sense is not clear. Other sources (al-Mubarrad, *al-Kāmil*; Ibn Manẓūr, *Lisān al-ʿArab* s.v. *Ḥ-B-B*) have Mushriq instead of Murshaq.

601 Q Āl ʿImrān 3:31, the normal form being *yuḥbibkum*; according to other sources (e.g., al-Mubarrad, *al-Kāmil*), Abū Rajāʾ read *yaḥibbakum*. Abū Rajāʾ ʿImrān ibn Taym al-ʿUṭāridī died 105/723–24.

602 A poem is very often compared to a string of pearls; the Arabic for "stringing," *naẓm*, also means "versifying, making poetry."

603 He speaks of his love. Both poems are found in the old anthology *al-Mufaḍḍaliyyāt* (see Lyall's annotated translations, *The Mufaḍḍalīyāt*, ii, 327–41).

604 These lines and the following four lines are from the first-mentioned poem. Rabīʿah is the beloved's clan; Tharmadāʾ, its location uncertain, is apparently far away. Several pre-modern commentators suggest this could mean that the "well" is a grave: she will never come back and die in Tharmadāʾ.

605 Literally, "frown."

606 Instead of "their ailments" one could interpret it as "diseases caused by women." A medieval commentator glosses it as "women's characters."

607 The poem was composed on the occasion of a battle (the Battle of ʿAyn Ubāgh) that took place in AD 554 between the Ghassānid king al-Ḥārith al-Aʿraj and the Lakhmid king al-Mundhir ibn Māʾ al-Samāʾ of al-Ḥīrah. The poet's brother Shaʾs had been taken prisoner and the poem closes with an appeal to al-Ḥārith to free him. The petition was successful.

608 In *khabaṭṭa* the *t* of the suffix has been assimilated to the *ṭ* of the root; it would be difficult to do otherwise, although the Sheikh seems to take a different view. Here the word is spelled with *ṭṭ*, although the usual spelling would be *khabaṭta*.

609 For yet another interpretation, see Sells, *Desert Tracings*, p. 18: "It'll take you up and spin you around."

610 The long vowel *ū* is analyzed (and written) as *uw*.

611 All available sources have *yahdī*, which makes sense, unlike *yahdhī* ("he raves[?]").

612 An allusion to the opening of his *Muʿallaqah*: "Wake up girl, get your bowl, give us our morning drink!" (what follows makes it clear that wine rather than milk is intended).

613 The rhyme word, *jaraynā*, jars; all other lines end correctly in *-īnā* or *-ūnā*.

614 The number of verses in ʿAmr's *Muʿallaqah*, in the current redactions, fluctuates between 93 and 115.

615 See, e.g., Q Anʿām 6:70, Yūnus 10:4 and passim.

616 Referring to the second line of ʿAmr's *Muʿallaqah*: "(Wine) mixed, as if containing saffron, / when the water mingles with it; hot."

617 The former explanation derives *sakhīnā* from the root *S-Kh-Y*, with a pronominal suffix *-nā*, the latter from the root *S-Kh-N*.

618 Line 1 mentioned "the wines of al-Andarīn"; Qāṣirīn (not mentioned in the poem) is also said to be a place in Syria. The often-discussed ambiguity of the word *sakhīnā* is surely unintentional and it is obvious that it means "hot."

619 Such as "forget."

620 Kaʿb ibn Māmah and the poet Ḥātim al-Ṭāʾī, both pre-Islamic, are proverbial for their generosity. On this idiomatic use of *wa-lā* in comparisons, which acquires the sense of "even more than," see, e.g., Wright, *Grammar*, ii, 333.

621 The following verse is from his *Muʿallaqah.*

622 Some commentators think that the "wild ass" is an allusion to a particular tribe; they also think that the words "vassal" and "protectors" (both from the root *W-L-Y*) here stand for "kinsmen."

623 The poem rhymes in *-āʾū*, but one verse ends in *samāʾī.*

624 The rhyme words are *Ẓamyā* and *aḥyā*, although strictly speaking they should both end in *-aʾ*, with glottal stop (a consonant). A final glottal stop, when not followed by a vowel (as in al-Ḥārith's poem) tends to disappear.

625 The imperative *ʿish* ("live!") has a short *i* because a long vowel in a closed syllable is not normally allowed in Arabic phonology. With the addition of the emphatic suffix *-an* the long *ī* should be restored; but this would be unmetrical here.

626 The second vowel in *tashaʾ* (of the verb *shāʾa - yashāʾu*) is short only because of the closed syllable. With the addition of the feminine suffix the length should be restored, which, again, would not scan here.

627 Leaving a she-camel with some milk in the udder was supposed to make them conceive. Rather, says the poet (in a following verse), the milk should be offered to guests; after all, the animal might be stolen from you before it gives birth.

628 Letting a camel die in this manner may have been a kind of sacrifice; it was seen as an indication that the pre-Islamic Arabs believed in the Resurrection.

629 The word *buhm* is explained in the text as meaning *ghurl*, "uncircumcised (pl.)." This is a mistake on the part of al-Maʿarrī, based on a misinterpretation of a hadith in the collection of Aḥmad ibn Ḥanbal, according to which the Prophet said that people at the Resurrection will be "naked, uncircumcised, and *buhm*," a word he then explains as "without having anything with them." This explanation, in its turn, is not confirmed by the dictionaries (the singular *abham* meaning "speaking a foreign language").

630 With Ṭarafah the Sheikh completes his series of meetings with the seven poets of the *Muʿallaqāt*. The *Muʿallaqah*, from which the five following lines are taken, is famous for its long and detailed description of the poet's camel.

631 Or more literally "nephew," *ibn akhī*. Does this mean that Ibn al-Qāriḥ and Ṭarafah are somehow related, belonging to the same tribe (Ḍubayʿah, Qays ibn Thaʿlabah)? The Sheikh's family seems to have been obscure (Blachère, *Analecta*, p. 432). Or is *akh* simply "friend," with *ibn* added because Ṭarafah died so young?

632 The *maysir* game is played with marked arrow shafts. The poet hopes for his arrow to "reply," i.e., to come out winning. "Scorched": to harden the shafts; "beside the fire": they are playing in winter.

633 Since the particle *an* ("that") is absent, Sībawayh reads *aḥḍuru*, indicative rather than subjunctive.

634 By al-Akhwaṣ al-Yarbūʿī (or al-Riyāḥī; d. ca. 50/670). The point is that the genitive *nāʿibin* ("croaking") can only be justified by an implied *laysa bi-* "is not."

635 This expression is unclear.

636 The meaning of the last line of this fragment (not found in Ṭarafah's collected verse) is unclear; there is a reference to the game of *maysir*.

637 Bint al-Shāṭiʾ is mistaken in thinking it was about a matter of rhyme (a form of *sinād*: in a poem with a rhyme ending in a consonant the preceding short vowels *i* and *u* may be freely used, but they should not be mixed with *a*, even though this is not uncommon in early poetry). Rather, it is about meter: the mixing, in the last foot of a verse or hemistich, of LL (*taʿṣir, kallam, murghim*) and SSL (*-ḥu yasar, -ba ṣamam, malikun*); cf. Ibn Qutaybah, *Shiʿr*, pp. 72, 102–3, on the *mīmiyyah* by al-Muraqqish.

638 Needless to say, the poets lived long before al-Khalīl.

639 i.e., his *Muʿallaqah*.

640 Q Jinn 72:15.

641 The verse is about a she-camel; it is said to contain three loan words from Persian or Greek.

642 See above, §7.3.

643 Literally, "when al-Munakhkhal will return," a proverbial expression for something that one does not expect to happen. Al-Munakhkhal al-Yashkurī, a pre-Islamic poet, was suspected by king al-Nuʿmān of al-Ḥīrah of having an affair with his wife, al-Mutajarridah (see above, §6.5). Al-Munakhkhal disappeared and was never seen again; perhaps he was buried alive.

644 Literally, "knotted." The sense is not wholly clear. Perhaps there is a connection with *ḥisāb al-ʿaqd/ʿuqad*, dactylonomy; or the origin has to be sought in magic or superstition, as the English "keeping one's fingers crossed."

645 The proverb is explained in different ways: either Darim was killed but his death was not avenged; or he was taken prisoner to be killed at the orders of al-Nuʿmān, but he died on the way.

646 The verse describes a pair of onagers; the male is so closely behind the mare that his head looks like a pack-saddle on her croup.

647 The normal form is *qasṭal*; lengthening the second produces a pattern normally found only for roots of the type $C_1C_2C_1C_2$, such as *zalzāl* ("earthquake").

648 Zuhayr is said to be short for Zuhayrah, a woman's name.

649 A play on words (*nasiya* "to forget", *nasā* "heel tendon").

650 From a long supplicatory ode addressed to an Umayyad prince; for a translation of the complete poem see Stetkevych, *The Poetics of Islamic Legitimacy*, pp. 121–28.

651 Literally, "O God, give (us) life!"

652 On the "rain stars" see above, *Gh* § 3.8.2.

653 Wine (*khamr*) being feminine in Arabic, such metaphors are rife in Bacchic verse.

654 "She" is an amour of the caliph, a Christian girl.

655 The word *daskarah* can mean "village, hermit's cell, tavern"; the last has been chosen in view of the caliph's character.

656 *Asarra* has two opposite meanings: "to keep secret" and "to divulge, reveal." The former does not make sense here (but the speaker may be intentionally equivocal).

657 Abū Sufyān (Yazīd's grandfather) led the victorious anti-Muslim forces at the Battle of Uḥud.

658 See above, *Gh* § 15.2.8.7 on the undecided battle of Ṣiffīn and its aftermath, which brought Yazīd's father to power.

659 A common nickname of the devil, as is the one that follows.

660 Animals are slaughtered at the Muslim "Feast of Sacrifice" (*ʿīd al-aḍḥā*) or "Major Feast" (*al-ʿīd al-kabīr*).

661 Part of the Muslim call to prayer. The motionless standing of wild asses or onagers and the braying of the male are often depicted in Bedouin poetry.

662 A proverb, explained with the story of a man who angrily broke his new bow, thinking he had repeatedly missed his target in the dark, only to discover the next morning that he had killed five onagers. To spite himself he cut off his thumb.

663 The grammarians have discussed the unusual accusative used for the vocative, and the form *awāqī* (from **wawāqī*).

664 The verse is quoted in Sībawayh's grammar; as the commentaries explain, the subject of "knocked down" is an implied "the horses," meaning "our cavalry." The second half may indicate the closeness of kinship (inbreeding as a reason for boasting of nobility).

665 The beginning of a lament on the death of his brother.

666 Several early poets were nicknamed after a rare or striking word they used.

667 A proverb. Lubad was the name of the last of the seven long-lived vultures of the legendary sage Luqmān, who was promised a lifetime spanning the consecutive lives of the birds.

668 Muraqqish was promised marriage to his cousin Asmā', but during his absence she was married to another. Upon his return he was told she had died. Having found out the truth he went on his way to her, together with a servant of Ghufaylah. Too weak to proceed, he was left in a cave and the man told others that Muraqqish had died. Asmā', in her turn, discovered the truth and found her lover, who soon afterward died in her presence.

669 A famous collection of pre- and early Islamic odes (126 in one recension), compiled by al-Mufaḍḍal al-Ḍabbī (d. 164/780 or a few years later). A complete, richly annotated translation was published by C. J. Lyall.

670 Twigs of the *arāk* tree (for which Na'mān, not far from Mecca, was famous) were used to clean the teeth and massage the gums.

671 The younger Muraqqish was the lover of Fāṭimah, daughter of King al-Mundhir ibn al-Nuʿmān of al-Ḥīrah. She ordered Hind bint ʿAjlān, her servant, to bring him to her.

672 Janāb ibn ʿAwf, a friend of Muraqqish, insisted on secretly taking his place with Fāṭimah one night. When Muraqqish gave in at last, and Fāṭimah became aware of the matter, she broke with Muraqqish.

673 "The two bitter things" have been explained as "poverty and old age," or "old age and disease," or "poverty and nakedness."

674 The following line is taken from the famous ode attributed to him called *Lāmiyyat al-ʿArab*, although the second/eighth-century poet and transmitter Khalaf al-Aḥmar is said to have fabricated it; opinions are still divided.

675 The line is from a passage about a wolf answered by other wolves; the standard version has "He complained, they complained; and then he turned, they turned. . ."

676 *Simākī* is apparently rain "caused" by the rain stars called al-Simāk, which are associated with the sign of Libra (September/October).

677 Translation uncertain.

678 The Qur'anic word *al-furqān* (of uncertain meaning, see R. Paret, entry "Furḳān" in *EI2*) is here used for the Qur'an itself. The following verse is Q Ṭā Hā 20:115.

679 The roots are different (*'-N-S* "human", *N-S-Y* "forget") but especially in some derived forms they can be confused.

680 Abū Tammām.

681 Q Baqarah 2:199.

682 Q Ḥajj 22:55. Standard Arabic would be *al-bādī* (the word has also been interpreted as "Bedouin, dweller in the desert").

683 One would expect it to be *unaysān*, which could not be confused with the root *N-S-Y*. Obviously, the Basrians are correct in rejecting the etymological connection between "human" and "forgetting," even though the Sheikh does not follow them.

684 An image for something that cannot be gotten rid of.

685 These lines are often quoted and ascribed to Adam, theologians being on the whole more gullible than philologists.

686 Presumably Abel's.

687 *Malīḥī* instead of *malīḥū* produces a faulty rhyme.

688 i.e., reading *bashāshata l-wajhu l-malīḥū* (even though normal syntax requires *bashāshatan*).

689 *ʿAmru lladhī* should in normal syntax be *ʿAmrun-i lladhī*. This ʿAmr is better known as Hāshim, "the bread crumbler;" he was the Prophet's great-grandfather. The epithet "Hāshimī" has been used through the centuries until today by those claiming descent from him. In most sources the verse is attributed to Ibn al-Zibaʿrā.

690 cf. Q Zumar 39:32: «But who does greater wrong than he who lies against God and denies truth when it comes to him?»

691 cf. Q Nūḥ 71:17–18, «And God has made you grow from the earth; then He will make you return to it.»

692 There is a pre-Islamic tale about a snake ("She of the Rock") who killed a man but afterward struck a deal with his brother, agreeing to pay him a dinar every other day as blood money. Al-Nābighah al-Dhubyānī refers to the story in the poem quoted below, which is paraphrased by al-Maʿarrī.

693 This seems to be the sense; the normal meanings of *man kafara* and *muʾmin* are "he who is an unbeliever" and "believer," respectively, and probably play a part here as well.

694 The brother's grave.

695 Taking *al-barr* to refer to God; alternatively, "for a righteous person there is a watchful eye."

696 Q Anʿām 6:96. Variant readings crept in as a result of the early transmission of the Qur'an, aurally or in a script originally without diacritical dots (distinguishing between particular consonants) or vowel signs, which were introduced later. To put a halt to the proliferation of variants a limited number (seven or ten) of versions were recognized as canonical. The differences are mostly insignificant, without any serious consequences for the interpretation.

697 Q Āl ʿImrān 3:41.

698 Unlike al-Ḥasan's version, Abū ʿAmr's is one of the canonical seven.

699 Through Ethiopian from Greek *euangelion* ("evangel"); it occurs twelve times in the Qur'an.

700 Q Nisā' 4:1.

701 Q Ibrāhīm 14:22.

702 Q Fāṭir 35:43.

703 Imru' al-Qays, *Dīwān*, p. 122; having revenged his father's murder he is no longer bound to the oath of abstention that he had sworn.

704 Pronouncing it as *ashrab*ᵘ, with a furtive vowel, the word counting as two long syllables rather than one long followed by two short.

705 The verses, also found in Sībawayh's grammar, are attributed to Abū Nukhaylah (second/eighth century).

706 *Ṣāhi*, though going further in shortening *ṣāḥibī* ("my friend"), is common and allowed, unlike *ṣāḥib*.

707 The meter does not require this balance and the final foot may be LLSL or SLSL.

708 Al-Mutanakhkhil.

709 In this meter SLSS (*maʿāriya*) is considered a fuller form than SLL (*maʿārin*), but both are allowed.

710 In this opening verse of the poem *ʿalāmātin* ("marks") and *ka-taḥbīri l-* ("like woven patterns of") are both SLLL instead of SLSSL.

711 Or possibly "she," taking the woman to be the subject of *talin* rather than the wine.

712 The verse is from his *Muʿallaqah.*

713 Bint al-Shāṭi' ascribes them to Majnūn Laylā but they are not in his collected verse. The third line is found in the *Dīwān* of Ibn Muqbil.

714 Unidentified, as is the following one.

715 With the last, rare word (*ʿuthmān*) the author no doubt alludes to the killing of the third caliph ʿUthmān in 35/656, an event that lies at the root of serious rifts in early Islam.

716 Imru' al-Qays; the lines are from his *Muʿallaqah.*

717 In the story connected with the poem the poet sees some girls, including his beloved ʿUnayzah, bathing in a pool; he takes away their clothes and returns them only after they have let him admire their charms. Then he slaughters his camel and regales them on the meat.

718 In the *Muʿallaqah* the girls throw chunks of raw meat to one another, after the poet has slaughtered his camel. The rare word *tharmad,* a bitter herb, may have been chosen because the verb *tharmada* means "to undercook meat."

719 All of them *rajaz* poets from the first/seventh and second/eighth centuries.

720 There is a short lacuna in the text; the following words between square brackets must be supplied.

721 This saying of the Prophet is found in the Hadith.

722 The "leader" could be al-Khalīl or else Sībawayh (d. ca. 177/793), in whose *Kitāb* Ru'bah is often quoted.

723 In the following purple passage the Sheikh employs rhymed prose and again displays his fondness of obscure words, not imitated here.

724 The Sheikh apparently condemns the use of the lowly meter for the lofty genre of eulogy and for the *qaṣidah* form (in which praise of the patron is often preceded by a camel description).

725 Q Ṭūr 52:23.

726 cf. Q Wāqiʿah 56:18–19, in a description of Paradise: «a cup from a spring; their brows will not be throbbing, to them no befuddling».

727 cf. Q Wāqiʿah 56:23.

728 Q Yūnus 10:10.

729 i.e., Ibn al-Qāriḥ's letter; the reply follows in Volume Two.

Glossary of Names and Terms

(Names are given as they appear in the text. Where necessary, a fuller version of them is given in parentheses).

abārīq pl. of *ibrīq* (q.v.).

ʿAbd Allāh ibn (al-)ʿAbbās see Ibn (al-)ʿAbbās.

ʿAbd Allāh ibn Jaʿfar (d. 80/699 or some years later) nephew of the fourth caliph, ʿAlī, known for his generosity; friends with several famous singers, including Budayḥ, who was his *mawlā* ("client").

ʿAbd al-Malik ibn Marwān (r. 65–86/685–705) Umayyad caliph.

ʿAbd al-Malik ibn Qurayb (d. ca. 216/831) famous philologist better known as al-Aṣmaʿī; specialist in ancient Arabic language, lore, and poetry; rival of Abū ʿUbaydah.

ʿAbd al-Munʿim ibn ʿAbd al-Karīm ibn Aḥmad (Abū Yaʿlā) judge known as al-Qāḍī al-Aswad ("the black judge") who lived in Aleppo in the author's time.

ʿAbīd (ʿAbīd ibn al-Abraṣ al-Asadī; first half of the sixth century AD) famous pre-Islamic poet.

Abū "father of."

Abū l-ʿAbbās Aḥmad ibn Khalaf al-Mumattaʿ (Abū l-ʿAbbās Aḥmad ibn Khalaf ibn ʿAlī al-Maʿarrī, known as al-Mumattaʿ, dates unknown) a man of letters and poet from Aleppo; a pupil of Abū l-ʿAlāʾ, who composed elegies on his death (Ibn al-ʿAdīm, *Bughyat al-ṭalab*, pp. 725–30).

Abū ʿAbd Allāh al-Ḥusayn ibn Jawhar (executed in 401/1011) Fatimid general; son of Jawhar, the conqueror of Egypt for the Fatimids.

Abū ʿAbd Allāh ibn Muḥammad ibn Rizām al-Ṭāʾī al-Kūfī (fl. 340/951) anti-Ismāʿīlī polemicist.

Abū ʿAlī al-Fārisī (d. 377/987) important grammarian born in southern Iran, active in Aleppo and Baghdad.

Abū ʿAmr ibn al-ʿAlāʾ (d. ca. 159/776) philologist from Baṣra, one of the earliest scholars who systematically collected early poetry; also a famous Qurʾan reciter.

Abū ʿAmr al-Shaybānī (d. ca. 213/828) a lexicographer from Kufa.

Abū l-Aswad al-Duʾalī (d. ca. 69/688) a minor poet famous as the alleged founder of Arabic grammatical studies in Basra; the report is probably spurious.

Abū l-ʿAtāhiyah (d. 210/825) a poet famous for his ascetic, world-renouncing poetry.

Abū Bakr (r. 11–13/632–4) one of the earliest converts, the father of ʿĀʾishah who became the Prophet's favorite wife; the first caliph.

Abū Bakr ibn Durayd (d. 321/933) an important lexicographer as well as a poet; he died at a very advanced age.

Abū Bakr ibn Mujāhid (Aḥmad ibn Mūsā ibn Mujāhid; d. 324/936) influential Baghdadi specialist in the Qurʾanic textual variants.

Abū Bakr Muḥammad ibn ʿUbayd Allāh al-ʿArzamī (d. after 133/750) minor poet from Kufa.

Abū Bakr al-Shiblī (d. 334/945 in Baghdad) early mystic; a follower of al-Ḥallāj for a while but turned against him at the latter's trial.

Abū Dhuʾayb poet of Hudhayl; a younger contemporary of the Prophet who participated in the early conquests.

Abū l-Faraj al-Zahrajī nothing is known about him; the text notes that he was the state secretary at the court of Naṣr al-Dawlah.

Abū Ḥafṣ al-Kattānī (Abū Ḥafṣ ʿUmar ibn Ibrāhīm al-Kattānī; d. 390/1000) Qurʾanic scholar from Baghdad.

Abū l-Ḥasan ʿAlī ibn ʿĪsā (d. 334/946 at an advanced age) a vizier under the caliphs al-Muqtadir and al-Qāhir, known for his righteousness and learning.

Abū l-Ḥasan ʿAlī ibn ʿĪsā al-Rummānī see Rummānī, ʿAlī ibn ʿĪsā al-.

Abū l-Ḥasan al-Maghribī, ʿAlī ibn al-Ḥusayn (killed in 400/1009) the father of al-Wazīr al-Maghribī, who held offices under Sayf al-Dawlah in Aleppo and later in Cairo.

Abū l-Hindī (d. ca. 132/750) poet from the late Umayyad period known for his Bacchic verse.

Abū l-Ḥusayn al-Khayyāṭ see Khayyāṭ, Abū l-Ḥusayn al-.

Abū ʿĪsā (d. 209/824–25) a son of Hārūn al-Rashīd; he was a bit of a rake.

Abū Kabīr al-Hudhalī, ʿĀmir ibn al-Ḥulays (d. probably early seventh century AD) poet of Hudhayl; little is known about him. Apart from some fragments only four odes of his have been preserved, all with the same opening words.

Abū Manṣūr Muḥammad ibn ʿAlī al-Khāzin (d. 418/1027) librarian of the *Dār al-ʿilm* ("House of Learning"); Abū l-ʿAlāʾ knew him during his sojourn in Baghdad and addressed an ode to him.

Abū l-Murajjā apparently a benefactor of the Sheikh or the author; perhaps he is Sālim ibn ʿAlī ibn Muḥammad al-Amīr Abū l-Murajjā al-Ḥamawī, mentioned in Ibn al-ʿAdīm's *Bughyat al-ṭalab*.

Abū Muslim (d. 136/754) the propagandist and organizer of the revolution that brought the Abbasids to power in 132/749–50; his former employers had him murdered.

Abū Nuwās al-Ḥakamī (d. ca. 200/814) one of the greatest and most versatile poets, famous especially for his Bacchic poetry and love lyrics (mostly on boys); associated with the caliph al-Amīn, Hārūn al-Rashīd's son, and dying shortly after him.

Abū l-Qāsim al-Maghribī, al-Ḥusayn ibn ʿAlī (d. 418/1027) known as al-Wazīr al-Maghribī (his family came from North Africa, but it seems he was born in Aleppo), a man of letters, the only one to escape the massacre of his family (a line of high officials and viziers under the Fatimids) in 400/1009, during the reign of the "mad" caliph al-Ḥākim; he held several offices. Ibn al-Qāriḥ had been his tutor but after the family fell from grace he satirized and criticized al-Maghribī in a poem.

Abū l-Qaṭirān al-Marrār ibn Saʿīd al-Faqʿasī (d. middle of second/eighth century) poet.

Abū Saʿīd al-Sīrāfī (al-Ḥasan ibn ʿAbd Allāh al-Sīrāfī; d. 368/979 in Baghdad) judge and grammarian from Sīrāf in Persia.

Abū Ṭālib (d. AD 619) the Prophet's paternal uncle and the father of ʿAlī; he looked after Muḥammad when he became an orphan in early childhood and protected him when Muḥammad's preaching evoked opposition and persecution, even though he himself did not convert to Islam.

Abū Tammām (Ḥabīb ibn Aws, d. ca. 231/846) a very important poet from the Abbasid period who composed odes on leading personages including Caliph al-Muʿtaṣim but also excelled in other genres; noted for his often difficult, rugged diction and a highly rhetoricized style full of rather far-fetched metaphors, plays on words, and "intellectual" conceits. He compiled a very influential, thematically arranged anthology of pre- and early Islamic poetry, called *al-Ḥamāsah* (*Zeal*, after the first, "heroic" chapter).

Abū l-Ṭayyib see Mutanabbī, al-.

Abū l-Ṭayyib al-Lughawī (ʿAbd al-Wāḥid ibn ʿAlī Abū l-Ṭayyib al-Lughawī, i.e., "the lexicographer"; d. 351/962) lexicographer and grammarian.

Abū ʿUbādah see Buḥturī, al-.

Abū ʿUbaydah (d. 210/825) famous philologist, specialist in ancient Arabic language, lore, and poetry; rival of al-Aṣmaʿī.

Abū ʿUmar al-Zāhid (Abū ʿUmar Muḥammad ibn ʿAbd al-Wāḥid; d. 345/957) devoted pupil of Thaʿlab, hence known as Ghulām Thaʿlab, "Thaʿlab's servant."

Abū ʿUthmān al-Māzinī (d. 246/861 or some years later) a philologist from Baṣra.

Abū ʿUthmān al-Nājim (Abū ʿUthmān Saʿd (or Saʿīd) ibn al-Ḥasan al-Nājim; d. 314/926) minor poet, friend of Ibn al-Rūmī.

Abū Zayd (Abū Zayd al-Anṣārī; d. 214 or 215/830–1) grammarian and lexicographer.

Abū Zubayd (d. first half of the seventh century AD) Christian poet who died without converting to Islam.

ʿĀd mentioned in the Qur'an as an Arab tribe who, in ancient times, disobeyed the prophet Hūd; God consequently destroyed them by means of a "roaring wind" or a drought. They are traditionally located in Hadramawt; the historical background is obscure.

Adhriʿāt place in Syria.

ʿAdī ibn Rabīʿah better known by his nickname Muhalhil ("he who weaves [poetry] finely)", he is one of the earliest known poets and credited with producing the first *qaṣīdah*s or odes; said to be an uncle of Imru' al-Qays. His poems deal mostly with the protracted feud between the tribes of Taghlib and Shaybān known as the "War of Basūs," caused by the murder of his brother Kulayb (see, e.g., Nicholson, *Literary History of the Arabs*, pp. 55–60).

ʿAdī ibn Zayd al-ʿIbādī (d. ca. AD 600) pre-Islamic Christian poet from al-Ḥīrah famous for his descriptions of wine.

afāniyah a tree.

Afshīn, al- (d. 226/841) commander under al-Muʿtaṣim, of Iranian extraction, who had suppressed a dangerous revolt by Bābak; having been in secret correspondence with Māzyār, he was accused of apostasy in a show trial in Sāmarrā and left to starve to death.

Afwah al-Awdī, al- (d. ca. AD 570) a pre-Islamic poet.

Aḥmad ibn al-Ḥusayn see Mutanabbī, al-.

Aḥmad ibn Khalaf al-Mumatta' see Abū l-'Abbās Aḥmad ibn Khalaf.

Aḥmad ibn Yaḥyā al-Rāwandī (d. probably in the middle of the fourth/tenth century) he turned from the "rationalist" Mu'tazilah to "heresy" (*zandaqah*) and skepticism, rejecting the idea of prophethood and attacking the Qur'an; there are reports that he renounced this at the end of his life. Parts of his works have been preserved.

Aḥmad ibn Yaḥyā Tha'lab see Tha'lab.

Ahwāz, al- town in Khuzistan (now in Iran) close to Basra; it had extensive sugar plantations.

'Ajjāj, al- (d. after 99/717) poet famous for his poems in *rajaz* meter; the first to use *rajaz* for longer poems and odes. On account of his extremely rich diction he is quoted very often by lexicographers.

Akhfash al-Awsaṭ, al- see Sa'īd ibn Mas'adah.

Akhṭal, al- (d. ca. 92/710) with Jarīr and al-Farazdaq, one of the three great poets of the Umayyad period. Even though he was associated with the court of several caliphs, eulogizing 'Abd al-Malik and others, he was a Christian, like many other of his tribe, Taghlib, in early Islam; he also excelled in Bacchic scenes. In the protracted poetic battle between Jarīr and al-Farazdaq he sided with the latter.

Ākil al-Murār ancestor of Imru' al-Qays and name of a pre-Islamic Arab dynasty in Central Arabia.

'Alī see 'Allī ibn Abī Ṭālib.

'Alī ibn al-'Abbās ibn Jurayj al-Rūmī see Ibn al-Rūmī.

'Alī ibn Abī Ṭālib (killed in 40/661) cousin and son-in-law of the Prophet, the husband of the latter's daughter Fāṭimah; he became the fourth Caliph and was murdered after a reign of five years.

'Alī ibn al-Ḥusayn son of al-Ḥusayn, the principal martyr of Shi'ite Islam (he died in 61/680 at Karbala) and one of the sons of 'Alī and Fāṭimah; 'Alī, like his father, is a Shī'ite imām.

'Alī ibn 'Īsā, Abū l-Ḥasan see Abū l-Ḥasan 'Alī ibn 'Īsā.

'Alī ibn 'Īsā al-Rummānī see Rummānī, 'Alī ibn 'Īsā al-.

'Ālij place whose location is a matter of disagreement.

'Alqamah ('Alqamah ibn 'Abadah; sixth century AD) pre-Islamic poet connected with the court of the Arab Lakhmid rulers in al-Ḥīrah.

'Alwah a place in Najd (Central Arabia).

Āmid place now called Diyarbakır, in S.-E. Turkey.

ʿAmr ibn Aḥmar al-Bāhilī (first/seventh century) poet born in the pre-Islamic period who died after the coming of Islam; he is said to have died at a very advanced age, perhaps during the caliphate of ʿAbd al-Malik (65–86/685–705).

ʿAmr ibn Kulthūm (sixth century AD) poet of one of the seven *Muʿallaqāt*, which is his only famous poem.

ʿĀnah place on the Euphrates in Northern Mesopotamia associated with wine production.

ʿAntarah (ʿAntarah ibn Shaddād, ʿAntarah al-ʿAbsī; d. ca. AD 600) famous pre-Islamic poet and warrior, son of an Arab of the tribe of ʿAbs and a black slave mother called Zabībah, therefore considered a slave according to pre-Islamic custom, until he acquired his freedom by his courage in battle; the author of one of the seven *Muʿallaqāt*. Later he became (as ʿAntar) the hero of a vast, fantastic, and extremely popular epic in sub-standard Arabic, recited by oral narrators; ʿAntarah, Sulayk, and Khufāf are known as the "Ravens."

ʿArzamī, al- see Abū Bakr Muḥammad ibn ʿUbayd Allāh.

Aʿshā, al- (Maymūn ibn Qays) al-Aʿshā means "the Night-blind, the Nyctalope"; of the tribe of Bakr, one of the great pre-Islamic poets. He was probably a Christian.

Aṣmaʿī, al- see ʿAbd al-Malik ibn Qurayb.

Aswad ibn ʿAbd Yaghūth, al- a contemporary of the Prophet.

Aswad ibn Maʿdīkarib, al- possibly a mistake for Abū l-Aswad Yazīd, son of Maʿdīkarib, one of the leaders of the Kindah tribal confederation.

Aswad ibn al-Mundhir, al- a hero eulogized by the poet al-Aʿshā, the brother of the last king of the Lakhm dynasty.

Aswad ibn Yaʿfur, al- (d. toward the end of the sixth century AD) poet; only a few of his odes have been preserved.

Aswad ibn Zamʿah, al- a contemporary of the Prophet, whose son was killed at Badr in AD 624.

Aws (Aws ibn Ḥajar; said to have died shortly before the Hijra (AD 622)) a pre-Islamic poet admired for his hunting scenes and descriptions of arms and manly virtues.

Awzāʿī, al- (d. 157/774) Syrian jurist, founder of a school of Islamic law superseded by other schools.

Bāb al-Ṭāq a large quarter, named after the arch (*ṭāq*) of the palace of Asmāʾ, the daughter of the founder of Baghdad, Caliph al-Manṣūr.

Bābak (Pāpak in Persian; d. 223/838) leader of the anti-Islamic and anti-Arab Khurramī movement in Azerbaijan, active since 201/816–17 and finally defeated by al-Afshīn in 222/837; he was cruelly executed in Sāmarrā the following year.

Bāhilī, al- see ʿAmr ibn Aḥmar.

Bakrī, al- see al-Aʿshā.

Banū l-Dardabīs a fanciful name of a tribe of the jinn; the word *dardabīs* is given various meanings by the lexicographers ("calamity," "old man," "old woman," "love charm," and "penis").

Barāqish place in Yemen.

Barmakids or *Barmecides* (descendants of Barmak) a family of very powerful viziers in the early Abbasid period; they fell spectacularly from power during the reign of Hārūn al-Rashīd.

Bashshār ibn Burd (Abū Muʿādh; executed 167/783 or 784) an important Arabic poet, called the "father of the modern poets"; proud of his Persian descent; the first great Arabic poet who was not an Arab; he excelled in many poetic genres. Though famous for his "courtly" love poems, he was notorious for his suspected heretical, Manichaean beliefs, which may have led to his execution at the orders of the caliph al-Mahdī.

Basīl presumably Basil (Basileos) II Bulgaroctonos ("Bulgar-slayer," r. AD 976–1025).

Battī, al- (Abū l-Ḥasan Aḥmad ibn ʿAlī al-Battī; d. 403/1013) *kātib* ("state secretary") at the court of Caliph al-Qādir, man of letters and wit.

Baysān (adj. Baysānī) a town in the Jordan Valley, famous for its wine.

Bayt Raʾs place in Syria, near Aleppo.

Bishr (Bishr ibn Abī Khāzim) a pre-Islamic poet, some eight hundred of whose verses are preserved.

Buḥturī, Abū ʿUbādah al- (d. 284/897) important Abbasid poet.

Camel-herd, The see ʿUbayd ibn al-Ḥuṣayn al-Numayrī.

Chosroes (Persian Khusraw, Greek Chosroes, Arabic Kisrā) the name of several Sassanian emperors in the pre-Islamic period, and often standing for any Sassanian king, just as Qayṣar/Caesar stands for any Roman or Byzantine emperor.

colocynth a plant with pungent and very bitter fruit, used as a laxative and for various other medical purposes.

Dahnāʾ, al- a very long (some thousand kilometers) strip of sand desert in Arabia, connecting the Nafūd in the northwest with the "Empty Quarter."

Dardabīs, Banū l- see Banū l-Dardabīs.

Dārīn port in Eastern Arabia, where Indian musk was imported.

Dawmah or *Dūmah* probably Dūmat al-Jandal, an oasis between Medina and Damascus.

ḍaymurān a kind of tree.

Dhāt al-Raḍm a place in northern Arabia.

Dhū Ḥusam a wadi in Najd.

Duʾalī, al- see Abū l-Aswad al-Duʾalī.

Ḍubayʿah a branch of the tribe of Qays ibn Thaʿlabah; the name means "little hyena."

Dūmah see Dawmah.

fālūd, fālūdhaj from Pahlavi (Middle Persian) *pālūdag* ("strained"), a sweet made of flour and honey.

Faqʿasī, al- see Abū l-Qaṭirān al-Marrār.

Farazdaq, al- (Hammām ibn Ghālib; d. ca. 110/728) usually called al-Farazdaq ("Bread Morsel"); was with al-Akhṭal and Jarīr one of the great poets of the Umayyad period, famous for his many panegyric poems on caliphs and others, and feared for his satire. He and Jarīr exchanged a lengthy series of lampooning poems (*naqāʾiḍ*).

Fārisī, al- see Abū ʿAlī al-Fārisī.

Farrāʾ, al- (Abū Zakariyyā Yaḥyā ibn Ziyād al-Farrāʾ; d. 207/822). Important grammarian of the "school of Kufa."

Fāṭimah the Prophet's daughter and ʿAlī's wife, the mother of al-Ḥasan and al-Ḥusayn, through whom all descendants of the Prophet trace their descent.

Fūrah, al- Yāqūt, *Muʿjam al-buldān* has al-Qurrah (s.v. al-ʿUmayr and al-Qurrah); it is said to be a monastery.

Fustat (al-Fusṭāṭ) the "Old Cairo" of today, founded by the Arab conquerors in the first half of the first/seventh century.

ghalwā a perfume.

Gharīḍ, al- (d. ca. 92/716–17) a famous singer from the Umayyad period.

Ghayl, al- (or al-Ghīl, according to some). Location near Mecca.

Ghulām Thaʿlab see Abū ʿUmar al-Zāhid.

Ghumayr al-Luṣūṣ Yāqūt calls it ʿUmayr al-Luṣūṣ in his *Muʿjam al-buldān* s.v. al-ʿUmayrah and al-Qurrah, where it is said to be a village near al-Ḥīrah or al-Qādisiyyah.

Ḥabīb ibn Aws see Abū Tammām.

habīd explained as "colocynth" or its seeds.

Ḥādirah al-Dhubyānī, al- (Quṭbah ibn Aws ibn Miḥṣan; d. early in the seventh century AD) pre-Islamic poet who was known as al-Ḥādirah ("the broad-shouldered," i.e., "the frog").

Ḥakamī Abū Nuwās, al- see Abū Nuwāṣ.

Ḥākim, al- (r. 386–411/996–1021) the controversial Fāṭimid caliph who at some stage claimed divinity; he was notorious for his capricious behavior and bloodshed. After his disappearance (apparently having been murdered) the cult of his person gave rise to the Druze religion.

Hakir (or *Hakr*) according to the sources, a place, or a palace, or a monastery; it is located in Yemen, or forty miles south of Medina, or a Roman name . . . in other words, nobody knows.

Ḥallāj, al-Ḥusayn ibn Manṣūr al- (d. 309/922 in Baghdad) very famous early mystic, cruelly executed, accused of blasphemy and heresy.

ḥamāṭah 1. a tree; 2. its fruit; 3. heartburn; 4. blackness or bottom of the heart.

Ḥāmid ibn al-ʿAbbās (d. 311/923) vizier during the trial of al-Ḥallāj.

Ḥamzah ibn ʿAbd al-Muṭṭalib (d. 3/625). The Prophet's uncle; he was killed at the battle against the Meccans at Uḥud.

Ḥamzah ibn Ḥabīb (d. 156/772). One of the seven canonical readings of the Qur'an goes back to him.

harīsah a dish of minced meat and crushed wheat, pounded together.

Ḥārith ibn Hānī' ibn Abī Shamir ibn Jabalah al-Kindī, al- distinguished himself at the battle of Sābāṭ (a place near Ctesiphon) during the early conquests, in 16/637.

Ḥārith ibn Kaladah, al- the oldest known Arab physician; he studied at Gondeshapur in Iran and was a contemporary of the Prophet, surviving him by a few years. The sources ascribe to him a series of recommendations on medicine, diet, and hygiene.

Ḥārith al-Yashkurī, al- (al-Ḥārith ibn Ḥillizah al-Yashkurī; d. ca. AD 570) of the tribe of Yashkur; a pre-Islamic poet, author of one of the *Muʿallaqāt*, an ode he extemporized, so the story goes, in the presence of ʿAmr ibn Hind, the ruler of al-Ḥīrah.

Ḥasan al-Baṣrī, al- (al-Ḥasan ibn Abī l-Ḥasan Yasār) (d. 110/728) a famous theologian and Qurʾan reciter from Basra frequently quoted with approval by almost all later schools, especially the Sufis.

Ḥasan ibn ʿAlī al-ʿAskarī, al- (d. 260/874) the eleventh of the twelve imams of the Twelver Shiʿah (all being descendants of the Prophet through his daughter Fāṭimah, her husband ʿAlī ibn Abī Ṭālib being the first).

Ḥasan ibn Rajāʾ, al- (al-Ḥasan ibn Rajāʾ ibn Abī l-Ḍaḥḥāk) an official in Baghdad and Khorasan (now in Eastern Iran and Afghanistan) under the caliphs al-Maʾmūn and al-Muʿtaṣim.

Ḥasanī, al- apparently a local governor.

Hāshim a leading figure in the Quraysh, great-grandfather of the Prophet.

Ḥassān ibn Thābit converted to Islam around the time of the Hijra (AD 622) and forcefully supported Islam with eulogies on the Prophet and invective against his opponents; his pre-Islamic and even some "Islamic" poems contain passages describing wine.

Haylān place in Yemen.

hazaj 1. a meter; 2. a rhythmical mode.

ḥiḍb male snake; other meaning: bottom of the heart.

Ḥimyar pre-Islamic kingdom in Yemen, overthrown by the Christian Ethiopians in the sixth century AD.

Hudhayl a tribe that produced many poets; their poetry was collected in the third/ninth century and forms the only preserved instance of a collective, tribal *dīwān* (a *dīwān*, or collected verse, is normally of an individual poet); a recurrent theme in their poetry is honey gathering.

Ḥujr ibn ʿAdī al-Adbar distinguished himself at the battle of Sābāṭ (a place near Ctesiphon) during the early conquests, in 16/637.

Ḥumayd ibn Thawr al-Hilālī (d. ca. 90/709) poet born in the pre-Islamic period who died after the coming of Islam, apparently at an advanced age; he is famous especially for his animal descriptions.

Ḥusayn ibn Jawhar see Abū ʿAbd Allāh al-Ḥusayn ibn Jawhar.

Ḥusayn ibn Manṣūr al-Ḥallāj, al- see Ḥallāj, al-Ḥusayn ibn Manṣūr al-.

Ḥuss, al- a place in Syria, near Homs; cf. Yāqūt, *Muʿjam al-buldān,* s.v. and mentioned in a well-known Bacchic epigram by Abū Miḥjan al-Thaqafī;

but ʿAdī's verse is quoted in the entry "al-Khuṣṣ," said to be a place near al-Qādisiyyah.

Ḥuṭay'ah al-ʿAbsī, al- (Jarwal ibn Aws, of the tribe of ʿAbs) a younger contemporary of the Prophet and a major poet notorious for his invective skills (which he used for extortion); also noted as a miser and a lukewarm Muslim; nicknamed al-Ḥuṭay'ah (a word with several meanings but usually interpreted as "the dwarf" or "the ugly runt").

Ibn (al-)ʿAbbās, ʿAbd Allāh (d. 68/687) a cousin of the Prophet and ancestor of the Abbasid caliphs (the dynasty having been named after him); he is considered the founder of Qur'anic exegesis.

Ibn Abī ʿAwn (executed in 322/934) a man of letters, the author of a work on comparison in poetry, usually called *Kitāb al-Tashbīhāt* (*The Book of Similes*).

Ibn Abī Du'ād, Aḥmad (d. 240/854) judge of great power under al-Ma'mūn and al-Muʿtaṣim.

Ibn Aḥmar see ʿAmr ibn Aḥmar al-Bāhilī.

Ibn Durayd see Abū Bakr Ibn Durayd.

Ibn Durustawayh (d. 347/958) grammarian and lexicographer.

Ibn Ḥājib al-Nuʿmān (d. 423/1031) civil servant and anthologist.

Ibn Jawhar see Abū ʿAbd Allāh al-Ḥusayn ibn Jawhar.

Ibn Khālawayh, Abū ʿAbd Allāh al-Ḥusayn ibn Aḥmad (d. 370/980 in Aleppo) lexicographer, grammarian, and Qur'anic scholar from Hamadhān.

Ibn Misjaḥ (d. ca. 96/715) the Meccan singer was the founder of the new "art song" modeled on Byzantine and Persian music.

Ibn Mujāhid see Abū Bakr ibn Mujāhid.

Ibn Muqbil see Tamīm Ibn Ubayy.

Ibn al-Rāwandī see Aḥmad ibn Yaḥyā.

Ibn Rizām see Abū ʿAbd Allāh ibn Muḥammad ibn Rizām al-Ṭā'ī al-Kūfī.

Ibn al-Rūmī, ʿAlī ibn al-ʿAbbās ibn Jurayj (d. 283/896 in Baghdad) one of the most important Abbasid poets; his grandfather Jurayj ("George") was a Byzantine (Rūmī); his superstitiousness is often mentioned.

Ibn al-Ṣāmit (d. probably shortly before the Hijra) pre-Islamic tribal leader and poet in Medina.

Ibn al-Sammāk (Abū l-ʿAbbās Muḥammad ibn Ṣabīḥ; d. 183/799) ascetic and preacher from Kūfa.

Ibn Surayj (d. 96/714 or some years later) famous singer of the early Islamic and Umayyad periods.

Ibrāhīm ibn al-Mahdī (162–224/779–839) son of the caliph al-Mahdī; a gifted musician, poet, and cook.

Ibrāhīm al-Mawṣilī (d. 188/804) a leading musician, composer, and courtier in the time of Hārūn al-Rashīd; of Persian origin.

ibrīq (pl. abārīq) 1. jug; 2. "radiant" (graceful) girl; 3. shining sword.

Ilāl (read by some as Alāl or Ulāl) watering place on the pilgrims' route to Mecca.

Imru' al-Qays (d. in the middle of the sixth century AD) son of a prince of a tribal federation led by the tribe of Kindah; the most famous pre-Islamic poet and also the poet of the most famous of the *Muʿallaqāt*.

Isḥāq ibn Ibrāhīm (d. 235/850) son of Ibrāhīm al-Mawṣilī who followed in his father's footsteps; in addition to being the leading singer and composer of his time he wrote books on music and was also a poet.

Iyās ibn al-Aratt (Iyās ibn Khālid al-Aratt) rather obscure poet, quoted a few times in Abū Tammām's famous anthology *al-Ḥamāsah*.

jaʿdah described as "a curly plant growing on river banks" or "a green herb growing in mountain passes in Najd," etc.

Jadhīmah a legendary pre-Islamic king of Iraq who killed his two inseparable friends while drunk, bitterly repenting afterward; later killed by Queen al-Zabbā' of Palmyra, who may be (partially) identified as Zenobia.

Jadīs legendary Arab tribe.

Jafnids pre-Islamic Arab dynasty in Syria.

jāhiliyyah "ignorance", pre-Islamic period.

Jamīl (Jamīl ibn Maʿmar; d. 82/701) poet of the ʿUdhrah tribe; famous for his love poetry on Buthaynah, who was forced to marry another.

Jannābī, al- (Abū Ṭāhir al-Jannābī, d. 332/943–44) the leader of the Qarmaṭī movement in eastern Arabia, from where he raided southern Iraq and, notoriously, Mecca, where he killed pilgrims and took away the Black Stone in 317/930; it was returned only after some twenty years.

Jayfar the Splendid nothing is known about him; perhaps he is the same as Jayfar ibn al-Julandā, the "king of Oman," who converted to Islam at the time of the Prophet.

jinn (sg. jinnī, jinnee) jinnees, "genies" demons (good or evil).

Jirān al-ʿAwd al-Numayrī (ʿĀmir ibn al-Ḥārith) a poet of the tribe of Numayr, said to have lived in early Islamic and early Umayyad times; Jirān al-ʿAwd is a nickname, meaning "leather whip made from an old camel stallion," an expression he used in a poem in which he threatens his two wives with whipping them.

Jurhum legendary Arab tribe.

Jurhumī, al- (Muʿāwiyah ibn Bakr) of the ancient Arabian tribe Jurhum, who according to traditional lore reigned in Mecca in the time of the Arabian prophet Hūd.

Kaʿb (Kaʿb ibn Mālik; d. ca. 50/670) a poet; he opposed Islam at first but to save his life he composed a celebrated ode in praise of the Prophet; it came to be known as the "Mantle Ode," after the mantle that Muḥammad gave Kaʿb as a sign of his favor. He converted before the Hijra.

Kafr Ṭāb a town between Maʿarrat al-Nuʿmān and Aleppo.

Karkh, al- the part of Baghdad west and south of the original "Round City" founded by Caliph al-Manṣūr.

Kattānī, al- see Abū Ḥafṣ al-Kattānī.

Kawthar, al- a river in Paradise whose name means "Abundance."

Khadījah (d. AD 619) the first wife of Muḥammad, who was her third husband; mother of Fāṭimah; the Prophet's first supporter.

Khalaf al-Aḥmar (d. ca. 180/796) poet and *rāwī* (transmitter) of early poetry.

Khalīl ibn Aḥmad, al- (d. 160/776, 170/786, or 175/791) one of the founders of Arabic grammar and lexicography; the discoverer of the science of prosody; the author, or rather the *auctor intellectualis* or instigator, of the first Arabic lexicon, called "the letter *ʿayn*," after the first letter in his rearrangement of the alphabet; teacher of Sībawayh.

Khansāʾ, al- (b. between AD 580 and 590 and d. after 23/644, having converted to Islam) generally considered the greatest female poet in Arabic; her fame rests on her numerous elegies for her two brothers, Ṣakhr and Muʿāwiyah, the former having died before the coming of Islam.

Khayyāṭ, Abū l-Ḥusayn al- (ʿAbd al-Raḥīm ibn Muḥammad al-Khayyāṭ; d. prob. before 300/912) Muʿtalizite theologian and jurist from Baghdad.

Khāzin, al- see Abū Manṣūr Muḥammad ibn ʿAlī.

Khufāf ibn Nadbah al-Sulamī (died during the caliphate of ʿUmar (between 13/634 and 23/644)) called Ibn Nadbah after his mother who was a black slave; poet and warrior. ʿAntarah, Sulayk, and Khufāf are known as the "Ravens."

Khuṣṣ, al- said to be a place in Syria famous for wine; or a place near al-Qādisiyyah (in Iraq); or a noun meaning "wine shop."

Khuṣūṣ, al- a place near al-Ḥīrah, on the Euphrates.

Kindah a large tribal confederation that dominated central Arabia in the fifth and early sixth centuries AD.

Kisāʾī, al- (d. 189/805) grammarian and specialist in the Qurʾanic text; like many other Arabic grammarians, he was of Persian descent.

Kuthayyir (d. 105/723) poet famous for his love poetry on ʿAzzah, and therefore often called Kuthayyir ʿAzzah ("Kuthayyir of ʿAzzah").

Labīd a famous pre-Islamic poet who converted to Islam.

Lakhm, Lakhmids a pre-Islamic Arab dynasty ruling in al-Ḥīrah in Iraq (ca. AD 300–600), vassals of the Persian Sassanids.

Laṣāf watering place on the pilgrims' route to Mecca.

Maʿadd ibn ʿAdnān the legendary ancestor of the North Arabs.

Maʿarrat al-Nuʿmān the town in Syria where Abū l-ʿAlāʾ was born and died, and which gave him the epithet al-Maʿarrī.

Maʿbad (d. ca. 125/743) famous singer of the early Islamic and Umayyad periods.

Maghribī, al- see Abū l-Ḥasan al-Maghribī and Abū l-Qāsim al-Maghribī.

Mahdī, al- (r. 158–69/775–85) Abbasid caliph whose reign was marked by the persecution of "heretics" (*zanādiqah*).

Malatya place in eastern Anatolia.

Mālik an angel, the chief guard of Hell.

mandal wood a kind of wood from India, used as incense; Mandal is said to be a place in India (perhaps Mandal in Rajasthan, India).

Mani (Mānī, Manes, Manichaeus; executed AD 274 or a few years later) the founder of the dualist religion called Manichaeism after him, which enjoyed great popularity in the Sassanian empire and beyond.

maradah (sg. marīd) an evil form of jinn.

Marrār, al- see Abū l-Qaṭirān.

Marw al-Rūdh place in Khurāsān (modern Afghanistan).

Marzubānī, Abū ʿAbd Allāh al- (Muḥammad ibn ʿImrān al-Marzubānī; d. 384/994) prolific literary scholar and anthologist from Baghdad; wrote a (lost) book on the poetry of the jinn, said to have contained over one hundred folios. Several of his other works about poetry have been preserved.

Māṭirūn a place near Damascus.

Maymūn ibn Qays see Aʿshā, al-.

Mawṣilī, al- see Ibrāhīm al-Mawṣilī.

maysir an ancient Arab gambling game in which portions of a slaughtered camel were divided by shuffling marked arrow shafts.

Mayyāfāriqīn town in eastern Anatolia.

Māzinī, al- see Abū ʿUthmān al-Māzinī.

Māzyār, (al-) (d. 225/840) Qārinid ruler of a principality in Ṭabaristān, became a Muslim when he sought the help of Caliph al-Ma'mūn; involved in a rebellion during the reign of al-Muʿtaṣim. He was defeated and executed in 225/840.

Muʿallaqah (plur. Muʿallaqāt) an old collection, made in the second/eighth century, of seven celebrated long odes (*qaṣīdah*s) from the pre-Islamic period, among them odes by Imru' al-Qays, ʿAntarah, Ṭarafah, Zuhayr, and Labīd, who was the youngest and who died at an advanced age in the early Islamic period; the term *al-muʿallaqāt* seems to mean "the suspended (poems)" but the true meaning is obscure and the story that they were hung in the Kaaba is a later fiction.

Mubarrad, al- (Muḥammad ibn Yazīd al-Mubarrad; d. 285/898) famous grammarian.

Muḍar one of the two most important confederations within the "North Arabian" tribes according to the genealogists; also the ancient ancestor of the Arabs for whom the confederation was named.

Muhalhil, al- see ʿAdī ibn Rabīʿah.

Muḥammad ibn ʿAlī al-Khāzin see Abū Manṣūr Muḥammad ibn ʿAlī al-Khāzin.

Muḥammad ibn Ḥāzim (Muḥammad ibn Ḥāzim al-Bāhilī; end of the second/eighth and the beginning of the third/ninth century) poet notorious for his satire; the sources maintain that his professed frugality and abstinence were feigned.

Muḥammad ibn Yazīd see Mubarrad, al-.

Muḥassin al-Dimashqī, al- probably al-Muḥassin ibn al-Ḥusayn ibn ʿAlī Kawjak (d. 416/1026), copyist, man of letters, minor poet.

Mukhabbal al-Saʿdī, al- (d. ca. AD 640) a poet of the early Islamic period from central Arabia.

mulḥid a somewhat vague term for heretics, atheists, and all those who deviate from orthodoxy (the technical term for an apostate from Islam is *murtadd*).

Mumatta', al- see Abū l-'Abbās Aḥmad ibn Khalaf.

Muraqqish al-Akbar (the Elder), al- both the proper name ('Amr, or 'Awf, or Rabī'ah) and the nickname (Muraqqish or al-Muraqqish) of this early pre-Islamic poet are disputed; the younger Muraqqish was his nephew. Both became the hero of a love romance.

Mushaqqar, al- a fortress in eastern Arabia, held by a Persian governor in pre-Islamic, Sassanian times.

Mutajarridah, al- the wife of the pre-Islamic king al-Nu'mān ibn al-Mundhir; al-Mutajarridah is a nickname and means "she who stripped [herself], the denuded woman."

Mutanabbī, Abū l-Ṭayyib Aḥmad ibn al-Ḥusayn al- (d. 354/965) though controversial in his own day, he is by many considered to be the greatest Arabic poet of Islamic times; also highly regarded by al-Ma'arrī; he excelled in panegyrics, often skillfully combined with self-praise. Al-Mutanabbī earned his sobriquet, "the would-be prophet," when, in his late teens, he was involved in a kind of revolutionary movement, which led to his arrest in Homs (Syria)—not Baghdad—in 322/933.

Mutanakhkhil, al- pre-Islamic Hudhalī poet.

Nabhān ibn 'Amr ibn al-Ghawth ibn Ṭayyi' ancestor of a clan of the tribe of Ṭayyi', called Banū Nabhān after him.

Nābighah al-Dhubyānī, al- (sixth century AD) poet active at the court of the Lakhmid kings of al-Ḥīrah and the Ghassānid rulers in Syria; he is considered one of the greatest Arabic poets.

Nābighah al-Ja'dī, al- (d. ca. 63/683) poet born in the pre-Islamic period; a supporter of 'Alī ibn Abī Ṭālib, he was banished in old age to Isfahan by 'Alī's rival and successor as caliph.

Nadbah the mother of Khufāf al-Sulamī.

Naḍr ibn Shumayl, al- (d. ca. 204/820) expert in grammar and lexicography.

Nahshal ibn Dārim a tribe belonging to the large tribe of Tamīm.

Najāshī al-Ḥārithī, al- (Qays ibn 'Amr nicknamed al-Najāshī, "the Negus," on account of his dark color or because his mother was Ethiopian) a contemporary of Ibn Muqbil; he composed invective poetry on the latter. He fought with 'Alī at the Battle of Ṣiffīn (37/657).

Najd the central Arabian plateau.

Nājim, al- see Abū ʿUthmān al-Nājim.

Najrān place in northern Yemen.

Naʿmān, al- a wadi in the Hijaz between Mecca and al-Ṭāʾif.

Namir ibn Tawlab al-ʿUklī, al- (d. before 23/644) a poet who was born in the pre-Islamic period and who converted to Islam; he was praised for the purity of his language and style.

Naṣr al-Dawlah (Abū Naṣr Aḥmad ibn Marwān, r. 401–53/1011–61) Marwānid ruler of Mayyāfāriqīn and Diyār Bakr, in northern Syria and northern Mesopotamia.

Naṣrids pre-Islamic Arab dynasty in Iraq.

Nuʿmān ibn al-Mundhir, al- (r. ca. AD 580–602) the last king of al-Ḥīrah, subject of stories and poems.

Numayrī, al- see ʿUbayd ibn al-Ḥuṣayn al-Numayrī.

Nuṣayb (Nuṣayb ibn Rabāḥ; d. ca. 111/729) son of a black slave woman, a poet; he composed eulogies on Umayyad caliphs and princes.

parasang the ancient Greek form of a Persian measure of length, between three and four miles (Parthian *frasakh*, Middle Persian *farsang*, Arabic *farsakh*).

Qafūṣ said to be a place (location unknown) from which incense is imported.

qaṣīṣ. a plant described in *Lisān al-ʿArab*, not very helpfully, as "a plant at whose stems truffles are found."

Qayl ibn ʿItr (or ibn ʿUnuq) said to have been among ʿĀd's deputation to Mecca, where they had gone to pray for rain.

Quraysh the tribe of the Prophet Muḥammad.

qurūf (sg. qarf) described by the dictionaries as a leather container tanned with bark of the pomegranate tree, in which meat is stored that has been boiled with aromatic herbs.

Quṭāmī, al- (d. ca. 101/719) a poet from the Umayyad period.

Quṭrub (d. 206/821) a grammarian from Baṣra.

Rabāb, al- a woman's name often found in early Arabic love poetry.

Rabīʿah one of the two most important confederations within the "North Arabian" tribes according to the genealogists.

Rabīʿat al-Faras ("Rabīʿah of the Horse") the eponymous ancestor of Rabīʿah acquired his nickname because he inherited his father Nizār's horses, as legend has it.

Rāʿī, al- see ʿUbayd ibn al-Ḥuṣayn.

rajaz the simplest and presumably oldest poetic meter; it resembles the Greek or Latin iambic meter and is considered to be of lower status. Many specialists in *rajaz* studded their verse with rare words; as a consequence their verses are very often quoted as lexicographic evidence.

ramal 1. a meter; 2. a rhythmical mode.

Ramlah a major town in Palestine.

Rashīd, al- the caliph Hārūn al-Rashīd.

Ru'bah ibn al-'Ajjāj (d. 145/762) with his father al-'Ajjāj among the most famous *rajaz* poets; on account of their extremely rich diction they are quoted very often by lexicographers.

Rummānī, 'Alī ibn 'Īsā al- (Abū l-Ḥasan 'Alī ibn 'Īsā al-Rummānī; d. 384/994) grammarian, Qur'anic scholar, and literary theorist from Baghdad.

Sa'd (Sa'd ibn Abī Waqqāṣ; d. between 50/670–71 and 58/677–78) early convert and conqueror of Iraq.

Sa'd al-Dawlah (r. 356–81/967–91) Ḥamdānid ruler of Aleppo; son of Sayf al-Dawlah.

Ṣafā, al- ("the Stony Ground") a low mound at Mecca, which plays a role in the rituals of the Hajj.

Sa'īd ibn Mas'adah (d. ca. 215/830) better known as al-Akhfash al-Awsaṭ; a grammarian; he also wrote a treatise on metrics.

Ṣakhr al-Ghayy (Ṣakhr ibn 'Abd Allāh) pre-Islamic poet of Hudhayl, counted among the *ṣa'ālīk* or "outcast, brigand" poets; he acquired his epithet al-Ghayy ("going astray") because of his dissolute nature.

Ṣāliḥ ibn 'Abd al-Quddūs (executed ca. 167/783) preacher and poet from Basra.

Sanad, al- location near Mecca.

Ṣanādīqī al-Manṣūr, al- (rebelled in 270/883–84, as al-Ma'arrī says (*Ghufrān*, Part Two)). Al-Ṣanādīqī means "the box maker"; he was possibly identical with Abū l-Qāsim al-Najjār ("the carpenter"), a Shi'ite extremist who is elsewhere named as Rustam ibn al-Ḥusayn ibn Ḥawshab; see *EI2*, vi, 438–39, "Manṣūr al-Yaman" (W. Madelung).

Ṣanawbarī, al- (d. 334/945) Syrian poet famous for his poetry on gardens, flowers, and spring.

Ṣarīfīn (or *Ṣarīfūn*) see Yāqūt, *Mu'jam al-buldān*, s.v.; a place in Iraq.

Ṣarkhad place in Syria.

Sawādah ibn 'Adī the son of the pre-Islamic poet 'Adī ibn Zayd; the word *sawādah* means "black patch."

Sawdah bint Zamʿah ibn Qays she was Muḥammad's second wife and survived him by thirty-two years; the word *sawdah* means "patch with black stones."

Sayf al-Dawlah (r. 333–56/944–67) Ḥamdānid ruler of Northern Syria, renowned for his campaigns (not always successful) against the Byzantines and the literary splendor of his court in Aleppo; he owes his fame in large part to a series of odes by al-Mutanabbī.

Shalmaghān village between Basra and Baghdad.

Shammākh ibn Ḍirār, al- poet of the Banū Thaʿlabah ibn Saʿd ibn Dhubyān born in the pre-Islamic period who died after the coming of Islam.

Shanfarā al-Azdī, al- a pre-Islamic poet, one of the *ṣaʿālīk* or "outcast, brigand poets"; the famous ode called *Lāmiyyat al-ʿArab* is attributed to him, although the second/eighth-century poet and transmitter Khalaf al-Aḥmar is said to have fabricated it; opinions are still divided.

Shaybānī, Abū ʿAmr al- see Abū ʿAmr al-Shaybānī.

Shibām place in North Yemen associated with wine production (not to be confused with the more famous town of that name in South Yemen).

Shibl al-Dawlah (Nāṣir ibn Ṣāliḥ Shibl al-Dawlah; r. 420–9/1029–38) Mirdāsid ruler of Aleppo at the time al-Maʿarrī wrote his *Epistle of Forgiveness.*

Shiblī, al- see Abū Bakr al-Shiblī.

Sībawayh (d. 177/793) author of the first and by far the most important Arabic grammar. Like many other Arabic grammarians, he was of Persian descent.

Sīrāfī, al- see Abū Saʿīd al-Sīrāfī.

storax (lubnā) a vanilla-scented resin used as incense, medicine, or perfume.

Suḥaym (killed ca. 40/660) known as ʿAbd Banī l-Ḥaṣḥāṣ ("the slave of the tribe of Banū l-Ḥaṣḥāṣ"), of Ethiopian descent (Suḥaym means "Blackie"); a poet who was killed for his too-explicit verses.

Sulakah, al- the mother of Sulayk.

Sulamī, al- see Khufāf ibn Nadbah al-Sulamī.

Sulayk (or al-Sulayk) called Ibn al-Sulakah after his mother, a black slave, he was a pre-Islamic "outcast, brigand poet"; ʿAntarah, Sulayk, and Khufāf are known as the "Ravens."

Suwayd ibn Abī Kāhil a poet, a contemporary of the Prophet; Suwayd literally means "little black one."

Suwayd ibn Ṣumayʿ a minor poet.

Ta'abbaṭa Sharrā (Thābit ibn Jābir) one of the legendary "outcast, brigand poets"; friend of al-Shanfarā. His strange nickname ("He took evil under his arm") is explained in various anecdotes.

Tabālah said to be a place in Yemen.

Tamīm ibn Muqbil see Tamīm ibn Ubayy.

Tamīm ibn Ubayy ibn Muqbil al-ʿAjlānī (d. after 35/656) poet born in the pre-Islamic period who died after the coming of Islam.

Ṭarafah ibn al-ʿAbd attached to the court of ʿAmr ibn Hind at al-Ḥīrah; he died young. Having angered the king he was sent with a "letter of Uriah" containing his own death warrant (cf. 2 Sam. 11).

Ṭayyi' an important Arab tribe.

Thabīr a mountain near Mecca.

Thabrah watering place on the pilgrims' route to Mecca.

Thamūd frequently mentioned in the Qur'an, is a legendary Arabian tribe or people who were destroyed because they disobeyed God and his messengers; often mentioned in connection with ʿĀd.

Tinnīs a town (now in ruins) in Egypt, on a small island near the eastern part of the Nile Delta.

ʿUbayd ibn al-Ḥuṣayn al-Numayrī (d. ca. 96/714) poet nicknamed al-Rāʿī al-Numayrī, the "Camel-herd," for his many descriptions of camels and other animals.

Uḥud place not far from Medina; also the location of a battle between the Muslims and the Meccans, who were victorious; it was only a temporary setback for the Muslims.

ʿUmānī, al- (Muḥammad ibn Dhu'ayb al-ʿUmānī; d. during Hārūn al-Rashīd's caliphate (170–93/786–809)) poet; he did not come from Oman, as his name would suggest, but acquired his nickname on account of his sallow complexion (perhaps a result of jaundice).

ʿUmar ibn al-Khaṭṭāb (r. 13–23/634–44) the second caliph.

Umm "mother (of)."

Uqayshir al-Asadī, al- (first/seventh century) poet from Iraq known for his bohemian behavior and love of wine.

ʿUrwah ibn Masʿūd al-Thaqafī (d. 9/630) one of those who brokered the truce between the Prophet and the Meccans in 6/628 at al-Ḥudaybiyah, a village near Mecca.

ʿUrwah ibn al-Ward (second half of the sixth century AD) pre-Islamic poet.

ʿUtbah ibn Ghazwān (d. 17/638) an early convert to Islam, founder of the city of Basra.

ʿUthmān ibn Ṭalḥah al-ʿAbdarī a member of Quraysh, who held the hereditary office of guarding the Kaaba in pre-Islamic times.

Waḥshī ("Savage") an Abyssinian slave fighting with the Meccans at Uḥud.

Wajj another name of al-Ṭāʾif.

Walīd ibn Yazīd, al- (r. 125–6/743–4) Umayyad caliph notorious for his dissolute behavior; a good poet.

wars a yellow dye.

Warsh (ʿUthmān ibn Saʿd; d. 197/812) transmitted one of the seven canonical readings of the Qurʾan from his teacher Nāfiʿ al-Laythī (d. ca. 169/785).

Wazīr al-Maghribī, al- see Abū l-Qāsim ibn ʿAlī ibn al-Ḥusayn al-Maghribī.

Yabrīn place in central or eastern Arabia.

Yaʿrub the son of Qaḥṭān, ancestor of the South Arabs; his name is etymologically connected with ʿArab, and he is said to have been the first to speak Arabic (there are different views).

Yashkur a tribe in al-Yamāmah.

Yashkurī, al- see Ḥārith al-Yashkurī, al-.

Yathrib the old name of Medina.

Yazīd ibn al-Ḥakam al-Kilābī (d. ca. 105/723) poet from the Umayyad period; he should have been called al-Thaqafī ("of the tribe Thaqīf") rather than al-Kilābī.

Yazīd ibn Muʿāwiyah (r. 60–64/680–3) the second Umayyad caliph, known for his hedonism and love of wine; among Shiʾites his reputation is particularly bad because al-Ḥusayn, their principal martyr, was killed during his reign. He favored the arts and composed poetry.

Yūnus ibn Ḥabīb (d. 182/798) grammarian.

Zabībah the mother of ʿAntarah.

Zāhid, al- see Abū ʿUmar al-Zāhid.

Zahrajī, al- see Abū l-Faraj al-Zahrajī.

Zanj blacks originally from East Africa; widely exploited as slaves on plantations in southern Iraq.

Zibriqān ibn Badr, al- a poet and tribal leader, called al-Ḥuṣayn but nicknamed al-Zibriqān ("brilliant full moon") on account of his handsome appearance; after his conversion to Islam he was appointed tax collector for his tribe, Tamīm.

zindīq (pl. zanādiqah) someone professing Islam but having heretical (often Manichaean) beliefs.

Zuhayr ibn Abī Sulmā al-Muzanī it is said that he died at an advanced age in AD 609, just before the Prophet began to preach his message. Famous pre-Islamic poet; father of Kaʿb, poet of the famous "Mantle Ode."

Zuhayr ibn Masʿūd al-Ḍabbī a pre-Islamic poet, not to be confused with Zuhayr ibn Abī Sulmā.

Bibliography

al-ʿAbbāsī, ʿAbd al-Raḥīm. *Maʿāhid al-tanṣīṣ*. 2 vols. Cairo: al-Maṭbaʿah al-Bahiyyah, 1316/1898–9.

ʿAbd al-Raḥmān Bint al-Shāṭiʾ, ʿĀʾishah. *Abū ʾl-ʿAlāʾ al-Maʿarrī*. Cairo: al-Muʾassasah al-Miṣriyyah al-ʿĀmmah, [1965, date of preface].

———. "Abū ʾl-ʿAlāʾ al-Maʿarrī." In *ʿAbbasid Belles-Lettres*, edited by Julia Ashtiany et al., 328–38. Cambridge: Cambridge University Press, 1990 (The Cambridge History of Arabic Literature).

———. *Qirāʾah jadīdah fī Risālat al-Ghufrān*. Cairo: Jāmiʿat al-Duwal al-ʿArabiyyah, 1970.

al-Ābī, Abū Saʿd Manṣūr ibn al-Ḥusayn. *Nathr al-durr*, edited by Muḥammad ʿAlī Quranah. 7 vols. Cairo: al-Hayʾah al-Miṣriyyah al-ʿĀmmah, 1980–90.

Abū l-ʿAtāhiyah. *Dīwān*, edited by Shukrī Fayṣal. Damascus: Dār al-Mallāḥ, n.d.

Abū Ḥātim al-Sijistānī. *Al-Muʿammarūn*, edited by Ignaz Goldziher. In Ignaz Goldziher, *Abhandlungen zur arabischen Philologie, 2. Theil*, Leiden: Brill, 1899.

Abū Nuwās al-Ḥasan ibn Hāniʾ. *Dīwān*, edited by Ewald Wagner. 5 vols. + 2 vols. Index (vol. 4 edited by Gregor Schoeler). Wiesbaden: Franz Steiner, Berlin: Klaus Schwarz, 1958–2006.

Abū Tammām. *Dīwān*, edited by Muḥammad ʿAzzām. 4 vols. Cairo: Dār al-Maʿārif, 1976.

Abū ʿUbayd al-Bakrī. *Faṣl al-maqāl fī sharḥ al-amthāl*, edited by Iḥsān ʿAbbās and ʿAbd al-Majīd ʿĀbidīn. Beirut: Dār al-Amānah, 1983.

———. *Simṭ al-laʾālī fī sharḥ Amālī al-Qālī*, edited by ʿAbd al-ʿAzīz al-Maymanī. 3 vols. Beirut: Dār al-Kutub al-ʿIlmiyyah, 1997 (repr. of ed. Cairo, 1936).

Ahlwardt, Wilhelm, ed. *The Divans of the Six Ancient Arabic Poets*. London, 1870, repr. Osnabrück: Biblio Verlag, 1972.

al-Akhfash al-Aṣghar. *Al-Ikhtiyārayn*, edited by Fakhr al-Dīn Qabāwah. Damascus: Majmaʿ al-Lughah al-ʿArabiyyah, 1974.

Asín Palacios, M. *La Escatología musulmana en la Divina Comedia*. Madrid: E. Maestre, 1919.

———. *Islam and the Divine Comedy*, translated by H. Sutherland. London: J. Murray, 1926.

al-ʿAskarī, Abū Hilāl. *Jamharat al-amthāl*, edited by Aḥmad ʿAbd al-Salām. 2 vols. Beirut: Dār al-Kutub al-ʿIlmiyyah, 1988.

———. *Kitāb al-ṣināʿatayn al-kitābah wa-l-shiʿr*, edited by ʿAlī Muḥammad al-Bajāwī. Cairo: ʿĪsā al-Bābī al-Ḥalabī, 1971.

ʿAbd al-Qādir al-Baghdādī. *Khizānat al-adab wa-lubāb lisān al-ʿarab*, ed ʿAbd al-Salām Muḥammad Hārūn. 13 vols. Cairo: Dār al-Kātib al-ʿArabī / al-Hay'ah al-Miṣriyyah al-ʿĀmmah, 1967–86.

al-Bākharzī. *Dumyat al-qaṣr*, edited by ʿAbd al-Fattāḥ al-Ḥulw. 2 vols. Cairo: Dār al-Fikr al-ʿArabī, 1968, 1971.

al-Baṭalyawsī. *Sharḥ al-ashʿār al-sittah al-jāhiliyyah*, edited by Nāṣīf Sulaymān ʿAwwād. 2 vols. Beirut – Berlin: Klaus Schwarz, 2008 (Bibliotheca Islamica, 47).

Blachère, Régis. "Ibn al-Qāriḥ et la génèse de *l'Épître du Pardon* d'al-Maʿarrī." *Revue des Études Islamiques*, (1941–46): 5–15; also in his *Analecta*, Damascus: Institut Français, 1975, 431–42.

Brockelmann, Carl. *Geschichte der Arabischen Litteratur*, 2. Aufl. 5 vols. Leiden: Brill, 1937–47.

al-Buḥturī. *Dīwān*, edited by Ḥasan Kāmil al-Ṣayrafī. 5 vols. Cairo: Dār al-Maʿārif, 1972–78.

Bürgel, J. C. "Les deux poèmes autobiographiques du démon Khaytaʿūr dans 'l'Épître du pardon' (*Risālat al-ghufrān*) d'Abou l-ʿAlā' al-Maʿarrī." *Arabic and Middle Eastern Literatures*, 2 no. 1 (1999): 109–54.

Cerulli, Enrico. *Il «Libro della Scala» e la questione delle fonti arabo-spagnole della Divina Commedia*. Vatican City, 1949.

Continente Ferrer, J. M. "Consideraciones en torno a las relaciones entre la *Risālat al-Tawābiʿ wa-l-Zawābiʿ* de ibn Šuhayd y la *Risālat al-Gufrān* de al-Maʿarrī." In *Actas de las jornadas de cultura árabe e islámica*, 1978. Madrid: Instituto Hispano-Árabe de Cultura, 1981: 124–35.

Dechico, Michel. "La Risāla d'Ibn al-Qāriḥ: traduction et étude lexicographique," Thèse pour le Doctorat de 3e Cycle. Paris: Université de Paris III, Sorbonne Nouvelle, 1980 [also contains an edition of the Arabic text].

al-Dhahabī. *Tārīkh al-Islām: Ḥawādith wa-wafayāt 221–30*, edited by ʿAbd al-Salām al-Tadmurī. Beirut: Dār al-Kitāb al-ʿArabī, 1991.

———. *Tārīkh al-Islām: Ḥawādith wa-wafayāt 441–50, 451–60*, edited by ʿAbd al-Salām al-Tadmurī. Beirut: Dār al-Kitāb al-ʿArabī, 1994.

EI2 = Encyclopaedia of Islam, New [= Second] edition. Leiden: Brill, 13 vols. 1960–2009.

al-Farrā'. *Maʿānī l-Qur'ān*, edited by Aḥmad Yūsuf Najātī et al. 3 vols. Cairo: al-Dār al-Miṣriyyah, 1955–72.

Gabrieli, Francesco. "Al-Walīd ibn Yazīd: il califfo e il poeta." *Rivista degli Studi Orientali*, 15 (1935): 1–64.

al-Ghazālī. *Iḥyā' ʿulūm al-dīn*. 5 vols. Cairo: Maktabat al-Mashhad al-Ḥusaynī, n.d.

Gibb, H. A. R. *Arabic Literature: An Introduction*, second (revised) ed. Oxford: Clarendon Press, 1963.

Hamilton, Robert. *Walid and his Friends: An Umayyad Tragedy*. Oxford: Oxford University Press, 1988 (Oxford Studies in Islamic Art, VI).

al-Harrās, ʿAbd al-Salām. "*Risālat al-Tawābiʿ wa-l-zawābiʿ* wa-ʿalāqatuhā li-*Risālat al-Ghufrān*." *Al-Manāhil*, 9 no. 25 (1982): 211–20.

al-Ḥātimī, Abū ʿAlī Muḥammad ibn al-Ḥasan. *Al-Risāla al-Mūḍiḥah*, edited by Muḥammad Yūsuf Najm. Beirut: Dār Ṣādir, 1965.

Heinrichs, Wolfhart. "The Meaning of *Mutanabbī*." In *Poetry and Prophecy: The Beginnings of a Literary Tradition*, edited by James L. Kugel. Ithaca: Cornell University Press, 1990: 120–39, 231–39.

Hogan, Jenny. "Dunes Alive with the Sand of Music." *New Scientist*, 18 (Dec. 2004): 8.

Ibn ʿAbd Rabbih. *Al-ʿIqd al-farīd*, edited by Aḥmad Amīn, Aḥmad al-Zayn, and Ibrāhīm al-Ibyārī. 7 vols. Beirut: Dār al-Kitāb al-ʿArabī, 1983 (repr. of ed. Cairo, 1948–53).

Ibn Abī l-Iṣbaʿ. *Taḥrīr al-taḥbīr fī ṣināʿat al-shiʿr wa-l-nathr wa-bayān iʿjāz al-Qurʾān*, edited by Ḥifnī Muḥammad Sharaf. Cairo: Lajnat Iḥyāʾ al-Turāth al-Islāmī, [1963].

Ibn Abī Yaʿlā. *Ṭabaqāt al-Ḥanābilah*, edited by Muḥammad Ḥāmid al-Fiqī. 2 vols. Cairo: Maṭbaʿat al-Sunnah al-Muḥammadiyyah, 1952.

Ibn al-ʿAdīm. *Bughyat al-ṭalab fī tārīkh Ḥalab*, edited by Suhayl Zakkār. 10 vols. Damascus: no publ., 1988.

———. *Al-Inṣāf wa-l-taḥarrī fī dafʿ al-ẓulm wa-l-tajarrī ʿan Abī l-ʿAlāʾ al-Maʿārrī*. In *Taʿrīf al-qudamāʾ bi-Abī l-ʿAlāʾ* [q.v.], 483–578.

Ibn al-Anbārī, Abū l-Barakāt. *Nuzhat al-alibbāʾ fī ṭabaqāt al-udabāʾ*, edited by Ibrāhīm al-Sāmarrāʾī. Beirut: Maktabat al-Manār, 1985.

Ibn Ḥijjah al-Ḥamawī. *Khizānat al-adab wa-ghāyat al-arab*, edited by Kawkab Diyāb. 5 vols. Beirut: Dār Ṣādir, 2001.

Ibn Ishaq. *The Life of Muhammad: A Translation of Ishāq's* [sic] Sīrat Rasūl Allāh, translated by A. Guillaume. Oxford: Oxford University Press, 1955.

Ibn al-Jawzī. *Al-Muntaẓam*, edited by Muḥammad ʿAbd al-Qādir ʿAṭā and Muṣṭafā ʿAbd al-Qādir ʿAṭā. Beirut: Dār al-Kutub al-ʿIlmiyyah, 1992.

Ibn Jinnī. *Al-Khaṣāʾiṣ*, edited by Muḥammad ʿAlī al-Najjār. 3 vols. Cairo: Dār al-Kutub al-Miṣriyyah, 1952–56.

Ibn Khallikān. *Wafayāt al-aʿyān*, edited by Iḥsān ʿAbbās. 8 vols. Beirut: Dār al-Thaqāfah, 1968–72.

Ibn Manẓūr. *Lisān al-ʿarab*. 20 vols. Cairo: al-Dār al-Miṣriyyah lil-Taʾlīf wa-l-Tarjamah, n.d. (repr. of ed. Būlāq, 1300–8/1883–91).

Ibn Qutaybah. *Kitāb al-Maʿānī l-kabīr fī abyāt al-maʿānī*. Hyderabad: Dāʾirat al-Maʿārif al-ʿUthmāniyyah, 1949.

———. *Al-Shiʿr wa-l-shuʿarāʾ*, edited by Aḥmad Muḥammad Shākir. Cairo: Dār al-Maʿārif, 1966–67.

———. *ʿUyūn al-akhbār*. 4 vols. Cairo: Dār al-Kutub, 1925–30.

Ibn Rashīq. *Al-ʿUmdah fī maḥāsin al-shiʿr wa-ādābihi wa-naqdih*, edited by Muḥammad Muḥyī l-Dīn ʿAbd al-Ḥamīd. 2 vols. repr. Beirut: Dār al-Jīl, 1972.

Ibn al-Rūmī. *Dīwān*, edited by Ḥusayn Naṣṣār. 6 vols. Cairo: Dār al-Kutub, 1973–81.

Ibn Sallām al-Jumaḥī. *Ṭabaqāt fuḥūl al-shuʿarāʾ*, edited by Maḥmūd Muḥammad Shākir. Cairo: Dār al-Maʿārif, 1952.

Ibn Shuhayd. *The Treatise of Familiar Spirits and Demons by Abū ʿĀmir ibn Shuhaid al-Ashjaʿī, al-Andalusī*, Introd., transl., and notes by James T. Monroe. Berkeley etc.: University of California Press, 1971.

Ibn Yaʿīsh. *Sharḥ al-Mufaṣṣal*. 10 vols. Cairo: Maktabat al-Mutanabbī, n.d.

al-Ibshīhī. *Al-Mustaṭraf fī kull fann mustaẓraf*. 2 vols. Cairo: Muṣṭafā al-Bābī al-Ḥalabī, 1952.

al-Iṣfahānī, Abū l-Faraj. *Al-Aghānī*. 24 vols. Cairo: Dār al-Kutub / al-Hay'ah al-Miṣriyyah al-ʿĀmmah, 1927–74.

al-Jāḥiẓ. *Al-Bayān wa-l-tabyīn*, edited by ʿAbd al-Salām Muḥammad Hārūn. 4 vols. Cairo: Maktabat al-Khānjī, 1968.

———. *Al-Ḥayawān*, edited by ʿAbd al-Salām Muḥammad Hārūn. 8 vols. Cairo: Muṣṭafā al-Bābī al-Ḥalabī, 1965–69.

Jones, Alan, ed., trans. and comm. *Early Arabic Poetry, Volume One: Marāthī and Ṣuʿlūk Poems*. Reading: Ithaca Press, 1992. *Volume Two: Select Odes*. Reading: Ithaca Press, 1996.

al-Jundī, Muḥammad Salīm. *Al-Jāmiʿ fī akhbār Abī l-ʿAlāʾ al-Maʿarrī wa-āthārih*. With annotations by ʿAbd al-Hādī Hāshim. Damascus: al-Majmaʿ al-ʿIlmī al-ʿArabī, 1962.

[al-Kalbī], Werner Caskel. *Ğamharat an-nasab: Das genealogische Werk des Hišām ibn Muhammad al-Kalbī*, I: Tafeln, II: Register. Leiden: Brill, 1966.

al-Khaṭīb al-Baghdādī. *Tārīkh Baghdād*. 14 vols. Cairo: Maktabat al-Khānjī, 1931.

Kratschkovsky, I. "Zur Entstehung und Komposition von Abū 'l-ʿAlā''s *Risālat al-ghufrān*." *Islamica*, 1 (1925): 344–56.

Kremers, Dieter. "Islamische Einflüsse auf Dantes «Göttliche Komödie»." In Wolfhart Heinrichs, ed. *Orientalisches Mittelalter* (Neues Handbuch der Literaturwissenschaft, Bd. 5), Wiesbaden: Aula-Verlag, 1990: 202–15.

Lane, Edward William. *An Arabic-English Lexicon*. 8 vols. London: Williams and Norgate, 1863–77.

Laoust, Henri. "La vie et la philosophie d'Abou-l-ʿAlāʾ al-Maʿarrī." *Bulletin d'Études Orientales*, 10 (1934–44): 119–58.

Lucian. *Chattering Courtesans and Other Sardonic Sketches*, translated with an Introd. and Notes by Keith Sidwell. London: Penguin, 2004.

Lyall, Charles. *The Dīwāns of ʿAbīd ibn al-Abrās of Asad, and ʿĀmir ibn aṭ-Ṭufail, of ʿĀmir ibn Ṣaʿṣaʿah.* Cambridge: E. J. W. Gibb Memorial Trust, 1913.

al-Maʿarrī, Abū l-ʿAlāʾ. *al-Fuṣūl wa-l-ghāyāt fī tamjīd Allāh wa-l-mawāʿiẓ*, edited by Maḥmūd Ḥasan Zanātī. Cairo: Maṭbaʿat Ḥijāzī, 1938, repr. Beirut: al-Maktab al-Tijārī, n.d.

———. *Al-Luzūmiyyāt (Luzūm mā lā yalzam)*, edited by Amīn ʿAbd al-ʿAzīz al-Khānjī. 2 vols. Cairo: Maktabat al-Khānjī, 1924.

———. *Risālat al-Ghufrān*, edited by ʿĀʾisha ʿAbd al-Raḥmān "Bint al-Shāṭiʾ." 9th ed. Cairo: Dār al-Maʿārif, 1993 [the basis of the present translation; 1st edition 1954, based on her doctoral dissertation, University of Cairo, 1950].

———. *Risālat al-Ghufrān*, edited by Ibrāhīm al-Yāzijī. Cairo: al-Maṭbaʿah al-Hindiyyah, 1903.

———. *Risālat al-Ghufrān*, edited by Kāmil Kaylānī (Kīlānī). Cairo, Dār al-Maʿārif, [1943].

———. *Risālat al-Ghufrān*, edited by Mufīd Qumayḥah. Beirut: Dār Maktabat al-Hilāl, 1986.

———. *Risālat al-Ghufrān*, edited by ʿAlī Ḥasan Fāʿūr. Beirut: Dār al-Kutub al-ʿIlmiyyah, 2001 [not consulted].

———. *Risālat al-Ghufrān*, edited by Muḥammad al-Iskandarānī and Inʿām Fawwāl. Beirut: Dār al-Kātib al-ʿArabī, 2011.

[———] — Abou' l'Ala de Maarra. *Le Message du Pardon*, translated by M.-S. Meïssa. Paris: Librairie Orientaliste Paul Geuthner, 1932.

[———] — Abul Ala' Al Maʿarri. *Risalat ul Ghufran: A Divine Comedy*, translated from the Arabic by G. Brackenbury. Cairo: al-Maaref, n.d. [preface dated 1943].

[———] — Abûl-ʿAlâ al-Maʿarrî. *L'Épître du pardon*, trad., introd. et notes par Vincent-Mansour Monteil. Paris: Gallimard, 1984.

———. *Paradies und Hölle. Die Jenseitsreise aus dem «Sendschreiben über die Vergebung».* Aus dem Arabischen übersetzt und herausgegeben von Gregor Schoeler. München: C. H. Beck, 2002.

———. *L'epistola del perdone. Il viaggio nell'aldilà*, cura e tradizione di Martino Diez, Torino: Nuova Universale Einaudi, 2011.

———. *Risālat al-Malāʾikah*, edited by Muḥammad Salīm al-Jundī. Beirut: Dār Ṣādir, 1992.

———. *Zajr al-nābiḥ: Muqtaṭafāt*, edited by Amjad al-Ṭarābulusī. Damascus: Majmaʿ al-Lughah al-ʿArabiyyah, 1982.

Margoliouth, D. S. "Abū 'l-ʿAlāʾ al-Maʿarrī's Correspondence on Vegetarianism." *Journal of the Royal Asian Society*, 1902: 289–332.

al-Marzūqī. *Sharḥ Dīwān al-Ḥamāsa*, edited by Aḥmad Amīn and ʿAbd al-Salām Hārūn. Repr. Beirut: Dār al-Jīl, 1991.

Massignon, Louis. *Essay on the Origins of the Technical Language of Islamic Mysticism.* Notre Dame, Indiana: University of Notre Dame Press, 1997.

al-Masʿūdī. *Murūj al-dhahab*, éd. Barbier de Meynard & Pavet de Courteille, revue et corrigée par Charles Pellat. 7 vols. Beirut: al-Jāmiʿah al-Lubnāniyyah, 1966–79.

al-Maydānī. *Majmaʿ al-amthāl*, edited by Naʿīm Ḥusayn Zarzūr. 2 vols. Beirut: Dār al-Kutub al-ʿIlmiyyah, 1988.

Merali, Zeeya. "Dune Tune: The Greatest Hits." *New Scientist*, 17 Sept. 2005: 11.

Montgomery, James E. *The Vagaries of the Qaṣīdah: The Tradition and Practice of Early Arabic Poetry.* [Cambridge:] E. J. W. Gibb Memorial Trust, 1997.

Moreh, Shmuel. *Live Theatre and Dramatic Literature in the Medieval Arabic World.* Edinburgh: Edinburgh University Press, 1992.

al-Mubarrad. *Al-Kāmil fī l-lughah wa-l-adab*, edited by ʿAbd al-Ḥamīd Hindāwī. 4 vols. Beirut: Dār al-Kutub al-ʿIlmiyyah, 1999.

The Mufaḍḍalīyāt: An Anthology of Ancient Arabian Odes compiled by al-Mufaḍḍal, edited by Charles James Lyall. *Vol. II: Translation and Notes.* Oxford: Clarendon Press, 1918.

al-Mutanabbī. *Dīwān*, edited by F. Dieterici. Berlin: Mittler, 1861.

Nagel, Tilman. "The *Risālat al-ghufrān* and the Crisis of the Certainty of Faith." In *Proceedings, 10th Congress [of the] UEAI, Edinburgh, 9–16 Sept. 1980*, edited by Robert Hillenbrand, Edinburgh: Union Européenne des Arabisants et Islamisants, 1982: 55–60.

Nicholson, Reynold A. *Literary History of the Arabs.* London, 1907, repr. Cambridge: Cambridge University Press, 1966.

———. "The Meditations of Maʿarrī." In Reynold A. Nicholson, *Studies in Islamic Poetry.* Cambridge: Cambridge University Press, 1921, repr. 1979: 43–289.

———. "Persian Manuscripts attributed to Fakhru'ddīn Rāzī with a Note on *Risālatu 'l Ghufrān* by Abū 'l ʿAlā al-Maʿarrī and other MSS in the same collection." *Journal of the Royal Asiatic Society* (1899): 669–74.

———. "The *Risālatu 'l-Ghufrān* by Abū 'l-ʿAlā' al-Maʿarrī." *Journal of the Royal Asiatic Society* (1900): 637–720, (1902): 75–101, 337–62, 813–47.

al-Nushshābī (or Nashshābī), Asʿad ibn Ibrāhīm al-Irbilī. *Al-Mudhākarah fī alqāb al-shuʿarā'*, edited by Shākir al-ʿĀshūr. Baghdad: Dār al-Shu'ūn al-Thaqāfiyyah al-ʿāmmah, 1988.

Osman, Hassan. "Dante in Arabic." *Annual Reports of the Dante Society*, 73 (1955): 47–52.

al-Qifṭī, al-Ḥāsan ibn ʿAlī (Ibn). *Inbāh al-ruwāh ʿalā anbā' al-nuḥāh*, edited by Muḥammad Abū l-Faḍl Ibrāhīm. 4 vols. Cairo: Dār al-Fikr al-ʿArabī, 1986.

al-Qurashī, Abū Zayd Muḥammad b. Abī l-Khaṭṭāb. *Jamharat ashʿār al-ʿarab.* Beirut: Dār Ṣādir, 1963.

Reckendorf, H. *Arabische Syntax.* Heidelberg: Carl Winter, [1921], repr. 1977.

al-Ṣafadī. *Al-Wāfī bi-l-Wafayāt*. 30 vols. Beirut - Wiesbaden – Berlin: Franz Steiner – Klaus Schwarz, 1931–2005.

Saleh, Moustapha. "Abū 'l-ʿAlāʾ al-Maʿarrī (363–449/979–1057): bibliographie critique." *Bulletin d'Études Orientales*, 22 (1969): 133–204; 23 (1970): 197–309.

al-Ṣanawbarī. *Dīwān*, edited by Iḥsān ʿAbbās. Beirut: Dār Ṣādir, 1998.

Schoeler, Gregor. "Abū l-Alāʾ al-Maʿarrīs Prolog zum *Sendschreiben über die Vergebung*." In *Islamstudien ohne Ende. Festschrift für Werner Ende zum 65. Geburtstag*, edited by Rainer Brunner et al. Würzburg: Ergon Verlag, 2002 (Abhandlungen für die Kunde des Morgenlandes, Deutsche Morgenländische Gesellschaft, LIV, 1): 417–28.

———. "Die Vision, die auf einer Hypothese gründet: Zur Deutung von Abū 'l-ʿAlāʾ al-Maʿarrīs *Risālat al-Ġufrān*." In *Problems in Arabic Literature*, edited by Miklós Maróth. Piliscsaba: The Avicenna Institute of Middle Eastern Studies, 2004: 27–41.

Sells, Michael A. *Desert Tracings: Six Classic Arabian Odes by ʿAlqama, Shánfara, Labíd, ʿAntara, Al-Aʿsha, and Dhu al-Rúmma*. Middletown, Connecticut: Wesleyan University Press, 1989.

al-Shirbīnī, Yūsuf. *Yūsuf al-Shirbīnī's Brains Confounded by the Ode of Abū Shādūf Expounded*, translated by Humphrey Davies. Leuven: Peeters, 2007.

Sībawayh. *Kitāb Sībawayh*. 2 vols. Cairo: Dār al-Ṭibāʿah, 1318/1900–1.

Smoor, Pieter. *Kings and Bedouins in the Palace of Aleppo as reflected in Maʿarrī's works*. Manchester, 1985 (*Journal of Semitic Studies*, Monographs, 8).

———. "al-Maʿarrī." In *Encyclopaedia of Islam*, New [=Second] Edition, vol. V, Leiden: Brill, 1986: 927–35.

Stetkevych, Suzanne Pinckney. *The Poetics of Islamic Legitimacy: Myth, Gender, and Ceremony in the Classical Arabic Ode*. Bloomington, Indiana: Indiana University Press, 2002.

Strohmaier, Gotthard. "Chaj ben Mekitz – die unbekannte Quelle der Divina Commedia." In Gotthard Strohmaier, *Von Demokrit bis Dante*. Hildesheim, Zürich, New York: Georg Olms, 1996: 449–65.

al-Sukkarī. *Sharḥ ashʿār al-Hudhaliyyīn*, edited by ʿAbd al-Sattār Aḥmad Farrāj. 3 vols. Cairo: Dār al-ʿUrūbah, 1965.

al-Ṣūlī, Abū Bakr Muḥammad ibn Yaḥyā. *Akhbār Abī Tammām*, edited by Khalīl Maḥmūd ʿAsākir et al. Cairo: Lajnat al-Taʾlīf, 1937.

al-Suyūṭī. *Bughyat al-wuʿāh fī ṭabaqāt al-lughawiyyīn wa-l-nuḥāh*, edited by Muḥammad Abū l-Faḍl Ibrāhīm. repr. Beirut: Dār al-Fikr, 1979.

———. *Al-Muzhir fī ʿulūm al-lughah wa-anwāʿihā*, edited by Muḥammad Aḥmad Jād al-Mawlā et al. 2 vols. Cairo: Dār Iḥyāʾ al-Kutub al-ʿArabiyyah, n.d.

Taʿrīf al-qudamāʾ bi-Abī l-ʿAlāʾ. Cairo: al-Dār al-Qawmiyyah, 1965.

al-Tanūkhī, al-Muḥassin. *Nishwār al-muḥāḍarah*, edited by ʿAbbūd al-Shāljī. 8 vols. Beirut: Dār Ṣādir, 1971–73.

al-Thaʿālibī. *Tatimmat al-Yatīmah*, edited by Mufīd Muḥammad Qumayḥah. Beirut: Dār al-Kutub al-ʿIlmiyyah, 1983.

Tibbets, G. R., and Shawkat M. Toorawa. "Wāḳwāḳ. 2(b). The tree." In *The Encyclopaedia of Islam*, New [=Second] Edition, vol. XI, Leiden: Brill, 2002: 107–08.

Ullmann, Manfred. *Der Neger in der Bildersprache der arabischen Dichter*. Wiesbaden: Harrassowitz, 1998.

Usāmah ibn Munqidh. *The Book of Contemplation*, translated by Paul M. Cobb. London: Penguin, 2008.

Wagner, Ewald. "Sprechende Tiere in der arabischen Prosa." *Asiatische Studien*, 45 (1994): 937–57.

Walther, Wiebke. Review of Schoeler's translation of *Risālat al-Ghufrān*. *Zeitschrift der Deutschen Morgenländischen Gesellschaft*, 157 (2007): 225–28.

WKAS = *Wörterbuch der klassischen arabischen Sprache*. Bearbeitet von Manfred Ullmann. Wiesbaden: Harrassowitz, 1970–2009.

Wright, O. "Music." In A. F. L. Beeston et al. (eds), *Arabic Literature to the End of the Umayyad Period*, Cambridge: Cambridge University Press, 1983 (The Cambridge History of Arabic Literature): 433–59.

Wright, W. *A Grammar of the Arabic Language*, 3rd ed. rev. by W. Robertson Smith and M. J. de Goeje. 2 vols. Cambridge: Cambridge University Press, 1896–98.

Yāqūt. *Muʿjam al-buldān*. 7 vols. Beirut: Dār Ṣādir, 1995.

———. *Muʿjam al-udabāʾ*, ed Aḥmad Farīd Rifāʿī. 20 vols. Cairo: 1936–38, repr. Beirut: Iḥyāʾ al-Turāth al-ʿArabī, n.d.

Yarshater, E. "Zuhāk." In *Encyclopaedia of Islam*, New [= Second] Edition, vol. XI, Leiden: Brill, 2002: 554–55.

al-Zabīdī, Murtaḍā. *Tāj al-ʿarūs*, edited by ʿAbd al-Sattār Farrāj. 40 vols. Kuwait: Maṭbaʿat Ḥukūmat al-Kuwayt, 1965–2001.

al-Zamakhsharī. *Asās al-balāghah*. Beirut: Dār Ṣādir, 1979.

al-Zamakhsharī. *Rabīʿ al-abrār*, edited by Salīm al-Nuʿaymī. 4 vols. Baghdad: Maṭbaʿat al-ʿĀnī, 1967–82.

al-Zamakhsharī. *Tafsīr al-kashshāf ʿan ḥaqāʾiq ghawāmiḍ al-tanzīl*, edited by Muḥammad Mursī ʿĀmir. 3 vols. Cairo: Dār al-Muṣḥaf, 1977.

Further Reading

Main pre-modern sources for al-Maʿarrī's life

Most of the following and many other shorter passages are also found in two compilations of biographical material on al-Maʿarrī: *Taʿrīf al-qudamāʾ bi-Abī l-ʿAlāʾ*, and Muḥammad Salīm al-Jundī, *al-Jāmiʿ fī akhbār Abī l-ʿAlāʾ*. For bibliographical details see the Bibliography.

al-Thaʿālibī (d. 429/1038), *Tatimmat al-Yatīmah*, p. 16.

al-Khaṭīb al-Baghdādī (d. 463/1071), *Tārīkh Baghdād*, iv, 240.

al-Bākharzī (d. 467/1075), *Dumyat al-qaṣr*, i, 129–37.

Abū l-Barakāt Ibn al-Anbārī (d. 577/1181), *Nuzhat al-alibbāʾ fī ṭabaqāt al-udabāʾ*, pp. 257–59.

Ibn al-Jawzī (d. 597/1201), *al-Muntaẓam*, xvi, 22–27.

Yāqūt (d. 626/1229), *Muʿjam al-udabāʾ*, iii, 107–218.

(Ibn) al-Qifṭī (d. 646/1248), *Inbāh al-ruwāh ʿalā anbāh al-nuḥāh*, i, 81–118.

Ibn al-ʿAdīm (d. 660/1262), *Bughyat al-ṭalab fī tārīkh Ḥalab*, pp. 863–913.

———, *al-Inṣāf wa-l-taḥarrī fī dafʿ al-ẓulm wa-l-tajarrī ʿan Abī l-ʿAlāʾ al-Maʿarrī, in Taʿrīf al-qudamāʾ bi-Abī l-ʿAlāʾ*, pp. 483–578.

Ibn Khallikān (d. 681/1282), *Wafayāt al-aʿyān*, i, 113–16.

al-Dhahabī (d. 748/1348), *Tārīkh al-Islām: Ḥawādith wa-wafayāt 441–50, 451–60*, pp. 198–220.

al-Ṣafadī (d. 764/1363), *al-Wāfī bil-Wafayāt*, vii, 94–111.

ʿAbd al-Raḥīm ibn ʿAbd al-Raḥmān al-ʿAbbāsī (d. 963/1556), *Maʿāhid al-tanṣīṣ*, i, 48–52.

Editions of *Risālat Ibn al-Qāriḥ* and *Risālat al-Ghufrān*

Ibrāhīm al-Yāzijī, ed. Cairo: al-Maṭbaʿah al-Hindiyyah, 1903.

Kāmil Kaylānī (Kīlānī), ed. Cairo: Dār al-Maʿārif, [1943].

Michel Dechico, "La Risāla d'Ibn al-Qāriḥ: traduction et étude lexicographique," Thèse pour le Doctorat de 3e Cycle, Paris: Université de Paris III, Sorbonne Nouvelle, 1980 [also contains an edition of the Arabic text].

Mufīd Qumayḥah, ed. Beirut: Dār Maktabat al-Hilāl, 1986.

ʿĀʾisha ʿAbd al-Raḥmān Bint al-Shāṭiʾ, ed., 9th ed. Cairo: Dār al-Maʿārif, 1993 [the basis of the present translation; 1st edition 1954, based on her doctoral dissertation, University of Cairo, 1950].

Muḥammad al-Iskandaranī and In'ām Fawwāl, eds. Beirut: Dār al-Kātib al-ʿArabī, 2011.

ʿAlī Ḥasan Fāʿūr, ed. Beirut: Dār al-Kutub al-ʿIlmiyyah [not consulted].

Translations of *Risālat Ibn al-Qāriḥ* and *Risālat al-Ghufrān*

Abou' l'Ala de Maarra. *Le Message du Pardon*. Tr. M.-S. Meïssa. Paris: Librairie Orientaliste Paul Geuthner, 1932.

Abul Ala' Al Maʿarri. *Risalat ul Ghufran: A Divine Comedy*. Tr. from the Arabic by G. Brackenbury. Cairo: al-Maaref, n.d. [preface dated 1943].

Abûl-ʿAlâ al-Maʿarrî. *L'Épître du pardon*. Trad., introd. et notes par Vincent-Mansour Monteil. Paris: Gallimard, 1984 (also contains a translation of *Risālat Ibn al-Qāriḥ*).

Abū l-ʿAlāʾ al-Maʿarrī. *Paradies und Hölle. Die Jenseitsreise aus dem Sendschreiben über die Vergebung*. Aus dem Arabischen übersetzt und herausgegeben von Gregor Schoeler. München: C. H. Beck, 2002 [For a study and translation of the Preamble, see Gregor Schoeler, "Abū l-Alāʾ al-Maʿarrīs Prolog zum *Sendschreiben über die Vergebung*," in Rainer Brunner et al., ed., *Islamstudien ohne Ende. Festschrift für Werner Ende zum 65. Geburtstag*, Würzburg: Ergon Verlag, 2002 (Abhandlungen für die Kunde des Morgenlandes, Deutsche Morgenländische Gesellschaft, LIV, 1), pp. 417–28 (translation pp. 422–28)].

Abū l-ʿAlāʾ al-Maʿārrī. *L'epistola del perdone. Il viaggio nell'aldilà*. Cura e tradizione di Martino Diez. Torino: Nuova Universale Einaudi, 2011.

Some modern studies

ʿAbbūd, Mārūn. *Zawbaʿat al-duhūr*. [Beirut:] Dār al-Makshūf, 1945.

al-ʿAbd, ʿAbd al-Ḥakīm ʿAbd al-Salām. *Abū l-ʿAlāʾ al-Maʿarrī wa-naẓrah jadīdah ilayh: Tamḥīṣ naqdī ḥaḍārī wa-fannī*. 2 vols. Alexandria: Dār al-Maṭbūʿāt al-Jadīdah, 1993.

ʿAbd al-Raḥmān ʿĀʾishah "Bint al-Shāṭiʾ". *Abū l-ʿAlāʾ al-Maʿarrī*. Cairo, [1965, date of preface], also published as *Maʿa Abī l-ʿAlāʾ fī riḥlat ḥayātih*. Beirut: Dār al-Kitāb al-ʿArabī, 1972.

———. "Abū l-ʿAlāʾ al-Maʿarrī." In Julia Ashtiany et al. (eds), *ʿAbbasid Belles-Lettres*. Cambridge: Cambridge University Press, 1990 (The Cambridge History of Arabic Literature), 328–38.

al-ʿAlāyilī, ʿAbd Allāh. *Al-Maʿarrī dhālika l-majhūl*. Beirut: Manshūrat al-Adīb, 1944.

ʿAlī, ʿAdnān ʿUbayd. *Al-Maʿarrī fī fikrihī wa-sukhriyyatih*. Amman: Dār Usāmah, 1999.

ʿAlī al-Dawlah, Nādiyā. *Naqd al-shiʿr fī āthār Abī l-ʿAlāʾ al-Maʿarrī*. Damascus [s.n.], 1998.

al-ʿAqqād, ʿAbbās Maḥmūd. *Rajʿat Abī l-ʿAlāʾ*. Cairo: Dār al-Hilāl [1966].

Asín Palacios, M. *La Escatología musulmana en la Divina Comedia*. Madrid: E. Maestre, 1919; translated by H. Sutherland as *Islam and the Divine Comedy*. London: J. Murray, 1926.

ʿAwaḍ, Luwīs. *ʿAlā hāmish al-Ghufrān*. Cairo: Dār al-Hilāl, 1966.

Bāshā, ʿUmar Mūsā. *Naẓarāt jadīdah fī Ghufrān Abī l-ʿAlāʾ*. Beirut: Dār Ṭlās, 1989.

Blachère, Régis. "Ibn al-Qāriḥ et la génèse de *l'Épître du Pardon* d'al-Maʿarrī." *Revue des Études Islamiques*, 1941–6: 5–15, also in his *Analecta*, Damascus: Institut Français, 1975, 431–42.

Brockelmann, Carl. *Geschichte der Arabischen Litteratur*. 2. Aufl. Leiden: Brill, 1937–47, I, 254–55, Suppl. I, 449–54.

Cerulli, Enrico. *Il «Libro della Scala» e la questione delle fonti arabo-spagnole della Divina Commedia*. Vatican City: Bibliotheca Apostolica Vaticana, 1949.

Farrūkh, ʿUmar. *Ḥakīm al-Maʿarrah*. Beirut: Dār Lubnān, 1986.

Grotzfeld, Heinz. "*wa-ʿallama Ādama l-asmāʾ kullahā* „und er lehrte Adam alle Namen" (Sure 2:31). Spekulationen über Adams Sprache im arabisch islamischen Mittelalter." (Farewell Lecture, University of Münster, 25 June 1999). Münster: Universität Münster, 1999.

Ḥabābī, Fāṭimah al-Jāmiʿī. *Lughat Abī l-ʿAlāʾ al-Maʿarrī fī Risālat al-Ghufrān*. Cairo: Dār al-Maʿārif, 1988.

al-Ḥakīm, Suʿād. *Abū l-ʿAlāʾ al-Maʿarrī: Bayna baḥr al-shiʿr wa-yābisat al-nās*. Beirut: Dār al-Fikr al-Lubnānī, 2003.

al-Hāshimī, Muḥammad Yaḥyā. *Lughz Abī l-ʿAlāʾ*. Aleppo [s.n.], 1968.

Ḥimṣī, Muḥammad Ṭāhir. *Abū l-ʿAlāʾ al-Maʿarrī: Malāmiḥ ḥayātihī wa-adabih*. Damascus: Dār Ibn Kathīr, 1999.

———. *Madhāhib Abī l-ʿAlāʾ al-Maʿarrī fī l-lughah wa-ʿulūmihā*. Damascus: Dār al-Fikr, 1986.

Ḥusayn, Ṭāhā. *Dhikrā Abī l-ʿAlāʾ*. Cairo: Maṭbaʿat al-Wāʿiẓ, 1915.

———. *Tajdīd dhikrā Abī l-ʿAlāʾ*. Cairo: Dār al-Maʿārif, 1922.

———. *Maʿa Abī l-ʿAlāʾ fī sijnih*. Cairo: Maṭbaʿat al-Maʿārif, 1944.

Kennedy, Philip F. "Muslim Sources of Dante?". In Dionisius A. Agius and Richard Hitchcock, eds., *The Arab Influence in Medieval Europe*. Reading: Ithaca, 1993, 63–82.

Khuraybānī, Jaʿfar. *Abū l-ʿAlāʾ al-Maʿarrī rahīn al-maḥbisayn*. Beirut: Dār al-Kutub al-ʿIlmiyyah, 1990.

Kratschkovsky, I. "Zur Entstehung und Komposition von Abū 'l-ʿAlā''s *Risālat al-ghufrān*." *Islamica*, 1 (1925): 344–56.

Kremers, Dieter. "Islamische Einflüsse auf Dantes «Göttliche Komödie»." In Wolfhart Heinrichs, ed., *Orientalisches Mittelalter* (Neues Handbuch der Literaturwissenschaft, Bd. 5). Wiesbaden: Aula-Verlag, 1990, 202–15.

Laoust, Henri. "La vie et la philosophie d'Abou-l-ʿAlāʾ al-Maʿarrī." *Bulletin d'Études Orientales*, 10 (1934–44): 119–58.

al-Mallūḥī, ʿAbd al-Muʿīn. *Difāʿ ʿan Abī l-ʿAlāʾ al-Maʿarrī*. Beirut: Dār al-Kunūz al-Adabiyyah, 1994.

Margoliouth, D. S. "Abū 'l-'Alā' al-Ma'arrī's Correspondence on Vegetarianism." *Journal of the Royal Asian Society*, (1902): 289–312.

al-Maymanī al-Rājakūtī, 'Abd al-'Azīz. *Abū l-'Alā' wa-mā ilayh*. Cairo: al-Maṭba'ah al-Salafiyyah, 1925.

Nagel, Tilman. "The *Risālat al-ghufrān* and the Crisis of the Certainty of Faith." In *Proceedings, 10th Congress [of the] UEAI, Edinburgh, 9–16 Sept. 1980*. Edited by R. Hillenbrand. Edinburgh, 1982, 55–60.

Nicholson, Reynold Alleyne. "The Meditations of Ma'arrī," = Chapter II of his *Studies in Islamic Poetry*. Cambridge: CUP, 1979, 43–289 [also contains many verses from *Luzūm mā lā yalzam*, in Arabic and English].

Rizq, Ṣalāḥ. *Nathr Abī l-'Alā' al-Ma'arrī: Dirāsah fanniyyah*. Cairo: Dār al-Thaqāfah al-'Arabiyyah, 1985.

Saleh, Moustapha. "Abū 'l-'Alā' al-Ma'arrī (363–449/979–1057): bibliographie critique." *Bulletin d'Études Orientales*, 22 (1969): 133–204; 23 (1970): 197–309.

al-Sāmarrā'ī, Ibrāhīm. *Dirāsāt fī turāth Abī l-'Alā' al-Ma'arrī*. Amman: Dār al-Ḍiyā', 1999.

———. *Ma'a l-Ma'arrī al-lughawī*. Beirut: Mu'assasat al-Risālah, 1984.

Schoeler, Gregor. "Die Vision, die auf einer Hypothese gründet: Zur Deutung von Abū 'l-'Alā' al-Ma'arrīs *Risālat al-Ġufrān*." In *Problems in Arabic Literature*. Edited by Miklós Maróth. Piliscsaba: The Avicenna Institute of Middle Eastern Studies, 2004, 27–41.

Smoor, P. "al-Ma'arrī." *Encyclopaedia of Islam*, New [=Second] Edition, vol. V (Leiden, 1986), 927–35.

———. *Kings and Bedouins in the Palace of Aleppo as reflected in Ma'arrī's works*, Manchester: University of Manchester, 1985 (*Journal of Semitic Studies*, Monographs, 8).

Strohmaier, Gotthard. "Die angeblichen und die wirklichen orientalischen Quellen der ‚Divina Comedia.'" In Gotthard Strohmaier, *Von Demokrit bis Dante*. Hildesheim, Zürich, New York: Georg Olms Verlag, 1996, 471–86.

———. "Chaj ben Mekitz – die unbekannte Quelle der Divina Commedia." In Gotthard Strohmaier, *Von Demokrit bis Dante*. Hildesheim: Wissenschaftliche Buchgesellschaft, 1996, 449–65.

al-Ṭarābulusī, Amjad. *Al-Naqd wa-l-lughah fī Risālat al-Ghufrān*. Damascus: Jāmi'at Dimashq, 1951.

Taymūr, Aḥmad. *Abū l-'Alā' al-Ma'arrī*. Cairo: al-Maktabah al-Anjlū al-Miṣriyyah, 1940.

'Uthmānī, Yūsuf. *Al-Ihtimāmāt al-lughawiyyah fī āthār Abī l-'Alā' al-Ma'arrī*. Tunis: Kulliyyat al-'Ulūm al-Insāniyyah wa-l-Ijtimā'iyyah, 2005.

Zaydān,'Abd al-Qādir. *Qaḍāyā l-'aṣr fī adab Abī l-'Alā' al-Ma'arrī*. Cairo: al-Hay'ah al-Miṣriyyah al-'Āmmah, 1986.

Index

If no death date is given, this is because it is unknown or because the person is legendary or fictional. Book titles are listed under *Kitāb*.

About the NYU Abu Dhabi Institute

The Library of Arabic Literature is supported by a grant from The NYU Abu Dhabi Institute, a major hub of intellectual and creative activity and advanced research. The Institute hosts academic conferences, workshops, lectures, film series, performances, and other public programs directed both to audiences within the UAE and to the worldwide academic and research community. It is a center of the scholarly community for Abu Dhabi, bringing together faculty and researchers from institutions of higher learning throughout the region.

NYU Abu Dhabi, through the NYU Abu Dhabi Institute, is a world-class center of cutting-edge research, scholarship, and cultural activity. The Institute creates singular opportunities for leading researchers from across the arts, humanities, social sciences, sciences, engineering, and the professions to carry out creative scholarship and conduct research on issues of major disciplinary, multidisciplinary, and global significance.

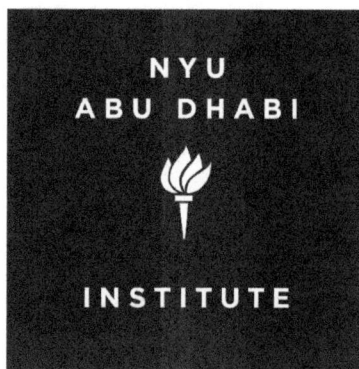

About the Typefaces

The Arabic body text is set in DecoType Naskh, designed by Thomas Milo and Mirjam Somers, based on an analysis of five centuries of Ottoman manuscript practice. The exceptionally legible result is the first and only typeface in a style that fully implements the principles of script grammar (*qawāʿid al-khaṭṭ*).

The Arabic footnote text is set in DecoType Emiri, drawn by Mirjam Somers, based on the metal typeface in the naskh style that was cut for the 1924 Cairo edition of the Qur'an.

Both Arabic typefaces in this series are controlled by a dedicated font layout engine. ACE, the Arabic Calligraphic Engine, invented by Peter Somers, Thomas Milo, and Mirjam Somers of DecoType, first operational in 1985, pioneered the principle followed by later smart font layout technologies such as OpenType, which is used for all other typefaces in this series.

The Arabic text was set with WinSoft Tasmeem, a sophisticated user interface for DecoType ACE inside Adobe InDesign. Tasmeem was conceived and created by Thomas Milo (DecoType) and Pascal Rubini (WinSoft) in 2005.

The English text is set in Adobe Text, a new and versatile text typeface family designed by Robert Slimbach for Western (Latin, Greek, Cyrillic) typesetting. Its workhorse qualities make it perfect for a wide variety of applications, especially for longer passages of text where legibility and economy are important. Adobe Text bridges the gap between calligraphic Renaissance types of the 15th and 16th centuries and high-contrast Modern styles of the 18th century, taking many of its design cues from early post-Renaissance Baroque transitional types cut by designers such as Christoffel van Dijck, Nicolaus Kis, and William Caslon. While grounded in classical form, Adobe Text is also a statement of contemporary utilitarian design, well suited to a wide variety of print and on-screen applications.

About the Editor-Translators

Geert Jan van Gelder was Laudian Professor of Arabic at the University of Oxford from 1998 to 2012. He has published widely on classical Arabic literature in Dutch and English, particularly on the history of poetics and criticism and on literary themes as diverse as food, the hammam, and incest. His books include *Beyond the Line: Classical Arabic Literary Critics on the Coherence and Unity of the Poem* and *Of Dishes and Discourse: Classical Arabic Literary Representations of Food.*

Gregor Schoeler was the chair of Islamic Studies at the University of Basel from 1982 to 2009. His books in the fields of Islamic Studies and classical Arabic literature include *The Oral and the Written in Early Islam*, and *Paradies und Hölle*, a partial German translation of *The Epistle of Forgiveness.*